MW00769831

FOR EUROPE

0 11557 03581 0

The Stackpole Military History Series

FOR EUROPE

The French Volunteers of the Waffen-SS

Robert Forbes

STACKPOLE
BOOKS

This book is dedicated to my father, Albert Forbes.
I still miss you.

English edition © 2006 by Robert Forbes

Published in paperback in 2010 by
STACKPOLE BOOKS
5067 Ritter Road
Mechanicsburg, PA 17055
www.stackpolebooks.com

FOR EUROPE, by Robert Forbes, was published in 2006 by Helion & Company Limited. Copyright © 2006 by Robert Forbes. Paperback edition by arrangement with Helion & Company Limited. All rights reserved.

Original edition POUR L'EUROPE: THE FRENCH VOLUNTEERS OF THE WAFFEN-SS published by the author in 2000.

No part of this book may be reproduced or transmitted in any form or by any means electronic or mechanical including photocopying, reprinting, or on any information storage or retrieval system, without permission in writing from Helion & Company Limited.

Cover design by Tracy Patterson

Printed in the United States of America

10 9 8 7 6 5 4 3 2 1

Library of Congress Cataloging-in-Publication Data

Forbes, Robert.
  For Europe : the French volunteers of the Waffen-SS / Robert Forbes. — Pbk. ed.
    p. cm. — (Stackpole military history series)
  Originally published: West Midlands, England : Helion, 2006.
  Includes bibliographical references.
  ISBN 978-0-8117-3581-0
  1. Waffen-SS. Franzvsische SS-Freiwilligen-Sturmbrigade—History. 2. Waffen-SS.
Waffen-Grenadier-Division "Charlemagne," 33—History. 3. World War,
1939–1945—Regimental histories—Germany. 4. Soldiers—France—History—20th
century. I. Title.
  D757.85.F67 2009
  940.54'134308941—dc22
                                    2008045322

Contents

Acknowledgments

This book started life with the aim of bringing the story of the French volunteers of the Waffen-SS to an English language audience, a story which had been evoked by the likes of Saint-Loup and Mabire in French. Many have asked why. Quite simply, there is little in English about the French volunteers of the Waffen-SS and I wanted to write the book I wanted to read. Originally, I had intended to repeat the story told by Saint-Loup and Mabire, but the book took on a new life as I received generous assistance and advice from many veterans, as well as many knowledgeable correspondents.

Specifically I wish to thank veterans Robert Soulat, Robert Blanc, Michel de Genouillac, Raymond Mercier and François Faroux, who continues to put a smile on my face even in my darkest of times. I owe all a debt of gratitude for their time and generosity.

I am also indebted to the following veterans of 'Charlemagne' who assisted me: André Bayle, Yann de Brangelin, Georges Blonet, Jean Castrillo, Maurice Comte, Noël Cornu, André Doulard, Henri Fenet†, René Forez†, Jean Fronteau, Robert Girard, Henri-Georges Gonzales, Jean Grenier, Jean Halard, Daniel L.G., Robert Lacoste, François de Lannurien, Louis Levast, Jean Malardier, Christian Martret†, Jean de Misser, Paul Pignard-Berthet, Jean-Louis Puechlong†, Yves Rigeade†, Philippe Rossigneux, Pierre Rusco†, Marc Santeuil, Jean Sepchant, Yvon Trémel, Jean-Louis Vaxelaire.

Others requested anonymity. I have respected their wishes. But you know who you are.

This revised edition includes new material relating to the French N.S.K.K., which was provided by François Faroux and Henri Raga. Sadly Henri has now passed away.

N. I. provided me with her rather unique and interesting story as a French nurse of the Waffen-SS.

Pierre Duthilleul added a personal insight into the BILOM.

Historian Henri Mounine also assisted me, providing much information and many new leads. He read and edited my original manuscript three times. And although we went our separate ways after the publication of the original English edition he still deserves mention. In late 2005 I was shocked to learn of his untimely death. My thoughts go out to his wife and children.

Through historian Eric Lefèvre, I gained an understanding of the *Milice française* [French Militia] that my original manuscript lacked. He also provided me with much biographical information.

Also, I thank Christa Cuthbertson, who for seven months in 2004 came into my life. It was a time I will never forget. 2005 came and went and love tore us apart again and again, for 'in this world we are afraid of what we truly love'.

Assistance also came from Wilfrid of Helion & Company, Chris Gorgon and Goth proofreader Lorraine Smith. Thank you all.

My thanks I also extend to the following friends and family who have supported me through the last few years: my stepmother Rhoda, my brother Sean,

Clint Chapman of Infest, Rachel Strayer, Ian Oxley, Peter Duncombe, Marcus Andrews, Chris D'Arcy, Mike Taylor, Sarah Orrow, Claire, Matt and Jade McCartney, and the two 'Wembley Warriors' Kevin Howson and Dinker Pandya.

Lastly, despite all the trouble the book brought me, I still remain proud of it. And more importantly I believe my father, who died before its publication, would have been proud of me as well as the book. Sometimes, this thought alone spurred me on to complete the book. And that is why the book remains dedicated to my father.

Introduction

29th April 1945, the holocaust of Berlin:[1]

A little before midday, in Saarlandstrasse, I [Uscha. Malardier] fetched under fire a machine gun that its crew, granddads of the Volkssturm, who had abandoned it during a mad rush withdrawal, did not seem in any great hurry to go and collect. Thereupon, feeling like a hero, I volunteered to remain as the file closer in the course of a withdrawal along Friedrichstrasse. The majority of my section stayed with me.

My platoon, which withdrew thanks to a lull, was set on some moments later by two machine guns whose positions I located immediately. Without taking time to clear my throat, I yelled out at the top of my voice so as to be heard over the fracas around me: "MG *en batterie*! Fire at will at the two machine gun positions fifty metres in front of us". As in the majority of its interventions, the MG 42 did not have to spit out its 1300 rounds per minute; very quickly the enemy fire stopped, either our lads had hit the bull's eye or Ivan thought that it would be better to withdraw before the irresistible [MG] 42. I then gave the order to rejoin the platoon, but spotting some twenty paces from us a group of Kalmouks emerging from a porch, as peacefully as if they were going for a walk, I took time to send them the *bonjour d'Alfred* in the form of a Sturmgewehr burst of continuous fire. I saw them fall, but, immediately, from the same embrasure other rogues who had spotted me started to fire in my direction. Then, so as not to remain blocked there, considering I had done what I had to, I decided to withdraw in turn, by going through the courtyard of the building and that of the next one where I expected to find comrades. Alas! They had left already and as soon as I ventured a peep into the road it was Ivan who learnt of me rather than ours [who] were not opposite any more ... Thus, if I wanted to get out of this tight spot I had to beat a retreat through the back ways. However, before putting my plan into operation, I took several paces back inside the corridor to take cover as well as to observe methodically with binoculars the side of the road in my view, hoping anxiously to spot some friendly presence.

At that moment, a bit set back from the carriage entrance of a building next to that from where I had just been set on, I spotted Rostaing [his company commander] who, it seemed to me, was peacefully doing his exercises, slapping himself on the back and thighs. He was some metres from the enemy!

Although I knew of his legendary qualities of coolness and imperturbability I could not help but be a little astounded for several moments. Then, very quickly, on seeing the white and ochre cloud forming around him, I simply understood that he was shaking off the rubble dust in which his uniform was covered. In fact, afterwards, he told me that he had just been hit by a falling balcony.

When the fire resumed from the corridor next to that where he was trying to give back human form to the 'fellow of plaster' who had emerged from the rubble of the debris, Rostaing immediately interrupted his exercises. I saw him slip along the wall so as to place himself as close as possible to the enemy corri-

---

1   Letter to the author, 21/2/99, abridged.

dor. From the shelter of the dead angle, he threw a grenade into the doorway and ran in, Sturmgewehr spitting continuous fire. As soon as he entered I crossed the road and rushed in behind him, yelling out his name so as to warn him that I was coming to the rescue.

At first sight the corridor was empty, perhaps Ivan had cleared off before the grenade explosion. But no! Near the door opening onto the courtyard, I spotted a small Kalmouk whose arms were full of bottles and I don't know what provisions, peacefully coming through the cellar door. Having spotted us, he opened his mouth in surprise, let go of his spoils, and in less time than one could say it, fled through the double door left open to the courtyard ...

Then, from the far end of the courtyard, we heard voices; one could say a confab of at least ten Russians judging by the different tones of the voices. Therefore, to ward off a renewed attack, I took the pin out of a grenade and, taking cover against the wall, I opened the door and threw the gadget ... Then I sprayed the courtyard with some Sturmgewehr bursts. Unfortunately, as I discovered when I ventured a peep through the door, I had without doubt caused them more fright than real harm, having not thrown the grenade far enough, because they were taking off to the far end of the courtyard towards a way of withdrawal located beforehand—of which all good soldiers would make sure—where I saw them rush jostling each other, some hobbling, without a doubt hit in the legs by my fire.

I then looked for Rostaing and I spotted him on his knees in a corner of the corridor near the carriage entrance. Was he wounded? I approached him and discovered that he was bending over one of our comrades stretched out on the tiled floor in a pool of blood ... Before this awful sight, the idea suddenly came to me that it was perhaps us who had struck him down and it was with relief that I heard him murmur: "Ah! It's you, lads, I was expecting you!" I immediately recognised our comrade. It was Rosfelder, a brave Alsatian *adjudant*, who had not wanted his late thirties to make him an 'Etapenschwein'. Despite this handicap of age, he had managed to come to Berlin with 'his' youngsters. Rostaing spoke to him in a voice that I did not know he had, a voice that was low, soft, tender, almost imploring: "Hold on, old brother, we'll get you out of here, we'll get you back." Rosfelder, alas, who had been hit in the stomach, continued to lose a lot of blood that we could not stop. And now we know that he is going to die in several moments. He opened his mouth several times as if he wanted to speak to us, but we heard no longer any words that he seemed to want to tell us, and which only made his lips tremble in a spasmodic movement. Bent over him, we finally deciphered some words that he managed to articulate: "Meine Frau! Meine Frau!" Rostaing took his hand and pressed it into his, and me, eyes full of tears, I caressed with my trembling fingers his bloodless brow, very sticky with sweat. I felt at that point his head lift in one last start of life. Rostaing, who could not feel this movement from Rosfelder, whose strength revealed all his hopelessness as well as the last willpower to push back death, nevertheless saw on our comrade's face the full horror of this fight, and he could not, no more than me already, hold back the tears, nor control the sobs that nervously shook his body of *dur à cuire* [a 'tough nut'].

Both of us, then, to show better that we were not going to abandon him, we bent a bit closer over the one who had betrayed *soldatenglück* [the luck of a soldier] of which he had often spoke when evoking his long military career.

We bent over almost touching his face, our gazes fastened on his whose intensity, that I had trouble seeing through my tears, grew from moment to moment and became so unbearable that I had to force myself not to look away.

Some seconds went by which seemed to us very long, then his head fell back and on his lips, suddenly still, we could no longer read his moving supplication of "Meine Frau! Meine Frau!" I wiped his face with the back of my hand and my blurred eyes believe they saw his mouth part as if he was going to be able to confide to us distinctly his last message for the one with whom he had shared his life.

Leaving the body of Rosfelder where it lay Malardier and Rostaing went back to the fighting. The three of them were wearing the field-grey uniform of the Germany Army and collar insignia of the SS runes, but on their left sleeve was a *tricolore* shield. Yes, they were French. And they were volunteers serving with the Waffen-SS, the armed branch of the SS, which is not to be confused with the mainly political and bureaucratic Allgemeine-SS (General SS) or the SS-Topenkopfverbände (SS Death's Head Units) used to guard the concentration camps.[2]

This book is the story of the more than seven thousand Frenchmen like Rosfelder, Malardier, and Rostaing who served in the ranks of the Waffen-SS. Frenchmen of whom author Jean-François Deniau wrote[3]:

Les dates d'engagement des Français qui ont choisi de servir dans la SS mèritent réflexion: très tard, en 1944, alors que l'Allemagne a déjà perdu évidemment la guerre. Quant aux âges des volontaires, dix-huit à vingt ans pour la plupart.

2   While Totenkopf troops were assimilated into the Waffen-SS as the nuclei of new units or as reinforcements for existing units, it must be noted that at no time did Frenchmen of the Waffen-SS ever serve in any concentration or extermination camp.

3   Deniau, "*Mémoires de trois vies*".

CHAPTER 1

The Formation of the Sturmbrigade and the *Milice française*

The Defeat and the Armistice

In the summer of 1940, few would have expected the French Army, the 'greatest army in Europe', to be defeated by that of Germany, but it was and after only six weeks of blitzkrieg. It was a disaster. On 14th June 1940, the victorious German Army entered Paris, which had been proclaimed an open city days before. Christian de la Mazière, who would later serve with the French division of the Waffen-SS, said of the armies of Germany and France[1]:

> And Germany was triumphant. Wherever her armies went they were victorious. I must say that the German Army at that time made a great impression on young people. The sight of those German soldiers, stripped to the waist ... Let me remind you, if I may, that I am the son of a soldier, I am a soldier myself, and I had in me a great sense of responsibility, of hierarchy, discipline. A disciplined army is very important for people like us. For the first time we saw an army which was all we had dreamed ours might be. The French Army was made up of rather sloppy recruits, not exactly the kind of soldier that puts fear into the heart of the mob. It is a terrible thing to say, but it must be said. It is the truth.

On 17th June 1940, President Lebrun called upon Marshal Pétain, the eighty-four-year-old hero of Verdun, to form a new government. He accepted.[2] Within less than a week, on 22nd June 1940, to limit the disaster of the defeat, he had signed an armistice with Germany.

Compared to the fate suffered by other conquered nations, Czechoslovakia and Poland, and even the likes of Holland and Belgium, the armstice terms imposed on France seemed almost moderate. France was divided into two, separated by a demarcation line. The French government would have complete sovereignty over the unoccupied zone, the so-called 'free' zone, which consisted of some two-fifths of the country, and would also facilitate the administration of the occupied zone by the Germans. She was granted a Metropolitan army of one hundred thousand men. Moreover, her Navy and Empire remained intact and there was no mention of Alsace-Lorraine.[3]

The government installed itself at the town of Vichy in the unoccupied zone. Pétain enjoyed popular support from the French people. 'For the present, he was

---

1   Ophulus, "The sorrow and the pity", pages 49–50.
2   On 12th July 1940, Pétain named himself Head of the State.
3   Alsace-Lorraine was later annexed to the Reich. Also, *départements* Nord and Pas de Calais were placed under German military administration in Belgium.

the father who would protect them from the worst'.[4] He was adored. The cult of Pétainism grew swiftly. His picture was everywhere to be seen. He spoke of a 'National Revolution', a political programme to remake a new France, and in contrast to the parliamentary chaos of the Third Republic, which was made responsible for the shameful defeat and the present ruin of France, he would build an authoritarian state. Against the former republic's values of Liberty, Equality, and Fraternity, he preached those of Work, Family, and Country. To promote a new morality, he stressed discipline, order, and respect for authority.

Most members of the Vichy government adopted towards the Germans a policy of *attentisme*, 'wait and see'. Then, on 30th October 1940, days after meeting Hitler at Montoire and shaking hands, Pétain said on the radio:

> It is in all honour and in order to maintain the unity of France—a unity of ten centuries within the framework of the constructive activity of the new European Order—that I am today pursuing the path of collaboration ... This collaboration must be sincere ... Until today I have spoken to you in the language of a father. Today I speak to you in the language of a leader. Follow me. Put your faith in France eternal.

But what was the meaning of the term 'collaboration'? To Pétain, it signified joint arrangements between the occupiers and the occupied. It was a necessity to *éviter le pire*. Simply put, it was survival. He foresaw economic and administrative collaboration, which he said was inevitable, but not military collaboration.[5]

However, by early 1941, a number of nationalist political parties had emerged in the occupied zone, which desired a closer union with Germany than that envisaged by Vichy. The most important were the *Parti Populaire Français*, which was on the right of the political spectrum, and the *Rassemblement National Populaire*. They flayed Vichy for its continuing policy of *attentisme*.

The collaborationist parties were political rivals, constantly at war among themselves for political advantage. They were tolerated by the occupying power and, when it suited, supported.[6] They never represented a serious threat to Vichy.[7]

---

4   Dank, page 28.
5   Of note is that some historians (see E. Jackel, "*Frankreich in Hitler's Europe*"; A. Milward, "*The New Order and the French Economy*"; R.O. Paxton, "*Vichy France: Old Guard and New Guard, 1940–1944*") have concluded that it was first and foremost the French and not the Germans who wanted to collaborate.
6   It is interesting to note that 'German individuals or agencies supporting French collaborationist interests were often working for the promotion of their own careers or political importance' (Kingston, "*Collaboration in France*", page 54).
7   It was the Germans who kept the Vichy regime 'in power'. Arguably, Germany, which desired economic rather than political collaboration from France, had more 'need' of the Vichy regime than the collaborationist parties. Through Vichy and its civil servants, the French economy worked to support the German war effort. Indeed by the autumn of 1943, France had become the most important supplier of raw materials, foodstuffs and manufactured goods to Germany. Moreover, for the first two years of the Occupation, Vichy, through the Police, had kept order in France. Also, the Germans remained suspicious of the nationalist sentiment of some collaborationist parties.

The Paris collaborationist parties greeted with great excitement Hitler's attack on the Soviet Union on 22nd June 1941 and temporarily united to create the *Légion des Volontaires Français contre le Bolchevisme* (Legion of French Volunteers against Bolshevism), usually known as the LVF, to participate in the campaign. A purely 'private' affair, the LVF did not have the official support of Vichy, although Marshal Pétain did give it his personal blessing. In spite of the assurances that they had been given, the volunteers of the LVF soon found themselves in the *feldgrau* of the German Army and not in French uniform.

The N.S.K.K. Motorgruppe Luftwaffe[8]

There were, however, a smaller number of French citizens more willing to don the German uniform of the auxiliary transport corps N.S.K.K.[9] In 1941, Charles-Gilbert Robba, born on 30th January 1910, 'privately' enlisted in the N.S.K.K. and was trained at Vilvoorde, Belgium. He was then sent to Poland with a munitions convoy that 'melted away' en route like snow in the sun. Eight days later he was back at Diest, Belgium. 'More or less demobilised some [of his compatriots] returned to France as workers, the others vanished into thin air'.

During the winter of 1941–1942, an all-French unit of the N.S.K.K. with a German cadre was engaged on the Eastern front in the region of Leningrad. This is all the more surprising because the N.S.K.K. did not officially open its ranks to French volunteers until early 1942.

The prime mover was Pierre Costantini, the head of French political party *Ligue Française*. In the late summer of 1941, with great enthusiasm, he had set about forming a French branch of the Luftwaffe for the many airmen who had joined the LVF. This new formation was known as the *Légion des Aviateurs Français*, sometimes called the *Aviateurs Volontaires Français*. Costantini found it offices at first in 5, rue de la Chaussée d'Antin, Paris, a stone's throw from the headquarters of the *Ligue* and then, from November 1941, in 1, rue Godot de Mauroy, between La Madeleine and the Opera.

Costantini continued to lobby the Germans, wishing to see himself at the head of the squadron he intended to raise. The Germans responded by opening in 1, rue Godot de Mauroy[10] a recruiting office for a *Corps Automobile de Volontaires*

---

8   See Mounine, article "*Le bataillon français du N.S.K.K.-Motorgruppe Luftwaffe*". Since the publication of this article, Mounine has received a large number of unpublished papers. He has kindly shared a brief overview of these papers with the author.

9   On 1st May 1931, the N.S.K.K. (Nationalsozialistisches Kraftfahrkorps, the National Socialist Motor Transport Corps) was established from the N.S.A.K. (Nationalsozialistisches Automobil Korps, the National Socialist Motor Car Corps). At first a branch of the SA, the N.S.K.K. became an independent party organisation when the SA was reorganised after its entire leadership was purged in the Night of the Long Knives.

     In peacetime the mission of the N.S.K.K. was the promotion of motor transport and National Socialist ideology, as well driving and motor mechanics training. The war brought the N.S.K.K. new responsibilities, including the transportation of supplies and personnel, and the forming and training of Transport companies consisting of non-German personnel.

10   Presumably the *Légion des Aviateurs Français* was now dissolved or soon after.

Antibolcheviques [Motor Corps of Anti-Bolshevik Volunteers], soon redesignated the N.S.K.K. Motorgruppe Luftwaffe.[11] Recruits were required to sign on for the duration of the war.[12]

Apparently, the German decision to open the N.S.K.K. to French volunteers had more to do with propaganda than combat. *Capitaine* Troupeau, the *secrétaire général* of the *Ligue Française*, ran the recruiting office.[13] Troupeau was the brother-in-law of General Bridoux, Vichy's Secretary of State for War. Also of note is that the French N.S.K.K. attracted the attention of the French 2° *bureau* and the German Abwehr.[14]

Recruiting was conducted throughout the whole of France, but concentrated mainly in the occupied zone. The Pétainist and anti-Communist autonomous youth movement *Les Jeunes du Maréchal* [the Marshal's youth or young], which had only and paradoxically operated in the occupied zone, far from its namesake in Vichy, actively recruited French teenagers for the N.S.K.K. from among high schools and colleges.[15] Also, many recruits were ex-LVF.

On 21st July 1942, the first one hundred and fifty French recruits left Paris for the N.S.K.K. training centre at Vilvoorde, outside Bruxelles, where they were issued with uniforms and commenced basic military training. They wore the blue-grey uniform of the Luftwaffe with N.S.K.K. ranks and insignia, and on the upper left sleeve a tricolore shield surmounted by a double-headed axe, the

11   In the summer of 1940, the N.S.K.K. Regiment Luftwaffe was formed for the purpose of delivering munitions to forward airfields in France. Over the next three years this formation went under a variety of designations:
N.S.K.K. Transportregiment Luftwaffe   Autumn 1940 - December 1940
N.S.K.K. Transportbrigade   December 1940 - January 1942?
N.S.K.K. Gruppe Luftwaffe   January 1942 - 11th May 1942
N.S.K.K. Motorgruppe Luftwaffe   May 11th 1942 - July 1943
N.S.K.K. Transportgruppe Luftwaffe   July 1943
The Division also recruited volunteers from Belgium and The Netherlands. French N.S.K.K. volunter Faroux does not recall the conversion of N.S.K.K. Motorgruppe Luftwaffe into N.S.K.K. Transportgruppe Luftwaffe.

12   Lambert and Le Marec, "*Les Français sous le casque allemand*", page 71, and confirmed by French N.S.K.K. volunteers Raga (letter to the author, 16/9/2002) and Faroux (letter to the author, 2/10/2002). However, according to Littlejohn, "*Foreign Legions of the Third Reich vol. I*", page 161, volunteers were required to sign on for a minimum engagement of two years.

13   According to Littlejohn, "*Foreign Legions of the Third Reich vol. I*", page 161, Troupeau was the prime mover behind the formation of an official French section of the N.S.K.K.

14   For example, French N.S.K.K. volunteer Raga knew of two French moles.

15   Littlejohn, "*Foreign Legions of the Third Reich vol. I*", page 132. However, this is disputed by French N.S.K.K. volunteers Raga (letter to the author, 16/9/2002) and Faroux (letter to the author, 2/10/2002). Moreover, Faroux was a member of *Les Jeunes du Maréchal*. In fact, he learnt of the N.S.K.K. from a newspaper advertisement. One such newspaper advertisement ran as follows: "Calling all automobile drivers who understand and approve of the politics of collaboration for a new Europe united and pacified... driving licence holders or not..."

francisque.[16] The choice of the *francisque* may have been derived from the *francisque* of *Les Jeunes du Maréchal* or the *Ligue Française*. Eventually, the recruits were issued with weapons: French Army Lebel rifles!

By the end of 1942, a first company of about two hundred men, who were largely from the occupied zone, had been raised at Schaffen, some fifty kilometres east of Vilvoorde. Many were young and had enlisted out of a spirit of adventure and a taste for uniforms.[17] A second company of French recruits was subsequently raised at Diest, which was followed by a third. The French companies may have been grouped as a battalion.[18]

On 18th December 1942, the day he turned sixteen, François Faroux volunteered for the N.S.K.K. at the recruiting office in Paris. Although a member of *Les Jeunes du Maréchal*, he was not politically motivated. He needed to get away from home. And with no skills to his name and no job, he chose to sign up for the army rather than enter religion. Moreover, he wished to give the lie to the horror stories of German atrocities on which he had grown up.[19] His father, who had sympathies with the P.P.F., did not disagree with his son's decision.

Faroux was dispatched to Bruxelles by train and arrived on 12th January 1943. More than six months of recruit training were to follow at Vilvoorde, Diest, Schaffen, and Grammont, west of Bruxelles. The drilling was hard, the discipline tough, and the rations poor. He received rifle and anti-tank weapons training. Most of the instructors were German. A few were from Alsace. Most were convalescents. He recalls heated, sometimes violent political arguments between the supporters of Doriot, Déat, *Croix de Feu*[20] and even some former Cagoulards or so they claimed. He did not get involved. He was too young for all of that. Besides his main worry was food, describing the daily rations as 'plain ridiculous' for a growing lad of sixteen.

In March 1943, Faroux swore an oath of loyalty to Hitler. This made him proud, describing the oath as the 'consequence of his engagement'. At the end of March, he attended a training course for medical orderlies at Forest, a suburb of Bruxelles. It was a veritable refuge for homosexuals and all too quickly did he understand why he had been sent there! Thus to keep his virtue intact, each evening after soup, he returned to sleep with his 'Column'.[21] Thankfully the course only lasted two weeks, after which he was promoted to the rank of Obersturmmann.

---

16   French N.S.K.K. volunteer Raga was welcomed into the N.S.K.K. at Vilvoorde by a French Sturmführer who referred to the tricolore badge by saying: "It is a piece of French territory that you wear on your arm!"

17   Mabire, page 39.

18   An N.S.K.K. battalion contained three companies (Kompanien).

19   One such story was that the Germans would cut off the hands of the civilian population.

20   Founded in 1928, the *Croix de Feu* [Cross of fire] grew under the charismatic de La Rocque, a retired Lieutenant Colonel, to number some half a million members by the time it too was banned in 1936. Thereupon the CF became the Parti Social Français, the P.S.F. The CF was more right wing than fascist.

21   An N.S.K.K. Company contained ten columns (Kolonnen).

Meanwhile, on 2nd February 1943, the nineteen-year-old Henri Raga volunteered for the N.S.K.K. He came from a nationalist and military family, but was shaped by the events that marked France from 1936 up to his enlistment.

Raga's reaction to the defeat of June 1940 was one of incomprehension and sadness. He desired to fight, but *Maréchal* Pétain, who he respected, was doing his utmost to keep France out of the conflict. In July 1940, with some comrades of his age, he tried to reach the 'free' zone from where he hoped to travel and join the Army in England or failing that the one in Africa, but could not cross the guarded demarcation line.

As time passed Raga became less and less anti-German; French pre-war propaganda had started to wear thin. The German attack on the Soviet Union on 22nd June 1941, which made him realise that this new conflict engaged the whole of Europe, turned him into a Germanophile.

Raga remained troubled. He regarded his life as mediocre and morally uninteresting, while much of the European youth was fighting for an ideal. In August 1942, he enlisted in the French Navy. It was a family tradition. His father had more than twenty years service in the Navy. But the 'sabotage' of the French fleet in November 1942 freed him from all sentimental connections and he now took the time to think about his next move, no longer distracted by filial respect.

He made contact with the LVF but came away disappointed because he believed the LVF to be the French Army of old, to which he had no inclination, and also the influence of the political parties of the day within the LVF was too great. Indeed, the officers and NCOs he met were more concerned about the political party to which he belonged rather than his reasons for enlistment and personal convictions. Ironically, he was not a member of a political party. And nor were his parents.

Then he contacted the N.S.K.K. which seemed to fit his aspirations better. He told his parents. They were disorientated. His father took the prospect of his son in a German uniform badly and his mother feared for his life, but they still gave him moral support.

On 9th February 1943, he left Gare du Nord, Paris, for Vilvoorde, Bruxelles, where he met and made friends with François Faroux. At the start of March 1943, he was sent to Schaffen and was assigned to the forming 3rd Company, 6th Regiment[22], otherwise the 3/6. He fully expected to join the other French N.S.K.K. companies in Russia, the 1st Company had been in Russia since January and the 2nd Company had just left for Russia[23], but they were returned to Diest at the end of March 1943. One reason for the return of the 2nd Company was the condition of the equipment passed to it, which had been abused and run into the ground by its previous owners![24] Thereupon the personnel of both the 1st Company and the 2nd Company had the choice to continue or work in German factories. In this way, very few men of the 2nd Company chose to 'fight on'.

Around the same time as the return of the French companies from Russia, the French battalion was reorganised as the 2nd battalion, 4th Regiment[25], otherwise the II/4, under the command of Staffelführer Joseph Seigel. Company 3/6 became

22   The 6th Regiment was formed in April 1942.
23   They were put at the disposal of Luftgau Rostov/Don.
24   Correction to the original English edition.

Company 4/II under Kompanieführer Sturmführer Hans Ströhle. The remaining personnel of Companies 1/6 and 2/6 were used to form Company 5/II.

Henri Raga was assigned to the 3rd Column of the 4th Company under Kolonneführer Truppführer Rupp (known as 'Riton') and François Faroux to the 4th Column of the 4th Company under Frenchman Kolonneführer Hauptscharführer Soyer, who was one of the very few French *chefs*. André Henriot, the son of Philippe Henriot, who would later become Vichy's Minister of Information, also 'soldiered' in the 4th Company. He and Faroux were good friends [and would remain so after the war].

To Raga, Rupp was hard, but fair and open. He recalls the time Rupp assembled the Column and had translated (he did not speak a word of French): "I am Prussian and I don't like the French." The Frenchmen replied to him: "That's lucky, we don't like the Prussians." Then there was the time Staffelführer Seigel organised a competition between the barrack rooms one Sunday morning. The prize was a radio set. Raga recounts:[26]

> Truppführer Rupp came into our barrack room about one hour before the inspection: beds not made, the barrack room not swept, nothing put away! Rupp, self-effacing, did not even react. The officers arrived, led by the Staffelführer, the door opened, and behind every one Rupp, anxious, preparing himself for the worst of reprimands when he heard 'Fine, perfect, very good' said by the Staffelführer. After the officers left, he entered the barrack room and this is what he saw: an enlargement of a photo of the Staffelführer in a quite beautiful frame placed on a table covered with a blanket and several small flowers around the photo. He looked at us all, smiled, and left us saying: "Great swindler." Of course our barrack room won the radio set.

Like Faroux, Raga found the training at Schaffen hard, explaining that the weather was miserable and that there was little to eat. Things improved when he was dispatched to Grammont late April 1943.

In July 1943, when Rupp left to join the Wehrmacht, he had requested a transfer, the members of his Column clubbed together to offer him a gold-rimmed amber cigar holder. He was touched. They would miss him.

Faroux and Raga would both serve with the N.S.K.K. for 'the duration of the war'. However, some Frenchmen viewed the N.S.K.K. as little more than a stepping stone to their ultimate goal of joining the Waffen-SS.

In early March 1943, French N.S.K.K. of a company at Vilvoorde began to 'desert' to Waffen-SS barracks or nearby recruitment centres. Among them were Boulmier, Delsart, Fayard, Labourdette, Le Meignan, Martret, and Robba.[27]

---

25   According to Raga, letter to the author of 19/9/2001, the French battalion inherited the designation of the 2nd battalion, 4th Regiment from a Dutch battalion disbanded after a tour of duty in Russia.

26   Letter to the author, 19/9/2001.

27   Robba was the first Frenchmen to volunteer for the French unit of the Waffen-SS. Promoted to Oberscharführer, he was attached to SS-Ausbildungslager Sennheim and ran the 'Germ. SS-Werber' section. Detached to the SS-Hauptampt [Main Office], on 14th April 1944 he attended SS-Junkerschule Tölz. Promoted to Untersturmführer, he commanded one of the mortar platoons of the 8/57 of

Martret volunteered for the Waffen-SS because his family was on good terms
with the Germans, he and his family was anti-bolshevist and he had a great interest
in military life. The SS had fascinated him ever since the day he had been present at
the parade of elements from SS Division 'Totenkopf' in the streets of Vierzon. The
sight of motorcyclists with leather raincoats was etched in his memory. He did not
belong to any political party or movement. His father, however, had been a
member of the once popular, but short-lived right-wing *Solidarité Française* (SF).[28]

In the end, after a war of words between the N.S.K.K. and the Waffen-SS, this
transference was encouraged; an SS representative came to Vilvoorde and appealed
for volunteers.[29] Of the twenty men of Costabrava's 'group',[30] fifteen decided there
and then to enlist in the Waffen-SS. In fact, seventeen-year-old *Niçois* Fernand
Costabrava was the first to sign up. A militant in the *jeunesses doriotistes*,[31] he had
enlisted in the N.S.K.K. following the death of François Sabiani[32] because he was
too young to join the LVF.

Those Frenchmen volunteering for the Waffen-SS from the N.S.K.K. and at
the recruiting centres of SS-Ersatzkommando Bruxelles and Antwerpen were first
sent to SS-Ausbildungslager (otherwise called SS-Vorschule) Schotten in the scenic
setting of a chateau. As its designation suggests, Schotten was a training and preparatory depot whose primary role was to welcome the volunteers to the Waffen-SS
and then form them into a convoy which could then be sent on to a unit or a
training establishment. Thus, most volunteers passed through Schotten within a
matter of weeks, unless they were unlucky enough to arrive there just after a convoy

'Charlemagne', following which he again joined the staff of the SS-HA. He
worked with Gamory-Dubourdeau. During the battle of Berlin he led a
kampfgruppe of German SS men in the quarter of Moabit. Captured by the
Russians, handed over to the French authorities, he was condemned to ten years
hard labour and stripped of his French nationality with *interdiction de séjour* (an
order denying access to specified places). He died on 20th March 1993.

28   Launched in June 1933 by millionaire François Coty, an anti-Communist, the
Solidarité Française claimed a total membership of 315,000 in December 1933.
However, its fall was just as dramatic and by June 1934, because of financial
problems and internal dissension, the SF was in shambles. During that period it
was, according to police authorities, the largest right-wing movement in France.
After 1934 the SF limped on with a hardcore of militants. Banned in June 1936
as a paramilitary league, the SF reconstituted itself as the *Amis de la Solidarité
Française* [the friends of French Solidarity]. Like all of the other major French
right-wing parties of the interwar period, the SF had its own uniformed 'shock
troops'.

29   Mabire, page 42. Curiously, both Faroux and Raga do not recall the Waffen-SS
approaching them.

30   Ibid. The designation of 'group' was probably an N.S.K.K. 'column' of 28 men.

31   Mabire, page 38. The *jeunesses doriotistes* was presumably the *Jeunesses Populaires
Française* (J.P.F.), the youth branch of Jacques Doriot's *Parti Populaire Français*
(P.P.F.).

32   François Sabiani, the son of the leader of the P.P.F. in Marseille, was killed on 2nd
June 1942 while serving with the LVF on the Eastern Front. He became the first
'hero and martyr' of the P.P.F. on the Eastern Front.

had left. No more than two companies were ever present at Schotten at any one time.

In the short time available to the training personnel at Schotten to prepare the volunteers, the former 'Leibstandarte' NCOs and officers could do little more than issue their 'pupils' with an assorted range of equipment, begin their physical (sports) training programme and enlighten them on close order drill. But the volunteers noted that they were still without weapons.

By SS standards, the depot 'regime' was very relaxed; each and every day the volunteers could go out into the town. Indeed, one Frenchmen, a Ch'timi[33], recalled that 'after eight days at Schotten some even obtained permission to return home in the North to settle some family matters'. The departure of his convoy was marked by 'a ceremony full of the usual decorum' organised in a Flemish town.[34] Later he reflected about Schotten: "A life of luxury compared to what awaited us at Sennheim."

From Schotten, the French volunteers were sent on to SS-Ausbildungslager Sennheim near Cernay in Alsace. Sennheim was the name given to Saint-André Institute (or school) built after the Great War as an orphanage housing handicapped children and the mentally sick, but now employed as a training camp.

By early July 1943, some fifty N.S.K.K. deserters had arrived at Sennheim. They were incorporated into international companies of Germanic volunteers. Under the watchful eye of German, Flemish, and Dutch NCOs, they underwent basic training.

And yet there was still no official agreement between Vichy and the German authorities authorising recruitment of French volunteers by the Waffen-SS, despite some political activity of late.

The Waffen-SS

The notion of foreign volunteers was not new to the Waffen-SS. The victories of 1940 provided the Waffen-SS with a vast new recruiting ground and volunteers were accepted from the so-called 'Nordic' countries of Norway, Denmark and Sweden, and from the 'Germanic' areas of North Western Europe such as Holland and Flanders. In this way, the Waffen-SS formed two new regiments, 'Nordland' and 'Westland'.

The German attack on the Soviet Union on 22nd June 1941 brought offers of military support from most of the occupied countries, as well as from the Independent State of Croatia, and neutral Spain. On 29th June, Hitler gave his approval to the formation of legions of foreigners who wished to participate in the 'European crusade against Bolshevism'. The Waffen-SS was made responsible for the legions from the Germanic countries and the Wehrmacht for those from the Non-Germanic countries, including France.

By 1943, faced with huge losses on the Eastern Front, Germany was in need of fresh manpower. On 30th January 1943, Hitler authorised the recruitment of French volunteers by the Waffen-SS. The French volunteers were to form a regiment by the name of *Karl der Grosse* [Charlemagne]. RF-SS Himmler was instructed accordingly.

33   A Ch'timi is a native of the *Pas-de-Calais* and the adjoining *Départment du Nord.*
34   In fact, each departure was marked in a different Flemish town.

However, for the past two years since the very start of the occupation, a small number of individual French citizens had already been serving in the ranks of the Waffen-SS. During 1942, many of those who volunteered their services enlisted as 'Flemings born in Northern France', hence called Ch'timi. Of the estimated three hundred 'private enlistments', many served with premier Waffen-SS divisions 'Totenkopf' and 'Wiking'. At least two Frenchmen served with 'Leibstandarte Adolf Hitler'.

In the spring of 1943, various German agencies in France raised the matter of a French regiment of the Waffen-SS. SS officials representing Brigf. Oberg, the Höhere SS und Polizeiführer[35] in France, contacted and discussed the matter with different French groups, including Darnand's *Milice française* and Doriot's *Parti Populaire Français* (P.P.F.). However, only Doriot was ready to commit himself to this new formation.

For his part, Otto Abetz, the German ambassador to Occupied France, discussed the matter in what has been described as a prudent manner with a number of officials of the Vichy Government who were friends of his. Secretary of state Marion and Ambassador de Brinon did not dismiss the idea of a 'pure SS regiment' but preferred to see the creation of a regiment that would belong to a French institution, that of the *Légion des Volontaires Français contre le Bolchevisme* (LVF). Undoubtedly such a solution would give Vichy some influence, if not control, over the new regiment. Needless to say, this was not the official 'welcome' that Oberg had wished to hear.

While continuing to seek a mutual political solution with Vichy, Brigf. Oberg pressed ahead with the recruitment of French volunteers for regiment *Karl der Grosse*.

A recruiting office, called Ersatzkommando Frankreich der Waffen-SS, was opened at 24 avenue du Recteur-Poincaré in Paris. It was run by SS-Hstuf. Alfred Nikles. SS-Schtz. Jean Balestre, the former chief of the ultra-collaborationist Vichy youth movement *Les Jeunes du Maréchal* (the Marshal's Lads) who had deserted the cause of the N.S.K.K. for that of the Waffen-SS, worked out of the same office as a *referent* (reporter) for Ergänzungsstelle der Waffen-SS Frankreich.[36]

---

35   As the head of the SS and police, the HSSPf was responsible for internal security.

36   Balestre would later claim that he enlisted in the 'German Army' on the order of 'his *chefs* of the Resistance' and that his role was to help Jews to escape. He further claims that in 1944 he was arrested by the Germans as he was about to dynamite the Waffen-SS recruiting office and sent to Dachau. However, in response, if he was caught red-handed in the act of dynamiting the Ersatzkommando Frankreich der Waffen-SS in Paris, the Germans would have undoubtedly sent him before a firing squad rather than to Dachau. In addition, some sources have a less honourable explanation for his arrest. Nevertheless, after the war, on his repatriation to France, he was denounced, arrested and interned at Fresnes prison in Paris for two years. Yet, when the *Cour de justice* judged his case, he was exonerated of collaboration; testimonials from the Minister for war veterans, from the Minister for the Armed forces and from the Minister for Defence revealed that he had been resisting since 1942. (*Le Point* No 736, October 1986.)

Towards 1000 hours on Monday 15th March 1943, André Bayle from Marseille, aged only sixteen and a half, stepped into Ersatzkommando Frankreich der Waffen-SS and volunteered for the European Waffen-SS.

European in outlook, Bayle wanted to defend Europe from the Reds, the enemy of Europe, and from the Anglo-Amercians, who were also anti-European. In 1936, he attended the Olympic Games in Berlin with his parents and was totally seduced by what he saw in Germany, including Hitler, who had only been in power for some three years. 'The population seemed happy in a grandiose, organised and clean environment. Pensions were already instituted, as well as Social Society. Calm reigned'.[37] This was in contrast to the economical and political chaos back in France. He blamed the Popular Front government for the moral decline of the country and for her defeat in May 1940. Nevertheless, he did not belong to any political party.

He was proud of the Colonial Empire and the Navy, which the armstice 'safeguarded', but the brutal English attack on the Navy at Mels-el-Kebir, the aborted assault on Dakar, and the seizure of colonies in Central Africa were not the friendly acts of a former ally. In this way, they 'deprived France of the defence of its empire, leaving it to the mercy of the firstcomers: the English and their loyal supporter de Gaulle'.[38]

A Sea Scout, Bayle had wanted a career in the Navy, but that was out of the question after the fleet was scuttled at Toulon on 27th November 1942. He was stunned that the sailors had not fought to the bitter end, like so many before them. They had 'spoilt' their honour and that of the French Navy and no excuse could absolve them.[39]

With Toulon, the time had now come for Bayle to act and participate in the war of his generation. Attentisme was not for him. On the morning of 10th March 1943, he saw some young French workers leaving for Germany and thought to himself: "Why them and not me? I'm off!" He rallied to the camp of Europe, a united Europe against Bolshevism, which the Waffen-SS best represented.

After the formalities, Bayle was sent to Clignancourt barracks. Two days later, he left for Sennheim in Alsace. Also among the first to volunteer and sign up for the duration of the war was Henri Kreis, not yet 18 and of Swiss origin.

One French volunteer said of his decision to enlist:[40]

In 1940, the German soldiers had filled me with admiration and horror. In 1943, they began to inspire pity in me. I knew that they were facing the entire world and I had a feeling that they were going to be defeated.

After Stalingrad and El Alamein, we hardly ever saw any more tall blond athletes. In the streets of Paris, I passed pale seventeen or eighteen year old adolescents with helmets too large for them and old Mausers of the other war. Sometimes also old men with sad eyes. We called them mockingly: the *Bismarck-Jugend* ...

37   Bayle, "*De Marseille à Novossibirsk*", page 12.
38   Bayle, "*De Marseille à Novossibirsk*", page 33.
39   Bayle, "*De Marseille à Novossibirsk*", pages 38-39.
40   François Delatour, "*Historia No 32*", page 118.

> But suddenly reappeared small groups of soldiers true to the legend. Tall, silent, solitary, [with] both hardened and childish features. They returned from hell and the Devil was their only friend. On their collar the two 'flashes of lightening' of the Waffen-SS.
>
> I knew that the French were not admitted to this 'Germanic elite'. But I refused to be respected [any] less than a Norwegian or a Dutchmen. Why would I not have the right to fight in what I knew to be the best army in the world?
>
> When I learnt that Degrelle's Walloons were going over to the SS, I guessed that the doors were going to open for us as well. I was among the first to enlist …

Notably, the French volunteers were registered as Walloons because the Vichy Government had still not approved the recruitment of French volunteers by the Waffen-SS.

Vichy gives its rubber stamp of approval

In mid June 1943, Reich ambassador Rudolf Schleier officially informed Pierre Laval, the head of the Vichy Government[41], that the creation of a Waffen-SS regiment of French volunteers would now begin. He also pressed Laval to ensure for this regiment 'the same concessions as those in force for the LVF'.[42] Laval agreed. Also, during the discussions they had about the subject of the formation of the Waffen-SS regiment, mention was made of the *francisque* as collar insignia.

Finally, on Wednesday 22nd July 1943, Laval passed Law No 428 concerning voluntary service in anti-Bolshevist formations. The Law consisted of three articles and read as follows:[43]

Article 1	The French are allowed to enroll voluntarily in French units formed by the German Government (Waffen-SS) for the purpose of fighting Bolshevism outside of France.
Article 2	The members of this unit who actually fight outside state [national] territory shall be entitled to all the benefits promised to the *Légion des volontaires français contre le bolchevisme*.
Article 3	This law shall be published in the *Journal Officiel* and be enforced as a State law.

Thus, for the first time, French volunteers could 'officially' enlist in the Waffen-SS and in a wholly French unit.

Volunteers were required to be physically fit for the demands of military training, a minimum height of 1.65m, and between the ages of seventeen and forty. Those of Jewish blood as well as those who had 'incurred a *condamnation infamante*'[44] were excepted.

---

41   In fact, from April 1942, Laval was, if not in title, the real head of the State.
42   Cited in a telegraph that Minister Schleier sent to Berlin on 20th June 1943.
43   "*Europäische Freiwillige Im Bild*", page 301, with slight modifications.
44   A sentence involving exile or a loss of civil rights.

That same day, a *Comité des Amis de la Waffen-SS* was established under the chairmanship of Paul Marion, the Vichy Minister of Information. One role of the *Comité des Amis de la Waffen-SS* was to organise a vigorous propaganda campaign for recruitment.

The response was a flurry of activity at the various recruitment centres across the country.[45] On 6th August 1943, a press conference announced that more than 1,500 volunteers had already come forward for the medical.[46] And yet, curiously, the press conference noted that they had come forward 'without the slightest propaganda'.

To 'tidy' the paperwork of those 'Frenchmen' who had already enlisted, the Waffen-SS authorities had them sign their enlistment papers again.[47] No longer were they Walloons.

Party politics

Many of the initial volunteers after the publication of Vichy's statutory 'seal of approval' were adherents of the Paris-based collaborationist political parties. Of the first 'official' convoy of French volunteers of the Waffen-SS to arrive at SS-Ausbildungslager Sennheim in early August 1943, half were members of the *Jeunesse franciste*, the youth branch of Marcel Bucard's *Parti Franciste*.

Founded on 29th September 1933, the trappings and ideology of the *Parti Franciste* was modelled upon Italian Fascism rather than German Nazism. Openly declaring itself fascist, the *Parti Franciste* dreamed of a *deuxième révolution française* where 'order would eventually prevail over liberty, the national *corps* and the hierarchic society over individualism, [and] the totalitarian State over all the forces of dissolution'. Like other French political parties of the right, the *Parti Franciste* also adopted a blue shirt whose shade was the lightest of all. Its party militia was known first as the *Corps Franc*, then in 1943 renamed the *Légion Franciste*.

Party leader Marcel Bucard, born in 1895, was a highly decorated World War One veteran who remained haunted by the *esprit du front*. His military background, as well as his incendiary speeches captivated his adherents. His hold over them was total. Originally destined for the priesthood, his Catholic background had undoubtedly appealed to those of a more religious disposition. Indeed some *cérémonies francistes* were adorned with Catholic pomp. Bucard's personal bodyguard, termed the *Main Bleue* (Blue Hand), had been made 'responsible for keeping agitators at a good distance'.

In the summer of 1943, during the *camp des Mille* gathering at Semblançay, near Tours, Bucard had tried to dissuade several tens of his *francistes* from volunteering for the Waffen-SS, but had met with little response. Indeed, 'Bucard had magnified his memories of a former combatant so much that the young *francistes* now believed that nothing could replace military glory, whatever the uniform'.[48]

---

45   Besides the Ersatzkommando Frankreich der Waffen-SS in Paris, volunteers could enlist at the Kommandos der Ordnungspolizei in Angers, Bordeaux, Châlons-sur-Marne, Clermont Ferrand, Dijon, Limoges, Lyon, Marseille, Montpellier, Nancy, Orléans, Poitiers, Rennes, Rouen, Saint-Quentin, and Toulouse.

46   Newspapers reported the very same figure. See *Le Petit Parisien* of 8th August 1943.

47   Bayle, "*De Marseille à Novossibirsk*", page 46-48.

48   Mabire, "*La Brigade Frankreich*", page 50.

For some, the downfall of Mussolini and Fascism had been their final motive for enlisting in the Waffen-SS. Even so the *francistes* promised to wear their blue shirt of France under their Waffen-SS uniform! Pierre Bousquet and Henri Simon were two such *francistes* Bucard could not talk out of volunteering for the Waffen-SS.

Pierre Bousquet and his whole family had joined the Party before the war. As the years passed, his importance within the Party grew and by the time he volunteered for the Waffen-SS he was a member of its *Bureau national* and the leader of the *conseil* national of the *Jeunesse franciste*. This was a far cry from when he was a young kid selling the party newspaper in the streets. Although he hailed from Alsace, he was *tricolore* and in 1939 was a *Sergent aviateur* ready to do battle with the Germans. To Bousquet, the poor performance of the French Army against the Germans in 1940 was a crushing blow and after that debacle 'he no longer believed in the French Army'.[49]

The crushing defeat also turned the world of Henri Simon upside down. Born in 1919 in Lorraine, he was raised in 'the cult of heroic patriotism'. Despite the pacifist words of the primary school teacher, he dreamt about the stories of *assault à la fourchette* [assault with 'pig-sticker' fixed]. Besides, his first name of Henri was in memory of an uncle, a *sous-lieutenant d'infanterie*, who had fallen in combat in Alsace.

By the age of twelve, Simon was already interested in politics and a reader of *L'Action Française* [the newspaper of the right wing movement *L'Action Française* headed by Charles Maurras].Little by little, the thoughts of Maurras impregnated his spirit. The Stavisky scandal and the bloody night of 6th February 1934[50] reinforced his disgust for parliamentary democracy.

In 1938, Simon enlisted in the French Navy, becoming a *quartier-maître des fusiliers-marins* [a leading seaman in the Marines]. Of the defeat, he would never forget the picture of a *capitaine de cor-vette* [a lieutenant commander] 'clearing off with the flag in a oil cloth' or that of 'an officer of a ship's crew, a former hero of Dixmude, who was crying his eyes out because he had lost his bags'.[51] This spectacle of such abandon and such refusal of community interest aroused in him contempt towards his compatriots. At heart, he was still the young boy who admired the *poilu*[52] of the 14/18 war.

Defeat also brought captivity, but he was out within one month after he volunteered to work for the Germans. Fluent in German, Henri Simon became an interpreter and worked for the *Militärverwaltung* [the administrative arm of the *Militärbefehlshaber in Frankreich*—the military command in France] at the city port of Lorient, Brittany. A nationalist through and through, he clashed with Breton separatists and, on one occasion, got into a fight with Dutch

49   Mabire, "*La Brigade Frankreich*", page 50.
50   As a result of the financial scandal, the Right had taken to the streets and, with the Communists fighting side by side, attempted to storm the Chamber of Deputies and bring down the Republic. The insurrection was defeated by a handful of Police at the cost of 16 dead and 655 wounded.
51   Mabire, "*La Brigade Frankreich*", page 51.
52   *Poilu* translates as hairy; while on active service French privates did not shave. *Poilu* is the French equivalent of 'Tommy' in the British Army.

Schutzkommando of the Organisation Todt guarding a *Breiz Atao*[53] meeting. For this, he was punished with one month's imprisonment.

And then, one day during the summer of 1941, while passing through square Alsace-Lorraine, Simon came upon the office of the *Parti Franciste*. On display was a *grand* portrait of a robust man sporting a chestful of military decorations, 'proof valorous acts during the war of his elders'. Simon stood there in awe of this man on the portrait who was, of course, Marcel Bucard, the leader of the *Parti Franciste*. Thereupon Simon became a *franciste*. He went on to run a *section départementale* in the West. He later reflected that the portrait of Marcel Bucard became the 'most deciding object of his destiny'.[54]

Convinced that France was slipping into civil war, Simon had no desire to police his countrymen and thus volunteered for the Waffen-SS.

Pierre Bousquet and Henri Simon were on the first official convoy of French Waffen-SS volunteers to arrive at Sennheim. On this same convoy were volunteers from the *Jeunesse Nationale Populaire* (J.N.P.), the *Jeunesses Populaires Française* (J.P.F.), *Les Jeunes de L'Europe Nouvelle* (J.E.N.), and *La Ligue des Jeunes de France et de l'Empire*.

The *Jeunesse Nationale Populaire* was the youth branch of the *Rassemblement National Populaire* [National Popular Rally]. Established by Marcel Déat on 1st February 1941, the R.N.P. brought together former Socialists and trade unionists with former combatants of the *Union Nationale des Combattants* (U.N.C.), as well as members of Deloncle's *Mouvement Social Révolutionnaire* (M.S.R.).

Although most of the executive members of the RNP were of leftist persuasion, the new movement actually promoted a National Socialist programme. For them, socialism was essentially anti-Marxist.

As for Marcel Déat himself, he began political life as a socialist. The First World War, in which he distinguished himself, leaving as a *simple soldat* and returning as a *capitaine* with *la Légion d'honneur* and five citations, also made him a pacifist. In the post war years, he went into teaching. He became the president of the *Fédération des étudiants socialistes* [Federation of socialist students]. 1926 saw him stand as a candidate of the socialist *Section Française de l'Internationale Ouvrière* [French section of the Workers' International] and enjoy electoral success.

In 1933, Déat called for a revision of Marxism that he labeled Neo-Socialism. To defeat fascism, he argued that the S.F.I.O. had to abandon all talk of class struggle and win middle-class support. Also he no longer advocated parliamentary

---

53   Literally 'Brittany always', this slogan became the title of a Breton separatist review in 1927 and, later, the title of a Breton separatist newspaper. The last issue of '*Breiz Atao*', 27th August 1939, had prophesied French military defeat and that France 'would then have to resign itself to making concessions and collaborating with the Axis, or be subjected in turn to the coup de grâce.'

54   Cera, "*Les raisons de l'engagement de volontaires francais sous l'uniforme Allemand*", page 129. The notion that Simon came to *francisme* after the armistice is also recounted by Mabire, "*La Brigade Frankreich*", page 51. However, in contrast, according to Gaulois, "*Der Freiwillige*", 10/97, Simon joined the *Parti Franciste* at a young age. So which is it? The present author remains undecided. Curiously, all three sources had face-to-face interviews with Simon.

democracy as a means of bringing about socialism, but dictatorship. This, of course, was heresy to the vast majority of members of the S.F.I.O. He was expelled. A number of like-minded 'neo-socialists' left with him to form their own party, the *Parti socialiste de France*. Déat became its *secrétaire général*. He was still anti-Fascist.

From January to June 1936, Déat held office as a cabinet minister, but the 1936 elections and the parliamentary failure of the *'néos'* and his own personal failure before a Communist marked the start of his shift toward the right. In 1939, he got himself elected *député* for Angoulême on a ticket that called itself the 'Anti-Communist Rally'. And yet his famous editorial *mourir pour Dantzig* of 4th May 1939, which argued to plunge Europe into war because of Danzig 'was going a bit too far', placed him in the ranks of the 'Pacifists'.

Then came the war and defeat. Déat now emerged as an enthusiastic supporter of Hitler, National Socialism and collaboration. He was sincere, but ambitious. He believed in the 'revolutionary mission of Germany' and his programme advocated the rebuilding of a France integrated in the 'new Europe'. In this way, France would restore its greatness and legitimate influence. He argued that 'the material necessity compelled Collaboration'. However, during the late summer months of 1940, he failed in his efforts to convince Marshal Pétain to establish a *grande parti unique* [large single party] as a means of integrating France into Hitler's 'new European Order'. His hopes disappointed, he went off with his typewriter to Paris from where he sniped at the Vichy regime in his editorials. Months later, for want of this *grande parti unique,* he formed his own, the *Rassemblement National Populaire*.

The R.N.P. had its own uniformed shock troops, known as the *Légion nationale populaire* (L.N.P.). In its ranks were many militants of Deloncle's M.S.R. party. A red tie was worn, which, according to Déat, was 'a souvenir of Socialism'. In 1943, the L.N.P. was renamed the *Milice nationale populaire* (M.N.P.).

In the autumn of 1941, the internal conflict between Déat and Deloncle, who wanted to take control of the R.N.P., came to a head. Déat removed Deloncle. In this way, the R.N.P. lost much of the right-wing support and militancy Deloncle had brought to it. In 1942, Déat tried once more to form a single party, the *Front Révolutionnaire National* (F.R.N.). The refusal of Doriot to integrate the P.P.F. was a blow to the success of the F.R.N.

Although he enjoyed little support from the Germans Déat continued to call for greater collaboration with Germany. According to one commentator[55]: "He would serve them [the Germans]. He would give them his soul."

Membership of the R.N.P. as a whole is difficult to estimate, but is generally believed to have been between 20,000 and 25,000. It had one rival, the *Parti Populaire Français* (P.P.F.).

The *Jeunesses Populaires Française* was the youth branch of the *Parti Populaire Français* (P.P.F.). Of all the Paris-based collaborationist parties, the P.P.F. was, by far, the largest. Its leader was Jacques Doriot, born on 26th September 1898 in Bresles, near Beauvais. In 1915, at the age of seventeen, he left home. Thereafter Saint-Denis became his home and, in time, the seat of his political triumph.

Doriot also started political life as a socialist, joining the *Jeunesses Socialistes de France* [Socialist Youth of France] in 1916, but four years later he became a 'convert' to Communism. A superb orator, he enjoyed a spectacular rise through the

---

55   Delperrié de Bayac, page 59.

Communist Party (PCF). By 1924, he was at the head of the *Jeunesses communistes* [Communist Youth] and a member of the Central committee of the party, but he was also in prison at la Santé, Paris, for antimilitarist activities. His release came in May 1924 when he was elected to parliament after a most brilliant election campaign.

1929 saw Doriot first break with Communist doctrine and discipline. In favour of co-operation with the Socialists on the common problems of the rights of workers, he found himself shunned by the 'top brass'.[56] He withdrew from the leadership. Nevertheless, he was re-elected to the Chamber of Deputies as a Communist and, in 1931, became the Mayor of Saint-Denis.

In February 1934, the party sent its militants into the streets to fight alongside Rightist organisations against the government. One reason for this call to action was 'a desire to exhibit a display of force against what was called the 'Social-Fascism' of the Socialist Party'.[57] But Doriot still saw the Socialists as allies in the war against Fascism. He was vocal. By June 1934, the party could no longer tolerate his heresies and expelled him for indiscipline. And yet, one month later, the party adopted the policies of Doriot by signing an agreement on 'unity of action' with the Socialists. He was bitter. And so began his march to personal power. He became a most virulent anti-Communist.

On 22nd June 1936, some two years after his expulsion from the PCF, Doriot officially created the *Parti Populaire Français* (P.P.F.). His platform for the new political party was Socialistic, nationalistic, and peculiarly French. Strangely enough, his power base was the Communists of Saint-Denis, most of who were disaffected with the party because of its rigid discipline. Also, unemployment was rife.

The P.P.F. was a great success and, by 1937, had an estimated 200,000 supporters. With Doriot at the helm, the party continued to drift to 'international Fascism'. His hold over the party was absolute.

In 1938, to 'save the peace', the P.P.F. decided to support Hitler's demand on Czechoslovakia. For the nationalists in its ranks, this decision was the final straw. Resignations tore apart the party. In this way, the P.P.F. all but disappeared as a political force of the Right.

At the start of hostilities Doriot was posted to the *24e Régiment Régional de Garde* at Senalis with the rank of *sergent-chef*. He would be cited at the *ordre de l'Armée* and be awarded the *Croix de guerre avec étoile de vermeil*.

The overwhelming defeat and occupation of 1940 brought unexpected prosperity to Doriot, even if Vichy held him 'at arm's length' and German support was slow in coming. Restricted to the Occupied zone, the P.P.F. did operate in the Unoccupied zone under the title of *Mouvement Populaire Français* (M.P.F.). The P.P.F. was only allowed to operate in the Unoccupied zone with 'authorised status' from 28th December 1941, by which time Doriot was in German uniform.

On 22nd June 1941, the day Hitler attacked the Soviet Union, Doriot, who was attending the first P.P.F. congress of the Free zone in Lyons, said: "France cannot simply be a spectator in the decisive battle which has begun and whose issue

56   Dank, "*The French against the French*", page 49.
57   Ibid.

will determine the fate of the entire continent." He proposed the raising of volunteers to fight with the Germans on the Eastern front.

Déat of the R.N.P. and Deloncle of the M.S.R. also came forward to advocate a legion of French volunteers. Accordingly, on 7th July 1941, the leaders of the collaborating parties, including Doriot, met at the Hotel Majestic in Paris to launch a *Légion anti-bolchévique* that was later renamed the *Légion des Volontaires Français contre le Bolchevisme* (LVF). Doriot encouraged his militants to enlist. He too donned the German uniform to fight the Bolshevik beast.

In the early days, the greatest single faction to make up the LVF was from the MSR. That changed in April 1942 when Deloncle ordered his men home. The P.P.F. then became pre-dominant. Indeed, the fanion of the I. Battalion bore the arms of Saint-Denis.

Ambitious, Doriot still lived in hope of coming to power. However, his short-term aspirations were dealt a blow on 21st September 1942 in a letter from Ribbentrop to Otto Abetz: to maintain social order in France, Hitler preferred Laval to Doriot. Undeterred, he held a 'Congress of Power' in Paris from the 4th to the 8th of November 1942. 7,200 delegates attended. However, they may have represented no more than 25,000 members. When Laval banned its closing ceremony at the Velodrome d'Hiver the delegates, in a show of force, paraded along the Champs-Elysées, clashing with the police.

The recruitment of French volunteers for the Waffen-SS offered Doriot one more opportunity to find favour with the German authorities and perhaps political power. The P.P.F. promised to send 600 men into the Waffen-SS. Many were from its youth branch, the *Jeunesses Populaires Française.*

The J.P.F. was founded in May 1942 under the presidency of 'Vauquelin' [real name des Yvetots] when its predecessor, the *Union populaire de la Jeunesse française* (U.P.J.F.), had joined forces with a number of smaller youth organisations. The J.P.F. was against communism, capitalism, Jews, described as 'the direct causes of the degeneracy of our people' and 'instruments of propagation of capitalism', Freemasons and those responsible for the war. With a rallying cry of *'Tenue, Force, Audace'*, the J.P.F. wanted to rebuild France and 'fight on the same front as the German youth, against Bolshevism, the common enemy … '[58]

The *Les Jeunes de L'Europe Nouvelle* (J.E.N.) was the youth branch of the *Groupe Collaboration.* Although equally collaborationist in its political stance, the *Groupe Collaboration* differed from the R.N.P. and the P.P.F. in so much as its aims were principally cultural/intellectual rather than political. European in outlook, with a strong spiritual ethos, this organisation 'supported the moral regeneration which the National Revolution was to bring to a Europeanised France'.[59] In its support for an alliance between France and Germany, the *Groupe Collaboration* arranged lectures, screened German films, promoted German literature, and organised public discussions and other social events. Authorised to function in the Unoccupied zone on 29th December 1941, its middle class and wealthy membership may have peaked at the significant total of 100,000 by mid-1943. Its popularity some commentators have ascribed to its theoretical non-political aspect.

58   Vauquelin, *"Discours de fondation des J.P.F."* (Les documents de la Jeunesse, 1942)
59   *"Collaboration in France"*, page 67.

Less reserved in its pro-German attitude was its youth branch *Les Jeunes de L'Europe nouvelle* [The Youth of The New Europe] founded at the start of the new school year of 1942. Indeed, some sections were even attached to the S.D. and armed for active duty against the resistance. Its creator and chef was Jacques Schweizer, a barrister and pre-war *Jeunesse patriote* (Patriot Youth) militant.[60]

La Ligue des Jeunes de France et de l'Empire was the youth branch of the *Ligue Française*. Headed by Pierre Costantini, a highly decorated World War One pilot, the *Ligue Française* was anti-British[61], anti-Semitic and anti-Bolshevik. The *Ligue* had few adherents, perhaps some 2,000 to 3,000 in October 1941.

A student by the name of Charles Laschett, born on 2nd March 1920, was the sole representative of *Le Front Franc* which was violently anti-Semitic and pro-German. His father, Maurice, figured among those in charge of this 'party' numbering only several hundred adherents. Party leader Jean Boissel was a severely disabled World War One veteran. His son Jean-Jacques Boissel volunteered and served with the N.S.K.K.

Few were the number of volunteers who were not adherents of a political party, but even they spoke of similar, if not the very same, motives for enlisting. For one volunteer, the international Waffen-SS offered an opportunity to find his dream of European Socialism:

My father was a (primary school) teacher. An honest and simple bloke with ideas of his milieu: socialism, peace and Europe … Thanks to him, I discovered Romain Rolland and Germany. I believed the most important thing was to get along among neighbours.

I joined the 'youth hostels'. I discovered there the open air, the sun, friends who came from other countries with their guitars and their songs, and friendship.

I was mobilised in 1939. I waged war in an atmosphere of disorder and cowardice which would not stop until the defeat … I returned to my region, a small sub-prefecture on the banks of the Loire. My father still continued to read *L'Oeuvre*, just like before the war. He admired Marcel Déat. I found he was right sometimes, but the masquerade imitated from the Germans did not really tempt me. Those coloured shirts, those shoulder-belts, those *bérets basques* that seemed to me small and mean, in a word French. What interested me was Europe. Not Germany, Europe. [And] Socialism that spanned a whole continent.

I was still not a militarist, but I believed we had to win the war against the communists who I had never liked, and against the capitalists I had always detested. The LVF did not tempt me because of its *tricolore* side. And besides it had too many regulars and *doriotistes*. In the Waffen-SS, I hoped to find an international army and a sort of socialism in poverty, courage and voluntary discipline.

Some volunteers were from the *1er Régiment de France* (1er R.d.F.). Created by Law No 413 of 15th July 1943, published in the *Journal Officiel* of 28th July 1943, the 1er R.d.F. was, in the words of Laval of 15th June 1943, 'the promise and hope

---

60   François Mitterrand, the one time president of France, was also a member of the *Jeunesses Patriotes*.

61   Following the aggression of the 'hereditary enemy' at Mers-el-Kébir, Costantini declared war on England.

of our new army'; France had been without an army ever since the dissolution of the Armistice Army on 27th November 1942. The 1er R.d.F., however, was placed under the authority of the head of government and not the head of State.

The ranks of the 1er R.d.F. filled with former cadets of military schools Saint-Cyr, Saint-Maixent, Poitiers, Versailles and Saumur whose studies had been cut short by the dissolution of the Armistice Army. Also, such was the influx of students into the 1er R.d.F. that the press dubbed it the *'régiment des bacheliers'*.[62] Jews and freemasons were refused admission to the regiment.

Even though agreements were made between the SS-Hauptamt and the 1er R.d.F. to facilitate the engagement of men in the French Waffen-SS,[63] few 'went over'.

At Sennheim, the French volunteers were assigned to the 1st Company under the command of SS-Ostuf. der Reserve Martin Laue, a former minister in the Reformed Church. Laue had declared to the French volunteers upon their arrival at Sennheim: "To serve France was a duty, but to serve Europe in the Waffen-SS is an honour!"

The 1st platoon was almost exclusively made up of 'deserters' from the N.S.K.K.

On 18th August 1943, Hitler authorised the establishment of the 'Französische SS-Freiw. Grenadier Regiment'. The French SS Volunteer Grenadier Regiment was to have a structure of two battalions, each with four companies. In addition, and notably, the regiment had two infantry gun companies and two anti-tank gun companies.[64]

One month later, the Führer hoped to form a Regiment and a Division of French volunteers.[65]

By SS-FHA order of 22nd October 1943[66], which numbered all Waffen-SS formations and infantry regiments into a numerical sequence according to their chronological dates of formation, the French Regiment became the '8. Franz. SS-Freiw. Gren. Rgt'.[67] Curiously, the order lists the French Regiment under 'Brigaden und Sturmbrigaden'. This suggests that the French Regiment, although it still carried the designation of a regiment, had Brigade status.

Shortly after, on 12th November 1943, the SS-FHA again ordered the renumbering of the Waffen-SS infantry regiments and the 'Franz. SS-Freiw. Rgt' became the 'Franz. SS-Freiw. Rgt 57'.[68] Notably, this time the French Regiment appeared under 'Regimenter'.

---

62   The French word *bachelier* describes a person who has passed the *baccalauréat* [secondary school examination giving university entrance qualification].

63   See report with reference SAM/36003, CARAN.

64   See the undated chart, Yerger, "*Waffen-SS Commanders Krüger to Zimmermann*", page 168. Normally, each infantry regiment had one infantry gun company and one anti-tank company.

65   See SS-FHA, Amt II Org.Abt. Ia/II Tagesbefehl Nr.1297/43 geheim Kommandos 16.9.1943.

66   SS-FHA Amt II Org.Abt. Ia/II Tgb. Nr. 1574/43 g.Kdos, 22.10.43, Anlage 3: III. Brigaden und Sturmbrigaden.

67   However, "*Cloth Insignia of the SS*", page 491, shows the same designation, but without the number.

French recruits continued to arrive at Sennheim. By September 1943, they had filled out the 2nd Company under SS-Oscha. Lang. Notably, the majority of the new intake arrived from Germany. Some were former POWs.

Months earlier, in July, German authorities earmarked a sum of 100,000 Reichsmarks to finance the recruitment of French workers and POWs in Germany for the Waffen-SS.[69]

One such prisoner to volunteer was the thirty-five-year-old Lucien Hennecart.[70] After having tried and been disappointed by all the pre-war French fascist parties, he became a 'Hitlerian'.[71] Nonetheless, when war came, he immediately rallied to the flag. To him, 'France is France'. During May 1940, this convinced fascist fought the Germans, but his old F.M. was no match for the tanks and airplanes of the enemy.

Made a prisoner because somebody senior put his hands up for him, Hennecart ended up in a Stalag in Germany. Behind barbed wire, he was not attracted to either de Gaulle or Pétain. He believed the former was too far away and the latter too weak. Indeed, he wrote to Brasillach[72]: "The war is lost, but I would like to die with weapons in my hands."

Becoming a free worker,[73] Hennecart now found himself in a kommando, but soon tired of 'pushing a wheelbarrow'. Learning that prisoners could enlist in the Waffen-SS, he decided to see 'how it was going on the other side of the barbed wire'.[74]

It could be said that Pierre Ruche was an idealist, coming to the Waffen-SS years after he first tried to gain admittance:

> I did not belong to any political party but from my fourteenth year I was already won over by the cause of National Socialism and before that I had always been a germanophile. I was nevertheless a monarchist but not of *Action Française*.
>
> I had no desire to make war or play at soldiers. It was quite simply the call of blood and race. Since 1815 I was descended from a Prussian who, wounded,

68   SS-FHA Amt II Org.Abt. Ia/II Tgb. Nr. II/9542/43 geh, 12.11.43, Anlage 4: III. Regimenter.

69   Bundesarchiv, Potsdam, R55-1237.

70   See Mabire, page 67, and the anonymous autobiography "*Plutôt au front qu'au stalag*" ['rather at the front than in the stalag'], "*Historia No 32*", page 119. And although the latter is anonymous, there is some similarity between the two.

71   Mabire, page 67.

72   Brasillach was a journalist who wrote for the Fascist Parisian newspaper *Je Suis Partout*.

73   From early 1943 prisoners of war could volunteer to become *Freiarbeiter* (free-workers). Vichy was against this change of designation because the prisoners were no longer protected by their status.

74   "*Plutôt au front qu'au stalag*", "*Historia No 32*". In contrast, according to Mabire, page 67, Hennecart was told that he did not have the right to enlist in the Waffen-SS. However, this did not deter him. And so he took the train to Görlitz where there was a Waffen-SS recruiting office. The rest was just a formality. Or was it? A Gestapo agent was now waiting for him outside. So was it to be the Waffen-SS or back to the stalag? Already a *SS-Freiwillige*, he was not sent back to his stalag.

remained at Paris and got married there. Thus I could not be anything else, for better or for worse …

I never believed at all that I was a fanatic. I simply believe I was a convinced National Socialist. My enlistment was not only the sole product of my germanophilia and my support without restriction for National Socialist ideology more of a great admiration for the Führer. Whereas even [SS-Uscha. Philippe] Merlin[75] [of Abteilung IV, ideological training] had ambitions for France (not for the Republic, nor tricolore …)

From the start I had requested my integration into a purely German unit but paradoxically my impeccable knowledge of the German language stopped me. They had need of me as an interpreter. Thus I ended up by only having personal relations with the Germans. The French eventually regarded me as such and all too quickly as a 'fanatic'.

My enlistment in the SS dates from 1941. In France, on holiday in a small charming village whose name I forget there was billeted an SS unit whose commander played chess with me and of which a very young SS-Ustuf. (Ernst Ritter of Magdeburg) came for walks with me to practice French. It was over a game of chess that I asked the commander if I could enlist in his unit. It took three weeks for his reply: "Today impossible, but later, soon, you can".

His presence at Sennheim was brief, ending when he was posted to SS-Ergänzungsstelle Nordost at Königsberg. Ruche believes that Merlin was responsible for this. Because of his impeccable German he found himself in great demand, even by camp commander SS-Oberführer Fick, when Merlin was not available. This situation was not agreeable to Merlin, who wanted to remain the only German speaker at Sennheim.

Not all recruits were idealists like Ruche. Some were victims of blackmail. Ending up in the suburbs of Vienna, an S.T.O.[76] worker explained:[77]

[It was] an idiot job. A nasty ambience. The majority of the workers were Polaks. People I can't stand. The only distraction, on Sunday: walks along the Danube. With a friend, a lad from Levallois[78], we found ourselves two small, kind 'birds'. But it was forbidden to frequent with German females, especially if they were engaged to soldiers at the front. One day the feldgendarmes fell on us. We ended up at the Gestapo. It seemed that we were 'defilers of the race'. A right fine mess. We risked years of work camps. Arrived a bloke in uniform who told us everything could be sorted out. We just had to enlist and they would forget about it. Thus, rather than end up in the nick, we both signed …

S.T.O. worker Camille Rouvre was also blackmailed into joining the Waffen-SS.[79] One day at the factory he was caught by his foreman making love to a young German girl. When the foreman started to bawl him out in German he lost

75 See Mounine "*Cernay*", pages 318-322.
76 On 16th February 1943, under a law instituting the *Service du Travail Obligatorie* (S.T.O.) Laval and the Vichy government made labour service obligatory for all French males born in 1920, 1921 and 1922.
77 "*Historia No 32*", page 119.
78 A suburb of Paris.
79 See "*Levée d'écrou*", pages 125-126.

his temper and punched him in the face. Two Gestapo agents and a policeman arrived and threatened him with the concentration camp. Then an Oberscharführer of the SS arrived who spoke very good French. This NCO told him that he could only avoid the concentration camp by enlisting in a French formation of the SS, adding that if this formation was not to his liking he could return to France. Rouvre signed up on 13th January 1944. Two days later, he was accompanied to Sennheim.

There were also some romantics among the volunteers. To them, the Waffen-SS offered a gigantic adventure that no French political party could and also a break with the world around them. One such volunteer, a romantic seventeen-year-old philosophy student who had discovered National Socialist Germany through the bearded prophet Alphonse de Châteaubriant[80] and his book *Gerbe des forces*, explained:[81]

> I was against the bourgeois order, that of my parents and my teachers. I believed in all the myths of revolution and youth. My enlistment in the Waffen-SS was above all a rupture with the old world. I wanted to scandalise, why deny it? I have to say I succeeded perfectly …

In September 1943, nineteen-year-old Jean de Misser arrived at Sennheim in the uniform of the N.S.K.K. In May of that year, he had signed up for the N.S.K.K. and was sent to Vilvoorde, Belgium. But as soon as enlistment in the Waffen-SS was made official for Frenchmen he left the N.S.K.K. for the Waffen-SS. He wanted to be a *combattant contre le bolchevisme* in an elite unit. He did not belong to any political party and nor did his parents.

At Sennheim, de Misser was assigned to the 1st platoon of the 5th Company commanded by German SS-Ostuf. Sommer. He noted:

> My instructors were in the image of the Waffen-SS: European. My section commander was a Flemish Rottenführer and my platoon commander a Oberscharführer from Luxembourg.

At Sennheim, all commands were given in German. Many struggled with the language. Laue, whose mother was French, helped out by giving German lessons.

On 13th September 1943, in the somewhat poignant setting of the former chapel, the 1st Company swore the oath of loyalty to Adolf Hitler.

Political affiliations faded. One October day, SS-Ostuf. Sommer assembled the 5th Company and explained to them that the time to make the final decision had come. They were free to leave if they so wished, but if they chose to remain the Waffen-SS they would have to give up questions of politics and religion. Some fifteen men left.

That same month, the 5th Company swore the oath of loyalty to Hitler. According to de Misser, it was a *cérémonie grandiose*.

---

80   A Christain intellectual, but also a champion of collaboration and an admirer of Hitler, Châteaubriant headed the strongly spiritual and Europeanist *Groupe collaboration*. Châteaubriant also published the weekly newspaper "*La Gerbe*" which had one of the largest circulations of the collaborationist newspapers or magazines.

81   "*Historia No 32*", page 116.

The French *freiwillige* felt less and less French, but for all that they did not become German. They felt born into a new European army.[82] Indeed, they were not willing to embrace some 200 of their own countrymen, for the most part from the south, who arrived in October 1943. To them, these newcomers, including several officers, represented those who had fled shamefully before the Germans in 1940.

Joseph Darnand

Many of these new volunteers were from Joseph Darnand's *Milice française*. His story and that of the *Milice* is closely entwined with the formation of the French Sturmbrigade of the Waffen-SS and, at a later date, the French Division of the Waffen-SS.

Joseph Darnand was born on 19th March 1897 in Coligny, the son of a railway worker. In 1915, at age seventeen, he volunteered for the Army, but was rejected; he was too sickly. It was a terrible blow for him and years later he admitted that he 'cried with anger'. He was not a man to give up and finally on 8th January 1916 he was declared fit for service and joined the *35e regiment d'infanterie*. It seemed that he had found his true vocation and quickly rose to the rank of sergeant. Found where the action was hottest, in thirteen months of combat he won six citations, including two '*à l'ordre de l'Armée*', and the Belgium *croix de guerre*, picking up two wounds in the process.

On 14th July 1918, Darnand, now of the *366e regiment d'infanterie*, took twenty-four prisoners, including a Lieutenant Colonel, during a raid on the German lines. The subsequent interrogation of the prisoners revealed an impending German attack that was smashed. For his exploit, Darnand won the *médaille militaire* [Military Medal] which he received six days later from Pétain in person. This event, according to some commentators, led to a lifelong devotion to the Marshal. Later, in 1926, Darnand was to receive the *Légion d'honneur*. President of the Republic Poincaré even lauded Darnand as one of 'the artisans of victory'.

After the war *adjudant* Darnand hoped for a commission at *École militaire d'infanterie de* Saint-Maixent but his superiors, who appreciated his military virtues but doubted his intellectual abilities, dissuaded him with the assurance that he would have a choice. This assurance came to nothing and it was this deception that embedded the seeds of his hatred of this Republic. On 30th September 1919, he enlisted again, this time for two years. He ended up in Syria and saw action in Cilicie,[83] before returning to France. Realising that he would never be commissioned, he left the army on 26th July 1921 a very bitter man. He was burning to take his revenge. In Nice he set up and ran a highly successful trucking business that became one of the principal means of transportation from the Southeast.

The years between the World Wars saw Darnand drift from one Rightist group to another but it was only in Eugène Deloncle's *Comité Secret d'Action Révolutionnaire* (CSAR), otherwise known as *La Cagoule* ('The Hooded Ones'), that he finally felt at home among men in his own mould. Men whose hatred of the

82   Mabire, page 71.
83   Cilicie is a region of Turkey along the northern border of Syria which was under a
      French mandate at the time.

present government of Léon Blum and its communist supporters was as strong as his. He was soon the head of the CSAR in Nice.

Convinced that France was now in danger of a communist takeover, which was its call to action, the CSAR and its action squads were responsible for a series of political murders during 1936 and 1937. Darnand became actively involved in gunrunning from Italy to the Côte d'Azur, which his lorries then distributed throughout France.

This gunrunning activity led the CSAR to murder Maurice Juif at Imperia in Italy. A trafficker and go-between for the sale of arms, Juif 'had not been playing fair'. Darnand's complicity in this murder is not known but the subsequent investigation brought about his arrest on 14th July 1938. He found himself in the dock accused of plotting against State Security, gunrunning and criminal conspiracy.

While in prison Darnand was visited by a young reserve officer by the name of Jean Bassompierre. Strapped up tight in his uniform, *sous-lieutenant* Bassompierre came to show Darnand his 'affection' and 'his loyalty in misfortune'. The two men got on well and would soon become close friends.

Born on 23rd October 1914 in Honfleur, Bassompierre studied at the *lycée* Jeanson-de-Sailly before going on to receive his *Diplôme de Sciences Politiques* at the university of Paris. While a student in the Latin Quarter of Paris he became a militant of the right-wing movement *Jeunesses Patriotes* (Patriot Youth).[84] Bassompierre made a name for himself at the time of the Stavisky scandal participating in anti-parliamentary and anti-semitic demonstrations. Two years later, the University suspended him for six months after he disrupted with a teargas a lecture by Dr. Jèze, a sworn enemy of the extreme French right. Before the League of Nations, Dr. Gaston Jèze had condemned Mussolini's aggression against Négus Hailé Selassié of Ethopia.

Politically, after leaving the *Jeunesses Patriotes*, Bassompierre was drawn to the CSAR.[85]

An ardent patriot, Bassompierre rallied to the flag. In 1936, he attended *école d'officiers de réserve* [EOR] training and graduated, one year later, as a *sous-lieutenant de réserve* [reserve 2nd Lieutenant]. That same year, Deloncle, the leader of the CSAR, made the young officer responsible for detecting any possible communist infiltration in his regiment. It was also Deloncle who put the young idealist in contact with Darnand.

Darnand's service record earnt him the court's leniency and, after six months in detention, he was granted bail on 16th December 1938. Seven months later, the case against him was dismissed through lack of evidence. Darnand's strong defence case and the fact that war was looming are often cited as the reasons behind the prosecution's decision to drop the case rather than any failure on their part.

---

84 In 1924, Champagne magnate Pierre Taittinger, the deputy for Paris, founded the *Jeunesses Patriotes*. It would remain a significant force on the French right to the mid 1930s.

85 According to Giolitto, page 537, Bassompierre became one of the first adherents of the CSAR with the number 180. However, his name does not appear on the list of CSAR members later seized by the Police. Nevertheless, he did work actively for the CSAR.

When war broke out *lieutenant de réserve* Darnand was mobilised to a rear area assignment as a transport officer in the *6e demi-brigade de Chasseurs Alpins*. Irked, the forty-two-year-old Darnand demanded combat duty and was rewarded with being assigned to the *24e bataillon de chasseurs* of the *29e division d'infanterie*. He and his good friend Lieutenant Agnély obtained authorisation from the general commanding the *29e D.I.* to form a *corps franc*—a sort of commando unit whose role was to penetrate German lines in order to gather intelligence. Agnély commanded. Darnand was second in command. In February 1940, the troops of the *corps franc* were greatly surprised to be armed with Italian Beretta sub machine-guns seized from the clandestine CSAR arsenal!

On 8th February 1940, Darnand's commanding officer and friend, Agnély, was killed while on a night patrol at Forbach. Darnand and three volunteers returned to the village under fire and brought back the body of his comrade. For this *coup de main*, Darnand was awarded the *rosette d'officier de la Légion d'honneur* and given command of the *corps franc*.

During the remainder of the so-called 'Phoney War' Darnand continued to distinguish himself time and again by his courage and his audacity. When the Battle of France came he was in constant action with his *corps franc* and was taken prisoner on 19th June 1940 at La Motte-Beuvron, in Sologne. By that time, he had been awarded two further bronze palms for his *Croix de Guerre*.[86]

In August, Darnand escaped from his POW camp at Pithiviers. Returning to Nice, he began to plot revenge against the Germans. Soon after Bassompierre joined him. He too now wanted revenge.

During the war, Bassompierre served as a Lieutenant in the *74e bataillon de alpin de forteresse* [Alpine Fortress Infantry] on the Alpes front, commanding an outpost at Conchetas, near Saint-Martin-Vésubie. On 20th June 1940, the Italians attacked. In heavy fighting, they were contained everywhere. Among the artisans of this defensive victory was Bassompierre. He fought bravely and was awarded the *Croix de Guerre* with one gilt star.[87] On the 25th, after the armistice, he even defied orders and blew up an ammunition dump. In this way, he showed himself to be 'the best officer of his *régiment*'.[88] When he separated from his men he told them not to be afraid to look the occupying forces in the face because 'we are not beaten'.

Demobilised on 15th August 1940, Bassompierre returned to Nice where he met Darnand. He said of this meeting of similar minds:

> We agree at once; we want to continue to serve France; we still have a govern-ment; this one speaks to us of National Revolution, prestigious words which restore hope to us. For it is obvious that our military disaster is above all due to the total incompetence of a regime which is loathed by all honest people. We all hope for a bit of moral decency and social justice. A noble task awaits us: to show the world that we have not become a nation of slaves, that we are still a great country at the head of an intact empire and commanding the most modern navy. The Marshal urges us to undertake this great task; we give

86   A bronze palm indicates a citation in an Army dispatch.
87   A gilt star indicates a citation in a Corps dispatch.
88   Ch. A. Colin, "*Sacrifice de Bassompierre*".

ourselves to him heart and soul, to him who is the symbol of a France that does not want to or can not die.

On 29th August 1940, the Vichy Government announced the formation of the *Légion française des Combattants* (Legion of War Veterans) to unite the numerous existing war veterans' organisations. Its president was Pétain and its secretary-general Xavier Vallat. The nationalist Legion exhibited adoration of the Marshal and with its anti-German sentiments dreamed of revenge. Indeed, the Legion was not allowed to function in the Occupied Zone. As such, the Legion can not be considered collaborationist.

After very favourable advice from Pétain, Vallat chose Darnand to run the Legion in the department of the Alpes-Maritimes raised on 6th October 1940. A convinced *maréchaliste*, he agreed. His friend Bassompierre became the *Secrétaire général*. To him, the Legion seemed the source of French revival. At a later date, he went on to become the *secrétaire régional* for the region of Marseille.

After Petain's public statement that he had 'entered in all honour in the way of collaboration', Darnand, blinded by his devotion to Pétain, fell into line like the good soldier he was. That devotion was intensified when he was summoned at the end of the year to see Marshal Pétain and told to continue his work in the Legion and denounce the enemies of the New Order. The Marshal told him: "I do not like Jews, I detest Communists and I hate Freemasons."

At the same time Darnand was also wholeheartedly involved in the *Groupes de Protection* created at Vichy by Colonel Groussard, François Méténier and Doctor Martin. Colonel Groussard wrote: "My task will be to create the nucleus of an anti-German intelligence service under the guise of a subsidiary police force." As well as being anti-German in nature, the *Groupes de Protection* were anti-Gaullist, but very *Maréchal, nous voilà*. In its ranks were many former *cagoulards* and that included Darnand. In many ways, the *Groupes de Protection* could be regarded as one of the first French 'underground' movements.

The *Groupes de Protection* were made up of two distinct branches: the armed military branch and the civilian branch, the *Centre d'Information et d'Études*. When the Italian authorities refused the formation of the *Groupes de Protection* in the department of Alpes-Maritimes, Darnand was appointed *chef de la 15e region du Centre d'Information et d'Études* on 11th November 1940. However, Darnand resigned his post the following month to devote himself entirely to the Legion. But in that short time Darnand had armed with weapons furnished in secret by the French Army and trained some two hundred and fifty men. More importantly, many *chefs* of the *Groupes de Protection* would become future *Milice* dignitaries. They included Joseph Lécussan at Toulouse and Jean-Baptiste Géromini, a former *sous-lieutenant* of the *24e bataillon de chasseurs alpins* (24e BCA), in the Var.

The German invasion of Russia in June 1941 compounded Darnand's commitment to collaboration. By the late summer of 1941, he had become disillusioned by the unwieldy and the unreliable Legion, which had proved slow to give up its anti-German sentiments and the idea of revenge. He was in need of real revolutionaries.[89] Thus, in August 1941, together with other senior members of the

---

89   Delperrié de Bayac is not the only source to comment that Darnand was also in need of a party (see page 96).

Legion, including Bassompierre, he created in the Alpes-Maritimes Department the *Service d'Ordre Légionnaire* [the Order Service of the Legion], the SOL.[90]

The SOL remained a private organisation until the Vichy Government gave its official blessing in January 1942. Named as the *Inspecteur général du SOL*, Darnand relocated to Vichy. He surrounded himself with friends. And again by his side was Bassompierre. He was in charge of Propaganda. In the months that followed, the SOL spread throughout the unoccupied zone, inaugurated at Annecy on 13th and 14th June 1942, then at Lyon on 11th and 12th July 1942 ... Membership of the SOL was probably a little over 15,000.[91]

The SOL was an integral part of the Legion, but differed in every aspect. Entry to the SOL was limited to those who were naturalised citizens, aged between twenty and forty-five and not Jewish nor members of a secret society. Also, recruits were required to undergo and pass a three-month period of probation that included physical training, political education and practical training in the techniques of the maintenance of order. In this way, the recruits would come to know of what was expected of them and sign up 'with full knowledge of the facts'. [And, of course, if the recruits were found wanting their applications could be rejected.]

Once recruited, members of the SOL were given the title of 'Knight of the New France' and assured that this new knighthood 'would draw from the past the strength to build the future'. Their suit of armour was the 'beret of our chasseurs, the khaki shirt of the French Army and a black tie, as a sign of mourning for the Homeland'.[92] On the left arm a white edged black brassard was worn and on the upper right arm heraldic unit insignia of the district of origin.

And what was the doctrine of the SOL? It was based entirely on twenty-one points codified by three friends of Darnand: Jean Bassompierre, Dr. Durandy, and Noël de Tissot. The points were a series of slogans that positioned the SOL politically against gaullist dissidence, Jewish leprosy, Bolshevism, and pagan freemasonry. Equally the SOL was for French unity, Nationalism, French purity and Christian civilisation. But what did this mean in practical terms? Its regulations called for the SOL to maintain good order at Legion gatherings, as well as meetings organised by the government. This was deemed as 'very easy, but necessary' and excellent training for more important and difficult tasks. One such task was to provide assistance for the repression of public demonstrations against Marshal Pétain and the Vichy government. Another such task for the political 'shock troops of the National Revolution', as for the Legion of French Combatants, was the surveillance of the population. In short, the SOL was 'to guarantee on all occasions the functioning of the public services'.

So how was the SOL going to transmit its message, ensure the triumph of the National Revolution and stop the enemies of the new regime? Firstly, through the personal qualities of its membership. Their life, their attitude and their outward

---

90   Delperrié de Bayac, page 96 and Darnand, speech to the *Haute Courte de Justice*, 3rd October 1945 (Delperrié de Bayac, page 97). Curiously, according to Lambet and Le Marec, page 117, Marcel Gombert, Darnand's right-hand man, created the SOL without the knowledge of Darnand.

91   Conclusion reached by Giolitto, "*Histoire de la Milice*", page 78. Also see Delperrié de Bayac, page 146.

92   Bassompierre, "*Frères enemis*", page 127.

behaviour had to be beyond reproach. They had to be the living embodiment of the Marshal's motto 'Work, Family, Country'. They had to have a 'spirit of strict discipline' and obey orders without question even when their sense and necessity were hard to understand. Its members had to be a veritable rock of order and discipline, and must 'never let despair invade their soul'. Secondly, a SOL circular read that the National Revolution was not about guns or fists, but method and organisation, and not about destroying but building, although this did not rule out the use of force. But the SOL was unarmed. In the final analysis the SOL was the 'young and dynamic force of the Legion' and perhaps *une troupe de choc de réserve.*[93] But Vichy had no need of the SOL because the *gendarmerie, la garde mobile* and the police were loyal to the regime and they alone could protect France from what little internal disorder there was.

On 28th June 1942, a delegation of the *comité central* of the *Légion Tricolore* left Paris for Poland. Darnand was at its head. On 1st July, at the camp of Kruszyna, the delegation visited the 1st battalion of the *Légion Tricolore.*[94] Darnand brought with him a message from Benoist-Méchin, *secrétaire d'Etat* to the *chef du gouvernement*, which spoke of defending French interests as well as a European cause.

It was this visit that convinced Darnand of the greater Russian threat to Europe than that posed by Germany to French national integrity. Thereupon, as a man of action, he saw it his duty to encourage SOL adherents to sign up for military duty on the Eastern Front in the *Légion Tricolore*. In this way, he drew even closer to aligning himself with the German cause in Europe.

That October, Darnand admitted that his values and ideals were not shared by most French people but declared: "We are determined to save France despite public opinion and against it if necessary … "

The Milice française

On 19th December 1942, Hitler summoned Laval and demanded the creation of a police/security force to be used against the growing Resistance groups in France. The SOL was to be the nucleus of such a force. On 5th January 1943, Marshal Pétain announced the transformation of the SOL into the *Milice Nationale*. He granted this new formation a 'certain amount' of autonomy from the Legion in order to facilitate its task as 'the advance guard for the maintenance of order inside French territory in co-operation with the police'.

Weeks later, Law No 63 of 30th January 1943, published in the *Journal Officiel* on the 31st, renamed the *Milice Nationale* the *Milice française* [French Militia] under the presidency of Laval. The *Milice française* was described in the annex to article 2 of the law establishing its creation as being 'composed of volunteers morally ready and physically capable not only of supporting the new state by their action, but also to assist in the maintenance of internal order'. The law also

93   Delperrié de Bayac, page 113.

94   On the 22nd June 1942, the *comité central* of the LVF (*Légion des Volontaires Français*) transformed the LVF into *La Légion Tricolore*. On 18th July 1942, *La Légion Tricolore* was created by Law No 704, which was published in the *Journal officiel* on 17th September 1942.

required that members of the *Milice* be French by birth, not Jewish, nor belong to any secret society, and be volunteers.

A ceremony held in Vichy on 1st February 1943 saw Darnand appointed the secretary-general of the *Milice française*. Laval spoke stressing once again the danger Bolshevism was to Europe. To prevent his country suffering this misfortune, he wanted France to understand that it must be at one with Germany. It is not known if Darnand shared this view but he did see saving France from the danger of Bolshevism as a fundamental part of the revolutionary task of the *Milice*. Indeed, one member of the organisation is recorded as saying that the greatest pleasure of a *Milicien* would be 'to wash his hands in the blood of communists'!

The fight against Bolshevism was but one expression of the political mission of the *Milice* defined by the twenty-one points of the SOL, which it adopted as its own. The *Milice* had to be the best advert for Vichy and the National Revolution. It would attack poverty and hunger, the consequences of defeat. It would curb the black market. It would revive and purify the Arts, and 'protect French intellectual heritage'.[95] Indeed, according to Philippe Henriot, the Vichy Secretary of State for Propaganda and Information, the *Milice* would 'return a soul to France'. Nevertheless, '*La Milice a pour première tache d'abattre le Communisme*'.[96]

The *Milice* also adopted many other attributes from the SOL. The marching song of the SOL, *Le Chant des Cohortes*, became *Le Chant de la Milice*. The *Milice* mirrored the SOL's adminstrative organisation. The *Milice* retained the SOL's three-month probation period. At the end of the period of probation, successful new recruits swore the following oath:

> I undertake upon my honour to serve France, even to the sacrifice of my own life. I swear to devote all my strength to the triumph of the revolutionary ideal of the *Milice française* whose discipline I freely accept.

The general regulations of the *Milice* stated that it was not an organisation in which one could enter or leave on a simple nod. A new recruit could only be accepted by a *chef départemental* subject to the approval of the *secrétaire général*. Resignations could only be pronounced by the *secrétaire général*. In this way, recruits for the *Milice*, like those for the SOL, had to 'understand the importance of their enlistment'.

That was not all the *Milice* and SOL had in common. The *Milice* carried forward the same morality and discipline outlined for membership of the SOL. According to Darnand, *Miliciens* were 'not vulgar henchmen stupidly in love with violence' nor 'mad youngsters only longing to play with the revolver'. They were militants not mercenaries. Darnand saw the *Milice* establishing itself through its loyalty, its honesty and its asceticism, and the *Milicien* as being not only revolutionary in word, but also in action. Article 45 of the *Milice* general regulations remarked that no *Milicien* must take advantage of his position for personal vengeance. Even Pétain set out his own tone for the *Milice*, suggesting that the organisation could win the heart of the population by showing 'an example of discipline and an unblemished private life'.

95 Some commentators have even described the *Milice* as the lofty successor to the Armistice army disbanded in November 1942.
96 Darnand, speech of February 1943.

The *Milice française* was composed of four branches; the *Miliciens*; the *Avant-Garde Milicienne* (the Youth branch); the *Franc-Garde* (the Free Guard); and *Les Miliciennes* (the Womens branch).

The *chef* of the *Avant-Garde* was *Capitaine* Jean-Marcel Renault, the co-founder of the 'recognised' youth movement *Jeunesse de France et d'Outre Mer* [The Youth of France and Overseas] in January 1941. Born on 4th May 1912 in the Nièvre, he had to abandon his preparartory studies for the 'Arts and Métiers' when his father died and find work instead. In 1931 he joined the Merchant Navy. In 1935 he started his career as an officer in the Air Force, working his way up through the ranks. From 17th May to 6th June 1940 he commanded *escadrille de chasse de nuit* 2/13 [night fighter squadron 2/13][97] and distinguished himself against the Germans in Belgium. He was cited twice. Ever since this sincere and ardent patriot had been 'literally hypnotised by German efficiency and force'.[98]

In November 1941 Renault succeeded Henry Pugibert at the head of the *Jeunesse de France et d'Outre Mer*, which had claimed a membership of 30,000 one month before. The J.F.O.M. was present at most meetings, rallies and *prestations de serment* organised by the *Légion française des combattants* and the SOL.

To fill the ranks of the *Avant-Garde*, Laval put to Renault that he encourage members of his former movement to enlist in the *Milice*. According to Renault, only one in ten would come across from the J.F.O.M. to the *Milice*.[99] The sixteen-year-old Georges Garrot, a sincere supporter of Marshal Pétain's National Revolution, passed from the J.F.O.M. to the *Avant-Garde*. His involvement consisted for the most part of parading in the streets. He would serve later with the French Division of the Waffen-SS.

Georges Cazalot, born on 8th September 1927, joined the *Avant-Garde* during the summer of 1943 thanks to his school sports teacher Charpentier, also a *chef de la Milice*, who was highly respected by all. He had fought with the LVF on the Russian Front and been seriously wounded. His medals of the *Légion d'honneur* and the *Croix de guerre* with four *palmes* were testament to his bravery. Cazalot said of him[100]: 'Men like him are neeeded at the rear. They're as useful here to instruct, form, educate and advise the impatient *jeunes*'.[101] Two of Cazalot's classmates also joined up. Cazalot, however, wanted to be a *combattant de l'Ordre Européen* and intended to join the Waffen-SS as soon as he turned 17.

The creation of a *corps d'élite* called the *Franc-Garde* was announced by Darnand on 30th January 1943 and placed under the orders of Jean de Vaugelas. On 2nd June 1943, the *Franc-Garde* was sub-divided into the *Franc-Garde*

97   Lefèvre. This corrects Delpierré de Bayac, page 205, that Renault was an officer of *l'aviation d'assaut.*

98   Delperrié de Bayac, "*Histoire de la Milice*", page 205.

99   And yet according to Lambert and Marec, page 144, "*Organistaions, mouvements et unités de l'état francais*", the *Avant-Garde* 'was, especially in the South Zone, composed almost exclusively of the *jeunes* of the J.F.O.M. who had preferred to follow their *chef,* Jean-Marcel Renault who had given them the choice between the *Milice* or remaining with the J.F.O.M.'

100   Cazalot, "... *Et la terre a bu leur sang!*", page 17.

101   Captured by the resistance in late 1944, he was shot.

Permanente and the Franc-Garde Non-permanente. The first unit of the *Franc-Garde Permanente* was created at the camp of Calabres, near Vichy. The Permanent force, as the name suggests, were the 'regulars' who belonged to full-time units which were available for active duty anywhere in the Southern, unoccupied Zone. The Non-Permanent force consisted of 'part-timers' of older men who could be mobilised in the event of emergencies.

Darnand said of the *francs-gardes*:

> To create the *esprit de corps*, to obtain a very strict discipline and to show to all that the *Milice* is an organisation with nothing to hide, and finally to force those who wear it to appear without fear, the *francs-gardes* will wear a uniform.

As such the *francs-gardes* were the only *Miliciens* to wear full uniform. Its uniform retained much of the flavour of its forerunner, the SOL: khaki shirt (although civilian shirts were sometimes worn), black tie and dark blue trousers. However, the *type basque* beret of the SOL was replaced by the blue-coloured modèle 41 beret, worn *à la manière des chasseurs*, pulled to the right for men and to the left for officers. While on active duty a French (Adrian) army steel helmet was sometimes worn. The badge of the department/province to which they belonged was often worn on the left sleeve. In addition, the *Milice* emblem was worn on the beret and on the right breast pocket of the tunic and shirt.

The *Milice* emblem was a stylised gamma in a circle. The Greek letter gamma, the Zodiac sign of the Ram and thus a symbol of force and rebirth, reflected the revolutionary task of the Milice.

The *Franc-Garde* was organised along the hierarchical lines of the SOL: *Main, Dizaine, Trentaine, Centaine* and *Cohorte*. The smallest unit was the *Main*, consisting of four *franc-gardes* and a *chef de main*. Two *Mains* made a *Dizaine* and three *Dizaines* constituted a *Trentaine*, deemed the 'smallest lone unit to participate in the maintenance of order.' The largest unit was the *Cohorte*, made up of three *Centaines*. However, several *Cohortes*, depending upon their numbers and department configuration, could be grouped into *Centres*.

Regulations insisted that all *Franc-Garde* units had to be placed under the command of 'an officer proven in the military point of view and absolutely certain in the political point of view.' In addition, at every echelon throughout the *Milice, chefs* had to give their adherents political training.

The *chefs* and *cadres* of the *Milice* received their political and military training at various *Écoles de cadres* (training schools). The most celebrated was undoubtedly the *École nationale des cadres de la Milice* at the picturesque chateau de Saint-Martin d'Uriage. Established on 1st March 1943, the national school accepted its first entrants on the 25th of the same month. The political training was centred on the twenty-one points of its Manifesto and the military training on the strategic rudiments of the *guerre des maquis* and street fighting. In October 1943, the first *Chef de l'École d'Uriage*, by the name of du Vair, was replaced by de Vaugelas, the *chef régional de la Milice* at Marseille.

At first, there was great enthusiasm for the *Milice*. Large numbers of recruits stepped forward. Who were they? Militants of various past and present Right wing and far Right movements; ultra-Catholics; fanatical anti-Communists; anti-Semites; former members of the royalist *Action française*; and former serviceman. Indeed, some were from movements of the far Left. A good number, however, did not belong to any political party.

The *Milice* attracted recruits from all age groups and from all sections of the community. A high percentage of the men came from the urban lower middle and middle class, but a number also hailed from agricultural backgrounds. A high percentage of the *chefs* were from professional backgrounds or intellectauls. Some were former or serving officers and bearers of old noble names who were violently anti-Republican.

What compelled them to come forward? For the most part, they loved France, its people and its way of life. They feared and hated Communism. They supported the Marshal and the National Revolution. They wanted to save France from ruin by maintaining order and fighting Communism. They wanted to rebuild an independent France that was the master of its fate. Most had little regard for Nazi Germany and its policies. In a letter to a friend, a young recruit from the South-west had this to say about joining the *Milice*:[102]

> To tell you the truth we are determined, no matter what, to pull France out of the mess in which it is stuck, without any other help than only our arms, drawing our theories and our strength from what our country holds traditionally French. That is why you see me serving in the ranks of the *Milice*, and devoting my days to developing myself or even developing men capable of serving France ...

Nevertheless, not all were convinced idealists. Undoubtedly, the *Milice* attracted a small number of those in search of adventure. For some, the *Milice* meant employment, even clothes and lodging. The wages were good and very large payments were made for denouncements. Also, for some, the *Milice* became a means of avoiding deportation to Germany for labour service.[103]

The Summer of Crisis

On 24th April 1943, Paul de Gassowski, the *chef départemental adjoint de la Milice* of Bouches-du-Rhône, was assasinated in Marseille by the Resistance. Days later, also in Marseille, surgeon Buisson, the *chef régional adjoint*, was killed. These two murders marked the beginning of a ferocious campaign of assassinations of *Miliciens* and their families, and bombings of their property.

The situation soon became intolerable. Unarmed, the *Miliciens* could not defend themselves. Again and again Darnand went to President Laval, the nominal *chef* of the *Milice française*, and pleaded for arms. His insistent pleas fell on deaf ears. In point of fact, Laval had no intention, for political reasons, of arming a movement more loyal to Darnand than it was to him. Besides, at that time, he had no need of the *Milice*. The traditional forces of order were still loyal to the Vichy

---

102 "*Historia #40: La Milice-La collaboration en uniforme*", page 40. The unnamed author of this letter would end up in the uniform of the Waffen-SS and finish the war fighting with the French *Sturmbataillon* in Berlin where he was seriously wounded by a Russian grenade.

103 Some sources claim that, at a later date, courts offered petty criminals a choice of either serving a prison sentence or serving in the *Milice française*. However, Lefèvre vehemently denies this accusation.

government and he was of the opinion that they were sufficient to maintain order. Moreover, what then of the prospect of 'extremists of the right' with arms? To him, this was dangerous. Indeed, he was concerned that their actions might only inflame the Resistance to commit further excesses against Vichy.

Many *Miliciens* lost faith in President Laval. They reproached him for refusing them arms. On 26th June 1943, a *Chef départemental* reported:[104]

> If the men lack confidence, it is not in their *chefs*, it is in their possibilities of success: the underhand campaigns just like the indifference—if not the hostility—of the public powers discourages them.
>
> Generally they believe that our success is linked to that of the Axis and few are those who do not see Germany defeated.

Faced with a lack of government support and no prospect of arms, many members of the *Milice* now resigned. Recruitment also slowed.

On 13th July 1943, in a change of tack, Darnand tendered his resignation to Laval, explaining that the *Milice* did not have the means to fulfil its mission.[105] On the following day, Pétain refused the resignation and handed it back to him in person. He told Darnand: "You are my best and my most faithful soldier." Darnand said nothing. Moments later, Darnand said to his friends that he could not refuse Pétain.[106]

Deceived by Laval, Darnand now thought of switching sides to the Resistance. He contacted Colonel Groussard, the ex-*chef* of the *Groupes de Protection*, in Geneva.[107] When Groussard asked him to sign a declaration promising to serve under him against the Germans and to obey him under all circumstances, Darnand discontinued all negotiations.

---

104   Non-referenced document, CARAN, F1 A, 3747.

105   Pierre Cance also tendered his resignation.

106   Mabire, page 45, chapter "*Le serment au Führer*", "*Historia #40: La Milice-La collaboration en uniforme*". However, no other source confirms Pétain's praise of Darnand or Darnand's immediate reaction to the refusal of his resignation. Also of interest to note is that, according to Delperrié de Bayac, "*Histoire de la Milice*", page 202, Darnand was not serious about resigning. If true, this would suggest his resignation was little more than a political ploy, but the tone of his letter suggests otherwise.

107   According to Mabire, page 46, chapter "*Le serment au Führer*", "*Historia #40: La Milice-La collaboration en uniforme*", Darnand sent Cance, the *Délégué Général* of the *Milice*, to Geneva to contact Colonel Groussard. He spent several days with Groussard, but their negotiations soon came to an impasse. They could not agree on who posed the greater threat to France. For Cance, it was the Communists, and, for Groussard, it was the Germans. Thereupon, 'just in case', Groussard drew up a declaration for Darnand to sign, described as 'a token of rallying and almost of repentance'. However, according to Delperrié de Bayac, "*Histoire de la Milice*", page 202, the intermediary was a certain Louis Guillaume and Colonel Groussard sent Darnand, through him, 'two pieces of papers'. On the second sheet was written the declaration requiring the signature of Darnand.

Although he detested de Gaulle, Darnand then turned to London. Through ex-*cagoulard* friends of his in the Resistance, he offered his support to de Gaulle. There was no reply.

Cornered more than ever, with his *Miliciens* still being cut down, Darnand, a man of responsibility, went to the Germans whom he still regarded as '*Les Boches*'. For their part, the German authorities had always shown great hostility towards the creation of 'stand alone' French military forces. They greatly feared the *revanche* of the French. In addition, many *chefs* of the *Milice* drew their inspiration from Charles Maurras, the leader of the Royalist *Action française*, whose pre-war vehement anti-German sentiments were notorious and whose watchword was "France only".[108] Moreover, his ideology was taught as part of the *formation politique* of *Milice élèves* [students]. Nevertheless, times had changed. The Germans had need of men to participate in the European battle.

Darnand played the 'SS card.'[109] In August 1943, at the German embassy in Paris, he swore an oath of loyalty to Adolf Hitler and accepted the rank of Obersturmführer in the Waffen-SS.[110] This move was an unequivocal gesture to the Germans, Vichy, and his *Milice*.[111]

In early October 1943, Darnand, accompanied by high-ranking *Milice* chiefs Gallet and Roleau, met with Ogruf. Gottlob Berger, the Chief of the SS Main Office (the SS-Hauptamt) and the man in charge of Waffen-SS recruitment. This was the first meeting between Darnand and Berger.[112]

---

108 Throughout the war, Maurras would maintain an anti-German sentiment, although somewhat toned down. He wrote in his book "*La Seule France*" published in 1941: "We have only one slogan: France. We are not Germans or English. We are French. Only France or, if you prefer France only…"

109 Delperrié de Bayac, "*Histoire de la Milice*", page 206.

110 The rank Darnand accepted at the German embassy in Paris is often misquoted as Sturmbannführer. Bernd de la Fontaine, the 'adjudant' of Franz Riedweg, who was present during the swearing in ceremony, has confirmed in writing to historian Mounine that Darnand did accept the Waffen-SS rank of Obersturmführer. Besides, the SS rank of Obersturmführer was equivalent to his French Army rank of *lieutenant*. However, in the autumn of 1944, the SS rank of Sturmbannführer was conferred upon Darnand to give him certain parity with Doriot, his political rival who had received the honorary SS rank of Sturmbannführer.

111 Although Darnand would play no active role in the SS-Sturmbrigade, or later in 'Charlemagne', his Waffen-SS appointment should not be viewed as 'purely nominal' (Mabire, page 83). As such, at any moment, Darnand could have been called up for active service. Curiously, according to Ministry of Interior report MRU/14/35301 dated 18th December 1943, 'the German authorities had named him [Darnand] inspector of the French Waffen-SS'. This is simply not true. Perhaps its origin was wishful thinking publicly 'loose-cannoned' by Darnand that later became reported as fact.

112 Research provided by historian Lefèvre. This corrects the suggested dates of mid to late July 1943 that appear in all previous accounts of this meeting (Delpierré de Bayac, Mabire, and Lambert and Le Marec). As a result, this throws doubt on many details of the meeting recounted by Delpierré de Bayac. For example, on page 205, Berger asks Darnand what his position would be '*if* the French Waffen-SS unit *was created*' (author's italics). As such, the French unit of the Waffen-SS already existed.

The upshot of the meeting suggests an arrangement was reached whereby arms would be supplied to the *Milice* and its *Franc-Garde* in return for co-operation from its executive in recruiting members from its ranks for the newly formed French Waffen-SS unit.

And what of Berger's motives? Undoubtedly, he saw the *Milice* as an ideal source of recruits for the new unit, but the possibility also exists that the Germans had finally come to recognise the potential an armed *Milice* might have in combating 'terrorism' and maintaining order in France.

On 11th October 1943, eleven senior *chefs* of the *Milice* enlisted in the Waffen-SS.[113] And who were they?

The Officers[114]

The first *chef* to offer his services was Noël de Tissot from Nice, born on 22nd December 1914. A mathematics teacher by profession, he was of late unemployed. As a reserve artillery NCO,[115] he fought with great courage against the Germans in 1939–40, winning the *Croix de Guerre*, but ever since had harboured a deep sense of betrayal. Among the first to join the *Légion des Combattants*, he became the *secrétaire général* of *La Légion* in the Alpes-Maritimes department.

In August 1941, while *secrétaire général*, de Tissot was the subject of an 'opinion'[116] put together by the prefect of the Alpes-Maritimes department. The report remarked, generally, that he was aged 27 and married with a child. As for his politics, the report read that he had always been a member of some extreme right wing group and that now he was a P.P.F. militant. As for his personal qualities, he was reported 'serious, reflective, a hard worker and of perfect morality'. And yet some sources claim he was famed for his eccentricity.[117] The report, however, failed to mention that he was fanatically devoted to Darnand and was one of his closest colleagues.

De Tissot passed to the SOL and was appointed *secrétaire général* on 13th March 1942. Together with Bassompierre and Durandy he developed the doctrine of the SOL which was later transported to the *Milice*. When Darnand left Nice for Vichy he followed. It was he who imposed the gamma as the emblem of the *Milice* – Darnand would have preferred a 'stylised grenade'. On 4th February 1943, he was appointed principal private secretary to the *Secrétaire général de la Milice* [Darnand]. His role was to maintain co-ordination between the *Milice* high command and the central administration, but Laval mistrusted him.[118]

---

113 Delperrié de Bayac, "*Histoire de la Milice*", page 213.
114 According to Mabire, page 80, there was great enthusiasm among the *chefs* of the *Milice* to enlist and Darnand had to limit those wishing to enlist because he was in need of their services in France. Many, however, were not so ready to don the German uniform. To them, the 'internal enemy' remained the greater threat.
115 Giolitto, page 145. His rank was actually *maréchal des logis* equivalent to that of Sergeant in the British Army, which corrects Mabire, page 80, that de Tissot was a reserve artillery officer.
116 On 27th August 1941, prefects had been asked to 'give a verdict' on the members of the *comités départementaux de La Légion*.
117 For example, see Saint-Loup, page 17.

The next *chef* was Pierre Cance, from Bordeaux, a brewer and seller of beer,[119] born on 28th June 1907. As a reserve infantry *lieutenant*,[120] he saw action during the 'shooting war' and was decorated with the *Croix de Guerre*. The SOL *chef* at Béziers, he was appointed by Darnand, on 4th January 1943, the *Délégué Général* of the *Milice*, becoming responsible for its organisation. According to Mabire,[121] Cance was Darnand's right hand man who was 'more tempted through direct action than doctrine'.

Like Darnand, Cance had received his political education in the CSAR. Courageous and ambitious, this former International rugby player, with a matching physique, was a leader of men who inspired great confidence even if he was unrefined when he spoke. 'The emulation between Cance and de Tissot profited all, one with more strength, the other with more flexibility'.[122]

There was also Léon Gaultier from the Berry, born on 1st February 1915. As a member of the P.P.F. during the years of 1936 and 1937 he lectured with François Dochet in small villages of the Berry before tired workers and peasants 'in order to revive France'. Regarded as an intellectual, arts graduate Gaultier was working as an attaché in the Vichy Ministry of Information. He said of his decision to enlist: "This enlistment represented a considerable step. It was the realisation of our political will and our consideration of interior French politics."

Add to this Henri Joseph Fenet, the 24-year-old *chef départemental de l'Ain*, born on 11th June 1919 in Ceyzeriat, Department of Ain. The outbreak of the war found him as a student at the Paris University of Henry IV studying for the entrance exam to the *École normale Supérieure* [teacher training college]. Without hesitation he enlisted. He had no regrets about abandoning his university studies for military service. Months later, after attending the *École spéciale militaire* of Saint-Cyr, he was commissioned *Aspirant* (officer cadet)[123] and posted to the anti-tank company of the *3e division d'infanterie coloniale* (3rd Colonial Infantry division).

In the subsequent hard battles against the Germans Fenet was wounded twice and decorated with the *Croix de Guerre* for bravery. With defeat came shame and anger at the rotten politicians and senile generals who were responsible, ultimately, for the *debâcle*. For a while he thought about leaving for England, but was enticed away when Pétain spoke. He believed him and opted for Vichy.

118   According to Saint-Loup, de Tissot was an instructor at the *Milice École des cadres* (training school) at Uriage. This is not confirmed by any other source, although he may have given lectures there.

119   Research provided by historian Lefèvre. His trade has often been inaccurately recorded as agricultural engineer or engineer. According to Ministry of Interior report, WEZ 11/31306, dated 18th August 1943, Cance had been an entrepreneur at Montpellier 'where he had realised a rather tidy fortune'.

120   According to Mabire, page 80, Cance was a reserve *Captaine*. This is incorrect. In addition, according to Giolitto, page 145, Cance was a former *saint-cyrien* [military cadet of the Saint-Cyr academy]. This is incorrect. In fact, it was in 1929 that Cance was appointed *sous-lieutenant de réserve*. (Research provided by historian Lefèvre.)

121   Mabire, page 80.

122   Gaultier, "*Siegfried et le Berrichon*", page 149.

123   This corrects Landwehr, page 185, that by May 1940 Fenet held an officer's commission of Lieutenant.

Joining the Armistice Army, infantry *aspirant* Fenet was posted to Mauritania where he commanded a platoon of Senegalese *tirailleurs*. His posting was to his great satisfaction, for he had little interest in what was happening in France.[124] He craved purity and adventure.[125] The LVF was not for him. Nor the *Légion tricolore* which, according to him,[126] had all the defects of the old French Army.

In late autumn 1942, Fenet returned to metropolitan France to attend the *École militaire d'infanterie* of Saint-Maixent[127] relocated to Aix-en-Provence. He was still there in November 1942 when the Allies landed in French North Africa and the Germans invaded the free zone. On the 29th, he was demobilised with the rank of *sous-lieutenant* (2nd Lieutenant).[128] He returned home. He was now at a loss what to do. And then one day his father told him that the local *chef* of the SOL, a retired major, was going to hold a conference and that he had expressed a wish to meet him. Henri Fenet did not attend the conference, but he did make a point of meeting this retired major and it was this meeting that was to define his immediate pathway. The retired major told him:

> France needs young officers like you. For the moment, there is no longer a French Army, but we are trying to assemble decent people because any day there will be a new army. Do you wish to work with me?

Fenet was of the same opinion. He joined the SOL and then the *Milice française* on its creation. He became the *chef départemental de l'Ain*. After the German defeat at Stalingrad he came to realise that 'what he was doing in France was serving no purpose'.[129] Rather than combating the 'internal enemy', he now saw himself on the Eastern front defending Europe against Soviet invasion. In October 1943, he volunteered for the Waffen-SS.[130]

From the *École nationale des cadres de la Milice française* at Uriage came the instructor Jean Artus. Born on 4th April 1916 in Blaye, he studied politics at the Paris *École des sciences politiques*. Having obtained the *brevet* [certificate] *de préparation militaire supérieure* (PMS), he went on to attend *École d'officiers de réserve* [reserve officers school] training.[131] On 10th April 1939, he was commissioned with the rank of *aspirant* [officer cadet] and posted to the *24e bataillon de chasseurs alpins* (24e BCA). On 10th October that same year, he was made up to the rank of

124 "*Historia #613*", page 15. However, in contrast, according to Mabire, page 28, Fenet was exasperated by the political vacillations of the Vichy Government and its adopted *attentisme* [wait-and-see policy] towards Germany.
125 Mabire, page 28.
126 Ibid.
127 Like military school Saint-Cyr, its equivalent, Saint-Maixent formed regular officers, but its entrants were NCOs and reserve officers.
128 According to Landwehr, "*Charlemagne's Legionnaires*", page 185, on 29th November 1942, Fenet was released from a POW camp. This is incorrect
129 "*Historia #613*", page 15.
130 According to German records, Henri Fenet enlisted on 18th October 1943. That is one week later than that stated by Delperrié de Bayac. Was this an administrative error? Or perhaps his date of arrival at Sennheim?
131 Those who passed the yearlong *préparation militaire supérieure* attended, on call up for military service, *École d'officiers de réserve* [reserve officers school] training.

sous-lieutenant de réserve. During the winter of 1939–40, the 24e BCA put up Darnand's *corps franc*. Never would Artus forget the raids into the forest of Warndt. Demobilised, he joined the *Jeunesse et Montagne* (Youth and Mountain), the Air branch[132] of the Vichy *Chantiers de la Jeunesse* (a sort of State Labour Service).

Artus brought along with him his twenty-three-year-old friend Paul Pignard-Berthet who was also an instructor at the *Milice École des Cadres*. Paul Pignard-Berthet was born into a military family on 17th May 1920 near Annecy, Haute Savoie. His father was the commander of the 6th Battalion of the *1er Régiment Étranger d'Infanterie* in the Levant. He followed the phenomenal ascension of the National Socialist Third Reich with an anxiety tinged with admiration, while the 'democratic' powers floundered sterilely in their internal contradictions. Enlisting in November 1939, he attended the *École militaire de l'Infanterie et des Chars de Combat* (EMICC). Shocked by the morale and the dilapidated state of the equipment of the 'most beautiful army in the world', its debacle before the Germans in May 1940 came as no surprise to him. He was not bitter. He felt that many officers, although willing and well educated, had been suddenly thrust into this responsibility without any idea of command. He was not angry at those of his age, but at those 'puppets' who had declared war against Germany without being prepared for it and who had expected the infantry offensive of the Wehrmacht.

Commissioned with the rank of Aspirant in August 1940, Pignard-Berthet was posted as a *Chef de Groupe* to the *Chantiers de la Jeunesse* in the Pyrenees. Demanding to be returned to the Army, which was accepted because of his graduation from the EMICC, he joined the *27e bataillon de Chasseurs alpins*. He served with the 27e BCA for just one month before the Armistice Army was disbanded. He came to the SOL and then passed to the *Milice*.

Many reasons contributed to his final decision to enlist in the Waffen-SS; he could see that France was slipping inexorably into bloody civil war and did not want to end up firing on his fellow countrymen; he was in sympathy with Germany in general and with National Socialism because of its political and social successes; he had military ambitions; and in particular he feared the dangers of Bolshevism. He was of the opinion that this war could only be resolved on the Eastern front. Through his actions he hoped to see France regain a place of power within a preponderant Europe. And yet like so many of his comrades he had absolutely no idea about the precise nature of the Waffen-SS. His only information about this European army had been gleaned from hearsay and a few inconsistent written accounts. He honestly viewed his enlistment as a step into the unknown.

Pignard-Berthet also felt that there were other motives behind Darnand's political manoeuvres towards the Germans:

> Darnand sent us to the Waffen-SS, rather like hostages, revealing a sincere wish to collaborate, and, also, to acquire the necessary skills to fulfil the second function: internal and external security of the nation. A man of the traditional French right, he had gone through the Maurrasian school and remained fundamentally catholic. For him, politics was an intellectual and sentimental choice based on images corresponding more to vows than to realities. This the youn-

132 Cited in the *Journal Officiel* of 18th January 1941.

gest among us understood straight away ... National Socialism opened horizons to us going well beyond these concepts.

Not all would be so young. Albert Pouget, the Lozère *Chef départemental*, was born on 24th August 1902.[133] In 1929, reserve *sous-officier* Pouget of the 80° RI was commissioned *Sous-lieutenant de réserve*. In keeping with his appearance as an ecclesiastic, when asked by a recruitment officer why he was enlisting in the Waffen-SS he had replied: "For the Christian West!"

Also in his forties was Ivan Bartolomei. Born on 11th November 1898 near to Bordeaux, this career soldier had first enlisted aged eighteen in 1916 'for the duration of the war' and was demobilised after the war. Signing up again, he served with the rank of *sergent-chef*, then *adjudant*, in the *13e régiment de tirailleurs algériens*. He fought in the closing stages of the campaign in Morocco and his feat of arms on 17th July 1933 on the Haouja-N'oua brought him the *médaille militaire*, conferred by decree of 13th December 1933. In 1937, he ended this part of his military career when he retired as a *adjudant de chasseurs à pied* (a warrant officer in the Light Infantry).

In 1939, after finding himself overlooked by mobilisation, the forty-one-year-old Bartolomei called to order those responsible for this administrative oversight and left for war again. This time his rank was that of *Sous-lieutenant*. Appointed to a pioneer unit, he grew more and more bored as the Phoney War dragged on. Then the Blitzkrieg came to France. He was captured in Flanders on 4th June 1940.

Released as a World War One veteran, Bartolomei attempted to enlist in the LVF but his application was turned down 'through lack of places'! Joining the *Légion des Combattants*, he passed to the SOL, then to the *Milice*, and finally to the Waffen-SS.

There were other *chefs Milicien*: Emilien Boyer, born on 3rd April 1910 in Carcassone, who had just escaped unhurt from an assassination attempt; Pierre Crespin[134]; Jacques-Flavien de Lafaye, the *chef départemental de la Milice de l'Allier*, born on 26th April 1914; and Honoré de Lareinty-Kotchoubey de Tholozan.

One *Milicien* said of his pathway to the Waffen-SS:[135]

> I had always been what they call a man of order. I belonged to the middle middle class, that which puts money by, which goes to mass, and which doesn't like foreigners much.
>
> Before the war, I worked as a personnel manager in a small factory in the South-East. I joined Colonel La Rocque's *Parti social français*. I did not like much the lads of the *Action française* who I found too excited.
>
> In 39–40, I did my duty as a *officier de réserve*, but I was astounded at the frame of mind of the lads I had to command. Nobody wanted to fight. They only just managed not to be taken prisoner. The defeat seemed crushing to me.

---

133   His son Georges also served with the *Milice*. Captured at Estivareiles on 22nd August 1944, condemned to death on 15 September by the *cour martiale du Puy*, he was executed on 18th September.

134   Crespin was eventually promoted to W-Ostuf. and appointed the commander of the *Comp. de recrutement* (Mabire) of the *Franz. SS-Grenadier-Ausbildungs und Ersatz* Battalion, the training and replacement battalion of 'Charlemagne'.

135   "*Historia #32*", page 121. The Milicien in question was Pierre Cance.

I believed, with the *Maréchal*, that the most urgent thing to do was to give back to our compatriots the sense of duty, service and homeland. I am very '*révolution nationale*'. I became the local person responsible for the *Légion des combattants* and I led the *service d'ordre légionnaire* of the department. I found Darnand a very good bloke: hero of two wars, that counted a great deal to me. I made some speeches to encourage the most ardent of our men to leave for the *Légion Tricolore* or the *Phalange africaine*. I passed quite naturally from the SOL to the *Milice française*. I was not particularly pro-German or collaborationist. But I remained anti-Communist. When, at the end of summer 1943, they asked for *cadres miliciens* for the Waffen-SS, I thought that it was my duty to leave. How could I urge the others to join without going (there) myself? There I was caught up in the chain of events …

On 17th October 1943, from *la gare de L'Est*, Darnand saw off his *Miliciens* to Sennheim. Three days later on the 20th, true to their word, the Germans supplied the *Milice* with fifty submachine guns to arm its *Franc-garde*. Darnand continued to pay the quid pro quo; on 6th November 1943, in the pages of *Combats*, the *Milice* newspaper, he published an article, entitled *Alerte miliciens*, appealing for enlistment of *miliciens* in the Waffen-SS. He declared:

I am determined to take up arms a third time, beside all Europeans, to mutually defend our revolution and the future of our peoples. I will not do this out of despair nor out of bravado, I will leave with the conviction of serving the French cause more usefully than ever.

Darnand argued:

Europe is in danger. France is threatened with losing its independence. Our civilisation will be enslaved by triumphant Judaism or destroyed by Bolshevism. But nothing is lost if a large enough number of men face the fight …

Continuing, Darnand spoke of their fight on the interior front and its complement on the 'European battlefields'. Turning to the subject of France, he remarked:

France is a warlike nation; its grandeur will be restored through the heroism of its sons. Several of our comrades understood this a long time ago and have risked, for more than two years, their life on the Eastern front. A great number, at the time when the clever ones are going over to the Jewish camp, have just followed their example and reached the training camps where the French Division of the Waffen-SS is being organised. I have decided to join them when, in several months time, they go into the firing line.

Darnand followed this vibrant appeal with a series of personal appearances before mass-meetings of the *Milice*. At Limoges, he distinguished between his 'military' oath to Hitler and his 'political' oath to Pétain.
Later that month, Darnand said:[136]

The French SS are being recruited from the militants of the National Revolution. They will form a troop officered by French officers, firstly in the service of

136 Ministry of the Interior report NJP/1/35303, F1A 3747, CARAN, of 16th December 1943. However, the report makes no mention of where and when Darnand said this.

France and the European idea. The national socialist ideal constitutes the principal motive of their enlistment. It is for this ideal that they will fight on the Eastern Front. They are revolutionary militants whose ambition is to save France from the Communism and the anarchy threatening it.

On 28th November 1943, in Nice, Darnand spoke before an audience estimated at 1,200 strong. In the main, they were *miliciens*. His speech would last almost an hour. He evoked the sacrifices of the *Milice*, 33 dead and 25 seriously wounded since April, but proudly acknowledged that the last had already been avenged. He stormed that he no longer wanted them to sacrifice themselves in vain and then warned all enemies that they would pay for their crimes. He denounced the justice system for being too slow and stigmatised the magistrates who feared for their lives. He promised: "I will arm our troops. Today I bring to them the necessary arms! Our last martyrs will be avenged! Our enemies have been warned! We fight!"

This was war, civil war.

Darnand moved onto the theme of setting up a union of 'European nationalities against Bolshevism'. After announcing that a great number of *Miliciens* had already enlisted in the Waffen-SS, he said:

I too have enlisted. I have taken the oath. Soon, I will join them on the Eastern front, the only battle, when their training is finished. I am proud to tell our friends and enemies.

He attempted to justify his conduct, recalling his past in the two wars. He declared that the cause of France was linked to that of Europe and that the internal revolution would happen after victory. Finally he concluded:

We are proud to say that we are going to fight beside the Germans! It is a question of life or death! You will be hanged along with me, we will all be hanged if we do not know how to fight! Be resolute, together we will win!

The auditorium resounded to a storm of applause and cries of "Vive Darnand!" The whole room rose to its feet. Even those German officers present stood up and applauded.

And what was the response to Darnand's personal appeal for enlistment of *Miliciens* in the Waffen-SS? According to one Ministry of Interior report dated October 1943,[137] 200 *Miliciens* had signed for the Waffen-SS. By February 1944, again according to the Ministry of Interior,[138] the *Milice* had furnished the Waffen-SS with nearly 300 men.

The initial response must have come as a great personal disappointment to Darnand, for 'his' *Milice* in the autumn of 1943 numbered some 29,000 adherents of which 10,000 were 'active'.[139] However, of the 10,000 real militants, perhaps no more than one thousand were *francs-gardes*.[140] Therefore, it could be argued that

---

137 A non-referenced report, F1A 3747, CARAN.

138 Ministry of the Interior report ENE/3/35301, written 21st February 1944, CARAN.

139 Delpierré de Bayac, page 181, based on figures quoted by Francis Bout de l'An, the *directeur de la propagande de la Milice*.

the *Milice* had a very small pool of 'fit and young' men from which to draw recruits for the Waffen-SS.

From this response, one can conclude that the majority of *Miliciens* were not won over. Stubbornly they adhered to the idea that the greater danger was from the internal Communists and 'terrorists'. For some traditionalists, Darnand had gone too far. They left the *Milice*.

Ironically those *Miliciens* and *francs-gardes* who now took the field against the 'terrorists' were the most anti-German! The civil war proved brutal and bloody.

Also disappointed in his attempts to recruit for the Waffen-SS was Jacques Doriot, the leader of the P.P.F. By November 1943, the party had recruited from its membership fewer than 500 of the 600 men promised. Nevertheless, if it were not for the manpower demands of the S.T.O., the P.P.F. would have kept its promise.[141] Notably, a high percentage of those who continued to volunteer were from the P.P.F. Indeed, the following statistics concerning the political party affiliation of 163 recent French volunteers appeared in a German report of 8th December 1943:[142]

> 38% no party
> 20% P.P.F.
> 10% *Milice française*
> 9% Francisme[143]
> 4% R.N.P.
> 19% all other parties

Remarkably 'the headquarters of the Waffen-SS'[144] came to the P.P.F. 'cap in hand'. It demanded of the P.P.F. to find urgently from the members of its party doctors, vets, and medical and veterinary staff for the French unit of the Waffen-SS. Doctors and vets were promised officer ranks even if they had not served as officers in the French Army. An internal P.P.F. circular specified that 'medical auxiliaries of the Army and veterinary auxiliaries who in France are *adjudants* will be assimilated with the rank of *sous-lieutenant* into the French corps of the SS'.[145] The same circular stressed the 'extreme' importance that *le Chef*

140 According to Ministry of Interior reports LIA/6/31300, dated 10th May 1943, and WEZ 9/31301, dated 18th June 1943, the *Franc-Garde* numbered 920 men and 30 *chefs*. However, in a report dated 19th June 1943, Pierre Cance put the number of *francs-gardes* in the zone under Italian control at 6,809. Undoubtedly this figure is exaggerated.

141 The reason for not meeting its target is given in an undated report, see X.C.G./1/ 35302, CARAN.

142 A certain Stubaf. Zwickler wrote the report. Also of great interest is that the majority of the volunteers were from Paris and the adjoining Ile de France. (28% of the volunteers were from Paris and 9% from Ile de France.)

143 Considering that Bucard had ordered his militants not to enlist, this figure of 9% seems quite remarkable.

144 An undated report, see X.C.G. 1/1/35302, CARAN. Presumably 'the headquarters of the Waffen-SS' was the SS-Hauptamt.

145 Ibid. Curiously the report states that Darnand 'holds the rank of *Capitaine* and is the only French SS officer'. As such, this is incorrect.

[undoubtedly Doriot] attaches to 'the efficient participation of the Party in the organisation of the Waffen-SS … '

The 'sieve' of Sennheim

By 30th September 1943, about 800 French volunteers were undergoing selection (or training) at the camp of Sennheim.[146] However, out of the first 1500 French volunteers to attend Sennheim, less than a third were actually admitted into the Waffen-SS.[147]

According to a German communiqué[148], of those French volunteers who stepped forward for the Waffen-SS during the month of October 1943, 48% were students, farmers and young men between the ages of eighteen and twenty, 39% were workers and 13% had technical and industrial professions.[149] The communiqué also stated that the majority had never belonged to a political party.

Many of those classed as 'workers' were from camps in Germany and from the mines to the north of France. About one third of the volunteers were Parisians, followed by the Southerners who had grown in number and more vocal since the arrival of the *Miliciens*.[150] According to Ory,[151] a large number of *repris de justice* [ex-convicts] were present.[152] Admittedly there were various incidents while on leave. Pierre Ruche remembers:[153]

> Paul Delsart [pseudonym] hated me to death because I knew about him (while on leave he had attacked, pistol in hand, a chic bar in Paris, at the head of a small commando (group) of bandits disguised like him as SS. This idiot had badly miscalculated his coup: the bar was protected by the SD and the attackers ended up in Fresnes [prison] less than two hours later. At that time, my influence still carried a certain weight and Delsart sent me a 'desperate word' through a [female] friend. He begged me to plead his case, that he had been drinking, that there was nothing else for him to do other than commit suicide, etc … Anyway, he was 'part' pardoned and he never forgave me …

Ruche did not expect such behaviour from a NCO and platoon commander. The past of the recruits was investigated. Jacques Lorazo said of this:

146   Ory, "*Les Collaborateurs*", page 266, and Landwehr, page 30.
147   Mabire, page 87. Considering Germany's military situation at the time, reservations about this high 'reject rate' are unavoidable. Of course the possibility exists that those who did not meet the high standards required by the Waffen-SS were found alternative employment in another military or paramilitary arm of the Third Reich.
148   The German communiqué is reproduced in the French Ministry of Interior report X.C.G./1/35324, dated 13th December 1943 (F1A 3747, CARAN).
149   Indeed, according to Saint-Loup, page 31, 50% of Cance's 1st Battalion of the SS-Sturmbrigade were students.
150   Mabire, page 87.
151   "*Les Collaborateurs*", page 266.
152   Bayle, who served with the Sturmbrigade, takes great exception to this suggestion (letter to the author), but some members of the Sturmbrigade were dismissed when the volunteers' criminal records turned up at Neweklau.
153   Mounine interview with Ruch.

When I think about myself, just a simple volunteer, they went to the *quai des Hollandais* at Dunkirk to investigate me, which had well annoyed the family vis-à-vis the neighbours.

However, some convicts did slip through the net, but it is unlikely that many were present.

Some historians also claim that many volunteers had only been able to enlist by falsifying their date of birth. Undoubtedly, some did, but many? Again this is unlikely.

Recognising that the previous military experience of the former French Army officers could serve as a potential 'building block' from which to train the unit's future encadrement, though not rewarding it like the LVF, the Waffen-SS was to consider any volunteer with such credentials as an officer cadet. Thus, the encadrement, mainly drawn from the *Milice*, would prove to be considerably older than the majority of volunteers whose average age was between eighteen and twenty.

The *Milice* lost its monopoly on the encadrement to its Paris based rival, Doriot's *Parti Populaire Français*.[154] The designated Regimental commander, Lieutenant-Colonel Gamory-Dubourdeau, was from the P.P.F. For the moment, he did not disguise the fact that he saw his role as that of preventing Darnand's men from colonising the French Waffen-SS.

Pierre Ruch recalls:

The struggle between the French political clans was not secret, but open, avowed, strident and bitter. All considered the SS as a simple INSTRUMENT.

Although Gamory-Dubourdeau was the most senior and the highest-ranking former French Army officer to volunteer for the Waffen-SS, his selection as the Regimental commander at the grand age of fifty-eight does surprise. Perhaps one explanation for his selection is that the Waffen-SS authorities, who, undoubtedly, were well aware of his political fidelity, wished to play him off against the large number of officers from the *Milice*.

Born on 29th January 1885 in Ploudalmézeau, Brittany, Paul-Marie Gamory-Dubourdeau started his long military career in the Foreign Legion. In 1911, after attending the *École militaire d'infanterie de Saint-Maixent*, he graduated with the rank of *sous-lieutenant d'active* and was posted to the 2° RIC at Brest. He went on to serve with the Camel Corps in the Sudan and Tibesti. His career came to a less than illustrious end when he was demobilised in Morocco as an officer in the Supply Corps.

Haunted by politics, *lieutenant-colonel* Gamory-Dubourdeau joined the P.P.F. and went on to become the *Secrétaire adjoint* [assistant secretary] of the P.P.F. in Morocco. Nevertheless, he remained fiercely loyal to his Celtic homeland of Brittany and led a small autonomous group called *Le Roc breton*. His appearance of an 'aryan menhir was going to captivate the Germans'.[155]

---

154 The P.P.F. actually tried to undermine the *Milice* by infiltrating its own members as *Miliciens!*

155 Mabire, page 93.

Also from the P.P.F. was former student Joseph Pleyber, born on 19th September 1906. He came to the Waffen-SS in order to follow in the footsteps of Party leader Doriot who had gone to the Eastern front himself in the ranks of the LVF. Pleyber had been greatly encouraged to do so by his wife, a more ardent supporter of Doriot than he was.

The Corsican Dominique Scapula, born on 10th December 1906, was also a P.P.F. adherent.

Robert Lambert was a member of the *Parti Franciste*. Born on 10th February 1918, he had served in the *Spahis Marocains* with the rank of *Aspirant*.

The political origin of the following French officer cadets is not known:

> Lieutenant Henri Maud'huit, born on 6th August 1895
> Lieutenant Pierre Brocquart, a former pilot, born on 15th August 1916
> Lieutenant Jean Croisille, born on 2nd September 1894
> Edmond Fluhr, born on 29th September 1916
> Paul Pruvost, born on 9th January 1901
> Lopez
> Robert Roy, ex-N.S.K.K., born on 13th June 1904
> Alfred de Mandiargues, born on 3rd June 1920
> Pierre Wable, born on 4th February 1904

Of note is that the white-haired and rosy-faced Croisille, who was approaching fifty, had enlisted in the Waffen-SS with his two sons.

Separated from their men upon their arrival at Sennheim, the former French officers were quartered in maison Sordi, named after its former proprietor, near Sennheim station. Stripped of their former French Army rank, though granted 'promotion' to the rank of Oberscharführer in the interim, these officer candidates of the *Französisch Lehrgang* were tested and educated by their new world. The pace would be furious.

The training of the French officer candidates was placed under the overall supervision of Stubaf. Welbrock. Although an amputee, his legs having been smashed by a Soviet shell, he was a man of extraordinary energy and he got round in a barouche. Welbrock had fully embraced the Germanic revolution of the Waffen-SS that was only just beginning.

Ustuf. Reiche from SS-Ausbildungslager Sennheim, a former embassy attaché at Berne with a gift for languages, was assigned to supervise the French officer candidates on a personal basis. His fair hair and glasses gave him the appearance of a diplomat rather than that of a soldier.

Ustuf. Binder and Ustuf. Kopp were responsible for the political education of the French officer cadets.

Erich Kopp had been a card-carrying member of the NSDAP since 1928; he had received his party card from Goebbels in person. Before the war he served with the SiPo-SD at Freiburg-am-Breisgau. Very energetic, he spoke French well.

Flemish NCOs Uscha. Eeckhout, born on 31st January 1921 in Maldegem, and Uscha. de Lodere, supervised the military and technical training of the French officer cadets. Pignard-Berthet recalls that they received a warm welcome from the German cadres but, on the other hand, their relations were rather distant with the other volunteers, particularly with the Flemings. This contrasts with Bayle who remembers an excellent spirit reigning between the different nationalities.

At the beginning of October 1943, Gauleiter Robert Wagner paid the French officer cadets a visit. After inspecting the officer cadets who were still in civilian clothing, he asked if any among them had fought in the First World War. Only Jean Croisille came forward. The Gauleiter shook his hand and his hand alone. The others took this gesture of reconciliation very badly.

The group of officer candidates was joined by Doctor Pierre-Auguste Bonnefoy, born on 1st August 1908 in Belley, and by Abel Chapy, born on 7th January 1920. Both were from the *Milice française*.

Before the war Chapy was a militant 'among the leagues of the nationalist formations', including the *Jeunesses Patriotes* (Patriot Youth), and came to realise that his nationalism correlated with ideas advocated by National Socialism. Chapy has gone on the record as stating: "From his seizure of power, Hitler developed, as it were, ideas which were mine." Yet his sense of country and duty were such that he was moved to enlist. Thus, in 1938, aged eighteen, he signed up. He served in Morocco with the *Spahis* and then the *Chasseurs d'Afrique*.

Demobilised with the rank of *Aspirant*, Chapy felt great bitterness over having missed the battle for France and her subsequent defeat. Returning to France in 1941, 'it was with no light heart that he saw the Germans in his country'. Before secretly crossing the Demarcation line to return home, to his native Tours, Chapy contacted the Marseille SOL. Despite taking an interest in Déat's RNP and its breakaway party, Deloncle's MSR, he was not roused from his indecisiveness to sign up. That all changed in November 1942 when the opportunity to return to North Africa presented itself in the form of the *Phalange Africaine* raised by Laval and Darnand to defend French Tunisia against the Anglo-Americans. However, Chapy never got across to North Africa.[156]

An admirer of Darnand, Chapy finally crossed into the Southern zone and came to the *Milice*. Following attendance at its Uriage training school he returned to Tours and organised an underground *Milice Trentaine*, which in theory was still prohibited, being in the occupied Northern zone.

Because of his European and National Socialist convictions, Chapy also decided to volunteer when he heard that many *Milicien* cadres were leaving for the Waffen-SS.[157] There was another reason, that of Nationalism. He detailed:

> There were at that time in Alsace about one thousand young Frenchmen who had enlisted in the Waffen-SS and to whom it was essential to give French cadres. The reason? What would the sacrifice of thousands of Frenchmen have served if they had to be integrated in a German unit! For them, [it was an] absolute necessity to have French officers and fight as Frenchmen. It was quite obvious and important that this formation of young SS Frenchmen could bring by itself an advantage and a role to France. I add that it was essential that France could benefit from our battles and the prestige we were going to win on the Eastern front.

156   In fact, only a *détachement précurseur* of the *Phalange Africaine*, six high-ranking and senior officers, ever got across to North Africa. For a comprehensive history of the *Phalange Africaine*, see "*Les français sous le casque allemand*", page 59 to 67.

157   Mabire, page 87.

When asked by the recruiting officer what he was looking for in the Waffen-SS Chapy replied: "The Iron Cross. I need honour."

Chapy knew Lambert. They had both served in the *Spahis Marocains*.

In mid-November 1943, more officer cadets arrived. They included:

René Fayard, born on 17th May 1922
Pierre Hug, born on 24th January 1920
Henri Kreis, born on 2nd February 1923
Charles Laschett
Joseph Peyron, born on 1st June 1913
Potier

Fayard, Hug, Kreis, Laschett and Peyron were all selected from the NCO cadets *Lehrgang*.[158] That they should be considered Waffen-SS officer material is a remarkable achievement. None had previous military service in the French Army. Peyron, however, had spent some time with the Todt, but had not found what he was looking for. And Fayard was ex-N.S.K.K. Also of note is that Hug was the son of an Army colonel.

Potier was ex-LVF and was decorated with the Iron Cross, probably 2nd class.

Like all new recruits, the officer cadets received some form of sports uniform, perhaps the all black two-piece SS tracksuit with a circular black and white SS emblem on the left breast.[159] The fatigue uniform would follow and finally the *feldgrau* SS uniform. Chapy admitted that he shed some tears when he donned the field-grey for the first time and that he was not alone. He recalled that the former French officers and *aspirants* beside him 'were hardly smiling'.

For Fenet, the German uniform posed no problem, remarking[160]:

> There was no other possible uniform to fight against the Soviet Union. In a war that atrocious, there was no place for doubts.

The officer cadets' training was not solely physical. Ustuf. Binder and Ustuf. Erich Kopp took them for the *Weltanschauung*, the central tenet of National Socialism. Ustuf. Binder spelled out this 'world view' through lectures on the laws of heredity and the history of humanity according to racist laws. The enemies of National Socialism were clearly identified: Communism, egalitarianism, Freemasons, multiparty democracy, capitalism, Judaism and Christianity. The French audience was difficult and demanding. Indeed, many were very thankful for the rest from the otherwise physical demands of the day. But this *Weltanschauung* came as a shock to those like officer cadet Pignard-Berthet who saw in National Socialism a political party like those back in France.

SS-Ausbildungslager Sennheim 'sieved' the French officer cadets in the same way as all French recruits. For whatever reason at least two officer cadets 'dropped out' and returned to France.

From the start of October to the end of December 1943, between eighty and one hundred Frenchmen underwent NCO training. Almost all were from the 1st Company. Ustuf. Bastian, a Volksdeutsche from Eupen-Malmédy, Belgium,

---

158 Mabire describes Hug, Kreis, Laschett and Peyron affectionately as the Sturmbrigade's 'Four Musketeers'!

159 See two photographs that appear in Mabire's "*La Brigade Frankreich*".

160 "*Historia #613*", page 16.

commanded the NCO candidates *Lehrgang*. Seriously wounded in the face on the Eastern front, he wore a black patch across one eye. His *Spiess* was Oscha. Waldemar Holtorf.[161]

The French NCO candidates were billeted in Sennheim church hall. Notably, they became the first French SS Freiwillige to receive a rifle. The training was intense.

One incident the French NCO candidates of the *Lehrgang* had cause to remember well. Three times, a Norwegian instructor had them march past a local priest and thunder out "Heil Hitler!" Politely, each time, the priest had replied "Guten Morgen!" And, each time, the instructor did not acknowledge this. Reported, the incident was investigated. The arrogant Norwegian instructor was returned to his original unit.[162]

At the end of the course, only about a dozen trainees were promoted to the rank of Rottenführer and thirty or so to that of Sturmmann. Nevertheless, the number who had simply failed was only about half a dozen. The remainder became Oberschütze.

French recruits continued to arrive at Sennheim. One such recruit was Jean Halard, born December 1926 in the 14th department of Paris, who abandoned his college studies to enlist in the Waffen-SS. Ashamed of the military debacle in 1940, he wanted to show the Germans just how proud he was to be French. Moreover, his enlistment was a statement to the Germans that all Frenchmen were not cowards in the fight against Communism and also that they were not alone in this fight *pour l'Europe*. Notably, unlike many other recruits, he wholeheartedly believed in the ideology of National Socialism.

Leave was granted over Christmas and the New Year (22/12/1943–7/1/1944) for some one thousand volunteers. The exploits of some came to the attention of the German Military Administration in Paris that complained to Abteilung III [the justice section] of Sennheim camp. Those responsible, brought together in the 3rd Company at Weiler to continue their training, were investigated. The punishment meted out to them, however, was token. It was taken into consideration that all had rejoined their units rather than deserting which would have been easier for them.

Enter Skorzeny. French volunteers of the Waffen-SS were recruited for the SS-Sonderverband z.b.v. (and later the SS-Jagdverbände). The total number of Frenchmen who went on to serve in the ranks of Skorzeny's Special Forces is not known. However, between 25–28 February 1944, fifty-three Frenchmen at Sennheim were proposed for the SS-Sonderverband z.b.v.

On 22nd January 1944, the SS-FHA ordered that all non-German infantry regiments of the Waffen-SS (SS-Freiw.-Gren.Rgter) should have nationality as well as a progressive numeration within that nationality added parenthetically to their titles. In this way, the French Regiment became the Franz. SS-Freiw.Rgt.57 (französisch Nr.1).[163]

161 Identified by Mabire as Hans Ohlendorf.
162 Bayle, "*De Marseille à Novossibirsk*", page 54. Bayle was, in fact, one of the French NCO candidates present. Mabire recounts the 'same' incident, see pages 101-102, but curiously there are some major differences; French NCO candidate Bousquet replaces the Norwegian instructor, the priest does eventually reply: "Heil Hitler!", and no action is taken against Bousquet.

By early January 1944, French volunteers had filled six companies.[164] At the head of the 1st battalion (companies 1–4) was Swiss officer W-Sturmbannführer Hersche.[165]

Heinrich Hersche was born on 30th September 1889 in Zurich. He served in the Foreign Legion and the Swiss Army, becoming a Colonel. Before the war he commanded the cavalry school at Thun. He was a former member of the Swiss national horse-riding team. Going over to Germany, he joined the 3rd squadron of the SS-Kavallerie-Ersatz-Abteilung. On 1st December 1943, he joined the SS-Hauptamt and was found employment at Sennheim.

The training at Sennheim was hard and manoeuvres were often conducted with live-fire. Louis Blanchere said:[166]

> We were on manoeuvre towards Thann, [in an] undulating and wooded region, [and] a detachment of the Kriegsmarine[167] was holding a sector opposite—at a certain point the order was given to the latter to fire on us; we took cover on the ground and I found myself on a half-frozen stream—I threw myself on the ice, I broke it and I remained for quarter of an hour with icy water going over me—as I wished to realise if the danger was as real as they had told me, I took a stick in my hand and raised it 70cms from the ground; it was instantly broken by bullets which whistled all around us—three comrades were killed and five or six were wounded. The following week the same exercise was repeated.

Discipline at Sennheim was very strict. Two French volunteers, one of whom was a *Milicien* from Lyon, stole two geese, brought them back to their sleeping quarters and cooked them up. Unfortunately for the two men and de Misser, who witnessed the cooking, the geese belonged to the local NSDAP leader. There was an inquiry. The two thieves were caught and brought before a military tribunal. They were sent to SS-und Polizeilager Danzig-Matzkau. As for 'accomplice' de Misser, he was sentenced to fifteen days close arrest, but the punishment was not executed immediately, only in June 1944 when he was with the French SS-Sturmbrigade in Bohemia-Moravia, finding himself in Neweklau prison. Also, he had to forfeit promotion to Unterscharführer for one year.

In January, some one hundred French NCO candidates were sent to Unterführerschule der Waffen-SS Posen-Treskau, Poland (then Reich territory), for an eight week training course. Accompanying them were three German instructors.

On their arrival, much to their surprise, the French NCO candidates were greeted in French by their course supervisor, a young Walloon Oberjunker. In French, he ordered them to stand to attention but they did not react. A second

163   SS-FHA, Amt II, Org.Abt.Ia/II, Tgb.Nr. 166/44 g.Kdos of 22.1.1944.

164   Mabire, page 113.

165   Curiously, according to Mabire, page 113, in early January 1944, the first to enlist finally started their real military training and formed the first *bataillon de marche* and the last to arrive formed a training battalion under Hersche. This is unconfirmed.

166   Recorded in a non-referenced Ministry of the Interior report, dated 5th February 1944, F1A 3747, CARAN.

167   It should be noted that at no time did French volunteers of the Kriegsmarine, also trained at Sennheim, conduct manoeuvres with their compatriots of the Waffen-SS. (Personal conversation with Soulat.)

order, quickly followed by a third, was barked out in French. The French NCO cadets stayed as they were. They would only respond to orders in German!

The French NCO cadets were also surprised to meet Moslems on the same course who were dressed in the exact same uniform, but wearing an SS fez with the death's head and SS cap eagle. They were from the recently raised 13. Waffen-Gebirgs-Division der SS 'Handschar' (Kroatische Nr.1).

All the NCO cadets would receive section commander and even platoon commander training. Yet at the end of the training course only fifty of their number were promoted, for the most part, to the rank of Sturmmann.

Around the same time twenty-four French officer candidates, accompanied by Reiche and Binder, were dispatched to SS Junkerschule Tölz for a special abridged training course (1. *Sonderlehrgang für französische Offiziere*) that ran from 10th January 1944 to 4th March 1944.

Ustuf. Reiche, who spoke excellent French, went in place of Uscha. Eeckhout. On 8th March 1944, Eeckhout was transferred to 6. SS-Freiw. Sturmbrigade 'Langemarck'.

The French officer candidates were (in alphabetical order)[168]: Artus, Bartolomei, Brocquat, Cance, Chapy, Croisille, Fayard, Fenet, Fluhr, Gamory-Dubourdeau, Gaultier, Hug, Kreis, de Lafaye, Lambert, Laschett, Maud'huit, de Mandiargues, Peyron, Pignard-Berthet, Pleyber, Pouget, Pruvost, Scapula, de Tissot and Wable.

The course supervisor was SS-Hauptsturmführer Kostenbader, otherwise called 'Koko', holder of the Iron Cross 1st Class, who had transferred to Bad Tölz from a post at NCO school Posen-Treskau.

On their arrival at Bad Tölz, the French officer candidates found themselves 'demoted' from the rank of Oberscharführer to that of Unterscharführer. All would start from a 'level playing-field'.

Because the standard of German amongst the French officer candidates left much to be desired instruction was given in French. Also, the time spent learning German was increased by one hour per week to six. The French officer candidates were permitted to wear French medals and that included those won during the 1940 campaign. And, for the first time, the French tricolore flew with equal status to those flags of the other nations at Bad Tölz.

At the close of the course, the French officer cadets were commissioned as such:

Sturmbannführer: Gamory-Dubourdeau
Hauptsturmführer: Cance
Obersturmführer: Artus, Fenet, de Tissot, Pleyber, Croisille and Maud'huit
Untersturmführer: Brocquart, Bartolomei, Gaultier, Lambert, Pignard-Berthet and Scapula
Standartenoberjunker: Fayard, Chapy, Hug, Peyron, Kreis and Laschett

Of those that had served in the French Army, most bettered their former rank. Some promotions do surprise.[169]

168 The official report 'SS-FHA. Amt XI (2) Az: 36 o /Amt V/IIa Ref.6/Amt II/Org. IE/III/4 vom 26.1.44' actually spells four of the names incorrectly!!

169 The promotion of Cance to Hauptsturmführer and particularly that of de Tissot to Obersturmführer suggests that the Germans were 'looking after' some of the more

Found wanting, Pouget and Fluhr were 'promoted' to the rank of Oberscharführer.[170] For Pouget, promotion it was not. The equivalent French Army rank of Oberscharführer is *adjudant* and this NCO rank was below the commission of Lieutenant he once held in the French Army.

Presumably, de Mandiargues, Pruvost and Wable also received the rank of Oberscharführer. That is unless they were discharged.

As for de Lafaye, he refused to swear the oath of loyalty to Adolf Hitler and left the Waffen-SS. He returned to the *Milice*, becoming the *chef de la Franc-Garde du département de l'Allier.*

The end of the course also brought the news that Hauptsturmführer Kostenbader had just become an instructor to the French Waffen-SS regiment soon to be assembled in Bohemia-Moravia.[171]

After the training course at Bad Tölz the French SS officers went off for a weeklong stay (perhaps 4th March 1944 to 11th March 1944) at San Martino di Castrozza in the Italian Tyrol where they could initiate themselves into skiing or, if more experienced, perfect their skills. However, they paled before the Scandinavians.

While his fellow officers were away at Bad Tölz, Doctor Bonnefoy attended a training course at SS-ArztlicheAkademie [SS medical school] Graz. He was promoted to the rank of Obersturmführer.

Meanwhile, on 22nd February 1944, Breton nationalist Yvon Trémel, born in 1922, volunteered for the Waffen-SS at the Rennes recruiting office. He said of his formative years:

> I was not against the Germans. My teacher was not anti-German. I had friends who had been in Germany in 1938. They had been well received and well treated. In August 1939, for fear of war, they were advised that it would be better to go home. I was not in favour of war against Germany because I was a Breton nationalist, I had been a member of the PNB since 1937, and because of France's hypocrisy, summed up best by the expression 'do as I say and not what I do'. France had seized Alsace-Lorraine and yet it was complaining about the German occupation of Sudatenland. And the majority of Austrian people wanted the annexation. In France it was lies, lies.
>
> [I remember] a discussion with my half-sister, a teacher, who was married to a French officer of the Colonial Army. She had been in Senegal for two years. She was in favour of war. I was not. [It was] a lively discussion. She grabbed me. I took her by the arms and she fell on her knees. Her husband, who was present, did not say a word. A few weeks after the declaration of war she said to me that I was a traitor. This I did not accept. My mother sided with my sister. She was anti-Boche and anti-Nazi. I never used the word Boche. My mother and half-sister did.

influential and senior members of the *Milice*.

170   Edmond Fluhr was appointed *germanische SS Werber* (recruiting-sergeant) on 1st May 1944 and then posted on 2nd December 1944 to the *Franz. SS-Grenadier-Ausbildungs und Ersatz* Battalion, the depot and training battalion of 'Charlemagne'.

171   According to Mabire, page 163, Hauptsturmführer Kostenbader was promoted to Sturmbannführer soon after the end of this course. Bayle does not recall this.

I did not fight against the Germans in the 39–40 war. I was too young. And yet I had received mobilisation papers in 1939, but I was only seventeen and a half. I was morally and physically older than my age.

In May 1940, my schoolteacher told the class to return home to their families. I heard on the radio about the fighting on the Somme. [President] Renault said we are the strongest and we will win. And yet weeks later, catastrophe.

He tried to embark for England, but was thwarted by the speed of the German advance. He was impressed by the bearing and appearance of the German soldiers he met:

Suddenly a new German column stopped on the right side of the street. Ten or so Germans 'joined' us in a bar, asking for cigarettes, cigars and sweets. The owner, who was afraid, gave them everything. Suddenly the Germans said: 'How much?' Surprised, she gave them receipts and they gave her Marks. She gave them French change. Appel! The Germans left. The lady said: '*Ah bien ça alors!*'

I reflected. The Germans looked good. They were tall, strong and not hungry. And they were wearing good uniforms. And yet the newspapers and radios were reporting that the German soldiers were hungry and in paper uniforms. So this was not true. And they had paid too. Later we met more German soldiers and all were of the same good appearance.

Contact with the occupying German forces only accentuated his already strong German sympathies. He wanted to serve, but the 'French' LVF was not for him. He chose instead the European Waffen-SS. Sent to Sennheim, he trained with the 5th Company under SS-Hauptsturmführer Hartmann at Weiler. In June 1944, he was transferred to the 1st Company.

The Sturmbrigade

In March 1944, the French volunteers were ordered to form a motorised heavy artillery regiment with the title and number of 'Schw.Franz.SS-Freiw.Artillerie Rgt.(mot.) 500'.

The artillery regiment was to be organised as follows and with such field post numbers:

Headquarters and Headquarters Battery	Nr. 11 003
I. schw. Abt. (Heavy Battery)	Nr. 13 847
II. schw. Abt. (Heavy Battery)	Nr. 12 175
III. schw. Abt. (Heavy Battery)	Nr. 14 049
Artilleriekolonne (Artillery Column)	Nr. 13 847

In April 1944, an Observation Battery, field-post number 06 386, was added to the regiment.

For artillery training, the newly promoted French officers were dispatched to SS-Artillerieschule II Beneschau, one of the many training schools located within Truppenübungsplatz Beneschau, south of Prague.

In mid-March, at the conclusion of their training at Posen-Treskau, the French NCO cadets were sent to artillery school Beneschau.[172]

The French officers and NCOs alike had no enthusiasm for the artillery training. It was with sadness that the NCOs replaced their white epaulettes of the Infantry for the vermilion-piped epaulettes of the Artillery. In protest, many NCOs went sick or went down with the strangest of medical complaints. This seriously disrupted the training and came as a great surprise to the instructors.

The officers, for their part, protested in a manner more befitting their rank. Cance wrote to Darnand, Pleyber wrote to Doriot and the young Oberjunken wrote direct to RF-SS Himmler himself. Gamory-Dubourdeau went off to Berlin intent on 'having it out man to man' with Ogruf. Berger.[173]

Equipment, straight out of the factory, was supplied to the forming French Artillery Regiment: semi-tracked lorries, and 105mm and 155mm guns.

Several days after their arrival at Beneschau, the French officers were joined by Ostuf. Pierre Michel. He too had acquired his rank at the SS Junkerschule at Bad Tölz, but in a platoon of Germanic officer cadets. Regarded as a National Socialist fanatic, he was welcomed with some reservation. Born on 15th February 1919 in Paris,[174] Michel, a student engineer, entered the *Ecole spéciale militaire de Saint-Cyr* in 1938. On 2nd September 1939, he was commissioned as a *Sous-lieutenant d'active* and posted to the *503e régiment de chars de combat* (503° RCC). Years later, he joined the LVF, becoming the company commander of the 2nd Company. In late August 1942, he resigned. On 5th July 1943, after a stint in the N.S.K.K., he volunteered for the Waffen-SS. He brought along with him from the N.S.K.K. several like-minded illuminati.

Among the first Frenchmen to arrive at Sennheim on 2nd August 1943, Michel attended the officer cadets' course run from 1st September to 17th October 1943. Assigned to SS Ausbildungs-und Ersatz-Battalion 11 at Graz on 17th October 1943, he was sent to SS Junkerschule Tölz on the 20th, attending the 3. Lehrgang für germanische Offiziere.[175] He graduated with the rank of Obersturmführer.

Even with the arrival of Michel the French Sturmbrigade of the W-SS remained desperately short of officers. Stubaf. Gamory-Dubourdeau asked the P.P.F. to send urgently officers or *aspirants*, preferring those who had received their rank before the war.[176]

In late March or early April 1944, perhaps as a result of the protests, the French volunteers were formed into a Sturmbrigade[177] titled the

---

172 Curiously, Bayle, one such French NCO, does not speak of meeting the officers at Beneschau.

173 Mabire, page 160.

174 Potsdam archives. However, according to Mabire, page 161, Pierre Michel retained a great passion for his pagan homeland of Brittany.

175 Ibid.

176 Undated report, see X.C.G. /1/35302, CARAN. Presumably Gamory-Dubourdeau went to other French political parties with the same request. Or did he? The P.P.F. was his former party.

177 This does not appear to have become official until later, perhaps June or July 1944 (Bayle cites June 1944, and Klietmann and Littlejohn cite July 1944). Indeed, the French Heavy Artillery Regiment was not aborted until May 1944.

'Franz.-SS-Freiwilligen-Sturmbrigade' ['French SS Volunteer Assault Brigade'][178] or the 'Franz. SS-Sturmbrigade Nr. 8'.[179]

Told that they were leaving to form a Sturmbrigade, the NCOs literally jumped with joy. The 'sick' miraculously recovered. They had been SS-Kanonier for some three weeks. The NCOs went on to attend Panzer as well as Engineer training. In this way, they became 'ultra-trained'.[180]

The French SS-Sturmbrigade was now assembled in the village of Networschitz, several kilometres from Beneschau. More than 1,000 men arrived from SS-Ausbildungslager Sennheim.

To perform administrative duties, French-speaking 'German' personnel, many of whom were Alsatians or natives of Lorraine, were transferred to the forming French SS-Sturmbrigade. For the most part, they were furious about the posting, but all would knuckle down to their duties.

By early April 1944, five companies had been formed with such a command:

1st Company (infantry)	Maud'huit
2nd Company (infantry)	Artus
3rd Company (infantry)	Fenet
4th Company (heavy)	Michel
5th Company (PAK)	Pleyber

The infantry companies had more than 200 men each.

---

178   SS-FHA, Amt II Org. Tagesbefehl Nr. 2710/44 geheim Kommandos, Bayle (*"De Marseille à Novossibirsk"*, page 79), Klietmann, (*"Die Waffen-SS"*), and Ertel Heinz and Schule-Kossens Richard (*"Europäische freiwillige im bild"*).

179   Mounie (*"Cernay 40-45"*). However, the Sturmbrigade has appeared with a variety of designations; Lambert (*"Les Français sous le casque allemand"*) and Angolia (*"Cloth Insignia Of The Waffen-SS"*, page 491) cite the '8. Franz. SS-Freiwilligen Sturmbrigade'; Mabire cites the 'SS-Sturmbrigade Nr. 7 Frankreich'; and Saint-Loup cites the 'SS-Sturmbrigade Nr. 7'. In response to those titles carrying number 7, in September 1944, number 7 was officially allocated to the Dutch brigade 'Landstorm Nederland'. Therefore, its use by the French unit should be regarded with great suspicion. Moreover, the number 7 did not appear in the SS-Soldbuch nor on the identity disc of French SS volunteers. And yet certificates for medals won in Galicia show the use of number 7 (see Bayle, *"De Marseille à Novossibirsk"*, page 100), but are they post war? Furthermore, as far as many veterans are concerned, the French SS-Sturmbrigade never had the official number of 7. Nevertheless, the number 8 also cannot be found in the SS-Soldbuch nor on the identity disc of French SS volunteers.

Also, some sources name the Sturmbrigade 'Frankreich' (the German word for France). In response to this, at no time was the French Sturmbrigade ever officially called 'Frankreich' or even 'Brigade Frankreich'. However, 'Brigade Frankreich' was employed because many French SS volunteers could not report the full unit name in German! Even so the French SS volunteers often contented themselves with just saying 'Sturmbrigade'.

180   Bayle, page 79.

Maud'huit was quickly replaced by Ostuf. de Tissot at the head of the 1st Company. Later on, Ustuf. Pignard-Berthet was detached from the 2nd Company and assigned to the 1st Company with orders to take over the supervision of the training.

Officers and NCOs were also appointed to other positions of command in the various support and heavy units. Croisille went to the Headquarters services and Brocquart to Signals.

To supervise the continued training, Kostenbader placed a young German officer in each company. Some had combat experience. After some initial suspicion and friction between the French company commanders and their German supervisors, things were quickly smoothed out and they jointly set about the business of training.

As in many other non-German Freiwilligen Waffen-SS units, German NCOs were also brought in to various posts for their stabilising influence, but their number is unknown. Karl Rapp, a former member of the premier 'Leibstandarte SS Adolf Hitler' Division, served as *Spiess* (company sergeant major) in the 5th Company.

So what was the structure proposed for the French Sturmbrigade? Perhaps that of two battalions, each with three infantry companies, one heavy weapons company and one anti-tank company. And, in addition, brigade companies of Field Artillery, Light Flak, Heavy Flak and Assault gun.[181]

Command of the 1st Battalion went to Hstuf. Cance.[182]

The FLAK Company of the Sturmbrigade

On 1st April 1944, the 3rd Company left Sennheim to join the SS-Sturmbrigade. After journeying for three days, it arrived at Neweklau. The 3rd Company came with the tag of 'a sort of disciplinary unit'. This was not unfounded. In its ranks were a number of 'hotheads' whose exploits while on leave in France that Christmas and New Year had not gone unpunished. Nevertheless, this company, for all its ills, was well trained. It became the 6th Company of the Sturmbrigade.[183]

After some permutations, the 6th Company was designated the FLAK Company of the French SS-Sturmbrigade. German instructor SS-Ustuf. Jauss then asked Ostuf. Maud'huit to take command of this unit, and to organise its recruitment and training. In a matter of days, he set up the FLAK Company. And although some volunteers left to join the companies formed before their arrival, others did their utmost to fill the posts made vacant. In this way, the FLAK Company realised its full 'complement' of 1 officer, 36 NCOs, and 111 men. In total, 138 soldiers.

181   This was the structure of the 6. SS-Freiwilligen-Sturmbrigade 'Langemarck' as of
      June 1944. Notably, the first five companies formed for the French Sturmbrigade
      mirror the structure of a battalion. And yet the 1st Battalion that went to Galicia
      comprised three infantry companies and an anti-tank platoon, but this may have
      been more out of necessity and circumstances than planning. Also, Klietmann's
      claim to four battalions in formation in May 1944 appears very doubtful.
182   It is not known when he assumed command of the 1st Battalion.
183   Soulat, page 26.

Also 'on the books' of the FLAK Company were former French Army officers Crespin, Croisille, Roy, and Honoré de Lareinty-Kotchoubey de Tholozan. All held the rank of Oberscharführer and all were waiting to take up their appointment. Nevertheless, the rank and file of the FLAK Company never saw them.

Once formed, the FLAK Company began its training, but its personnel, 'as a direct consequence of the defeat of 1940', did not wish to serve under former French Army officers.[184] However, Maud'huit persevered and did his best, but on 22nd or 23rd April 1944 he was relieved of command and replaced by Führerbewerber Guignot, a former French Foreign Legion *Capitaine*, born on 20th September 1901.

To give Guignot support, the young, dynamic Oberjunker Fayard was assigned to the company and appointed the commander of the 1st platoon.

On 25th April 1944, the FLAK Company set out by civilian trains to Munich to attend a training course with the SS-Flak Training and Replacement Regiment. Arriving three days later on the 28th, the FLAK Company moved into barracks Freimann on Ingolstaderstrasse, which would be its home for the next three months.

Although the Germans endeavored to screen accurately each volunteer some of dubious loyalty and morality entered the ranks of the Sturmbrigade. While at Networschitz the Sturmbrigade received the criminal records of its recruits. All those who had received *condamnations infamantes* were expelled.

The Sturmbrigade also shed itself of those guilty of theft. In three months, some twenty volunteers, for the most part seasoned ex-criminals, were sent without a second thought to concentration camps. Among them was a common law criminal who, whilst on leave in France, had robbed some Jews.

Fenet came to suspect that a saboteur was disrupting his company. He was right. The saboteur was quickly exposed and arrested. The evidence against him was overwhelming: foolishly, he had kept a sort of diary of his acts of subversion. Fenet decided to have him sent to Prague for court martial. Until such time as he could be moved, he was kept under lock and key in a hut best described as ramshackle. The prisoner soon made his escape, but the guard from the same company by the name of Maurette calmly shouldered his rifle and shot him dead. Headquarters immediately promoted Maurette to the rank of Sturmmann! This precedent worried Fenet. Such was his concern that he had a message relayed to all his men that they were not to start taking pot shots at prisoners to gain promotion to Sturmmann!

Recognising that Networschitz's wretched conditions were paralysing the training and seriously affecting morale, Kostenbader managed to get the Sturmbrigade moved to Neweklau, some 10kms away, where the accommodation was better.

There was no respite at Neweklau, training continued day and night. Continuous drill. Continuous inspections. Route marches. Platoon maneuvers. Then company maneuvers. Then battalion maneuvers. And all were conducted with live ammunition. As a result some volunteers were injured and evacuated to hospitals

184   See Gaulois, article "*La SS-Französische Flakbatterie*".

in Prague, where they were treated by French nurses, also volunteers for the Waffen-SS.

Ostuf. Fenet came close to death in a 'live' exercise when his command post in a farmhouse was attacked by a *corps-franc* led by Oberjunker Kreis. A bullet actually went straight through the death's head on his cap!

Also, one beautiful, quiet Sunday a French SS volunteer writing to his family was accidentally killed by another cleaning his weapon nearby. His death was lamented.

Maurice Manfredi was wounded during the training at Neweklau. In 1942, this nineteen-year-old Marseillais volunteered for the paramilitary OT-SK (Organisation Todt-Schutzkommando) and served in Guernsey and Jersey. In September 1943, he volunteered for the Waffen-SS and was accepted after completing his training at Sennheim.[185]

Pignard-Berthet acquired the nickname of 'Tito', the partisan leader; following a night exercise with a *demi-compagnie* he had to set traps, in the manner of partisans, to break up the march of the battalion. Twice, acting on his own initiative, he brilliantly ambushed the units on the move whilst maintaining an elastic defence of a village in which his men had taken refuge.

As the weight of the volunteers dropped their morale heightened. The timely arrival of the French SS-Sturmbrigade at Neweklau had also contributed to the considerable rise in morale. And when Fenet learnt that a volunteer by the name of Vallebout, serving in the heavy platoon, had lied about his age to gain enlistment he offered him the opportunity to return home. Without hesitation the volunteer chose to remain with his comrades!

The Swiss connection

In April 1944, SS-Untersturmführer Büeler arrived at SS-Ausbildungslager Sennheim to pick up the reins of the 2nd Company.[186] Heinrich Büeler was born into a German-speaking Swiss family on 12th December 1901 in Cochin, the Indies. In 1907, he went to live with his grandfather in Winterthur. He studied law at the universities of Zurich and Hamburg, before attending La Sorbonne, Paris, for three semesters. Not surprisingly he was fluent in German, French and English.

At the age of twenty, Büeler joined the Communist youth. Some years later, he discovered National Socialism. Becoming a member of the *Front National*, he defended young Swiss National Socialists in court. He was soon considered an enemy of the state and, in June 1941, was arrested. The payment of a fine brought him his release. With his practice in ruins, he left Switzerland and crossed into Germany.

In October 1941, at the age of forty, Dr. Büeler decided to join the Waffen-SS. He underwent basic training at Sennheim. In April 1942, he was posted to the SS-Hauptamt in Berlin where he took up an administrative post

---

185   He was subsequently listed as missing-in-action with 'Charlemagne' in Pomerania, 1945.
186   Curiously, according to Mabire, page 114, Büeler commanded the 3rd and the 4th Companies.

in the Waffen-SS library department. In April 1943, he was awarded the KVK II.

In September 1943, Büeler attended the SS-Junkerschule at Bad Tölz. Graduating with the rank of Untersturmführer, he returned to Sennheim.

The _Spiess_ of the 2nd Company was SS-Oscha. Johann Neubauer, born on 31st December 1918 in Wels, Austria.[187]

In May 1944, André Doulard of the RNP enlisted in the Waffen-SS. He was born on 13th June 1921 in Geneva, but of French nationality. This connoisseur of jazz enlisted out of hatred for Communism, hatred born of Stalin's ban on jazz music and purge of musicians, and of the death of musician Parnakh in the Gulag. At Sennheim, he was assigned to the 1st Company.

Also in May 1944, up and coming Parisian actor Marc Sainteuil volunteered for the Waffen-SS and was accepted. His decision was all the more remarkable because he was a _résistant_ for the first two and a half years of the occupation, explaining that he had wanted to erase the shameful defeat.[188] But the geopolitical situation in 1944 was quite different to that at the end of 1940. He explained:

> It was no longer a matter of a Germanic Greater Reich dominating the whole of Europe. Germany needed the help of the countries of Western Europe no longer for a total victory enabling it to dictate its terms but to obtain, if the Anglo-American landing failed, a separate peace with the USA and England. This was not a utopia. Churchill was all too aware of the Soviet danger and wanted a landing in Greece in such a way to cut off the advance of the Soviet armies. Of course such a peace was only possible with the eviction of Hitler.
>
> Also, we were going more and more inexorably towards a disenchanted, senseless, [and] material world, a world without sorrow and a world without joy. Both my father and I were moral and spiritual 'human animals' who believed that it was the quality of the 'personal being' that counted. We were not politically minded.[189]
>
> The SS was the only means in existence through which I could start to realise my desire: to make the world enchanted and enchanting again. I wanted to pass in the road Egyptian, Greek, Khmer, Roman or Gothic statues. I wanted to be sitting in the Metro beside a Giotto, a Vermeer. I wanted to pay my taxes to an important person like Eschyle or Shakespeare. I was born immortal. I 'joined' the war so that everybody would know it. All this was for me simple and realistic.
>
> I enlisted against two materialisms: the collectivism of Marxism and the capitalism of the Anglo-Americans.

---

187 SS-Oscha. Johann Neubauer should not be confused with the SS-Ustuf. of the same surname who commanded the transport of the 1st Battalion of the French SS-Sturmbrigade in Galicia.

188 Curiously, during his time as a _résistant_, Sainteuil never heard of the word _résistant_ or De Gaulle.

189 In late 1936, at the age of sixteen, Marc Sainteuil had joined the P.P.F., which he saw as both a national and popular movement. Disappointed by the party's obvious lack of ideals and vision of the future, he resigned months later. Never again would he flirt with a political party.

Also he had become alarmed by the Gaullist government of Algiers behaving like the governments of the Third Republic that had led France to defeat in 1940.

There were a number of other reasons to help explain his decision to enlist. First, he had fond childhood memories of Germany. In 1936, his father, a prominent figure in the *Comité France-Allemagne* founded by former combatants of the 14–18 war in the spirit of reconciliation, took him to the Olympic Games held in Berlin as a present for his unexpected exam success.[190] The Games were a great success for Germany and he had never forgot the spirit of youth of the Germans. Also, like many, he respected Hitler for the way he had revived his people between 1933 and 1939. Then came the occupation. The discipline and bearing of the occupying German troops greatly impressed him. But that was in the past and so were the victories of 1940–41. Germany could no longer win the war by itself. He reasoned that Napoleon had employed the services of foreign volunteers. He wished to help and help in the ranks of the Waffen-SS, whom he described as *les forces vives* and viewed as an 'embryo of Europe'. The LVF, which he described as a 'patriotic French movement of struggle against Marxist communism', was not for him because he also wished to fight the 'supreme capitalism represented by the USA'.

Secondly, prominent authors and journalists such as Jacques Chardonne, Henry de Montheriant and Robert Brasillach, and sculptor Aristide Mailloi, regarded by Sainteuil as the greatest sculptor of the twentieth century, had committed to collaboration. Indeed, cultural life had continued to flourish under the occupation.[191]

Lastly, the possibility of victory was slim when Sainteuil enlisted in May 1944. And yet this did not dissuade him from enlisting. In fact, he felt that he should enlist regardless of the consequences, even if it meant defeat or losing his life. *Attentisme* was not for him.

Parents and friends alike were surprised by his decision. His mother cried. His father, who did not share his son's convictions, said to him: "If you believe that it is your duty, do it. I only ask that you go and see Benoist-Mechin." Benoist-Mechin was a Vichy Secretary of State and a good family friend. Thus, he went to see Benoist-Mechin who said to him: "Don't leave. What are the reasons? I cannot tell you." He left, thinking to himself: another one playing the *double-jeu*. This he described as lamentable.

He was sent to Sennheim. On or around 20th June 1944, he learnt of the landings in Normandy. He immediately circulated among his fellow French volunteers a petition to fight on the Normandy front with the proviso that under no

190   After the *coup de Prague* in 1938, his father, concerned that German foreign policy had become aggressive and a threat to France, shelved *Le Comité*. Moreover, his father was hostile to the anti-Christian character of National Socialism.

191   For example, the major philosphical work *"L'Etre et le Néant"* by Jean-Paul Sartre was published in 1943. The collaboration in the arts is the subject of many books, but not this one. Nevertheless, the enlistment of Frenchmen like Sainteuil should be placed and perhaps best understood within the context of this rich and intense cultural life.

circumstances were they to be engaged against French troops. 70 to 75 of the 200 French volunteers present at Sennheim at that time signed the petition. However, the others thought he was going too far or had enlisted to fight solely the Soviet Union and Communism. Nothing came of his petition or so he thought.

The wearing of the *feldgrau* posed him no problems. He was a soldier and as such was expected to wear a uniform. And as a soldier he had to obey his commanders. Thus, the oath he swore to Hitler, a direct link between the soldier and the supreme commander, only strengthened this obligation. Be that as it may, he and his comrades did not hero-worship the Führer. They believed that the 'Ein Volk, Ein Reich, Ein Führer' of 1933–1942 was well in the past. Moreover, the oath did not give them the feeling of having entered a kind of Hitlerian monastic order.

At the end of his training at Sennheim, instead of leaving with his comrades, he was assigned to the political department and made an instructor. This was a posting he did not want. Sent to Neweklau for NCO training, he was promoted to the rank of Unterscharführer, but the racism of the political training he found crass and refused to teach. He asked to be transferred to the Special Forces.

In May 1944, following ten days in officer school Bad Tölz, a number of French officer candidates entered SS-Panzergrenadierschule Kienschlag near Prague.[192] Martret was one such officer candidate. He was a graduate of NCO school Posen-Treskau. The platoon leader of the French officer candidates was SS-Ustuf. Kleindienst, who had once served with the premier Waffen-SS Division 'Leibstandarte Adolf Hitler'. Martret remembers him as a playboy. Although Kleindienst would often go into Prague late at night, he was always the first to report for duty the following morning!

In early June 1944, Martret interrupted his officer training to return home.[193] His parents—innocent civilians—had been killed on 26th April 1944, victims of an English bomber downed by FLAK. Thanks to Kleindienst, Martret, who only had a fatigue uniform, went home in a complete service uniform. His donning of the *feldgrau* for the first time left him unmoved except for, perhaps, a touch of pride in the wearing of the 'runes'.

Meanwhile, back in France, at 0930 hours on 13th June 1944, Otto Abetz, the German ambassador to Occupied France, met with Doriot, Déat, Bucard, Knipping (Darnand's *délégué du Maintien de l'Ordre en zone Nord*), de Brinon (the *président du Comité de la LVF*) and Marion (the *président des Amis de la Waffen-SS*). The French side took the lead, insisting that since the invasion 'all members of the LVF and the Waffen-SS wish to fight, not in Russia, far from their homeland, but on French soil, to defend their homeland against the internal and foreign enemy'.[194] Abetz

---

192 The number of officer candidates that entered SS-Panzergrenadierschule Kienschlag may have been fifteen.

193 Strangely enough, Martret arrived in Paris on 6th June 1944.

194 Telegram from Abetz to Ribbentrop that same day (see Brunet, "*Doriot*"). And yet, according to Delperrié de Bayac, "*Histoire de la Milice*", pages 381 to 383, Abetz took the lead, calling on all the *groupements nationaux* to agree to fight in Normandy. Continuing, Abetz 'saw in the units that could be formed in this way a start point of a future Franco-German military alliance'. Then, and importantly, it was Abetz who called for the return of the LVF and for the

supported this request, noting that the French volunteers would probably fight with more zeal 'for their very existence against their mortal enemies, the gaullists, and against their Anglo-American allies'. However, support was not forthcoming from the military authorities and all such plans were soon abandoned.[195]

As of 30th June 1944 the Sturmbrigade had a total troop strength of 1,688 [30 officers, 44 NCOs and 1,614 men], but this figure would seem to reflect only those French volunteers on hand at Neweklau and not those undergoing training at Sennheim or at any other training establishment. Indeed, by the end of January 1944, two sources agree that 2,480 Frenchmen had enrolled in the Waffen-SS[196] and, by that August, the figure was 3,000.[197]

Introduced for wear in July 1944 was the official SS 'tricolore' sleeve shield.[198] This sleeve shield differed noticeably from its official LVF counterpart with curved sides and the word 'FRANCE' at the top. However, privately made insignia was worn prior to its official introduction and it is considered extremely likely that this practice continued. According to regulations from the SS-FHA, the national sleeve shield was to be worn on the left sleeve directly under the SS sleeve eagle. However, most wore the shield on the forearm. Strangely enough, when the first French sleeve shields (unquestionably the official SS pattern versions) were received it was the German instructors who were first to sport them, whereas the Alsatian NCOs held out for as long as possible.[199]

Discipline remained harsh. During a sweep for enemy paratroopers, Rottenführer Simon, a platoon commander in the 2nd Company who had attended NCO school Posen-Treskau, found himself before a charging doe. He did not hesitate to shoot it down. As punishment he had his command taken from him and was transferred to the 2nd Battalion.[200]

'immediate return of the 'Sturmbrigade des Waffen SS'.

195   Delperrié de Bayac, "*Histoire de la Milice*", pages 381-383. And yet, according to Mabire, pages 183-184, at the end of June 1944, the French officers learnt that the Sturmbrigade was to be sent to France and employed against the maquis. Incensed, Stubaf. Gamory-Dubourdeau gave them his word that they would be employed as soldiers and not 'cops', and on the Eastern Front and nowhere else. He kept his word. He created such a fuss at the SS-Hauptamt (the SS Main office) that the order was revoked. So had the SS-HA actually entertained the idea of employing the Sturmbrigade as an auxiliary police force on its own soil against its own countrymen? This will probably never be known.

196   See Ory, "*Les Collaborateurs*", page 266, and Neulen "*An Deutscher Seite*", page 110. Curiously, according to Burrin, "*La France à l'heure es Collaborateurs*", by January 1944, some 6,000 Frenchmen had volunteered for the Waffen-SS of which one half had been accepted.

197   Saint-Loup, page 31, and although this figure is not dated, the engagement of the 1st Battalion of the French SS-Sturmbrigade before Sanok in August 1944 is talked about in the very same breath. Furthermore, Littlejohn repeats the figure of 3,000 (see "*Foreign Legions of the Third Reich vol. 1*", page 159).

198   Angolia, "*Cloth Insignia Of The SS*".

199   Mabire, page 173.

200   Transferred to the 2nd Battalion, Simon did not go to Galicia. He was later transferred to the Engineer Company of 'Charlemagne'. Much to his regret, other

On that same sweep, men from the 4th Company went hunting even though it was prohibited. This became known and 'went all the way up to Prague'. Company commander Ostuf. Michel was put under close arrest. As punishment, Michel had his command taken from him[201], the NCO candidates of this company had to give up any idea of promotion, and all were fined twenty marks!

There were other events worthy of note.[202] Picture the scene of Oberjunker Kreis of the 5th Company standing in the middle of a road, with his legs wide apart, watching over his platoon conduct an exercise in crossing a road under enemy fire. Suddenly behind him came the sound of a car horn. He paid the car no attention and continued on with the exercise that lasted some time. With the exercise finished, he turned round and waved the car on. It was only then that he realised that no less a person than the Reichsführer-SS himself was in the car! Kreis presented his men to Himmler who then drove off to Neweklau. Now expecting the worst on his return to barracks, Kreis drew out the training. When he did finally venture back awaiting him was an order to report at once to Hstuf. Kostenbader. Far from being reprimanded, Kostenbader passed on to him Himmler's congratulations! There was an article in the regulations that prohibited the passage of vehicles across an exercise in progress.

By July, the 7th Company had begun to form. Ustuf. Pignard-Berthet received its command, but it was an appointment he accepted only on condition that he left for the front at the head of the 1st platoon of the 1st Company, which he had trained.

In late July,[203] the Sturmbrigade received the order to make ready a battlegroup for employment on the Eastern Front.

The battlegroup formed was based on the 1st Battalion of the Sturmbrigade under the command of Hstuf. Cance. The battalion was composed of three combat companies under de Tissot, Artus and Fenet and a support (heavy) company under Pleyber.[204] The composition of the heavy company still remains unclear although it did include Oberjunker Kreis' PAK platoon and the so called Panzervernichtungstruppe, a close combat tank destruction unit, apparently of platoon strength.[205]

The 1st Battalion was heavily reinforced, although the precise nature of that reinforcement is also unclear. Before its departure, those elements of the 1st Battalion not quite up to scratch were replaced by some of the best volunteers arriving from Sennheim.[206]

Before the 1st Battalion was deemed as combat ready it had to undergo a manoeuvre under the critical eye of an impressive group of Waffen-SS Gruppenführer. The results were very favourable. After the manoeuvre, a grand parade was held at Neweklau. At its close Hstuf. Kostenbader called together the

reasons kept him from going to Pomerania and Berlin. Bayle wrote: "In this way, Simon's voluntary service became sterile."

201   According to Mabire, page 179, Michel was transferred to a depot. This must be a reference to Greifenberg, the LVF's depot, for the Sturmbrigade had no depot. However, when Michel appeared at Greifenberg he did so at the head of a company of the 2nd Battalion. Arguably, as a result of this incident, he was transferred to the 2nd Battalion as a company commander and later his company was sent to the depot to continue its training.

French SS volunteers and congratulated them for the first and last time. He added
that of all the SS Freiwillige he had trained the French had been the best.

202   The first edition of this book also recounted the affair of Bussang pass, which can be
      found in both the pages of Saint-Loup (see "*Les Hérétiques*", pages 42-44) and Mabire
      (see "*La Brigade Frankreich*", pages 439-422), but really does beg belief. Because of
      this it has now been relegated to a footnote.
          According to Saint-Loup, following an alert in July 1944, a *compagnie de marche* of
      Frenchmen, Norwegians, Flemings and Dutchmen was hastily formed at Sennheim
      under Stubaf. Hersche to defend Bussang pass from American paratroopers.
      Although they did not find any American paratroopers, they did surprise and capture
      forty armed masquisards (members of the maquis) without a fight. Lined up in the
      main square of Thillot, a village at the foot of Bussang pass, Hersche informed them
      that since they were *francs-tireurs* they would be shot according to regulations.
      Suddenly changing his mind, Hersche asked all those who wanted to join the
      Waffen-SS to take one step forward. Thirty-five maquisards did so. Hersche
      screamed at the five who had stood fast to get lost and not to fall into his hands again!
      This he repeated several times. Of the forty, ten now remained. Concluding, Hersche
      told them to go and join their new comrades and to try and fight with a little more
      energy than earlier!
          The arrival of the maquisards at Neweklau aroused great curiosity. Assigned to
      Ostuf. de Tissot's 1st Company, they would serve loyally when the time came in
      Galicia.
          However, Mabire is not in full agreement. He replaces Hersche by a 'Prussian'
      Hauptsturmführer. He names the village Le Tillot. He numbers the masquisards
      captured at nearly 100. He numbers the masquisards determined to enlist in the
      Waffen-SS at 30 or so. And he states that the former masquisards would serve in
      Pomerania.
          In reply to both Saint-Loup and Mabire, a local historian of Le Thillot has
      stated there was no such incident and there was nowhere near the same number of
      franc-tireurs in Le Thillot and the surrounding area as found in the 'story'. However,
      one villager did volunteer for the Waffen-SS, but that was before the summer of
      1944. (Research provided by Mounine, letter to the author.)
          Also, Pignard-Berthet, at that time a platoon commander serving with de
      Tissot's 1st Company, does not recall the systematic incorporation of former
      maquisards into the company (letter to the author).
203   Mabire, page 186. Specifically, according to Mounine, letter to the author of 21/1/
      98, it was on 28th July 1944 that the French SS-Sturmbrigade received the order
      to make ready a reinforced battalion for Galicia.
204   Mabire, page 185.
205   Prior to going into action, the Panzervernichtungstruppe of the Heavy Company was
      attached to de Tissot's 1st Company. In the fighting that ensued no other
      elements of the Heavy Company, except for the PAK platoon, are mentioned.
      Thus, Pleyber may have been left with nothing more than a company in name to
      command. Indeed, the command of the Heavy Company appears to have been
      left vacant when he went across to the 2nd Company. Also, the
      Panzervernichtungstruppe was probably armed with hand held anti-tank
      weapons Panzerschreck and Panzerfaust.
206   Pignard-Berthet, letter to the author.

Elation for one officer and disappointment for another marked the days running up to the departure of the 1st Battalion for the Eastern Front. Hstuf. Cance appointed Oberjunker Chapy to the command of the Panzervernichtungstruppe and, despite the unit lacking the necessary equipment required for its role, Cance intended in the meantime to use this unit as a sort of *corps-franc* for the Battalion. Chapy was elated.

The officer disappointed was Ostuf. Artus. Cance summoned Artus, commanding the 2nd Company, and after praising him as one of his best officers, told him that he would be staying behind at Neweklau to serve as Stubaf. Gamory-Dubourdeau's assistant and to oversee the formation of the 2nd Battalion of the Sturmbrigade. Cance reasoned that Artus would be the heart of the 2nd Battalion, as such its real commander. Concluding, Cance assured Artus that soon he would join the 1st Battalion at the front with the new recruits from Sennheim. Ustuf. Gaultier became the new commander of the 2nd Company.[207]

Before the departure for the Eastern Front the *Amis de la Waffen-SS* visited the French volunteers. With them they brought reasonable quantities of sardines and French wine. Also the short stay of thirty young French nurses of the Waffen-SS is fondly remembered. One such French nurse was Nelly, who recalls that they received a warm welcome. She said of her enlistment[208]:

In June 1940, I had just turned nineteen. My family and I supported Marshal Pétain, the hero of the 1914 war. The armistice had just been signed when I met a young German NCO of the Wehrmacht; for both of us it was love at first sight. His regiment stayed six days at Moulins. When we separated he asked my parents for permission to correspond with me; he spoke rather good French. My father was Flemish and very pro German, thus no dificulties in that respect all the more so because he was very much on the right.

In 1941 his regiment was stationed at Brest. On 15th April, he came to my parents to spend part of his leave (unauthorised) and we were engaged. Claus was of Danish origin. Back home, in Schleswig-Holstein, he had taken steps so that we could marry, but it was still not possible.

On 26th August, he left for Russia. Claus taught me what National Socialism was and told me before we separated: "If I die in this war (he had a premonition) think always that I died not only for my country, but also for yours, for Europe." On 4th February 1942, he was killed at Smolensk. He had just turned twenty-four and I was twenty-one. It was his mother who had informed me. I was out of my mind with grief. Then a friend of my father suggested I join the J.E.N. where his daughter was. We became very good friends. It was here that I regained a little the strength of life without him, among soldiers who came to the J.E.N.

Then there were enlistments, several of our comrades joined the Abwehr and the Waffen-SS, and when I was told that women could enlist in

207 According to Bayle, "*De Marseille à Novossibirsk*", page 91, Gaultier was nicknamed 'Play-Boy' because of his presence and elegance. However, in 1944, the expression 'Play-Boy' was not in common use. Therefore, he may have acquired this nickname at a later date.
208 Letter to Jean Castrillo, 26/10/2004.

the German Red Cross I was one of the first, we must have been three or four from the J.E.N. In 1943, it must have been towards the end [of the year] that we had signed our enlistment in the German Red Cross in the offices of the Waffen-SS in Paris, in the 16th [district] I think. On 2nd November 1943, we left for Belgium, to Spa, for training. I had no previous training as a nurse.

Like all those joining the Waffen-SS, Nelly also swore an oath of loyalty to Hitler. For her, the oath represented 'loyalty to our engagement, to the fight against Bolshevism and especially to Europe'. She wore the uniform of the German Red Cross and on her coat lapel a J.E.N. badge.

On 9th February 1944, she left Spa for Germany, continuing her training at Nieder Weisel hospital, curiously a civilian hospital. The air raids on nearby Frankfurt left the hospital with 'much work' and Nelly with thoughts for the victims and also of retaliation, hoping that the Germans would bombard England likewise, because that 'is the only way they will understand'. In this 'first test' some of her comrades were found wanting. In a letter to her parents she expressed her determination to continue:[209]

> If we leave for Russia it is through ideals and we know very well the life that awaits us, I assure you that I prefer to be in a Lazarette and in a big city than being at Nieder Weisel. We are not in the German Red Cross to avoid the alerts and the bombardments. Believe me that I might have some hard days ahead, but never will I regret the path I have chosen and I want to fight until victory, in the difficult moments the memories of Claude will always support me.

Nelly was at Nieder Weisel for some three months, afterwhich she was sent to Berlin for an exam. Passing the exam, she was then posted to an SS hospital in Prague.[210] She was one of eight such French nurses there. The wounded SS soldiers were surprised that the nurses attending them were French, but very happy to have them, all the more because the French nurses amused them greatly, being unable to speak German fluently. Moreover, Nelly spoke German with a French accent!

There were no more than sixty French nurses of the Waffen-SS.

Finally, on 29th July 1944, the reinforced 1st Battalion of the French SS-Sturmbrigade under Hstuf. Cance left Neweklau on foot for Beneschau railway station. The very next day the battalion boarded trains and departed. Destination: the Eastern front.[211]

The strength of the reinforced 1st Battalion of the French SS-Sturmbrigade is reported as 20 officers and 980 other ranks.[212] Only the

209 Nelly, letter to her parents, 22/3/1944.
210 According to Bayle, "*De Marseille à Novossibirsk*", page 87, the French Waffen-SS nurses would also leave for the Eastern Front. This is not correct.
211 Mabire, page 198. However, according to Saint-Loup, page 38, and repeated by Littlejohn, page 161, the date of departure was 18th July 1944 which would put the arrival of the 1st Battalion at the front much earlier than most sources agree upon.
212 Bayle, "*De Marseille à Novossibirsk*", page 121, and confirmed in correspondence to the author, 1997. Mabire uses a figure that fluctuates between 1,000 and 1,200.

nucleus of the 2nd Battalion, apparently several hundred volunteers in two companies (perhaps the 5th and 7th), was now left at the virtually deserted Neweklau. The training of the 2nd Battalion continued under Hstuf. Kostenbader.

CHAPTER 2

The Sector of Sanok

The military situation in Galicia

On 13th July 1944, the 1st White Russian Front and the 1st Ukrainian Front went over to the offensive and inflicted a series of body blows on the German Army Group designated as North Ukraine. To begin with, on the 16th, the German XIII Corps was encircled. Then, on the 18th, the Russian 1st Guards Tank Army, striking between the Fourth and First Panzer Armies, reached Rava Russkaya. Also on that same day the Third Guards Tank Army passed north of Lwów while the newly committed 4th Tank Army closed in on the city from the east. The city would finally fall a week later.

22nd July was disastrous for the 4th Panzer Army. To the North, the 1st White Russian Army punched through Chelm in the morning and by nightfall elements were beyond Lublin, some 40 miles away. In addition, to the South, not only was the gap between the 4th Panzer Army and the First Panzer Army now thirty miles wide, but the spearheads of the 1st Guards Tank Army had reached the San river near Jaroslaw against no resistance. In danger of being outflanked and encircled, 4th Panzer Army reported to Army Group that it could only save itself by immediate withdrawal behind the Vistula and San rivers. Two days later, on 24th July, the 3rd Guards Tank Army and Cavalry-Mechanised Group Baranov had also approached the San on the stretch between Jaroslaw and Przemysl.

When the 4th Panzer Army finally received permission to withdraw on 25th July 1944 it was too late. The Russians already had bridgeheads across the Vistula and on that day the 1st Guards Tank Army and the 3rd Guards Tank Army burst across the San between Jaroslaw and Przemysl and fanned out. While the 1st Guards Tank Army stabbed north-west toward an open stretch of the Vistula on both sides of Baranów, the 3rd Guards Tank Army pushed south-west toward Krosno, west of Sanok.

To try and plug the gap between the 4th Panzer Army and 1st Panzer Army, the 17th Army was activated late July 1944 and initially provided with two and half divisions. By 31st July, its headcount had risen to five 'divisions'. That day marked the first signs of the Russian offensive faltering as the Armies outran their supply lines and also the first day of a counterattack by Army Group North Ukraine aimed at clearing the entire San-Vistula triangle. Although both the 17th Army and 4th Panzer Army made gains, the counterattack petered out in two days, with little disruption to the Russians. Throughout early August 1944 the Russians continued to advance through Krosno, Sedziszów Mlp, Mielec and Sanok in the area of the 17th Army. It was to this 'fluid' front in Galicia, Southern Poland, that the 1st Battalion of the French SS-Sturmbrigade was sent.

The preliminaries

On 5th August 1944, after a weeklong journey by rail without incident, the Battalion finally arrived at the town of Turka. Situated between Sambor (or Sambir in Ukrainian) and Uzhgorod, near to the source of the Dnestr, Turka was some ninety kilometres east of Sanok. The troops disembarked. Their first priority was to clean their weapons which was quickly carried out. Towards the end of the afternoon, the three grenadier companies set off on foot. They marched for some six hours through the hills of the Beskides before bivouacking for the night. Each company set up in a 'hedgehog' around which the engineer platoon under Oscha. Lopez, a Pied Noir[1], erected barbed wire entanglements. Before nightfall Cance assembled his officers to inform them that the Battalion would be fighting with the 18. SS-Freiwilligen-Panzer Grenadier Division 'Horst Wessel' in a sector to the west of Sanok. On the following morning, the officers told their men in turn of this attachment.

At 1000 hours, the companies marched off again due north in the direction of Sanok. The vehicles started out in turn escorted by the tracked vehicles of the PAK platoon. They climbed hill after hill. The dust and the heat soon became unbearable. Their bodies were covered in sweat. Their equipment and weapons became heavier and heavier and dug into their flesh. Their singing gradually ceased.

They came to a 'real' road that was nothing more than a gullied earth track. They were passed by ambulances and columns of Russian prisoners dressed in dust-coloured rags going to the rear and by convoys of vehicles and tanks from the Waffen SS, on which rode its exhausted infantry support, going back up to the front. The battalion covered some fifty-five kilometres before stopping at last around midnight in a bombed-out village surrounded by forest. And there were no stragglers! Patrols went out as this area could longer be termed 'friendly'.

During the night Ostuf. Bonnefoy, the Battalion's chief medical officer, went off in an ambulance to attend to a local who had been knocked down by a German vehicle. The ambulance was soon back and a stretcher was brought out. Even though the local actually turned out to be a partisan who had blown a leg off while laying a mine, Bonnefoy had him evacuated to a military hospital. He was strictly adhering to his moral responsibility as a doctor to save life.

Ironically, for the rest of the night, the partisans made a nuisance of themselves around the bivouac. The French volunteers warded them off with machine-guns, their first shots fired in anger.

Outside of the bivouac a greater danger lurked in the night: mines. A lorry carrying ammunition in which Oberjunker Peyron was travelling ran over a mine, but he was lucky enough to escape with only minor injuries.[2]

That night Cance decided to attach Oberjunker Chapy's platoon from the heavy (support) company to de Tissot's 1st Company.

1   An Algerian-born Frenchman or, more generally, a North-African European.
2   Mabire, page 229. However, according to Bayle, "*San and Persante*", the same incident came to pass on 13th August 1944, Peyron's 2nd platoon/2nd Company was actually travelling in the lorry, and Peyron was left stunned by the explosion; he had not been wearing his helmet and had bashed his head.

'Horst Wessel' sent lorries to speed up the arrival of the desperately needed French reinforcements.

The journey by lorry on the following day, 7th August 1944, took the Battalion across anti-tank ditches, streams and the San river, all spanned by makeshift bridges, to another nameless village where the French SS volunteers accommodated themselves for the night. The front was near now.

No movement is reported by Mabire on 8th August 1944. Gunfire and mortar explosions could now be heard. Sanok could be seen with binoculars. On the evening of the 8th, Cance was paid a visit by Obf. Trabandt, the commander of 18. SS-Freiwilligen-Panzer Grenadier Division 'Horst Wessel', who explained to him just how serious the situation was and that it was deteriorating hourly. To the west of Sanok a huge hole had been torn in the lines held by the Wehrmacht. SS-Kampfgruppe 'Schäfer' of 18. SS-Freiwilligen-Panzer Grenadier Division 'Horst Wessel' had been called in to deal with the breach.

SS-Kampfgruppe 'Schäfer' was based on SS-Panzergrenadier-Regiment–40 and led by SS-Stubaf. Ernst Schäfer, a Knight's Cross holder, although it seems that Trabandt was in direct command of the SS-Kampfgruppe. Formed as a result of the Russian offensive of June 1944, the SS-Kampfgruppe had been rushed to Southern Poland where it had been in constant action ever since.

By 8th August, despite committing in vain all his last reserves, Trabandt had still not managed to completely plug the breach and the left flank of his sector was still wide open. Indeed, now faced with the Russians attacking through his left flank and the strength of his infantry companies reduced to 40, 30 and as little as 25 men, Trabandt felt he would no longer be able to hold onto his present positions. Thus it was with great relief that he welcomed the arrival of the 1st Battalion of the Sturmbrigade with some 1,000 men. One official wartime source lists the 1st Battalion of the French SS-Sturmbrigade as the IV. Battalion of SS-Kampfgruppe 'Schäfer'.[3]

Trabandt asked Cance to engage a company straightaway. Ostuf. Fenet's 3rd Company was put at his disposal. It assembled and set off immediately. Reporting to the headquarters of the SS-Kampfgruppe, Fenet was given concise orders by Trabandt: firstly, to try and establish contact with friendly troops to the left of the positions of the SS-Kampfgruppe, and, secondly, if unable to do so, then to cover its left flank. Also, because the situation was so confused, Fenet was told to await dawn before starting out. In the meantime, the French Company was held in reserve.

Morning came, bringing with it a slight delay for the 3rd Company impatient to get going. Fenet did not waste the 'time now on his hands'. He asked his NCOs to remind the men of how to handle safely the panzerfäuste they had just drawn.[4]

The demonstrations were interrupted by another piece of rocket equipment in the armoury of the German Army, the Nebelwerfer. When a nearby battery

3   According to Mounine, letter to the author, the French Sturmbrigade was the 'IVth Bataillon des Kampfgruppes der 18. SS-Div'. This is not confirmed by any other source.

4   The launching tube of the panzerfäuste actually carried the words 'Achtung! Feuerstrahl' (Beware of Jet flame) to protect the unwary user from the potentially dangerous jet of flame that extended rearwards from the tube when fired. In fact some men had actually been burnt alive by the rearwards flame.

opened up the Frenchmen immediately dived to the ground; they had never heard the Nebelwerfer firing before.

The 3rd Company finally set off mid-afternoon on 9th August 1944 and advanced across terrain that alternated from open to woods. Suddenly the Company came to a stretch of open ground that it could not possibly avoid without considerable delay. Ostuf. Fenet decided to push straight on and gave the appropriate orders. As the first Frenchmen started across this stretch, Russian guns and mortars opened up and shells soon started to rain down. Zigzagging and advancing by successive dashes as if on exercise, the company made it across at the cost of only two casualties: both were slightly wounded.

As soon as the two wounded were dressed, Ostuf. Fenet pushed on and soon made contact with the SS company holding the extreme left of the SS-Kampfgruppe's front. Commanded by Ustuf. Tämpfer, the last surviving officer, this company, once 200 strong, had been hit badly and now stood at only 20 men. Tämpfer had just beaten off another attack and had dispatched a patrol to reconnoitre the ground opposite his positions. Before continuing, Fenet decided to await the return of this patrol. Some hours later, the patrol was back, reporting that it had 'found nothing'.

Concluding that it now seemed impossible to establish contact with neighbouring friendly troops, Fenet set about carrying out the second part of his orders. Setting off again, his company soon took up a covering position that sealed off a small valley. Fenet ordered patrols from the 1st platoon under Ustuf. Lambert into a hamlet opposite, while the rest of the company dug in. Their positions received sporadic mortar fire. The patrols reported back that the sector was infested with Russians who seemed to be growing in strength. Night fell. More patrols were dispatched. Two orders in quick succession, the first to prepare to leave the position that was countermanded by the second, were the only events in an otherwise quiet night for the company.

On the following day, a dawn patrol from the 1st platoon of the 3rd Company into the same hamlet drew fire. Section commander Sturmmann Delattre was killed outright. After silencing the Red snipers, the patrol returned with the body. Platoon commander Ustuf. Lambert buried him. Sturmmann Delattre was the Sturmbrigade's first killed in action.

On 9th August 1944, while the 3rd Company was undergoing its baptism of fire, the rest of the battalion, according to Mabire, spent the whole day on a frustrating succession of marches and partisan alerts.[5] The two companies marched for twelve hours non-stop. Throughout the day patrols were sent into reported partisan-occupied villages and yet all returned with no sightings.

The first brush with the partisans came after nightfall. One tractor of Kreis' PAK platoon, which had broken down crossing a river, was fired upon. Fortunately nobody was hurt. The village from which the shot came was surrounded and searched, but again no partisans were found. Back on its way again, far worse was to follow for the PAK platoon when one of its men, Courcol, standing up in his

---

5   Curiously, according to Bayle, "*San et Persante*", page 51, the whole battalion was already in line. It received enemy fire. The 2nd Company took its first casualty; French SS Freiwillige Quinton was seriously wounded. His leg was partly severed.

tractor, was half decapitated by barbed wire strung across the road. And still there was no sign of the partisans.

10th August 1944 and the 2nd Company

On 10th August 1944, the 1st Company and 2nd Company went into line. They had orders to capture Dundynce and establish contact with the 208th Infantry Division in the area to the west of Pielnia.[6]

By midday, the two companies were well into Dundynce forest and under intermittent mortar fire. Separating, de Tissot's 1st Company moved off to the left and Gaultier's 2nd Company to the right. Led by Oberscharführer Charles' platoon and Gaultier himself, the 2nd Company advanced towards the edge of the forest. Despite a skirmish with unidentified enemy forces and gunfire still ringing out, Gaultier decided to press on in order to carry out his orders to the letter.

Reaching the edge of the forest, Gaultier gave orders to Bartolomei to support the attack of the 1st Company to dislodge the Russians from the forest opposite. Ahead of Gaultier was a hill that would serve as an excellent observation post, but to reach it a stretch of exposed ground had to be traversed. Somewhat recklessly, Gaultier, accompanied by Bartolomei and a section of men, ventured across this stretch of ground and were suddenly caught in the open by Russian mortars that marked the beginning of a ferocious bombardment. Many were hit. Gaultier was seriously wounded in the chest and the loins. He was dragged back to cover, continuing to give orders and asking for Bartolomei to take his place. He was evacuated.[7]

Taking what cover could be found when the bombardment begun, Bartolomei was soon awake to another danger as any movement he made was greeted by a sniper's bullet. Thus it took him an hour to crawl back to the edge of the forest where he discovered that the 2nd Company had moved on. All alone, pistol in hand, he wandered around the forest for three hours before stumbling upon a German sentry who directed him to his unit.

Ustuf. Bartolomei now took command of the 2nd Company. One third of the company was missing. However, not all of those missing were casualties. The platoon under Uscha. Lefèbvre[8], which had joined a German unit[9], reappeared

6   Tieke and Rebstock, "*Im Letzten Aufgebot*", page 44. Unfortunately Mabire does not record what exact orders the two companies had received, but implies that they were to relieve front-line units of the Wehrmacht. And as the companies advanced, it seems they passed the very units they were due to relieve, which had evidently pulled back too early. Ustuf. Pignard-Berthet, the commander of the 1st platoon of the 1st Company, was particularly critical of this untimely withdrawal which did not bode well. Also, Mabire cites the premature withdrawal of the Wehrmacht units as a contributory factor to the failure of the French Battalion that day.

7   Gaultier's wounds were such that he would play no further part in the war.

8   Incorrectly, Mabire, page 265, identifies Lefèbvre's platoon as the company's 'heavy' platoon with mortars and heavy machine-guns. However, the possibility exists that he became its commander after Bartolomei's presumed 'death' or by chance in the chaos that followed the bombardment.

9   According to Saint-Loup, page 20, the platoon ended up among the Waffen-SS of 'Horst Wessel'.

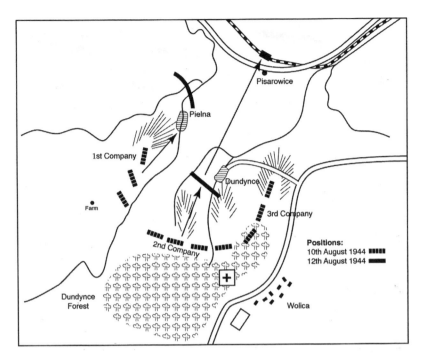

Map 1: The sector of Sanok, 10-15 August 1944: The charge of the Sturmbrigade
Based on Saint-Loup, page 32, Tieke and Rebstock, and de Morville, article *"Galicie
1944"* (see magazine "39-45" #87), although the last source shows that Dundynce fell to
the 2nd Company on 12th August 1944.

three days later. During its absence from the battalion, it stopped several Russian
attacks, which might explain why Lefèbvre returned with the Iron Cross.[10]

Bartolomei received a visit from Cance. The battalion commander seemed
concerned. The cause of his concern was the 1st Company that had been badly hit.
Three-quarters of its cadre was already out of action.

10th August 1944 and the 1st Company

For its part, the reinforced 1st Company, on separating from the 2nd Company,
also advanced to the edge of Dundynce forest, but along a gully that afforded it
shelter from the Russian bombardment. Its objective (as defined by Mabire) was a
farm atop a hill that lay beyond a huge cornfield, but the gully opened out at the
edge of the forest.[11]

10   Mabire, page 265. However, according to Saint-Loup, page 20, Lefèbvre's platoon
      'disappeared' after the attack on the 12th and reappeared two days later with some
      Iron Crosses.
11   Undoubtedly this is the very same hill referred to by Tieke and Rebstock to the
      south-west of Pielnia on which the 1st Company was caught by Russian defensive
      fire.

First to heave themselves out of the gully and make their way across the corn-field to no or little enemy fire were the men of the 1st platoon under Ustuf. Pignard-Berthet. Accompanying the platoon were the company commander Ostuf. de Tissot and the company doctor Uscha. Jonquière.[12] When they arrived near the farm they saw a horse roaming about. De Tissot started to draw water for it from a well, but this humane gesture seemed to serve as a trigger that unleashed the response from Russian gunners and infantrymen alike. The first to be killed was Jonquière who had gone to the head of the 'scouts' (and who was possibly pushing beyond the farm with them).[13]

The 1st platoon attempted to manoeuvre, but was blown to pieces before it even had the opportunity to fire a single shot. Ustuf. Pignard-Berthet was wounded twice and out of action, as were his three section commanders, Atama, Cran and Jacquot, and his assistant Million-Rousseau, who had only been trans-ferred to the platoon just as the 1st Battalion was going up to the front.

Next to 'jump off' was Hug's 2nd platoon. Then came Mulier's 3rd platoon and Kaster's 4th (heavy) platoon. A warm reception greeted each platoon as it jumped off. The 2nd platoon, advancing to the left of the 1st platoon, suffered exceedingly heavy losses. There were dead and wounded everywhere. Hug was seri-ously wounded, as was Mulier. All was confusion.

Now it was the turn of the platoon under Chapy to jump off, but he delayed its entrance into this abattoir until he had personally spoken to de Tissot. As he made his way across the cornfield to the farm he had to dive for cover again and again. He found de Tissot in the farm. De Tissot gave him a situation report. It was not good. Not only was his company badly hit and disorganised, it was all alone, having no contact with friendly units to the left nor to the right where Gaultier's 2nd Company was supposed to be. Moreover, through a lack of defensive artillery support, the Russians could be seen massing in the valley below in readiness to attack once their barrage had finished.

De Tissot and Chapy urgently set about deploying the Company. On the right spur, the 3rd platoon under Unterscharführer Carre, Mulier's assistant. In the centre, around the farm serving as a command post, Kaster's heavy platoon and the remnants of the 1st and 2nd platoons. Chapy's platoon was assigned to the wooded left spur. Returning to his men, Chapy brought them out and across the cornfield to their position with the loss of only two wounded. One of those wounded, section commander Uscha. Dupin, a former legionnaire of the LVF, refused to be evacuated and rejoined his men.

The Russians approached. The machine-guns of the Frenchmen started rattling.

Chapy went to his map case and discovered that he was lucky not to be wounded; a piece of shrapnel had cut through his large map of Europe and his message pad, only to be stopped by his curvometer that it had crushed.

12   Incorrectly, Tieke and Rebstock, "*Im Letzten Aufgebot*", list Jonquière as serving in the 2nd Company.

13   According to Lupo, "*Levée d'écrou*", page 129, Uscha. Jonquière was killed by mortar shrapnel and according to Mabire, page 270, a sniper put a bullet through Jonquière's head. Incorrectly, Tieke and Rebstock, "*Im Letzten Aufgebot*", record that Jonquière was 'only' wounded.

By 1900 hours, the Russian fire had eased off, though it had become more accurate and shell after shell now ripped into the farm. Later, at an unrecorded time, de Tissot gave the order to pull back to Dundynce forest, however the order never reached Chapy and his platoon. Three runners carrying the order were sent to him by de Tissot, but unfortunately the first two were wounded and the third could not get through.

In the meantime, concerned about his growing isolation and the depletion of ammunition, Chapy sent a runner to the farm who got through and reported back that it was deserted. Only then did Chapy realise his predicament and to make matters worse he had just spotted three Russian tanks not far from his position. He gave the necessary order and his platoon disengaged and hurried off towards the forest. It was now getting dark. A sense of loneliness prevailed. It seemed as though the 1st and 2nd companies had disappeared into thin air. They did chance upon several German soldiers from the Wehrmacht, also lost, who did not know the whereabouts of the headquarters of the French Battalion. Chapy searched on and finally came across comrades from Oberjunker Peyron's platoon who directed them to the southern edge of Dundynce where H.Q. was believed to be.

Battalion H.Q. had been set up in a log dug-out to the south-west of Dundynce forest between two hills, near to the road leading to Sanok and near to the village of Wolica where the field hospital of the 'Horst Wessel' Division was located. Throughout that first day of combat it could be remarked that Battalion H.Q. resembled and served more as a first-aid post than a command post. Dr. Bonnefoy and his orderlies had been busy treating the wounded since early afternoon. There had been a constant to and fro of ambulances and lorries evacuating the wounded from the Battalion's first-aid post to the field hospital at Wolica.

'By the close of play', Hstuf. Cance was furious. The day had been most unsatisfactory. Casualties had been heavy, especially among the cadre. That day, according to Mabire, the Sturmbrigade lost one company commander, six platoon commanders and about twenty section commanders. Altogether, about twenty volunteers were killed. Specifically, the 3rd Company's casualties were one killed and two wounded.[14] Tieke and Rebstock, for their part, record that five volunteers from the 2nd Company were killed and that over sixty wounded passed through the hands of Dr. Bonnefoy and his orderlies. Bayle cites sixty dead and wounded. Whatever the exact figures may have been, it is evident that the French SS Freiwilligen had paid a heavy price for their baptism of fire. If truth were told, the French battalion had not covered itself with glory.

Cance now decided to keep the 3rd Company on its present positions, send the 2nd Company back up to the front line and keep the 1st Company in reserve due to its crippling losses. Chapy's platoon was held in reserve near the command post. The next day he planned to counterattack.

11th August 1944

On the whole, 11th August 1944 passed rather uneventfully for the 1st Battalion. Appreciating that the exhausted Battalion still required time to rest, accustom itself

14   However, Mabire gives no total figure for those wounded. The ratio of dead to wounded is normally put at one to five and this ratio would yield a figure of around one hundred wounded.

to its surroundings and reorganise following the terrible blood-letting of the previous day, Cance had no other choice than to postpone the counterattack planned for that day. Instead the 2nd Company was called upon to send out patrols. One patrol led in person by the new company commander, Untersturmführer Bartolomei, clashed with the enemy approximately 500 metres from his command post, but this time the Frenchmen came out on top. Twenty Russians were killed. Mabire nicely sums up the outcome of the clash by saying: 'Bartolomei had just equalised the score'. Bartolomei hoped to do even better during the counterattack being prepared for the 12th.

According to Bayle, far from just sending out patrols that day, the 2nd Company repulsed a major Soviet attack and inflicted heavy losses. Bayle continues that the Soviets then attempted, and in vain, to outflank the 1st Company with tank support.

The Frenchmen were on the receiving end of a Russian ruse. They welcomed into their positions some young children who had appeared from Russian lines. The children were trembling with fear or so it seemed. They were sent to the rear. Unbeknown to the Frenchmen, they discreetly slipped back to Russian lines. And thanks to their little spies, the Russians were able to bombard the French positions systematically and with precision.

That same day, the PAK platoon attempted to set up one of its three guns on an exposed hill in the sector of the 3rd Company (Mabire) or 2nd Company (Tieke and Rebstock) and immediately drew heavy Russian fire. The gun was destroyed, one of the gun crew was killed and five were seriously wounded. What a disaster! The gun had not even fired a single shot.

Trabandt, Schäfer and a German colonel from the Wehrmacht came to congratulate Cance and the French volunteers on their bearing and courage, while lamenting their inexperience.

12th August 1944

The attack on 12th August 1944 to align the front to the Cracow/Sanok railway was to be led by SS-Kampfgruppe 'Schäfer' and the 1st Battalion of the French SS-Sturmbrigade, and was promised massive artillery and Nebelwerfer support. The initiative for this attack seems to have come from Oberführer Trabandt and was authorised by Hermann Balck, commander in chief of the 4th Panzer Army.[15]

The battle plan drawn up for the French battalion called for the 2nd Company to lead the attack, followed by the 1st Company, and for the 3rd Company to safeguard the right flank of the battalion's disposition (and hence the left flank of the front held by SS-Kampfgruppe 'Schäfer'). H-hour was fixed for midday.

During the morning the German and French SS soldiers moved up to their starting positions on the edge of Dundynce forest. One hour before the attack, the German artillery opened up. According to Saint-Loup, the 2nd Company charged off (in every sense of the word) ahead of H hour and its men ran so fast that the supporting artillery had to immediately lengthen its fire so as not to hit them! Saint-Loup remarks that the Russians withdrew before this irresistible attack,

15   Mabire, page 295. However, there is a question mark against this as SS-Kampfgruppe 'Schäfer' appears to have been under the 17th Army and not the 4th Panzer Army.

leaving absolutely nothing behind them, no equipment, no wounded and no dead. The 2nd Company suffered no losses.

In contrast, according to Mabire, the 2nd Company took prisoners and the 1st Company even attended to Russian wounded, much to the surprise of a Wehrmacht officer. Also treated were wounded of 'Horst Wessel'. Of note is that one 'patient' thought to be German was in fact French. Enlisting as an Alsatian, he ended up serving in the 2. SS Panzer Division 'Das Reich'. Wounded on the Eastern front, he was evacuated to Lwów hospital. At the end of his convalescence he found himself incorporated into SS-Kampfgruppe 'Schäfer' and fighting on this Galician front 'on fire'.

Tieke and Rebstock do shed more light on the actions of both the 1st Company and the 2nd Company on the day of the 12th.[16] After storming the Russian front line the 2nd Company captured the village of Dundynce, but was thrown out. The 1st Company, equally successful in storming the Russian front line, took Pielnia and held it against Russian counterattacks.

From artillery observation posts, officers of 'Horst Wessel' and commanders of neighbouring Wehrmacht divisions followed the attack. The latter were surprised to learn from Oberführer Trabandt that this attack was conducted by the French SS-Sturmbrigade placed of late under his command. In this way, according to Bayle[17], they 'learnt of the efficient presence of French volunteers facing Bolshevism and *pour L'Europe*'.

As for the 3rd Company, although it was to protect the right flank of the battalion's disposition, Fenet ordered his men to advance and take up position from where they could support their comrades of the attack companies. In so doing, the 3rd Company revealed itself and was shelled savagely by mortars and artillery, yet it somehow managed to maintain its support through the 'storm of steel'.

The day's satisfactory proceedings for the 3rd Company were marred by a self-inflicted injury and while this particular individual from Couvreur's platoon got his wish to be evacuated, a court martial and the concentration camp awaited him. Nobody would miss him.

At 2100 hours, according to Saint-Loup, Bartolomei received the order to hand over the conquered positions to troops of the Wehrmacht. The 2nd Company then took up position on a rocky height to the south of the 3rd Company. In contrast, according to Mabire, the 2nd Company spent the night out in the field, 'sharing their holes with Russian corpses', and was relieved around midday on the following day.

The French Battalion was cited in the despatches of 'Horst Wessel' and in the OKW communiqué of that day.

13th August 1944

Outside of burying the dead, the battalion's units rested.

14th August 1944

In the early morning, the 2nd Company took up residence in former Russian positions on a hill from where German combat troops could be seen advancing towards

---

16   This is not confirmed or contradicted by Saint-Loup or Mabire.
17   Bayle, "*De Marseille à Novossibirsk*", page 97.

enemy positions that they took easily. The 2nd Company received some sporadic mortar fire that was of no consequence.

The command of the 2nd Company changed hands once again.[18] Owing to his deteriorating health, Ustuf. Bartolomei, old 'Barto', who was in the late forties, asked to be relieved of his command. Since his arrival at the front, Bartolomei had only managed to hold out by dint of will. Ostuf. Pleyber, the 'heavy company commander', to all intents and purposes 'unemployed', was given the command of the 2nd Company. This gunner inspired little confidence among the infantrymen.[19]

Russian artillery continued to inflict casualties. Needlessly caught in the open, Oberjunker Chapy was wounded by shrapnel, but turned down evacuation, and his assistant, Oberscharführer Grossman, was killed outright.

In need of an 'efficient assault platoon'[20] to support a tank attack on Pisarowice, a village located alongside the Cracow-Sanok railway, the Germans came to the French battalion. Bartolomei and Cance chose the 2nd platoon of the 2nd Company, that of Oberjunker Peyron, because of its competence and its dynamism over the past few days: it had particularly distinguished itself on the 12th. For the mission the platoon was brought up to full strength, that is to say three sections of twelve men each, plus two radio operators.[21]

At nightfall, after receiving final instructions delivered by Chapy, the 2nd platoon of the 2nd Company set out. With the platoon was Pleyber, the new company commander. Inexplicably, the two officers had told the NCOs and the men nothing of the mission. The platoon would march till daybreak on the 15th.

15th August 1944

On 15th August 1944, units of the French battalion saw action and achieved success.

In the early hours of the 15th, Stubaf. Schäfer of 'Horst Wessel' called upon the French battalion to help a neighbouring company of his Kampfgruppe cut off by partisans. Ustuf. Kammer, the company commander, had asked his regiment for help, but Schäfer went straight to the Frenchmen.[22]

18   Bayle, "De Marseille à Novossibirsk", page 99. However, Mabire records the change of command of the 2nd Company one day earlier (page 303).

19   Ibid, page 99.

20   Bayle, letter to the author 19/3/97.

21   According to Mabire, page 309, this attack was Hstuf. Cance's last effort to reach the Cracow/Sanok railway line because he was expecting an order to be relieved on the 15th. This is not wholly accurate. See Bayle, "De Marseille à Novossibirsk", page 99. Moreover, Mabire gives little detail of this attack in "La Brigade Frankreich" (although this omission was rectified in later editions). This attack was confined solely to the 2nd platoon of the 2nd Company and was not an entire company action as intimated by Mabire, and Tieke and Rebstock.

22   According to Bender and Taylor, Volume Four of the "Waffen SS", page 174, Schäfer only turned to the French-men because he had no men available. As such this sentiment is not expressed by Mabire. Arguably, Schäfer only called upon the Frenchmen because they were closest.

The 1st Company supplied Chapy's platoon for the rescue mission, which set off immediately and managed to cut its way through two kilometres of hostile terrain to reach Kammer's Company just after daybreak.

Kammer's situation was not good. Pinned down by machine-gun and mortar fire, his company had suffered many killed and many wounded. It was no stronger than Chapy's platoon. Kammer's position was not good. The company was dominated by a height, occupied by the partisans, some one hundred metres away. Because of this the break-out hinged upon the capture of the height.

Bayonets fixed, around one hundred screaming French and German soldiers of the Waffen-SS raced towards the height, from which the enemy hurriedly fell back. Although the rest of the rescue mission proved delicate, Chapy brought Kammer and his Company safely back. Not one further man was lost.

When a volunteer reported to Chapy that he had lost two boxes of ammunition and a machine-gun barrel crossing a road Chapy ordered him to return and collect them. The volunteer hesitated, but went on his way after Chapy grabbed a rifle. The volunteer was back minutes later with the recovered items and Chapy then offered him a conciliatory cigarette.

The 2nd platoon of the 2nd Company also saw action.[23]

By daybreak, after a night of many inexplicable and pointless detours, the platoon had covered some seven kilometres 'eastwards' (Saint-Loup) or a matter of kilometres (Bayle), but the officers now seemed lost. A halt was ordered along a road in a sort of basin bordered by cornfields. Although gunfire and the noise of clanking armour could be heard, the front seemed far away. The weather was splendid. As Peyron and Pleyber went off to a nearby village in ruins to find their bearings the platoon deployed itself leisurely and lazily.

Shots that rang out from the east suddenly shattered the peace, but the platoon remained untroubled by this development. At that same moment Peyron and Pleyber came running back from the village, shouting in alarm "The Russians! The Russians!" which could not be made out at first. They pointed to the Russians surrounding the platoon through the cornfields bordering the road to the east. The men quickly equipped themselves again and regrouped. Without any order being given, the Frenchmen fixed bayonets and watched over the cornfields. Hit in the hollow of his shoulder, a young grenadier went down beside Uscha. Bayle and died without a noise.

Ordered forward by Peyron, the platoon followed him into the cornfields. The Frenchmen started to run. They broke the encirclement at bayonet point and their momentum carried them further forward. The Russians fled. The very young volunteer Sacoman was killed. Others fell, wounded or dead. The Germans were quick to provide artillery and mortar support, but the Frenchmen were running so

---

23 Bayle, "*De Marseille à Novossibirsk*", page 99 to 103. However, Tieke and Rebstock provide a slightly different version of events. After Pisarowice fell to the '2nd Company' the Russians counterattacked from two directions. Surrounded, the '2nd Company' broke out to the south-west, swung north, then advanced to the level crossing west of the village and dug in. And it was during this break-out that Oberjunker Peyron and *freiwillige* Trévisan were killed. In response to Tieke and Rebstock, the author has used Bayle's account because he was an eyewitness.

fast that they were hit by their own rolling fire support, which could not keep up with them!

The charge continued through increasing enemy and friendly fire. The Frenchmen broke into the village of Pisarowce. They were held up by a machine-gun in a grove. Trévisan from Marseille was hit in the back by shrapnel from a friendly mortar and called out for help. Uscha. Bayle went to him, but was ordered away by Peyron with the words: "It's not your job!" Bayle left Trévisan who slipped into a stream where he died moments later.

Peyron attacked the machine-gun nest with five others. Hearing an incoming mortar salvo, Uscha. Bayle held back the others, but Peyron continued to rush forward alone. Oberjunker Joseph Peyron, whose ambition was to become the political theoretician of the French Waffen SS, was killed instantly by mortar shrapnel which also destroyed the Russian machine-gun position. He was the first French Waffen-SS officer to be killed in action.[24]

Uscha. Bayle now took over the command of the platoon and, despite the absence of firm orders, he sensibly continued to charge forward. After ejecting the Russians from Pisarowice, the platoon took up defensive positions on a nearby level crossing over the Cracow-Sanok railway to the west of the village.

The time was about 1000 hours. It was only then that Uscha. Bayle thought about their isolated and very precarious situation. They were without officers, orders, or means of communication and were only lightly armed. They would not be able to repel the inevitable Russian counter-attack.

A Panzer Major, whose tanks were now approaching the platoon's positions, came and asked to speak to the person in charge of this small knot of troops. Uscha. Bayle immediately presented himself and gave his name, rank and unit. The Panzer Major smiled and congratulated the Frenchmen on their 'Blitzkrieg', explaining that they had reached the objective and that he was supposed to have supported their attack! Henceforth, Bayle's nickname was 'Blitzkrieg'.

The Panzer Major asked Uscha. Bayle for his *Soldbuch* so he could propose him for the Iron Cross 2nd Class. Directed by the German officer to a radio antenna among the ruins of Pisarowice some three hundred metres away, Bayle was able to make radio contact with the headquarters of SS-Kampfgruppe 'Schäfer' as well as Hstuf. Cance who was there quite by chance. After making a resumé of the action and detailing his precarious geographical situation, Bayle received orders from Cance to withdraw and rejoin the battalion.

At 1800 hours (Saint-Loup) or 1500 hours (Bayle), the platoon handed its position over to panzer-grenadier of the German 'armoured Regiment' and, in two groups taking different routes, pulled back to Wolica where the battalion was assembling. Bayle led one group and his good friend Bruhat the other.

From Marseille, Raymond Bruhat was anti-Communist. He was a supporter of Pétain and Europe. He was not affiliated to any political party, even though his parents worked for Simon Sabiani, the vice president of the P.P.F. and Doriot's right hand man.[25] On learning of the death of Sabiani's son with the LVF on the

24   According to Bayle, "*De Marseille à Novossibirsk*", page 103, Peyron had been a little deaf ever since his earlier brush with death when a mine blew up a lorry in which he was travelling (see page 77). Consequently, he may not have heard the incoming mortar salvo. Besides, 'he persisted in not wearing his helmet'.

Eastern front, he had made it his duty to enlist in the Waffen-SS. Bayle wrote: "In this way, he continued the engagement of Sabiani's son by honouring his sacrifice, while thanking the Father."

Both groups somehow met up on the way back and shortly after made contact with the Battalion. Of the 40 who had set out on the mission, only 25 returned.

On the following day, the bodies of those killed on the 15th, including that of Joseph Peyron, were brought back and laid to rest. The dead were buried in a clearing near the village of Wolica.[26]

Now that the so-called Sanok pocket was sealed, the units of the French SS-Sturmbrigade returned the sector to the Wehrmacht. The Waffen-SS and the Wehrmacht 'passed each other without a word'[27], which would seem to suggest that the often uneasy relationship between the two had manifested itself again.

As the platoons filed into Wolica the Sturmbrigade counted its losses.

Mabire records the losses of the 1st Company as 60, the 2nd Company as 50 and the 3rd Company as 20 dead or wounded.[28] These figures conflict with those from Saint-Loup who lists the losses as 35, 30, and 20 respectively.[29] Elsewhere Saint-Loup states that the battalion now had a strength of less than 800 men.[30] This implies that the battalion lost in excess of 200 men.[31] Total losses were therefore 85 or as high as 200. However, the first figure does not include the losses of the PAK platoon and the support services, whereas the latter might.

As for the wounded, few, if any, would later return to duty with the battalion while still in Galicia.

25   Sabiani was also a former Communist. Before joining the P.P.F. in 1936, he had his own party, Socialist Action, and been the mayor of Marseille.

26   Saint-Loup, page 38. However, Bayle, in a letter to the author dated 19/3/97, stated that he is not so convinced that it was Wolica, but did add that it could easily have been.

27   Mabire, page 314.

28   See Mabire, pages 314-315.

29   See Saint-Loup, page 40.

30   See Saint-Loup, page 51.

31   This is the same figure Landwehr advances (see page 39). Undoubtedly, Landwehr's source was Saint-Loup.

CHAPTER 3

The Sector of Mielec

A new mission and a new sector

Several days of rest and reflection followed for the battalion. With the exception of the 3rd Company, Cance was greatly worried by the rashness of his battalion and in particular by the impulsive company commander of the 1st Company, de Tissot, who 'lacked real military experience'.[1] To calm down de Tissot, Cance called upon Bartolomei, back to health after several days of rest, and appointed him to the 1st Company as a platoon commander.

Cance made a number of other changes. Ostuf. Pleyber was returned to the PAK and Ustuf. Lambert was moved from the 3rd Company to the command of the 2nd Company.[2]

On 17th or 19th August 1944,[3] the 1st Battalion of the French SS-Sturmbrigade was transported by lorry to the sector of Mielec, one hundred kilometres north-west of Sanok. Also switched to this sector was SS-Kampfgruppe 'Schäfer'. Apparently the French Battalion still came under its command. On the night of its arrival the French Battalion went into line.

A vast sector of front-line along the river Visloka, south of Sandomierz, on the SS-Kampfgruppe's right flank was entrusted to the battalion. Its frontage varies from source to source and was possibly as long as 15 kilometres but definitely not the 2 kilometres noted by Bender. Relieving seasoned troops of two Wehrmacht companies (Bayle) or a Wehrmacht battalion (Saint-Loup), this time things went much more smoothly for the French battalion than previously at Sanok. But, to cover this sector, Cance had to spread out his companies thinly on the ground and some of de Tissot's platoons were expected to take over almost one kilometre of front! Saint-Loup records a deployment of sixty men per kilometre. Radio communication was made almost impossible by this gullied and wooded region. Moreover, the river Visloka could not be considered a serious natural obstacle and could easily be forded. It would be a gross understatement to describe the battalion's disposition as unfavourable although thankfully this sector seemed peaceful enough. In the past fifteen days there had been only one wounded. However, strong concentrations of enemy artillery had been observed to the north-east and south-east of Mielec.

Battalion headquarters was established in the hamlet of Zaborce.

---

1   Mabire, page 321.
2   Saint-Loup, page 49. In contrast, according to Mabire, page 359, Cance assigned Lambert to the 2nd Company to assist Pleyber. His departure displeased Fenet who considered him an excellent officer and hard to replace. Oscha. Quicampoix took up the command now left vacant in the 3rd Company.
3   Bayle, Landwehr, Saint-Loup, and Tieke and Rebstock cite the 17th and Mabire the 19th.

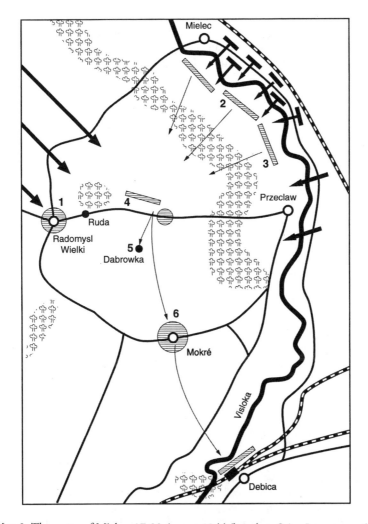

Map 2: The sector of Mielec, 17-22 August 1944 (based on Saint-Loup, page 69).
1. On the 20th, the PAK platoon of the Sturmbrigade defends Radomysl Wielki. 2. In
the late afternoon of the 20th, the three companies of the Sturmbrigade in position along
the river Visloka withdraw. 3. The 1st Company is the last to withdraw. [The author has
assumed that the 1st Company held the right flank of the battalion's disposition. See
Tieke and Rebstock map page 51]. 4. On the 21st, the 3rd Company, hit hard during
the night of the 20th/21st, takes up a position to the left of the crossroads held by
elements of the Sturmbrigade under Oberjunker Chapy and Ostuf. Le Marquer. As
ordered, the French hold until 1900 hours and then withdraw south. 5. On the 22nd,
elements of the 1st Company under Oberjunker Chapy join SS-Kampfgruppe 'Schäfer'
at Dabrówka. They are committed to the fighting and give a good account of themselves.
6. On the 22nd, the Sturmbrigade fights to the death at Mokré. All officers are killed or
wounded. The survivors withdraw south and assemble at or near Debica.

For some, the next two days proved relatively peaceful. Uscha. Bayle spent his time sleeping or on patrol. The only danger his men faced was from friendly mortar fire falling short. On one occasion an enemy lookout, sat on the high branches of a tree peacefully smoking, made a friendly sign his way.

Indeed, troops of the Wehrmacht and the Red Army fraternised in the late evening when the Soviets came to bathe and swim in the Visloka. Cigarettes, chocolate and uniform buttons were exchanged.[4]

In contrast, the sector of the 1st Company was under constant sniper fire, and sporadic machine-gun and mortar fire.[5]

Towards midnight on the night of 19th/20th August 1944, the 'peace' of the past days was shattered when Soviet artillery bombarded Wehrmacht positions to the left and the right of the French battalion.

The hurricane of fire intensified with the coming of dawn[6] and the entrance of batteries of Katyusha rockets, known as 'Stalin Organs'. The earth trembled, the forests shook and the 'fires set ablaze the whole horizon'. Even though the French Battalion was for the present spared this devastating barrage, it still suffered losses from random shelling. Ustuf. Bartolomei was wounded by shrapnel and evacuated. Uscha. Carre took over the command of the platoon again.

Radomysl Wielki

At 0700 hours on Sunday 20th August 1944, Cance received a telephone call from Stubaf. Schäfer: "Tanks have broken through to the north-east. Send your anti-tank platoon at once to Radomysl."[7] Off went Oberjunker Kreis and the PAK platoon.[8] He had about thirty men with him. Arriving at Radomysl at 0900 hours, Kreis received orders to hold the town at all costs until 1600 hours or die trying.[9]

---

4   Saint-Loup, page 51. Of note is that members of the French SS Battalion may have also been present at these exchanges (see Landwehr).

5   Mabire, pages 325–326.

6   Mabire, page 329. However, according to Saint-Loup, the Russians unleashed the bombardment at dawn on the 20th.

7   Saint-Loup, page 53, repeated by Landwehr, page 41. Tieke and Rebstock record slightly different wording but the meaning is the same (see page 53). However, according to Mabire, page 335, Oberjunker Kreis had arrived in a panic-stricken Radomysl the previous evening. Attentively, from dawn, he followed the approaching cannonade. This would seem to suggest that Kreis and his PAK platoon were at Radomysl more by chance to guard this major town, described as an 'important centre of communication', than sent there in reaction to the Russian offensive.

8   There is no agreement on the armament at the disposal of the PAK platoon. According to Tieke and Rebstock, page 53, and Landwehr, page 42, Kreis had three anti-tank guns. In response to this, the PAK platoon had already lost at least one gun in the fighting that had just gone. And, in contrast, according to Mabire, page 335, Kreis had left his two remaining anti-tank guns at the disposal of 'Horst Wessel' and his men had drawn panzerfäuste.

9   Saint-Loup, page 54. However, according to Mabire, page 338, Kreis received orders to hold until 1900 hours, but Mabire does not specify as to when Kreis received them. Perhaps Kreis received a number of different orders.

He had to smile at the pompous title of 'Kreiskommandant [battle commandant] of Radomysl' bestowed upon him.

Empowered, Kreis commandeered all personnel and equipment retreating through Radomysl. With the assistance and 'gentle persuasion' of six formidable Feldgendarmes, his command had grown in size to around one hundred men with the support of a Sturmgeschütz before the Russians attacked at midday exactly.

Infantry attacks came in first. Kreis was everywhere. The defenders held their ground. Eventually they may have faced a whole Soviet infantry regiment.[10]

Just after 1500 hours, Soviet tanks entered the battle.[11] The defenders fought back with panzerfäuste. Minutes later, the first tanks were blazing, but the defenders had paid a great price and now conducted a fighting withdrawal from house to house. They made a stand in the cemetery.

Faced with another tank attack, the defenders seemed lost when their supply of panzerfäuste ran out. Just at that moment, as if by miracle, a German formation of Stukas appeared and pounced like hawks on the Soviet tanks. Direct hit after direct hit. Explosion after explosion. Saved!

The afternoon seemed without end. Desperately the defenders clung to the cemetery.

The ending at Radomysl was either one of victory or one of good military sense.

According to Mabire[12], at 1830 hours, arrived German reinforcements of infantry and even several panzers. Stubbornly the Soviets came again with tanks. The defenders were still holding the cemetery when 1900 hours came and went. Oberjunker Kreis welcomed the passing hour with great relief. It meant that he had fulfilled his orders which, according to Mabire, were to hold until 1900 hours.

Soon after, panzerfaust in hand, Oberjunker Kreis boldly confronted a Soviet tank. Both man and steel giant fired almost simultaneously. He was seriously wounded. And yet he still noted that his aim had been true. The Soviet tank was burning.

Pulled under cover by his men, Kreis ordered section commander Nisus to take command of the PAK platoon. He grew delirious. The pain was too much and the prospect of losing an arm too horrible. He wanted to commit suicide.[13] More German reinforcements arrived. The situation stabilised. The PAK platoon had held Radomysl to the bitter end. This was victory.

However, according to Tieke and Rebstock, far from standing fast, Oberjunker Kreis had to give the order to pull back when the promised reinforcements did not materialise.[14]

10   Mabire, page 337. Presumably based on the eyewitness account of Kreis.
11   According to Landwehr, page 42, the defenders faced and 'hurled back' a Soviet tank regiment. This is doubtful.
12   See Mabire, pages 337 to 341.
13   He was evacuated to a military hospital in Vienna where he quickly regained his appetite for life.
14   See Tieke and Rebstock, page 53. Tieke and Rebstock continue that the defenders fell back along the Radomysl-Przeclaw road to the west of Ruda where they were

By its defence of Radomysl, the PAK platoon brought time for the remainder of the Sturmbrigade and for part of SS-Kampfgruppe 'Schäfer' whose situation, gloomy enough as it was, could have been considerably worse if Radomysl had passed into enemy hands earlier. Nevertheless, in combat there is always a price to pay and in this case that price was the decimation of the PAK platoon.

The most terrible night

Let us now return to the French SS companies in position along the river Visloka. All knew that they too would find themselves on the receiving end of the hurricane of fire the Russians had unleashed over the positions either side of theirs. The wall of explosions neared. Suddenly the bombardment was upon them. It was hell. Shells screamed down. The ground trembled from the blasts. Trees were ripped to pieces. Telephone lines were severed. And how long did the barrage last before it moved on? Minutes, perhaps hours, but for those sheltering from death, its end could not come soon enough.[15]

Soviet snipers now targeted the runners. Two from the 2nd Company were mortally wounded in the space of several minutes. Each platoon closed up.

In the late afternoon of 20th August 1944, because of the deteriorating situation to the northeast, Obf. Trabandt, the commander of 'Horst Wessel', ordered Hstuf. Cance to disengage the three companies of the French battalion with the utmost urgency from their positions along the river Visloka to a position defined by the line Radomysl-Pouby-Przeclaw.[16]

Oberjunker Chapy was called to see company commander Ostuf. de Tissot. When they were alone together de Tissot confided to him: "We've been encircled since this morning."[17] He explained that the Russians had steamrollered through Wehrmacht lines to the 'north and the south of their lines'. Also, he had received orders from battalion to withdraw at 1800 hours.

At the designated time the companies disengaged. Pushed by their commanders, the exhausted men quickly made it to the forest without too much interference. Then came a short period of rest during which night fell. Hstuf. Cance summoned the three company commanders who, like their men, had not slept for two days. The plan of action and the order of march was fixed. The first echelon would be Lambert's 2nd Company, including the headquarters group and Lopez's engineer platoon, followed by Fenet's 3rd Company and then by de Tissot's 1st Company bringing up the rear.

The platoons set off one after another into the darkness of the night and were immediately swallowed up. In order of march the echelons slipped through the burning hamlet of Dzilec.[18] Chapy's platoon, the rearguard, formed a defensive 'hedgehog' position to the east of the hamlet. Although the hamlet came under increasing mortar and artillery fire, no Russians had been spotted yet, but they were

integrated into the defence line of Battalion Riepe of SS-Kampfgruppe 'Schäfer'. This may well be true. Curiously, there is no mention of Kreis' wounding.
15   Remarkably, no casualties are reported.
16   Saint-Loup, page 54.
17   Mabire, page 331.
18   Saint-Loup, page 55.

thought to be everywhere. A runner finally brought the rearguard the order to withdraw.

The 2nd Company

The 2nd Company reached its assigned positions, only to find the Russians already there. Battle ensued. In the darkness, confusion set in. The 2nd Company shattered and its survivors retreated south. The Russians followed up. In vain did Bartolomei,[19] who was wounded in the leg by a bullet, attempt to round up the 2nd Company. Some groups gave battle. Outgunned and outflanked, they were forced to withdraw.

Hit in the legs, *Freiwillige* Lowandovski of Polish-French descent refused to be evacuated and asked for a machine-pistol to die fighting for 'his' country. The retreating men heard the machine-pistol bursts and then counted the single shots from the P38 sidearm he had on him. After a pause the last shot rang out. Had he chosen to take his own life with his last bullet rather than accept capture?[20]

Marching with Bartolomei were some thirty survivors of the 2nd Company. Convinced that they had at last outdistanced their pursuers, they stopped. It was now that a Russian patrol intervened. Uscha. Bayle saw the Russians slip into the nearby forest with one of his comrades, seized while attending to nature's needs.[21]

Presently, the Frenchmen came under fire. No casualties are reported.

'To facilitate the withdrawal', Bartolomei decided to separate the thirty survivors with him into two groups, one under himself and the other under Uscha. Bayle. The village of Mokré, where Cance was to set up battalion headquarters, was indicated as the meeting point. The two groups went their separate ways. By morning, the group led by Bartolomei had joined battalion headquarters.

During the night of 20th/21st August 1944, battalion headquarters withdrew to Ruda and then 800 metres further to another village.[22]

19   Presumably Bartolomei was now back with the 2nd Company.
20   Saint-Loup implies that the wounded man kept the last bullet 'for his own personal use'.
21   The captured soldier was known by sight to Bayle, but not by name.
22   Soulat, *"Histoire des volontaires français dans l'armée allemande 1940–1945"*. However, according to Tieke and Rebstock, page 54, as dawn of 21st August 1944 broke, Cance arrived with the battalion at Dabrówka Wislocka. This seems possible and probable. However, the same source goes on to say that Cance received orders from Schäfer to go to Mokré and hold the village for twelve hours. In response to this, no other source confirms the same timing for this order. Tieke and Rebstock continue that when Cance arrived at Mokré with seventy men of the battalion [presumably headquarters personnel and the engineer platoon] he discovered that the Russians were already 'in residence'. The French attacked and promptly ejected them. While possible, again no other source confirms that Cance had to fight for Mokré.

The 1st Company

Last to set off, the 1st Company followed a badly gullied dirt track for some time before coming to a stop when the track crossed a road. Nearby was a small bridge spanning a dry stream and beyond that a village which seemed deserted. The rest of the battalion seemed to have vanished without a trace. The night was heavy with mystery and danger. Uncertainty overtook company commander Ostuf. de Tissot. Unsure of which direction to take, he sent out patrols to reconnoitre the vicinity. Some were dispatched in the direction of where the positions of the 2nd Company were thought to be.

While awaiting the return of these patrols, de Tissot heavily fortified the crossroads and rested his exhausted company in the village. Silence descended. The patrols began to return. Nothing had been found. By midnight, two scouts still had not returned.

Sat on the bridge, Chapy and de Tissot awaited the return of the last scouts. They heard the sound of snoring, went to investigate and found a machine-gunner fast asleep. He was harshly awoken. De Tissot then told Chapy to go and inspect the other posts just in case the other men were asleep as well. They parted company. Chapy went first to the cottage serving as a command post and then on to the village where he awoke other lookouts fast asleep. Apparently de Tissot went back to sit on the nearby bridge.

On hearing a convoy approaching the crossroads from the east, Ostuf. Nöel de Tissot went to meet it. Unexpectedly, the convoy was not civilian, but Soviet. Suddenly, gunfire from the post at the eastern edge of the village rent the night. More gunfire followed. Then grenade explosions. Mortars joined in. De Tissot disappeared into the night and was never heard from again.[23]

Chapy heard the gunfire and raced back up the village towards the crossroads. On the way, in the light of a mortar being fired, he spotted a Russian soldier and fired at him. Once at the crossroads he came across Oscha. Kaster, commander of the heavy platoon, who told him that de Tissot had ordered a withdrawal westwards and that he had already departed. Chapy went to the command post and had the company assemble immediately. It abandoned all heavy equipment. Chapy led the 1st Company out of the village and at first northwards, reasoning that the Russians, once they had reorganised, would surely continue westwards along the road.

Liaison officer Rouvre, occupying a barn with seven other men, was woken from sleep by the sound of gunfire. He heard voices. He could not make out the language, but it was not German or French. He wiped the sleep from his eyes only

---

23   According to Mabire, page 379, a French Freiwillige from the 1st Company named Rouvre, who later managed to make it back to French lines, recounted that during the violent firefight at the crossroads de Tissot was killed. This is incorrect. According to "*Levée d'écrou*", page 136, which recounts the story of Rouvre, he learnt the sad news of de Tissot's disappearance when he made it back to French lines, following his capture and subsequent escape. He cried. He described de Tissot as a *grand chef* and the best officer of them all. Lastly, according to Tieke and Rebstock, page 54, de Tissot was wounded before being captured and then shot by the Russians.

to see three weapons pointing at him. He got up and raised his arms. Brossard, who was beside him, did not get up and was shot dead.

To alert his comrades in the barn and in another building to the presence of Russians, he risked his life to shout out a warning. This warning saved the thirty-five men of Carre's platoon, but his comrades in the barn chose to surrender rather than fight it out.

The seven prisoners were taken to a courtyard. Pinte, who spoke some words of Russian, was taken to see a Soviet commissar in his headquarters. He returned, announcing that the commissar had told him that they were to be taken to a field and there shot. One of them started to cry. Rouvre encouraged him as best he could, telling him that as long as there was life there was hope.

The Russians, nine men and an officer who may have been the commissar, escorted the prisoners to a field. One Russian was shouldering two spades. Rouvre alerted his comrades to save themselves when he gave the signal. The prisoners were made to sit two by two and back to back. The Russians stood in a circle around them. When Rouvre saw the Russians raise their weapons he shouted: "*En avant!*"

Rouvre charged straight ahead. He punched the Russian in front of him with 'all his force of instinct of self-preservation', sending him reeling. He glanced back to see his comrades also in flight. Jumping into a thorn bush, he fell into a pond. This may have saved his life, for bullets whistled above his head. He swam across the pond, which was some fifty metres across, and ran off, avoiding two or three farms on the way where the enemy had to be. He heard gunfire to his left. Some two kilometres on, he crashed out in a potato field to get his breath back.

Rouvre would eventually make it back to French lines, not before he had been captured again and had escaped again. Of the other prisoners, only Pierre Simon also made it back. The others were never heard from again. They were Darnaud, Grossard, Pinte, Van-de-Put, and an unknown medical orderly. Rouvre was welcomed back with open arms by comrades from his company, which Oberjunker Chapy, almost single-handedly and with a good deal of fortune, had managed to extricate from the clutches of the Soviets.

Silently, the company made its escape from the village along a sunken lane lined with hedges. Things went well until two Soviet cavalrymen on the banks of the sunken lane blocked the escape route. Covered by Chapy, the company slipped past in the shadow of the hedge.

Chapy went to the head of the survivors of the 1st Company. Gnawed by fear, the company wearily marched on in complete silence. The village blurred. The hedgerow became open fields which posed greater danger. Guided by Chapy, who was without a map, the company kept going through fields and marshes.

Suddenly, the company came under machine-gun fire. The French SS troops advanced towards this MG which they distinctly recognised as German. A voice called out to them in Russian, rooting them to the spot. Chapy shrank from the risk of pushing straight on and bore further west.

Finally, the company came across a road and Chapy decided to head westwards along the roadside ditches. The night was still like thick ink. After several hundred metres a machine-gun burst stopped the company in its tracks. It was a German MG again. They were careful. This time the machine-gun was actually manned by their compatriots. The 1st Company had made it back and it was all thanks to Chapy.

The 1st Company had just come across a hedgehog position manned by twenty men from various units under Ustuf. Le Marquer. The hedgehog position was centred on a crossroads to the east of Ruda and possibly along the Radomysl-Przeclaw road. Cance's command post was situated in a small hamlet one kilometre away and could be contacted by field telephone.

Speaking to Cance, Chapy's first concern was for his company commander, de Tissot, of whom he asked news. Cance had none but did agree to Chapy's request to go and search for de Tissot and told him to take all available elements of the 1st Company. That amounted to between sixty and one hundred men which was too few to break through the Russian lines and too many to infiltrate. Thus, the search was doomed to fail.

With Chapy marching in the lead platoon, the 1st Company set out in the direction of Mielec. They were hungry, thirsty, exhausted and scared. Only the prospect of extricating their *chef* and other missing comrades drove them forward. It was still not light.

The search collapsed very quickly. Half an hour after setting out, the 1st Company ran into about twenty Russian troops who had suddenly emerged from the mist. Chapy's submachine-gun was the first to speak. More and more Russians emerged from nearby woods. The 1st Company now found itself opposite a strong Soviet battalion supported by anti-tank guns. Chapy responded by sending a runner to Cance for orders.

Presently, the 1st Company came under heavy fire and was pinned down. The air was filled with the whine of shrapnel and bullets in all directions. Chapy's good fortune continued; he escaped injury when a bullet blew off his cap and when his helmet was 'holed'.

Day broke. Exposed, the 1st Company came under heavier and more accurate fire. Le Marquer gave what support he could from afar, but the Russians had outflanked the 1st Company and were infiltrating towards the crossroads held by him.

A runner brought Chapy orders to pull back to the crossroads.[24] If the cross-roads fell, the battalion's disposition would be irrevocably disrupted. The 1st Company disengaged without a hitch. Chapy was the last to leave.

Back at the crossroads, Chapy called up Cance and received orders from him to hold the crossroads at all costs until 1900 hours. Chapy requested reinforcements and Cance promised to send him all that he still had to hand.

On the morning of 21st August, one company from SS-Pz.AA 18 (Panzer-Aufklärungs-Abteilung 18) was ordered to counterattack on Przeclaw and also to release de Tissot's encircled 1st Company to the north. Although the Kradschützen (reconnaissance troops) courageously battled it out, they were unable to reach the target or render assistance to their trapped French comrades.[25]

---

24   Mabire, page 357. However, according to Saint-Loup, page 62, with a heavy heart, Chapy gave the sensible and necessary order to fall back.

25   Tieke and Rebstock, page 54.

The 3rd Company

If the night of 20th/21st August 1944 was terrible for the 1st Company, it was worse for the 3rd. And yet the night had started promisingly enough when the 3rd Company made it to its assigned position near to or in the village of Pouby[26] and promptly dug in.

The first Soviet attack, launched by a Guards battalion, hit the 3rd Company around dawn and was repelled in hand-to-hand fighting. Soon after, Soviet mortars and anti-tank guns picked up from where its infantry had left off. The heavy bombardment caught Laschett's platoon badly positioned. Laschett went in person to company headquarters and received permission from Fenet to fall back and align his platoon with that of Quicampoix.[27]

The Russians came again across the same ground. Once again, they were beaten off in hand-to-hand fighting, but Quicampoix and his 1st platoon were now out of position. Thereupon he went to company headquarters to ask for permission to align his platoon. This was duly granted, but on the understanding that the 'mortar platoon' [the 4th platoon under Couvreur] was not to be exposed. However, instead of aligning itself, Quicampoix's platoon actually fell back, turning up hours later at Cance's headquarters!

The disappearance of Quicampoix's platoon from the defensive line exposed Couvreur's platoon just as the Russians launched their third attack.[28] Struck violently, Couvreur's platoon scattered, abandoning its mortars. Laschett's 2nd platoon was encircled.[29] It fought furiously. By dawn, it was pinned down and unable to extricate itself.

An attempt was made to rescue Laschett's platoon by headquarters staff under Uscha. Hennecart, but was beaten back. Three times Ostuf. Fenet attempted to prise open the Soviet ring around Laschett's platoon and three times he was repelled, with heavier and heavier losses.[30] The end came all too soon for Laschett's platoon that was forced to surrender when its ammunition ran out.[31]

At midday, Ostuf. Fenet gave the order 'to fall back and break through to Mokré'.[32] He now had no more than fifty men with him—two platoons had disappeared and one was lost.[33] He too left behind him seriously wounded who did not wish to delay the march of the survivors. Schütze Charpentier was left with a pistol and a flask of water.

---

26   According to Saint-Loup, page 59, its designated position was Pouby and according to Mabire, page 359, 'a line of defense not far from the village of Poreby'.

27   Saint-Loup, pages 64 to 66.

28   Saint-Loup, page 72. However, according to Mabire, pages 367 and 368, Fenet still had Quicampoix's 1st platoon with him.

29   Saint-Loup, pages 71 and 72. However, according to Mabire, page 361, Laschett's platoon found itself isolated and encircled as a result of 'a lack of liaison between the units'.

30   Mabire, page 367.

31   Oberjunker Laschett would die later in the Soviet camp at Tambov in the first weeks of 1945.

32   Saint-Loup, page 73.

33   Mabire, page 368.

The survivors of the 3rd Company took up a position to the left of the cross-roads held by Chapy and Le Marquer whom Cance had reinforced with Lopez's engineer platoon. They too were ordered to hold, at all costs, until 1900 hours.

The battle continued to rage. Chapy was everywhere, an inspiration to all. In dribs and drabs men from all units made it back to the makeshift 'defence line' whose base was the crossroads. All had the same word on the Russians. They were everywhere.

The Russians brought up anti-tank guns and mortars and all too soon the Frenchmen came under a continuous hail of fire. The earth was ploughed up. The slightest careless movement brought injury or death. Any object 'sticking out the ground was riddled with shrapnel'.[34] All units counted dead and wounded. Oscha. Lopez was wounded.

The Russians closed to within five hundred metres, but the Frenchmen continued to hold them at bay with machine-gun fire. The defenders' ammunition dwindled dangerously. Indeed the term 'poor man's war' held good for them.

Continually cut, the telephone lines would only be kept repaired at the cost of wounded and killed. Brennion's men performed miracles to keep pace with the rate at which the Russians destroyed their work. Boyer's runners were almost all wounded or killed. French SS *freiwillige* Ferraud disappeared carrying a message from Cance to Fenet. He was never heard of again. Boyer's Kübelwagen, carrying ammunition and provisions for the hard pressed troops, was destroyed by a PAK shell. Pleyber was wounded and evacuated.

1900 hours was fast approaching. The 2nd Company[35] pulled back and the 3rd prepared to follow it. The Russian pressure increased. Machine-guns raked the French lines. Suddenly, gunfire was heard to the rear. Battalion headquarters was engaged in a heavy defensive battle against Russian units that had infiltrated the sieve-like 'defence line'. Cance just evaded capture. All headquarters personnel had to fight. They were delivered by the timely arrival of the disengaging 3rd Company which swept the area of Russians and formed a hedgehog position around the command post.

The seriously wounded had to be evacuated. Oscha. Boyer had them loaded onto a large car found abandoned. At that very moment, SS-Ostuf. Wagner of 'Horst Wessel' turned up and had a small 75mm infantry gun attached to the rear of Boyer's vehicle. A lorry was totally emptied of all its contents and filled with men who were all armed with a machine-gun or machine-pistol, and well stocked with ammunition. This 'armoured battering ram' led the way for those on foot behind it in columns on each side of the road. All told, the Frenchmen and Germans of Battalion Hoyer counted some one hundred men.

When the Russians tried to intercept this Franco-German battlegroup of company strength they were met by intense fire and scattered. With the wounded loaded onto the vehicles, the battlegroup continued on [probably southwards]. The dead were abandoned 'out of necessity to save the greatest possible number of men'.[36]

34   Mabire, page 381.
35   Presumably the 2nd Company had been reorganised. It would have been missing the group led by Bayle making its way to Mokré.
36   Bayle, "*San et Persante*", page 80. Tieke and Rebstock record, on page 56, a very similar break-out and add that the small convoy had only covered two kilometres

The small convoy came to a plain. To the right, some five kilometres away, was the village of Mokré. And to the left was the village 'sheltering' the *train de combat*[37] of the battalion. Soon after, the small convoy arrived in Mokré.

1900 hours could not come soon enough for the 1st Company on the verge of being overwhelmed. The Russians were now less than three hundred metres away. The crossroads and the hamlet were still under a continuous hail of fire. The minutes passed. The Soviets tried to turn the Frenchmen, but Uscha. Carre was quick to spot and eliminate the threat.

Finally, at 1900 hours, and not a minute before, the 1st Company withdrew. The survivors, no more than thirty, provided themselves with covering fire by walking backwards, firing from the hip. There was no panic.

Le Marquer led the survivors to the small hamlet 'housing' battalion headquarters. Chapy brought up the rear. The hamlet was burning. Cance and some headquarters staff were still there. They joined Le Marquer and the survivors of the 1st Company. Leaving the hamlet, they plunged into the relative safety of the woods. Night came. Totally exhausted, they staggered southwards like automatons. Gunfire rent the night. Fear gripped them. They started to run.

Tired of withdrawing, two unknown machine-gunners from the 2nd Company stayed behind to fight it out. Their sacrifice brought fifteen valuable minutes for the pursued. Harassed by Russian patrols, the survivors swept aside all in their path and managed to make contact with German forces. They collapsed on the ground under the watchful eye of several Sturmgeschütze. Thus, at high cost, they had fought their way to freedom, temporary though it proved to be.

By the evening of 21st August 1944, the 1st Battalion of the French SS-Sturmbrigade counted 300 combat-fit men at the very most. Each combat company now had the strength of only fifty men.

Once more into the breach

Cance called together his company commanders and passed on to them orders he had just received from 'Horst Wessel'. Quite simply the French battalion was to occupy new defensive positions and stop the Russians.[38]

Cance set about deploying his battered and bruised battalion. First he drove Fenet to his position to await his 3rd Company. Then he organised Lambert's 2nd Company. After wishing Lambert good luck he came to the 1st Company. He instructed Chapy to position the 1st Company between the 3rd Company on the left and troops of SS-Kampfgruppe 'Schäfer' on the right. At the sound of a

before it encountered Russians.

37   A French military term that describes the logistical elements, motorised or even horse-drawn, that accompany into battle a unit at least of battalion strength. As such, there is no English equivalent.

38   Other than being south of those just vacated the exact location of these new defensive positions is not known. According to Tieke and Rebstock, page 55, during the night of 21st/22nd August 1944 Ustuf. (sic) Chabert (sic) and the remnants of the 1st and 3rd companies of the French Sturmbrigade reached their own lines near Mokré. Here they were integrated into their battalion that had established defensive positions south of Nagoszyn to the right of 1st Battalion/SS Panzer-Grenadier-Regiment 39.

fusillade Cance jumped into his Kübelwagen and drove back to the command post where he would be needed most.

In vain did Ostuf. Fenet wait for his company. Eventually he met up with a group of German soldiers from the Wehrmacht and together they fought off wave after wave of Russians. Morning came. He was still without his company and battalion had not been in contact. His situation was no different from that of his German comrades. So they continued to hold their ground and return blow for blow. In the end the continued Soviet pressure told and they now found themselves outflanked.

At 1300 hours on 22nd August, the Wehrmacht soldiers and Ostuf. Fenet withdrew and made for the small town of Debica to the south. They came across a road and hid as Soviet motorised columns passed by. Incredibly a column of German vehicles then appeared. They raced to the roadside to make their presence known. A lorry stopped for them. They clambered aboard.

Suddenly overcome by a terrible tiredness, Fenet fell asleep. He had gone without sleep for two days and two nights.

The lorry took Fenet and the Wehrmacht soldiers all the way to Debica, where he was incorporated into the mixed Kampfgruppe 'Muller' made up of men from the W-SS, the Wehrmacht and the Military Police. At the head of a group of infantrymen, gunners and engineers,[39] he participated in the defence of Debica. However, he was soon wounded by a piece of shrapnel in the shoulder and, against his wishes, evacuated.[40]

After Cance's hurried departure, the 1st Company cautiously advanced into the dark woods, but found neither the 3rd Company nor Schäfer's SS troops, just Russians. Once again the Russians seemed everywhere. Chapy heard the sound of engines. They had to be Russian. In the hope of finding friends, he decided to head towards the sound of the fusillade he had heard just as Cance was giving him orders.

In this way, Chapy and the 1st Company came to a village and the encircled survivors of two platoons of the badly shot-up 3rd Company. At their head was Oscha. Quicampoix. For the past hour, he and the two platoons had been walking round and round the village in search of a way out that the Russians did not have covered. There were none. Hence, he had come to the conclusion that they were completely encircled.

Staying put, Chapy had the village prepared for all-round defence. In support were two FLAK guns manned by the Wehrmacht, but with few rounds left to expend.

With what little ammunition the defenders had, they managed to keep at bay the inquisitive Soviet patrols. Nevertheless, they continued to receive harassing mortar fire.

39   Mabire, page 407. However, according to Saint-Loup, page 86, repeated by Landwehr, page 50, Ostuf. Fenet led a platoon in Kampfgruppe 'Muller'.
40   Mabire, pages 405 to 408. Curiously, on pages 80 and 81, Saint-Loup places Ostuf. Fenet at Mokré for at least part of the day of the 22nd. Nevertheless, on page 86, Saint-Loup confirms the presence of Fenet at Debica.

Not wishing the village to become a trap, Oberjunker Chapy decided that they would have to get out. He was convinced that by dawn it would be too late. He told Quicampoix of his decision. He was in full agreement.

Just before dawn on 22nd August 1944, the French SS troops assembled, broke out of the village and marched to the sound of gunfire. They encountered no resistance. Unbeknown to them, the Soviets had pulled back during the course of the night.

They pressed on. Sporadic mortar fire continued to fall. Diving to the ground, they were showered with dirt. Day broke. The countryside seemed empty.

Eventually they ran into reconnaissance elements of SS-Kampfgruppe 'Schäfer' who directed them to Stubaf. Schäfer at the village of Dabrówka, some five kilometres away. Here Chapy was welcomed by Schäfer who told him that he had need of him to bolster his severely depleted command.[41] Yes, the situation was desperate. Schäfer had just dispatched all clerical and support staff to plug another hole in the collapsing front.

Pointing to his mapboard, Schäfer instructed Chapy to hold a position east of Dabrówka. Resupplied, the eighty French SS soldiers of the 1st and 3rd companies, heavily laden with ammunition, immediately set forth. Suddenly, they found themselves before some thirty German soldiers of the Wehrmacht who had abandoned their weapons and were fleeing the battlefield. At their head was a Major. Raising their weapons, the Frenchmen turned them round.[42]

Chapy 'moved into' the abandoned positions and made contact with troops of the SS-Kampfgruppe on both flanks. Hours later, the Frenchmen drove off a strong Soviet patrol with intense fire. Mortar fire then rained down on their positions. The first wounded were evacuated.

Fierce fighting flared up around Dabrówka. The Frenchmen and the Germans were outnumbered at a ratio of one to ten. Soviet assaults died under the fire of machine guns and machine pistols. Soviet tank attacks were broken up and beaten off by Sturmgeschütze. The Soviet air force made an appearance and machine-gunned the village. German FLAK answered and brought one down. Casualty lists mounted.

The SS-Kampfgruppe managed to send a platoon to reinforce the Frenchmen and, in the afternoon, to relieve them with a company totalling thirty very young and exhausted men.

Returning to Dabrówka, the Frenchmen could content themselves with another job well done. Once again they had plugged another hole left by the Wehrmacht.

Following another Soviet air attack, Chapy went to Schäfer for new orders. He found him sheltering in a hole under a lorry. Schäfer duly honoured him with field promotion to the rank of Untersturmführer (as well as, according to Saint-Loup, the Iron Cross).

41   Guarding the entrance to Dabrówka were two PAK guns whose previous owner may have been the PAK platoon of the Sturmbrigade.

42   Mabire alleges that machine-gunners of the SS-Kampfgruppe deliberately fired on this 'unit of runaways' when it returned to the front-line, killing some (see Mabire, page 399).

Mokré

In the meantime Lambert's 2nd Company also became locked in fierce battle. Deployed in the hamlet north of Mokré during the night of 21st/22nd August, the 2nd Company was attacked in the early hours of 22nd August. The Russians were too strong and broke into the northern part of the hamlet. They fortified the isbas they occupied.

To light up the night, Lambert had incendiary bullets fired into the thatched roofs of the isbas, which were soon ablaze. The fire spread quickly and as the Russians tried to evacuate the burning isbas they were mown down by MGs. Others sought refuge in isbas in the southern part of the hamlet held by the French. They were hunted down and dispatched with pistol and entrenching tools.

The very success of Lambert's strategy was his undoing, for the fire continued to spread. He had to withdraw.[43]

Withdrawing to new positions, the 2nd Company came across a Russian standing at a crossroads. He was wearing a mixture of Russian and Wehrmacht uniform. He had no papers on him and, on the orders of Lambert, a Sergeant executed him as a spy.

When the 2nd Company was in place Cance questioned Lambert about the Hiwi [a Russian auxiliary 'serving' in the German Armed forces] he had left at the crossroads to direct them along the correct route! Cance had posted many such Hiwis to guide the French stragglers back.

The Russians came again. Outflanked once again, the Frenchmen had to retreat once again.

Hit in the legs, a Sturmmann from Brittany beseeched his platoon commander, Hennecart, to put him out of his suffering. 'In the name of a higher charity', Hennecart administered the coup de grâce.[44]

Early on the foggy morning of 22nd August 1944, a hedgehog position was formed around the village of Mokré from survivors of the 2nd Company and rearward personnel scraped together and fed into the front line; at most one hundred men.[45] The defenders included the small group of the 2nd Company led by Uscha. Bayle that good fortune had brought safely to Mokré that morning.

Exhausted, the fifteen-strong group led by Bayle had begun to dig in for the night of 21st/22nd August near a road when Russian lorries appeared. The Russians stopped and noisily set up camp on the other side of the road. The night and a haze were literally all that separated the two!

Moments later, a Russian patrol, in single file, quietly walked straight through the French positions and joined their comrades on the other side of the road. Incredibly the patrol did not raise the alarm. Bayle put this stroke of good fortune down to the Russians thinking they had seen the bodies of dead men in their holes when in fact they were sound asleep! 'The Frenchmen spent the night in the light of enemy flares and the constant hubbub of their chitchat'.[46]

---

43   Saint-Loup, pages 76-77. However, Uscha. Bayle is incorrectly placed with Lambert.

44   Saint-Loup, page 80.

45   Mabire, page 409. According to Bayle, "*San et Persante*", page 81, the defenders of Mokré numbered 60 divided between three groups under Le Marquer, Reiche and Fenet.

Before daybreak, the Frenchmen left their Russian 'neighbours' and continued on their way through dense fog that made the going very difficult. Incredibly they stumbled upon a roadsign showing the way to Mokré. And the village was only three kilometres away!

Through the thickening fog they marched. And, quite by chance, they came to the command post of the battalion. Bayle reported to Cance. The battalion commander was surprised to see him, all the more so when Bayle showed him which way they had come, because he was convinced that 'they were totally encircled'. He ordered Bayle to take up position.

In the early morning hours, Hstuf. Cance and Ustuf. Lambert discussed the subject of counterattacks to 'loosen the Russian vice'.[47] Cance was back and forth between the front line and his command post, a hovel, which increasingly came under attack from Russian patrols that had slipped past the French resistance points. And it was here that Cance received his first wound of the day, a bullet in his left arm. No sooner was he bandaged up than he received orders from Schäfer to defend Mokré for twelve hours. Assembling his remaining officers, Cance conveyed the orders to them, adding they would carry them out to the last officer!

Then the Russians came. Ustuf. Lambert went to the head of a platoon and counterattacked. Violent hand-to-hand fighting raged with bayonet and trenching spade. The Russians broke, but the battle soon continued. The 2nd Company melted away in this inferno, but held the ground retaken from the enemy.

Hit by mortar shrapnel in the abdomen, Ustuf. Lambert suddenly keeled over. The French SS men quickly gathered round their mortally wounded company commander and fended off the Russian hordes. Informed, Cance was soon on the scene. Shouldering Lambert, he brought him back through enemy fire to Mokré. Dr. Bonnefoy raced over, but could do nothing for him except try and make him comfortable. Lambert asked for the Iron Cross [which was later sanctioned]. Minutes later, he died in the arms of Dr. Bonnefoy.[48]

Oscha. Schoulowski was seriously wounded. Having asked for a pistol and a cigarette, he committed suicide on the approach of the Russians. One of Croisille's two sons, who had been at Posen-Treskau, was killed. Machine-gunner Mamet was killed changing position. Oscha. Pouget may have also met his death at Mokré.[49]

46   Bayle, page 117.

47   Mabire, page 409.

48   Saint-Loup, page 83 and Mabire, pages 412-413. However, on the fall of Mokré, according to Boyer's citation for the Iron Cross 1st Class, he transported the body of the mortally wounded Ustuf. Lambert, as well as two seriously wounded soldiers, to the first aid post. This would suggest that Lambert's last moments were perhaps not quite so dramatic.

49   Mabire, page 411. However, there are, at least, two other versions of where Pouget met his death. According to Saint-Loup, page 62, in the early hours of 21st August 1944, Pouget, listed as the heavy platoon commander of the 1st Company, went in search of the missing Ostuf. de Tissot. He was never heard from again. Secondly, according to Bayle, "*San et Persante*", page 79, Pouget went off with a small group to

Hstuf. Cance went back to the battle and was wounded again when a grenade exploded at his feet. It left him dazed, but again he had escaped serious injury.

Hordes of Russians continued to surge forward. For hours the battle ebbed and flowed. Ostuf. Le Marquer was everywhere. No sooner had he averted danger at one 'quill' of the hedgehog than he was dashing off to another where danger was arising.

Hennecart was wounded and evacuated.

Once again the Russian artillery thundered and the mortars screamed. Isbas went up in flames and plumes of black smoke spiralled into the sky. Reiche, Binder and Le Marquer were blown to pieces in the farmhouse used as a command post.[50]

The end at Mokré

In the afternoon the situation at Mokré began to look ugly. Not only were the defenders running out of ammunition, but also they had no anti-tank weapons to combat the Russian tanks that had just been sighted. If they were to offer continued resistance they needed to be resupplied and fast. Orderly officer Ustuf. Scapula went speeding off in a Kübelwagen to the battalion's supply train located at Debica. With him were four others. They got through to Debica.[51] As soon as the Kübelwagen was stacked high with ammunition they started back. There was not a minute to lose.

Approaching Mokré, the Kübelwagen came under enemy infantry and mortar fire. Against all the odds, a bullet struck the nose cone of a panzerfaust attached to the bonnet for ease of use in the event of a chance meeting with enemy armour. In the resulting explosion the German driver and Ustuf. Scapula were killed outright. The three Frenchmen in the rear jumped out and defended themselves against the Russians who had just appeared. Of the three, only Sturmmann Mesqui would make it back to French lines. His two compatriots, named as Savaiau and Barthet,[52] who he last saw crawling some fifty metres from the Russians, were never heard from again.

As a result of the loss of the Kübelwagen the fire from the defenders of Mokré gradually diminished. They now only fired when they were sure of hitting their target. There was no longer any organised resistance, just isolated pockets of small groups. Overwhelmed and crushed, the ultimate fate of many of these

---

destroy or capture a Russian anti-tank gun in the village of Ruda. He was killed and the group decimated.

50   Bayle, "*De Marseille à Novossibirsk*", page 119. Bayle was an eyewitness. Incorrectly, both Mabire and Saint-Loup recount that Le Marquer, out of ammunition, was seen to fall in hand-to-hand fighting. Moreover, Saint-Loup puts his death in the afternoon. Furthermore, according to Tieke and Rebstock, page 56, Binder, Le Marquer and Reiche fell during the break-out from Mokré. This also has to be incorrect.

51   According to Saint-Loup, page 85, Ustuf. Bartolomei, who had been evacuated along with the *train de combat* to Debica, shook hands with Scapula during the brief turnaround. However, Mabire has Bartolomei serving as a nurse in the first aid post at Mokré (see Mabire, page 410).

52   Saint-Loup, page 85.

French groups will never be known. Despite the Frenchmen stubbornly contesting each and every inch of ground, the Russians had grown too strong and broke into Mokré itself. There was bloody hand-to-hand fighting in the blazing village.

Once again a grenade landed at the feet of Hstuf. Cance. This time, he was not so lucky. Seriously wounded in the knee, he was evacuated to Bonnefoy's first aid post. Thus, the Frenchmen had fought to their last combat officer, but they had held Mokré for twelve hours.

Oscha. Boyer now took over.[53] With the handful of men left to him he beat off two enemy attacks. He also had many wounded evacuated by car to the first aid post to the rear.

Finally, the defenders received orders to withdraw to the farm containing battalion headquarters[54] where they tried to regroup to face the Russian tanks, accompanied by infantry, closing in 'for the kill'. Clearly, this was the end.

The courtyard of the farm was full of dead, including Reiche, and seriously wounded. Learning of the tank attack, the wounded were gripped by panic. Some tried to run off, but they could not keep on their feet.

Pounding the farm with every kind of weapon, the Russian tanks approached. There was no cover for the wounded lying out in the farmyard. Few, if any, escaped death.

The defenders fled from the farm.[55] Oscha. Boyer was the last to leave the battlefield.[56]

Chased by bullets and shells, the survivors came to German assault guns camouflaged behind stacks of straw, but they were not engaging the enemy. They were to learn later that the assault guns had totally exhausted their ammunition and were awaiting replenishment. They pressed on. They now passed

53   Regarding this, Boyer's citation for the Iron Cross 1st Class reads that he took over the command of the battalion at 0900 hours, at which time his *chef de bataillon* [Cance] was seriously wounded and all other offices were dead or wounded. But, according to Mabire, page 417, and Saint-Loup, page 85, Cance was wounded for a third time and evacuated after holding Mokré for twelve hours. This time difference the author has not been able to explain. Also, according to Bayle, "*De Marseille à Novossibirsk*", page 119, shortly before the end at Mokré, Ustuf. Reiche confided to him the command of those still left. This too the author has not been able to explain, although it should be recalled that the battle appears to have been fought in great chaos.

54   A conclusion drawn by the author from Bayle, "*De Marseille à Novossibirsk*", page 119 and correspondence to the author.

55   Bayle, "*De Marseille à Novossibirsk*", page 120. However, according to Mabire, page 417, the French SS troops received orders to disengage and then 'withdrew in small groups, trying to delay the Russians again'. In response to this, Bayle, one of the last defenders of Mokré and perhaps the only able-bodied NCO left as the end neared, does not recall any such orders (correspondence to the author, 1997). Also, according to Bayle, the withdrawal was much more chaotic than that depicted by Mabire and little, or no, resistance was offered by the survivors as they retreated to Debica.

56   Cited in his citation for the Iron Cross 1st Class. However, according to Bayle, "*San et Persante*", page 82, Boyer was evacuating wounded by car when Mokré fell.

Army troops launching a counterattack. They gave the Frenchmen a friendly wave.

Quite by chance the survivors met the *train de combat* of the French battalion. 'Croisille asked for news of his [two] sons but they preferred to keep silent'.[57]

At or near Debica, the survivors from Mokré took up position. Here they met comrades from the 1st and 3rd companies under Chapy.

Orders were received to move to a forest location seventeen or eighteen kilometres from Tarnów on the road from Debica to Tarnów.[58] Lorries transported the survivors to the forest location where they met a very small precursory detachment of reinforcements from the 2nd Battalion of the Sturmbrigade.[59] Now they could rest.

The *train de combat* finds itself in trouble

However, the fighting was still not over for some elements of the battalion. On the afternoon of 24th August 1944, its *train de combat* of twenty lorries, carrying French and German wounded, found itself encircled.[60] Gunfire could be heard closing in from the north and the south, shells were pursuing the convoy from the east, and Russian troops had cut the road ahead to Tarnów.

Ostuf. Croisille called together the other officers present. Deciding upon a ruse, he hoped to draw off the Russian troops blocking the way westwards by creating diversions on the flanks. He ordered Ostuf. Dr. Bonnefoy to direct the diversion to the north and Ostuf. Maud'huit[61] that to the south. His orders to them were concise: "Assemble all available machine-guns … All combat-fit men … Intense fire for ten minutes and withdraw!"

Bonnefoy assembled the clerks, drivers, lightly wounded, and combat-fit men. Maud'huit assumed command of a platoon. They deployed and opened up on the Russian units across the plain gently descending westwards. Maud'huit fought like a man possessed and when one of his machine gunners was hit he immediately took over.

Immediately, and just as Croisille had hoped, the Russians 'bought' the ruse and relaxed their grip on the road to Tarnów to reinforce those 'under attack'. The first lorries of the convoy sped off.

Withdrawing to the convoy, Maud'huit was hit and wounded by mortar shrapnel, but a member of his platoon rushed over, shouldered him and threw him onto the last lorry of the convoy.

At breakneck speed the convoy now belted westwards, sweeping aside weak parties of Russians and dodging artillery fire. Miraculously it made it through.[62]

57   Bayle, "*De Marseille à Novossibirsk*", page 121.
58   Bayle, "*San et Persante*", page 85. These orders were probably received on the evening of 22nd August 1944. Undoubtedly the move would have come soon after.
59   Bayle, "*San et Persante*", page 85.
60   This begs the question what was the *train de combat* of the French battalion doing so near to the front some two days after its combat elements were moved to Tarnów? Unfortunately, the author still has no satisfactory answer to this question. Perhaps it was performing work for 'Horst Wessel'.
61   Mistakenly, Landwehr identifies Maud'huit with the rank of Untersturmführer.

Tarnów

At Tarnów, Ostuf. Croisille reorganised the command of the battalion as follows:[63]

> 1st Company: Ostuf. Maud'huit
> 2nd Company: Ustuf. Bartolomei
> 3rd Company: Oberjunker Chapy

The combat companies were now only of platoon strength. Indeed, the casualty balance-sheet made very grim reading. Every combat officer had either been killed or wounded. In point of fact, both Chapy and Bartolomei had been wounded, but refused evacuation!

Of the estimated 980 French SS troops engaged some two weeks before, Mabire cites '130 killed, 50 or so missing, and more than 660 wounded'. Saint-Loup cites that 140 men and NCOs came back and that 'all the others were either dead, wounded or missing'. Bayle also cites that there were 140 survivors of which about one hundred were slightly wounded. Tieke and Rebstock list the appalling losses as 90 killed, 660 wounded and 40 missing out of 900 French *freiwilligen* engaged. This figure of 900 could be a genuine mistake for 980 or refer to the actual total troop strength of the French SS-Sturmbrigade at the beginning of its second phase of fighting in Galicia. Landwehr records 130 other ranks killed, 661 other ranks wounded and 40 men missing. These figures, which differ little, represent a most terrible bloodletting.

Of those Frenchmen captured, sadly many were summarily put to death.[64] Years of rigorous Soviet imprisonment awaited the others from which few would return.

Even at the rear death struck. *Freiwillige* Artiganave, Boyer's orderly, drowned in a nearby river. He had fought bravely on the battlefield.

On 24th August 1944, the 1st Battalion of the French SS-Sturmbrigade was cited in the divisional orders of 'Horst Wessel'.

Days later, the survivors paraded for Obf. Trabandt who passed on his congratulations and those of General Graesler, Balck's assistant.[65]

The Frenchmen now had to part from 'Horst Wessel'.[66] The survivors were to be sent to the towns of Bruss and Schwarnegast in the former Danzig corridor

---

62   Saint-Loup, pages 86-87. It should be noted that Landwehr also writes of this same action, see pages 50-52, but the differences are many. Convinced that Landwehr used Saint-Loup as a source, the author chose not to repeat the rewriting of Landwehr. In addition, no other source confirms this action. This is curious.

63   Bayle, "*De Marseille à Novossibirsk*", page 125. In contrast, Mabire places Oberjunker Chapy at the head of the 1st and Oscha. Lefèvre at the 3rd (see Mabire, page 424). Furthermore, Saint-Loup also places Chapy at the head of the 1st (see Saint-Loup, page 92).

64   See Mabire, page 380, and Saint-Loup, page 68.

65   Saint-Loup, pages 92-93. Notably, no other source confirms this parade for Trabandt.

66   Curiously, according to Mabire, page 424, the Frenchmen could not stay with the 'Horst Wessel' because they were missing too many officers and NCOs.

where the French SS-Sturmbrigade was to be amalgamated with the LVF to form a new French unit of the Waffen SS.

A number of soldiers would receive awards.[67] Among the recipients of the Iron Cross 1st class were Pierre Cance, Henri Kreis, Robert Lambert and Marc Godillon. Among the recipients of the Iron Cross 2nd class were André Bayle, Emilien Boyer, Henri Fenet, Lefèbvre, and Camille Rouvre (1st Company).

On 1st September 1944, the 1st Battalion of the French Sturmbrigade left Tarnów railway station for the former Danzig corridor. Oberjunker Chapy was no longer with the battalion. He was actually under arrest for murder!

Chapy

The ill feeling that had developed between the combatants of the French battalion and the personnel of the Verwaltung [Supply Corps] came to a head at Tarnów.[68] So infuriated was Chapy when it came to his attention that the supply personnel were interfering with the belongings of the wounded and dead he confronted and warned a certain Unterscharführer Eglé of the Verwaltung. The Alsatian Eglé was a known trafficker.[69] That same day, a grenadier handed Chapy a letter to read from a wounded soldier of the 1st Company hospitalised in Bohemia-Moravia. The wounded soldier wrote that Eglé had refused to take him to the first-aid post. Chapy, who had had enough, decided to take matters into his own hands.

In the presence of a number of witnesses,[70] Chapy summarily executed Eglé and had him buried. He then reported his execution of Eglé to Croisille, Maud'huit and Bonnefoy who were at a total loss what to do. They did nothing. Chapy later reported that Eglé had disappeared. But Ostuf. Danke, the German commander of the Verwaltung, went to the headquarters of SS-Kampfgruppe 'Schäfer' and reported the true nature of Eglé's 'disappearance'.[71]

---

67   Sources differ as to the number of awards as well as the date of the awards. According to Saint-Loup, page 93, Obf. Trabandt left in his wake 40 Iron Cross, of which 29 were awarded posthumously. According to Bayle, "*De Marseille à Novossibirsk*", page 124, in conjunction with Ustuf. Bartolomei, the NCOs 'prepared the citations'. In this way, that September, nominations for over 100 awards of the Iron Cross, including many posthumously, went forward. Moreover, Bayle does not recall a distribution of Iron Cross at Tarnów (correspondence with the author). Lastly, according to Mabire, page 424, 58 Iron Cross were awarded, including many posthumously. And 20 were presented with little ceremony on 10th November 1944 at Wildflecken (Mabire, "*La Division Charlemagne*", page 169).

68   According to Mabire, page 429, the survivors blamed Ostuf. Danke, the German commander of the Verwaltung, for not keeping them sufficiently fed. This seems unfair. The situation was fluid.

69   Incorrectly, Mabire identifies Eglé as German.

70   According to Mabire, page 431, Chapy was accompanied by Belanger, Quarru (a pseudonym) and Delagarde (a pseudonym), all from the 1st Company. However, according to Bayle, "*San et Persante*", page 85, Chapy had four accomplices; Carre, Patt, Mercier and de Bonnegarde.

71   According to Mabire, page 435, Danke had much to cover up.

On 28th August 1944, Chapy and the onlookers were arrested and questioned.[72] Joined by three other Frenchmen of the 1st Company[73], they were sent to
Tarnów and then onto a military prison at Cracow.[74]

Months later, Chapy was brought before a military court, not from the new
French formation, but from the 28. SS-Freiwilligen Grenadier Division
'Wallonien'. Found guilty, he was sent to the Waffen-SS military prison at
Dachau.[75]

After the 'departure' of Chapy, Uscha. Lefèbvre,[76] whose younger brother was
also serving with the Sturmbrigade, became the commander of the 3rd Company
at Tarnów.

Command roster of the reinforced 1st Battalion of the 'Französische SS-Freiwilligen-Sturmbrigade' in Galicia August 1944

Commander:	Hauptsturmführer Pierre Cance (wounded 22nd Aug'44)
	Obersturmführer Jean Croisille (at Tarnow)
Aide-de-camp:	Untersturmführer Scapula (killed 22nd Aug'44)
H.Q. platoon:	Obersturmführer Jean Croisille
	Oscha. Emilien Boyer
Engineer platoon:	Oberscharfuhrer Lopez (wounded)
German liaison officer:	Untersturmführer Reiche (killed 22nd Aug'44)

72   Details of the arrest conflict. According to Mabire, page 435, six military
      policemen of 'Horst Wessel' arrested Chapy and the three other Frenchmen.
      Then an ugly situation arose when Chapy was surrounded by NCOs of the
      Verwaltung who were in turn ringed by armed Frenchmen from all three
      companies. Nevertheless, the situation was quickly diffused by Chapy himself.
      According to Bayle, "*San et Persante*", page 86, the 'arresting officers' were Oscha.
      Boyer and Uscha. Lefèbvre.

73   Mabire, page 436. However, there is little accompanying detail about the three.
      Thus, the possibility exists that they were not involved in the execution of Eglé.

74   Mabire, page 438. However, in October 1988, Chapy told Mounine that he was held
      in fortress Warsaw. And yet it was Chapy himself who provided Mabire with the
      details of his adventures.

75   What became of Chapy is irreconcilable; according to Mabire, page 438, and
      Landwehr, Chapy's case would only be reopened upon a personal order from
      Reichsführer-SS Himmler himself. In response, Bayle states that this is simply not
      true (correspondence to the author). Mabire continues that Chapy would be set free
      in the last days of the war. Landwehr adds that Chapy then saw action against the
      Americans in a mixed kampfgruppe with Hitler Youth and others. Again, Bayle states
      that this is simply not true (correspondence to the author), noting that Chapy was
      liberated from prison by the Americans and then arrested and locked up again by the
      French authorities (see Bayle, page 86). And yet, in October 1988, Chapy told
      Mounine that he was at large in Hamburg from late 1945 to early 1946 (Mounine,
      correspondence to the author).

76   Mistakenly, Mabire records Lefèbvre's rank as Oscha. which was the rank he would
      attain in 'Charlemagne'.

German liaison officer: Untersturmführer Binder (killed 22nd Aug'44)
Medical Officer: Obersturmführer Bonnefoy
Signals: Oberscharführer Schoulowski (killed 22nd Aug'44)
Transport: Obersturmführer Henri Maud'huit (to 1st
                         Company at Tarnow)
                         Untersturmführer Gustav-Adolf Neubauer

1st Company

Commander: Obersturmführer Nöel de Tissot (Missing in
                         action 21st Aug'44)
                         Oberjunker Abel Chapy (to 3rd Company at
                         Tarnow)
                         Obersturmführer Henri Maud'huit
Medical officer: Unterscharführer Jonquière (killed 10th Aug'44)
1st Platoon: Untersturmführer Pignard-Berthet (wounded 10th
                         Aug'44)
                         Unterscharführer Riot
Assistant: Million-Rousseau
2nd Platoon: Oberjunker Pierre Hug (wounded 10th Aug'44)
3rd Platoon: Oberscharführer Mulier (wounded 10th Aug'44)
                         Unterscharführer Carre
                         Untersturmführer Yvan Bartolomei (takes over on
                         17th, wounded on 19th)
                         Unterscharführer Carre
4th (Heavy) Platoon: Oberscharführer Kaster
Attached Platoon: Oberjunker Abel Chapy
Assistant: Oberscharführer Grossman (killed 14th August
                         1944)
                         Unterscharführer Belanger

2nd Company

Commander: Untersturmführer Léon Gaultier (wounded 10th
                         Aug'44)
                         Untersturmführer Yvan Bartolomei (evacuated
                         14th Aug'44)
                         Obersturmführer Pleyber (to PAK 16th Aug'44)
                         Untersturmführer Lambert (killed 22nd Aug'44)
                         Untersturmführer Yvan Bartolomei
1st Platoon: Unterscharführer Lefèbvre (to 3rd Company)
2nd Platoon: Oberjunker Joseph Peyron (killed 15th Aug'44)
                         Unterscharführer André Bayle
3rd Platoon: Oberscharführer Charles
4th (Heavy) Platoon: Untersturmführer Yvan Bartolomei (company
                         commander 10th August '44)

3rd Company

Commander: Obersturmführer Henri Fenet (wounded 22nd
                         Aug'44)

	Oberjunker Abel Chapy (arrested 28th Aug'44 at Tarnow)
	Unterscharführer Lefèbvre
1st Platoon:	Untersturmführer Lambert (to 2nd Company 16th Aug'44)
	Unterscharführer Quicampoix
2nd Platoon:	Oberjunker Laschett (captured 21st/22nd Aug'44)
3rd Platoon:	Unterscharführer Delsort
4th (Heavy) Platoon:	Oberscharführer Couvreur

Anti-tank Platoon

Commander:	Obersturmführer Pleyber (to 2nd Company 14th Aug'44)
Anti-tank Platoon:	Oberjunker Henri Kreis

CHAPTER 4

The *Légion des Volontaires française contre le bolchevisme*

The meeting of two very different worlds[1]

On a hot and sultry Saturday very late August 1944, one company of the 2nd Battalion of the French Sturmbrigade of the Waffen-SS disembarked at Greifenberg railway station. Commanded by SS-Ostuf. Michel, the company was made up of many volunteers aged seventeen and some as young as sixteen. They were disconsolate about not having gone to Galicia with the 1st Battalion.

They marched off. Haughtily they sang the German marching song *Panzerlied* whose words they all knew by heart. They came to Greifenberg barracks, the same barracks at which the remaining French volunteers of the *Légion des Volontaires Français contre le Bolchevisme* (LVF) under the command of General Puaud had been stationed since 18th July 1944.

From the barracks, the bored French legionnaires of the LVF watched the newcomers arrive. Such was the spectacle the newcomers were putting on that they assumed they were German. That was until they caught sight of the tricolore badge on the left sleeve of their tunic. This surprised them.

The Frenchmen of the Waffen-SS drew up. They awaited the order to dismiss. The Frenchmen of the LVF surrounded them and mocked. Ostuf-Michel made his way to a group of officers, including the 'French Captain who commanded the depot'[2], and saluted. They returned his Nazi salute half-heartedly. He immediately admonished them!

Later that day came the first contact between the youngsters of the Waffen-SS and the 'elders' of the LVF. The SS men were so shocked by the legionnaires. The legionnaires were ragged. Some were even wearing Russian fur 'papachas' and gaudy scarves. Indiscipline was rife. Their language was coarse and lewd. The NCOs swore at their men in Russian. And yet the decorations and ribbons on their uniforms did not lie. All were veterans of Russia. Some had been on the Eastern front since the terrible winter of 1941.

That night, the SS men went to bed early whereas the legionnaires went into town. Without question there was a great gulf between the Frenchmen of the Waffen-SS and the LVF.

Next morning, a Sunday, LVF Chaplain Verney celebrated mass in the great ground floor canteen of the barracks. Also in the congregation were the SS men.

---

1   See Mabire, pages 61-66, and Saint-Loup, page 126-128.

2   Mabire, page 63. Undoubtedly this 'French Captain who commanded the depot' was *capitaine* Cartaud. And yet, according to Saint-Loup, page 127, Colonel Puaud, the LVF commander, greeted Michel, but there was no warmth in his welcome. This is unlikely; Puaud may have been away in Berlin.

They were there out of curiosity. In silence, they too listened to the words of Verney whose nickname was 'Mickey'.

Born in 1902 in Franche-Comté, Albert Verney was ordained a priest in 1929. Working his way up through the ranks, he was appointed *sous-lieutenant de réserve d'infanterie* on 13th August 1938. From 1938 to 1940, he served in the *chasseurs à pied*. In 1941, he volunteered for the LVF with orders on him from Archbishop Besançon. He commanded the mortar platoon of the 12th (heavy) Company of the III. Battalion. In 1942, he returned to France. One year later, he was back with the LVF as a chaplain.

Suddenly, Ostuf. Michel appeared at the doorway to the canteen and shouted 'Antreten!' His men reacted immediately and dashed to the entrance. In their haste, they knocked over tables and chairs, and pushed aside the legionnaires. Michel now yelled 'Panzeralarm!' Quickly, he briefed them. It was an improvised exercise. He then ordered them to assemble in five minutes time in the square in full combat kit. They obeyed and rushed off.

Now missing part of his congregation, Verney brought mass to a quick end. The legionnaires rushed to the windows just in time to see Michel's company going through the main gates of the barracks.

According to rumour, the LVF was to be amalgamated with the French Sturmbrigade of the Waffen-SS. If this amalgamation was to have any chance of success, the legionnaires of the LVF had much to learn about the ways of the Waffen-SS, and, in return, the volunteers of the SS had much to learn about the history and the traditions of the LVF.

The *Légion des Volontaires Français contre le bolchevisme* (LVF)

On Sunday 22nd June 1941, Nazi Germany invaded the Soviet Union. The French collaborationist parties greeted the unheralded invasion with great excitement. That same day, Doriot, the *chef* of the P.P.F., proposed publicly the creation of a legion of French volunteers to 'participate by the side of the soldiers of Europe in the decisive battle against Bolshevism'. He went to the Vichy Government and the Germans. The same idea also came to Déat, the *chef* of the R.N.P., and Deloncle, the *chef* of the M.S.R. The two of them, who were furious that Doriot had left them behind the day before, went in turn to the Vichy government and the Germans.

The Vichy government was cautious, stating in an official communiqué of 1st July that no objection would be raised to Frenchmen enlisting 'to participate in the European struggle against Communism'.

On 6th July 1941, Otto Abetz, German ambassador in Paris, met with party *chefs* Bucard, Costantini, Déat, and Doriot, and told them that Hitler had agreed to the principle of a legion of French volunteers.[3] The day before Abetz had received a telegram from Minister Ribbentrop saying that the Reich agreed 'to enlist French nationals as volunteers in the struggle against the Soviet Union'. And yet Hitler had showed little enthusiasm when the idea of a French legion first came before him. He had no need of such 'foreign brothers', expecting a quick victory over the Soviet Union. Also, since June 1940, he had had a very poor opinion of the fighting quality of the French soldier. Nevertheless, he was finally won round by

3   Mabire and Lefèvre, "*La LVF*", page 67.

the propaganda benefits to be gained from having a French contingent in the united European crusade against Bolshevism. However, he did set three conditions: the legion must be born of a 'private' initiative and not a government decision; enlistment would be restricted to no more than 10,000, later upped to 15,000; and the Vichy Government must not demand anything in return. And so was born the *Légion des Volontaires Français contre le Bolchevisme*.

On 7th July 1941, the party *chefs* met with the German military at the Hotel Majestic in Paris. Some military matters were discussed. There was little or no common ground. However, out of this meeting came the creation of a *comité central de la LVF*. Deloncle was named president.

On the following day the first recruiting office was opened at 12 rue Auber, Paris [9th district], in the former building of the Soviet travel agency Intourist. That same day, newspaper *L'OEuvre* announced that Alsatian General Hassler would command the LVF. Undoubtedly this came as a surprise to Hassler who had not been approached beforehand. He refused the command. He wanted nothing to do with the LVF. He did not want to take a command side by side with the Germans. He had only one leader, the Marshal, and one flag, the tricolore flag. Besides, he was still at the disposal of the Vichy government's Ministry for War and, as such, could not accept the command without formal authority.

On 18th July 1941, a mass meeting of militants of the political parties was held at the Vélodrome d'Hiver, a large glass-roofed sports stadium on rue Nélaton, Paris. It was the first such meeting in Paris. Estimates of the audience vary from 8,000 to 15,000. One-quarter of them were women. Some militants were already wearing a tricolore armband with the letters LVF. One such militant at the meeting with an LVF tricolore armband was Raymond Mercier. He would later enlist in the LVF.

The militants heard their leaders speak in turn.

From the podium, Doriot proclaimed France's determination to recover the glory of French arms in Russia after Napoleon's disaster and swore to accompany the first volunteers into combat.

Deloncle was next to speak and the last. He announced the formation of an LVF division consisting of a regiment of heavy and one of light tanks, a motorised artillery regiment and a squadron of aircraft. He concluded: "Europe is on the march, nothing will stop it!"

Volunteers were required to be of aryan origin, physically fit, between the ages of 18 and 45 years, and to have already completed their military service.[4] For officers, the age limit was raised to 50.[5] The minimum height was one metre sixty. Also, there was no place in the LVF for POWs.

The volunteers were promised again and again by the likes of Déat that they would fight in French uniform. The volunteers were told that the Legion had the approval of Marshal Pétain.

Volunteers stepped forward in their thousands. Even so some claim that Déat and Deloncle ordered six hundred of their militants to enlist or be kicked out of the party.

4   Mabire and Lefèvre, "*La LVF*", page 89.
5   Mabire and Lefèvre, "*La LVF*", page 94. However, according to Giolitto, page 39, officers were to be no older than 40.

The Germans turned over *caserne* [barracks] Borgnis-Desbordes, 16 avenue de Paris, Versailles, for the use of the LVF.

On the 20th August 1941, the press announced that Colonel Labonne would now assume command of the LVF. He was sixty years of age. A product of Saint-Cyr, he served with *tirailleurs sénégalais* in the Sudan, Senegal and Morocco. In 1918, he commanded the 1st battalion of the prestigious *régiment d'infanterie coloniale du Maroc* on the Western front. In the pre-war years, he held a number of desk jobs, retiring as the military attaché in Turkey. In the 'shooting war', he commanded the *18e régiment de tirailleurs sénégalais* in Tunisia. Some have claimed Colonel Labonne had little field experience as a commander. This is unfair. If anything, he was a little 'rusty'. He was an intellectual and a distinguished military historian of the Napoleonic period.

In late August 1941, the first group of volunteers was called up. They reported to *caserne* Borgnis-Desbordes on the 27th. That same day, a parade was held at which a number of German and French dignitaries, including Déat and Laval, were present. A French flag was raised as the *Marseillaise* was sung. The atmosphere was one of celebration. For many of those present, this day seemed to be the start of a new era.

Unexpectedly, the Germans invited the French dignitaries to inspect the barracks. The inspection was brief. Then they left. As they entered the gateway out onto avenue de Paris a man fired five times at point-blank range. Laval and Déat were hit, but lived. The would-be assassin was, in fact, a volunteer of the LVF. Disgusted by the actions of the collaborationists, he had joined the LVF with the express intention of killing a prominent collaborator in an attempt to rouse the French from their apathy.[6]

On 28th August, the volunteers went before German Army doctors. 1,679 were seen and 800 were rejected, mainly for poor teeth.

On 3rd September, the LVF received its flag.

The following day, the first LVF contingent of 25 officers and 803 other ranks left *caserne* Borgnis-Desbordes for the Deba training camp in Poland. Among them was P.P.F. leader Doriot. He was one of the few political party leaders to keep his promise to go with the first volunteers into combat.[7]

The train journey to Deba lasted four days. The officers were met on the platform by *capitaine* Casabianca, Colonel Labonne's *adjoint*. He was wearing a German Army uniform. The reaction was, of course, one of surprise and, for some, one of indignation.

The first contingent would form the I. Battalion.

On 20th September, 127 officers and 769 men departed Paris for the same destination. They would form the II. Battalion.

---

6   The assassin was called Paul Colette. However, Laval himself saved Colette from the death sentence. He did not wish to make a martyr of him. In the early 90s, Colette was decorated with the *Légion d'Honneur.*

7   Mabire and Lefèvre, "*La LVF*", page 177. Confirmed by Mercier, who left with the first contingent (letter to the author, 6/9/2001). He saw Doriot on soup duty, with a mess tin in each hand. Incorrectly, according to Littlejohn, page 149, Doriot went with the second contingent on 20th September.

The volunteers

The volunteers ranged in age. Some were as young as 15 years of age. On the other hand, Callas de Gournay was 57.

The volunteers came from all walks of life.

The motives were varied. Those of anti-Communism and 'the need to realise, through himself, the reality of his thoughts' drove Pierre Soulé to enlist in August 1941. An announcement of support from a Papacy official swept away the last scruples he might have had. Besides, he wanted to 'help Marshal Pétain in his mission'.

Pierre Soulé was born in May 1916 in Bordeaux. His father was the co-founder of the Communist Party at Bordeaux, but when he left 'these monsters' they murdered him. Ever since he had considered Communism as a horror. In 1936, as a *scout de France*, he left for Spain on a bicycle for a month-long holiday. It was there that the 'horrible crimes' committed by the Republicans drove him towards armed struggle.

In 1937, Pierre Soulé returned home to France to do his military service and was assigned to the *126e Régiment d'Infanterie* at Brive. Since Napoleon the First, the *126e* had been wrapped in tradition. Two years later, he was plunged into war. He saw action in the ill-fated French offensive of September 1939 and was wounded in the region east of Deux-ponts in a 'corner infested with German pillboxes'.

After a month of hospitals, Soulé was sent on leave to convalesce. He was still in his uniform caked with German mud and in his trousers cut by the doctors. He was without shoes. At the end of October, he returned to the *126e* in Alsace.

In February 1940, Soulé was called upon, because of his 'Spanish interlude', to train soldiers in anti-tank warfare. It was farcical. A mock-up tank of wood was used. The only weapon at their disposal was the old and ineffectual 25mm anti-tank gun. He also noted that a number of officers aged between 40 to 60 were incapable of climbing aboard the tank to attack it with grenades or magnetic mines. Like many, he realised that France was unprepared for war.

In May 1940, the *126e* was sent to Tergnier on the Saint-Quentin canal. Soulé volunteered for the *groupe franc* of his battalion and was accepted. Patrols along the canal brought about the capture of two prisoners, but also the loss of a comrade who fell into the water. And then the retreat began. The *126e* saw constant action to the end. On 25th June 1940, the *126e* followed orders and laid down its weapons near Bellac and Limoges. Soulé was proud that his regiment, still in battle order, was one of the few to have fought to the very end. Because of this he wore with glory and honour the *Croix de Guerre* that Marshal Pétain awarded to all the men of the *126e*. Subsequently, he was demobilised. He returned to nothing.

In August 1941, Pierre Soulé finally learnt that Germany was fighting against 'Russian dictatorship' and that French volunteers were being accepted for this fight for 'European humanity'. He enlisted in the LVF.

Not unexpectedly, many of the volunteers, approximately one in three, were idealistic militants of the collaborating political parties. Many were those from the M.S.R. and the P.P.F.

Raymond Mercier was from the *Jeunesses Nationales Populaires* (J.N.P.), the youth movement of the R.N.P. He was the J.N.P. *chef de section* for the XIX°

arrondissement (district) of Paris with some thirty adherents. The LVF offered him the opportunity to contribute to the destruction of the Bolshevik scourge – his father had fought with the French Army sent to Siberia in 1919 – and to show that 'those of 41' were not unworthy of their fathers.

Called Raymond to preserve the memory of an uncle of the same name killed on the field of honour, Mercier was brought up in the cult of the soldiers of 1914–1918. He 'missed' the 1939–1940 war; he belonged to the class of 1941, which was not called up. He had wanted to join up, but his mother was opposed; he was a minor and had need of her permission.[8] Nevertheless, he too had expected a long war and 1941 would bring his call up for military service. Defeat came sooner. For him, the defeat of 1940 was the end of a world.[9] He was tempted to try and join the British army, but was dissuaded by the shameful sight of the flight of the state-employed teachers who had abandoned the children entrusted to them. He now thought it necessary not only to rebuild his country, but also reconstruct it. The question was how?

The collapse of May-June 1940 was both military and political. Regarding the latter, Mercier said: "To speak of our old political parties was derisory".[10] The time had come for a break with the past. His friends all agreed with him about a revival built on a national solidarity more or less authoritarian and more or less socialist. However, when it came to external politics, they were divided. As for Mercier, he approved of the politics of Montoire. So when the *Rassemblement National Populaire* (R.N.P.) was created, he found that it 'responded perfectly to his perspective'; in its internal policy, the R.N.P. was a union of former militants of the left with esprit national and former militants of the right with the spirit of social progress, and, in its foreign policy, the R.N.P. was unequivocal in support of the politics of collaboration. He joined the R.N.P., but was then attracted to the *Mouvement Social Révolutionnaire* (M.S.R.) which corresponded more to his personal leanings. Thus, he passed to the M.S.R.[11] and yet he retained his position within the J.N.P. as the *chef de section* for the XIX° *arrondissement* of Paris.

Of an anticommunist tradition, he welcomed the news of the German invasion of Soviet Russia. The subsequent creation of the LVF filled him with joy because political combat became military combat. In this way, 'his generation was freed from the obsession of 'those of 14' who had been heroes'. And so it was with enthusiasm that he went and applied for enlistment in the LVF at the recruiting office on rue Auber. This time his mother had not opposed his 'going to war'. She had given her written permission, even though she positively disapproved of his 'collaborationism' and was scandalised by his decision to enlist.[12]

8   His father had died in 1936.
9   According to Mercier, 'French people today cannot imagine what we felt' (letter to the author, 5/10/01).
10   Letter to the author, 5/10/01.
11   It should be recalled that the M.S.R. was one element of the R.N.P.
12   Without approving in the slightest of his enlistment his mother and elder brother would correspond with him to the end.

Parental permission was not the only obstacle Mercier had to overcome. To gain admittance to the LVF, he needed to have done his military service.[13] Otherwise he might end up as a groom or a farrier and this he did not want. He wanted to fight. So he went to the central office of the M.S.R. and asked for an audience with party chief Eugène Deloncle who, as president of the LVF, would have influence. Dr. Landrieu, Deloncle's 'orderly officer', received him. He took Mercier's case in hand. They talked. Mercier sold himself that as a student at the Faculty of Law and at the Sorbonne 'he had to know how to write and could be of more use as a journalist than a kitchen hand'. Journalist Jean Fontenoy, the *chef de la propaganda du R.N.P.* who was to head the war correspondent unit of the LVF, had need of young and determined collaborators. Thus, 'the problem was resolved'. Nevertheless, for Mercier, this was 'the means to an end' and there was no question of him joining Fontenoy.

On 27th August 1941, Mercier was recruited into the 3rd Company of the I. Battalion of the LVF.

Georges Blonet was also from the R.N.P. He said of his reasons to enlist:

Before the war, militant in the *Jeunesses socialistes* of the S.F.I.O. (the French section of the International worker). Marxist, pacifist, fighting against the rearmament of my country, I regretted in 1936–38 that I was too young to join the International Brigades in Spain.

Shocked by the signing of the German-Soviet pact in 1939, which was approved by the French Communist party, then shattered by our defeat, [and] disgusted by the conduct and the lies of our rulers and governments of the Third Republic after the armistice, it was for me the 'turn-around'.

Behind Marshal Pétain, the way of collaboration seemed to me the best means of allowing France to recover and to have the possibility of regaining its place in Europe in case of a German victory.

At the start of 1941, I joined the R.N.P. (I would leave in 1943 for Francisme.) What attracted me to the R.N.P. was its pro-European socialist commitment. The start of the German war against the U.S.S.R., which betrayed us in 1939, changed for me the stakes in the conflict. I could no longer be a passive spectator to this war.

The LVF offered me the possibility to act and to overcome the humiliation of having been defeated. I enlisted and left with the first contingent.

The volunteers were from all political horizons. *Adjudant* [warrant officer] R. wrote to his father that 'he hoped France would emerge from its great misfortunes thanks to the French National Socialists'.[14] However, few volunteers regarded themselves as National Socialists. In April 1942, *Lieutenant* C. wrote to his family that 'we're working for a new Europe'.[15]

Many, perhaps one third, of the volunteers were career soldiers. One such career soldier was Yves Rigeade from Bordeaux. From 1936 to 1938, he served with the *26e Régiment d'infanterie* (R.I.) at Nancy and, from 1938 to 1939, with the *149e Régiment d'infanterie de forteresse* (R.I.F.) on the Maginot line. When war

---

13   Later this stipulation was dropped.

14   "*Les Volontaires Français sous l'uniforme Allemand*", page 84.

15   Ibid, page 80.

broke out he was transferred to the *132e R.I.F.* Taken prisoner at Colmar in June 1940, he escaped the following month. Thereupon he rejoined the *26e R.I.* then stationed in his region. His reaction to the defeat of May 1940 was one of disbelief. In his eyes, France had the best weapons, the best officers and the strongest army in the world and yet it had been defeated in ten days. It was a catastrophe. Before this *debâcle* he felt such an overwhelming sense of helplessness.

In August 1941, Yves Rigeade volunteered for the LVF. He was a supporter of Marshal Pétain and a traditionalist[16] who wanted to preserve civilisation from Communism. He saw his enlistment in the LVF as a continuation of the struggle against the greatest enemy of civilisation he had begun as a militant of the pre-war *Jeunesses patriotes*. He left with the second contingent to Deba.

On 1st October 1941, twenty-year-old Jean Fronteau volunteered for the LVF. He was a supporter of the National Revolution and Marshal Pétain. He was neither a militant of a political party or a career soldier. He had volunteered for Army service, but was declared unfit, even as an auxiliary, because of excessive short sight in one eye. This defect he had had since birth. Disappointment overwhelmed him.

From the sidelines, Fronteau looked on as France went to her defeat. He blamed the *Front populaire* government, the Communists and the English for sabotaging the French Army. He believed that the English who had disembarked in such a cowardly way at Dunkirk had abandoned France. His attitude towards England hardened after the incidents at Mers-el-Kebir in July 1940 and Dakar in September 1940. In this way, he came to realise that the real enemy of France, its hereditary enemy, was England and not Germany. Thus, when the LVF was created, he saw this as a means, albeit indirectly, of fighting against England, the allies of Soviet Russia.

Jean Fronteau was not alone in his reasoning. He encountered in the ranks of the LVF many former French sailors who, disgusted by the behaviour of their allies of 1939, wanted to avenge their murdered comrades.

Also recruited into the ranks of the LVF, as with every army, were adventures, fugitives on the run from the authorities, the hungry, and the unemployed.

In total, the LVF received some 13,000 applications to join. Of these, some 6,000 were accepted. And over 3,000 were recruited in the first three months of its existence.

Broken promises

At Deba, two unpleasant surprises awaited the French volunteers of the LVF. They had to don the German uniform and take an oath of loyalty to Hitler.

Because France was not at war with the Soviet Union[17] the Germans would not entertain the idea of sending the French volunteers to the front in French uniform. This was, of course, strictly in accordance with the international rules of land warfare that 'require volunteers from non-belligerent countries to wear the uniform of the army in which they were fighting'. However, the LVF was permitted to wear French Army khaki at home. A dark blue uniform is also

16   To this day, Rigeade remains a traditionalist.
17   Following the German invasion of the Soviet Union, France did break off diplomatic relations with the Soviet Union, but did not go to war.

reported as sometimes being worn in France. Only a tricolore shield inscribed with the word 'France' or an early version with 'LVF' (probably of French origin) worn on the upper right arm would distinguish their nationality.

On 5th October 1941, the first two LVF contingents swore an oath of loyalty to Adolf Hitler. Some refused. They felt betrayed. They were sent to prison where several of them perished.[18]

On 12th October, the third LVF contingent of 21 officers, 125 NCOs and 498 men arrived at Deba. The newcomers swore the oath of loyalty to Adolf Hitler on the 19th.

On 22nd October, the LVF, designated by the Germans *Infanterieregiment 638 des Heeres* (IR 638), was ordered to Smolensk, Russia.

The LVF was transported by rail to Smolensk. The headquarters staff left Deba on 28th October, the I. Battalion (companies 1–4) on the 29th, and the II. Battalion (companies 5–8) on the 31st. 2,352 men were deployed.

The first elements of the LVF arrived at Smolensk on 1st November. It was bitterly cold and snow was on the ground. The last elements arrived on the 5th, during which time it had got colder and colder. The *légionnaires* lacked winter clothing.

In temperatures as low as minus forty degrees below zero, the LVF continued on foot to the front before Moscow. The *légionnaires* suffered from cold and hunger. Some 400 dropped out before trucks from the VII. Corps eventually 'collected' them.

On 19th November, the LVF was attached to the German 7th Infantry Division of the VII. Corps. Five days later, the I. Battalion of the LVF entered the front line. Moscow was only seventy kilometres away. The men had to spend the nights out in the open. The cold became terrible. There were more casualties from frostbite than enemy action, but the frost also struck at the troops' weapons, unprotected by anti-freeze lubricants. Machine pistols and machine guns were rendered unreliable.

On 30th November, the eve of the attack by the I. Battalion, Colonel Labonne read out a telegram from Marshal Pétain, part of which read as follows:

> In taking part in this crusade which Germany is leading, thus acquiring a right to the gratitude of the world, you are helping to protect us from the Bolshevik peril: thus, it is your country that you are protecting, while at the same time saving the hope of a reconciled Europe.

Yet despite this personal blessing from Pétain the LVF still remained a purely 'private' enterprise and had no official status. The creation of a legion of French volunteers had been looked on favourably by the Vichy Government, but ever since it had adopted an air of ambiguity toward the LVF.

On 1st December, the I. Battalion attacked towards the village of Djukowo. It took some ground, but suffered 12 killed and 55 wounded. On 3rd December, the II. Battalion entered the front line. However, so numerous were the losses from frostbite that the Germans doubted the value of the LVF and quickly relieved it.[19]

18   Indeed, according to Danke, page 195, they were immediately sent to punishment
      battalions.
19   The I. Battalion was relieved on 6th December and the II. Battalion on the 8th.

The cost to the LVF of front line duties from 24th November to 8th December was over 500 casualties, including 44 killed.[20]

Caught up in the great Russian counter-offensive before Moscow, the LVF retreated to Smolensk. From there it was pulled back to a camp at Kruszyna, Poland, for reorganisation. The two battalions were emerged into one. This became the new I. Battalion.

Few had good words to say about the combat performance of the LVF. Reich minister Goebbels wrote that 'the Frenchmen had in no way distinguished themselves on the Eastern front'. This is unfair. The LVF was ill equipped against the cold Russian winter and many of its troops had received little or no training.[21]

March 1942 saw the removal of Colonel Labonne from command and the cessation of front line duties for the LVF.

Meanwhile, a new III. Battalion (companies 9–12) was formed at Deba from the four contingents to arrive between December 1941 and February 1942.[22] It had a total strength of approximately 1,400 men of which 200 were coloured (North African Arabs). The command of the III. Battalion went to Colonel Ducrot.

One constant thorn in the side of the LVF was the bitter rivalry that existed between the militants of the M.S.R. and the P.P.F. In April 1942, the Germans told the Frenchmen to renounce all political activity or leave the LVF. The majority of those from the M.S.R. now took the opportunity to return to France. In this way, the P.P.F. became predominant. However, the purge thinned the ranks of the LVF; the total strength of the I. Battalion fell to some 750 officers and men, and, of the 1,400 officers and men of the II. Battalion at Deba, only 624 remained.

Now with no overall French commander, the two battalions of the LVF were employed separately and exclusively on anti-partisan operations to the rear of Army Group Centre.

On 26th January 1942, Jean Malardier, who was born on 1st October 1919 in the 13th department of Paris, enlisted in the LVF. Before the war he was not a militant of a political party. Underweight when called up for military service he was placed in the *service auxiliaire*. In June 1940, he was called up again, but it was too late for him to meet the Germans on the field of battle. For him, defeat came as no surprise:

> Being interested in military and political questions since the arrival in power of the Front Populaire in 1936, [and] much to the alarm of my employers (la Société Lyonnaise de Dèpots et de Credit in Lyon) and my family circle, I foresaw defeat. Now I jumped at the opportunity to denounce the flaws of our

20   A further 20-25 would later die of wounds received.
21   For example, the fourth contingent of 3 officers and 224 men and NCOs to arrive at Deba was sent direct to the Eastern front without having fired a single shot or participated in a single exercise.
22   The 5th contingent left Versailles on 1st December 1941 with 942 volunteers. The 6th contingent left on 15th December with 200 volunteers. The 7th contingent left on 5th January 1942 with 102 volunteers. The 8th contingent left on 19th February with 181 volunteers.

democratic system and its allegiance to Anglo-Saxon politics whose first prin-cipal, I recall, was always the humbling of Europe.

Malardier did not pass to the Armistice Army.

He became a supporter of Marshal Pètain, recognising in him 'the man lawfully vested with all the powers by the representatives of the Third Republic'.

Of his decision to enlist in the LVF, he said:

> It seemed evident to me that the German attack on Russia justified itself out of the necessity to push back, as far as possible, the eastern frontiers of Europe threatened by Slav expansionism. Thus I jumped at the opportunity which was offered to all European people to share in this action ... I believed and I believe Napoleon more than ever that: "Europe will be federated or Cossack". On the philosophical plane I felt none of the difficulties many of my comrades reported.

After completing his training at Kruszyna, Poland, Malardier was posted to Russia and assigned to the Headquarters Company of the I. Battalion.

In spring of 1942, Henri-Georges Gonzales enlisted in the LVF at Marseille, his place of residence. He enlisted 'out of a spirit of adventure, out of ideals, for he had a visceral hatred of Communism, and also out of friendship for Simon Sabiani', the Marseille mouthpiece of the P.P.F. 'His political leader', as he described Sabiani, was virulently anti-Communist.

Gonzales travelled up to the Versailles barracks of the LVF in the company of André Juin, also an inhabitant of Marseille. They became close friends and, although they would serve side by side for years in the 2nd Company of the I. Battalion of the LVF and later in the Engineer Company of 'Charlemagne', Gonzales never got to learn of Juin's reasons for enlisting.

At Versailles, Gonzales underwent a medical examination and passed. There-upon he exchanged his civilian clothes for a French Army uniform. Although he wanted to fight Communism 'in the colours of his homeland', he realised that this was out of the question because the Germans were abiding by the international rules of land warfare.

While based at Versailles, Gonzales visited Paris for the first time. He was a little ashamed to see the city overrun with disorderly servicemen of the German Army, but he never questioned his decision to enlist. He would fight with them against those that had become the common enemy.

From Versailles, Gonzales was sent to the camp at Kruszyna near Radom, Poland, where he received three months intense training. Then came the moment to swear the oath of loyalty to Adolf Hitler. The ceremony was full of incident as Gonzales remembers:

> The company was formed in a square. A German General, whose name I have forgot, pulled out his sabre and after some minutes of oratorical palaver asked us to swear an oath of loyalty.[23] At that moment the whole group to which I belonged left the ranks as a sign of refusal. The General choked and ordered the German instructors to surround us. And they shut us up in a building whose doors and windows were nailed up. The following morning, a German sergeant

23   The German general was General der Infanterie Halm.

came and asked us if we had changed opinion. 'No!' half replied. 'Yes!' replied the other half to which I belonged. Some days after these events we left for Russia.

As for those who continued to refuse, they were sent to work in salt mines in Silesia.

On 10th May 1942, the III. Battalion of the LVF left Deba for the front. It was attached to the 221st Security Division operating south-east of Smolensk. From 20th May to 20th June 1942, the III. Battalion was engaged in an anti-partisan operation. When Colonel Ducrot proved incapable of command he was removed and replaced by *Capitaine* (later Major) Demessine.

La Légion Tricolore

Meanwhile, back in France, with the approval of the Vichy Government, the LVF was transformed into *La Légion Tricolore*. The principal architect of this politically inspired move was Benoist-Méchin, the young Vichy Secretary of State to the *Chef de gouvernement*.

A brilliant intellectual, Jacques Benoist-Méchin was a 'man of letters in his books, in his speech, and in his life'.[24] In 1938, he published the monumental *Histoire de l'armeé allemande* which was favourable towards the German Army, triumphant Nazism and Hitler.

Benoist-Méchin wrote on 17th November 1941:

> A defeated country can take up three positions, against its conqueror, for its conqueror, or with its conqueror. I am against, as indeed France has shown herself to be against, the first position, because in a whole succession of circumstances she has not reacted. On the other hand, France is not agreed to be for the conquering power. I am a partisan of the third formula: with the conqueror.

A partisan of a New Europe in which France would play an important role thanks to its colonial Empire, Benoist-Méchin worked hard for military co-operation with Germany. Born of this was his idea of *La Légion Tricolore* modelled on the Spanish Blue Division. In April 1942, when Laval returned to power, Benoist-Méchin was tasked with the creation of *La Légion Tricolore*.

President Laval had much to gain from the creation of *La Légion Tricolore*. He would then have at his disposal a new Legion that could be employed in France against the Resistance and in Africa against those colonies that had gone over to de Gaulle. Moreover, through *La Légion Tricolore*, he hoped to control not only the 'ultras' of Paris, but also Joseph Darnand and the SOL. He knew that they could 'not remain uninvolved in a government initiative which corresponded to their views and ideal'.[25]

Benoist-Méchin went about the creation of *La Légion Tricolore* with great enthusiasm and formed a team of collaborators in his own image. On 21st June 1942, he entered into dialogue with a Wehrmacht officer, Colonel Mayer, the Chief-of-Staff of Generalmajor Matsky. Benoist-Méchin proposed that *La Légion*

24   Robert Aron, page 281, "*The Vichy Regime 1940-1944*".
25   These words are actually those of Darnand from his speech at Lyon on 12th July 1942.

Tricolore take the form of a miniature French Army with its own logistics and that it would fight in German uniforms, but be authorised to wear the French uniform in the rear. Mayer seemed receptive and concluded the dialogue with the words: "I think your projects will be accepted by General Matsky."[26] Benoist-Méchin was now of the opinion that he finally had German approval for the creation of *La Légion Tricolore*.

On the following day, the 22nd June, the *Comité central de la LVF* [central committee of the LVF], meeting at hotel Matignon in Paris, announced the dissolution of the LVF and its transformation into *La Légion Tricolore*. Statutes for the *La Légion Tricolore* were agreed unanimously. Under Article 6, Benoist-Méchin became the president of the *Comité central de la Légion Tricolore* which replaced the *Comité central de la LVF*. Named to sit on the central committee of *La Légion Tricolore* were Doriot, Deat and Costantinin from the central committee of the LVF, Darnand, the *inspecteur* of the SOL, and Jean-Marcel Renault, the *chef* of the J.F.O.M.

According to Article 3 of its statutes, *La Légion Tricolore* 'can be engaged on any front where the national interest is at stake'.

The new central committee then turned to Laval and the Vichy government for approval to transform the LVF into an official military force with the name of *La Légion Tricolore*.[27] Approval was, of course, forthcoming.

German Ambassador Otto Abetz and SS-Brigadeführer Oberg, the high commander of the SS and the German Police in France, were also quick to come out in support of *La Légion Tricolore*.

On 6th July 1942, General Bridoux, the Vichy Secretary of State for War, put his name to a circular that authorised officers and men of the metropolitan Armistice Army and the transitional Army in North Africa to enlist in *La Légion Tricolore*.

The following day, a Ministry of Interior circular called upon the *préfets* to support the recruiting offices for *La Légion Tricolore* and to encourage those civil servants expressing a desire to enlist.

However, it was not until Law No 704 of 18th July 1942, published in the *Journal officiel* on 8th August 1942, that the Vichy government finally gave its official support to *La Légion Tricolore*.

General Galy was appointed the *Commissaire Général de la Légion Tricolore*.

Edgar Puaud[28]

In July, a depot for *La Légion Tricolore* recruits from the Unoccupied zone and French North Africa was opened at Guéret near Vichy. Colonel Puaud was appointed to command them.

26   Cited by Mabire and Lefèvre, "*La Legion Perdue*", page 168.
27   According to Littlejohn, "*Foreign Legions of the Third Reich: volume I*", page 155, it was on 24th June 1942 that the controlling committee of the LVF sent Prime Minister Laval a memorandum proposing that the LVF be taken over as an official military force... However, as such, the controlling committee of the LVF no longer existed.
28   The author wishes to express his thanks to Eric Lefèvre for the information concerning Puaud.

Born on 29th October 1889 in Orléans, Edgar-Joseph-Alexandre Puaud joined the Army in 1909. In May 1914, *sergent* Puaud of the *133e régiment d'infanterie* was 'recognised eligible' for attendance at the *école militaire d'infanterie de Saint-Maixent*. However, because of the threat of war, he never got to go to the military school. On 5th August 1914, the Ministry of War decided that those NCOs recognised eligible for the military schools of Saint-Maixent, Saumur, Fontainebleau, Versailles and Vincennes were to be promoted to *aspirant* (published in the *Journal officiel* on the 8th). This included Puaud.

On 1st September 1914, Puaud was promoted to *sous-lieutenant à titre temporaire*. By the end of the war, he held the rank of *capitaine à titre définitif* and his chest was ablaze with medals. He was the proud holder of:

The *Croix de guerre* with seven citations, including two *à l'ordre de l'armée*
The *Croix de guerre des T.O.E.* with two bronze stars
The *Légion d'honneur*
(The *médaille des evades* instituted by law in 1926 for the *guerre* 1914–1918)

After the war Puaud served with the *13e bataillon de chasseurs mitrailleurs* (BCM) of the *armée du Rhin* [army of the Rhine]. From 1926 to 1937, he served in Morocco, obtaining three more citations. His posts were many and some were administrative. Notably he served with the *1er régiment étranger* [Foreign Legion] from 1926 to 1927 and with the *3e régiment étranger* from 1934 to 1937. In 1934, he was promoted to *chef de bataillon*.

In 1937, *chef de bataillon* Puaud was posted to Tonkin and the *5e régiment étranger*.

He returned to France in 1940[29] and, after the armistice, 'picked up' the command of the camp of Septfonds, in the Tarn-et-Garonne, where he did his utmost to protect the foreign volunteers, including many of Germanic origin, sought by the German authorities.

He went on to command the *3e bataillon du 23e régiment d'infanterie*, garrisoned at Montauban. A witness who served under *Commandant* Puaud described him as a '*super anti-collaborateur*'. Indeed, he refused to shake hands with the German officers of the armistice commission who came to inspect his weapons arsenal. Like many, he dreamt of revenge and had hidden a weapons cache in Montech forest to use against the 'Boches' when the time came.[30]

In July 1942, Puaud, the patriot, enlisted in *La Légion Tricolore*. After the departure of Lieutenant-Colonel Tézé, Puaud became the *Commissaire Général adjoint* of *La Légion Tricolore*.[31] Promotion followed to Lieutenant-Colonel and, then, on 25th November 1942, to that of Colonel. In early 1943, he became the *délégué général de la LVF* in France.

From hope to despair

Joseph Darnand, the Inspector-General of the SOL, threw his considerable weight behind the new Legion. At a ceremony held in Lyons on 12th July, Darnand stated

---

29   According to Ory's "*Les Collaborateurs*", Puaud returned from Indo-China in May 1940 to do battle with the Germans. As such, this remains unconfirmed.
30   See H.L., page 134, "*Historia #32*".
31   Roch, page 170.

that 'whereas the activities of the SOL would be confined mainly to France, *La Légion Tricolore*, should the necessity arise, would fight on the side of the Axis in Europe and in Africa'. With serious words heavy with meaning, Darnand told his adherents that they had to be represented in *La Légion Tricolore* and that they 'will prove in its ranks that they are sons of France agreeing to every sacrifice as soon as the homeland demands it'.

Jean Bassompierre, along with a handful of other SOL *chefs*, volunteered for *La Légion Tricolore*. Before coming forward, Lieutenant Bassompierre had hesitated. A traditionalist, he was anti-German but 'he had always been anti-Communist'. Darnand had spoken to him about the fate of Poland 'which had been fully absorbed by a tyrannical conqueror' and explained that France must not suffer the same fate. Darnand added that these 'new barbarians from Asia' had to be prevented from submerging one day 'our old continent'. The anti-Bolchevist struggle and the independence of France in the eventuality of a German victory were the reasons that silenced Bassompierre's lingering scruples. Before leaving, with the approval of Laval, he held propaganda meetings at Nice, Marseille, Toulouse, Lyon, Limoges, in the principal cities of the Southern zone. Received by Marshal Pétain, Bassompierre was embraced and told: "You are the youth of France."

On 18th July 1942, the Vichy government officially recognised the *Croix de Guerre Légionnaire*, the LVF's private decoration. On 10th August, a governmental decree stated that volunteers for *La Légion Tricolore* would receive French Army rates of pay, enjoy French Army pension rights and be allowed to wear the French uniform.

On 27th August 1942, a number of ceremonies were held in Paris to mark the first anniversary of the formation of the LVF. The first ceremony was at cathedral Notre-Dame, where mass was celebrated in memory of the dead of the LVF. Among the dignitaries present were Admiral Platon, representing the head of state, Ambassador de Brinon, representing the head of government, Secretary of State Benoist-Méchin, and Otto Abetz, German Ambassador to France.

The next ceremony was held in la cour d'honneur de l'Hôtel des Invalides in the presence of various representatives of the Maréchal, the services, and the head of government, as well as three members of the central committee of *La Légion Tricolore*, including Darnand. Colonel Puaud read aloud the names of the dead. General Galy presented a number of awards. Among the recipients of the *croix de guerre légionnaire* were LVF Chaplain Jean de Mayol de Lupé and Colonel Labonne.

In the afternoon, Benoist-Méchin and General Galy went to Suresnes hospital to present awards to seriously wounded *légionnaires*. At the same time, Colonel Puaud, accompanied by six *légionnaires*, laid three wreaths on the Tomb of the Unknown Soldier.[32]

However, *La Légion Tricolore* was not well received by the high command of the Wehrmacht, the Oberkommando-der-Wehrmacht [Armed Forces General Headquarters], more simply O.K.W. On 17th September 1942, the Wehrmacht officially

---

32   Many sources state that on 27th August 1942 *La Légion Tricolore* was inaugurated at
      the Tomb of the Unknown Soldier in Paris. This is incorrect. There was no such
      inauguration.

informed the Vichy Government that it was not prepared to accept an autonomous Legion into its midst.[33] Also, on that same day, Generalfeldmarschall Keitel, the Chief-of-Staff of O.K.W., gave an unfavourable opinion on the project.[34]

As for Hitler himself, he ordered *La Légion Tricolore* to be disbanded[35] and it was by Law No 1113 of 28th December 1942, signed by Pierre Laval and published in the *Journal officiel*. The prospect of a French-controlled unit that the Wehrmacht could not prevent from being withdrawn from Russia was intolerable. The French volunteers had to remain under German authority.

Besides, from the outset, the Legion had been forged on an 'illusion', on a 'false impression'.[36] The source of the misunderstanding stemmed from the meeting on 8th July 1942 between Colonel Mayer and Benoist-Méchin. The opinion of Mayer had been taken as a guarantee and approval from the German military authorities, but later it came to light that Mayer was solely on a fact-finding mission and had 'no mandate to promise in the name of the German headquarters'.[37]

On 5th October 1942, *La Légion Tricolore* had reported its strength at 54 officers, 118 NCOs and 595 men (including 105 Moroccans), but what now for its recruits? They were offered the option of returning to civilian life or transferring to the resurrected LVF. Nine officers, including Bassompierre, Boudet-Gheusi, Obitz, Panné, Schlisler and Wagner, and eighty men took up the latter.

That same month, *Capitaine* Boudet-Gheusi left Versailles for the training camp at Kruszyna. It was not long before he was 'in the field' with the I. Battalion. *Capitaine* Bassompierre followed him.

On donning the German uniform for the first time, Bassompierre later admitted to shedding a tear. He only managed to overcome his repugnance by repeating to himself the following words of Marshal Pétain to the *légionnaires* of the LVF: "You protect the same frontiers of France from Bolshevism by going to fight far from your homeland."

One or two days before Christmas day 1942, Bassompierre arrived at the village of Wydriza to take over the command of the 2nd Company of the I. Battalion. Henri-Georges Gonzales was appointed his orderly.

In early January 1943, Major Panné of *La Légion Tricolore* replaced Major Demessine at the head of the III. Battalion of the LVF.

February-June 1943

In early February 1943, the III. Battalion of the LVF was put at the disposal of the headquarters of the 2nd Panzer Army. Later that same month, on the 11th, the Vichy Government, through Law No 95, finally recognised the LVF as an official organisation 'having public utility'.

On 30th May 1943, the day he turned eighteen, Jean Grenier enlisted in the LVF. He said of his decision to enlist:[38]

33   Ory, page 245.
34   Delperrié de Bayac, page 138.
35   Littlejohn, *"Foreign Legions of the Third Reich: volume I"*, page 156.
36   Delperrié de Bayac, *"Histoire de la Milice"*.
37   General Galy, October 1942.
38   Letter to the author, 12/4/98, abridged.

I always wanted to enlist in the French Army, at the time the LVF was a French Regiment and we hoped to be victorious. It must be put in context; we wanted to serve … I enlisted on the advice of a French field officer, a friend of my parents. I was their only son. I waited to my eighteenth birthday, 30th May 1943, to enlist in the LVF; yet my father did not really approve, then my parents were very proud. I had been thinking of this idea for a long time, belonging to the *amis de la LVF*.

My motives were also political and philosophical because the national and domestic enemy was atheistic Communism and Bolshevism. I believed in the New France of Marshal Pétain, the new Europe. This battle was for me an obvious fact. As France was not at war with the URSS, to fight in the uniform of the Wehrmacht posed me no problem.

Moreover, my father was a *combattant volontaire* of 14–18, a volunteer in 39, a prisoner in 40, liberated in 42 as a former combatant of 14–18, [and] he came back with the evident idea that France and Europe could only be reborn with Marshal Pétain and Germany, like the great majority of French people at the time. Furthermore, the context of the time, contrary to what is said today, was that the great majority of French people accepted the politics of the Marshal …

In June, the I. Battalion, under *commandant* Simoni, and the III. Battalion were reunited under General Oschmann's 286th Security Division in the region of Mogilev and Orsha. The reconstituted II. Battalion was added to the LVF's order of battle. The overall command of the LVF was now entrusted to Edgar Puaud who the Vichy Government had just made up to full Colonel. However, many regarded the larger than life 'Monseigneur' Jean Count de Mayol de Lupé, the General Chaplain of the LVF, as its real commander.

Monseigneur de Mayol de Lupé[39]

Jean de Mayol de Lupé was born in Paris on 21st January 1873, the seventh child of an ultra-legitimist family. His father, comte Henri de Lupé, after being in the service of the King of Naples, had returned to fight for France in 1870. His mother, Elisabeth de Caracciolo-Girifalco, was born into the Neapolitan aristocracy. Aged seventeen, Jean entered the Benedictine abbey of Ligugé in the province of Poitou and on 10th June 1900 was ordained a priest of the Benedictine Order.

In 1914, he was mobilised as a military chaplain in the *1re division de cavalerie* and was captured on 28th September 1914. Freed and repatriated as an ecclesiastic on 16th October 1916, he volunteered again for front-line duties and arrived back at the front with the *33e D.I.* on 16th March 1917. He then served with the *9e chasseurs à cheval.* He saw action in the Champagne and in the sector of Verdun and was badly wounded in 1918 at Esmery-Hallon (Somme). Following the war he continued to serve as a military chaplain and went to Bessarabia, Bulgaria, Syria, where he was made a *chevalier de la Légion d'honneur,* and finally Morocco. After a long illness, he was discharged from military service in 1927 as a *capitaine* with a disability pension of 40%.

On 17th October 1934, he was made a canon by the powerful chapter of the cathedral of Lucera in Italy. From that day forward he was entitled to the position

39   See Bail, article *"Monseigneur"*, *"Historia No 32"*.

of Roman Prelate to his Holiness and the honorary title of Monsignor which he valued greatly. His aristocratic ancestry, his diplomatic talents and his knowledge of languages were recognised as the perfect credentials of an envoy and he was assigned a number of cultural missions. In 1934, he went to Munich on behalf of the *ministère de l'Éducation nationale*. He went back with a certain professor Lichzmann and was introduced to various German personalities including some dignitaries of the new regime. And so began his 'conversion' to National Socialism. In 1938, he attended the Nuremberg Rally where he met and began a friendship with professor Otto Abetz who years later would become the German ambassador to occupied France. That same year, such was the esteem in which the military and political authorities held him that he was made an *officier de la Légion d'honneur*.[40]

In August 1939, the *2e bureau* appealed to his great sense of patriotism by asking him to go to Italy to gauge Mussolini's attitude in the event of a Franco-German war. He agreed and met with important ecclesiastic and secular personalities in Rome and Naples. On his return, he reported that Italy, in the event of war, would side with the enemy.

When war came Mgr. de Mayol de Lupé requested to get back into harness as a stretcher-bearer on account of his age. Cardinal Verdier prevented him from doing so. The German victory left him heavy at heart and determined to have nothing to do with the German authorities. Abetz visited him, and while the conversation was courteous, it was without warmth. However, the arrest of some of his close friends and acquaintances prompted him to appeal to the German authorities for their release. The Germans did respond to his request, although not all were released, but in return asked him to become the General Chaplain of the LVF. He refused, but agreed, nevertheless, to spend a month in an untitled capacity with the LVF and to bless its first detachments based in Poland.

On his return, he learnt that the situation of one of his friends still held captive, Mme Simonnet, had not improved. Then another friend, Pierre d'Harcourt, was arrested. He intervened on his behalf as well as that of many Jewish families, but the Germans repeated their blackmail demand for him to become the General Chaplain of the LVF.

Undecided, Mgr. de Mayol de Lupé went to canon Jourdain, a declared enemy of the Germans, who told him not to hesitate as it was a question of French lives. He then wrote to Cardinal Sibilia in Rome asking for advice and permission, which was duly granted. Still beset by misgivings about donning the field grey uniform, he also consulted with Cardinal Suhard, who reassured him by replying: "Come on, it's only a contingency!"

The decision of Mgr. de Mayol de Lupé to become the Chaplain of the LVF was also borne of his anti-Bolshevism. He too viewed the attack on the Soviet Union as a religious crusade against atheist Bolshevism. Indeed, many prominent Catholics had come out strongly in support of the LVF. And so Mgr. de Mayol de Lupé became the General Chaplain of the LVF. He brought with him his secretary Henri Cheveau, born on 2nd August 1907 in St. Cloud, who would follow him to the end.

40   To be considered for promotion to *officier* in the order of the *Légion d'honneur*, it is necessary to have been a *chevalier* of this same order for at least eight years. Also, promotion to *officier* has to be merited.

For the next three years, with his pastoral cross hanging on his chest, Mgr. de Mayol de Lupé fought 'his' battle alongside his legionnaires. He won both classes of the Iron Cross and was wounded twice in combat. His photograph appeared frequently not only in the Paris press, but in the German magazine *Signal* whose front cover he even made, accompanied by the legend: "From the *Légion d'honneur* to the Iron Cross". And yet, being a royalist of the old regime, he refused to wear the LVF tricolore badge from which OKW had to exempt him. Indeed, he was authorised to place on his car a white pennant decorated with the fleurs-de-lis.

In a letter to the Führer dated 18th April 1942, Mgr. de Mayol de Lupé asked again for the release of Mme Simonnet, Harcourt and fourteen prisoners from his village, claiming that they were all ardently Franco-German. He also asked the Führer to honour the agreement made that for each legionnaire who had enlisted one prisoner of war would be released. But he also revealed in this letter that he was proud to have sworn an oath to him.

In June 1943, Mgr. de Mayol de Lupé wrote:

> The world must choose: on the one hand Bolshevist savagery, [an] infernal force; on the other hand Christian civilisation. We must choose at all costs. We can not loyally remain neutral any longer! It's Bolshevist anarchy or Christian order.

Linking Adolf Hitler and Christ on the basis of anti-communism, Mgr. de Lupé finished his sermons pledging dual allegiance to 'our Holy Father the Pope and to our venerated Führer Adolf Hitler'. His burning loyalty to National Socialism, which he freely interpreted in his own way, was unquestionable.

Admired by friends and even by those that ridiculed him in private, he enjoyed the confidence of the legionnaires and surprisingly 'managed to fascinate Himmler and the members of his staff'.[41] He was a 'tough guy' who understood the life of the soldier and did not worry about prudishness.

August 1943-February 1944

On 27th August 1943, the second anniversary of the formation of the LVF, the Legion received a new Colour from General Bridoux, the Vichy Secretary of State for War, at a ceremony in the *Cour d'Honneur* at the *Hôtel des Invalides*, Paris. The Colour, symbolically of the 1879 regulation pattern for all French Army regiments, bore the legend HONNEUR ET PATRIE which appeared on French regimental Colours and the battle honours of 1941–1942 DJUKOWO and 1942–1943 BÉRÉSINA.

In early September 1943, Michel de Genouillac enlisted in *La Légion Tricolore*.[42] Born on 13th July 1921 near the small village of Concoret, Brittany, he attended the military academy of La Flèche and, in May 1940, passed the written entrance examination for the *École Spéciale Militaire de Saint-Cyr*. Weeks later, France went to her

---

41   De la Mazière, page 56.

42   Curiously, at this time, *La Légion Tricolore* ceased to exist. When questioned about this, Michel de Genouillac confirmed to the author that he enlisted in *La Légion Tricolore* and not the LVF. One possible explanation for this is that the French authorities were using the 'front' of the *La Légion Tricolore* as a means of recruiting for the 'less attractive' LVF.

defeat. In September 1940, at Valence, after learning that he was not one of the few to gain admittance to Saint-Cyr relocated to Aix-en-Provence, he resumed his studies. Finally, in October 1941, he entered Saint-Cyr.

On 25th November 1942, de Genouillac graduated, receiving the rank of *sous-lieutenant*. His branch was the cavalry. Four days later, on the dissolution of the Armistice Army, he was demobilised. He returned home, where he waited for instructions that would never come. Months later, tired of waiting, he decided to request his enlistment in *Les Chantiers de la Jeunesse*. Assigned to Groupement 7, 'the Proud', he was entrusted with the command of camp 3, established in the mountains of Clergeon, above Rumilly in Haute Savoie. The months passed by. He had much time to reflect. By July 1943, he could no longer tolerate this inaction when the war was entering a decisive phase and decided to enlist in *La Légion Tricolore*. Thereupon, he wrote to the Vichy *Sécretariat à la Guerre* requesting authorisation to enlist. This only came in September. He then left *Les Chantiers de la Jeunesse* which was disintegrating anyway.

De Genouillac's decision to enlist stemmed from a melting pot of reasons: the partisan war and its excesses disgusted him, to him it was a return to barbarity; he did not want to participate in operations in France which could not fail to set him against Frenchmen of good faith, often sharing the same ideals as him; he had sworn an oath of loyalty to Marshal Pétain, and still felt bound to this oath (which was regarded as a sacred undertaking at that time); the atmosphere of the 'Government of Algiers' dom-inated by Communists and Gaullists did not encourage him to join his compatriots who were already there; to him, Communism was the most redoubtable enemy of his country and 'our' civilisation; and since the Germans were losing the war the symbolic help that he would bring to them on the Eastern front would not delay the liberation of his country.

On 1st October 1943, de Genouillac left for the training centre of Kruszyna in Poland. He arrived days later. At the end of his training period, he was sent to Russia, where he arrived on 1st April 1944. He was assigned to the 3rd Company of the I. Battalion.

Philippe Rossigneux and Jean Mailhe also came to the LVF from the *Légion Tricolore*.

Philippe Rossigneux was born in June 1919 in St. Cloud, the 16th department of Paris. He enlisted at the end of 1938 for three years in the Air Force. He did not see action against the Germans, explaining that 'the armistice came too early'! He said of the defeat of May 1940:

> Unfortunately defeat was 'deserved' through a lack of military preparation and because of the almost general 'defeatism' in some political classes. I would have left for England if I had had the opportunity.

After the Armistice he was sent to Senegal, where he served out his contract. Returning to France, he enlisted in the Armistice Army with the rank of *caporal-chef*. He attended EOR training. The invasion of the Free Zone by the Germans in November 1942 returned him to civilian life. Out of religious anti-Communism, this devout catholic enlisted in *La Légion Tricolore*. This brought him promotion to the rank of *sous-lieutenant*. He went across to the LVF in which he held a number of posts as a platoon commander, becoming in June

1944 (or perhaps as late as July 1944) Puaud's orderly officer. He was not a militant of a political party; he was (and still is) a monarchist.

Jean Mailhe was born on 9th September 1912 in Reims. He served France loyally in the *1e Régiment Étranger d'Infanterie* (1 R.E.I.) with the rank of *Aspirant* and fought against the Germans in Tunisia in 1943. Captured and brought back to France, he volunteered for *La Légion Tricolore*. Transferring to the LVF, he served in the 6th Company of its II. Battalion.

Both Rossigneux and Maile were later awarded the German Kriegsverdienstkreuz (War Merit Cross) 2nd Class.

In September 1943, while on leave back home in Marseille, Henri-Georges Gonzales visited Simon Sabiani, his mentor and good friend. Gonzales brought with him a photo of Sabiani's son, François, in his coffin on a Russian cart. [François was killed on 2nd June 1942 serving with the LVF.] Demoralised, Gonzales revealed to Sabiani his intention not to go back to Russia. They had a long conversation about this. In the end Sabiani managed to convince him to return. So back he went to his comrades of the 2nd Company of the I. Battalion. He was without regrets. Such was his destiny he would later reflect.

In October 1943, the Legion's artillery detachment was disbanded and its personnel relocated to the IV. Battalion (companies 13–16) which was in formation. The IV. Battalion was eventually added to the Legion's order of battle in April 1944. However, only the 13th Company was raised, which was sent to Russia in May 1944.

In November 1943, *Commandant* Bridoux arrived in Russia to replace *Capitaine* Bassompierre at the head of the I. Battalion of I.R. 638 (LVF). Born 16th November 1911 in Versailles, Eugène-Marie-Jean Bridoux was a product of the celebrated *École spéciale militaire de Saint Cyr*. His branch was the cavalry. He made 'soldiering' his career. During the battle of France he served with the *10e Cuirassiers* commanded by a certain Colonel de Gaulle and was wounded twice, winning the *Légion d'Honneur*. In defeat, he went across to the Armistice Army. He was one of the few *officiers d'active* to serve in the LVF and, as if to prove his military prowess, within a matter of months he was decorated with the Iron Cross 2nd Class.[43] Notably, his father was the Vichy Secretary of State for War.

In the spring of 1944, the LVF became the interest of the politicians again. Doriot attempted to have the LVF brought back to France to fight the maquis and drive the traitors from Vichy. For the first time, the German authorities took the decision to bring the LVF back, but pressure from Laval and de Brinon had the decision reversed.[44]

Throughout February 1944, the three battalions of the LVF took part in a major anti-partisan sweep in the forest of Somry. The sweep was code-named 'Operation Morocco' in honour of Colonel Puaud. On the 18th, *Commandant* Panné was killed. He had been on leave but flown back to personally conduct the operation at the Germans' request. *Capitaine* Berret succeeded him at the head of the III. Battalion.

At the conclusion of 'Morocco', its German planners deemed the operation a great success; an OKW communiqué credited the LVF with the destruction of 41 partisan camps and 1,000 blockhouses, the killing of 1,118 partisans and the

---

43   Bridoux was awarded the Iron Cross 2nd Class on 17th March 1944.
44   Brunet, "*Doriot*".

capture of 1,346 partisans. As 'recognition' for its success, Puaud was awarded with the Iron Cross 2nd class on 20th February 1944. Accolades were also forthcoming from the Vichy Government. On 1st April 1944, he was promoted to the rank of *Général de Brigade* and, on the 4th, awarded the *commandeur Légion d'Honneur*.[45] However, the Germans authorities did not recognise his new rank and still regarded him as holding that of Oberst.

'Their finest hour'

In late June 1944, the entire LVF regiment was assembled at Bobr to be transported back to France. Hours before the planned departure, it suddenly found itself called to action again when Army Group Centre's weak front crumpled under the Red Army's all-out summer offensive.

On 25th June 1944, the I. Battalion and two companies of the III. Battalion,[46] in total around 600 men, under Major Bridoux took up a position covering the bridge that carried the strategic Minsk-Moscow highway over the river Bobr, fifty kilometres east of Borisov.

Over the next forty-eight hours of bitter fighting the French Kampfgruppe, supported by Stuka, five Tiger tanks and a unit of SS-Police equipped with 75mm anti-tank guns[47], managed to check attack after attack.

Caporal-chef Malardier of the I. Battalion distinguished himself at Bobr. When the supply system broke down he volunteered to go to the rear and bring up a convoy of critically needed ammunition and supplies for the hard-pressed battalion. Into a hail of enemy fire he dashed. Some considered the fire impassable. Would he get through? Although wounded, he reappeared with the convoy. He was mentioned in dispatches and proposed for the Iron Cross 2nd Class.

On the morning of 27th June, the Frenchmen were relieved. They pulled back to a new defensive line before Borisov.

The battle of Bobr was undoubtedly the LVF's finest hour. Upwards of forty Soviet tanks (and as many as fifty-seven according to Rusco) lay wrecked in front of the French positions, but Rusco records that more than half of those Frenchmen engaged were killed or missing. This figure seems exaggerated; Mabire puts the French 'casualties' (presumably those killed) at forty; Lambert cites 41 dead and 24 serious wounded; and de Genouillac cites around twenty killed. Testimony to the fighting qualities of the LVF came from no less a source than a Soviet communiqué that spoke of their forces being stopped by the pointless sacrifice of 'two French divisions'!

There was no respite for the exhausted and hungry LVF legionnaires holding the position several kms from the town of Borisov that crossed the river Bérésina. This time, without heavy support, they found themselves easily overwhelmed and broken up by Russian tanks. They withdrew to Borisov or failing that attempted to cross the river Bérésina by any means possible. Many were killed. Many

---

45   Research provided by Mounine.

46   The two companies of the III. Battalion present at Bobr did not actually take up front line positions. The III. Battalion was only represented by Seveaux's *section de chasse*.

47   Indeed, according to Rostaing, the 'Waffen-SS Polizei Regiment' handed over three of its 75mm anti-tank guns to the LVF.

disappeared. Mercilessly harassed by the Soviet airforce and closely pursued by its ground forces, they continued to retreat.

The dispersed units of the LVF were assembled at Moritz Lager, south of Minsk. Colonel Puaud gave orders to leave in small groups and reach Vilno, Lithuania, then Greifenberg, Pomerania.

For those groups that did make it to Greifenberg each and every one had a different story to tell of the journey.[48] En route, some became involved in fighting. One such group, that of *Sous-Lieutenant* de Genouillac and part of the *section de commandement* of the 3rd Company, participated in the fighting at Rakov and Volodzyn before arriving at Lida from where it embarked for Greifenberg on one of the last trains.

At the end of July 1944, elements of the LVF left depot Greifenberg for a camp situated at Altwarp on the west bank of the Oder. In August, they were transferred to a training camp at Saalesch (Zalesic), near Bruss.

Rumours at Saalesch were rife. According to one rumour, the LVF was to be repatriated to France to fight the maquis. Opinion was divided. For his part, *Caporal-chef* Gonzales was not in agreement; he did not volunteer for the LVF to end up fighting his own countrymen.

According to another rumour, the LVF was to be amalgamated with the French Sturmbrigade of the Waffen-SS. The rumour appeared to have some foundation when the FLAK Company of the French Sturmbrigade arrived at Saalesch.

Meanwhile, back at Greifenberg, the depot quickly filled again with French legionnaires of the LVF; stragglers returning from Russia, those who had been delayed returning from leave, and the return of those who had 'deserted' to serve in other branches of the German Army. And then Michel's company of the Sturmbrigade joined them. So was the LVF to be amalgamated with the French Sturmbrigade of the Waffen-SS? The answer to that question was yes.

---

48   Rusco suggests that the Legion was finally assembled at a French monastery in
      Kaunas where it rested before being transported by rail to Greifenberg on 15th July
      1944. This is incorrect.

CHAPTER 5

The Formation of 'Charlemagne'

The birth

The decision to amalgamate the LVF and the Sturmbrigade into a single Waffen-SS formation was undoubtedly that of Reichsführer-SS Himmler.[1] And to this new formation, he also intended to transfer all Frenchmen serving with the Kriegsmarine and the Schutzkommando of the Organisation Todt, more simply the SK.

On 10th August 1944, the SS-FHA ordered the formation of Waffen-Grena-dier-Brigade der SS 'Charlemagne' (franz. Nr.1) at SS-Truppenübungsplatz [SS-training area] 'Westpreussen'.[2] What is interesting is that the brigade was also known as the Französische Brigade der SS.[3]

The command of this new French brigade of the Waffen-SS went to Oberst Puaud of the LVF and presumably he was told of this when he met Himmler in Berlin.[4] At this meeting Puaud categorically assured Himmler that all his men, without exception, had agreed to enter the Waffen-SS.[5]

On 1st September 1944, Puaud was promoted to Oberführer.[6] On the same day, as though a gesture of farewell, 127 French and German personnel of the LVF were proposed for the Kriegsverdienstkreuz 2. Klasse (KVK II). [The decorations would be awarded three months later.]

1   Of note is that most foreign volunteer units in German service were eventually absorbed into the Waffen-SS. For some units, however, the transfer was largely theoretical.

2   SS-FHA, Amt II Org. Tgb. Nr.2710/44 g. Kdos, 10th August 1944 and Yerger, "*Waffen-SS Commanders Krüger to Zimmermann*", page 167.

3   SS-FHA Amt II Org.Abt. Ia/II Tgb. Nr. 12000/44 geh, 1st August 1944 and SS-FHA Amt II Org. Abt. Ia/II Tgb. Nr. 3614/44 g. Kdos, 11th October 1944. It is interesting to note that different authors have cited this designation, but with various dates of introduction and employment. For example, according to Roch, page 41, the designation of Französische Brigade der SS was employed from early August 1944. According to Bayle, page 77, from 10th August 1944. According to Klietmann, from September 1944 to November 1944. Also, the Verordnungsblatt der Waffen-SS, 1st December 1944, redesignated the Französische Brigade der SS as the Waffen-Grenadier-Division der SS 'Charlemagne' (franz. Nr. 1).

4   Although the date of this meeting is not known, late August or early September would not seem unreasonable.

5   *"Entretien avec le général Krukenberg"*, *"Historia" #32"*, page 131. Needless to say, Puaud had not consulted his legionnaires about entering the Waffen-SS. Thus, the question has to be asked: why did Puaud give Himmler this assurance? The answer to that question will never be known, but had Puaud hoped to gain some advantage, personal or political, from such an assurance? Contrary to what has often been said and written about him, Puaud was not a soldier who sought promotion at all costs. Indeed, at the end of his last leave, saying goodbye to his wife, he told her: "My duty is to be beside my men!"

The LVF depot at Greifenberg in Pomerania now became that of the brigade and home to the 5. Franz.Ausb.u.Ers.Kdo., also designated the Franz. SS-Grenadier-Ausbildungs und Ersatz-Bataillon (the French SS-Grenadier Training and Replacement Battalion).[7] Command of the battalion went to Swiss SS-Obstubaf. Hersche.[8]

On 10th September 1944,[9] Puaud arrived back at Saalesch. He was in the uniform of a Waffen-SS Oberführer and wearing the Iron Cross first class. Before his assembled legionnaires he told them that he had seen RF-SS Himmler in Berlin. According to Puaud, the RF-SS 'knew all about the heroism they had shown during the retreat from Russia'. Because of this, the RF-SS had decided to exempt them from swearing a new oath and to admit them with their ranks into the Waffen-SS.

Puaud then added that the tradition of the LVF would remain and that 'this incorporation was only administrative'. Of the incorporation, he had this to say:[10]

> It will permit the creation of a complete French Division, which will participate in the fight on all fronts, and I asked the Reichsführer that the division 'Charlemagne' be admitted to participate in the counter-offensive that will recapture France from the Anglo-American armies.

In response to this, sources and documents vary as to the status, the title, and the naming of this new French formation. Indeed, it has appeared with the following designations:

6   Although the rank of Oberführer was not equivalent to Puaud's Vichy Government recognised rank of *Général de brigade*, the rank of Oberführer did represent promotion from his German recognised rank of Oberst (Colonel) whose equivalent Waffen-SS rank was that of Standartenführer.

7   Mounine, "*Cernay, 40-45*", page 313. However, of interest to note is that Mercier, who served in a temporary administrative capacity with one of the training companies, can only recall the designation of Franz. Ausbildungs und Ersatz-Bataillon der SS. Also, the date Ersatz Kommando Franz. I.R. 638 was renamed is unclear. According to Roch, "*La Division Charlemagne*", page 50, the Franz. SS-Grenadier-Ausbildungs und Ersatz-Bataillon was formed at Greifenberg in early September 1944. And yet, curiously, on 1st August 1944, the SS-FHA reported the Franz. SS-Gren.Ausb.u.Ers.Btl., Greifenberg/Pom as the Ersatztruppenteil for the Franz. Brigade der SS (SS-FHA, Amt II/Org.Abt.Ia/II, Tgb.Nr.II/12000/44 geh).

8   Hersche was promoted to Obersturmbannführer der Reserve on 21st June 1944. He left Sennheim on 10th August 1944 to take command of the Franz. SS-Grenadier-Ausbildungs und Ersatz-Bataillon at Greifenberg.

9   Mabire, page 81.

10   Labat, page 255. However, according to Mabire, who also recounts Puaud's speech that day, see pages 81-82, Puaud further stated that the legionnaires had been admitted into the Waffen-SS on 1st September 1944 (which is incorrect) and would keep their commanders and flag. Regarding the employment of 'Charlemagne', Puaud stated: "The Reichsführer promised me that it ['Charlemagne'] will participate in the coming counteroffensive, which will free France from the allies of international Bolshevism." (Ibid.) Clearly, both the Reichsführer and Puaud were convinced that the legionnaires would fight against the Western Allies.

Französische Brigade der SS
Französische SS-Brigade
Waffen-Grenadier-Brigade der SS 'Charlemagne'[11]
Waffen-Grenadier-Brigade der SS (franz. Nr. 1)[12]
Waffen-Grenadier-Brigade der SS 'Charlemagne' (franz. Nr. 1)[13]
SS-Sturmbrigade 'Charlemagne'[14]
Waffen-Grenadier Division der SS 'Charlemagne' (Französische Nr.1)[15]

11   Appears on reports produced by the Brigade dated 10th and 11th of October 1944 (see page 11 and 14 of issue # 87 of "*39-45 Magazine*") and reports from concentration camp Stutthof dated 30th and 31st of October 1944. Also, Mercier of Fahrschwadron A saw this designation used (letter to the author, 23/1/2002). Furthermore, there is the report from the Rekrutenkompanie [Recruit Company] at Leisten dated October 1944 (also on page 11 of issue 87 of "*39-45 Magazine*") that is headed with the designation Waffen-Brigade SS 'Charlemagne'. The omission of the word 'Grenadier' was probably nothing more than a simple error because that of Waffen-Grenadier-Brigade der SS 'Charlemagne' also appears on the same report. And, lastly, Littlejohn in "*Foreign legions of the Third Reich: Volume I*" cites that the new formation was known as the Waffen-Grenadier-Brigade 'Charlemagne' (page 169). His omission of 'der SS' was probably little more than an oversight, for on page 161 of the same book we read: 'In September 1944 Himmler announced that the Assault Brigade and the LVF were to be amalgamated as a Waffen-Grenadier-Brigade of the SS…'

12   Angolia, "*Cloth Insignia of the SS*", page 491. Angolia dates this designation to September 1944, but adds that the name 'Charlemagne was added shortly thereafter.

13   See SS-FHA, Amt II Org. Tgb. Nr.2710/44 g. Kdos, 10th August 1944, SS-FHA, Amt II Org.Abt. Ia/II Tgb. Nr. 4213/44 g. Kdos, 13th November 1944, and the Waffen-SS promotions list of 30/1/45, with specific reference to the November 1944 promotions of Doriot to Hstuf. and then to Stubaf. Again it is interesting to note that different authors have cited this designation, but again with various dates of introduction and employment. Bayle cites, page 77, from 13th November 1944 to 10th February 1945. In "*Cloth Insignia of the SS*", Angolia cites, page 491, from September 1944 to February 1945. "*Europäische freiwillige*" gives from September 1944 to November 1944 (page 286). Klietmann cites from September 1944 to November 1944 (pages 285 to 289). Landwehr appears to repeat Klietmann, citing, page 56, for the duration of the early formation period, defined as a little more than two months, thus from September 1944 into November 1944.

14   Appears on a short report dated 14th October 1944 from concentration camp Stutthof. In response to this report, the individual who wrote it probably did so in ignorance of the correct title of 'Charlemagne'. Therefore, this title should be discounted.

15   According to Klietmann, the designation Waffen-Grenadier Division der SS 'Charlemagne' (Französische Nr.1) was employed from November 1944. Also see Verordnungsblatt der Waffen-SS, 1st December 1944. And yet the designation Waffen-Grenadier-Brigade der SS 'Charlemagne' (franz. Nr. 1) was still in use early February 1945 (see the official documentation dated 1.2.45 that is reproduced on page 134 of "*San et Persante*"). Moreover, Soulat, then serving with the Headquarters Company of the Brigade, does not recall any such conversion (personal conversation).

Notably, few of the designations are supported by orders emanating from the SS-FHA in Berlin. For example, the use of Waffen-Grenadier-Brigade der SS 'Charlemagne' appears to have been widespread, but is unsupported. However, in summary, from August 1944 until February 1945, the French formation was titled the Französische Brigade der SS, the Waffen-Grenadier-Brigade der SS 'Charlemagne' and [perhaps lastly] the Waffen-Grenadier-Brigade der SS 'Charlemagne' (franz. Nr. 1).

Much has been said of the name 'Charlemagne'.

According to Mabire,[16] in late September 1944, when *Milice* chief Darnand met Ogruf. Berger of the SS-Hauptamt in Berlin to discuss issues around the future deployment of the *Miliciens* into the Waffen-SS, Darnand floated the idea of naming the French unit of the Waffen-SS 'Jeanne d'Arc' [Joan of Arc]. To him, the name sounded *catholique et français toujours*. Berger did not commit himself.

Mabire states elsewhere[17] that the name of 'Jeanne d'Arc', in memory of a similar named unit that had served on the side of Franco in the Spanish Civil War, was under consideration, but was dropped in favour of 'Charlemagne'. Landwehr explains[18] that the name of 'Charlemagne' was chosen over that of 'Jeanne d'Arc' because 'Charlemagne' was a 'pan European Germanic hero' while Joan of Arc was too provincially French and orientated towards the Catholic religion.

Delperrié de Bayac recounts[19] that, in early October 1944, Darnand left again for Berlin. This time it was Brigf. Krukenberg who received him. During the initial negotiations, Krukenberg told Darnand that RF-SS Himmler had decided that the new unit would receive the name of '*brigade Charlemagne*'. Days later, Berger took Darnand to meet Himmler at Birkenwald. The meeting lasted some two hours. His host spoke of 'Charlemagne'.[20]

On the weekend of the 7th and 8th of October 1944, Darnand met Brigf. Krukenberg once again. In a letter to RF-SS Himmler, reporting on the favourable talks between himself and Krukenberg, Darnand wrote that the insignia and name of the French Brigade was 'Charlemagne'.[21]

Lastly, by an order from the Führerhauptquartier of 1st October 1944, which has recently surfaced[22], the French Waffen-Grenadier-Brigade der SS was awarded the name 'Charlemagne'.

In conclusion, during this political 'merry-go-round', the French side appears to have had little or no input into the choice of the name of 'Charlemagne',

---

16   See Mabire, page 122.

17   See the photograph section of "*La Division Charlemagne*".

18   Landwehr, "*Charlemagne's Legionnaires*", page 56.

19   Delperrié de Bayac, "*Histoire de la Milice*", page 568.

20   Ibid. However, according to Giolitto, "*Histoire de la Milice*", page 476, Himmler was still undecided at this point between 'Jeanne d'Arc' and 'Charlemagne'.

21   See pages 122-124 of the present book.

22   An example of this FHA order was recently Internet auctioned and sold by the seller as original. However, some have questioned the authenicity of the order and the auctioned example. Unfortunately, the author has not seen the auctioned example and thus must refrain from passing comment, even if 'Charlemagne' was in use with 'Waffen-Grenadier-Brigade der SS' as early as October 1944. See above.

although it raised no objections to its 'imposition'. Arguably, the pan-European Germanic Emperor was a perfect symbol of Franco-German union.

The Brigade (and later the Division) was based on two grenadier regiments with the initial titles and numbers of Grenadier-Regiment 1 and Grenadier-Regiment 2.

By SS-FHA order of 11th October 1944[23], the non-regimental units of the Franz. Brigade der SS received the number 57. This same order showed the Brigade as having two regiments with the titles and numbers of Franz.Freiw.Gren. Rgt der SS 57 and Franz.Freiw.Gren.Rgt.der SS 58.[24] These changes may have only appeared on paper. The designations Grenadier-Regiment 1 and Grenadier-Regiment 2 were still very much in use 'in the field' as late as 27th October 1944.[25]

The two grenadier regiments were later renamed Waffen-Grenadier-Regiment der SS 57 (franz. Nr. 1) and Waffen-Grenadier-Regiment der SS 58 (franz Nr. 2).[26]

Thus, the principal elements of the French brigade can be summarised as follows:

Stab der Brigade
Waffen-Grenadier-Regiment der SS 57 (franz. Nr. 1)
Waffen-Grenadier-Regiment der SS 58 (franz. Nr. 2)
Waffen-Artillerie-Abteilung der SS 57
SS-Pionier-Kompanie 57
SS-Panzerjäger-Abteilung 57
SS-Nachrichten-Kompanie 57
SS-Feldgendarmerie Trupp 57

The French Sturmbrigade was the nucleus for Waffen-Grenadier-Regiment der SS 57 while the LVF was that for Waffen-Grenadier-Regiment der SS 58.[27] The I. Battalion of the LVF was used as the base for the 1st Battalion of Waffen-Gren. Regt der SS 58, otherwise the I/58. The III. Battalion of the LVF was used as that for the 2nd Battalion of Waffen-Gren. Regt der SS 58, the II/58. The II. Battalion of the LVF was broken up and its men used to strengthen the two combat battalions of Waffen-Gren. Regt der SS 58. The PAK Company of the

23 SS-FHA Amt II Org. Abt. Ia/II Tgb. Nr. 3614/44 g. Kdos, 11th October 1944.

24 The exact date on which the regiments took on the 'Freiw' designation is not known. Roch gives the same date of the order.

25 Wartime documentation in the author's collection.

26 The exact date on which the regiments took on the 'Waffen' designation as well as the nationality in brackets after the title has again been difficult to determine. Roch gives 1st December 1944 (based upon Verordnungsblatt der Waffen-SS, 1st December 1944). However, the final and full designations Waffen-Grenadier-Regiment der SS 57 (franz. Nr. 1) and Waffen-Grenadier-Regiment der SS 58 (franz. Nr. 2) were definitely in use by the middle of November 1944 (wartime documentation in the author's collection). Thus, the possibility exists that the regiments took on the designations Waffen-Grenadier-Regiment der SS 57 (franz Nr. 1) and Waffen-Grenadier-Regiment der SS 58 (franz. Nr. 2) when or soon after the Brigade was transferred to Wildflecken.

27 Please note that the final designations of the Grenadier Regiments are used hereafter.

LVF became the 10th Company (anti-tank) of Waffen-Gren. Regt der SS 58, otherwise the 10/58.

The LVF also populated the Artillery battalion, the Headquarters Company, the Engineer Company and the two transport columns [as well as the Panzerjäger battalion at a later date].

General Puaud, finding himself left with a number of old LVF NCOs of little use, took the inititaive in forming a small platoon of some twenty such veterans he called the 'Gendarmerie de Brigade'. This was in addition to the military police of SS-Feldgendarmerie Trupp 57.

The reaction of the legionnaires to the transfer to the Waffen-SS was mixed.

For *sous-lieutenant* Rigeade of the 3rd Company and *adjudant-chef* Rostaing of the III. Battalion it was the continual battle against the communist danger threatening Europe that was paramount and not the uniform worn. Rostaing still felt bound to his oath of loyalty and remarked in his book that if, like some, he did a bunk before defeat he could never again look at himself in the mirror while shaving.

Caporal-chef Malardier, who passed from the Headquarters Company of the I. Battalion/LVF to the Headquarters Company of Waffen-Gren. Regt der SS 58, embraced his integration into the ranks of the Waffen-SS.

This too was the reaction of *Caporal* Sepchant[28] when transferred from the engineer platoon of the Headquarters Company of the LVF to the engineer platoon of the Headquarters Company of Waffen-Gren. Regt der SS 58.

In 1941, Sepchant had enlisted in the LVF 'for fear of seeing Europe submerged by Bolshevism' and 'in the hope of a durable reconciliation with the hereditary enemy who, after having inflicted on us the most crushing defeat in our history, had spared us'. And now, some three years later, the very same motives, 'reinforced by the habit of fighting beside our German comrades', led him to accept the Waffen-SS with open arms. However, two of his comrades, who regarded the Waffen-SS as out-and-out hostile to the Catholic Church, refused to be transferred.[29]

Sergent Mercier was at the Ersatz Kommando of the LVF at Greifenberg when he learnt that the LVF was passing to the Waffen-SS. It was with great satisfaction that he greeted his transfer to the SS, for it corresponded exactly to his idea of things of the time. He wore the distinctive SS runes before it was made compulsory.

Sergent Blonet of the 3rd Company regarded the transfer of the LVF to the Waffen-SS as a 'sign of confidence in all foreign volunteers after the assassination attempt on Hitler and a sign of defiance towards the Wehrmacht'. Also, he approved of the 'maintenance of the difference between the LVF and the Sturmbrigade by the creation of two distinct regiments'. In this way, each unit would retain its *esprit de corps* and cohesion.

Sous-lieutenant de Genouillac of the I. Battalion does not recall his real reaction when he learnt of being assigned to the Waffen-SS. However, certain thoughts were prevailing in his mind at that time; he was not given any choice; a soldier has to obey his commanders; the only possibility was to continue the battle to the end

28   Pseudonym as used by Mabire.
29   Sepchant names the two T. and R.

and 'the uniform in which he would be buried mattered little'. Besides, the prospect of being incorporated into an elite unit where he would be well trained and well equipped did not displease him.

Caporal-chef Gonzales of the 2nd Company was discontented. He had no desire to serve in the ranks of the Waffen-SS. All the same he 'marched'.

Sergent Fronteau was transferred from the PAK Company of the LVF to the 10/58. His reaction to the transfer was one of betrayal. He explained:

> We lost our flag, we were no longer a French unit of the Wehrmacht with exclusively French officers and commands, but Frenchmen dragooned into a Division whose name was French alone. There was no regard for our contracts of enlistment.

Nevertheless, the contracts of the LVF officers were respected. In this way, between fifteen to twenty officers chose to leave the German Army, but the majority refused to abandon the legionnaires under their command. Between forty and forty-five officers transferred to the Waffen-SS.[30]

The officers alone had the right to choose. As a NCO, *Sergent* Fronteau did not. This angered him all the more. Nevertheless, he too marched.

In total, no more than seventy-five legionnaires of the LVF, including two NCOs, decided to resist the transfer to the Waffen-SS. This figure is all the more surprising considering the predominant French disposition and trappings of the LVF. But the legionnaires' weariness after up to three years of combat on the Russian front is cited as a contributory factor to their apparent reluctance to fight the inevitable. Moreover, many of the major 'figures' within the LVF had come out strongly in support of the transfer. And that included the larger than life Mgr. de Mayol de Lupé.

To de Lupé, the transfer from the Wehrmacht to the Waffen-SS was of no cause for concern. In fact, in his opinion, 'National Socialism reflected the will of God and the SS was its armed arm'. Indeed, de Lupé needed little pushing to compare the Reichsführer-SS Heinrich Himmler to the Archangel Saint Michael![31]

For all his prestige, Mgr. de Mayol de Lupé could still not convert the seventy-five legionnaires of the LVF who refused to be remustered to the Waffen-SS. Indeed, one of their number called Richter[32] who was the son of a general, stole de Mayol de Lupé's horse and deserted.[33]

30   Roch, page 49.

31   Mabire, page 75.

32   De Genouillac, correspondance to the author throughout 1997. According to Saint-Loup, de Villefranche stole de Mayol de Lupé's horse. This is incorrect; de Villefranche was killed on 13th June 1944 in Russia. *Elève-officier* Noell identified his body.

33   According to Saint-Loup, page 141, the horse-thief was stopped two or three days later by Feldgendarmerie on the frontier of Eastern Prussia. Sent to SS and Police camp Danzig-Matzkau, he was brought before a court and condemned to death! The news of his execution surprised the LVF, especially at a time when desertions were part of daily life. In fact, the horse-thief was actually accused of deserting to the enemy for which there was no pardon. This execution added another powerful argument to Puaud's armoury on which he could draw when he attempted to convert

In desperation, Puaud summoned Renardeau,[34] the 'ringleader', and offered him the choice of either transferring to the Waffen-SS or being sent to a concentration camp. Renardeau still refused to embrace the Waffen-SS. A few days later, the riled Puaud, true to his word, sent him and the other 'reprobates' to Konzentration-Lager [concentration camp] Stutthof, near Danzig.[35]

Among the 'reprobates' were Pierre Soulé and Norbert Désiré of the 10th Company/III. Battalion. As a political soldier, Soulé could not accept the order to pass from the LVF to the Waffen-SS because it totally changed the ideals for which he was fighting.

As for Norbert Désiré, a black *Martiniquais* [inhabitant of Martinique], despite wanting to join the Waffen-SS, he was refused admission because of the colour of his skin.[36]

Of importance to note is that Puaud had the 'reprobates' transported to Stutthof the day before the arrival of SS-Brigf. Krukenberg to take up post as Inspector of the French W-SS. Puaud said nothing of this to Krukenberg. Clearly he was anxious to hide from Krukenberg the refusal of some legionnaires to enter 'Charlemagne'.[37] But Mgr. Mayol de Lupé did say something. One or two days after the arrival of Krukenberg, Mgr. Mayol de Lupé told him of the plight of these legionnaires. Thereupon Krukenberg ordered his Intelligence officer, SS-Hstuf. Schmidt, to go to the concentration camp with a view to liberating them and sending them onto arbeitslager [work camp] Wilhelmshagen,[38] run by Frenchmen. That same evening, Schmidt informed Krukenberg that his orders had been carried out.[39]

Krukenberg then concluded the matter by rebuking Puaud who, in his eyes, had overstepped his authority and acted without any formal process. But this was not quite the end of the matter; unbeknown to Krukenberg, Puaud still

the legionnaires opposing the passage to the Waffen-SS. In response to Saint-Loup, de Genouillac, who served with the LVF, knew Richter well and cannot recall his capture yet alone his execution. This suggests that Saint-Loup is incorrect.

34   Pseudonym.
35   Saint-Loup, page 143. However, according to Mabire, page 83, they were sent to Danzig-Matzkau (which was a SS and Police camp, and not a concentration camp as stated by Mabire).
36   Of note is that while in the concentration camp Désiré was decorated with the KVK II.
37   This conclusion is reached by Krukenberg in his letter to Saint-Loup, 18/3/65.
38   Krukenberg, letter to Saint-Loup, 18/3/65. However, according to Saint-Loup, page 143, the transit camp was at Willemshagen (sic).
39   Ibid. However, according to Saint-Loup, the concentration camp commander, after studying the dossiers of the legionnaires, proved sympathetic towards their refusal to join the Waffen-SS and on the following day dispatched them to the work camp. And yet it should be recalled that Krukenberg learnt that 'his orders had been carried out' which he probably understood to mean that, on his orders, the legionnaires had been sent to the work camp. Of course the possibility exists that when Schmidt reported back to Krukenberg, he choose to conceal the fact, for whatever reason, that the camp commander had already decided to send the 'reprobates' to the work camp or had already dispatched them there.

'gave instructions against some of these legionnaires'.[40] Five of them ended up in concentration camp Sachsenhausen. In this way, 'Puaud kept his promise'.[41] In February 1945, Renardeau was transferred to concentration camp Mauthausen.[42]

Estimates vary of the number of LVF legionnaires transferred into the French Waffen-SS; Littlejohn, Landwehr, Soulat and Bayle cite 1,200 or about 1,200; de Genouillac cites no more 1,500; Mabire cites 2,000; and Roch cites 2,100 (minus the 15 to 20 officers and 75 men who refused to transfer).

The command of Waffen-Gren. Regt der SS 58 went to *Commandant* Bridoux of the LVF. He had a touchy character that did not win him friends. Nevertheless, the Germans near to him held him in high esteem because of his military training and bearing. It is said he even quoted them passages from the memoirs of Hindenburg.

Although required to wear the W-SS pattern *tricolore* shield on the left upper arm, many former LVF men continued to wear their former Wehrmacht *tricolore* shield on the right upper arm. Sometimes the former LVF shield was worn with the word 'France' turned inwards to conceal it.

Enter the Kriegsmarine

The LVF legionnaires were not the only French volunteers to be transferred to the French Waffen-SS without consultation. The somewhat mute reaction of the legionnaires to their transfer contrasted to that of the first French contingents of the Kriegsmarine and the Naval Police. Theirs was vocal. Bayle talks of a riot, Mabire of a revolt, and Saint-Loup of a mutiny. However, there was no such mutiny, yet alone a riot, but only 'a very limited show of discontent'.[43] So what happened?

In the late evening of 17th September 1944, the French Kriegsmarine volunteers of the 2nd Company of Schiffsstammabteilung 28 arrived by train at Greifenberg station. Waiting on the platform were French volunteers of the Waffen-SS. It was then that they realised that they had been simply transferred to the Waffen-SS. Some grumbled, but discipline prevailed. They went into barracks.

By parade next morning, after a night of great debate, the French volunteers of the Kriegsmarine were split in two. A small number assembled in the *feldgrau*, but the majority remained in blue. Indeed, some of those willing to pass to the Waffen-SS were even wearing its insignia, its epaulettes, and its belt! As for those who wished to remain 'sailors', encouraged by legionnaires of the LVF present, they shouted out their protest, but their demonstration soon quietened down.

---

40   Krukenberg, letter to Saint-Loup, 18/3/65. Indeed this only came to light on the publication of Saint-Loup's "*Les Hérétiques*".

41   Saint-Loup, page 144.

42   Landwehr states that those LVF legionnaires rejecting Waffen-SS service were firstly sent to a penal unit and then to a construction battalion on Brigf. Krukenberg's orders. This is unconfirmed.

43   Confirmed by Mercier, who witnessed the 'sailors' arrive at Greifenberg (letter to the author, 21/9/2001).

In order to calm the former Kriegsmarine volunteers, headquarters dispersed them to different local villages to help the farmers harvest the potato crop.[44]

So what prompted the French volunteers of the Kriegsmarine to react in such a manner? *Matrose* [rating] Soulat, one such French volunteer of the Kriegsmarine transferred without consultation to the Waffen-SS, explained that they felt angry because their officers had not provided them with any prior explanation. The age-old hostility that has existed between the Navy and the Army world over could also explain this reaction. Uscha. Mercier, a former legionnaire of the LVF who witnessed the sailors arrive at Greifenberg, said of speaking to some of them:

> They told me that their vocation was 'the sea' and nothing else. One of them said to me that he had been a naval officer and agreed to be a simple rating, but not an infantryman. A German NCO said to them 'but there are no ships any more', to which one replied 'then put us in the merchant navy'.

They were Navy through and through. And yet they had little history to talk of and few traditions to uphold. Indeed, the tricolore arm shield,[45] held so dear by the legionnaires of the LVF, does not appear to have been worn by their compatriots serving in the Kriegsmarine. Also of importance to note is that the French volunteers of the Kriegsmarine were not recruited for a wholly 'French unit' like that of the LVF or the SS-Sturmbrigade. Thus, their transfer to a 'French unit' may well have been another source of complaint.

It was only in February 1944 that the Kriegsmarine had begun to appeal for French volunteers on an official basis, although before this date a number of individual 'private' enlistments had certainly been accepted from the traditional sea-going regions of Brittany and Normandy. Law No 159 of 17th March 1944 (published in the *Journal officiel* of 18th March 1944) supplemented that of the 22nd July 1943 with the addition of 'the arrangements apply to those who enlist in the Kriegsmarine'.

The main Kriegsmarine recruiting office for French volunteers was located in Boulevard des Alliés (sic), Caen, Normandy. The Kriegsmarine even continued its

---

44   Soulat, correspondence to the author 1997-98. There are, however, different versions of how the Kriegsmarine volunteers 'came to be calmed'. According to Mabire, page 103, the wind of 'revolt' died down days later, which was assisted in part by the removal of the agitators to 'concentration camp' Danzig-Matzkau. According to Saint-Loup, pages 125-126, it was Chaplain Verney, who came to the assistance of the Kriegsmarine volunteers. Firstly he calmed the riot and then heard the grievances and demands of the Officers and NCOs. Puaud was contacted, but only promised them a court martial and the concentration camp. Thereupon, Verney alerted the influential Mgr. de Mayol de Lupé and, following his intervention, the 'leadership of the LVF' finally gave way to the demands of the Kriegsmarine volunteers 'to choose freely between civilian life and the Waffen-SS'. Rostaing cites, page 146, that it was only the threat of seeing themselves hauled before a court martial that quashed the mutinous behaviour of the sailors. In response to Mabire, Saint-Loup and Rostaing, they are all incorrect (Soulat, correspondence to the author 1997-98, and see Mabire, page 111).

45   Under German regulations, foreign volunteers were permitted to wear an arm shield in their national colours.

campaign to recruit Frenchmen for 'the Atlantic defence of France and Europe' after the Anglo-American landing in France and relocated its main recruiting office to 2 bis Rue du Havre, Paris.

After the medical, French Kriegsmarine recruits were gathered at Caen and then sent on to Alsace and SS-Ausbildungslager Sennheim for basic training with Schiffsstammabteilung 28 (SStA 28). The command structure of SStA 28 was as follows:

Commander:	Fregattenkapitän Dr. Schneider (to March 1944)
	Fregattenkapitän Schroeder
Adjutants:	Oberleutnant Dr. Bruckmann
	Oberleutnant Frischauf
Administration:	Leutnant Battenfeld (to December 1944)
	Oberleutnant Benz
Medical services:	Marine-Oberstabsarzt Dr. Goebel

Eleven training companies of Kriegsmarine recruits of different nationalities were formed under the tutorship of SStA 28:

1st Company	KorvettenKapitän Wellner	Mixed
2nd Company	Kapitänleutnant Hoffmann	Mixed
3rd Company	Oberleutnant zur See Hoech	French
4th Company	Kapitänleutnant Dr. Bruckmann	Estonian and Latvian
5th Company	Oberleutnant zur See Hahn	Estonian and Latvian
6th Company	Oberleutnant zur See Polck	French
7th, 8th, 9th and 10th Companies	?	The 7th was Volksdeutsche
11th Company	Kapitänleutnant Wilhelm	Mixed

In general, the recruit's training lasted a period of six to eight weeks and concluded with the solemn swearing in ceremony. During this period the emphasis was on physical training and on mastering the rudiments of the German language. Besides, no weapons and little equipment was available with which to train. Even so, the volunteers trained hard, very hard, under the watchful eyes of their instructors who were all decorated German NCOs carrying wounds. The results were good. If proof were needed of this, there is the time General Hardtmann made an impromptu visit to Sennheim.

After watching an exercise of Naval Companies, General Hardtmann expressed the wish to inspect a little closer those of the company who had most impressed him. When he questioned some of them, to his great surprise, he received no response: none of the 3rd Company of the SStA 28 (French volunteers) could speak German. Turning to the Kommandeur accompanying him, General Hardtmann said:

I have been in the Army for more than thirty years and I started under Emperor Guillaume as a young 2nd Lieutenant in the 4th Guards Artillery Regiment at Potsdam. I can only tell you that your Frenchmen manoeuvre as well as the companies of the Prussian Guard which I had the honour of commanding in the past!

Apart from in the canteen, the French volunteers of the Kriegsmarine had no contact with their countrymen of the Waffen-SS.[46]

At the conclusion of this training period the Kriegsmarine volunteers were immediately forwarded to various garrisons in Germany—including Duisburg, Varel and Mannheim—for weapon and specialist naval training. This further period of training lasted some three months in which they perfected their 'trade' by manoeuvring small boats on lakes or rivers. Thereupon, the French Kriegsmarine volunteers received an assignment aboard a naval unit. Most assignments, if not all, were to the Baltic fleet[47] and on the smaller vessels in the armoury of the Kriegsmarine.

Only the French Kriegsmarine volunteers of the first four companies of SStA 28 served aboard and, in some cases, saw action at sea. Initially, there were no French NCOs or officers, but it was in combat that some Frenchmen received their first rank.

Well over one thousand Frenchmen are said to have served in the Kriegsmarine, but the figure of two thousand found in some sources is considered doubtful. One such Frenchman who volunteered for and served in the Kriegsmarine was *Matrose* Robert Soulat.

Born in January 1920 in Paris, Soulat had not completed his secondary education when he enlisted in a *Régiment de Tirailleurs Tunisiens* in November 1938. He was stationed in France at La Roche sur Yon and then Fontenay-le-Comte. By April 1939, he held the rank of *Caporal.* When the Germans invaded he played his part in the defence of his country and was captured on 20th May 1940 between Valenciennes and Cambrai by the 7th Panzer Division. Sent to Stalag VIII-C at Sagan, Germany, it was here that he learnt of the Armistice. His reaction was one of profound sadness but not of surprise. Even so he was relieved that the French population was now spared the horrors of war. In February 1943, he was repatriated.

The *Parti Franciste* had brought about Soulat's liberation from captivity; he had been a member of this nationalist party since November 1934 and, on several occasions, had met Bucard, its leader, whom he greatly admired and respected. Although the party asked nothing of him in return, it made it obvious that on his homecoming a political gesture was expected from him on its behalf. But, on the month of his homecoming, compulsory labour service was made obligatory for French males born in 1920, 1921 and 1922 under a law instituting the *Service du Travail Obligatoire* (STO). Soulat, born in 1920, fell into this category and the

---

46   Indeed, some from both sides recall no contact whatsoever. This lack of contact appears to have no other reason other than that the volunteers of the KM and the W-SS occupied two distinct annexes of Sennheim.

47   These assignments suggest that the Kriegsmarine had no wish to place its French volunteers in a situation where they might find themselves fighting the Allied forces.

French bureaucrats of the STO, aware that he had just returned, proposed to post him to a foundry at Puteaux. He carefully thought over his next move.

Over the past three years of captivity, the Germans, in most cases, had treated him decently and thus he had no reason not to work on their behalf. And although the STO had been kind enough to propose a French posting, Soulat did not want to work in a foundry. He wanted work that was agreeable to him. Then there was the party to consider. This twenty-three-year-old knew that he could not remain neutral. Thus, on 13th March 1943, he volunteered for the Organisation Todt as a uniformed Baufernsprecher (fitter-telephonist).

Until the end of 1943, Soulat's posting was Paris. Then it was Mamers where he still was early May 1944. The intensification of the Allied air attacks led him to believe that the Invasion was imminent and he chose to take up arms again. Because he had no desire to experience once again the daily suffering of the Infantry, he volunteered for the German Kriegsmarine on 15th May 1944 at the Caen recruiting office. In fact, he was not looking forward to finding himself on water; he could not swim!

At Sennheim, Soulat underwent his basic training in the 6th Company of Schiffsstammabteilung 28. He was surprised to make the acquaintance of anti-militarists. He made friends with Pierre Soulier who had served with the OT-SK in Russia in 1943.

On 30th June 1944, the 6th Company was sworn in. The following day, the first of July, the company visited the hill of Hartmannsweilerkopf, the scene of fierce fighting during the First World War. One of the French Kriegsmarine volunteers found the grave of his father killed there in 1915. Their presence on this ground in the uniform of the enemy of yesterday was full of symbolic meaning, marking the desire, once and for all, to put an end to the hostility cultivated between their two countries.[48]

The 6th Company was sent to Duisburg, quartered in the FLAK barracks of Duisberg-Wannheim and renumbered the 2nd Company. Days later, the new company commander, Oberleutnant zur See Hochhaus, arrived.

One day, instructor Bootman Fleming asked the 'sailors' of the 2nd Company if they would be happy to be engaged in the west as *infanterie de marche* with their present officers. He was deafened by an ovation of overflowing enthusiasm and had to calm them down using all of his authority. Nevertheless, nothing came of this.[49]

On 16th September 1944, the 2nd Company left Hamm by rail. According to their German officers and NCOs, the French sailors were now bound for a naval depot on the Baltic Sea. One day later, the train pulled into Greifenberg station.

The 2nd Company was among the first French contingents of the Kriegsmarine transferred without consultation to the Waffen-SS. Soulat greeted his transfer with little enthusiasm rather than with open hostility. But it was clear to him that the coming fight, either on land or at sea, would be against Russia and that was a fight he preferred to that in his homeland, for he had no wish whatsoever to fight against his fellow countrymen.

48   The memoirs of Robert Soulat.
49   Ibid. The date of this incident was probably early September 1944.

When the time came for the French Kriegsmarine volunteers to exchange their blue naval uniforms for the *feldgrau* almost all kept their beret band as a souvenir of their time in the Kriegsmarine.

On 28th September 1944, some two weeks after their arrival at Greifenberg, those French volunteers of the Kriegsmarine transferred to the Waffen-SS, including Soulat and his friend Serge Vincenti from Catalan, were relocated by train to training area 'West Prussia', around Konitz, in the Danzig corridor. Arriving at the small town of Bruss, they disembarked and set off on foot to Saalesch, six kilometres away. Night had fallen by the time they arrived. Saalesch was the journey's end for one half of them. The others were sent on to Leisten (with the Polish name of Lesno). And yet their quarters were not actually in the village, but a further two kilometres away at the camp of Waldlager. Finally, the 'sailors' found rest on straw in accommodation delightfully described as 'hovels'.

The very next morning, Soulat was awoken by Rttf. Labrousse. Thus began his transformation and that of his comrades into grenadier of the Waffen-SS under Oberjunker Martret.[50]

The Kriegsmarine also recruited a naval police unit of French volunteers to guard the U-Boat base at La Pallice, near La Rochelle. The unit was called the Kriegsmarinewerftpolizei La Pallice (roughly the Navy Wharf Police of La Pallice), abbreviated to KMW. The first volunteers were wounded soldiers discharged from the LVF, followed by adherents of political parties M.S.R., P.P.F. and Franciste. Some were STO who preferred to do their time in this unit rather than in Germany. On 30th June 1944, the German commander of the U-Boat base gave the men of the KMW the choice of defending the base or joining the LVF in Germany. Some of those who left found their way into 'Charlemagne'. The KMW numbered some 200–300 men.[51]

Of the French contingents of the Kriegsmarine transferred to the Waffen-SS, only a handful, at most five or six men, were dismissed during the 'weeding out' in October 1944.[52] Thus, between 1,000 and 1,200 former French volunteers of the

---

50   According to Soulat, letter to the author, 16/7/98, the KM volunteers at Waldlager were formed into two strong (Zuge) platoons under Oberjunker Martret and Brazier, with Brazier probably assuming the command of the two because of his seniority. Matret, however, remembers things differently, stating that at Waldlager he was at the head of the *Wach-und Ausbildungskompanie* and that at no time was he a *chef de section* of KM volunteers (personal discussion with Martret). Furthermore, according to Matret, at Waldlager the KM volunteers were placed into the forming *Wach-und-Ausb.Kp.* Curiously, Soulat, one such KM volunteer was only told on his arrival at Wildflecken months later that he was now with the *Wach-und-Ausb.Kp.* (letter to the author). Thus, the possibility exists that the KM volunteers were not told of their placement until such time as they had proved themselves worthy of the *Wach-und-Ausb.Kp.*

51   Similar 'guard' units of naval police may have been recruited for other U-Boat bases. There is even a suggestion that French naval police fought at Saint-Nazaire against the British commando raiders.

52   Soulat, letters to the author, 8/12/97 and 3/1/98. However, according to Saint-Loup, page 126, the first French contingents of the Kriegsmarine transferred to the Waffen-SS were offered the alternative of returning to civilian life. In this way, twenty

Kriegsmarine and the Naval Police actually went on to serve in 'Charlemagne'.[53] They were assigned to all units, but large numbers served in the following:

The Wach-und Ausbildungskompanie der Inspektion (the guard and education company of the Inspection)
The Signals Company
The Medical Company
The Engineer Company

Also, many former members of the Kriegsmarine served in the headquarters staff of the regiments and battalions.

5% of Waffen-Gren. Regt. der SS 58 was ex-Kriegsmarine.[54]

Four former members of the Kriegsmarine were assigned to the FLAK Company of the Brigade. They included Strmm. Grimaldi who would later receive the Iron Cross 2nd Class 'for acts of war in the KM'.[55]

The special forces

'Some of the new SS men were from the French section of the Army's celebrated Brandenburg Division'.[56] The number of French *Brandenburgers* that joined 'Charlemagne' probably totalled only a handful.[57]

The auxiliary forces

Frenchmen serving with the paramilitary formations of the German war machine were also absorbed into the Waffen-SS. It is estimated that some 2,000 to 2,300 Frenchmen of the Schutzkommando of the Organisation Todt [or simply the SK] and the Technische Nothilfe ('Teno') served in 'Charlemagne'.[58] And yet little is known of when and where they were placed into 'Charlemagne'. Also not known is their reaction to this. Presumably it too was one of disgruntlement.

per cent of the first French contingents of the Kriegsmarine transferred to the Waffen-SS chose to leave Greifenberg as 'free workers'. In response to this, whilst at Greifenberg, Soulat does not recall any such offer nor the departure of so many of his comrades. Indeed, according to Soulat, the five or six discharged in October were the only such former volunteers of the Kriegsmarine to leave 'Charlemagne'.

53   Mabire and Bayle, "*San et Persante*", page 125. The author has dismissed Littlejohn's figure of 640, "*Foreign Legions of the Third Reich: vol. I*", page 170, undoubtedly based on the strength of the first French contingents of the Kriegsmarine recorded by Saint-Loup minus the twenty per cent of those released.

54   Lefèvre, cited in "*La Division Charlemagne*", Roch, page 51.

55   "*Encadrement de la FLAK*", unpublished.

56   Littlejohn, "*Foreign Legions of the Third Reich: vol. I*", page 170. Formed in early 1943, the 8th Company of the 3rd Regiment was largely French. It operated on French soil.

57   Arguably, in September 1944, when the Brandenburg division was relieved of its duties as a special operations unit and transformed into a motorised panzergrenadier division, most French *Brandenburgers* chose to join the commando units of the Waffen-SS commanded by Skorzeny rather than 'Charlemagne'.

58   It should be noted that the figure of 2,000 represented a fraction of those Frenchmen actually employed in these paramilitary formations.

In 1941, the *Schutzkommando* [Protection Command] was formed by the Organisation Todt[59] to guard its building sites against theft and sabotage and to supervise its 'employed' workers. Personnel of the SK wore a brown uniform with black shoulder straps and black ties. To fill its ranks, the SK turned to the recruitment of foreign volunteers because most physically fit German males were already serving in the armed forces. Many Dutch, Flemings, Walloons and, to a lesser extent, French volunteered for the SK. French volunteers wore on the upper right arm a tricolore shield surmounted by the word 'FRANCE' in a yellow cogwheel on a dark blue, or black, background.[60]

Among the Frenchmen to volunteer for the SK was Roger Vigny. 'Captivated by Nazi doctrine, the launching of operation 'Barbarossa' prompted him to enlist. He did so in September 1942 after having falsified his papers; he was in fact only sixteen years old!'[61] With a contingent of French volunteers, he left for the SK training school at Pontivy, Brittany, in October 1942. He recalled:

59   In 1938, when tasked by Hitler with the construction of the Westwall, Fritz Todt, the Generalinspektors für das deutsche Strasenwesen [Inspector general of German roads], responded by mobilising some one thousand private construction firms. This army of workers Hitler christened Organisation Todt. On 4th September 1939, Fritz Todt declared 'that the OT would function in wartime as a fortress construction organisation, employing building firms organised on military lines'.

When war came, OT personnel served on all fronts. Their roles were varied; from building bridges, often under fire, to repairing roads damaged in the fighting; from the construction of harbour facilities to dams in marshy regions; from the running of oil-extraction facilities in Estonia to collective farms in the Ukraine. Indeed, the OT became responsible for all construction projects behind the front lines.

In late 1941 OT Einsatzgruppe 'West' was formed to supervise the nine Oberbauleitungen units operating in France, Belgium and the Netherlands. Located at Lorient, then 33, avenue des Champs Elysées, Paris, OT Einsatzgruppe 'West' was tasked with the realisation of the *'Atlantikwall'*, the so-called Atlantic Wall, a defensive system of fortification units stretching along the Atlantic coastline of German occupied Europe. Needless to say, it was a massive undertaking requiring steel, concrete and manpower.

By 1942, OT Einsatzgruppe 'West' was employing 112,000 German and 152,000 French workers, including 17,000 North African Arabs. Although many French workers were employees of firms under OT contract or genuine volunteers, others had joined to save themselves from deportation to Germany or in order to escape from poverty. Thus, for some, the Organisation Todt was little more than a point of refuge. Also many of the large numbers of non-French workers in France could hardly be described as volunteers. And yet, in November 1942, members of the OT were granted full armed forces status.

By 1943, 'West' had grown to 18 Oberbauleitungen and now numbered 291,000 workers of more than twenty nationalities. For the first time, in its ranks were allied prisoners-of-law. As well as fortifying the Mediterranean coast, OT labourers now repaired the increasingly bombed and sabotaged railway network.

60   This national shield may have only been introduced for wear late 1943; Frenchmen Roger V. and Castrillo, who volunteered for the SK September 1942 and early 1943 respectively, did not wear the French national shield.

61   See Mounine, *"Les Français Schutzkommandos de l'OT"*.

The welcome was rather friendly and courteous from the officers and NCOs responsible for our training. That same evening we were handed a sheet on which appeared every command in German translated into French as well as the names of our instructors, all Frenchmen with the rank of SK-Rottenführer or SK-Kameradschaftsführer. They advised us to do our utmost to learn the contents quickly. The following morning, we received training overalls, a personal weapon, helmet, belt, cartridge belt … The ammunition would be distributed to us later. The training was rigorous: it was similar to that followed by all infantrymen. The training course lasted about a month or longer if it proved necessary. At the end, our recompense was the issue of the epaulettes: black with a white border. They were presented after the swearing in ceremony performed on the 'golden flag' of the OT (a swastika ringed by a cogwheel), the company in a U formation in the barracks square. We then received the khaki uniforms of the OT and we marched through the streets of Pontivy, led by the band and the flag.

The next day the postings began. Vigny was posted to Saint-Malo and then Cherbourg. In September 1943, one year after joining up, while on leave, bored of the monotony and the routine of guard duties and convinced that there was no opportunity of promotion for Frenchmen, he decided to hand back his Soldbuch and uniform. However, he did not give up the fight and enlisted in the Speer Legion, another German paramilitary formation.

In January 1943, the twenty-eight-year-old Roger Mariage entered the SK. Previous, with the rank of *sergent*, he had fought with the LVF and been seriously wounded. The SK gave him the NCO rank of SK-Haupttruppführer and made him an instructor at Pontivy.

On 9th April 1943, the SK training school was relocated from Pontivy to a former camp for German POWs at La Celle Saint-Cloud, outside Paris. By upgrading its facilities, the camp was converted into a model training school. The instructors were from the Waffen-SS.

Most, if not all, of the French collaborationist political parties actively recruited volunteers for the OT and its SK. Numerous *Francistes* enlisted in the various branches of the OT. At the start of 1943, a two hundred strong uniformed contingent of Déat's *Rassemblement National Populaire* enlisted in the SK. The P.P.F. was also well 'represented' in the SK. And orders from the P.P.F. brought loyal party member Jean Castrillo to the SK.

Born in December 1922, Jean Castrillo was the son of a businessman. His father, a French resident since 1907, was of Spanish origin.[62] His mother, who was born in Paris, was of Alsatian, Flemish and Dutch origin. Politically, his parents were Falangists.[63]

In 1936, the year the P.P.F. was founded, his father went into business in Saint-Denis, which became the power base of the P.P.F., and struck up a friendship with novelist Drieu La Rochelle, who supported the P.P.F. Before the year was out, his father had entered the P.P.F. and the fourteen-year-old Jean the *Union populaire de la Jeunesse française*, the youth branch of the P.P.F.[64]

---

62   He only took French nationality in 1940.

63   During the Spanish Civil War two cousins were shot in Madrid by communist forces under General Miaja. One of them was a fervent Falangist.

Castrillo served the party as best a young militant could, selling newspapers and billposting. He attended party meetings. He heard Doriot speak, of whom he said: "A remarkable orator and organiser, a workaholic, with great leadership qualities and great personal courage." The young Castrillo was devoted to Doriot and the party.

From June 1940 to October 1941, Castrillo attended secondary school, passing his *baccalauréat*. He remained politically active. Like his father, by now the head of the P.P.F. for the XIX° *arrondissement* of Paris, he greatly admired Pétain. The family supported the German led crusade against Communism and believed that Germany needed help, although it was not yet a question of Jean volunteering for the LVF, populated by the P.P.F., and leaving for the Eastern front.

Castrillo followed very closely the debut of the LVF on the Eastern Front. When François Sabiani, the son of Simon Sabiani, the 'proconsul of the P.P.F. for Marseille', was killed at the front he hailed him as a hero. Thus in June 1942 he decided to volunteer for the *Chantiers du Maréchal* whose training instructors belonged to the P.P.F.

Posted to camp des Châteliers near Orléans, Castrillo received one month's instructor training under the supervision of a NCO of the LVF, who had been wounded during the winter of 1941–42 before Moscow and invalided out of the service. At the conclusion of the one-month *stage*, in receipt of his *diplôme de moniteur des Chantiers de la Jeunesse*, he left for the 'lumber' camp at Méry ès Bois in the Cher[65], where he was put to work clearing the tree plantations of Sologne. By now it was late August 1942.

Castrillo soon found himself in trouble. Along with a youngster of the R.N.P. and a former sailor, anglophobe since Mers el Kebir, he led a mutiny against the criminal activities of the *chefs* of this camp, for they were openly trafficking, buying and selling on the black market, and helping themselves to the recruits' food coupons. With the three 'crooks' locked up, the mutineers requested the Chantiers' headquarters at Orléans to come and investigate.

The following morning, four cars arrived from the *préfecture* of the Loiret with an official from the Chantiers. The newcomers talked with the mutineers. They were all smiles. A lorry of *gardes-mobiles* then arrived. The three ringleaders of the mutiny, which included Castrillo, were arrested and sent to a forced labour camp at Vouzeron in the outer suburbs of Vierzon.

Contact with the outside world was forbidden, but at the beginning of November 1942 Castrillo was granted permission to write to his father. At the request of his father the party now came to the rescue. Vauquelin de la Fresnay, head of the J.P.F., obtained from Doriot permission to go and see Otto Abetz, who ordered the French authorities to release him because he had not stood trial. A car sent by the party collected him.

On his return to Paris, Castrillo attended the P.P.F. 'congress of power' at cinema Gaumont Palace, which opened on 4th November 1942 and ran to the 8th. Under the *tribune d'honneur* was a huge banner which read 'Vichy betrays'. He recalls the speeches of both Doriot and Simon Sabiani, the 'proconsul of the P.P.F.

64   The UPJF later became the *Jeunesses Populaires française* (J.P.F.).

65   The camp was installed in the family chateau of De Lesseps, a name made famous by an ancestor who had conceived and constructed the Suez Canal.

for Marseille', who exhorted the youngsters of the party to follow the example of his son François. Henceforth 'his decision was taken' and, at the request of the party, volunteered for the SK. He considered himself a political *engagé* [enlisted man or volunteer] through and through. Because he was not yet twenty, he could not leave without consent from a parent, which his father gave him.

Castrillo was dispatched to La Celle Saint-Cloud and placed into the French training company. The training under company commander Mariage was hard. On 28th May 1943, shortly after the conclusion of recruit training, Castrillo's company swore an oath of loyalty to Hitler as 'commander of European armies'. Black epaulettes were issued.

Castrillo was then granted three days leave, after which he left for Norway in a company composed of equal numbers of Dutch and French volunteers with German officers and NCOs, all of Saxon origin. The Dutch were for the most part members of the youth branch of the N.S.B. (National-Socialist Movement) led by Mussert. Half of the French were apolitical and half were, like Castrillo, from the J.P.F. Many of the recruits had joined to avoid forced labour in Germany or out of a taste for adventure. Only two or three of Castrillo's compatriots were really politicised. One, a young Belgian residing in France, would later join Degrelle and the Walloon Division of the Waffen-SS.

Transported by road to Denmark, the company sailed for Oslo on a cruiser of the German Navy. It was assigned to protect a 'top secret' industrial complex south of Bergen, which Castrillo would later learn was involved in nuclear research.

Norway was no longer a quiet tour of duty. Castrillo received his baptism of fire when the company participated in an operation against Norwegian Resistance forces north-east of Bergen. The operation lasted three weeks.

In October 1943, the company was engaged against British commandos who had landed not far from the complex. This was a much more serious test. The British fought fiercely, but were rounded up one after the other. Some two hundred British were taken prisoner. The losses suffered by the SK company were heavy: five dead, ten seriously wounded, and twenty slightly wounded, which included Castrillo, for which he received the wounded badge.

On 14th November 1943, the company was relieved. Hopes of leave were dashed when the company was transported across the Baltic Sea on a Norwegian vessel to the port of Memel, where it remained on security duties alongside Latvian Police until April 1944. Castrillo, promoted to SK Mann 1. Klasse in November 1943 and then to SK-Rottenführer in March 1944, recalls a very friendly population, which was warmly anti-Communist. It was a home from home.

On his return to France, Castrillo was granted one month's leave. As to be expected he went to the headquarters of the P.P.F. at 10 rue des Pyramides, Paris, where he received a warm welcome, but also news of the death of two of his comrades of the J.P.F. with the LVF on the Eastern Front. Barthélemy, one of the leading figures in the party, took him into his office and congratulated him on his service record. Castrillo then asked him to facilitate his transfer to the LVF. There was no question of this because Doriot now had need of men in France to take the fight to the terrorists. Castrillo left the SK. He would later serve with 'Charlemagne'.

The French volunteers of the SK also served in Germany, Yugoslavia and Estonia, where a company of French SK was 'almost totally destroyed during the summer of 1943'.[66]

By 1944, the SK was also guarding POWs, criminals and concentration camp inmates serving in OT detachments. With the liberation of France, the French SK volunteers fled to Germany, and the great majority were transferred to the Waffen-SS and sent to Wildflecken. In this way, René Binet, a former member of the *Parti communiste français* and perhaps one of the most well known Frenchmen of the SK, found himself serving in 'Charlemagne'.[67]

In March 1945, all SK companies were disbanded. There may have been as many as 3,000 French volunteers of the Schutzkommando.[68]

Also absorbed into the Waffen-SS were French volunteers of the Technische Nothilfe (Technical Emergency Corps) or 'Teno'. The primary war role of 'Teno' was to repair breakdowns in vital public services. The 'Teno' recruited French technicians, but faced competition from a rival, the Organisation Todt. Thus, the number of Frenchmen in 'Teno' is believed to be small.

Like their compatriots in the French N.S.K.K., the French 'Teno' volunteers were subordinate to the Luftwaffe and wore its grey-blue uniform with black 'Teno' ranks and insignia. It is not known whether or not the French 'Teno' volunteers were permitted to wear some form of national insignia, but it is considered very likely. Also not known is the actual number of French 'Teno' volunteers who went on to serve in 'Charlemagne', but they could not have amounted to more than a handful.

Frenchmen serving as Hilfswilligen [perhaps best translated as 'voluntary helpers'][69] or Hiwis also came to 'Charlemagne'. Perhaps the most remarkable was René-Jean Bourget.[70] In 1941, at the age of sixteen, he enlisted in the LVF. He served with the 2nd Company. On 4th October 1942, he was caught in a partisan ambush and seriously wounded. Such were his wounds that he had his right leg amputated. He received the wounded badge silver. In 1943, he was demobilised. Nevertheless, on 6th June 1944, he volunteered his services once again. Assigned to the 21st Panzer Division, he 'rode shotgun' on supply columns. Then came action with a *Panzerschützen* unit in Alsace before entering 'Charlemagne'.[71]

'Chalemagne' also 'welcomed' into its ranks French agents of the *Selbstschutzpolizei*, 'Self Defence Police', organised by the German Police in the spring of 1943 to assist in the fight against terrorism. Agents were recruited from the *jeunes* of the collaborationist movements and received police, sabotage and radio training at Taverny. In February 1944, the Germans extended the offer of training to members of the political parties authorised in the occupied zone and

---

66   Mabire, page 24. Curiously, according to Lambert and Le Marec, page 143, a French SK company was entirely annihilated in Latvia.

67   It should be noted that at least three persons with the name of René Binet served in 'Charlemagne'.

68   Bayle, "*De Marseille à Novossibirsk*", page 147.

69   For example, Jean de S.C. served with the 17. SS-Panzer-Grenadier-Division der SS "Götz von Berlichingen".

70   Pseudonym as employed by Lefèvre and Mabire "*La Légion perdue*", page 228.

71   In February 1945, he too would go to Pomerania with 'Charlemagne'.

those willing to 'take sides with the French and German police to maintain order in case of unrest'.[72] The best students could remain at Taverny to become *permanents* [literally 'paid officials'] of the SPP. In the months of April and May 1944, three Kommandos of these full-time *permanents* were sent to Dijon, Toulouse and Rennes. There were some 150 *permanents*, although the Germans planned to install 50 per department. Before it closed its doors, some 5000 *jeunes* had passed through Taverny. Not all were French. They included Italians, Russians, Arabs, and Flemings. After Liberation, some *permanents* of the *Selbstschutzpolizei* found their way into 'Charlemagne'.

Some sources state that the bulk of the French N.S.K.K. was absorbed into the Waffen-SS.[73] This is not correct. Nevertheless, individual Frenchmen may have 'deserted' the N.S.K.K. for the Waffen-SS, but their number, if any, would have been small.

In the summer of 1943, some French Columns 'ran missions' connected with the building of V1 sites in Northern France. From December 1943 to the end of November 1944, the headquarters and the three companies (4–6) of the French battalion of the 4th Regiment of N.S.K.K. Transportgruppe Luftwaffe were stationed in Italy. There were a number of desertions.

Meanwhile, back in France, the N.S.K.K. continued to compete with rival military and paramilitary organisations for its 'fair share' of French recruits, but its efforts appear to have reaped little reward. Even the allied invasion of France did not deter the N.S.K.K. and 'Gruppe TODT' from attempting to recruit drivers, mechanics and electricians for a French section. Volunteers had to be aged 18 to 50 and in very good health.

In early December 1944, the French battalion was posted from Italy to Denmark. The 4th Company was employed on guard duties. On 28th January 1945, at Odense, battalion commander Staffelführer Seigel first announced the existence of 'Charlemagne'. Thereupon, ninety per cent of the Frenchmen volunteered to join the Brigade, but were only 'rewarded' with three days of intensive exercise!

The battalion was reorganised into two groups.[74] In late February 1945, one group was dispatched to Hungary.[75] The rail journey lasted almost a whole month. Obersturmmann Faroux's Kolonnefführer, French Sturmführer Györ, who was Hungarian born, disappeared after crossing into Hungary. Equipped with trucks, the group was deployed towards Lake Balaton. There were supply and fuel problems. Each soldier was given a jerrycan and a rubber hose, and told to siphon fuel wherever possible from knocked out trucks and tanks.

The front was not continuous. Obersturmmann Faroux had two brushes with the Russians. He would never forget the time his convoy was ambushed a few kilometres west of Vezprem. He jumped out of the cab, took up position under the truck and started to return fire. The German Luftwaffe driver, who took his time to

---

72   Lambert and Le Marec, "*Les Français sous le casque Allemand*", page 205.

73   For example, see Littlejohn, "*Foreign Legions of the Third Reich: vol1*", page 165.

74   The battalion may have been reorganised into a 'headquarters' and two companies numbered 4 and 5 (Faroux, letter to the author, 14/8/2001).

75   This group dispatched to Hungary may have counted one half of the battalion, which may have been organised as two companies (Ory, page 265).

take cover, was shot dead and collapsed beside him. The Russians then withdrew. From that day forth he would count each day as a blessing.

Then there was the time Faroux was engaged in anti-tank combat.[76] The date was late April 1945, the location was west of Lake Balaton and the situation was Panzeralarm. Armed with a panzerfaust, he was commandeered by a German Army officer, incorporated into an emergency anti-tank unit, and sent on foot in search of enemy tanks, which had cut the road to the rear. The lead elements made contact, destroying one tank. The Russians withdrew, but there was no doubt that they would be back. And they were one hour later. Faroux made use of the bushy terrain to approach to within panzerfaust range, took aim at a tank and fired, but nothing happened. Fortunately, he was not discovered. Losing another tank and with the dark setting in, the Russians withdrew.

The group retreated into Austria by way of Deutschkreuz, a few kilometres south of Sopron, but was now no more than a kolonne, having 'melted like butter in the sun'.[77] The crew of NSKK-Scharführer Tregouboff, a white Russian in his fifties, and Faroux soon found themselves alone. On 7th May 1945, they learnt that many German soldiers had surrendered. The following day, they abandoned their truck, changed into civvies and walked west.

On 31st March 1945, the second group left Denmark for Hungary. At Flensburg the Frenchmen met some volunteers of the *Britisches Freikorps* [British Free Corps]. The convoy continued through Berlin, then onto the smouldering ruins of Dresden and then westwards. On 18th or 19th April 1945, the group disembarked at Gmünd in the Sudetanland. To celebrate the Führer's birthday on the 20th, the Frenchmen men paraded for the authorities and local population of Gmünd. The journey resumed the next day. After passing through Linz and Graz, the convoy arrived at Salzburg on the evening of 26th April. The following morning, a violent air raid destroyed Salzburg station. A tank convoy, which had been given priority over the French convoy and was occupying its place, was smashed. The French convoy suffered no damage, but two German NCOs, who were former Foreign Legion and spoke French perfectly, were killed. This, however, was the journey's end. On 29th April 1945, the group was demobilised by Hauptsturmführer Ströhle.[78]

Estimates of the number of Frenchmen who served with the N.S.K.K. range from 2,000 to 10,000.[79] Also, several Frenchmen are known to have become officers in the N.S.K.K.

---

76   According to Littlejohn, "*Foreign Legions of the Third Reich: vol. I*", page 165, '…in the closing months of the war one French NSKK unit fought in Hungary against the Russians as an anti-tank formation'. As such, this is not correct.

77   Faroux, letter to the author, 5/9/2002.

78   A small group of eleven made their way on foot to Innsbruck and from there crossed into Northern Italy via the Brenner pass. A truck then took them to Bolzano, arriving on 3rd May 1945. Their meal at the local *Soldatenheim* was interrupted by SS-Oscha. Rossfelder, a former N.S.K.K. volunteer, who proposed that they join the *Lehrgang* organised at Gries for French SS volunteers of 'Charlemagne' so that the fight against Russia might be continued with the Americans! They thanked him, but declined his proposal. They had other plans on their mind.

Workers

To swell the ranks of 'Charlemagne', the Waffen-SS tried to attract new recruits from among the large number of French workers in Germany. One of those involved in the recruitment drive was Swiss-born André Doulard who, in mid August 1944, after the conclusion of his recruit training at Sennheim, had been posted to the SS recruiting office in Stuttgart. He toured Bavaria speaking to French workers and not once was he insulted. Wearing full SS uniform, the Frenchmen took him for a German and the Germans for a Frenchmen!

The recruiting campaign took Doulard to Göttingen, Heidelberg, Mannheim, Stuttgart, Karlsruhe, Ulm, and Sigmaringen. He arrived at Mannheim just after a daytime air raid. It was frightening. The workshops had not been hit, but the dinning halls had been razed to the ground. Palpable was the hate for the Americans that filled the French workers. Here he also spoke against the terror raids.

At Sigmaringen, Doulard met many of the French exiled personalities; the chief editor of the *journal 'la France'* whose son had enlisted in the Waffen-SS; Laval; and Marcel Déat. On 30th October 1944, he held a meeting in the town's cinema. It was full to bursting. His arrival in full uniform made a strong impression. No sooner had he begun to speak than there was a power cut. Contrary to what he expected, from the audience there was not a sound, not a yell, not a whistle or an insult, just silence. When the power came back on he continued to speak, explaining the goal of 'our combat'. He included slogans heralded by Léon Degrelle in the *grand* speech he gave in April 1944 at the Palais de Chaillot, Paris.[80]

And what was the result of the recruiting campaign? The workers came to see him to sort out small problems they had with their foremen. This he did. But few volunteered there and then. And of those who did volunteer, half were 'false'; such volunteers knew full well that the medical examination would find them unfit for military service, but the enlistment process would take some ten days and that meant some ten days 'on holiday' away from life in the factories!

On 4th November 1944, Doulard was posted to the SS-Hauptamt in Berlin.

The FLAK Company of the Sturmbrigade

From 28th April 1944 to 28th July 1944, the FLAK Company was on a training course at Munich. Each morning, FLAK Company commander Führerbewerber Guignot, called *Capitaine* which was his former rank in the French Foreign Legion, led the company onto the training ground and handed it over to the German instructors. For the rest of the day he would look on. At no time was he ever involved

---

79 Littlejohn cites 2,000 ("*Foreign Legions of the Third Reich: vol 1*", page 165) and Saint-Loup 10,000 (page 124). Also of note is that some authors state that there were seven French companies (Littlejohn, "*Foreign Legions of the Third Reich: vol 1*", page 161, and Ory, "*Les Collaborateurs*", page 265). As such this is not correct. Only three companies operated at any one time.

80 After the meeting Doulard spoke with Déat for an hour. Déat spoke of the certainty of final German victory. On a large wall map, he explained how the European troops were going to attack, encircle and defeat the Allies. Also, he spoke of the V-10!

in its training or in its internal running! Nevertheless, he appeared at meal times. His 'lack of interest' was of little concern to the Germans who were in awe of the dazzling row of medals he wore proudly on his tunic.

Absent from the FLAK Company were platoon commanders Fayard, Ouvre and Mary. They were on a platoon commander's course.

At Munich, the French volunteers actively participated in the defence of the city against the Anglo-American 'terror' raids. On one occasion their barracks was bombed, but they struck back by shooting down some American aircraft. Several times, after the all clear, the FLAK Company was also employed to repair railway bridges near its barracks (Notbrücke).

The assassination attempt on the life of Hitler on 20th July 1944 brought about a memorable day of drama and activity for the FLAK Company. Tanks of the Waffen-SS appeared throughout the city; in fear of an attempted Putsch by the Heer, the RSHA had ordered them onto the streets. German Waffen-SS soldiers left barracks Freimann to surround the barracks of the Heer, the Luftwaffe and even those of the Vlasov Army! As for the French FLAK Company, orders were received from the Kommandeur of Freimann to protect the barracks. Taking up a 'hedgehog' position around the outside of the buildings, they waited …

On 28th July 1944, after completing its training, the FLAK Company left Munich for Pomerania. The next day, it disembarked at the small town of Bruss (now Brusy) in the former Danzig corridor and was quartered in a camp.

At Bruss, the FLAK continued to train, albeit without weapons, under the supervision of Oberjunker Fayard. As for Guignot, he was impassive as ever. Some time after, with elation, the FLAK received its full allocation of heavy and light weapons, and vehicles.

On 17th August 1944, the FLAK Company was moved to Saalesch, several kilometres from Bruss, and quartered with LVF units, who greeted its arrival with surprise and contempt. The LVF considered the FLAK as 'fanatical Nazis'.[81] But the forced cohabitation led to curiosity and then sympathy. For its part, the FLAK was not without admiration for the veterans of the Russian Front 'who recounted their adventures'.

The end of the Sturmbrigade

The FLAK Company was one of the first units, if not the first unit, of the SS-Sturmbrigade to arrive in Pomerania.[82] In late August 1944,[83] the skeletal 2nd

81   Article "*Le Schreiber*" (unpublished).

82   Personnel of the arriving French Sturmbrigade were assigned to SS-Panzer-Grenadier Ausbildungs-und Ersatz bataillon 35 (see the *Soldbuch* of Fenet and that of Pierre J. which appears on page 9 of "*39-45 magazine*", issue number 89). SS-Panz.Gren.Ausb. u. Ers. Btl. 35, based at SS Training area 'Westpreussen' in Bruss, may have been the responsible Ersatz unit for the French Sturmbrigade before the formation of 'Charlemagne' and its Franz. SS-Grenadier-Ausbildungs und Ersatz-Bataillon.

83   The date of arrival of the 2nd Battalion at Schwarnegast is unclear; according to Mabire, page 54, "*La Division Charlemagne*", days after its own arrival, the 2nd Battalion expected the survivors of the 1st Battalion [who arrived on 5th September 1944]. This dates the arrival of the 2nd Battalion to either late August or early

Battalion of the SS-Sturmbrigade [no more than two companies] was transferred from Neweklau to the hamlet of Schwarnegast[84] west of Bruss (Brusy) and north of Könitz (Chojnice).

Although the SS-Sturmbrigade commander Gamory-Dubourdeau had not been with the 1st Battalion in Galicia, he was promoted to Obersturmbannführer as a 'reward' for its impressive performance.

In August 1944,[85] 'in a fit of excessive indulgence',[86] Ostubaf. Gamory-Dubourdeau promoted FLAK Company commander Guignot to Hauptsturmführer and placed him in command of the 2nd Battalion of the SS-Sturmbrigade. St.Ob.Ju. Fayard was slotted into the vacancy Guignot left behind and St.Ob.Ju. Pierre Vincenot, who was ex-LVF, succeeded Fayard at the head of the 1st platoon.

One of the first actions of Fayard as the new FLAK Company commander was to accelerate the pace of the training. Thus, for up to ten hours a day, the men of the FLAK Company trained and trained hard. Heavy emphasis was placed on learning the mechanics of their weapons.

From the LVF the FLAK inherited a young Russian boy by the name of Nicolas Samassoudov. He became its mascot and Fayard even promoted him to the rank of Sturmmann! He would serve with his 'adopted parents' of the FLAK Company to the end.

On 5th September 1944, the one hundred and forty survivors of the decimated 1st Battalion joined the 2nd Battalion at Schwarnegast.

A trickle then followed of those who had recovered from wounds received in Galicia.

In this way, some 1,000 or 1,100 men of the two battalions of the SS-Sturmbrigade were placed into 'Charlemagne'.[87]

      September 1944. However, according to Saint-Loup, pages 94-96, Gamory-Dubourdeau (and presumably the 2nd Battalion) had been at Schwarnegast 'for several weeks' before the arrival of the 1st Battalion.

84   All sources refer to Schwarnegast. However, this is possibly a misprint for Schwornigatz (Swornegacie in Polish).

85   According to Soulat, page 26, Fayard took over from Guignot in August 1944. Thus, the author has reasoned that Guignot was promoted to Hauptsturmführer and placed in command of the 2nd Battalion of the Sturmbrigade that same month. Articles "*Le Schreiber*" (unpublished) and "*La SS-Französische Flakbatterie*" also suggest his date of promotion and transfer as August 1944. However, according to a non-referenced wartime command roster of 'Charlemagne', Guignot was promoted to Hstuf. on 1st July 1944. (Then again this said document does contain many errors.)

86   Mabire, page 135. Furthermore, the suggestion is made that Guignot's promotion to Hstuf. and his appointment to the command of the 2nd Battalion stemmed more from a shortage of officers than his ability. In fact, this may well be true. Firstly, his promotion cannot be attributed to attendance at and graduation from an SS officer training school. Secondly, after the terrible blood letting in Galicia, the SS-Sturmbrigade was definitely short of officers and, in particular, officers with either the training or ability to discharge command effectively at battalion level.

87   Littlejohn cites 'about 1,000'. Bayle cites 1,100.

In early September, six 'French training companies'[88], numbering over one thousand men, arrived at Greifenberg from SS-Ausbildungslager Sennheim.[89] The convoy commander was SS-Ostuf. Laue. Some of the 'evacuees' were assigned to the Franz. SS-Grenadier Ausbildungs-und Ersatz bataillon to complete their training. Most went to the forming Waffen.Gren. Regt der SS 57 at Schwarnegast, Bruss and Leisten.

One such 'evacuee' from Sennheim was Parisian student Jean-Louis Vaxelaire. At the end of May 1944, days before the *embarquement* in Normandy, the twenty-year-old volunteered for the Waffen-SS. His parents had told him to wait and do nothing, but he could not sit by and see Germany continue to suffer in isolation without showing his solidarity. For his ideals were those of Germany. He believed that Germany would, if victorious, create a new Europe. And if Germany was defeated then he could console himself with his show of solidarity. As for regrets, he has none, but he remains convinced to this day that he would have regretted making a decision not to enlist.

On his arrival at Sennheim, Vaxelaire was assigned to the 2nd Company of Ustuf. Büeler. Billeted in a villa in the village of Weiler some ten kilometres from Sennheim, he counted himself lucky when one night the empty villa across the river was bombed from the air and totally destroyed. And yet the villa occupied by him and two companies of French W-SS volunteers was not touched. It seemed to him that the bombers had been fed the wrong intelligence.

On one occasion, Vaxelaire and his company, on manoeuvre in the field, were granted a rest period in the shade of cherry trees. Hungry, the men could not resist the bountiful fruit and gorged themselves. Soon after, back on their way, they started to fall out with stomach pains. The cherries which had begun to ferment was their undoing. In this way, the whole company was incapacitated!

On 8th September 1944, Vaxelaire and a 20–30 strong group of men went in search of *résistants* in the neighbourhood of Sennheim. One French W-SS volunteer was hit in the head by a bullet.

At the end of September, while en route by train to Greifenberg, Vaxelaire witnessed one French W-SS volunteer commit murder. At one stop, a French POW insulted a group of W-SS volunteers. One of them was so enraged that he shot the French POW dead.[90]

At Greifenberg, Vaxelaire was assigned to the Stammkompanie [depot company] of the Franz. SS-Grenadier Ausbildungs-und Ersatz-bataillon. In this way, he found himself on administrative duties with three or four others recording the new arrivals. He went on to attend a *Lehrgang* run at Greifenberg after which he was promoted to Sturmmann.

Also 'evacuated' from SS-Ausbildungslager Sennheim to Greifenberg and the Franz. SS-Grenadier Ausbildungs-und Ersatz bataillon was a certain Jacques Evrard. Born in May 1924, he volunteered for the Waffen-SS in June 1944 after

---

88   Mabire, "*La Brigade Frankreich*", page 442.

89   Of note is that some French volunteers of the Waffen-SS remained at Sennheim until its final evacuation on 28th November 1944.

90   After the war, the French *gendarmerie* investigated this murder. The outcome of its inquiry is not known to the author.

the Allied landings in Normandy. He was a militant of the P.P.F. By volunteering for the Waffen-SS, he was seeing his political commitment through to the end.

As previously noted, the SS-Sturmbrigade was used as the base for Waffen-Grenadier-Regiment der SS 57. The command of the new regiment went, of course, to Ostubaf. Gamory-Dubourdeau. He was soon able to form eight companies at full strength.[91] Some of the company commanders were; Albert; Bartolomei; Philippe Colnion, born on 8th July 1926; Hennecart; Labourdette; Million-Rousseau; and Jean Marie Stehli[92], a Swiss national, born on 21st March 1918.[93] With the exception of Bartolomei and Hennecart, all were young and of late had graduated from SS-Panzergrenadierschule Kienschlag with the rank of Oberjunker.[94]

Faced with amalgamation, the W-SS volunteers of the SS-Sturmbrigade had no crisis of conscience. But many felt great disappointment at seeing their fellow countrymen of the LVF, the Kriegsmarine and the various paramilitary organisations admitted so readily into the Waffen-SS. They, this 'new race of Franco-Boche' which the legionnaires of the LVF called the W-SS volunteers of the SS-Sturmbrigade, had undergone months of rigorous selection and hardship before being accepted into the Waffen-SS.

Furthermore, the W-SS volunteers of the SS-Sturmbrigade were concerned that many of their own kind now incorporated into the Waffen-SS lacked proper military training. They knew that to withstand the brutal shock of life and combat on the Eastern Front the newcomers had to be both physically and mentally tough. They doubted that the same level of training afforded to them could now be afforded to the new 'volunteers'.[95]

Without exception, all former members of the French SS-Sturmbrigade in 'Charlemagne' continued to wear the standard SS runes right collar insignia and

91   Mabire, pages 90-91.
92   Stehli was at the head of the 1/57. According to Saint-Loup, page 161, Fenet had him relieved of his command. Puaud later appointed him the *officier de justice* of 'Charlemagne'.
93   Cited by Mabire, page 135, as of mid-October 1944. Also listed as company commanders are Boyer, Brazier and *Matres* [Martret]. In response to this, Boyer did not succeeded Stehli at the head of the 1/57 until 28th October 1944 and was only in post for just one week. Brazier probably succeeded Boyer. As for Martret, by mid-October 1944, he was at the head of the Wach-und Ausbildungskompanie which was not one of the organic companies of Waffen-Gren. Regt der SS 57.
94   In total, ten Frenchmen graduated with the rank of Oberjunker from this class (Roch, page 49).
95   In addition, on page 129 of "*San et Persante*", Bayle points out that the newcomers to the W-SS could no longer be screened because what military or criminal records they might have had were back in France which, by now, was largely liberated. This would suggest that there may have been some concern that the newcomers from military or paramilitary formations whose standards he describes as 'more flexible' actually had criminal records that at another time would have prevented their entry into this elite corps. In response to this, it does seem doubtful that the military and paramilitary formations at which Bayle is directing his comments would recruit persons with criminal records at the expense of their reputation.

the SS regulation pattern national shield (or privately made versions of the national shield). As per the regulations of 15th April 1944,[96] most, if not all, now started to wear the national shield directly under the SS eagle.

In mid-October, after paying a brief visit to Ulm to speak to Darnand about the problems faced by the enlistment of his exiled *Miliciens* into 'Charlemagne', Ostuf. Fenet arrived at Schwarnegast. In his absence, he had been placed in command of the 1st Battalion of Waffen-Grenadier-Regiment der SS 57, the I/57. He was alarmed to hear that Hstuf. Guignot was in command of the II/57.

The German Inspection

The formation and training of 'Charlemagne' continued in various locations throughout the Danzig corridor under the watchful eye of the Inspektion der französischen SS-Verbände (InF)[97] [Inspection of French SS units (infantry)] located at Leisten. At the head of the German Inspection was Brigadeführer und Generalmajor der Waffen-SS Gustav Krukenberg. In his capacity as Inspector or Inspector General he reported directly to the Reichsführer-SS Himmler who gave him a free hand to carry out his role. In theory, the role of Krukenberg to oversee the formation of 'Charlemagne' differed from that of Puaud, but in reality it was Krukenberg who served as its behind the scenes commander. In this way, Puaud's position became essentially nominal.

Although regarded as an archetypal Prussian, Gustav Krukenberg was in fact born in Bonn on 8th March 1888. His father was a doctor and a professor at Bonn University. His mother was the daughter of archaeologist Alexander Conze. After passing his *Abitur*, he attended university to study law and economics, gaining a doctorate in law. He saw his career as that of a military attaché.

In 1907, Krukenberg joined the Army as a Fähnrich with the 6th Guards Field Artillery Regiment 76. On 1st April 1909, he was commissioned as a reserve Leutnant. Two years later, he switched to active duty. Then came World War One. His wartime posts were many. He served as an Ordnance Officer to the 3rd Guards Division, then as an adjutant to the 6th Guards Infantry Brigade and then as a corps Ia. In 1918, after attending general staff training at Sedan, he became a Hauptmann (Captain) and a member of the Army General Staff. By the end of the war, he was the recipient of various decorations, including both classes of the Iron Cross. That of the Iron Cross 1st Class was pinned on him by Kaiser Wilhelm II.

The post war years saw Krukenberg serving as Oberquartiermeister-Adjudant [Senior quartermaster adjutant] in the war history unit of the General Staff.[98] He

96   The Verordnungsblatt der Waffen-SS of 15th April 1944. By order of the RF-SS Himmler, the national shield of units of foreign volunteers was to be worn 1.5cm below the national emblem.

97   SS-FHA, Amt II Org. Tgb.Nr.4212/44 g.Kdos auf Befehl des Reichsführer SS am 10.10.1944. It should also be noted that the Inspection has appeared under numerous titles. For example, according to Mabire, page 148, Brigf. Krukenberg was assigned as General-Inspektor der französischen Verbände der Waffen SS. According to Giolitto, page 389, Krukenberg was named as Inspector of the units of French volunteers of the Waffen SS. Also, Landwehr speaks of an Inspectorate of the French Waffen-SS (see page 60, "*Charlemagne's Legionnaires*"). In response to Mabire, Giolitto and Landwehr, all are unsupported by official documentation.

disapproved of the 1920 'Kapp Putsch'[99] and found himself in conflict with General Hans von Seeckt, the Commander–in–Chief of the Reichswehr, the 100,000-man post-war army, who wished to distance the officer corps from any political view. Later that year, Krukenberg returned to civilian life and joined the civil service.

From June 1920 to the end of January 1922, Krukenberg served as the principal private secretary to successive Foreign Ministers Simons and Dr. Rosen.[100] He participated in the formulation of the Treaty of Rapallo that was signed in 1922.

From 1922 to 1923, Krukenberg was active as a representative of the Reichsverband der Deutschen Industrie [National Federation of German Industry]. He attended the world economy conference held in Genoa. Moving to the private industry, he worked as a director for a German company in Holland from 1924 to 1925.

In 1926, Krukenberg went to Paris as part of the German delegation to the Deutsch-Französischen Studienkomitees [German-French study committee or German-French relations study commission].[101] He returned five years later with a passion for France.

Joining the NSDAP (number 1,067,635) on 1st April 1932, Krukenberg served as a spokesman for the National Radio-Broadcasting Commission in the cabinets of von Papen and von Schleicher. With Hitler's election he became an Under State Secretary in the Propaganda Ministry. He would have continued 'to climb up the ladder' if it was not for a 'difference of opinion' with Josef Goebbels, the Reich Propaganda Minister, which led him to resign his position and go back into private business.

On 30th May 1934, Krukenberg was accepted into the Allgemeine-SS with the number of 116,685 and assigned to the 6.SS-Standarte in Berlin. On 9th November 1936, he was commissioned with the rank of SS-Untersturmführer. More Allgemeine-SS promotions followed and, by 30th January 1939, he held the rank of SS-Hauptsturmführer.

In 1939, Major d.R. [reserve Major] Krukenberg was recalled to full-time Army service.[102] On 28th July 1940, he won a clasp to his WW1 Iron Cross 2nd class. From August 1940 until February 1941, he was assigned to the Senior Armed Forces Commander for the Netherlands. He then went to Paris as a General Staff officer. In 1943, he became the Chief-of-Staff of Wirtschafts-inspektion Mitte [Economy Inspection Centre] which covered occupied White Russia.

On 1st December 1943, Oberstleutant Krukenberg transferred from the Wehrmacht to the Waffen-SS with the equivalent rank of SS-Obersturmbannführer d.R. and spent the first month with Panzer Training and Replacement Battalion 1. On 17th January 1944, he was appointed as the Chief-of-Staff of the V. SS Gebirgs-Korps [Mountain Corps]. This also brought him promotion to SS-Standartenführer on the 20th.[103] On 7th May 1944, Corps commander Gruppenführer Phleps wrote to Himmler requesting the transfer of Krukenberg.[104] On 19th May 1944, Krukenberg was relieved of his command.[105]

---

98   According to Bayle, page 153, in the post war years, Krukenberg served as a staff officer in Brigade Reinhard.

99   On 13th March 1920, the Ehrhardt brigade, one of the many armed units of the nationalist Freikorps [Free corps] of demobilised right-wing troops, occupied Berlin

And yet on 9th May 1944, he received promotion to SS-Oberführer d.R. From 19th May to 25th June 1944, he served as Chief-of-Staff of the VI.Waffen-Armee-korps der SS (Lettisches).

On 25th July 1944, Krukenberg took up post as Waffen-SS Commander-in-Chief for the 'Ostland' (Befehlshaber der Waffen-SS 'Ostland') based in Riga, Latvia. For two months, until the cessation of the post on 23rd September 1944, he was actively involved in the mobilisation, training and reformation of Latvian Waffen-SS units, Latvian Police Battalions and Latvian Border-Guard Regiments. In early August 1944, he briefly succeeded Ziegler as Chief-of-Staff of the III. (Germ.) SS-PanzerKorps.

In that same period, Krukenberg also led Kampfgruppe 'Krukenberg' of SS-Kampfgruppe 'Jeckeln' on anti-partisan duties, winning a bar to his WW1 Iron Cross 1st Class on 26th October 1944.

Then, on 23rd September 1944, RF-SS Himmler named Krukenberg as Inspector of the French W-SS and promoted him to the rank of SS-Brigadeführer und Generalmajor der Waffen-SS. Two days later, on the 25th, he took up post.

Krukenberg was an excellent choice as Inspector. He spoke the French language impeccably, had an excellent understanding of the French people, and had previous experience working and serving with foreign volunteers.

Krukenberg did not underestimate the task before him, fully recognising that if he did not strike hard and fast then the 'wound' of French internal politics in 'Charlemagne' would hinder, if not irreparably damage, its formation and endanger the spirit of Camaraderie.

And what of the soldiers Krukenberg had to mould into a Waffen-SS formation? He thought that the legionnaires of the LVF were 'more hardened, but too undisciplined' and 'often exhausted by three years of combat and their difficult retreat'. As for those soldiers of the French SS-Sturmbrigade, he had some concerns about their political traits and said of this:[106]

to establish Dr. Kapp, an ultra-right monarchist bureaucrat, as chancellor. The Reichswehr did not intervene.

100   Georgen, "*Sur les traces du Sturmbataillon de la Division Charlemagne*", part 1, page 21. However, according to Landwehr, page 187, he became a 'bureau chief' in the Foreign Ministry and, according to Yerger, page 42, he was the ministerial office head for the Ministry of Foreign Affairs.

101   See Landwehr, page 187.

102   Krukenberg had been a Major d.R. since 1st October 1938.

103   Otto Kumm, "*Prinz Eugen*", page 106 (English edition) and Mabire, page 150. However, Krukenberg recalls in "*Historia #32*" that he had the rank of Oberführer when appointed as the Chief-of-Staff of the V. SS Mountain Corps. Unfortunately, Krukenberg is mistaken. Also, Landwehr, page 188, "*Charlemagne's Legionnaires*", repeats this same mistake.

104   This was, undoubtedly, as a result of a clash between Phleps and Krukenberg.

105   Otto Kumm, "*Prinz Eugen*", page 115 (English edition). Yerger dates his replacement one day earlier (see page 43.)

106   *Entretien avec le général Krukenberg*, "*Historia #32*", page 136.

They no longer believed in France or Germany: they spoke of a 'European nation'. For my part, I still did not believe the time had come for such an undertaking.

In fact, Krukenberg wanted the volunteers to 'remain French and not be SS men speaking French'. Thus, there was no question of promoting National Socialism.

Krukenberg set high standards for the French volunteers:[107]

The honour of the French flag and the prestige of the French soldier must remain the supreme law, not only in combat, but also in behaviour towards the German civilian population.

It was a question of national pride.[108] He understood the psychology of the French volunteers. Respected, Krukenberg was not liked by his German subordinates.[109] Krukenberg was also the holder of both classes of the Kriegsverdienstkreuz (KVK). Married in September 1912, Krukenberg and his wife had two daughters, born in 1920 and 1924.

Brigf. Krukenberg had at his disposal a thirty-strong Inspection, including SS-Ostuf. Jauss. Born on 12th December 1921 in Göppingen, Hans Robert Jauss had enlisted in the Waffen-SS aged seventeen. Decorated of late with the German Cross in Gold after distinguishing himself in action in Estonia, he was made responsible for the training of the French Oberjunken of Waffen-Gren. Regt. der SS 57. He wore several 'tank destruction' badges, denoting the single-handed destruction of an enemy tank.[110]

There was also SS-Ustuf. Rohrer who supervised the training of the PAK companies. Although only twenty, he was highly qualified having spent the last three years on the Eastern front. He was the holder of the Nahkampfspange [Close Combat Clasp] in silver.

Many other German personnel served in 'Charlemagne'. Their exact number is not known. Many, if not all, of the German Heer personnel of the LVF transferred to the Waffen-SS. For example, all of the German interpreters of the Brigade Headquarters Company were from the E.M.L.A. [*Etat-Major de Liaison Allemand*, the German liaison headquarters] of the III/638.

German personnel were found in the Engineer Company (including Edgar Becker, born on 14th Feb. 1925; Gustav Sachse, born on 31st August 1912; and Karl Sanner, born on 29th May 1920)[111] and the Medical Company (including Johan Adlgasser, born on 13th October 1908 and Wilhelm Sack, born on 6th December 1925).[112]

---

107 Soulat, "*Histoire de la Division Charlemagne*", page 15.

108 By appealing to their national pride Krukenberg believed that the Frenchmen would fight better, *Entretien avec le général Krukenberg*, "*Historia #32*", page 136.

109 Saint-Loup, page 153.

110 One silver badge was awarded for each tank destroyed. Four such badges could be worn, but for five kills, a gilt badge was worn in their place. For more than five kills, additional silver badges could be added.

111 Missing In Action was the fate of all three.

112 Both are also listed as Missing In Action.

Not all of those with the SS prefix to their rank were actually of German origin. SS-Uscha. Adam Wagner, born on 12th March 1911, was a Volksdeutsche from Hungary. He was on the German liaison staff to Waffen-Gren. Regt der SS 57.[113] SS-Uscha. Hans Wagner was Alsatian. He was a Schirrmeister [Technical sergeant major] in the I/58.

The initial training courses[114]

At the end of September 1944, about a dozen (de Genouillac) or twenty (Mabire) former officers of the LVF, were sent to the SS-Unterführerschule at Lauenburg (Lebork) for a company commander's training course.[115] Among the officers were Baudouin, Defever, Falcy, Fatin, de Genouillac, Laffargue, Rigeade and Wagner. The course lasted one month and proved too demanding for four or five of their number. Good friends Falcy, de Genouillac and Rigeade, who had successfully completed the course, rejoined the French brigade at Wildflecken camp on 11th November 1944.

In September or October 1944, the engineer platoon of Headquarters Company/Waffen-Gren. Regt der SS 57 as well as that of Headquarters Company/ Waffen-Gren. Regt der SS 58 were dispatched to SS-Pionierschule Hradischko, one of the many training schools located within Truppenübungsplatz Beneschau, south of Prague, Bohemia-Moravia. Their escort to Hradischko was SS-Rttf. Thiel, born on 7th February 1911 in Berlin.[116] At Hradischko they came into the 'care' of SS-Ustuf. Thomas. He spoke good French and had nothing but good things to say of France. Notably his young assistant with the rank of SS-Unterscharführer was from Alsace or Lorraine. He too spoke perfect French without any trace of an accent. SS-Ustuf. Hans von Twistern, who looked barely twenty-years-old, 'administered' political education. He spoke no French. His means of communication became a rather old interpreter who wore the uniform of the Heer and not that of the Waffen-SS. Although the interpreter admitted that he was not a National Socialist, he had not let himself slide into defeatism.

The field training was all too real. W-Strmm. Sepchant of the engineer platoon of the Headquarters Company/Waffen-Gren. Regt der SS 58 had this to say of the 'bunker busting':[117]

… but what most impressed us was the initiation into the role played by the engineers in the clearing of fortified lines. As far as I can remember, the case-mate to be neutralised was subject to a violent bombardment first. Under what still remained of the barbed-wire entanglements, an engineer, among the most

113 Listed as Missing In Action in Pomerania, February 1945.
114 According to Mabire, page 70, one hundred NCOs of the former LVF attended a Waffen-SS school. But where were they? Was it Lauenburg? Perhaps Bütow?
115 Mabire suggests that this was a calculated move by the German authorities to deprive the LVF of its influential *encadrement* which might have proved troublesome about the disbandment of the LVF and the absorption of its personnel into the French Waffen-SS. This might be true, but is impossible to prove.
116 Roland Thiel, whose profession was teaching, later disappeared in the hell of Pomerania, February 1945.
117 Gaulois, article *"Pionierarbeit"* (as yet unpublished).

daring, slid a concentrated charge (geballte Ladung) placed on a long board. Immediately after the explosion he informed his comrades that the way was clear ('Hier Gasse!'). Those rushed into the breach. One of them blinded the embrasure with a flame-thrower. Another placed on the turret the hollow charge (Hohlladung) which was going to pierce it.

All these manoeuvres were terribly dangerous, and more than one engineer sacrificed himself 'für Führer, Volk und Vaterland' before having seen the case-mate explode, but as Ustuf. Thomas put it: That's when the awards of the EK I are won first time!

Another training exercise required the engineers to lie down around holes, five metres in diameter and one metre deep, in which five kilograms of gelignite was exploded.

The training course at Hradischko would last some two months.

Thirty officer candidates, for the most part ex-LVF, including Poupon, Douroux, Coste, Maisse, and Garrabos, were sent to SS-Panzergrenadierschule Kienschlag.

In early October 1944, about thirty French NCO candidates departed to the SS-Unterführerschule at Bütow in Eastern Pomerania for a three month long course.[118] One such candidate was Obergrenadier de Misser, who was ex-Sturmbrigade. The training was arduous.

Integration

In October, at Leisten, the anti-tank company subordinated to the Brigade's Panzerjäger Battalion began to form. Importantly, the men were from the French SS company of Ostuf. Michel and the gradés [NCOs] from the LVF. One such NCO was adjudant Hérin. This was the first attempt to fuse elements of the SS-Sturmbrigade and the LVF into a sole unit but would it succeed? The worst fears of Brigade Headquarters were not realised. Concessions were forthcoming from both camps; the 'old' LVF NCOs commanded alternately in German and French, and the young French SS volunteers started to sing the 'Panzerlied' in French. There would be no serious problems.

Each regiment had one anti-tank company and they too were at Leisten for anti-tank training. Oscha. Julian commanded the anti-tank company of Waffen-Gren. Regt der SS 57 and Capitaine Rémy that of the Waffen-Gren. Regt der SS 58. The two of them had nothing in common.

A former Milicien, Julian was 'completely moulded by the harsh SS discipline'.[119] He was a survivor of the battles in Galicia. As for Capitaine Rémy, described as good-natured, he was ex-LVF.

Born in 1910 in Tarare, Rhône, Henri Léon Rémy was drawn to serve France on the 'high seas' rather than on solid ground. In the Navy, he acquired the rank of Enseigne de Vaisseau de 1ére Classe [lieutenant]. It was with the equivalent German Army rank that he entered the LVF. Trained in Poland at Kruszyna, then at Demba, he was posted to the II/638 as officier-adjoint to chef de Bataillon Tramu. At the conclusion of Operation Morocco, February 1944, he was proposed for the

---

118   De Misser, correspondence to the author.
119   Mabire, page 145.

Croix de Guerre Légionnaire. Weeks later, at the end of March 1944, *commandant* Tramu entrusted to him the command of company 6/638 which was stationed at Scheplewitschi in a sector considered the most dangerous. By all accounts, company 6/638 was in very poor shape; demoralised and 'without spirit', it was composed of very young soldiers who had not seen action before. However, in weeks, through the personal leadership of Rémy, the company became the best in the battalion. He was tireless; he went on all patrols and operations. He received several citations for his *Croix de Guerre* and was proposed for the Iron Cross 2nd Class and promotion to *Capitaine.*

Julian and Rémy, and the men they commanded, were from 'two different worlds', but soon bonded.

However, not all were so willing to embrace integration or the discipline of the Waffen-SS. During the month of October 1944 the brigade purged itself of 184 men to Konzentration-Lager [concentration camp] Stutthof. 109 men were transported from Bruss on the 13th, arriving at KL Stutthof on the 14th,[120] and a further 75 men were despatched on the 30th. Their origin is worthy of note: most were ex-LVF, ten or so were ex-Sturmbrigade and five or six were ex-Kriegsmarine. Their charge sheets speak of indiscipline, heavy drinkers, theft, absence without leave, homosexuality, physical and moral ineptitude, and participation in preparations to desert. One of those purged was a former maquisard who was now regarded as dangerous. Another was a Jew. He had arrived at SS-Ausbildungslager Sennheim late June 1944.

From Stutthof, some were moved to SS-und Polizeilager Danzig-Matzkau. Others went to Arbeits-Lager [work camp] Wilhelmshagen and the life of a civilian. Some would remain at Stutthof.

Also, the esprit de corps and the harsh discipline of the former Sturmbrigade that its NCOs tried to instil did not sit well with the LVF veterans who, it is said, prided themselves on their slovenliness and bawdiness. Sometimes, this led to tension between the two.[121]

The Panzerjäger Battalion

Hstuf. Jean Boudet, called Boudet-Gheusi, commanded the Panzerjäger Battalion of 'Charlemagne'. Born on 26th July 1904 in Tarbes, he studied law at the *Faculté de droit d'Aix-en-Provence.* Armed with the *brevet de PMS,* he attended EOR training. In 1930, he was promoted to *sous-lieutenant de réserve* and posted to the elite *22e bataillon de chasseurs alpins* (22° BCA). After the defeat of 1940 he joined the Legion, then the SOL, becoming the *chef* of the department of Alpes-Maritimes. Responding to Darnand's appeal, he volunteered for *La Légion Tricolore* in 1942. On 15th August 1942, he was promoted to the rank of *Capitaine.* After the *La Légion Tricolore* was disbanded, he went on to serve with the LVF on the Eastern front.

On paper, the so-called 'Heavy' or 'Heavy Weapons' Battalion comprised 1 anti-tank company, 1 FLAK company, 1 assault gun company[122], and 1 escort

---

120 On the 14th, KL Stutthof confirmed the arrival of 105 men belonging to the 'French Legion'. Two are known to have escaped en route.

121 One former French officer of 'Charlemagne' commented to the author that accounts written of late have blown this tension out of all proportion.

platoon. Except for the anti-tank company that had its full complement of twelve towed 75mm anti-tank guns, the battalion was desperately short of equipment. Drivers did not have trucks, signallers did not have field telephones, and the assault gun company under Ostuf. Michel did not have the promised fourteen assault guns.[123] Also promised and not delivered were ten heavy 'Tiger' tanks. And to make matters worse, Boudet-Gheusi failed to 'stamp his authority' on the FLAK Company at Saalesch.

Wildflecken

At the beginning of October, Strmm. Vaxelaire was posted from Greifenberg to Truppenübungsplatz Wildflecken in Western Germany to serve as an instructor. Here the French brigade was to continue its training.

Set in the picturesque setting of the wooded Rhön massif, Truppenübungsplatz Wildflecken had been built in 1936 for the German Army.[124] All roads led to a central square, Adolf Hitler Platz. Around the square were the various functional and administrative buildings, including camp headquarters. Near the *Lagerkommansantur* stood a high stone column. Atop was a winged eagle with a wreathed swastika in its claws. Among the firs and the larches stood the barracks constructed of stone and wood that could each house two entire companies.

In late October 1944, the entire French brigade, no more than 5,000 men, was assembled at Bruss and dispatched to Wildflecken.[125] The first convoy left Bruss at 1400 hours on 26th October 1944 and stopped some fifty hours later at Brückenau railway station. All disembarked. Wildflecken camp was about half an hour's march away.

On 31st October 1944, the FLAK Company left Bruss. Two days later, it disembarked impeccably at Brückenau.

In late October 1944, officer B. arrived at Wildflecken from France. He had attended military cadet academy La Flèche and then military school Saint-Cyr, but his studies were cut short by the 'second disaster' of November 1942. He went on

122 According to Mabire, page 145, the company was to be fitted out with Sturmgeschütze.

123 Mabire, page 530. Curiously, the same author notes on page 145 that the Assault Gun Company was awaiting twelve assault guns. In response to this, an assault gun company had a theoretical establishment of fourteen and so the author has used fourteen.

124 According to de la Mazière, page 35, near the camp entrance was a large arch supported by two pillars on which was inscribed the Waffen-SS motto 'My Honour is Loyalty'. This is unlikely. Wildflecken was an Army camp and not a Waffen-SS camp, although Waffen-SS troops were also trained there.

125 Mabire and Soulat, "*Historique de la Division Charlemagne*", page 1. However, de la Mazière, a new recruit to the French Waffen-SS, recounts that upon his arrival at Wildflecken in early October 1944 he met Zimmermann, Krukenberg and Puaud in person, and encountered sections of the French Sturmbrigade and members of the first LVF echelon. But de la Mazière, a *Milicien*, actually arrived at Wildflecken with the *Milice* in early November 1944. For whatever reason, he rewrote the date of his arrival.

to work for the Vichy Government. He was admitted into the Waffen-SS and 'Charlemagne' with his equivalent former rank in the French Army, that of Oberjunker. Stubaf. Bridoux, the commander of Waffen-Gren. Regt der SS 58, who knew of B. and of his situation, sent for him and entrusted to him the command of the anti-tank company of the regiment (which is often numbered the 10th Company and abbreviated the 10/58[126]). In this way, B. replaced *Capitaine* Rémy, who in the words of B. 'was political, but not a soldier and not in control of the company', which might explain why the company had become of concern to Bridoux.[127] Besides, B. had been schooled in the art of anti-tank warfare. He accepted his new command with much enthusiasm.

Upon entering the anti-tank company, B. was greeted with indifference, not opposition. However, he was quick to make an impression, served well by his physical attributes; he stood one metre 82 and had a strong voice. After some initial reservations, the NCOs followed him. Problems subsided, so much so that when Oscha. Girard assumed command of the company he met no problems.

Walter Zimmermann

At Wildflecken, the German Inspection was joined by SS-Staf. Zimmermann. He was well known to Brigf. Krukenberg.[128] They had served together in the V. SS Gebirgs-Korps.

Walter Zimmermann was born on 1st October 1897 in Meissen, Saxony. His father was a postal secretary. On 2nd September 1914, he joined the Army. In the years that followed he worked his way up through the ranks. He saw service in Lithuania, Poland and France. He won the Iron Cross 2nd Class. In March 1918, he became an officer candidate and that October was commissioned as a Leutnant d.R. with Pionier Bataillon 241.

On 1st August 1932, Zimmermann joined the NSDAP. His number was 1,378,990. Months later, on 3rd January 1933, he volunteered for the Allgemeine-SS. His SS number was 59,684. He was assigned to the Engineer platoon of the 46.SS-Standarte in Dresden. In November 1935, he moved to the recently formed Pioniersturmbann of the SS/VT and, on the 16th, was commissioned with the rank of SS-Untersturmführer. From October to December 1937, he was on a posting with the engineering section of the SS-HA (Main Office). After a stint with the Nachrichtensturmbann, he served with the staff of the SS/VT inspection and then the Kommandoamt der Waffen-SS in an advisory capacity, where he remained until January 1941. By now, he held the rank of SS-Sturmbannführer.

On 20th January 1941, Stubaf. Zimmermann took command of the SS-Pionier-Ersatz-Bataillon. On 30th January 1942, he was promoted to SS-Obersturmbannführer. In April 1942, he became the first commander of SS-Geb. Pionier Bataillon 7 of the 7. SS-Freiwilligen-Gebirgs Division 'Prinz

---

126 See Mabire. However, of note is that the regimental commander never used the
     designation 10/58 for the anti-tank company, nor did B. and nor did Girard who
     would later command the company.
127 Also, Rémy may have been demoralised.
128 Undoubtedly Krukenberg had requested the services of Zimmermann.

Eugen'. On 31st January 1943, he won a clasp to his World War One EK II. Klasse and, on 15th June 1943, the EK I. Klasse. He was also the recipient of the order of the crown of King Zvonimir that Ante Pavelic, the Plogavnik [leader] of Croatia, awarded him for keeping open the strategic roads of Croatia. From July 1943, he served as the Korpspionierführer [Corps engineer leader] of the V. SS-Freiw.-Geb.-Korps. On 20th April 1944, he was promoted to SS-Standartenführer. Then, in late September, he was placed in reserve.

On 31st October 1944, SS-Staf. Zimmermann was posted to the French Brigade of the Waffen-SS at Wildflecken. He came as its Ausbildungsführer [Training leader].

Zimmermann spoke French fluently. He carried on him a dictionary of French slang. On its cover he had drawn a tricolore.[129] Although his reputation as a cold and rather severe man instilled fear among the French trainees, he did have a charming and affable side.[130]

On one occasion, when challenged by a guard, Staf. Zimmermann had been without the password and immediately found himself against a wall with a bayonet in his back. He remained in that position for half an hour before being shown in to see Hstuf. Roy, the guard's company commander. Much to Roy's surprise, Zimmermann actually congratulated them both for 'conscientiously applying orders'.[131]

Zimmermann was one of the few Germans serving with 'Charlemagne' who wore the French national shield. In fact, he wore that of the LVF.

Many surprises awaited Strmm. Vaxelaire at Wildflecken, none more so than the person in the next bed to his who had the typically Jewish name of Cohen![132] Nevertheless, there was nothing in a name. Many, for obvious reasons, had enlisted under *noms de guerre*. One volunteer, an electrician by trade, enlisted and served under the British name of Jack Greenhalgh.[133] However, he was certainly of French nationality; he had seen previous military service in the Armistice Army.

---

129   The author has seen the dictionary.

130   Marotin, "*La Longue Marche*", page 46. According to Soulat, "*Histoire de la Division Charlemagne*", page 4, Zimmermann was the most popular German officer among the volunteers because of his diplomacy and his knowledge of Parisian slang.

131   Gaulois, article '*Mein Freund Georges*'.

132   Also of interest to note is that a volunteer by the Jewish name of Goldstein served in the 1st Company of the LVF.

133   Volunteers with British names had served in the LVF. One was Alexander Hill. Another was Richard Ryding, who was well known to Mercier. Of French nationality, 'Dick' also had British blood in him. He was perfectly bilingual and spoke with a very slight niçois accent. P.P.F. militant, he had enlisted in the LVF at the end of 1941. However, the Germans were opposed against his going to Russia and assigned him to office duties with the Ersatz Kommando at Breslau, then Kruszyna. Ryding told Mercier that he admired the shrewdness of the Germans who feared a dangerous individual like him going to a lost corner of Russia, but entrusted to him the most confidential dossiers of the regiment (Mercier, letter to the author, 24/9/2001).

Later, quite by chance, Vaxelaire was surprised to meet an old school friend. They had been together in the same class at *lycée* Carnot. Since then they had lost contact and each of them had no idea that the other had enlisted. As it turned out they met only the once. The name of Vaxelaire's friend was Robert Blanc. He had arrived at Wildflecken with the *Milice*.

CHAPTER 6

'Charlemagne' Welcomes the
Milice française

The Miliciens arrive

O n 5th November 1944, the *Miliciens* arrived at Wildflecken[1] and made their way to Adolf Hitler Platz in French dark-blue and khaki uniforms 'with berets pulled down over one eye'.[2] They carried captured British Sten guns, as well as 'Smith and Wesson' and American 'Colt' revolvers. At their head marched *Capitaine* Jean Bassompierre[3] and at the head of the first *Cohorte* was *Capitaine* Émile Raybaud.[4]

The air of the *Miliciens* was unashamedly very anti-German. Yet was this not the same *Milice* that over the past year had become closely identified in the popular mind with the Nazi cause?[5]

1   According to Saint-Loup, page 145, the *Miliciens* marched to the *chasseur* step. Some units of *franc-gardes* may have, but the majority marched to the *pas normal de l'armée française*. The *chasseur* step is very fast and requires particular training. Robert Blanc, who arrived at Wildflecken with the *Milice*, said of the step: "My unit marched to the *pas normal de l'armée française*. Otherwise, I assure you I would have remembered it!"

2   De la Mazière, page 53.

3   According to Mabire, page 168, *Capitaine* Bassompierre was wearing his former Wehrmacht field grey uniform with the tricolore badge of the LVF. This is unlikely. Bassompierre was a *milicien* through and through. He would not have 'deserted' his men in this way.

4   According to Mabire, Raybaud was wearing all his decorations. This is not true. Mabire continues on page 171 that when Raybaud collected his Waffen-SS uniform his chest was covered in decorations won in action against the Germans. This too is not true. In fact, at no time did Raybaud wear decorations in the *Milice* or in the Waffen-SS, letter from Raybaud to Mabire, 3/11/74, and for good reason; the *croix de guerre avec palms*, awarded to Raybaud at the end of the 39-40 war, was not sanctioned following the intervention of his corps commander, Cdt. Carolet, because Raybaud had dissociated himself from his former military comrades when the Armée Secrète was formed and joined the *Milice* instead.

5   There is great debate on whether or not the *Miliciens* entered Wildflecken defiantly singing '*Sambre et Meuse*' and '*La Madelon*'. For the most part, this version is confirmed by the professional authors but is not substantiated by eyewitness accounts nor Léfèvre. However, René Forez, a *franc-garde*, remembers that '*Sambre et Meuse*' and '*La Madelon*' were sung on their entrance but remarked that this was not to defy the Germans. He explained that they were singing in French because they did not know any German songs. Curiously, according to Mabire, page 168, the *Miliciens* also sang the *Panzerlied* because 'they were proud to enter an assault unit'.

The Maintenance of Order

On 4th December 1943, Marshal Pétain was handed an ultimatum from Hitler that demanded greater action against the resistance and that Déat, Henriot and Darnand be brought into the Vichy government. Pétain bowed to these demands, though he held out against the appointment of Déat whose attacks on Vichy in *L'Oeuvre* had infuriated him.

On 30th December 1943, Darnand was named Secretary General for the Maintenance of Order. This post replaced that of the Secretary General of the Police. Two days later, on 1st January 1944, Darnand and Henriot took up their duties. On the 10th of that same month, Darnand was granted full powers over 'all the police forces; all bodies and formations that assure public security and the internal safety of the state'.

Ten days later, on the 20th, Law No 38, signed by Pierre Laval, conferred new powers on Darnand. Under this new law, Darnand was authorised as the Secretary General for the Maintenance of Order to establish court-martials at the request of *intendants de police* to judge immediately those individuals caught in flagrante delicto committing 'assassination or murder, and attempted assassination or murder'.

As such, this new law suspended the judicial guarantees under Common Law. The proceedings were closed; the accused was not permitted a defence counsel; there was no right of appeal and the sentence, invariably execution, was discharged immediately.

To protect the identity of the three-judge panel, chosen by Darnand as 'the Secretary General for the maintenance of order', no transcripts were written up and the verdict was often left unsigned or signed illegibly. It is often alleged that *chefs* of the *Milice* frequently carried out this mockery of justice, but few of the judges were ever identified!

That same month, in the pages of *Combats*, the *Milice* newspaper, Darnand proclaimed: "Do not be afraid of being only small in number. Throughout history from time immemorial it was always the handful of men who have forced destiny." Destiny now awaited the *Milice* in the Haute-Savoie.

In January 1944, Darnand initiated a police campaign against the maquis of Glières in the Haute-Savoie. He nominated Colonel Lelong of the gendarmerie as the *directeur des opérations*. He had at his disposal 19 *pelotons* [platoons] *de gendarmerie*, 12 *escadrons* [platoons/squadrons] *de gardes mobilies* and, finally, 5 *escadrons de groupes mobiles de réserve* (GMR). In all, some 2,200 men.

The results of the campaign were so disappointing that Darnand sent in some 700 to 800 *Miliciens*, including some 400 *francs-gardes permanents*.[6] The *Milicens* were organised into two ad hoc battle units. The *2° unité de la Franc-Garde* (or *2° unité de Franc-Gardes*), commanded by Jacques Dugé de Bernonville, consisted of units (probably *centaine* sized) under Di Constanzo, Mongourd, Perrin and de Bourmont.

Darnand appointed *Commandant de la Franc-Garde permanente* de Vaugelas to take command of the *Milice* forces engaged in Haute-Savoie 'against the

---

6   Delperrié de Bayac, page 320. Remarkably, one source, which shall not be named, records that some 7,000 to 8,000 *Miliciens* were actually sent in!

outlaws'.[7] Born on 2nd January 1913 in Paris, Jean de Vaugelas attended the *École de l'Air*.[8] In 1939, he was promoted to *sous-lieutenant de réserve*. His war was rather lacklustre as an administrative officer.[9] 1942 brought him promotion to *lieutenant*. Subsequently he served in Vichy's *Chantiers de la Jeunesse*, but had to leave 'through lack of adapting himself to the state of spirit of this organisation'.[10] He joined the *Milice* while still in its infancy and brought his two brothers along with him.

Proving to be a born leader, de Vaugelas enjoyed a meteoric rise through the ranks of the *Milice*. He became the *chef régional* at Marseille and then, after the departure of du Vair, the *Chef de l'école* of the *École des Cadres* at Uriage. In Feb. 1944, he took a more active role in the fight against the resistance when he left Uriage to take command of the forces of the *Franc-Garde* participating in the Maintenance of Order operations in the Haute-Savoie.

A monarchist, de Vaugelas was not sentimentally or ideologically pro-German. A commander, he did not tolerate theft or breaches of discipline. This intelligent, sometimes insolent officer had character and presence, and was held in great esteem by all which somewhat displeased Darnand and the political wing of the *Milice*. Although his relationship with Darnand was often strained, he was ardently devoted to the *Milice*.[11]

At Glières, de Vaugelas was ably assisted by two career officers, *Capitaine* Victor de Bourmont and *Capitaine* Émile Raybaud.

Born on 5th May 1907, Victor de Bourmont was the great grandson of Louis, comte de Ghaisnes de Bourmont.[12] In 1927, he entered the celebrated *École spéciale militaire de* Saint-Cyr. Two years later, he graduated as a *sous-lieutenant d'active* in the infantry. On 25th December 1938, he was promoted to *Capitaine*. By now, he was serving in a Tunisian Tirailleur Regiment.[13] Taken prisoner in 1940, he

7   See de Vaugelas' *citation à l'ordre de la Nation* published in the *Journal Officiel* of 8th July 1944.

8   According to Mabire, page 118, Jean de Vaugelas was thrown out of the *École de l'Air* after refusing to reply to a coloured officer. In a letter to the author, 20/3/97, Lefèvre states that this is untrue.

9   Research provided by Lefèvre. This corrects Giolitto's portrayal of de Vaugelas during the 1939-40 war, see page 171, as a lieutenant in a *escadrille combattante* [fighting squadron].

10 *Achives nationales* F 60 514.

11 According to Delperrié de Bayac, page 320, de Vaugelas had another side to his character. At the end of March 1944, after the attack on the plateau of Glières, he summarily executed a prisoner, a veteran of the 27 e BCA. Later, when speaking of the execution with a *Milicien*, also of the 27 e BCA and who knew the person in question, de Vaugelas told him: "What a pity. I thought he was a Communist." For him, a Communist was not a human being.

12 Ghaisnes de Bourmont, who was made a *Maréchal de France*, went over to the enemy on the eve of the battle of Ligny in 1815. He served the Restoration, becoming Charles X's minister of war in 1829, and commanded the expedition that seized Algeria for France in 1830, although he later fell into disgrace.

13 Research provided by Lefèvre. This corrects Mabire, page 115, that de Bourmont was serving in 1939 as a regular lieutenant in a Moroccan Tirailleur Regiment.

volunteered one year later to fight in Vichy Syria. By the time he was released, the fighting was as good as over. He went instead to the Armistice army. On its disbandment he passed to the *Milice*, attracted more by its military trappings than its political doctrines. He became the *chef régional* at Lyon. He was a monarchist and a legitimist. Although at times moody, he was loved by his men. Small in stature, he was overshadowed by Raybaud.

Born on 3rd July 1910[14] in Trans, Émile Raybaud attended the *École spéciale militaire de* Saint-Cyr between the years of 1930–1932. Graduating as a *sous-lieutenant d'active* in the infantry, he was posted to the elite 20e BCA (*bataillon de Chasseurs alpins*) at Antibes. On 1st April 1940, he was promoted to *Capitaine*. Two months later, he found himself on the Somme with his division, the *40e Division de Chasseurs*, fighting the Germans. In defeat, he joined the Armistice Army.[15]

Although not politically orientated, *Capitaine* Raybaud was a fervent supporter of Pétain's National Revolution that promised to rejuvenate France. He too came to the *Milice* after the Armstice Army was disbanded and, in April 1943, became the *Directeur Adjoint* [assistant director] at the *École des Cadres de la Milice* at Uriage. He worked well with *directeur de l'école de* Vaugelas and, in February 1944, he left his post at Uriage to join de Vaugelas as his Chief-of-Staff for the Maintenance of Order operation in Haute-Savoie.[16]

A soldier Raybaud had been and a soldier he would remain. Side by side on his tunic, he wore the gamma of the *Milice française* and the hunting horn of the *Chasseurs alpins*. A traditional officer, he had much in common with de Bourmont. They both had nothing but contempt for the thugs, policemen and opportunists recruited of late to the *Milice*. They had little interest in political intrigues and were wary of the *partisans de la collaboration* and also of the *cagoulard* stance of some *chefs* of the *Milice*. Devoted to their men, they did not shun their responsibilities whatever the circumstances. Raybaud and de Bourmont epitomised the 'professional' side of the *Milice*.

However, the *gendarmes* of the *gardes mobilies* and the GMR at Glières did not regard the *Miliciens* as professionals, but amateurs, worse still amateurs of *style bravache*.[17] Indeed, relations between the *gendarmes* and the *Miliciens* were poor.

The combined French forces, which were in need of air support, could still not disperse the maquis by themselves. The Germans intervened and, on 26th March 1944, crushed the maquis on the plateau of Glières. The *Milice* was now relegated to the capture of isolated maquisards and the interrogation of the local population.

In a series of radio broadcasts, Philippe Henriot, the Vichy Secretary of State for Propaganda and Information, glorified the role of the *Milice* in this 'historic victory for French discipline and order' over an assortment of terrorists, assassins

---

14   Research provided by Soulat. However, according to a non-referenced wartime document of German origin, his date of birth was 19th May 1910.

15   As a serving officer in the Armistice Army, Raybaud is unlikely to have been a member of the *Légion Française des Combattants* (as cited by Mabire, page 115).

16   Research provided by Lefèvre. This corrects Delperrié de Bayac, page 249, repeated by Giolitto, page 171, that Raybaud succeeded de Vaugelas as the *Chef de l'École* when he left Uriage to take command of the forces of the *Franc-Garde* participating in the Maintenance of Order operations in the Haute-Savoie.

17   Delperrié de Bayac, page 322.

and cowards. Notably, not one word was mentioned of the German presence at Glières.

On 8th July 1944, the *Journal Officiel* of the French state mentioned de Vaugelas in dispatches. The citation explained that as the commander of the *Milice* forces engaged against the outlaws in the Haute-Savoie he had shown tireless ardour and exemplary courage which had filled with admiration his *chefs*, his comrades and his men. As a result, he had given his troops the impetus to successfully execute the final assault against the rebels on the plateau of Glières.

The Maintenance of Order operation against the maquis in the Haute-Savoie was the first of many such operations throughout the whole of France in which the *Milice* participated. The Limousin, where the maquis was great in number and active, was now targeted.

On 8th April 1944, de Vaugelas was appointed *directeur du Maintien de l'Ordre* to the administrative region of Limoges. This gave him authority over the Police and all Vichy forces in the Limousin. With him, he brought some two hundred *francs-gardes* who had just participated in the operation at Glières, *Capitaine* Raybaud,[18] who would be his assistant, and *Capitaine* de Bourmont.

The forces of the Maintenance of Order had a total strength of some 6,000 men. However, only the *Miliciens* were prepared to take the fight to the terrorists and they were small in number.

In April, the forces of the Maintenance of Order were organised into five groups; A, B, C, D, and E. *Capitaine* de Bourmont commanded Group E that comprised one *Franc-Garde Cohorte* and one GMR company. *Chef* Mongourd commanded one of the three *centaines* of the *Franc-Garde Cohorte*.

Outnumbered, the forces of the Maintenance of Order could do little more than contain the maquis.

On 7th June 1944, in response to the Allied landing in Normandy, Darnand mobilised the *Milice* in a radio speech he made to the *forces du Maintien de l'Ordre*. He stormed:

> The orders are clear. Consider as enemies of France the Franc-Tireurs and Partisans, the members of the so-called Secret Army and those bands of resistance. Attack the saboteurs, whether or not they have landed by parachute. Hunt down the traitors who are trying to sap the morale of our formations. Face them like the G.M.R. in Haute-Savoie, like the Garde in the Limousin scrub.

The maintenance of order operation in the Limousin went on. *Capitaine* Raybaud, who still believed in a German victory because 'morale is with us', succeeded de Vaugelas. Lieutenant Géromini replaced de Bourmont.

Following the collapse of the short-lived *Groupes de Protection*, Géromini resumed service with the Colonial Army and left for Senegal. He started out back to France less than one week before the Allied landings in North Africa. By the time he arrived back home, the Armistice Army no longer existed. He entered the *École d'administration militaire* (relocated to Marseille) where he became bored. Contacted by Darnand and asked to come over to the *Milice*, Géromini refused. Months later, Darnand was to try again and invited Géromini to Vichy. Darnand

---

18   According to Giolitto, Raybaud only left his post at the *École des Cadres* at Uriage in May 1944. However, this is incorrect (research provided by Lefèvre).

spoke to him of the *École des Cadres* at Uriage where veterans of the 24e BCA were or through which they had passed. Géromini hesitated. Darnand then asked: "Do you imagine that I want to betray France? France must be rebuilt. We will do a good job." Now troubled, Géromini still 'did not jump'. Darnand brought out his trump card: photos of the *franc-gardes* of the *Milice* 'with the flag'. Géromini saw *Chasseurs alpins*, his former branch in the Army. He was won over.

From the moment he arrived at Uriage, Géromini knew that his decision to join had not been misguided. 'He was seduced by the setting, the chateau on its spur, the ambience that reigned at the school: France to be rebuilt, the new knight-hood'.[19] However, of concern were the pictures of German and Waffen-SS soldiers pinned up by the *aspirants* and trainees in the bedrooms. He had them removed.

With regard the Germans, Géromini once said: "We have a duty to keep our distance. We must keep our dignity."[20] This he would do.

Of a fiery-nature, Géromini quickly proved troublesome to his superiors and the Germans during the Maintenance of Order operations in the Limousin. Four or five of his *francs-gardes* had enlisted in the Waffen-SS without his authorisation and when they were seen dressed in German uniforms he had them arrested. A high ranking SS officer came to see Géromini and ordered him to release the prisoners. This Géromini refused, retorting that his *francs-gardes* did not have the right to enlist in the Waffen-SS without first submitting their intentions to their commander. He won the day.

On 20th July 1944, Raybaud ordered Géromini to operate alongside the Germans against the maquis. He refused point-blank. Raybaud then replied: "You are the only one capable of preventing exactions from the Germans. It is your duty to go." Géromini agreed. A sincere patriot, he declared in 1967: "My idea was not to fight against Frenchmen and to limit the damage."

Three days later, Lieutenant Géromini saved thirty of his fellow countrymen at Eymoutiers from a German firing squad after the maquis had ambushed their column. On the following day, Géromini and one of his assistants intervened on behalf of a wounded terrorist who a German NCO was about to finish off. A fiery altercation developed. The German NCO called his men to his aid and Géromini did likewise. The two groups faced each other, with the wounded terrorist between them. A German officer was consulted who sided with Géromini, but later the Germans reproached Géromini for his incorrect attitude towards the German NCO and pressurised the appropriate French authorities to relieve him of his command.

On 25th July 1944, Raybaud was promoted *adjoint* to Dr. Rainsart, *chef de la Franc-Garde de zone Nord*.

From April to August 1944, between thirty and forty *francs-gardes* were killed in combat against the maquis in the Limousin.

Pour la Milice, justice

In the maintenance of order operations in the Haute-Savoie and the Limousin the *Milice* participated in great numbers and in the manner of regular military forces. Far more often the *Milice* operated alone in small numbers. They were employed to

19   Delperrié de Bayac, page 250.
20   Delperrié de Bayac, page 428.

search out, infiltrate and destroy resistance networks, round up and guard resistance suspects, and provide security for all kind of potential resistance targets.[21]

Occasionally, units of the *Franc-Garde* did find themselves on military operations fighting side by side with the German Police and Army against the maquis, but there was no common command. The *Franc-Garde* only operated under the control of the French authorities charged with the Maintenance of Order, the *intendants de police* who became *intendants du Maintien de l'Ordre* in April 1944, and possibly provincial *directeurs du Maintien de l'Ordre*. As such, *Milice* forces did not operate 'hand in glove' with the Gestapo, the SD or the German Police. In fact, the *Milice* and the German authorities usually regarded each other as a mutual enemy and co-operation between the two was frowned upon without prior discussion at 'high levels'![22]

The Maintenance of Order was but one role for the *Milice* and was not the sole responsibility of the *Milice*. Both Laval and Pétain ardently supported the *Milice* in its war against the 'terrorists'. Indeed, on more than one occasion, Pétain complimented the head of the *Milice* on his success in maintaining order.

To its credit, the *Milice* handed over its prisoners to the appropriate French authorities rather than to the German authorities. However, towards the end of the occupation, maquis prisoners were actually handed over direct to the Germans, but this practice was not commonplace and often resulted from the frequent release of prisoners and suspects by the French authorities. At times, refusal by the *Milice* to hand over prisoners provoked the Germans to seize them.

Accusations of wholesale torture, murder, extortion, rape and robbery are repeatedly levelled at the *Milice*. While there were isolated instances, this cannot be denied, the criminal outrages of the maquis and the resistance certainly surpassed those of the *Milice* in scale and brutality! Furthermore, unlike the maquis, *Miliciens* were held accountable for their actions and were severely punished for breaches of discipline.[23]

There were acts of revenge perpetrated by *Miliciens*, but this was in response to 'terrorist' outrages. Needless to say, every army at war has been guilty of acts of revenge. Assassinations of *Miliciens* were paid back in kind after November 1943 by which time thirty-three defenceless members of the *Milice française*, including a young woman and a priest, had already been murdered. However, this was the work of individual *Miliciens* and not a policy conducted by the *Milice* as a whole. Joseph Lécussan, the regional head of the *Milice* in Lyon, and other *Miliciens* acted on their own initiative and without orders when they murdered elderly Victor Basch, President of the League for the Rights of Man, and his wife in January 1944.

21   According to Sweets, page 95, 'the *Milice* operated in conjunction with German police or the strong-arm bands hired by the German Labor Service to track down individuals for deportation for work in Germany'. In response, *Milicien* Robert Blanc has 'never heard of this particular mission' (letter to the author, 4/12/2004).

22   For example, on two occasions, General Gleininger, the Feldkommandant at Limoges, formally requested the *direction du Maintien de l'Ordre* [the directorate of the Maintenance of Order] to sanction the intervention of the *Milice* and the forces of the Maintenance of Order and was refused.

23   For example, after raping a female prisoner, Jean Roger Thomine, a *Milicien*, was arrested by his superiors and ejected from the *Milice*.

When the bodies were found there was a card pinned to the clothes of Victor Basch that read: "Terror against Terror". For this brutal crime, Darnand dismissed Lécussan from the *Milice.*

The *chef de centre de la Milice* at Voiron, Isère, was a certain Jourdan. On the evening of 20th April 1944, two students entered his house, shot him down and his two bodyguards, and then proceeded to butcher four members of his family, including his daughter, aged fifteen months. The two students and their school supervisor, an accessory, were apprehended and shot by a *Milice* firing squad in front of twenty students and teachers from the same school.[24] Terror against terror.

On 28th June 1944, Philippe Henriot, the Vichy Secretary of State for Propaganda and Information, was assassinated at his Ministry of Information apartment in Paris. The *Milice* took reprisals. At Mâcon, for example, seven resistance suspects were executed. Also, the notable Republican Georges Mandel, Reynaud's former minister of the interior and leading member of the Third Republic who had opposed both the armistice and Pétain taking power, was murdered by a *Milicien* named Mansuy. It is not known who, or if anybody, gave Mansuy the order to kill Mandel, but it was neither Darnand nor Laval. He was probably acting alone. Again, terror against terror.

The *Milice française* as a whole, which numbered some 29,000 adherents at its peak, should not be judged, nor condemned, by the actions of a handful of a more violent and unsavoury disposition. More often than not, the *Milice* is portrayed as recruiting into its ranks the dregs of the French underworld and those who foresaw opportunities for booty and loot, but many of its recruits joined out of political commitment, considering themselves superpatriots who would save France from Communism and ruin. They were predominantly from the Right and the far Right but few were genuine National Socialists. A great number of *Miliciens* were, in fact, anti-German French Nationalists! Indeed, a maquis leader of the Secret Army wrote:[25]

> The majority of the *Miliciens* we captured were able to present their defence. Almost all protested their patriotism. Almost all recognised that they had helped the Germans. One said to me: "I'm anti-Communist. I believe the Communists are commanding you". Another declared to me: "You have won but Europe has lost. To save Europe we had to march with Hitler".

To be a *Milicien* in 1944 was to have the courage of one's convictions. The *Milicien* was isolated. The *Milicien* aroused the hostility of most French people. The *Milicien* risked personal harm and so did his family. It took genuine courage to stand up and be counted as a *Milicien*, more so after the Allied landing in Normandy. Georges Cazalot of the *Avant-Garde de la Milice, Centaine* 'Gascogne',[26] wrote of this situation:[27]

24   According to Delperrié de Bayac, page 296, the onlookers were later shipped off to Germany where nearly all would die in concentration camps. Some sources, however, dispute this chain of events.
25   Delperrié de Bayac, page 552.
26   This designation may not have been the official title of his unit, but was definitely used.

Almost one month ago the forces of invasion landed on the Norman coasts …
Parallel to this invasion the forces of subversion raised their head and left the
woods and mountains where until then they had carefully been hiding, only descending into the plains and the towns very cautiously and when absolutely necessary. Now the dogs are let loose. It's not only acts of sabotage and murder
attempts on isolated people and unarmed civilians, [but] ambushes on small detachments, kidnappings and assassinations of awkward notables or political opponents, indeed personal enemies who have nothing to do with the war or
politics, attacks on tobacconists – tobacco and wine are, it seems, the sinews of
the war for these bandits – and town halls to steal food coupons …

All these bandits spread through the countryside, pillaging and plunder-
ing, raping and burning, indulging themselves, [and] sowing terror. France
slowly sinks into anarchy. The majority of the *forces de police*, infiltrated, that
courage is not the first virtue, that the verb 'to serve' has been banished from the
list of their duties, wait to see which way the wind is going to blow, keep weapons at their feet when they don't go over to subversion, and wait to shout in
chorus with the victor.

Alone, courageous and lucid in this squall carrying along the homeland,
the *Milice* faces [up to] things and fights. It fights against this immense rotten-
ness spreading over us, against this havoc trying to submerge us and suffocate
us, against the decay of our Society, against Bolshevism, a suppurating cancer
gripping us and eating away at us.

Above all the *Milice* was a public utility French Association which was sanctioned and subsidised by a legitimate French Government. And notably it too, like
many other organisations of the State, sought to implement Pétain's National
Revolution in all sectors of public life. But it was a National Revolution that few
French people wanted.

The *départ*

In the last weeks of the occupation Darnand directed *Milice* units 'out in the field'
to seize hostages if the local population showed itself to be hostile. One source poi-
gnantly remarks 'it was if the *Milice* were operating on foreign soil'.[28] Even Marshal
Pétain, once an ardent supporter of the *Milice*, came out against its brutal methods
in a letter to Laval dated 6th August 1944, protesting:

> The *Milice* has gained a hideous reputation of using methods which I knew well
> when they were used by the Reds in Spain. I cannot pass over in silence the
> tortures inflicted on victims who are often innocent, in places which, even in
> Vichy, are less like French State Prisons than Bolshevik Chekas. By these
> methods, the *Milice* has succeeded in establishing an atmosphere of police
> terror which has been unknown in our country till today.

Faced with the prospect of German defeat in France, thousands of *Miliciens*
and their families fled towards the East. It was chaotic and desperate. They had no
illusions about their fate if they should fall into the hands of their countrymen. For

27   Cazalot, *"…Et la terre a bu leur sang!"*, page 15.
28   Sweets, page 96.

some, however, the evacuation was also an 'expedition'. This was the view of those from Bretagne.

Darnand sent *Commandant* of the *Franc-Garde permanente* de Vaugelas to Limoges to organise the evacuation of the encircled Vichy forces. As there was no longer any question of reaching Limoges by road, de Vaugelas arrived by plane. He was in the company of de Londaiz. Feverishly, he set about his task. At midday on 16th August 1944, a convoy of ninety-five vehicles, carrying between 400 and 500 *Miliciens*, and some 350 women and children, set off. Destination: the town of Guéret, approximately seventy kilometres away.

That same day, the convoy was ambushed twice, but managed to keep going, covering some twenty-five kilometres. On the following morning, the convoy stopped before trees placed across the road and was caught in strong crossfire: three *Miliciens* were killed and thirteen were wounded, including *chef de trentaine* Aumont. Unable to pass, de Vaugelas gave the order to turn around, but they now found the way back blocked. Encircled, de Vaugelas sent out a distress call that was received by the Germans at Limoges. Troops were promised to free the convoy. The *Milice* forces dug in.

On the 18th, little changed. Patrols were sent out which beat a hasty withdrawal after engaging.

Finally, on the 19th, the 2nd Schutzpolizei Company of Limoges came to the rescue. Assisted by the Germans, the convoy continued east and crossed the gorges of Taurion. Once on the other bank, they parted ways. Just outside Bourganeuf, the *Milice* convoy was ambushed again, losing vehicles to mines and mortars, but de Vaugelas and Géromini forced their way through to the town which was held by a small German garrison. Their roles reversed, the *Miliciens* were now able to render assistance to the Germans and beat off a maquis attack, but one third of their vehicles had been damaged or were in tow. It took days to repair them. Together the *Miliciens* and the Germans set off. Finally, on the 23rd, they arrived at Guéret. It had taken eight days to cover seventy kilometres.

'Toulouse' also had a narrow escape. On 10th August, de Perricot, the *chef régional* of 'Toulouse', sent messengers to the *chefs départmentaux* with orders to assemble. In the days that followed, his forces concentrated without serious incident. He then sent the women and children ahead by train under the command of Dr. Sailhant. The *Miliciens* set out by road with the Wehrmacht, SS and Gestapo.

Harassed from the air, dogged by delays and skirmishes, they came to Montpellier where de Perricot had the unpleasant surprise of finding the train that he had sent on its way from Toulouse days earlier. Although he did not have enough vehicles to take the women and children along, the Montpellier Red Cross agreed to give them protection. However, this protection was not extended to the *Miliciens* who stayed behind with the women and children. Dr. Sailhant and seven other *Miliciens* were shot days later.

The rest continued and reached the Rhône valley where the chaos only intensified. The *Milice* forces of 'Marseille' under the command of *chef régional* Dr. Durandy were already there. They went north. Machine-gunned and bombed non-stop by allied aircraft, 'Toulouse' split. The smaller group under de Perricot proceeded on the right bank to Lyon. Finally, they arrived at Belfort.

Not all proved able to escape. Many were overtaken by the liberation, unleashing the intense hatred the *Milice* had provoked in the overwhelming majority of the population. The retribution was swift and bloody. Many *Miliciens* and family members were arrested and summarily executed by the maquis or mobs. One *chef* of the *Francs-Tireurs et Partisans*[29] or F.T.P. declared:

> We did not take *Milicien* prisoners, especially at the start. They were executed as soon as they were captured. When we entered Lyon we shot about thirty.

A combined German and *Milicien* force was encircled at Estivareilles. After a brief fight, it decided to surrender. The Germans were treated as POWs whereas *chef départemental* Le Tellier, his wife, and twenty *Miliciens* were shot. They went to their death singing *La Marseillaise*.

Those *Miliciens* hauled before special tribunals, court martials or resistance courts were invariably and predictably sentenced to death and executed. When the *Milice* forces of 'Annecy' could not extricate themselves the *chef départemental* negotiated surrender terms with the *Résistance* who guaranteed that the *Miliciens* were to be treated as POWs. One hundred and thirty *Miliciens*, including a number of trainees from the *École des Cadres d'Uriage*, surrendered. Contrary to the resistance promise, the *Miliciens* were brought before a tribunal on which sat three members of the F.T.P. and two of the *Armée secrète*. Seventy-four of the *Miliciens* were condemned to death and the sentences were carried out on 24th August.

Suffice to say, author Delperrié de Bayac considered it difficult to find a city or village 'where there were *Miliciens* and where *Miliciens* were not executed in August or September 1944'.

In mid-September 1944, the great majority of the fleeing *Miliciens* were assembled at the camp of Natzwiller-Struthof, near the city of Schirmeck. There was great debate about the future. Many were those who now wanted to leave the *Milice*, but only thirty or so of their number slipped from the camp. Some would reach the Swiss frontier, where they were interned and then quickly handed over to French justice, while others were captured by the German police on the roads of Alsace and shot on the spot as 'deserters'.

Each day the French flag was hoisted over the part of the camp occupied by the *Miliciens*.

Darnand came to camp Struthof to take his *Milice* in hand. He started by reducing every officer to the ranks. Only those who had proved themselves received army ranks. In this way, some *chefs* fell into disgrace. Darnand was everywhere, bawling out those with incorrectly creased uniforms, those who could not properly present arms or those who looked sleepy-eyed. It was the guardhouse for those with a button missing or with dust in a rifle barrel.

One day, Darnand called together the *Miliciens* and announced to them that they were going to cross over into Germany and that their military training would continue under French command. He added that this crossing might not be final

---

29 The F.T.P. were the Communist *résistants* and although most F.T.P. groups only accepted orders from the French Communist Party they sometimes formed local alliances with the *Armée secrète*.

because the Reich was preparing a great offensive and the *Milice* would return to France with the Germans.[30] The reaction was mixed. For Marotin from the *Trentaine Alpine de Savoie de la Franc-Garde permanente*, exile was of no importance. In his words:

> The same fight still continued and the objective was the same as our enemies were still the same ... Thus I had no moral problems or uncertainties.

On the evening of 19th September,[31] the *Miliciens* left Struthof on foot and embarked at Schirmeck railway station. They crossed the Rhine that same day. Marotin wrote that 'they were now in a friendly country' and that 'there were no more terrorists'.[32] To celebrate, they emptied their guns into the air. On the 22nd, they arrived at Ulm on the Danube.

The companies disembarked in good order and went to a barracks and various schools. The 3rd *Cohorte* (Lyon) under *Capitaine* de Bourmont was quartered in a school in the heart of the city. The re-organisation, started at Struthof, continued. Discipline was very strict. Training resumed. Endless arms drills, parades, route marches and manoeuvres. *Jurys d'honneur* were set up to decide the cases of those *Miliciens* who 'had gone too far'. Some left the *Milice* before they were expelled.

Marotin was promoted to sergeant, one of the few appointments made in Germany, and proudly recalls that the papers were signed by the hand of Darnand. This earned him the comical and mocking nickname of '*Sergent de Darnand*'! Marotin remembers that the local population adopted them and made them feel as if they were still *chez nous*.

Around 5,000 *Miliciens*, mostly *franc-gardes*, were finally assembled at Ulm. For the most part, all still remained fiercely loyal to Darnand. At their head was Jean Bassompierre. A *Milicien* through and through, he too was devoted to Darnand. After *La Légion Tricolore* was dissolved, he went across to the LVF. Serving as a company commander in the I. Battalion with the rank of *Capitaine*, he received the Iron Cross 2nd Class. He was Battalion commander for a short time. In December 1943, he was appointed Puaud's Chief-of-staff, but Darnand, now Secretary General for the maintenance of order, also had need of him. In February 1944, Bassompierre was recalled by Darnand to organise the *Milice française* in the North zone as its *Inspecteur général*. His name is forever connected with the revolt of four thousand prisoners at *la Santé* Prison, Paris, on 14th July. Admittedly he led the suppression of the revolt, but the German authorities wanted to punish four hundred prisoners with execution and he alone managed to talk them down to no more than fifty executions.[33] On 16th August, he left France with the Parisian *cohorte des miliciens*.

---

30   Delperrié de Bayac, page 563. However, according to Voiron, page 117, "*Historia #40, La Milice*", Darnand left each free to decide according to their conscience, but invited all to follow him.

31   Blanc, corrections to the author, 2001. [Blanc has cause to remember this day well]. This corrects Mabire who cites on page 107 that on 21st September the *Miliciens* went over to Germany.

32   Marotin, page 36.

33   Two or three prisoners who were caught with weapons were executed immediately.

A *Franc-Garde Cohorte* of several hundred *Miliciens* under de Vaugelas was sent to Sigmaringen rather than Ulm. This *Cohorte* comprised those *Miliciens* that their *chef* had extricated from the maquis infested Limousin. Its mission at Sigmaringen, the seat of exiled French collaboration, was to uphold 'the armed presence of the *Milice* beside Marshal Pétain'.[34] But its presence could also be interpreted as a demonstration of Darnand's continued power before the impotent *'Commission Gouvernementale française pour la defénse des intérêts français en Allemagne'* (Governmental Commission for the defence of French interests in Germany, otherwise the French government-in-exile). Moreover, by now, Pétain had divorced himself from any political and official role and considered himself a prisoner of the Germans. On 1st October 1944, he refused to attend the raising of the tricolore over this French refuge and opted to stay in his bedroom. All the same, the ceremony went ahead with an honour guard partly supplied by the *Franc-Garde Cohorte*. Pétain had turned his back on the *Milice*. In turn, the *Miliciens* began to turn their back on their idol. Later, Pétain refused to allow a platoon of *Miliciens* to pay him tribute as he came and went from his chateau. He also refused to be guarded by them.

Work or fight?

But what now for the *Miliciens* in exile? Since their arrival at Ulm, rumour had it that all fighting Frenchmen were to be amalgamated in a special unit. Was there any truth in this?

At Ulm, Darnand and other French *chefs collaborateurs* met several times with SS officers to discuss the creation of what was to become 'Charlemagne'.[35]

On 1st September, Hitler summoned Darnand and other leading French collaborationists to talk about the creation of a new French government. During the meeting the Führer said to Darnand: "The men of the *Milice* died for a great cause, and, like those at Stalingrad, they did not die in vain." After listening to the translation, Darnand thanked him. No more was said about the *Milice* or its future. Nevertheless, the future of the *Milice* was a subject of conversation among high-ranking Nazi officials.

On 6th September, Darnand met with SS-Ogruf. Hofmann and was told that Sennheim camp could not accommodate the *Milice* because of a lack of space.

The following day, Gauleiter Wagner wrote that Darnand intended, after eliminating those unfit for military service, to integrate the *Milice* as an elite troop into the Waffen-SS or with German agreement as an autonomous French unit.[36]

At the end of September 1944, Darnand and SS-Ogruf. Berger of the SS-Hauptamt held preliminary discussions about the future of the *Milice*. Darnand was accompanied by his friend Henry Charbonneau who was of the opinion that the best course of action for the *Miliciens* was to enlist in the Waffen-SS and to go and fight the Reds on the Eastern front.

34   Mabire, page 117.
35   Eyewitness account of André Doulard [pseudonym] who acted as an interpreter (Mounine, correspondence to the author, 1999).
36   The addressee is an unknown Obergruppenführer (see Mounine, "*Cernay 40-45*", page 344).

Although Darnand and Berger had met several times before, Darnand was not at ease. He wished to keep the *Milice* intact for a future role when France was reconquered, but he realised that his *Miliciens* could not escape some form of mobilisation. And if or when his *Milice* disappeared, he would lose his trump card, in fact his only playing card.

Darnand was also concerned about the predominance of Doriot, his political rival. Although Berger assured Darnand that Doriot would have no role in the new French unit of the Waffen-SS, there was no mention of what his might be, if any.

Indeed, the meeting resolved little. Nevertheless, Darnand came away from the meeting certain that 'on entering the Waffen-SS, the *Miliciens* would not have to wear the runes on their uniforms, but an emblem created specially for them: a sword of *Jeanne d'Arc* surrounded with two *fleurs de lys*'.[37]

Beset by doubts, Darnand continued to hesitate about enlisting the *Miliciens* in the Waffen-SS.[38]

In early October 1944, when Brigf. Krukenberg received Darnand in Berlin, the real negotiations about the future of the *Milice* began. They would last weeks.

Brigf. Krukenberg announced to Darnand that RF-SS Himmler had decided to call this new French unit 'Charlemagne' and that the 'Frenchmen would not wear the SS insignia on their collar patch, but a sword like that of *Jeanne d'Arc*'.[39]

Darnand pressed for an answer about his future role in this new unit and also that of Doriot. The Germans could reassure him that Doriot would not be dominant in 'Charlemagne' and that Obf. Puaud was its commander.[40] However, this did not satisfy Darnand who suspected Puaud of being in league with Doriot.

On Saturday 7th and Sunday 8th October 1944, Darnand had discussions with Brigf. Krukenberg. In a letter to Reichsführer Himmler[41], Darnand wrote that the following 'questions of organisation' had now been agreed:

---

37   Roch, page 29. However, of note is that Mabire and Delperrié de Bayac also write of this same meeting, but do not confirm that Darnand came away with this understanding. According to Mabire, page 122, Darnand wanted his *Miliciens* to wear another device other than that of the SS runes, but that device is not specified.

38   According to Delperrié de Bayac, page 567, there was never any question of the *Milice* going over en bloc to the Waffen-SS!

39   Delperrié de Bayac, page 568. Note the use of the word Frenchmen rather than *Miliciens*. Thus, the possibility exists that the collar patch of the 'sword of Joan of Arc' may not have been only intended for former *Miliciens* in 'Charlemagne'. And yet, according to Littlejohn, page 172, 'Brigf. Krukenberg met Darnand's objections that his *Miliciens*, many of whom were devout Catholics, would refuse to wear the pagan runes of the SS, by saying they would not be called upon to do so but would have instead a sword like that of Joan of Arc'. This suggests that the collar patch of the 'sword of Joan of Arc' was only intended for former *Miliciens* in 'Charlemagne'.

40   Curiously, according to Delperrié de Bayac, page 568, the Germans indicated that 'Charlemagne' *would be* [author's italics] commanded by *Colonel* Puaud. [Mabire and Roch repeat as much at the meeting Himmler had with Darnand later.] In response to this, Puaud received the command of 'Charlemagne' as early as August. And that is, at least, one month before these negotiations! Also, Puaud held the Waffen-SS rank of Oberführer and the equivalent French Army rank of Oberführer is not that of *Colonel*.

The name of the Brigade was 'Charlemagne'.

The badge was the sword of Joan of Arc.

[*Milicien*] Officers and NCOs to be accepted into the Waffen-SS with the rank they held in the French Army.

The political and social committees of the LVF and Waffen-SS to be dissolved and that, in future, the questions within their domain he would settle as *Secrétaire d'Etat à l'Intérieur* and in his capacity as a member of the *commission gouvernementale française chargée de l'organisation des forces françaises nationales.*

They also agreed that the time was not right to form a pure *Milice* regiment because it might ignite the political differences. The idea of a pure *Milice* regiment was, in fact, that of Himmler. To Darnand and Krukenberg, the simplest solution seemed to maintain the two existing regiments, expand them to three battalions and divide the members of the *Milice* among the different units.

In the same letter, Darnand recognised that *Général* Puaud would command within the framework of a wholly independent military hierarchy while he 'would exercise his authority in agreement with Brigf. Krukenberg within the framework of his domain of political and social points of view over the French command of the unit'.

Of interest to note is that Darnand refers to himself again and again in no other role than that of a politician.

Soon after this letter, Darnand was received by RF-SS Himmler at his headquarters at Birkenwald. The meeting lasted two hours.

RF-SS Himmler spoke about the military situation, the secret weapons and assured Darnand that the 'V' weapons would not be used against Paris. He then questioned Darnand on the strength and motives of the various collaborationist political parties. He wanted to know the number of militants Doriot had with him in Germany. They spoke of Déat and his RNP, and Bucard and his *francistes*. Himmler then questioned him on the causes that had led to the failure of the collaborationist parties. Darnand was of the opinion that the collaborationist parties had failed because, in the eyes of Frenchmen, they appeared as 'movements in the pay of the occupier, in close collaboration with the Gestapo' and thus of rather little national character. Darnand could only see a movement gaining public support if it were purely French.

Himmler recognised that the Germans had made political mistakes in France and was critical of the lack of understanding shown by the German Ministry of Foreign Affairs and by the German ambassador in Paris. He declared that, in agreement with Hitler, he was prepared to support a purely national French movement which would keep its independence, its propaganda, its press, its radio and which would have sufficient broadness of outlook to assemble the Frenchmen in Germany and the opponents in France.[42] Then they came to the *Milice.*

41   Letter of 14th October 1944 from SS-Stf. Wagner to Dr. Brandt of the Personalstab RF-SS that reproduced and commented on the undated letter from Darnand to Himmler.

Himmler remarked that the *Miliciens* could not remain 'unoccupied' and presented Darnand with the following solution, perhaps better described as an ultimatum: one third of the *Miliciens* would have to enlist in 'Charlemagne'; another third, the oldest and those unfit for military service, would have to go to work in the factories of the Reich; and the last third were to remain in the *Franc-Garde* and form an autonomous unit.[43] As for the women and children of the *Miliciens*, these 'guests of the Reich' would be found accommodation with German families or in camps such as Siessen or Neckargmund.

Himmler then assured Darnand that the Frenchmen of 'Charlemagne' would remain under French command, have a French chaplain and never fight against the Western powers. He announced that they would now wear a tricolore shoulder badge and not the 'sword of Joan of Arc'.[44]

Without any real bargaining power, Darnand had little other choice than to 'admit defeat' and accept the solution put to him.

In closing, Himmler declared that Darnand was (or could be) 'the right man for the job' despite his strong nationalism. 'He pronounced the name of Doriot and differentiated between the politicians and those who fight. After spring, only those who fight will be valuable ... '[45] Moments later, Himmler said his last words and brought the meeting to an end.

Darnand returned to Ulm. He was disappointed—Himmler had made him no promises about his own future. Now, more than ever before, he was convinced that his revolutionary *Miliciens* would end up under the control of Doriot and his P.P.F. cadres in 'Charlemagne'. He had lost all or so he thought.

Days later, Berger invited Darnand to Berlin. Over dinner, in the company of Krukenberg, Berger promised Darnand the role of political leader in 'Charlemagne'. He added:[46]

> Thanks to your action within the Brigade, as well as thanks to your position close to all Frenchmen at present in Germany, I hope the brigade will soon become a division. Then we will create other divisions. In this way, your

42   Cited from an unpublished document by Darnand appearing in *"Historia #40, La Milice, la collaboration en uniforme"* and in Delperrié de Bayac, pages 568 to 569. Of note is that although word for word the two quotes are not the same, they do convey a similar message.

43   The *Miliciens* of the *Franc-Garde* unit were permitted to keep their French uniform, their French arms, their French flag, their French *chefs* and their French cadres. Arguably, the Reich did not have sufficient resources to uniform and arm them.

44   Delperrié de Bayac, page 568. However, according to Mabire, page 123, RF-SS Himmler assured Darnand that his *Miliciens* would wear the tricolore badge, but did not announce that the collar badge of the 'sword of Joan of Arc' had been dropped. And, curiously, the appearance of the 'sword of Joan of Arc' on the map of collar and sleeve insignia for foreign volunteers produced in February 1945 by the SS Propaganda Department would seem to suggest that it was not dropped.

45   Cited from an unpublished document by Darnand that appears in *"Historia #40, La Milice, la collaboration en uniforme"*. According to Mabire, *"La Division Charlemagne"*, page 124, Himmler is reported as saying: "We will win the war. And only those who fight will have the right to speak."

46   Delperrié de Bayac, page 570.

soldiers will have contributed to meriting the predominant place your country has always had in Europe.

Alarmed, Krukenberg intervened and explained that, for him, politics and military questions did not mix. Berger cut him short, saying that he knew what he was doing and that his decisions matched the thinking of Himmler. Overjoyed, Darnand warmly thanked Berger. Now he had to face his *Miliciens* and sell them the least unfavourable solution.

On 23rd October 1944, the *Miliciens* packed into a cinema at Ulm. *Chef* of the *Milice* Robert spoke first. He explained why 'Charlemagne' was forming and why a 'unification of all revolutionary French forces at present in Germany was necessary'. Alfonsi followed him. He spoke of the necessity of both a military and a political role for the *Milice*. Then Darnand spoke.

Darnand announced that 'after careful consideration' all *Miliciens* capable of bearing arms were to be enrolled into the French unit of the Waffen-SS, adding that 'only volunteers will be accepted'. He appealed to their spirit of *catholique et français toujours* when he spoke of their conditions of service: not only would they serve under French commanders, but they would be permitted to wear the tricolore badge, and they would be ministered by Catholic chaplains. He assured: "Under no circumstances will this French unit fight on the Western Front." Then he explained:

> We cannot live like layabouts in a Germany at war against Communism and plutocracy. Our duty is to fight or work … We fought in France. We will fight again by the side of the German armies against the same enemies.

Darnand pledged to continue the fight at their head and evoked sacrifice: "If need be, we will die together". He warned them that they must be ready for the political tasks that lay ahead on their return to France. He needed them to have strength and doctrine. Bitterly, he concluded: "The French people must understand that by your discipline and your faith you have been servants of your homeland".

When Darnand finished, his *Miliciens* stood up to a man and replied by striking up the *Chant de la Milice* with a fervour that brought tears to the eyes:

> Kneeling, we take the oath
> *Miliciens*, to die singing
> If need be for the new France
> In love with glory and grandeur
> All united by the same fervour
> We swear to remake France:
> Kneeling, we take the oath

Darnand sang along with his *Miliciens*. Moved, he did not attempt to hide his emotion. Once the meeting was over the *Miliciens* headed to a stadium for a parade organised by Bassompierre, the master of ceremonies, where Darnand reviewed his *Miliciens* for the last time. Before falling out, the *Miliciens* shouted out the *Chant des Adieux* ('song of the Farewells'). Then, with a tricolore flag at their head, they paraded through the streets of the city.

There was much discussion about Darnand's announcement. The reaction was mixed. Some were enthusiastic. Many volunteered. Many hesitated. Many were volunteered. Some protested.

Like most of his comrades, Robert Blanc of the Dijon *Franc-Garde* was enthusiastic about entering the Waffen-SS.[47] Darnand's announcement came as little surprise to him. There had already been talk of passing to the Waffen-SS. He had been hesitant, but that was before Jacques de Lafaye, one of the *chefs* of the Dijon unit, took him to meet French Waffen-SS officers Fenet and Bonnefoy over dinner at Hotel Bahnhof. The enthusiasm and spirit with which they evoked the battles of the Sturmbrigade in the Carpathians, the feats of their men, and the Waffen-SS in general removed his scruples of a family nature, which had stopped him from leaving much earlier for the Eastern Front. His father, an *officier de réserve des deux guerres* for whom he felt great respect and affection, had asked him never to wear the German uniform. In addition, he 'had no wish to lag behind his comrades'.[48] Of his *trentaine*, on which no pressure was exerted, only three or four refused to enlist.

The *3e Cohorte* under *Capitaine* de Bourmont volunteered for the Waffen-SS almost to a man.

However, many were not so willing to volunteer. They wanted to fight, but were not prepared to don the German uniform. Over and over again at meetings, Darnand and other leading *chefs* of the *Milice* attempted to sell the Waffen-SS. German officers spoke to them of the terrible new weapons that were reducing London to dust and that would ultimately guarantee them victory. Frenchmen of the former LVF and the Sturmbrigade came and extolled to them the merits and advantages of German military organisation. These efforts reaped little reward.[49]

On 30th October, in *la France* (a collaborationist *journal*), Pierre Cance, Darnand's former adjoint who had been wounded at the head of the SS-Sturmbrigade in Galicia, appealed to young Frenchmen 'to practise their politics on the battlefield'.

Jean-Pierre Lefèvre of the Paris *Franc-Garde*[50] wrote a letter to *Capitaine* Monneuse explaining that he did not wish to go over to the Waffen-SS because of religious as well as patriotic reasons. *Capitaine* Monneuse ripped up his letter and replied that it was the SS or striped pyjamas. After that, he signed on the dotted line as a volunteer.[51] He did not consider himself a volunteer but as mobilised![52]

---

47   Born September 1923, Robert Blanc joined the *Milice* in April 1944. He served first with the 'Students' *section* of the Paris *Franc-Garde*. When the *Franc-Garde* was mobilised he joined the *cohorte* stationed in Lycée Saint-Louis (boulevard Saint-Michel). Subsequently he responded to a call for volunteers to form a unit of *franc-gardes* at Dijon and left Paris for Dijon on 15th or 16th July 1944.

48   Blanc, letter to the author, 14/6/2001. Of those *Miliciens* that volunteered for the Waffen-SS, various authors have cited various reasons. According to Mabire, page 158, 'the overwhelming desire to remain together and not to abandon the struggle swept away the last doubts.' And according to de la Mazière, page 52, most of the young *franc-gardes* and their officers choose to be assimilated into the Waffen-SS because of their loyalty to their *chef*, Darnand.

49   According to Delperrié de Bayac, page 575, volunteers were few. Whereas, according to Mabire, page 157, 'the number of volunteers for the SS remained sizeable'.

Ordered to volunteer, *Franc-garde* Noël Cornu of the *école des cadres de la Milice* at La Chapelle en Serval obeyed.[53] For him, an order was an order. And an order was to be obeyed.

To those that protested, Darnand said: "What I cannot obtain through discipline and loyalty, I can obtain through force."[54] One by one they succumbed and fell into line.

The story of de Brangelin

Chef de trentaine de Brangelin went across to the Waffen-SS without protest. For him, 'the Waffen-SS was the only means of fighting against Bolshevism in October 1944'. Nevertheless, he was deeply unhappy that he would have to don the German uniform!

Born in Morocco in 1921, Yann de Brangelin spent his childhood in this French protectorate where his father was an official in Native Affairs. In late September 1939, he attended the military academy of La Flèche. He made friends with Michel de Genouillac who sat next to him in the classroom and whose bed was next to his in the dormitory. They had much in common. A passion for horse-riding was but one of their shared interests. [This was the beginning of a friendship that has lasted fifty years.]

The *débacle* of June 1940 distressed de Brangelin deeply. Thenceforth he bore a grudge against the Germans who had defeated and occupied his beloved France. But, by the same token, he raged at those French people responsible for the defeat: the members of Parliament, the Popular Front government, as well the Jews and the Freemasons. Also, he was fiercely critical of the British for their retreat from the Somme and their selfishness during the battle of Dunkirk. Continued British aggression at Mers-el-Kebir, then at Dakar and later in Syria only served to compound his Anglophobia.

In defeat de Brangelin continued to study at Valence, then at Algiers, for the entrance examinations to the *École Spéciale militaire de Saint-Cyr*.

Finally, in 1942, de Brangelin gained admittance to Saint-Cyr where he met again his good friend de Genouillac. His attendance at Saint-Cyr was brief, coming to an abrupt end by its closure in November 1942 after the German occupation of the Free Zone and the subsequent disbandment of the Armistice Army.

---

50   Born on 7th April 1925, Jean-Pierre Lefèvre joined the *Milice* in 1944. He served first with the Paris *Franc-Garde* and later in the two *Centaines* sent to Dijon. As such, he did not serve in the *cinquième cohorte* 'Dijon' as cited by Delperrié de Bayac, page 605.

51   No *Milicien* would end up in a concentration camp as a result of refusing to 'volunteer' for the Waffen-SS, but the threat was probably all too real.

52   According to Mabire, "*La Division Charlemagne*", page 159, Jean-Pierre Lefèvre was 'one of the most hostile' to the transfer to the W-SS. As such, this is not correct. Yes, he was hostile, but not 'hostile enough' to be expelled from the Division.

53   Cornu was also a member of the Vichy *Équipes Nationales* composed of young volunteers who were to protect and help those civilians threatened or touched by war. See Lambert and Le Marec, "*Organisations, mouvements et unités de l'état français, Vichy 1940-1944*", pages 233-246.

54   Delperrié de Bayac, page 576.

Demobilisation would have left him at a loose end if it were not for de Genouillac who invited him back to his parents. Weeks later, he left to try and reach North Africa via Spain. He did not get through, narrowly avoiding arrest and deportation. Where to now? Having learnt that de Genouillac was with the *Chantiers de la Jeunesse* in Haute-Savoie, he joined him. It was July 1943. For the time being, he felt at home in this patriotic and *marechaliste* [supporting the Marshal and the National Revolution] organisation which was never actively collaborationist, but more often anti-German.

At the end of 1943, de Brangelin decided to enlist in the *Franc-Garde* of the *Milice française*. He enlisted out of a love for France and a sincere hatred for Communism. He was disgusted by the blind bombardments of the Allies that claimed more French than German victims, and also by the cowardly acts of murder perpetrated in the name of the 'Resistance'. Thus, for him, the *Franc-Garde* was the best way of fighting the Communist peril aided and encouraged by the Allies.

Appointed *chef de trentaine*, de Brangelin was posted to Rouen in Normandy where he remained from May to August 1944. His role, above all, was that of an instructor and a recruiter. In this way, the *Trentaine* of the *Franc-Garde de Normandie* became a Centaine whose command went to de Brangelin and with it promotion to *chef de centaine*. Life as a *franc-garde* was perilous and de Brangelin counted himself lucky when an assassin's bullet missed him one day on stepping outside of his home.

His *Centaine*, which hated the Germans occupying France as much as the Allies bombarding her, did not participate in any Maintenance of Order operations for the simple reason that there were few, or no, maquis in Normandy. But the *franc-gardes* of his *Centaine* were occupied with helping the victims of the Allied bombardments and guarding the partly destroyed houses against theft. In this way, after an air attack, his unit prevented the sacking of the office of the *Banque de France* in Rouen.

At the beginning of August, de Brangelin received permission to go on leave to Paris, but during his absence his *Centaine* was ordered to withdraw to Paris. By chance, de Brangelin met one of his *franc-gardes* who filled him in. De Brangelin was indignant; this order to withdraw smacked of flight.

In Paris, through a female associate living where he was staying, de Brangelin and a good friend, de la Mazière, met with two rather mysterious men.[55] They explained that the Allied staff were concerned about the Communist-inspired elements in the Resistance which might start fighting for Paris before receiving any order. In this way, 'the Communists could seize power and proclaim France a socialist republic'. As the Paris police were due to go on strike, the Allies were now in need of 'convinced anti-Communists' to intervene and oppose the Communists if they were to act in the way feared.

De Brangelin was then questioned about his activities and ideals. As though satisfied, the two men asked him if he would continue the fight against Communism on the Allied side! And then they asked him if he could persuade the *Miliciens* under him, described to him as an important force, to rally to the Allied side in the

---

55   Little is known about these two men, although de la Mazière recounts that they were from London.

name of anti-Communism! He answered yes and yes. A meeting-place was arranged. The 'guests' left.

Thereupon, de Brangelin contacted about forty of his *franc-gardes* and asked them to assemble at a predetermined time in la place de la Concorde, Paris, at the foot of the statue of the city of Rouen. His men agreed to follow him without explanation. But one of them had no confidence in de Brangelin and informed the *État-major de la Franc Garde* of de Brangelin's plan to desert with part of the *centaine de Normandie*. Denounced, the *coup de main* was now doomed to failure.

When de Brangelin's armed *franc-gardes* arrived at the place de la Concorde they were intercepted by the Germans summoned by some *Milice* commanders. As for de Brangelin, one of his *franc-gardes* managed to join him and warned him of the danger. He then telephoned the *chef* of the *cohorte de la Franc Garde* to which he belonged. The *chef de cohorte* agreed to release and exculpate de Brangelin's men provided that he came to him and explained himself. He did just that.

The meeting with his superior proved stormy. Considering himself offended by the insulting words of his superior, de Brangelin slapped him in the face. Consequently, he was arrested and imprisoned.

Brought before a court martial, de Brangelin was sentenced to death by Bassompierre who did not even give him an opportunity to explain his point of view. No less a person than President Laval saved him from the execution squad; notified by some of de Brangelin's friends, Laval intervened and gave the order to have him released. It was Raybaud who received the order to release him and also to listen to him. At the end of the conversation, de Brangelin was free to leave the *Milice française* or continue. With bad grace, he agreed to continue, saying: "With this departure, we're taking the way to Germany and we're leaving the way free to the Communists to take power in France." Moreover, he had no wish to abandon his men.

Thus, *chef de centaine* de Brangelin returned to his unit that had actually been preparing to liberate him by force. Weakened by desertions, the *Franc-Garde de Normandie* was amalgamated with some *franc-gardes de Bretagne* to become the *Centaine de la Franc-Garde de Normandie-Bretagne*. The retreat began.

At a barracks near Nancy, de Brangelin received a visit from Darnand who asked him about the morale of his men. In response he stated that it was not good and then evoked the 'affair' of la place de la Concorde, even remarking that Darnand had put the *Milice* under the Germans' control. At no point did Darnand say anything, but Dr. Rainsart, his *adjoint*, also present, later made de Brangelin pay for his outburst: de Brangelin found himself transferred from his unit and demoted to *chef de trentaine*.

In Germany, de Brangelin was approached about returning to France as a saboteur. This he refused, preferring to fight Bolshevism as a soldier in uniform.

Then came the medical examination before SS doctors. Physical fitness was demanded. Some were rejected.[56] Vilbert of the Dijon *Franc-Garde*, who had been seriously wounded in 1940, was refused. He cried with rage.

The number of *Miliciens* who 'volunteered' for the Waffen-SS is now considered to be 1,800, of which 300 were 'sent back' at a later date.[57] Thus, some 1,500 former *Miliciens* went on to serve in 'Charlemagne'. With them were their battle

---

56   According to Mabire, page 157, those who did not want to enter the Waffen-SS
     could find the sympathetic ear of a French doctor.

proven leaders of de Vaugelas, Bassompierre, Raybaud, de Bourmont, de Londaiz, Dr. Durandy, Géromini and de Perricot.

Of those *Miliciens* left 'unemployed', some one thousand became workers and some 700 to 800—the youngest, the oldest, the physically unfit and the politically unreliable—were sent to Heuberg camp, near Sigmaringen, and formed into a battalion.

The *Miliciens* arrive at Wildflecken

On 4th November, after parading through the streets of Ulm for the last time, shouting out German military songs, *Milice* recruits for the Waffen-SS embarked at Neu-Ulm railway station. The following day, they arrived at Brückenau railway station, disembarked, reassembled, and marched off to the camp of Wildflecken.[58] They went into barracks.[59]

The *Miliciens* got a cool welcome. The Frenchmen wearing German uniforms ridiculed the *Miliciens* because they were dressed as French soldiers and had a tendency to brandish at the slightest thing their pistols and submachine-guns.[60] They told them that they looked like gangsters and cowboys. As for the *Miliciens*, 'they felt ill-at-ease by the appearance of Frenchmen in German uniforms who looked more German than the Germans'.[61]

57   Mounine and Lefèvre, correspondence to the author, 1997 and 1998, and Bayle, "*San and Persante*", page 125. Different authors, however, have cited different figures; 2,000—Mabire and Bassompierre; 2,500—Saint-Loup, Delpierré de Bayac, Voiron and de la Mazière.

58   Delpierré de Bayac, page 577, and de la Mazière, page 52. However, according to Mabire, page 166, as though in quarantine, the *Miliciens* waited several days near Brückenau railway station before making their entrance into Wildflecken. Marotin, a *franc-garde* who volunteered for the Waffen-SS, agrees that there was a delay before they entered Wildflecken. In his memoirs he wrote (see page 45): "Here we are billeted in wood huts at the foot of the mountain crowned by Wildflecken... The *franc-gardes* grow impatient. Now that the step is crossed, the decision is taken, they crave action and find it hard to understand this inaction." In response to this, *franc-garde* Blanc cannot recall any such wait at Brückenau. And *chef* Raybaud, in his letter to Mabire of 3/11/74, cannot recall any such 'quarantine', or even a period of some days, spent outside the camp. Nevertheless, the possibility exists that part of the *Franc-Garde* was stationed at Brückenau for a number of days.

59   According to Rostaing, page 152, the *Miliciens* made their way through the camp to Adolf Hitler Platz, where they formed a square and struck up *la Marseillaise*. Brigf. Krukenberg looked on phlegmatically. Beside him was his German shepherd. However, in response to this, Blanc, who arrived at Wildflecken with the *Milice*, does not recall going direct to Adolf Hitler Platz nor having sung there *la Marseillaise* (letter to the author, 2001), but added that *la Marseillaise* may have been sung out of his earshot.

60   According to Mabire, page 166, veterans of the Sturmbrigade and the LVF viewed with contempt those who only had known the Army of the defeat and the *Milice* of the civil war. Indeed, according to Krukenberg, quoted from Bayle, "*De Marseille à Novossibirsk*", page 154, because of Darnand's activity as *chef de la Police de Vichy*, they feared that the presence of the *Miliciens* would tarnish the reputation of those who had volunteered to fight only Bolshevism in the East. Such sentiments, however, remain unsubstantiated (various letters to the author).

The *Miliciens* crossed swords with the camp staff. The *Miliciens* switched the dormitory pictures of Hitler, which they moved to a quiet corner and turned face down, with those of their leaders, Darnand or Marshal Pétain. Aghast when they discovered this switch, the camp staff told the *Miliciens* to remove their offending French flags and 'decorations'. The *Miliciens* replied with threats that they would 'give them what for' if they tried to touch them. The camp staff prudently beat a hasty retreat.[62]

Two days after the arrival of the *Miliciens*, they were brought to Adolf Hitler Platz. The whole brigade was already assembled there. New recruits were sworn in and decorations were awarded. Blanc of the Dijon *Franc-Garde* was struck by 'the scale and the reverence of the ceremonial as well as by the look of our comrades'.

Although drafted into the Waffen-SS, the *Miliciens* were still required to swear an oath of loyalty to Hitler. Brigade headquarters agreed that Sunday 12th November 1944 was as good as any other day to conduct the ceremony.

Anticipating a wave of indiscipline, Krukenberg ordered the formation of a penal platoon officered by those 'chosen for their parentage with certain ruminants'.[63]

Enter Darnand and Cance

On 11th November 1944, Joseph Darnand arrived unannounced at Wildflecken in the uniform of a Sturmbannführer of the Waffen-SS.[64] He had come to take up his political role in 'Charlemagne' and attend the swearing-in of his *Miliciens* into the Waffen-SS. A secretary asked him for his *Soldbuch*.[65] This he did not have. The secretary explained to him that he could not be admitted into 'Charlemagne' without the appropriate paperwork. Darnand then asked for a room and a bed while the matter was cleared up. This was refused for the same reasons. Darnand got all the angrier. Informed of Darnand's arrival, Brigf. Krukenberg appeared. Undoubtedly, Krukenberg had calculated this confrontation.

Darnand declared: "I am a French Secretary of State and I ask for respect." Krukenberg replied: "Excuse me, I thought you were Sturmbannführer Joseph Darnand who has come to take his command. If you are Secretary of State Darnand, come."[66]

Krukenberg did not take his 'guest' to the officers' mess but to his personal villa outside the camp. Dinner was served during which Krukenberg fell over himself to be polite to Darnand, addressing him repeatedly as 'Mr. Secretary of State'.

Brigf. Krukenberg bluntly put it to Darnand that there was no political role or command for him in 'Charlemagne'. However, to reassure Darnand, Krukenberg confirmed that Doriot, Darnand's political rival, would also have no political role and no command in the brigade and that he would not even be coming to

61 Delperrié de Bayac, page 578.
62 Saint-Loup, page 150.
63 Memoirs of Soulat.
64 It should be noted that many sources state quite categorically that Darnand never donned the field-grey.
65 Mabire, page 173. Curiously, according to Delperrié de Bayac, page 579, the secretary asked Darnand for his 'certificate of cessation of pay'.
66 Delperrié de Bayac, "*Histoire de la Milice*", pages 579.

Wildflecken. Moreover, Doriot had drafted a letter to his militants asking them to refrain from political activity within the brigade and to do their duty as soldiers. Krukenberg then requested Darnand to do likewise. Thus, Darnand had won and lost. He had 'won' his battle against his rival by securing numerous positions of command for the *chefs* of the *Milice* throughout the brigade, but had lost the best elements of the *Milice* to the Waffen-SS. Worse still, his revolutionary militants were now divorced from their political origin.

Shortly after this tête-à-tête, Krukenberg recounted to *Capitaine* Renault, the French liaison officer to the German Inspection[67]:

> Darnand was very annoyed when I announced to him that there was no question of him receiving any command in 'Charlemagne', nor even of serving in it. He asked me if at least Pierre Cance could have an important command. I refused. We had managed to eliminate Doriot. There was no question of accepting Darnand in the Waffen-SS. We have had enough of the political quarrels from the Frenchmen. We want soldiers, not party leaders.

Years later, Brigf. Krukenberg reflected that Darnand took this rebuff better than he expected.

Despite his great disappointment, Darnand chose to stay on for the ceremony next morning at which his *Miliciens* would be sworn into the Waffen-SS.[68]

67   Delperrié de Bayac, "*Histoire de la Milice*", pages 580.
68   Delperrié de Bayac, "*Histoire de la Milice*", pages 579-601, and Mabire, pages 173-175 (which appears to have been based on Delperrié de Bayac's work). The memoirs of Soulat [reproduced in part by Mabire, pages 178-181] also confirm the presence of Darnand at the ceremony. However, Krukenberg recalled in *Entretien avec le général Krukenberg*, "*Historia #32*", page 133, that Darnand did arrive to assist in the swearing-in ceremony, but stayed for only a matter of hours. Also, in the article "*Problemes autour de la division Charlemagne*", Krukenberg wrote that Darnand 'arrived late and after the ceremony'. Furthermore, Darnand was fiercely critical of the fact that his men had not remained in a special separated unit and, above all, that the initial oath sworn to him was not satisfactory. Subsequently, Darnand expressed these two criticisms in a strongly worded letter to Ogruf. Berger of the SS-Hauptamt which also complained that the German Inspection had 'taken his last combatants' from him. On Himmler's orders, Darnand had to retract his letter. But aged 85 when interviewed for "*Historia*" and 92 when he wrote '*Problemes autour de la division Charlemagne*', Krukenberg recognised in the latter that the events were some 35 years old and that this length of time might have erased memories. Also, on 16th December 1944, Berger wrote to Himmler about Darnand and remarked that the *chef de la Milice française* had arrived at Wildflecken on 19th November 1944 only to be told that he was welcome as a Stubaf. but not as a *Secrétaire d'Etat*. The 19th was one week after the swearing in ceremony. So was Darnand at the ceremony or not? The author is convinced that he was. Darnand still saw a political role for himself and his militants in 'Charlemagne' and because of this he would not have let his faithful *Miliciens* be 'usurped' in this way without first putting in an appearance and putting up a fight. And what better time to appear than on the eve of the ceremony at which his *Miliciens* would be sworn into the Waffen-SS and pledge their allegiance to Adolf Hitler. Any later and Darnand would have been presented with a distasteful fait accompli.

Pierre Cance, Darnand's former assistant, also came to Wildflecken for the swearing-in ceremony of the *Miliciens*.[69] Brigf. Krukenberg greatly feared his return. He was all too aware that Cance was still a close friend of Darnand and still politically pre-occupied, but he could not readily exclude him without offending the former *encadrement* of the *Milice française* and also that of the SS-Sturmbrigade. Cance had been wounded in Galicia at the head of the 1st Battalion of the SS-Sturmbrigade, now held the rank of Sturmbannführer and, while convalescing at Sigmaringen, been designated to take up the command of Waffen-Gren. Regt der SS 57. Thus, Krukenberg trod lightly. Cance said of his reception:[70]

> I saw Krukenberg who invited me to dine with de Vaugelas. Krukenberg told me that he had no job for me and that I was expelled from the Brigade. Why? He believed that if I received the order to fight in the west, I might desert. I had a feeling of total uselessness. Krukenberg said that I was not physically fit to exercise a command. I had actually been wounded with the Sturmbrigade, but I had recovered. The following morning I went and had a medical examination and, as if by chance, I was declared unfit.

The doctor who carried out the medical examination and declared Cance unfit was Stubaf. Schlegel of the German Inspection. Undoubtedly, the German doctor was 'under the influence' of Krukenberg to declare Cance unfit because of his serious knee injury received in Galicia. Thus, with the greatest of tact, Krukenberg had got his way again. Cance was, of course, disappointed. He went on to become an instructor at annex Neweklau of SS-Junkerschule Kienschlag. His pupils were not French, but Latvian, Estonian and Wallonie.

The oath of loyalty to Hitler

By the eve of the swearing-in ceremony, some fifty *Miliciens* had made it known that they would not swear allegiance to Hitler. The ringleaders were, it seems, André Brilland[71] and some of his comrades of the *Avant-Garde*. All had attended the *école des cadres* [training school] at La Chapelle en Serval. Obf. Puaud called on Hstuf. de Bourmont to 'tear a strip off' the 'draft dodgers'.[72]

Hstuf. de Bourmont summoned Brilland first. However, he could not convince Brilland to move from his stand that he would never wear the German uniform or swear loyalty to Adolf Hitler till death. De Bourmont then gave Brilland the blunt choice of 'Charlemagne' or the concentration camp. His threat still did not convert Brilland who defiantly retorted: "I prefer to be guarded by the SS rather than wear their uniform. A question of principle." Continuing, Brilland spoke of Darnand's broken promises. He even questioned de Bourmont's honour.

---

69   Roch, "*La Division Charlemagne*", page 35, confirmed by Soulat, letter to the author, 20/2/98. This date of 'on or around' 12th November 1944 corrects that of the end of January 1945, cited by Mabire, pages 233, and thus also the idea that Stubaf. Cance was excluded from the Brigade when Ostubaf. Gamory-Dubourdeau left for Berlin.

70   Cited by Roch, "*La Division Charlemagne*", page 35.

71   Pseudonym?

72   Mabire, page 176.

Provoked to anger, de Bourmont called Brilland a saboteur and promised him that he would find himself in Danzig-Mazkau.

Rebuffed, de Bourmont went onto the others. All ended with the same outcome. The 'draft dodgers' were locked up in the camp prison, guarded by two former soldiers of the SS-Sturmbrigade.

Curiously, Oberjunker B. of the Panzerjäger Company of Waffen-Gren. Regt. der SS 58 refused to swear the oath of loyalty to Hitler and yet he was not punished.

Sunday 12th November 1944 started with mass celebrated by Monseigneur Mayol de Lupé in the stable. The *Miliciens* were all there. Once mass was over[73] they assembled on Adolf Hitler Platz for the swearing-in ceremony at 0900 hours. They were still wearing their dark-blue and khaki uniforms, and *basque* berets, but the arms they had brought with them to Wildflecken had long been confiscated on the orders of Brigf. Krukenberg.

Unit by unit, the whole brigade drew up around Adolf Hitler Platz for the ceremony. It was cold and snowing. In the centre of the platz stood a rostrum flanked on each side by an anti-tank gun, a mortar and a heavy machine-gun. From three flagpoles on the platz, in front of the 'Kasino', flew the tricolore, the black SS flag and the 'war flag of the Reich'.

Standing on the rostrum were Brigf. Krukenberg, Obf. Puaud, Darnand and Ostubaf. Léon Degrelle, holder of the Knight's Cross with 'Oak Leaves' conferred on him personally by Hitler and commander of the 28. SS-Freiwilligen-Panzer-Grena-dier Division 'Wallonien'. Behind them were the eighty or so officers of the brigade and those of the German Inspection.

Mgr. Mayol de Lupé spoke. He said that he had been a National Socialist since 1925. He continued:

> Stalin and Bolshevism represent Evil in the pure state. In the East, Good and Evil clash. You will participate in the battle against Evil in the ranks of the Waffen-SS. Be proud. Long live Führer Adolf Hitler! Long live our France-German homeland!

Both Brigf. Krukenberg and Obf. Puaud gave a short speech.

Then, four *Miliciens*,[74] including *Capitaine* Monneuse, a decorated veteran of 1914–1918 and 1939–1940 well into his forties, of late the *chef* of the *5e Cohorte de la Milice*, took the oath in the name of all present with the left hand on a sword held out by a German officer. The *Miliciens* repeated the oath in French, although 'the majority remained silent or mumbled anything'.[75] Furthermore, the *Miliciens* should have also raised their arm but the majority did not.[76] Many had a heavy heart.

---

73   In his memoirs, Soulat wrote that, after mass, Mgr. Mayol de Lupé gave a speech. Curiously, this speech was similar to that he gave later that day at the swearing-in ceremony (see Mabire, pages 178-179, and Saint-Loup, page 581). In response to this, the author does not know if Mgr. Mayol de Lupé gave just the one speech after mass or two similar speeches.

74   Soulat's memoirs. However, according to Mabire, page 179, it was three *Miliciens* who took the oath: a *franc-garde*, a NCO and *Capitaine* Monneuse.

75   Mabire, page 180.

76   Delperrié de Bayac, "*Histoire de la Milice*", pages 582.

For *Milicien* officer de Brangelin, his reaction to the oath was mixed:[77]

Admittedly I swore the oath without enthusiasm, but the Waffen-SS was an international European force. It was logical to recognise the authority of one military commander and only that of one military commander. The result was that I agreed to take the oath without any particular frame of mind …

Blanc of the Dijon *Franc-Garde* was not troubled by the oath. He explained:[78]

Having already agreed to fight under the command of the Fuhrer, which was a decision I had taken quite freely, it was normal that he could firmly count on me. In my mind, I swore the oath to him as the European *chef de guerre* (head of war), and not as the foreign Head of State.

The oath sworn that day was as follows:[79]

I swear to obey faithfully Adolf Hitler, commander of the Waffen-SS, in the struggle against Bolshevism, as a loyal soldier.

This oath was not that administered to the other French volunteers serving in the Waffen-SS. It was that of the LVF. Why was this? According to one source,[80] Brigf. Krukenberg doubted the attachment of the *Miliciens* to National Socialism and thus could not ask them to swear the *real* SS oath. However, Bassompierre has also been credited with having obtained the change of oath so as not to leave the door open for possible combat duty on the Western front.[81]

Immediately after the oath, the entire brigade, more than 7,000 men, sang the 'SS-Treuelied'. On the third verse everybody automatically came to attention. The officers saluted. Commands resounded. In the thickening snow the brigade now marched past the rostrum. At its head marched *Commandant* Bridoux. The *Compagnie d'Honneur,* heartily singing the 'SS marschiert', led the way. The companies of the two grenadier regiments and the service units of the brigade

---

77   De Brangelin, letter to the author, 7/1/98.

78   Blanc, letter to the author, 7/8/2001.

79   Memoirs of Robert Soulat [unpublished], repeated by Mabire, page 180. Of note is that, some days earlier, de la Mazière swore an SS oath that ran as follows: "I swear to you, Adolf Hitler, Germanic Führer and Remaker, to be true and brave. I swear to obey you and the leaders you have placed over me until my death. May God come to my aid."

80   Saint-Loup, page 151.

81   Cited by Pierre Giolitto, "*Histoire de la Milice*", page 492. However, according to one former French Divisional soldier, the Germans gave their word never to engage them against French troops without getting their agreement first. Unfortunately, the author has not been able to substantiate this arrangement, but if true, clearly, the Germans had not discounted the possibility of employing 'Charlemagne' against Anglo-American forces on the Western front. Indeed, this is all the more remarkable because Brigf. Krukenberg and RF-SS Himmler were totally opposed to its employment on the Western front. And although foreign minister von Ribbentrop was actually in favour of employing 'Charlemagne' on the Western front his viewpoint would have carried little or no weight with the then all-powerful Himmler.

followed. Then came the *Miliciens* singing 'Monika' or 'rubbish'. Soulat, who was present at the ceremony, simply remarked: "The charm was broken."

On seeing the 'good uniform' of the *Miliciens* parading before him, Ostubaf. Degrelle commented: "I would like to have those people with me."[82] Ambitious, he hoped to combine the Frenchmen of 'Charlemagne' with the Walloons, Flemings and Dutchmen serving in the Waffen-SS to form an army corps by the name of 'Occident'.[83]

On the command of 'head right', a platoon emphatically looked left, much to the embarrassment of those reviewing the parade. Many *Miliciens* did not know the German language.

During the ceremony Darnand's presence had paled before that of Ostubaf. Degrelle.[84] In fact, he practically went unnoticed. After the ceremony, Darnand briefly visited Fenet, a former *Milicien*, who now had nothing in common with his former leader.

Broken-hearted, Darnand left Wildflecken that night (or the following day), but not before he had asked his men to be, above all, soldiers. Darnand still lived in hope, but he no longer interested the SS hierarchy.

Several days later, Father Brevet, a nephew of Darnand and former chaplain of the *Milice*, turned up at Wildflecken to try his hand at talking round those *Miliciens* who had refused to swear the SS oath. He convinced over half to go over. Nineteen were left. Bassompierre tried next. He had no success.

82   Raybaud, letter to Bayle, 22/2/1992. Although the wording of the comment and the circumstances of its passing are different, the written interview with Raybaud in "*Charlemagne's Legionnaires*" confirms, as expected, that the comment was aimed at the *Milicens*. However, according to Saint-Loup, page 151, a similarly worded comment from Degrelle to Krukenberg was aimed at the Frenchmen as a whole rather than the *Miliciens* in particular.

83   Although Darnand appears to have been in agreement, the idea of an 'Occident' corps would come to nothing. Indeed, on 8/12/1944, Darnand wrote to Berger, the head of the SS-Hauptamt, stating his intention to resign his post of *Secrétaire d'Etat* from the *Commission Gouvernementale Française*, as well as requesting his transfer to 'Wallonie'. For his part, Degrelle hoped for Darnand's transfer in the expectation that he would bring with him a large number of his adherents who had just been incorporated into 'Charlemagne'. On 16/12/1944, Berger wrote to RF-SS Himmler about Darnand and warned him that 'in the eyes of many Frenchmen, Darnand had devalued himself through his widely-known project to join Degrelle' and in this way given a great political advantage to his rival Doriot. As for Degrelle's proposed 'Occident' Corps, Berger described its formation as being fraught with danger and its success doubtful. He explained that the 'antinomies between the French and the Walloons had still not been overcome' and that, even if the project were a success, 'Walloon will have drawn closer to France rather than to the Reich'. Although Berger stopped short of dismissing the project outright, 'reading between the lines', there is little doubt that he was not in favour of it. Himmler, undoubtedly, would have had similar reservations.

84   Of interest to note is that according to "*Charlemagne's Legionnaires*", page 90, Darnand wanted the place of honour at the ceremony, but this was given over to Degrelle. However, Delperrié de Bayac, one of many sources consulted, makes no mention of this.

On 15th November 1944, the nineteen *Miliciens* were taken from Wildflecken to Sigmaringen where, five days later, Darnand spoke to them in person. He persuaded a further eight to enlist in the Waffen-SS, but he was not prepared to punish the others for a show of French patriotism. Discharged, they put on civvies and went to work for the Reich.

The change of uniform

Meanwhile, back at Wildflecken, the *Miliciens* drew what uniform and kit was available, including old stocks of greenish coloured Italian overcoats that proved useless against the bitterly cold weather. Some even ended up clothed in the mustard-coloured overcoats of the SA or Organisation Todt. A steel helmet could not be found to fit Blanc of the Dijon *Franc-Garde*. Neither did he receive a mess tin!

Uscha. Mercier of Fahrschwadron A wrote that the clothing received by the *Miliciens* was 'one of the less glorious episodes'.[85] As a veteran of the LVF, he recalled the new uniforms, the new weapons, and the new equipment received in September 1941 at Deba. In contrast, the Germany Army of 1944 no longer had the means to dress its soldiers in a worthy manner. Indeed, one of Mercier's comrades, an NCO from the *Milice* of very stocky build, still did not have a uniform into which he could fit some two months later.

While most of the former *Miliciens* wore blank right collar insignia[86] some managed to acquire and wear the standard SS runes.

Now dressed in a Waffen-SS uniform, René Jean Forez of the *3e Unité de Franc Garde de Lyon* felt proud to be serving with a *grande unité européenne* in the continual battle against Soviet Bolshevism.

Franc-garde Cornu donned the *feldgrau* without heartache. That he should end up in *feldgrau* came as no surprise to him. Indeed, the 'slide' had begun years before when he was with the P.P.F.[87]

Towards the end of November 1944,[88] the *Milicien* contingent was assembled on Adolf Hitler Platz and, in a scene likened to that of a cattle market by Blanc of the Dijon *Franc-Garde*, divided up among the units of 'Charlemagne'.[89] Company commanders or their delegates came to 'fish' for men, exalting the charms and

85   Mercier, letter to the author 25/10/2001.

86   Soulat, letter to the author, 21/9/98.

87   Cornu joined the P.P.F. in 1941.

88   Blanc, personal conversation with the author, 2001.

89   Curiously, according to Mabire, pages 166-167, some senior officers of the *Milice* came to Wildflecken hoping to form a pure *Milicien* unit within the brigade. But de Vaugelas, who had become convinced that this move would only exasperate the already serious political infighting, reached agreement with Puaud and Krukenberg to help eliminate political strife. For his part, Krukenberg considered the prospect of a wholly *Milicien* unit as a 'factor of insecurity' for the entire brigade. In return for the splitting up of the *Milicien* personnel, de Vaugelas secured from Puaud and Krukenberg that *Milicien* officers would be placed in numerous positions of command throughout the brigade. This agreement he brought back to the other officers of the *Milice* who he won over with his arguments. In response to this, if true, clearly, Darnand had not told them of the agreement he had reached with Krukenberg to divide the members of the *Milice* among the different units.

merits of his unit or speciality. The patron of the Escort Company assured that it was the most exposed and was immediately filled up. Some decided on such and such unit to join a brother, or a cousin, or a comrade. As planned, *Franc-garde* Blanc followed the representative of Company 5/58. He and the company commander, Walter, were old friends. Blanc was accompanied by some of his closest comrades.

Francs-gardes from Limoges filled out the skeletal Assault Gun Company and those from Chambéry the 'heavy mortars'.[90] *Franc-garde* Marotin was assigned to Company 4/57 and then transferred to Company 8/57, becoming its armourer. *Franc-garde* Cornu, a medical student of more than three years, was assigned to Company 5/58[91] and then placed into the Medical Company. However, the majority of *Miliciens* became Waffengrenadier.

The *Miliciens* served in all units. The following units benefited the most:[92]

The Artillery Battalion

The Anti-tank or 'Heavy' Battalion

The two Supply columns

The Engineer Company

The Signals Company

The Medical Company

The Veterinary Company

Political infighting?

According to Mabire and Saint-Loup,[93] by the end of the day, the political infighting had intensified. Once the *Miliciens* were in their mixed dormitories they put up photographs, postcards, and, in pride of place, pictures of Darnand. The LVF legionnaires replied with pictures of Doriot or LVF badges, the *Francistes* with Bucard, and the Sturmbrigade veterans with the Führer. Even pictures of Mayol de Lupé, Puaud and the Reichsführer-SS appeared. Insults were traded between the factions. Mabire also records that broken noses, broken teeth and stabbings settled scores.[94]

Rostaing cites that fights between the various factions of 'Charlemagne' became quite common-place inside the camp and especially outside in the neighbouring small villages 'whose pubs welcomed the troops on leave'.

Brigf. Krukenberg was quick to clamp down on all political expression, except that of the Führer and Marshal Pétain, which appears to have been generally

---

90   Mabire, page 187. Presumably this refers to the organic heavy company of each grenadier battalion.

91   While Cornu was with the 5/58 his platoon commander was one Pierre Rusco.

92   According to Blanc, the Supply Corps was not popular.

93   See Mabire, pages 187 to 189, and Saint-Loup, page 154.

94   The exact nature and background of these scores is not made clear. They may have been non-political.

upheld, but political unrest was not completely suppressed. Morale was at a low ebb.

However, regarding the dissension and political infighting depicted by the likes of Saint-Loup and Mabire, many veterans have expressed genuine and great surprise.

Strmm. Marotin, the only *Milicien* in a small bedroom with six other NCOs, of whom five were from the SS-Sturmbrigade, recalls no such problems posed by their different origins. Moreover, while in 'Charlemagne', he had no inkling of these disputes. He commented that they were going to discover a camaraderie that was perfect.

Maurice Comte, who had arrived with the *Milice*, also recalls no such problems in his company, the 5/57, but much political discussion. Also serving in the 5/57 was *franc-garde* René Forez. Although he was the only one of his platoon to attend mass taken by Mgr. de Mayol de Lupé, he was never ridiculed about his choice. Among his platoon there was mutual respect.

Company commander Ustuf. Rigeade cannot recall any lasting or important disputes among the men of the 3/58 of whom about half were former legionnaires of the LVF (including thirty holders of the 'Ost medialle' [East Medal] who had served during the first winter campaign in Russia). The others were former *Miliciens*, about forty in number, ex-Kriegsmarine, ex-N.S.K.K., ex-SK der OK ... but none were from the Sturmbrigade. Although Rigeade felt proud to have been 'among the first to enlist', he had no taste for snubbing, denigrating, scorning or judging the others, nor their reasons to enlist, their path or their past choices. They were now in his Company and, in his own words, 'honour to them all'!

The 4/58 also comprised 'volunteers' from the LVF, the *Milice*, the Kriegsmarine and the SK der OK. Stamping his authority, company commander Ustuf. de Genouillac made it understood to one and all that his only concern was to make them into elite combatants, that their origin or political origin would play no part in this objective, and that he would not tolerate any disruption to the cohesion of the unit. The young *Miliciens*, recognising that they all had to learn how to be 'veterans', posed him no problems.

Assigned to Company 5/58, *franc-garde* Robert Blanc found himself in a platoon solely made up of *Milice* recruits, except for the section commanders and platoon commander-instructor Oscha. Walter. They were ex-LVF. Nevertheless, between the two camps there was no expression of political rivalry rather esprit de corps; those from the LVF subjected the *franc-gardes* to biting remarks, even some minor ragging, but this never degenerated into insults or fights. Things would calm down some months later. Besides, the new recruits wanted to know where the friendly 'pubs' were in the local villages! Of note is that Oscha. Walter remained above such 'political' problems.

Jean Castrillo of Company 5/58, who was ex-SK, recalls no such political infighting, even though the *Miliciens* from the Gers had trouble 'slipping' into the SS discipline.

In contrast, Ustuf. Martret had cause to remember well the *Miliciens* and their ill feeling towards the Waffen-SS. For example, one day, as Unterführer vom Dienst, he officiated in German to an audience of *Miliciens*. Noting that the *Miliciens* disapproved of his use of German, he argued that 'Charlemagne' was a unit of the Waffen-SS and, as such, German would be spoken. Continuing, he told them that they were neither French nor German, but European SS.[95]

"In our unit, we had no friction between former *légionnaires*, former SS, and former *miliciens*", said Uscha. Mercier of Fahrschwadron A.[96] However, the incorporation of the *Milice* into 'Charlemagne' had not pleased him at all. He had no sympathy with the *Milice* itself, but personal contact with the *Miliciens* completely changed his opinion. He immediately developed excellent relations with them. Some became his friends (and remain so). His comrades from the *Milice* expressed themselves freely in front of him. They spoke to him of the *départ* from France and of Ulm without ulterior motive, but were rather bitter when it came to evoking *chef* Darnand.

Transferred to the Headquarters Company, Soulat found himself among soldiers who were mainly ex-LVF. They warmly welcomed this young sailor. Moreover, there were never any problems because of origin.

Clearly, there was little or no political infighting. However, the integration of the *Miliciens* with their equivalent former French Army rank was greeted by concern and discontent.[97] Simply stated, many of the *Miliciens* were militarily untrained for modern warfare. Regarding this, Blanc, a *Milicien*, said: "We only knew guard duty and some 'operations', which despite a great willingness, did not us make soldiers." The *Miliciens* had much to learn and that included those who had formerly served in the French Army, for the training and tactics of the Waffen-SS were far removed from those of the French Army beaten in 1940. Furthermore, some *Miliciens* were too old and unfit for proper military service, and some were too political. Nevertheless, their courage was not doubted.

As a result of the integration of the *Miliciens*, a number of changes occurred in the higher positions. Ostuf. Fenet relinquished command of battalion I/57 to Hstuf. de Bourmont. Hstuf. Raybaud assumed command of battalion I/58.

Notably, Krukenberg intervened and told Puaud not to give Bassompierre any command. The reason for this has never been properly explained, although Krukenberg may have considered Bassompierre too political for command.

The junior ranks objected to the 'promotions' the *Miliciens* received. Those from the Sturmbrigade had 'suffered' one year of rigorous training before promotion to Sturmmann or Unterscharführer. Moreover, previous military service had not determined their promotion. In their eyes there was no substitute for the training received at Sennheim and Posen-Treskau. Additionally, *sergents* of the LVF, who had waged war for three years against the partisans and the Red Army to gain their strips, refused to obey eighteen-year-old *aspirants* of the *Milice* whose previous 'military' experience amounted to service in the *Chantiers de la Jeunesse*.[98]

---

95 Furthermore, according to Martret, the *Miliciens* wanted to wear the Gamma badge of the *Milice française* on their uniform (personal discussion). Was this just wishful thinking on behalf of the *Miliciens*? Unfortunately, the author does not have the answer, but it should be noted that some foreign nationalities serving with the Waffen-SS were permitted to wear badges of a political nature.

96 Mercier, letter to the author 25/9/2001.

97 For example, Uscha. Fronteau, who was ex-LVF, had no confidence in the abilities of the former officers of the *Milice* in front of the Russians. Nevertheless, he was not hostile to them.

98 Saint-Loup, page 156-157.

Despite nullifying the political threat Darnand and Doriot had posed, Krukenberg appears to have become concerned about the political activities of Puaud. In October 1944, Krukenberg was alarmed to hear that Puaud, on his own initiative, offered Marshal Pétain a *Garde d'Honneur* from 'Charlemagne'. [The Marshal immediately refused this move.]

Krukenberg said of another incident:[99]

> One day I entered his office. He [Puaud] clumsily tried to hide a circular among his files. He eventually showed me it: he was asking the cadres in the Division for those who were interested in *postes de préfet* after the victorious return to France.

Puaud was but one concern for Krukenberg. There was also the matter of the numerous 'desertions'. In less than one month, more than two hundred men, in groups of two or three, had 'deserted' to units going up to the front.[100] In this way, some of these French SS 'deserters' would actually end up serving in Waffen-SS Divisions 'Totenkopf' and 'Wiking'. And although Krukenberg would later describe the desertions as honourable because they wanted to fight, he was more concerned that 'they were very bad for the morale of their comrades' left behind.[101] No desertions in the true sense of the word are reported by any source.

Others employed more official channels to leave. Chansarel of the Kriegsmarine discovered a make-believe Belgian ancestry and managed to get himself transferred to Waffen-SS Division 'Wallonie'. Barat, also ex-Kriegsmarine, wrote to RF-SS Himmler in person, protesting that his skills as a torpedo technician could be better employed elsewhere. Days later, he received a reply from the private secretary of the RF-SS. To the great envy of many others, he obtained satisfaction and was transferred away.

Instructor Strmm. Vaxelaire wanted to leave the *bordel* [shambles] that was Wildflecken. He was hungry, full of lice, and disappointed that some of his compatriots were not willing to don the German uniform. Moreover, he felt undervalued as an instructor in the company commanded by Artus. In fact, his work was ridiculed.

99   "*Entretien avec le général Krukenberg*", "*Historia #32*", page 133.

100   Mabire, page 192.

101   "*Entretien avec le général Krukenberg*", "*Historia #32*", page 136.

1. Swearing-in ceremony of the LVF at Deba on 5th October 1941

2. Ustuf. Hans Reiche

3. Michel de Genouillac

4. Yves Rigeade of the LVF attending a Russian wedding

4b. Yves Rigeade and a friend, Berand, at the same Russian wedding in 1943

5. Wilhelm Weber

6. Jean Fronteau of LVF 1943

A two-man MG34 machine-gun team in a partially dug-in position. When mounted on a heavier tripod as pictured here, the MG34 could fire accurately over longer than normal distances in a support role. SCOTT PICK/SUMMIT PHOTOGRAPHICS

Somewhere on the vast Russian steppes, a lonely two-man MG42 machine-gun crew awaits the inevitable onslaught of Russian infantry and armor. Much improved over the MG34, the MG42 is considered by many to be the best machine gun of the Second World War, but its technical superiority was still not enough to stem the Allied forces. SCOTT PICK/SUMMIT PHOTOGRAPHICS

A lone sentry stands guard with his rifle, a KAR 98, and two stick grenades close at hand. SCOTT PICK/SUMMIT PHOTOGRAPHICS

A German tank crew examines a destroyed Russian T-34. The German Panther and Tiger tanks were superior to the T-34 in many respects—especially armament and armor—but the Russians were able to outproduce and ultimately outfight the Germans. SCOTT PICK/SUMMIT PHOTOGRAPHICS

German troops examine a 7.62-millimeter Russian Maxim heavy machine gun. With carriage and armored shield, the whole gun weighed up to 140 pounds, making it difficult to carry on the battlefield.

SCOTT PICK/SUMMIT PHOTOGRAPHICS

The war on the Eastern Front saw acts of barbarism committed against civilians as well as combatants. Several Russians have been hung by the Germans, guilty of the crime of being Jews or partisans, or perhaps as an example to cow the population into submission. SCOTT PICK/SUMMIT PHOTOGRAPHICS

A destroyed Russian T-34/76. German forces were initially shocked when they encountered the T-34 for the first time. With its sloped armor, 76.2-millimeter main gun, and incredible cross-country performance, the T-34 proved a deadly adversary.
SCOTT PICK/SUMMIT PHOTOGRAPHICS

A side view of a destroyed Russian T-34. The large road wheels and wide tank track gave the T-34 a distinct advantage in the snow and the mud, which, on the Eastern Front, meant a great deal. SCOTT PICK/SUMMIT PHOTOGRAPHICS

A decapitated statue of Lenin. Ideology and hatred marked the fighting on the Eastern Front to such an extent that not even symbols were immune to the destruction.
SCOTT PICK/SUMMIT PHOTOGRAPHICS

A funeral for an SS soldier. Elaborate ceremonies such as these became increasingly rare later in the war as the German retreat meant the dead were often left for the enemy to bury. SCOTT PICK/SUMMIT PHOTOGRAPHICS

CHAPTER 7

Greifenberg and the Franz. SS-Grenadier-Ausbildungs und Ersatz-Bataillon

L ocated at Greifenberg, the French SS-Grenadier Training and Replacement Battalion assisted in the training of recruits and provided replacements for 'Charlemagne'. Commanded by Swiss national SS-Ostubaf. Hersche,[1] the battalion was organised with three training companies and a number of other units.

When the Ersatz Kommando of the LVF was transformed into the French SS-Grenadier Training and Replacement Battalion *Sergent* Mercier of the *Compagnie de Dépôt* was automatically transferred to the Stammkompanie. Then made the temporary Rechnungsführer of one of the training companies, he was tasked with setting up its administrative structure.[2] As soon as his work was done, he left this post to a Volkdeutsche who held the rank of SS-Uscha. Health problems followed. He was sent to the SS-Erholungsheim at Bad Gleichenberg in Styrie where he spent some fifteen days.

In October 1944, all soldiers of the Stammkompanie had a medical examination.[3] Uscha. Mercier had his with Ostuf. Dr. Louis. The doctor suggested demobilising him as unfit for service. This did not correspond to his aspirations, but several of his comrades took advantage of this 'comfortable' way out from the SS. Mercier sought his own way out by requesting a transfer to the SS parachutists. He was refused on grounds of ill health. This transfer request he would later describe as a romantic gesture.

In mid-November 1944, after a long period of convalescence, Ustuf. Paul Pignard-Berthet arrived at depot Greifenberg and received the command of the Stammkompanie from W-Ustuf. Kipp.[4] The role of the depot company was

1   Hersche succeeded *Commandant* Cartaud of the LVF who had refused to pass to the SS.

2   Such was the confusion at the time of the transfer to the Waffen-SS that Mercier can no longer recall the name of the company commander. Moreover, he never saw the company commander. Nevertheless, he is convinced that it was not Ostuf. Michel who had been his company commander in 1942 when serving with the LVF. The Spiess was an old Feldwebel from the German training staff of the Ersatz Kommando. He had no idea of his function. He too may have only been temporary.

3   Mercier, letter to the author, 23/1/2002, although the date of the medical examination and the attendees are not confirmed.

4   A Luxembourg national, Jean Kipp enlisted in the LVF and served in the 1st Company under *Capitaine* Cartaud. He won the Iron Cross 2nd class. In 1943, Cartaud was transferred to Kruszyna to take command of the Ersatz Kommando. Kipp went with him. In early 1944, he was promoted to *Sous-Lieutenant*. After

twofold; in the first place, to 'process' (or bring into line) the new recruits and, secondly, to demobilise some of the more seriously wounded or those refusing to pass to the SS. In this way, the strength of the Stammkompanie was later reduced from over 800 men to 130.

At the end of November 1944, Hstuf. Schlisler, the *officier adjoint* of the battalion, left Greifenberg for Wildflecken to take command of Fahrschwadron A of 'Charlemagne'.[5] Schlisler took a small team with him. One of those he asked to remain on his team was Uscha. Mercier, who being very attached to him, had agreed without hesitating. Once again, he was touched by Schlisler's trust. [He would follow Schlisler to the end.]

With W-Hstuf. Schlisler's departure, the order of battle of the Franz. SS-Grenadier-Ausbildungs und Ersatz-Bataillon at Greifenberg was as follows:

Commander:	SS-Ostubaf. Hersche	
Assistant:	SS-Hstuf. Kroepsch	
Training officer:	SS-Ustuf. Schueler	
Office III:	SS-Ostuf. Dick	
Office IV/A:	W-Ostuf. Dr. Louis[6]	
Office VI:	SS-Ostuf. Zander	
1. Kompanie:	SS-Ostuf. Ludwig	(180 men)
2. Kompanie:	W-Ostuf. Michel	(180 men)
3. Kompanie:	SS-Ostuf. Allgeier	(180 men)
Stammkompanie:	W-Ustuf. Pignard-Berthet	(825 men)
Ausbildungszug:	W-Ostuf. Crespin	(430 men)

German officers Allgeier, Ludwig, and Schueler had all served as instructors at Ersatz Kommando I.R. 638. They too were transferred from the Wehrmacht to the Waffen-SS. Ludwig had been badly wounded in 1940 fighting the French and left paralysed in one arm.

At the end of December 1944, a Rekrutenkompanie (in French *compagnie de recrues*) was formed. Its command went to Ostuf. Crespin. The company was 450 strong.

In January 1945, Ustuf. Pignard-Berthet spent fifteen days at Wildflecken supervising a platoon of officer cadets. From Hstuf. Monneuse, the battalion commander of the I/58, he received the task of 'polishing up' the officer cadets and selecting those capable of attending Junkerschule Kienschlag.

While at Wildflecken, Ustuf. Pignard-Berthet also received personal instructions from Krukenberg to eliminate all those at Greifenberg whose morale would

passing his command to Pignard-Berthet, he promptly 'disappeared'. Like Cartaud, he too may have refused to pass to the SS.

5   Schlisler once confided to Mercier that General Puaud wanted him to take command of the IV. Battalion of the LVF, which was not raised because of the events of 1944 (Mercier, letter to the author, 9/10/2001).

6   Bayle, "*San et Persante*", page 147. Curiously, W-Ostuf. J.M. Louis, who came to the Waffen-SS from the LVF, was a trained doctor. And, as such, one would expect to find him at the head of Office IV/B, that of medical and sanitation, rather than Office IV/A, that of uniforms, footgear and rations. In any case, he survived the war and became a surgeon.

no longer withstand the new hardships or those who might exert a bad influence over their comrades. On his return, he carried out these instructions to the letter.

On 16th January 1945, the Ausbildungszug [Training platoon] was transformed into a kompanie of 250 men. Its command went to Ustuf. Pignard-Berthet. Hstuf. Flamand succeeded him at the head of the Stammkompanie.

CHAPTER 8

The Training of 'Charlemagne'

Dispersed throughout Europe

The Reich still had much to offer in the way of specialist training. The following were sent to military bases and training centres throughout Europe:

NCO candidates to SS-Unterführerschule Posen-Treskau or Paderborn

Officer candidates to annex Neweklau of SS-Junkerschule Kienschlag in Bohemia-Moravia

Engineers to SS-Pionierschule Hradischko in Bohemia-Moravia.

Signallers to SS-Nachrichtenschule Sterzing-Vipiteno in South Tyrol

Mechanics to Berlin

Medical orderlies to Stettin

Interpreters to the SS-Dolmetscherschule Oranienburg near Berlin

Company clerks to Breslau

The assault gun company and panzerjägers to Janowitz in Bohemia-Moravia

The personnel of the Infantry Gun companies, 9/57 and 9/58, to Breslau-Lissa

Artillery officers to SS-Artillerieschule Beneschau, Bohemia-Moravia

Artillerymen to Josefstadt, Bohemia-Moravia

The drivers of the horse-drawn vehicles to SS-Kavallerieschule Göttingen

Only the Waffengrenadier would stay put at Wildflecken for training.

In mid November, Rttf. Malardier of the Headquarters Company of Waffen-Gren. Regt. der SS 58, who was expecting promotion to Unterscharführer, and a number of other officer candidates departed to annex Neweklau of SS-Junkerschule Kienschlag. Also among the officer candidates were de Bouge, de Bazelaire, Bonnet, Dabadie, Dedieu, Fleury, Uscha. Fronteau of Company 10/58, Jacoby, de Lacaze, Lebrun, Moureu, Piffeteau, Soupault, Velay and Voiturier. They were a mix of former *Miliciens* and *Légionnaires* of the LVF.

In late November, Section commander Rttf. Gonzales and the Engineer Company were sent to SS-Pionierschule Hradischko, one of the many training schools located within Truppenübungsplatz Beneschau, south of Prague, Bohemia-Moravia.

On his transfer to the Engineer Company, Gonzales was surprised to learn that the parents of *Kompanieführer* Ostuf. Roger Audibert de Vitrolles were friends and neighbours of his! Because of this Gonzales is convinced that Audibert asked for him to serve in his company.

Audibert was elegant, but his monocled and very abrupt air reminded Gonzales of 'a certain aristocracy of French Army officers'. Nevertheless, Audibert was a ranker, promoted in the reserves to *sous-lieutenant* before the outbreak of war. With this same rank, Audibert was accepted into the LVF, arriving in the field in May 1943. Wounded in August 1943, he only returned to active service in early 1944 at the head of the 7th Company of the II. Battalion. He was still with the same company when the LVF was transferred to the Waffen-SS. He was a holder of the KVK 2. Klasse.

Rttf. Gonzales had cause to remember well his company commander's assistant, Ustuf. Maile. While in Russia with the LVF, he very nearly shot him dead! As for the circumstances, well, Gonzales admits that he was completely drunk at the time. Thankfully a comrade had punched him hard and put him out for the count before he could fire again. Maile bore him no malice.

Of his training at Pikowitz, Gonzales recalls the 'joys' of bridge building, weapons training, the placing of anti-tank mines and anti-personnel mines, and 'bunker busting'.

Physical training was, of course, emphasied. They lost weight and gained strength. Through this arduous training, some developed the sense of discipline that was lacking beforehand.

The training continued by night. Woken at all times of the night, Gonzales cannot forget how he and his comrades marched for kilometre after kilometre carrying two anti-tank mines on their back.

With each passing day, the engineers' proficiency improved. In addition, they began to move more and more swiftly and efficiently. Most were willing trainees, but some, for reasons best known to them, did not respond.

The training course at Pikowitz would last some three months.

In December, Strmm. Sepchant of the Headquarters Company/58 joined the French artillery officers at SS-Artillerieschule Beneschau. He acted as their interpreter.

The Frenchmen were part of a group that also included Flemish and Bulgarian officers. Notably, at the head of the group, for the period of the course, was Hstuf. Martin, not Hstuf. Havette, his senior[1] and the commander of the Artillery Battalion of 'Charlemagne'. One of the instructors had considered Havette incapable of exercising this function!

One day, the trainees noted a large rectangle left in white on a map. Curious, they asked what it was. The answer came: "We cannot tell you. When certain events happen, you will understand." In this way, the myth of the secret weapons was continued. Some would still believe in them to the end.

On his return to Wildflecken, Sepchant was given the job of translating German artillery regulations into French. Not an easy one without a technical dictionary!

Also in December, a number of officer candidates from the former Sturmbrigade, including Jacques Frantz, Piquemal, Trémel, and Viot,[2] returned from annex Neweklau of SS-Junkerschule Kienschlag. The course under Kleindienst had lasted some three months. Strm.-F.Bew. Trémel was assigned to the 3/57 under Ustuf. Counil.

1   Jean Havette was born on 12th December 1891.
2   Also on this course were brothers Gastine or Gastinel.

The role model of the *Compagnie d'Honneur*

New recruits, be they workers or prisoners of war, as well as those who had finished convalescing from wounds received on the Eastern front, continued to arrive at Wildflecken from Greifenberg. The reaping of Frenchmen serving in other formations of the German Army continued and together they swelled the ranks of 'Charlemagne'. Each regiment was now able to form two additional companies, called A and B. In his infinite wisdom, Puaud requested de Vaugelas to activate a third regiment, but the idea was dropped days later, which may be due in part to the protests from Fenet with support from de Vaugelas.[3]

On 16th December 1944, the strength of 'Charlemagne' stood at a total of 7,340. This strength probably included those in training schools.

By the middle of December 1944, Krukenberg was in a position to accelerate the military training. His training strategy revolved around the Wach-und Ausbildungskompanie der Inspektion (guard and education company of the Inspection) which he wished to forge into an elite unit and hence a role model for the other troops.

Brigf. Krukenberg had formed the Wach-und Ausbildungskompanie at Leisten soon after he assumed command of the Inspection. The company reported direct to the *Inspekteur* [i.e. Krukenberg]. Oberjunker Christian Martret, a graduate from SS-Panzergrenadierschule Kienschlag, was appointed its commander.[4] He was seventeen and a half and 'hailed from' the SS-Sturmbrigade.

At first, the Wach-und Ausbildungskompanie counted three platoons of thirty men each. It was bolstered by the incorporation of two platoons of former Kriegsmarine volunteers of the 2/28. They were transferred to the Wach-und Ausbildungskompanie because they knew how to march and parade like Germans.

At Wildflecken, former *Miliciens* were added. In this way, the Wach-und Ausbildungskompanie comprised all the constituent elements of 'Charlemagne', although the SS-Sturmbrigade and the Kriegsmarine were well represented. One platoon commander was Oscha. Charles of the Sturmbrigade.

A certain Unterscharführer by the name of Eugène Vaulot, who had come to the Waffen-SS from the 2/28 of the Kriegsmarine, made such an impression on Oberjunker Martret that he requested his promotion to Oberscharführer. This, however, the Inspection refused.[5]

At Wildflecken, trouble flared when a former *Milicien* was found in possession of a 2 Franc coin with a hole through it. This meant nothing to Martret, but to other former *Miliciens* it was a symbol of the maquis! They started to quiz the man with the coin. Nobody knew of him. So the question has to be asked: was the maquis trying to infiltrate 'Charlemagne'? Martret does not have an answer because, one or two days later, around the time of his promotion to Untersturmführer on 9th November 1944, a German officer by the name of Weber arrived. And who was Weber?

Wilhelm Weber was born on 19th March 1918 in Pivitsheide, Westphalia.[6] His father was a mason. After completing his basic education, he entered the Trade

---

3   Presumably these additional companies were broken up at a later date.

4   This was probably very late September 1944. Martret had only been out of Kienschlag a matter of days before he received this command.

5   Martret believes that he had the support of Ustuf. Patzak of the Inspection, but not that of Krukenberg.

School in Detmold. As a member of the Hitlerjugend, he received an altogether different education. From 1st April 1936 to 31st March 1937, he served with the RAD [Reichs Arbeitsdienst, the Reichs Labour Service] at Bad Salzuflen. On 26th June 1937, he joined the 1st Company of SS-Standarte 'Germania' in Hamburg. He would serve with 'Germania' until 1944.

By the time war broke out, Weber was a NCO in command of an armoured scout car. He served in the Polish Campaign of September 1939, winning the Iron Cross 2nd Class, in the Western Campaign of 1940, and then in Russia. By July 1941, he had worked his way up to the rank of SS-Oberscharführer and was now in command of a motorcycle reconnaissance platoon. From April 1942 to November 1942, he attended SS-Junkerschule Braunschweig, graduating with the rank of SS-Standartenoberjunker. Shortly afterwards, he was promoted to SS-Untersturmführer. Until 1944 he remained a platoon commander.

In August of 1944, leading a special SS Training Company in the defence of Riga, Latvia, Weber came to the attention of SS-Oberführer Krukenberg. He went on to command the 2nd SS Armoured Recce Training Company in Staumühle before Krukenberg requested his transfer to 'Charlemagne'.

In early November 1944, Ustuf. Weber came to Wildflecken. Brigf. Krukenberg assigned him to the Wach-und Ausbildungskompanie. He was to work together with Martret. However, Martret remembers well the first day Weber arrived. Weber walked straight into his office and started to go through his desk draws, as though the office and the kompanie was his. Martret exploded. The kompanie was his and his alone.

Martret and Weber continued to clash. The Inspection resolved the conflict by transferring Martret to the vacant post[7] of orderly officer of Waffen-Gren. Regt. der SS 57.[8] Although disappointed, Martret obeyed as a good soldier. Orders are orders. Besides, he preferred this post to any other in the regiment.[9]

Soulat also has cause to remember well the arrival of Weber: like all those who no longer satisfied the minimum height requirement for the Wach-und

6   According to Mabire, Weber was born three years later. This is incorrect.

7   This post was filled previously by Oberjunker Stehli.

8   Curiously, according to Mabire, page 203, when Kreis, now with the rank of Untersturmführer, arrived at Wildflecken following a long period of convalescence—he was wounded in Galicia with the Sturmbrigade—Krukenberg decided to appoint him the commander of the Wach-und-Ausbildungskompanie. However, like many from the Sturmbrigade, he felt ill at ease in 'Charlemagne' which was no longer their 'SS'. Several days after his appointment, Weber arrived. As the two of them held the same rank, had the same bad-tempered and stubborn personality, and insisted on being its sole commander, sparks flew. Brigf. Krukenberg intervened, promoting Weber to Obersturmführer, with effect from the 9th of November 1944, and dispatching Kreis as an instructor to annex Neweklau of SS-Panzergrenadierschule Kienschlag. In response to this, at no time was Kreis the company commander of the Wach-und-Ausbildungskompanie. (Personal discussion with Martret. Furthermore, in a letter to the author of 11/6/98, Soulat, a member of the Wach-und-Ausbildungskompanie while still in its infancy, does not recall Kreis as his company commander.)

9   Today, Martret remains very proud of having built the base of the Wach-und Ausbildungskompanie.

Ausbildungskompanie, Soulat was transferred out. And yet, before his arrival, Weber, who had heard good things of Soulat, had pulled a few strings to have him as his *putzer* [orderly]. Soulat went to the Headquarters Company, whereas most went to the Engineer Company and the Medical Company. Avinain took the place of Soulat. He too was former Kriegsmarine with service in the 6/28 at Sennheim and then in the 2/28 at Duisberg.

The minimum height for the Wach-und Ausbildungskompanie was one metre seventy (or one metre seventy-five).[10]

Louis Levast was assigned to the Wach-und Ausbildungskompanie because he met its height criteria: he was one metre 83 tall. Born on 13th November 1925 in Lyon, he had been shocked by the defeat of 1940 and left indignant at the illusions of French military power. From *Les Compagnons de France*, a Vichy Government approved youth movement in the Unoccupied zone, he was drawn to 'serve France against Bolshevism' in the ranks of the *Franc-Garde* of the *Milice*. Volunteering for the Waffen-SS, he was still impatiently awaiting his transfer when he arrived at Wildflecken with the *Milice* in November 1944.

Also assigned to the Wach-und-Ausb.Kompanie was Jean-Louis Puechlong, born on 20th February 1920 in Saint Foy-les-Lyon (four kilometres from Lyon). His father was a career soldier, who was wounded seven times during the course of World War One. While being treated for his seventh wound in a military hospital he met a nurse who would later become his wife. By the end of the war, he held the rank of lieutenant. He left the army in 1933. A royalist, he brought his son up in the 'spirit of war for the return of the King'.

Aged fifteen, Jean-Louis Puechlong entered the world of far right politics; he joined the *Jeunesses Patriotes*. He guarded its political meetings in Lyon and the surrounding region. Although a fervent patriot, he came to admire Italy. And then, in 1937, he accompanied a group of French scouts to a Hitler Youth camp in Bavaria. He was seduced by 'this active, patriotic youth, showing its will and its hope'. Nevertheless, it was with fear that he viewed the German menace becoming clearer every day.

In 1938, Puechlong enrolled in a Lyon university to study law, but in November 1939 he decided to enlist. He was posted to the *27e Régiment Tirailleurs Algériens* (R.T.A.). From January to mid-May 1940, he attended E.O.R. training at camp La Courtine and, upon graduation, was commissioned as a *aspirant* with the suffix *à titre temporaire*. His twelve days of combat for France were without glory and without merit! He was retreating with his battalion to the fortress of Pont-Saint-Esprit when he learnt of the appeal from Marshal Pétain to stop fighting.[11] He cried. It was terrible.

To Puechlong, the young nationalist, the defeat of France was a catastrophe. Today, he still believes that the war was lost in advance because France did not

10   Curiously, according to Mabire, page 202, this minimum height was applied from the start.

11   On 17th June 1940, Marshal Pétain announced to the country over the radio: "It is with a sad heart that I tell you today that we must stop fighting. I have this night approached the enemy and asked him if he is prepared to negotiate with us, as between soldiers and after the battle has been fought in all honour, means of putting an end to hostilities".

believe in it. This was evident from the Army's lack of preparation to its lack of equipment, and from the officers' lack of morale to their lack of will. Also, France was left spiritless before the will to conquer, the physical condition, and the morale of Germany.

Demobilised at the end of August 1940, Puechlong was assigned to *Groupement 15* of the *Chantiers de la Jeunesse* at Agay (Var); all men of his age, that of twenty which was the normal age of conscript service, were required by law to serve in the *Chantiers*. Over the next two years he rose through the ranks; at first *Chef d'atelier*, then *Assistant de chef de Groupe* and then *Chef de Groupe*. At the start of November 1942, he left the *Chantiers*.

On his return to Lyon, Puechlong took the advice of his father and joined the *Légion Française des Combattants*. Soon after, he passed to the *Service d'Ordre Légionnaire*. He may well have joined the *Milice française* if it was not for his call-up by the S.T.O. in March 1943. And although the avenue of joining the maquis was very much open to him as a means of escaping the S.T.O., he agreed to leave for Germany. To him, the S.T.O. was state law. Also, his father had advised him to leave so as to avoid any possible trouble for his younger brother, then aged 18.

Puechlong was assigned to the Messerchmitt A.G. factory complex at Augsburg-Haunstetten. As an interpreter in a work camp, he made a number of good contacts with fellow workers and then with the local German population. He grew to admire the will of the German people.

With politics still close to his heart, Puechlong organised a section of the S.O.L. in the region. In May 1943, he 'converted' to the *Milice française*. He was made responsible for the Gau [district] of Augsburg.

At the head of a thirty-strong contingent of civilian *Miliciens*, *Chef de centaine* Puechlong went out to spread the politics of Marshal Pétain to the kommandos of French POWs in the work camps. However, the German authorities did not always appreciate their political activity and there were some minor clashes.

Puechlong knew of the recruiting office for French volunteers of the Waffen-SS in Paris, but believed his work and that of his compatriots in the camps was more useful than military service.

Then came the Allied 'terror' raids on Augsburg and surrounding villages. Puechlong went to the help of the innocents. Today, he still recalls the flames, the screams, the phosphorous, trying to get up stairs on fire, and mothers, trapped, throwing small children and babies from third or fourth floor windows that the rescuers, despite their best efforts, could not catch. It was terrible.

And then one Saturday afternoon the Allied bombers came back and completely destroyed the KZ lager next to Puechlong's camp. More than two thousand were killed. Puechlong remains convinced that he and a friend escaped almost certain death at the camp when they went off to help the townspeople of Augsburg. This, he reasoned, was war, undoubtedly total war, but now he too wanted to wage war, a war that was not in the west against his compatriots nor his Allies of 1939, but a war against Russia and 'its invading tentacle of Bolshevism'.

In a gesture of European patriotism, he enlisted in the Waffen-SS. It was late June 1944. He explained:

> I also wanted to show a will of total war with those who appeared as though they wanted to defend, before this danger of an invasion of Europe by the Russians,

our ethics [and] our concern about remaining free in a Europe without restriction. This solidarity with Germany seemed to me the only guarantee of our future liberty. At that time the Waffen-SS was the surest means to fight against the Russian invader till the end.

Puechlong was posted to the Franz. SS-Grenadier-Ausbildungs und Ersatz-Btl. at Greifenberg. On his arrival in September 1944, he was assigned to the 1st Company of Ostuf. Ludwig. That November, he was transferred to Wildflecken. One metre seventy-eight tall, he too was assigned to the Wach-und Ausbildungskompanie der Inspektion.

The Wach-und Ausbildungskompanie was now almost two hundred-strong. With the help of some German NCOs, Weber reorganised the Wach-und Ausbildungskompanie into four platoons. At the head of the first platoon was Oscha. François Appolot and at that of the second was Uscha. Eugène Vaulot. Notably, the two of them were French volunteers of the Kriegsmarine who were serving in the ranks of the 2nd Company of the 28 SStA [2/28] when integrated into the Waffen-SS.

The twenty-strong sections were, for the most part, commanded by fanatical French Sturmmann who had been wounded in Galicia with the Sturmbrigade. An entire platoon, called Jugend [Youth], consisted solely of those under the age of eighteen. Indeed, in its ranks were some even under the age of sixteen. Because of their age they did not receive the daily ration of three cigarettes.

As his assistant Ostuf. Weber chose Oberjunker Jacques Pasquet who has been described as having been 'at various times the best athlete in Europe and, once, in the world'[12]. Indeed, in 1937, he won the title of Mr. Universe! The key position of *Spiess* (Company Sergeant-Major) went to Oscha. Klein, a Luxembourg national, whom Weber had brought with him.

After the reshuffle, Ostuf. Weber now set about moulding the *Compagnie d'Honneur* in his own image. An extraordinary individual, Weber did not ask anything of his men that he was not capable of himself.

The training programme was ferocious. Route marches of 30kms, 50kms and even 60kms. Endless arms drills. Endless combat training. Anti-tank training. Twenty-four hours a day in the freezing cold and deep snow. All commands were given in German and when Weber spoke it was never in French. He was sparing with compliments. Any error was punished with yet more exercise. Each and every day the volunteers united more and more. Their military background and political orientation became a thing of the past. They 'fought neither for France nor Germany, but for a Europe without inner borders, governed by their caste, subject to their law'.[13]

Predictably, the *Compagnie d'Honneur* was detested and taunted for being germanophile by the *Miliciens* and legionnaires. Yet its esprit de corps was envied throughout 'Charlemagne'. Gradually its volunteers were admired and emulated. In this way, Krukenberg's strategy started to pay dividends and he then made use of the company as a training tool.

12   De la Mazière, page 61.
13   Saint-Loup, page 210.

In December 1944, some twenty members of the *Compagnie d'Honneur*, including Puechlong and Levast, were sent to Paderborn for NCO training. They were attached to the 3. Unterführer Lehrgang Kompanie made up of two hundred trainees all hailing from different backgrounds in the Waffen-SS. The training was hard, recalls Levast, but on a par with that in the *Compagnie d'Honneur*.

The *Compagnie d'Honneur* was not the only unit regarded as personifying the SS spirit. The FLAK Company also burned with the same spirit that was born of Fayard, its commander, the embodiment and soul of the Company, appointed to Ustuf. on 8th October 1944, and also of the independence the Company enjoyed. Identifying more with the Germans, Fayard sought to evade any dealings with the French Waffen-SS hierarchy! To this end, official paperwork from the 'Schreibstude' [office] of the FLAK Company had always been headed with the legend "SS-Französische Flakbatterie"[14] and had never carried any reference to a superior corps. Indeed, much of the paperwork emanating from higher echelons, especially at Wildflecken, referred to Fayard as SS-Untersturmführer. In fact, the 'SS' prefix to rank was adopted by all rather than that of 'Waffen'. And yet they did not abandon their distinctive French characteristics. They all but considered themselves as an 'Army of occupation in Germany'!

As though in the image of the *Compagnie d'Honneur*, the FLAK Company was also truly cosmopolitan and integrated. There was no question of politics. If proof were needed, in early November 1944, when Ustuf. Fayard reorganised his *encadrement*, he brought in former *Miliciens* or *légionnaires* of the LVF. Of the opinion that platoon commanders Mary and Ouvre had grown too familiar, Fayard appointed former *Milicien* Hscha. Junquet to the head of the 2nd platoon and former *légionnaire* Uscha. Masson to the head of the 3rd platoon.

In the same reorganisation, Ustuf. Fayard managed to rid himself of the troublesome Rechnungsführer Hscha. Brillet, a former prisoner, to the PAK Company. Rttf. Jund (or Jundt), a placid Alsatian, succeeded him.

In addition, there was promotion of all from the rank of Rottenführer to Unterscharführer and of all from Sturmmann to Rottenführer. As for all those who had served in the FLAK Company since its creation, they received the rank of Oberschütze.

Around the same time, Std.Ob.Ju. Vincenot was transferred to the PAK Company. He was sorry to leave the FLAK Company. Ustuf. Fayard replaced him at the head of the 1st platoon[15] with former *Milicien* Uscha. de Montfort.

Waffen-Grenadier Regiment der SS 58

Stubaf. Bridoux, formerly of the LVF, had actively supported and encouraged its entry into the Waffen-SS three months before. However, since then, the com-

14 Indeed, according to Soulat, "*Histoire de la Charlemagne*", page 26, on 28th April 1944, the FLAK Company received final designation 'SS-Französische Flak-Batterie'. If this is correct, then the FLAK Company would have been the only French unit to carry the 'SS' and not the 'Waffen' prefix.

15 Articles "*SS-Französische FlakBatterie*" and "*Le Schreiber*" (unpublished). However, a document in the possession of the author headed "*Encadrement of the FLAK*" records de Montfort at the head of the 2nd platoon and Junquet at the head of the 1st platoon.

mander of Waffen-Grenadier Regiment der SS 58 had undergone a change of heart and now anxiously sought to ensure that the military rather than the Doriotist spirit of the LVF lived on. The reasons behind his change of heart and his subsequent abandonment of post after a visit from his father, General Bridoux,[16] are not known.[17]

Without informing anybody of his decision, Stubaf. Bridoux suddenly left Wildflecken[18] the day after his father had called on him.[19] Obf. Puaud attempted to hush up his disappearance as leave but Bridoux, the respected defender of Bobr, never returned. Nevertheless, Puaud was not angry to see his most dangerous rival, one of the few career officers serving in 'Charlemagne', disappear because some German officers of the Inspection would have been happy to see Bridoux oust him and take over.[20] As for Brigf. Krukenberg, although angry on hearing the news of Bridoux's departure, he remained level-headed and argued that he only wanted volunteers and 'not those who had joined the forces of the Reich out of ambitiousness'.[21]

Brigf. Krukenberg appointed Hstuf. Émile Raybaud the new commander of Waffen-Gren. Regt der SS 58. Confronted with the situation of being a *Milicien* in command of a regiment deemed Doriotist, Raybaud held officer and NCO

16   At the time of his visit to Wildflecken General Bridoux was concerned with military affairs and prisoners in Brinon's 'French Government in exile'.

17   Unfortunately, the instigating conversation between father and son is not known. However, Saint-Loup records Bridoux's growing unhappiness (see page 157): he was accused by his peers of belonging to Vichy's Deuxième Bureau and he thought he had uncovered a P.P.F. plot against him. However, to infer that his decision to abandon his post stemmed solely from these factors would be unreasonable, although they may have contributed.

18   Curiously, Landwehr states in "*Charlemagne's Legionnaires*" that, after meeting with his father, Stubaf. Bridoux then joined a Battalion of SS Regiment 57, but no other source substantiates this.

19   Saint-Loup, page 158. However, according to Mabire, pages 217-218, Stubaf. Bridoux left Wildflecken that same evening after summoning many former officers of the LVF and informing them of his decision. This came as a shock to those present—reported as Oscha. Girard, company commander of the 10/58 (Anti-tank), Ustuf. Rigeade, company commander of the 3/58, and Ostuf. Fatin, company commander of the 1/58—who were all very angry and felt a great sense of betrayal. They tried their best to convince him to reverse his decision, but failed. In response to this, Mabire is incorrect; in a letter to the author, 31/1/97, Rigeade states that Bridoux did not speak to him or to any other former LVF officers before departing. Nevertheless, Rigeade did say in the same letter that Mabire correctly reflected their feelings about the departure of Bridoux.

20   Cited by Soulat, "*Histoire de la Charlemagne*", page 89.

21   Mabire, page 219. However, Brigf. Krukenberg may have been much more involved; some thirty years after the event, Krukenberg declared that he had learnt that as soon as it was a question of going up to the front Obf. Puaud had intended to announce to him his dismissal of Bridoux. Thereupon, Krukenberg put Bridoux in the picture and advised him to leave without delay. (Cited by Soulat, "*Histoire de la Charlemagne*", page 89.) If true, a most re-markable revelation and one which could be interpreted as Krukenberg actually finding himself impotent before Puaud.

meetings and then assembled his whole regiment to appeal to them to drop politics and concentrate on preparing for battle. However, his appeal was not heeded by all. To curtail the political agitation of Ostuf. Auphan, his Intelligence Officer, who had built up a Doriotist network within the regiment, Raybaud had him transferred to Brigade Headquarters.

'Submissive son of the Church', Hstuf. Raybaud also sought the assistance of Mgr. de Mayol de Lupé in the depoliticisation of his regiment; the prelate still retained considerable influence over his former congregation of dear Legionnaires and reassured Raybaud that he would have no problems with them. And yet, his political problems were still not laid to rest. A network of French informers was uncovered feeding back the political thoughts of their comrades to a German officer of the Inspection who was close to Brigf. Krukenberg. Raybaud went straight to Krukenberg and demanded the cessation of this activity. The Brigadeführer actually had no knowledge of this activity and agreed to Raybaud's demand. In this way, Raybaud finally became the only political leader of the regiment.

To those officers and NCOs of his regiment that might have been surprised that their new *chef* was without any war decorations, Hstuf. Raybaud explained on the occasion of a meeting the circumstances around the *croix de guerre avec palms* awarded to him.

Waffen-Gren. Regt der SS 58 was made up of some 15% *Miliciens* and 80% legionnaires of the LVF. At the head of the 1st Battalion was Hstuf. Emile Monneuse. He was ex-*Milice*. And at the head of the 2nd Battalion was Hstuf. Maurice Berret. He was ex-LVF.

Courageous and devoted, Monneuse was a professional soldier with good military knowledge, but his age, he was well into his forties, sometimes got the better of him and his 'heavy responsibility'. He was the former *chef de la Franc-Garde de l'Ile-de-France*. His assistant was the very able W-Ostuf. Falcy who had previous military service with the *chasseurs alpins* and the LVF.[22]

Alfred Falcy was born in 1912. A ranker, he was commissioned *sous-lieutenant de réserve* in 1938. Four years later, with the same rank, he was serving with the LVF on the Eastern front. His position was *chef de section* [platoon commander] and his Company the 2nd [of the I. Battalion]. In late 1943, he received the command of the 2nd Company. When the LVF was transferred to the Waffen-SS its 2nd Company became the 2/58. Falcy remained at its head. Promoted to assistant battalion commander, he had to give up his 2nd Company to Ostuf. de Rose, also from the LVF, a command he would relinquish a little later to Ostuf. Géromini.

As for Maurice Berret, he was born on 28th July 1914. In 1936, he was admitted to the *Ecole spéciale militaire de Saint-Cyr*. On 1st October 1938, he was promoted to *Sous-lieutenant d'active* in the infantry and posted to the *23e régiment*

---

22   Although his exact role within the regiment remains unclear, de Genouillac believes that Falcy was the *adjoint* to the commander of the I/58. The suggestion has also been made that Falcy was even the *adjoint* to Raybaud, the regimental commander. Although Falcy was sufficiently qualified to hold either post, the author, in the face of no official documentation, has gone along with de Genouillac.

de tirailleurs algériens (23° RTA). He served with the same regiment from 1938 to 1940. In late 1941, Lieutenant Berret volunteered for the LVF. He was one of the few *officiers d'active* to serve with the LVF. He held various commands and, on 1st July 1943, was promoted to *Capitaine*. On 30th March 1944, he was awarded with the Iron Cross 2nd Class.

Hstuf. Raybaud placed Hstuf. de Perricot, one of his most trusted men, in command of the Headquarters Company. Born on 20th March 1893, Marc-Raoul de Perricot served first in the *infanterie métropolitaine* as a *officier de réserve*. On 30th March 1924, he was promoted to the rank of *lieutenant de réserve*. In 1935, he switched to the *service de santé* [health service], obtaining the rank of *pharmacien lieutenant de réserve* on 11th May 1938. A veteran of the Great War, he also served in 39–40.

In the years that followed de Perricot proved himself time and time again; in 1942 as the *chef* of the SOL for the department of Lot-et-Garonne; in 1943 as the *chef départemental* of the *Milice* for the same department; and, finally, in 1944 as the *chef régional* for 'Toulouse'. His two sons, who had also joined the *Milice*, were also now serving in 'Charlemagne'.

Raybaud's assistant was the ageing Ostuf. Marcel Baudouin, born on 11th May 1902 in Bt. Gereon. By October 1937, he held a commission of *lieutenant d'active* in the infantry.[23] After the French campaign he became a *commissaire de police*. In 1942, he volunteered for *La Légion Tricolore* and served as *adjoint* to *Commandant* Herchin, the *chef du dépôt* of Montargis. He later transferred to the LVF and served on the headquarters staff of the II.Bn. He was a holder of the Kriegsverdienstkreuz (War Merit Cross) 2nd Class.

The company commanders of the Waffen-Gren. Regt. der SS 58 were drawn from both the LVF and the *Milice*. Their tricolore spirit did not displease Raybaud. But the combat experience of the LVF officers was in striking contrast to that of the *Milicien* counterparts.

At the head of the 1/58 was Ostuf. Jean Fatin. He was an 'old hand' of the LVF who had come up through the ranks. He had served with the LVF on the Eastern front since the terrible winter of 1941. Like Fatin, the four platoon commanders of the 1/58 were LVF veterans of 1941. At the head of the 1st platoon was Oscha. Girard. At the head of the 2nd platoon was Oscha. Froideval from the south of France. His son was serving in the 1st platoon. At the head of the 3rd platoon was Oscha. Bonnafous, a former *gendarme*. And at the head of the 4th platoon (heavy) was Scha. Choumiline. A white Russian with a very strong Russian accent, he too had served in the French Army.[24]

At the head of the 3/58 was Ustuf. Rigeade. He too was an old hand of the LVF who had served on the Eastern front since 1941. For three years he served with the 3rd Company, working his way up through the ranks. On 1st April 1944, he was appointed *Sous-lieutenant* (2nd Lieutenant). From 20th May 1944 to 12th June 1944, while *Capitaine* Martin[25] was on leave, he had command of the 3rd

23   He probably gained his commission at the *école militaire d'infanterie de Saint-Maixent.*

24   Grenier, letter to the author, April 1998.

25   Martin became an Hauptsturmführer in 'Charlemagne' and the assistant commander of its artillery group.

Company. Following the hospitalisation of Martin on 24th June he again took over command. Three days later, on the 27th, he was wounded at Bobr and evacuated. In August 1944, he resumed command.

Three platoon commanders of the 3/58 were also LVF veterans who had served on the Eastern front since 1941. At the head of the 1st platoon was Oscha. Armani, a P.P.F. militant, born of a Corsican father and a Madagascan mother. At the 2nd platoon was Oscha. Stiffler. He too was a P.P.F. militant. He was a native of Nice. At the 3rd platoon was Oscha. Blonet. He was a *Franciste*. Uscha. Tartaglino commanded the 4th (mortar) platoon. He was a *Milicien* who had come to the company in November 1944. The *adjudant de compagnie* was Hscha. Perrigault. He was a former serviceman. He too was a veteran of 1941. He did not belong to any political party. By trade he was a professional draughtsman.

In late December 1944, Uscha. Blonet, who commanded an infantry platoon, was surprised that he was sent to Berlin for training to command a heavy machine-gun platoon. He believes that he was the only Frenchman on the course. His absence from his comrades was made all the more bearable by his friendship with an Austrian officer, his wife and his daughter living in Berlin. The German instructors, who were all war wounded and sometimes disabled, trained him in the use of heavy machine guns and also in anti-tank combat with the Panzerfaust and Panzerschreck. He witnessed numerous air raids on the city, which was already in ruins. In late January 1945, the course was interrupted by the arrival of the Russians at Kustrin, only some eighty kilometers away. In early February, fearing that he would be forcibly incorporated into a German unit for the defense of Berlin, he returned to Wildflecken without authorisation. On his return, he was promoted to the rank of Oberscharführer.

Ustuf. de Genouillac commanded the 4th (heavy) Company of battalion I/58. During the reorganisation of the LVF at Greifenberg he had been made responsible for the training of the 4th (heavy) Company of the I. Battalion which became the 4/58 in 'Charlemagne'. Three of his four theoretical platoon commanders were from the LVF; *élève-officier* Antoni Noell, who he had known in Russia, commanded a platoon of 80mm mortars; *Adjudant-chef* Bonnefous commanded a heavy machine-gun platoon; the young Jean Louis Martin commanded the second heavy machine-gun platoon. The last platoon commander, *élève-officier* Yann de Brangelin, one of his comrades from his French Army days, had arrived at Wildflecken with the *Milice*. In fact, after meeting de Brangelin quite by chance in the camp, de Genouillac had had him assigned to his company. His transfer had presented no problems. However, for the best part of the months December, January and February, the platoon commanders were away from their commands at officer training schools or on officer training courses. Some would not rejoin the company.

On one occasion de Genouillac found himself in front of Krukenberg for not returning to him a list of German songs sung by his company. This he had completely neglected to do. With three others, he was harshly rebuked.

Company 5/58 was under Ostuf. Georges Wagner, born on 22nd September 1919.[26] Wagner had also commanded its forerunner, the 9th Company of the III/

26   Various letters to the author from Blanc and Rusco, who both served in Company 5/
        58. This corrects Mabire, who cites Hscha. Walter as the company commander (page
        222). Also, according to Rusco, letters to the author of 2/98 and 5/3/98, it was in

638 (LVF). Two platoon commanders were ex-LVF. They were Pierre Rusco and Hscha. Edmond Walter, who was succeeded by Oscha. Blaise, also ex-LVF. It is said that Blaise had served with the Foreign Legion. One platoon commander was ex-SS. He was Uscha. René Maixandeau. Seriously wounded in Galicia with the French Sturmbrigade, he still walked with a limp. He commanded the heavy machine-gun platoon. The fourth platoon commander may have been ex-*Milice*.[27] The Company *Spiess* was Oscha. Both. He was ex-LVF. Hscha. Gobion, the LVF legend, was the company's armourer.

Blanc of Company 5/58, who was ex-*Milice*, noted that the ex-LVF cadre had a shared nostalgia for Russia and the Russians. They would often speak of the beauty of the scenery, and of the warm and confiding welcome of the peasants. Indeed, Blaise once confided that after the war he wanted to return to Russia and get a farm there. At the time, Blanc was surprised to hear this but, much later, he would understand.

Michel Saint-Magne, also from the LVF, commanded the 6/58. Before transferring to the Waffen-SS he had served in the 9th Company of the III/638 (LVF) with the rank of Feldwebel. Like Baudouin, he was a holder of the Kriegsverdienstkreuz (War Merit Cross) 2nd Class. Now he was at the head of a company that had few veterans. For the most part, the *encadrement* of its forerunner, the 10th Company of the III/638, had moved on. Nevertheless, *caporal-chef* Wassili, a former Russian partisan whom the 10th Company had adopted, served and served loyally in this new company.[28] He was deaf and dumb.

The commander of Infantry Gun Company 9/58 was Ostuf. Jean Français. His orderly was Robert Lacoste. One platoon commander was Oscha. Marcel Duchène. The three of them were inseparable. They had joined the LVF in 1943 at the same time, becoming good friends. They had served together in the same company of the LVF, the 5/638, and now, having passed to the Waffen-SS, they were serving together again in the same company.

The 9/58 was equipped with French 75mm mountain guns. The guns were horse-drawn.

Oberjunker B. commanded the Panzerjäger Kompanie of the regiment. The company comprised one panzerschreck platoon, one panzerfaust platoon, and one platoon (or battery) of three 75mm anti-tank guns, which were French and pre-war.

Of his platoon commanders, the company commander recalls that one 'had been with the LVF since 1941' [undoubtedly *Adjudant* Pierre[29]], two 'came from

early January 1945 that Wagner assumed command of the company. However, according to Blanc, letter to the author of 14/6/2001, when he was assigned to the company in November 1944 Wagner was at its head.

27 Curiously, Rusco recalls that Company 5/58 had three platoons. However, the author is convinced that it would have had four. Rusco commanded one platoon. Of the other two platoon commanders, he recalls one was ex-*Milice* and one was ex-SS [undoubtedly Maixandeau].

28 In this way, his homeland became the 10th Company of the LVF that had welcomed him. With a French tricolore on his arm, he was killed in Pomerania.

29 *Sergent* Fronteau, also transferred from the PAK Company of the LVF to the 10/58, was his assistant at Bobr. Pierre was killed late February 1945 at Heringen,

the recruitment drive in the POW camps', and the last 'came from the *Franc-Garde* of the *Milice*'.[30] All were apolitical, with the exception of Pierre who was former P.P.F. And all had previous military experience.

Oberjunker B. once incurred the displeasure of Brigf. Krukenberg, but he did bring it upon himself. He recalls:

> Brigf. Krukenberg came to inspect the company. Although it was risky, I presented the company in French and *à la française*, saluting the French salute. This did not please him and, before the men, he hurled reproaches at me in franco-german. He summoned me and started again. I did not move nor reply … and they did not take [my] command from me. He was not a spiteful man.

In December 1944, Oberjunker B. was selected for Kompanieführer training and attended an in-house Lehrgang supervised by SS-Hstuf. Jauss. The training lasted some four weeks. Jauss used B. as an instructor because of his interest in anti-tank warfare and weapons. During one such demonstration, Oscha. Charles met his death. Charles hailed from the Sturmbrigade and was wounded at the head of a platoon in Galicia. Accidents accompany realistic battlefield training with live fire, but Oberjunker B. is not convinced that Charles' death was an accident.[31]

Asked to explode a mine, B. and Charles took up position in a hole some six metres away. Suddenly and without reason, Charles left the hole and started to crawl towards the mine. B. tried to stop him by grabbing hold of Charles' trousers, but the fabric tore and came away in his hands. Charles was some three metres from the mine when he exploded it. He was blown apart. 'The snow was red and grey'.[32] It was B. who brought him back in a tent sheet. Thereupon, Charles' comrades tried to accuse B. of his death, but after a quick inquest Hstuf. Jauss cleared him.

Also and notably, for the duration of the course, B. continued to command and train the Panzerjäger Kompanie: he worked with the NCOs in the evening and at night, leaving them to carry out his orders in the day.

And yet more problems

A host of problems plagued the training. To begin with, there was the chronic shortage of food supplies. To supplement their meagre rations, some former legionnaires took to poaching, a habit they had picked up on the Eastern front. The disappearance of a calf in a nearby village led to an inquiry and the Military Police being brought in. Subsequently, it came to light that some Frenchmen had taken, slaughtered, cut up and eaten the calf in an almost 'magical ceremony'. Krukenberg was beside himself with rage. Puaud sent the culprits to a disciplinary company and sent out notes reminding units of 'SS ideals'.[33]

near Nordhausen, Germany, when American aircraft attacked one of the many convoys transporting 'Charlemagne' to the Eastern front.

30   W-Uscha. Soulié may have served as a platoon commander.
31   This is contrary to Mabire, see page 243. B. still wonders if despair 'got the better' of Charles and brought him to commit suicide.
32   B., letter to the author, 16/10/1999.
33   Saint-Loup, page 159. Curiously, de la Mazière recounts an incident on Christmas Day when Krukenberg came across pork being eaten in a dining-hall instead of the veal on the menu. The pork had been brought from a local farmer and smuggled into

The rations became so bad at one point that Ostuf. Fatin took his company back to the kitchens and gave the order to throw the contents of their mess tins across the kitchen. Ignoring the protests and the pleas of helplessness from the German cook, Ostuf. Fatin then ordered his company to occupy the kitchen until such time that the cook could come up with something edible to eat. And of course that did not prove too long! This was but one of many such instances instigated by the officers who shared the same meals as their men.

To stave off hunger, a platoon from Waffen-Gren. Regt der SS 58 assigned to remove horses that had died of impetigo fed on the rotting meat! Perhaps worse, some hungry grooms deliberately had their horse run down so as to get it put down by the veterinary surgeon and gorge themselves on the fresh meat.

Gren. Blanc and his comrades of Company 5/58 also went hungry. Conversations often returned to stories of meals. Such was their hunger that if they had been offered the choice between a snack and a good-looking woman, they would have chosen the snack! So as not to devour in the evening the entire bread ration, and thus have nothing left for the morning, Blanc confided his to a comrade on the understanding that no matter what he was not to give it back to him before the following morning. It was to Daniel L.G. that he confided his bread, and L.G. confided his to Blanc. This 'pact of bread' was never broken. This sort of communion was a symbol of the camaraderie existing between them.

There was also a shortage of equipment. What weapons were available were often rotated. The twelve 105mm guns for the Artillery group had still not materialised. The fourteen Jagdpanzers for Ostuf. Michel's Assault gun Company and the ten 'Tiger' tanks had still not arrived. Each regimental commander had a light cross-country vehicle at his disposal, but no petrol for it. Neither was there petrol for the ambulances and Weber was forced to requisition a horse-drawn carriage from a village to get a wounded soldier of the *Compagnie d'Honneur* to hospital. No horses were available to pull the anti-tank guns. There was a distinct lack of practice ammunition and even personal equipment like helmets, gloves, balaclavas, spades and field glasses.

Wildflecken itself was a problem. Although a modern training camp, it was, throughout the months of winter, covered with snow, sometimes two metres deep. Then there were the violent snowstorms. Indeed, according to Castrillo of Company 5/58, the weather was worse than that he had experienced with the SK in Norway. Such conditions made Wildflecken unsuitable for infantry training. Battalion and regiment manoeuvres proved impossible, as well as those in conjunction with its heavy units.

The snow gave somebody the idea of forming a scout-ski platoon. Blanc and L.G. of Company 5/58 were volunteered. Blanc was not asked if he was a good skier, which was not the case. In this way, they made the acquaintance of Lucien V. born of a French mother and a Thai father. He had been accepted into the ranks of the Waffen-SS when the LVF was disbanded and yet, previously, he had been denied, joining the LVF instead.

The training of the scout-ski platoon was in the hands of a former NCO of the *chasseurs alpins* by the name of Insabi (perhaps of Algerian origin). He was a

the camp. Obviously this was strictly forbidden and yet Krukenberg took no disciplinary action in this instance.

first-rate instructor. Almost every afternoon for a period of six weeks, the men trained. The skis provided, said to be of Norwegian origin, were not very solid and made control downhill almost impossible. The platoon was later disbanded.

One problem of lesser significance was the language barrier. Few were those who had full mastery of the German language. Indeed, in several units, the *Kompanie-Schreiber* [Company secretary] had little or no knowledge of German![34]

The Headquarters Company

Transferred to the Headquarters Company, Soulat found himself working to SS-Uscha. Max Micholski who, before the war, had worked as the head waiter on the Orient Express! Micholski spoke seven different languages. Of late, he had served with the Dtsch.Verb. Stab. III/Frz. I.R.638 [the German liaison staff of the III/638].

The Company commander of the Headquarters Company was W-Ostuf. Maud'huit. He reported to SS-Stubaf. Katzian, the German liaison officer.[35] Of Austrian birth, Katzian had fought with the Gebirgsjäger [Mountain troops] at Narvik, Norway, and in Crete. He too had served with the Dtsch. Verb. zum Frz. I.R. 638 and transferred to the French Brigade of the Waffen-SS.

In November or perhaps as late as early December 1944, SS-Stubaf. Katzian was succeeded by SS-Stubaf. von Lölhoffel.

In late December 1944, Hscha. Surrel succeeded Ostuf. Maud'huit at the head of the Headquarters Company.

Fahrschwadron A

Fahrschwadron A or Fahrschwadron I[36] began to take shape in November 1944 under the command of W-Hstuf. Schlisler. A veteran of the Great War, he had served France again in *la Légion Tricolore* and then the LVF. The assistant commander was W-Ostuf. Darrigade who had previously served with the *Milice*. The Spiess was W-Hscha. Goubin from the III. Battalion of the LVF.

Fahrschwadron A was organised with three transport columns (Fahrkolonne), an escort (or combat) platoon, and an independent platoon of administrative and support staff.[37] At the head of the transport columns were W-Oscha. Carbillet and W-Oscha. Bernand. The third *chef* is not known. Carbillet was ex-LVF and was one of two brothers serving with 'Charlemagne'.[38] Bernand and the unknown *chef* were ex-*Milice*.

---

34 For example, Soulat's *soldbuch* contains the spelling mistake of *Verselgung* for *Versetzung* (transfer) not once but twice.

35 The memoirs of Soulat. Because of this the possibility exists that the Headquarters Company took its orders from the German Inspection rather than from Brigade Headquarters as one would have expected. If true, this is surprising.

36 Confusingly, Mercier of Fahrschwadron A also saw used the designation of Waffen-Grenadier-Brigade der SS 'Charlemagne' Kolonne A Fahrschwadron.

37 Mercier, letter to the author, 9/10/2001, although unconfirmed. The independent platoon of administrative and support staff comprised among others the Spiess, the head clerk, the secretary, liaison officers, nurses, stretcher-bearers, armourers, farriers, vets, blacksmiths, the chief accountant, and cooks.

Uscha. Mercier, who made the journey from Greifenberg to Wildflecken with Goubin and Carbillet, was assigned to the independent platoon as Rechnungsführer.

One of the most colourful characters of Fahrschwadron A was *adjudant* Louis, who had been inherited from the Trésorerie of the I. Battalion of the LVF. Louis was a pathological liar. Because of his job within the Trésorerie he had acquired the nickname of baron Louis in memory of the Minister of Finance of Charles X and Louis Philippe. He let it be known that his personal fortune was considerable and included, among other small things, the Lido cabaret in Paris. There was the time a soldier reported saying 'I was told to go and see baron Louis', to which he put on a saddened expression and said 'They call me baron when I am a marquis!'

Nobody had ever seen Louis on horseback but his knowledge of equestrian terms let the connoisseur know that he had probably been a waiter or headwaiter in a restaurant frequented by riders. He always put off until the following day the formalities that he needed to do to obtain German nationality. In fact, he thought that it was his by right, being the grandson of a German general.

Louis was idle. Hstuf. Schlisler ordered Uscha. Mercier to go over the head of Louis to organise the support services, which he did. As befitting his status, Louis continued to do nothing.[39]

Fahrschwadron A also 'inherited' Grenadier Harnu. He had once held the rank of *adjudant-chef* and been the *adjudant de battaillon* of the I. Battalion of the LVF, but had got into disciplinary problems. Uscha. Mercier was asked by Oscha. Carbillet to take Harnu under his wing and appoint him to a post where he would not be ragged. Mercier had Harnu with him to the end.

Fahrschwadron A was also short of equipment, although it did receive some horse-drawn wagons bearing the inscription 'Carretta di Battaglione', which must have been scrapped before in the days of Garibaldi.

The Medical Company

W-Hstuf. Dr. Péribère was at the head of the Medical Company. Like many serving in the company, he too was ex-*Milice* and had 'volunteered' of late for the Waffen-SS. Nevertheless, nearly all of the officers and NCOs were German.

The Medical Company was quartered in barracks at the foot of Wildflecken camp. Medical staff learnt how to handle the panzerfäuste rather 'than the art of dressing wounds'.[40] Indeed, one former member of the company described it as a 'bloody shambles'.

Religion still plays its part

A regular sight at Wildflecken was Monseigneur de Mayol de Lupé riding a splendid chestnut thoroughbred. Invariably he carried a revolver on his hip and around his neck was a pectoral cross. But his presence reassured many young Catholics of the *Milice* who now found themselves serving in the Waffen-SS, which they regarded as an enemy of the Church.

38   Carbillet was a former editor for *Le Petit Dauphiné*, a regional daily newspaper.
39   In February 1945, when 'Charlemagne' left for Pomerania, Louis remained at Wildflecken. It is not known what became of him.
40   Cornu, correspondence to Mounine.

The riding school had been converted into a chapel and 'did good business'. Each Sunday afternoon, after mass, de Mayol de Lupé conducted a service for the few Protestants of 'Charlemagne'. Blanc of the 5/58 was there. He noted that the Monseigneur had very much mastered the liturgy of the Protestant form of worship and respected the spirit perfectly. On one occasion de Mayol de Lupé even addressed a Protestant congregation as 'the elite of Christianity'!

It is said the Monseigneur would have gladly converted the riding school into a Mosque, introduced Ramadan and summoned the faithful to prayer by the Muezzin call if there had been any Moslems in 'Charlemagne'.[41]

Brigf. Krukenberg himself recognised the important service the Monseigneur continued to play. After the war Krukenberg said of him:[42]

> You could say that he held the Division in his hand. I have to recognise that he was the one who helped me the most to unite the so disparate elements.

Father Lara also spread the word of god at Wildflecken.[43] Of Spanish origin, he had participated in the civil war in the ranks of the Nationalists. He came to the Waffen-SS from the *Milice*.

In early December, morale was raised by the announcement of the Ardennes offensive. Many like Uscha. Mercier of Fahrschwadron A were still not quite convinced of Germany's defeat. He believed in the new weapons. The *Miliciens* had told him of planes 'crossing the sky of Ulm like shooting stars'. He believed that the Ardennes offensive was only the start of the recovery.

With the coming of Christmas, morale dipped again. It was a Christmas of misery and loneliness, although an end of year 'review' did provide some comic relief. Much to the delight of the audience, Desrumeaux mimicked Ostuf. Defever. Defever was not amused. Both Desrumeaux and Defever were ex-LVF.[44]

A four-page booklet was distributed for Christmas. On the first page there was the music and words of the hymn 'He was born the Holy Child'.

On Christmas night, Mgr. de Mayol de Lupé celebrated the Nativity in the riding school. Nearly two thousand men, for the most part former *Miliciens*, were crowded together around the improvised altar. The aristocratic *Milice* hierarchy was there, but Puaud, Krukenberg and the officers of the Inspection were conspicuous by their absence. Assisted by Father Lara, Mgr. de Mayol de Lupé spoke of the birth of Jesus and concluded by asking the congregation to pray for 'our Führer' and for the 'final success of our crusade against atheistic Bolshevism, the enemy of Christ'! This religious ceremony did actually help to foster a sense of unity and purpose.

As for Brigf. Krukenberg, on Christmas night, accompanied by his blonde daughter in the uniform of the B.D.M, he visited the assembled FLAK Company.

On New Years Eve, the whole Brigade was assembled in the riding school around a gigantic fir tree to celebrate the old Germanic pagan festival of 'Yule' (or

41   De la Mazière, page 57.
42   "*Entretien avec le général Krukenberg*", "*Historia #32*", page 133.
43   His presence at Wildflecken may have only been fleeting (Blanc, letter to the author, 31/1/2001).
44   Jean-Marie Desrumeaux was among the first to join the LVF. He was present at Versailles on 27th August 1941 when Laval was shot.

the Winter solstice). The evergreen symbolised the life force in winter promising rebirth. Poems were read out, then followed by a story. Finally an officer lit one candle after another on the tree and dedicated each new flame to persons, living or dead. The highest candle was reserved for the Führer, but it would not catch light and fell to the ground. An omen? Before drawing the ceremony to an end, Krukenberg spoke briefly. Concluding, he evoked the oath sworn by all to the Führer and appealed to them all to remain faithful to the SS motto 'My honour is loyalty'.

The New Year of 1945

Comings and goings marked January 1945. On the 3rd, Brigf. Krukenberg gave the FLAK Company an operational mission: to participate in the anti-aircraft defence of Fulda from the nearby village of Bachrain.

Billeted on the locals, the FLAK Company quickly forged bonds with them. Ustuf. Fayard still had his horse with him. At Wildflecken, he had managed, and nobody quite knew how, to acquire a horse for his own personal use.

The liaison officer was monocled Luftwaffe Lieutenant Murmann.

While continuing to train, the FLAK Company fully played its part against the numerous Anglo-American air raids, shooting down some bombers. The FLAK Company then had to protect the baled out crews from the vengeful population.

From the 3rd, Hstuf. Fenet attended the 26th Lehrgang at Heer school Hirschberg in Mecklenburg. He received battalion commander's training. The course lasted until 10th February. He graduated with glowing feedback.

On 2nd January 1945, Hscha. Boyer, the commander of the regimental Pionierzug/Waffen-Gren. Regt der SS 57, and thirty men—fifteen men of his Pionierzug and fifteen men of the regimental Pionierzug/Waffen-Gren. Regt der SS 58—left Wildflecken for SS-Pionierschule Hradischko. The Pionierlehrgang, commanded by SS-Ostuf. Sapin of 'Wallonien', would last some two weeks. Here Boyer met Ostuf. Audibert de Vitrolles and Ustuf. Mailhé of the Engineer Company of 'Charlemagne' who were attending another Lehrgang. Sickness struck Boyer and he was in hospital for ten days (from 13th January to 23rd January 1945).

Meanwhile, on 5th January 1945, the fifty-strong Workshop Company under W-Ostuf. Maud'huit left Wildflecken for a training course. In its ranks was company secretary Strmm. Vaxelaire. He had been with the Workshop Company since its formation days before. He too had responded to a circular sent to all units requesting volunteers for the company.

At first Strmm. Vaxelaire believed that the Workshop Company was bound for Pomerania, but on the 8th it reached its destination of Berlin. Deloused, the company was sent on to barracks Lichterfelde-West, the home of Waffen-SS Division 'Leibstandarte SS Adolf Hitler'. Vaxelaire for one was glad to be away from the *bordel* of Wildflecken.

The destruction of Berlin and the suffering of its inhabitants deeply affected Vaxelaire. Each day, from his office, he watched the air raids. Each day, he noted how the first group of enemy bombers would pass over ahead in the same place. Each day, in reply, he saw explosions fill the sky. And, each day, he noted how the following groups of bombers would then turn to avoid the flak because they now knew its position.

However, his time at Berlin was not without moments of humour and surprise. He had to laugh at Ostuf. Maud'huit who, to impress the Germans, had put a nameplate of *Graf von Maud'huit* on his door! On one occasion, while eating out at a restaurant, he was surprised to meet a school friend. His surprise was all the greater at another restaurant where he met the housekeeper of a nearby household back in Paris. The two of them were in Berlin as civilian workers.

And yet his everlasting memory of Berlin was that of two German soldiers shot for desertion in the main courtyard of the barracks. Indeed, one of the soldiers was dressed up like a woman complete with robe and wig. But now he could not help wondering if this man was perhaps more lucky than him and his comrades of the Workshop Company.

The Waffen-Grenadier Regiment der SS 57

Back at Wildflecken, the command of Waffen-Grenadier Regiment der SS 57 became vacant when Ostubaf. Gamory-Dubourdeau left to take up a post at the SS-Hauptampt in Berlin. His old age and his deteriorating physical state of health had conspired against him to leave him commanding his regiment in nothing more than name only. To replace him, Brigf. Krukenberg called on Hstuf. de Bourmont to become the new commander of Waffen-Grenadier Regiment der SS 57.

Preferring to be called *Mon capitaine* and not by his SS rank, de Bourmont found himself in conflict with his orderly officer, Ustuf. Martret, who was SS to the core. Artus mediated. This 'French war' became known throughout the whole regiment and many sided with Martret.

Hstuf. de Bourmont had at his disposal two grenadier battalions of four companies each, an anti-tank company, an Infantry gun company and various regimental units. At the head of the 1st Battalion was Ostuf. Fenet and at the 2nd Battalion Hstuf. Obitz.

Born on 9th March 1908 in Lerouville, René-André Obitz attended the infantry *Ecole militaire de Saint-Maixent* and, in 1932, was promoted to *sous-lieutenant d'active*. He transferred from *La Légion Tricolore* to the LVF, where he served with the 1st Battalion[45], attaining the rank of *Capitaine*. On 23rd April 1944, he was awarded with the Iron Cross 2nd Class.

The commander of the Infantry Gun Company (9/57) was W-Ostuf. Robert Roy. A former *Capitaine de l'artillerie coloniale française*, Roy had come to the Waffen-SS in the summer of 1943 from the N.S.K.K.[46] He was a most remarkable character. He had a liking for good food, red wine and women. Indeed, legend has it that he smuggled his female conquests into Wildflecken in gun carriages! Although regarded as stubborn and bad tempered, he excelled as a gunner and could calculate firing distances without the use of a rangefinder. And he never made a mistake. He demanded that his subordinates call him *Mon Capitaine* rather than by his German rank and asked the Germans in his company to speak only in French! And yet he was a convinced National Socialist. Of late, he had been standing in for Fenet away on a training course. On 30th January 1945, he was

---

45   He probably joined the battalion in the field in January 1943.

46   According to Saint-Loup, page 176, Roy was languishing in an *offlag* when he volunteered for the Waffen-SS. In response to this, he probably went to the N.S.K.K. first.

promoted to the rank of Hauptsturmführer which was equivalent to his former French Army rank. Notably, he was promoted to SS-Hauptsturmführer and not Waffen-Hauptsturmführer.[47]

Ostuf. André commanded the Headquarters Company of Waffen-Gren. Regt der SS 57. He was a former *Milicien*. The Headquarters Company consisted of a reconnaissance platoon, a signals platoon, and a *Pionierzug* (engineers platoon). On 12th November 1944, Hscha.[48] Boyer received the command of the *Pionierzug* from Robert Lefevre. The *Pionierzug* numbered eighty men.

Ostuf. Labuze, also a former *Milicien*, commanded the anti-tank company.[49]

All of the grenadier company commanders came from the Sturmbrigade. Some had only graduated of late from Kienschlag.

Hstuf. de Bourmont brought onto his regimental staff his friend Ostuf. de Londaiz, also a regular officer and a *Milicien*. Born on 4th November 1919, de Londaiz was a convinced fascist who had fought on the side of the Falangists in the Spanish Civil War. In the *Milice*, he went from the rank of *chef de cohorte* to the post of *chef régional adjoint* at Lyon in June 1944. In August 1944 he had accompanied de Vaugelas to Limoges to organise the evacuation of the encircled Vichy forces.

Much is made of the fact that Waffen-Gren. Regt. der SS 57 was considered to be an ideologically 'pure' Waffen-SS unit. This is all the more remarkable considering that the origin of much of its personnel was not the Sturmbrigade. Indeed it seems that those who were not from the Sturmbrigade had assimilated themselves body and soul into this regiment. They had responded to what the veterans of the Sturmbrigade had to offer and that was esprit de corps and unit loyalty.

Nevertheless, Waffen-Gren. Regt. der SS 57 had its own problems. In January or February 1945,[50] the 'desertion' of a whole platoon from company 2/57 complete with MG 42 machine-guns and full kit sent Brigf. Krukenberg into a rage.

Led by its commander, the platoon had left Wildflecken camp in the early hours of the morning and marched, in order and in step, to Brückenau railway station where fake movement orders were produced and stamped as being in order. The 'desertion' was, in fact, aided and abetted by the whole company; the fake movement orders had been prepared by *Spiess* Montcarnie; Vincent and his section had been on guard duty at the camp entrance; Bayle and Mauclair had been on lookout in and around the barracks.

The Military Police soon found the 'deserters': they had joined Degrelle's 28. SS-Freiwilligen – Panzer-Grenadier Division 'Wallonien'. Brigf. Krukenberg

---

47   See the SS-Verordungsblatt of 30th January 1945.

48   Boyer was promoted to the rank of Hauptscharführer on 1st October 1944 for 'acts of war'.

49   His brother, a *Milicien de Limoges,* was captured by the F.T.P. and tortured to death.

50   This 'desertion' actually took place sometime after Bayle's arrival at Wildflecken camp on 2nd January 1945 (see *"De Marseille à Novossibirsk"*, pages 141-143) and was not in mid November 1944 intimated by Mabire and recorded by Landwehr.

wanted them back, but the SS-Hauptampt proved of no help to him. In the end, he had to resign himself to losing them to Degrelle whose prestige was high.

Among the 'deserters' were Strmm. Pierre Lemaire, Gren. Brousses, Gren. Eudes, Gren. Morineau, Gren. Ourgaud and Gren. Roland. They were attached to the Jungkompanie under the command of André Regibaud. Their new section commander was Uscha. Renard.[51]

More 'desertions' from Wildflecken, this 'camp of the Gauls', were planned by the entire former Sturmbrigade contingents of company 2/57 and of neighbouring companies when their turn for guard duty came around![52] Bayle let company commander Ostuf. Bartolomei into the secret in the hope that he would follow them, but the departure to Pomerania overtook Bayle and his fellow 'conspirators'.

Also of concern were some *Miliciens*. While most had responded to their new circumstances, some had not. On 20th January 1945, company commander Coutret was thrown out of 'Charlemagne' for having 'too much bad spirit'. This former *lieutenant de chasseurs alpins de réserve* and Darnand's former *chef de cabinet* had remained a staunch supporter of Darnand and the Marshal. Sturmbrigade veterans refused to obey him because he commanded in French. Demobilised at Greifenberg, he went to Sigmaringen where Darnand sent him to Heuberg camp and the autonomous *Milice* unit.

Coutret was not an isolated case. During January 1945, a total of fifteen officers, including Coutret and Guignot, were dismissed.

January 1945 also saw the completion of the in-house officer cadets' Lehrgang supervised by SS-Hstuf. Jauss and W-Ustuf. Pignard-Berthet. Among the officer cadets were B., Yann de Brangelin, de Bazelaire, Marcel Carlier, Maurice Comte, Jean de Lacaze, d'Oléon, Gerard de Perricot, Girel, Lapart, Pierre Méric and Terrel. They numbered more than twenty. Most, if not all, were former *Miliciens*.

At the end of the Lehrgang, most of the officer cadets went to Kienschlag where they should have attended a second Lehrgang supervised by Ustuf. Kreis, but this did not go ahead because of the rapid development of the war. Instead they received liaison officer training, lasting some fifteen days. They were taught tactics at the sand table, they were taught how to identify enemy weaponry and, from films and commentaries, they were taught the combat methods of the enemy (snipers, camouflage …).

The officer cadets returned to Wildflecken with the rank of Standartenjunker. The training had been too short to warrant promotion to that of Standartenoberjunker.

Std. Ju. Comte was assigned to company 5/57. Thanks to the 'political' classes[53] he attended as part of his officer cadet training he came to realise that it was no longer

---

51   According to Mabire, pages 192-194, nearly all of the French 'deserters' would fall or be wounded in the Ardennes offensive. In response to this, the fate of the six Frenchmen listed was as follows; Strmm. Lemaire was wounded on the Oder front on 22nd April 1945; Gren. Brousses fell in combat at Streesen on 4th March 1945; Gren. Eudes also fell in combat at Streesen on 4th March 1945; Gren. Morineau survived the war; Gren. Ourgaud was also killed at Streesen; and Gren. Roland survived the war. Also, 'Wallonien' did not see action in the Ardennes. Thus, none of the French 'deserters' fell in the Ardennes.

52   Bayle, "*De Marseille à Novossibirsk*", pages 141-143.

a question of France and its internal struggles, but the gestation of a new European order. This realisation is all the more surprising because his background was that of a masquisard. Moreover, he was not an adherent of any political party.

Maurice Comte was born on 21st August 1921. While studying at engineering school *Arts et Métiers* (this was from before the war to 1941) he had neither the time nor the spirit to indulge in politics. After the armistice, and despite a strong dislike of the occupying forces, he found the Germans correct, in fact, very different from the image portrayed later by the so-called 'official history'. However, at the beginning of 1943, when he was working in Grenoble, he was called up by the S.T.O. for forced labour in Germany. Not prepared to accept this eventuality, he fled, like many others, to the woods and hills, and joined the Maquis.

Comte served in the maquis company of *Capitaine* Stéphane, regarded as one of the few officers of high moral and military worth. But he was instinctively worried that the maquis, for the most part made up of workers, peasants and students, was led without explanation by a Communist minority, just like Stéphane himself. And then in July 1944 the course of his war as a *chef de section* in maquis Stéphane suddenly took a dramatic turn when, in stupid circumstances, he was taken prisoner by a patrol from the *École des Cadres de la Milice* at Uriage. Questioned, he told his captors nothing. They responded in kind by withholding his food. And yet six months later Comte was in the uniform of the Waffen-SS and being put through his paces in a *Lehrgang* of officer cadets. How did this come about? He explained:

> Stéphane organised a *coup de main* on Uriage château; *Milicien* officer Benezit was killed and two or three *Miliciens* were captured. Through the intermediary of a priest, one of the *chefs de la Milice* at Grenoble, Berthon, and Stéphane decided upon a meeting with a view to an exchange of prisoners. The meeting took place near Uriage in the middle of the woods. Stéphane and Berthon, whom I accompanied, talked and separated, not being able to decide without the agreement of their *chefs*. I returned to Grenoble with Berthon, still a prisoner, but treated correctly, but with a certain apprehension.
>
> The following day, back at Uriage in a car driven by Lieutenant Chabert, with political *chef* Giaume and two *Miliciens*, we were pursued, then accosted by a car of *resistants*, armed and commanded by Lieutenant Ranavalo (grandson of the last queen of Madagascar) who I had known before the war. Nobody fired. Chabert manoeuvred and escaped. We abandoned the car and set off in the direction of the château.
>
> I knew the region well. I led and proposed to my companions in adventure to go forward in the direction I indicated, and to cover them as a rearguard armed with a submachine gun. And we arrived at Uriage château to the general surprise of its occupants who saw me armed behind the four *Miliciens*, including Giaume.
>
> Immediately their attitude changed. I was still a prisoner, but 'on parole', perfectly free to do what I pleased in the château. I was treated as a comrade. Questioned by all, we started to exchange ideas and thus I came to know an-

---

53 The classes included such topics as history, the science of man and the creation of the world.

other perception of the world and another perspective of the problems of the moment.

The general withdrawal. I was still a prisoner on parole. Exchanges of opinions continued. And little by little, I realised that my ideas, my sentiments were very close to theirs, and that what they told me and what they thought of the problems of this world, were exactly what I felt without knowing why.

We arrived at the German frontier. De Vaugelas and other *chefs de la Milice* set me free, but offered me, without constraint, to stay with them ... I stayed.

Comte was not the only former maquisard to serve in 'Charlemagne'.

After his political 'conversion' he now wondered if sufficient time would be made available to instill the revolutionary ideas of a new European order. [The answer would be no.]

At the end of the in-house officer-cadets' Lehrgang at Wildflecken, Oberjunker B. and Oberjunker de Brangelin were sent to Janowitz, Bohemia, for anti-tank training.[54] They never arrived. After one week of being shunted back and forth through Bavaria and Bohemia, they returned to Wildflecken.

In the absence of B., Oscha. Girard was appointed commander of the Panzerjäger Kompanie of Waffen-Gren. Regt der SS 58. Some days after the return of B., Hstuf. Raybaud, with the agreement of B., posted him back to the Panzerjäger Kompanie to *renforcer le difficile commandement.* Still not ambitious to make a career for himself, B. became second in command.

As for de Brangelin, he was assigned as W-Hstuf. Monneuse's orderly officer.[55]

Rumours continued to circulate of the employment of 'Charlemagne' on the Western front against the Americans. There was universal uproar among the French SS volunteers. Such was the unrest that in the end Krukenberg had to put out a denial![56]

Morale nose-dived in January as Germany's military situation deteriorated: the Ardennes offensive had ended in a costly defeat and a Russian offensive had swept into East Prussia, Pomerania and Silesia.

Other factors affecting morale were a reduction in the already spartan rations, the cold, a spate of bloody accidents, and the tattooing of the blood group.

'Charlemagne' was plagued, or so it seemed, with stupid and bloody accidents. A sentry guarding men of the penal platoon fell on a patch of ice and his loaded rifle, pointing at them, went off. The sentry had neglected to put the safety catch on. One man was killed and another was wounded.

Then there was the armourer who foolishly tried to hammer free a shell that had become jammed in the breech of a PAK gun. The resulting explosion killed

54   Of note is that the two of them were graduates of Saint-Cyr. This might explain why they were sent to Janowitz rather than Kienschlag with the other officer cadets.

55   As for his new appointment, de Brangelin believes that it was none other than Monneuse himself who had asked for his transfer and, although they did not know each other that well, he also believes that Monneuse held him in high regard. (Letter to the author, 31/8/97.)

56   In December 1944, when 'it was a question of sending us to the Western Front', one former French Divisional soldier learnt that Mgr. de Mayol de Lupé had been to see Himmler, who had asserted that 'Charlemagne' would not be deployed to the west. This is unconfirmed and may have only been rumour.

two men and wounded several others. A further two grenadier's repairing damaged tracks in Fulda railway station were crushed to death by a locomotive.

The announcement of the tattooing of the blood group came as an unpleasant surprise to many. The tattoo was peculiar to the Waffen-SS and was simply an indication of blood group. This information was essential for wounded requiring a blood transfusion. However, this tattoo, which was intended possibly to save life, was viewed by many with disquiet because it could equally condemn prisoners to death. This tattoo would clearly identify them as members of the Waffen-SS and it was rumoured that the Russians examined the arms of wounded and captured for this distinguishing mark and summarily executed those bearing the brand. Even if the tattoo were removed there would still be a telltale mark left in the same area.

The tattooing of the blood group under the left arm started in early January 1945.[57] Some men had their blood group determined and tattooed when they gave blood for the wounded. Kompanie 3/57 was tattooed by Indian doctors of the Waffen-SS. Still one-quarter of all French SS men managed to avoid being tattooed.[58] Although a non-commissioned officer who should have set an example, Uscha. de la Mazière had made up his mind to evade being tattooed and managed to on the pretext of being urgently summoned to headquarters. All the same, he felt ashamed of 'this small act of betrayal', but reasoned that if he were hit by a bullet or by a piece of shrapnel in the left arm the medical orderlies would not find his blood group in the pulp left.

Those men away in various training schools stood the best chance of not being tattooed. In this way, Henri-Georges Gonzales of the Engineer Company, away at Hradischko, was lucky enough not to be tattooed. Oberjunker B. of the Panzerjäger Kompanie of Waffen-Gren. Regt der SS 58 openly refused to have the tattoo. This came to the attention of Stubaf. Raybaud. Nevertheless, Oberjunker B. went unpunished. And yet, in contrast, some viewed the tattoo as final proof their full integration into the Waffen-SS, 'a sort of magic sign of affiliation'.

Days after receiving the blood group tattoo, the volunteers were offered the opportunity to donate blood for those wounded at the front. In large numbers, they flocked to the collection points, but the blood they donated proved worthless—their blood was too poor. A report from the military doctors at Fulda read that 'the men are weak, overworked and anemic' and that their 'food is insufficient'. The subsequent fuss over this could not be overlooked and, as a result, rations were increased. An ironic conclusion considering that many, if not all, of the volunteers were only moved to donate blood in the first place because of the 'snack' offered to all blood donors.[59]

---

57   This date is implied by Mabire and confirmed by de Genouillac. The turn of de la
     Mazière and 'his' company [the PAK Company] to be tattooed came on the day after
     Christmas, although he states that the tattooing 'had been announced for
     November'. Rostaing is alone when he records the tattooing starting in November
     1944, on the 14th to be precise.
58   Mabire, page 245.
59   See Mabire, pages 245-246.

Company 5/58

In early January 1945, platoon commander-instructor[60] Hscha. Edmond Walter left Company 5/58 to become the company commander of the 7/58. Oscha. Blaise succeeded him.

Walter was a most remarkable individual. A bachelor of Philosophy,[61] he was married to a beautiful cinema actress. In 1942, aged twenty, he joined the LVF. One year later, having worked his way up through the ranks, he was an *adjudant*. A fanatical National Socialist, he seemed out of place among his 'tricolore' compatriots of the LVF. He was, according to Mabire, the embodiment of the 'political soldier' of the time.

Walter was an excellent leader of men and trained his men hard, very hard. Blanc of Company 5/58, who was trained by Walter, recalls that he once said to them: "I hope that you want to kill me, because it is normal that one should want to kill one's instructor." At times they did. From seven in the morning to seven in the evening, they trained outside in sub-zero temperatures. They were without gloves, as was Walter. He did not ask anything of his men that he himself was not prepared to do. Frequent bouts of dysentery did not slacken his effort.

Each evening, weapons inspection. If the instructor found a single grain of dust in the chamber of a rifle the whole platoon was given 20 minutes to prepare for a new inspection at which all rifles were checked again. It was just too bad if the grain of dust had changed rifle. This would continue until such time as it had disappeared.

Under Walter, the men learnt collective responsibility. If a single person slipped while marching on an icy road then the whole platoon was punished by the 'stand-up, lie down' drill, preferably in a ditch and in the nastiest mud. Again, if the instructor commanded 'Panzer von links' (tank on the left) and a single person took cover to the left of the road rather than the right then the whole platoon 'copped it'.

Walter once confided to Blanc: "Our strength lies above all in our camaraderie, because it is greater than anywhere else." It was this that Walter fostered. On one occasion, seeing that one of his men was hungry, he gave him part of his bread ration.

To toughen his men, he demonstrated that a hand grenade could be detonated atop his head, on his helmet, without harm to himself. Standing rigid, he showed that the grenade splinters traveled laterally and upwards, riddling the snow around his feet in an almost perfect circle. One time he forgot to secure sufficiently the chinstrap of his helmet, which the grenade blast brought down on his nose and caused to swell.

Walter never joked and did not accept such behaviour from others. One day, he reproached the men for not knowing how to sing well in chorus. One of their number, Bernardini, then murmured 'Sistine Chapel'. He found himself transferred at once to the Medical Company.

---

60   Blanc, letter to the author, 19/3/01. [Blanc was a member of Walter's platoon.] This corrects Rusco of the same company, who, in letters to the author of 2/98 and 5/3/98, stated that Walter took care of supply problems rather than matters of training.

61   Mabire, page 222.

Grenadier Blanc liked Walter. Many of his closest comrades did not. However, it was thanks to him that the men stood up well to the hardships of battle.

Both Uscha. Maixandeau and Junker der Waffen-SS Rusco[62] were capable platoon commanders.

Maixandeau was in many ways the opposite of Walter and this was undoubtedly the reason they got on well. Maixandeau had style, but not the appearance of a soldier. Very cultivated, he often came and chatted with the men about literature or the cinema.

Rusco was an 'old hand' of the LVF. Following in the footsteps of his father, who was a 1914–1918 combatant, he too became a militant in the right-wing *Parti Social Français* (P.S.F.) of Colonel de La Rocque.[63] Then came 1940 and defeat. He wanted to fight, but was too young.

On 2nd January 1942, having falsified his papers because his parents had refused to sign the *dispense* [certificate of exemption], Rusco joined the LVF. Why? 'He felt European'. He was of the view that France should 'disregard its nationalism by integrating itself into a greater European organisation, following the example of Germany'.[64]

Rusco went on to serve with the celebrated *section de chasse*. His transfer at the end of August 1944 to the Waffen-SS he described as 'the consecration of his ideas' and explained that 'he joined the Legion [the LVF] to fight Communism, but he discovered another reason to fight; the creation of a New Europe'.[65] From late August to mid December 1944, he attended SS-Unterführerschule [NCO school] Posen-Treskau and proved himself of NCO calibre. His arrival at Wildflecken coincided with his promotion to Uscha. and then Junker. He was posted to Company 5/58.[66]

In mid January 1945, Rusco was on the point of leaving for SS-officer school Kienschlag when Ostuf. Wagner managed to pull a few strings at headquarters to keep him with the promise that after three months at the front he would be promoted to the officer rank of Untersturmführer. Rusco was, of course, pleased. Weeks later, before leaving for Pomerania, he was promoted to Oberscharführer and appointed his assistant.

The morale of Company 5/58 was excellent. This was due in part to Jean Castrillo, who was ex-SK. He was a sort of morale officer and political officer all rolled into one, even though his rank was that of Grenadier. He was always able to raise a laugh, even at the toughest of times, and could comfort with a wink. Each evening, after returning from training and before dinner, he taught the history of National Socialism to the men sat on stools in the corridors of the company's

---

62   Pseudonym.

63   His father was a member of Colonel de La Rocque's right-wing *Croix de Feu* movement of war veterans that, after the ban on parliamentary pressure groups in 1936, became the *Parti Social Français*.

64   Rusco, "*Stoï*", page 17.

65   Mabire, page 243.

66   According to Rusco, page 249, as the only *gradé* present, he found himself the company commander for several weeks. However, this is not recalled by Blanc, but that is not to say that it did not happen.

building. He managed to keep the exhausted men interested by incorporating humour. His reputation grew and before long he was going to neighbouring companies. Roger Wyckaert, who, like Castrillo, was from the J.P.F. and had served with the SK, gave him a helping hand. Robert Blanc regarded Castrillo as a perfect comrade, a brother.

There was no talk of regrets and also no talk of defeat. This was in contrast to the companies wholly formed of young officers of the Wehrmacht also present at Wildflecken. They were being trained again as simple recruits, why the Frenchmen did not know. Blanc recalls:

> They [the young officers] did not like us: one day, our platoon, returning from an exercise, in marching order, crossed some of them; *adjudant* Blaise saluted them as per regulations, that is to say the raised arm. Not one responded to our salute. Blaise commanded 'platoon halt', stood in front of them and addressed them in German in a ferocious tone of voice, which sounded like a row, on the theme: we are French volunteers, we are fighting like you, have the correctness to respond to our salute. Which they did eventually, but clearly their hearts weren't in it.

The skeleton-like structure of the brigade started to flesh out late January with the return of those away on training courses. Not one of the thirty or so company clerks sent to Breslau would return to Wildflecken. They had been incorporated into the defence of the besieged fortress that would only capitulate on 7th May 1945, the same day on which General Jodl, the German Chief of Staff, signed the uncondi-tional surrender of all German forces. Most of the Frenchmen were killed.[67]

On 1st February 1945, all grenadier with at least two years service in the French Army or in German uniform were promoted to Rottenführer.[68] In this way, Soulat of the Headquarters Company, promoted to the rank of Sturmmann in December 1944, now found himself promoted to that of Rottenführer. Also promoted to Rottenführer was Strmm. Sepchant of the Headquarters Company/ 58.

A few days later, de Vaugelas, Raybaud and Boudet-Gheusi were promoted to Sturmbannführer. In fact, Raybaud continued to wear the insignia of Hstuf. while at Wildflecken and later in Pomerania. Of this, he explained that there were other more urgent concerns requiring his time and that of his staff.

But what of Hstuf. de Bourmont overlooked during this round of promo-tions? He was very piqued. Nevertheless, he too now seemed impatient to leave for the front, but which front? Marotin, like many former *francs-gardes*, still hoped that they would be leaving to liberate France alongside the German Army. However, for most, there was no question of this. And while this remained a topic of discussion, all knew with certainty that their departure was fast approaching.

On 7th February 1945, Uscha. Fronteau of the 10/58 returned to Wildflecken camp. For the past two months he had been away on a course at officer training

---

67   Correction to original edition of *Pour L'Europe* that stated that all the Frenchmen were killed.

68   Order SS-FHA B 12040/Amt V II b (7) Tgb. Nr 11/10835/44 geh. The automatic promotion was presented to them as a hierarchical benefit, as well as a financial benefit (de Genouillac, corrections to the author, 2000).

school Kienschlag. Exhausted from three long years in Russia with the LVF, he found the training mentally and physically demanding and elected to drop out before the graduation of his class. He hoped to return to Greifenberg for discharge, but was sent back to Wildflecken. On his return he reported to Brigf. Krukenberg. He explained the grounds for his decision, adding that he had little confidence in those officers of the *Milice* and the Sturmbrigade who had no experience of the Russian front. He also spoke of his regret that the *Miliciens* had been divided up among the two grenadier regiments. Of course, Krukenberg did not approve. Nevertheless, he acted humanely and sympathetically towards a demoralised veteran. Fronteau was posted back to the 10/58.

Ustuf. de Genouillac, the company commander of the 4/58, was transferred to the post of assistant battalion commander of the II/58. He was so devastated to leave the company he had formed that he did not regard his transfer as promotion. Nobody has ever fully explained to him the reasons behind his transfer to the II/58, but he was one of the few officers of Waffen-Gren. Regt der SS 58 who could understand and speak German in a comprehensible way. Perhaps Berret, the battalion commander of the II/58, a *officier d'active Saint-Cyrien* (a regular officer who had graduated from military school Saint-Cyr), preferred an *Adjoint* with the same training as him.

In this way, the vacant command of the 4/58 went to former *Milicien* André Tardan who in the opinion of de Genouillac 'had the makings of a good officer'. But, like many *Milicien* officers, Tardan did not have the necessary military training to enable him to fulfil altogether the role assigned to him. Only time and adequate training would have provided him with all the necessary skills.

From the Basque region, the Tardan family left France for Mexico around the turn of the century, built a hat factory and became very prosperous.[69] In 1940, André Tardan returned to France to do his military service. Attending *école d'officiers de réserve* training, he was commissioned a *éléve-officier de réserve*. Thereupon, he became caught up in the vortex of the Phoney War, the *débâcle*, and, after he was unable to return to Mexico, the National Revolution. He passed from the Armistice Army to the *Franc-Garde* of the *Milice française* and then to the Waffen-SS. Married, his wife lived in Paris.

Ustuf. Philippe Rossigneux was appointed the orderly officer of the II/58. Up to then he had been attached to the headquarters of Waffen-Gren. Regt der SS 58.[70]

In early February 1945,[71] Brigf. Krukenberg ordered Hstuf. Rémy[72] to go to depot Greifenberg in Pomerania and, from the ranks of the Franz. SS-Gren.-Ausbildungs und Ersatz-Bataillon, mobilise and take command of a Feldersatzbataillon [field replacement battalion]. Krukenberg had every

---

69   According to Saint-Loup, André Tardan's father was a multimillionaire!

70   His military training was non-existent and as such would not have permitted him to discharge effectively any other function than that of a staff officer.

71   To be more precise, 'several days before the departure of 'Charlemagne' for Pomerania' (Soulat).

72   The precise date of Rémy's promotion to Hauptsturmführer is not known, but may have been late January.

confidence in Rémy who had proved himself as a very capable company commander in the LVF.

By train, Rémy journeyed to Greifenberg via the Pomeranian city of Stargard (Stargard Szczecinski) which was the base of Himmler's limited 'Sonnenwende' offensive and thus a key Soviet target. On finding the railway line cut at Stargard, he returned to Wildflecken, thereby incurring the anger of Krukenberg who immediately sent Hstuf. Bisiau in his place.

Bisiau, for his part, managed to reach Greifenberg by train. His journey also took him via Stargard, but this time the railway system was running.

On 10th February 1945, the French Brigade of the Waffen-SS was ordered expanded to the 33. Waffen-Grenadier-Division der SS 'Charlemagne' (französische Nr.1).[73] On paper at least the order of battle of the 33. Waffen-Grenadier-Division der SS 'Charlemagne' (französische Nr.1) was as follows:

Stab der Division

Divisions Kampfschule

Waffen-Grenadier-Regiment der SS 57

Waffen-Grenadier-Regiment der SS 58

Waffen-Artillerie-Abteilung der SS 33

SS-Pionier-Kompanie 33

SS-Panzerjäger-Abteilung 33

SS-Nachrichten-Kompanie 33

SS-Ausbildungs-und-Ersatz-Batallion 33

SS-Feldgendarmerie-Trupp 57

SS-Feldpoststelle 57

The expansion from brigade to division status does not appear to have been widely communicated, if at all.[74] Many only learnt of the expansion postwar.[75]

---

73   RF-SS Feld-Kommandostelle, Adjutantur Tgb.Nr. 1698/45 geheim. This date of 10th February 1945 also appears in works by Bayle ("*de Marseille à Novossibirsk*", page 77) and Yerger ("*Waffen-SS Commanders, Krüger to Zimmermann*", page 167). However, according to an Allied Counterintelligence summary (Appendix E of "*Charlemagne's Legionnaires*"), the Division was formed on 1st February 1945, which is the same date Roch gives ("*La Division Charlemagne*", page 41).

74   Indeed, after the expansion to division, the internal paperwork of 'Charlemagne' still bore the legend 'Brigade' (see the paperwork for the promotion of Soulat to Rttf., "*San et Persante*", page 134). And 'Charlemagne' was still recorded as a brigade at the time of its arrival in Pomerania (see pages 19 and 35, "*Russo-German war: 25th January to 8 May 1945*").

75   Correspondence with many veterans of 'Charlemagne', 1997-2001.

The departure for Pomerania

On 11th February 1945, Cornu of the Medical Company left Wildflecken for driving training at Sbirow, near Pilsen, arriving some four days later. With him was Desrumeaux[76] who went for motor-cycle training. The driving school was in a former castle. Once or twice Cornu went into Pilsen. Life seemed normal and even beer was to be had. On 11th March, he left Sbirow. On the 17th, he arrived back at Wildflecken to find that, in his absence, 'Charlemagne' had left for Pomerania.

In February 1945, Uscha. Mercier of Fahrschwadron A was approached about leaving for officer IV/A training. Curiously, it was Oberführer Puaud who interviewed him in German to assess his level of knowledge of the language of Goethe. Along with several others, he passed this 'exam' and was told to be ready to leave for the training course, though details of the course were withheld. Weeks later, he found himself not in a training school, but in action.

On 15th February 1945, 'Charlemagne' was assembled in the shape of a horseshoe on Adolf Hitler Platz. The spectacle was impressive. In the centre of the horseshoe stood a platform from which Mgr. de Mayol de Lupé came to celebrate mass. Then the imminent departure of 'Charlemagne' to the front was confirmed.[77]

The following day, Rttf. Soulat, a member of the Headquarters staff, learnt that 'Charlemagne' was to leave Wildflecken for Pomerania the very next day![78] However, some preparations had been going on for the past two or three days that had led him to believe that the transfer of 'Charlemagne' was imminent.

'Charlemagne' was transferred to the east at the request of Krukenberg who had become concerned about the political intrigues of the likes of Laval, Doriot, and Darnand. He was now convinced that the French 'government in exile' at Sigmaringen was now seeking to bring the Division under its control and engage it, in full or in part, against the 'Western allied powers advancing on French territory'.[79] For him, this scenario 'would have been a catastrophe'. Yes, he later accepted that the training period was cut short,[80] but rather that than the unthinkable situation of Frenchmen fighting Frenchmen. And that was justification enough. Indeed, he was of the belief that if Frenchmen in German uniforms fought against their own compatriots then the German nation would have to accept the historic responsibility for it as well as sabotaging any kind of reconciliation between the two nations for an unforeseeable length of time.

On 17th February 1945, around 1400 hours, the first convoy of 'Charlemagne' left Brückenau station for Rummelsburg (Miastko), Pomerania.[81] More convoys followed that same day and continued over the next seven days. On the 18th, it was the turn of (elements of) Ostuf. Fenet's I/57. On the 21st, the ninth convoy left. It was under W-Hstuf. Monneuse. Aboard this convoy were companies 1/58, 2/58 and 9/58 as well as elements of the divisional headquarters, W-Ostuf. Bénétoux (office II/AB) and SS-Ustuf. Büeler (office VI), in a 'special' wagon.

As the ninth convoy was leaving Bruckenau station another convoy arrived from the Protectorate of Bohemia-Moravia. This was carrying the Engineer Company of 'Charlemagne' that had just completed its training at SS-Pionierschule Hradischko. In its care was a batch of 'Charlemagne' sleevebands[82] to be delivered to Wildflecken.[83] Notably, the engineers were

---

76   Jean-Marie Desrumeaux died in December 1998.

already wearing them on the left sleeve of their tunics.[84] This angered Krukenberg.[85]

On the 23rd, elements of Hstuf. Berret's II/58 boarded one of the last convoys, the sixteenth.[86] On board the same convoy were elements of the FLAK Company[87] and Ustuf. de Genouillac, the assistant battalion commander, armed

77   Rusco, "*Stoï*", page 253.

78   Soulat, letter to the author, 3/1/98. Curiously, according to Rostaing, "*Le Prix d'un Serment*", page 158, he learnt on 9th February 1945 that 'Charlemagne' would be leaving for Pomerania in two days time. However, if a member of the Brigade's Headquarters staff only learnt of the transfer on the 16th it's very doubtful that a member of the Headquarters staff of the II/58 learnt of the transfer one week before.

79   Krukenberg, cited by Soulat, page 15. However, no evidence exists, be it from World War II documentation or from credible witnesses, to substantiate the idea that the politicians of the French 'government in exile' at Sigmaringen wanted to have 'Charlemagne' engaged on the Western front. Moreover, according to Dank, "*The French against the French*, page 282, 'Doriot incurred the enmity of the R.S.H.A. through his refusal to permit the P.P.F. men enlisted in the French Waffen-SS (Charlemagne) Division to be used on the Western front'. The only enemy he recognised was Bolshevism. Arguably, Darnand, who had announced that *Miliciens* volunteering for the French unit of the Waffen-SS would not fight on the Western front, would have refused to permit the *Miliciens* serving in 'Charlemagne' to be used on the Western Front. Nevertheless, the fact remains that for whatever reason a political threat from the French government in exile at Sigmaringen seemed all too real to Krukenberg.

80   Ibid. And yet, in contrast, according to Mabire, page 256, in February 1945 (this date is implied), Brigf. Krukenberg informed the SS-Führungshauptamt that Brigade 'Charlemagne' had received sufficient training and requested that it should be engaged as soon as possible in Pomerania. Also, Landwehr remarks that 'on or about 15th February 1945, Brigf. Krukenberg decided that the training/formation process was finished, or as near to it as possible'.

81   'Charlemagne' departed to Rummelsburg not Hammerstein, for the word 'Charlemagne' can be found beside Rummelsburg on a situation map of Army Group Vistula dated 21st February 1945. According to Saint-Loup, page 170, as the advance party boarded the trains, 'Charlemagne' was bound for Rummelsburg or Hammerstein. And yet, on page 175, Saint-Loup writes into a conversation between Hstuf. Monneuse and Ostuf. Métais upon their arrival at Hammerstein that 'Charlemagne' should have been equipped at Rumelsburg (sic), but the Russians had already occupied it, which is incorrect.

82   This suggests that the sleevebands were probably manufactured in Bohemia-Moravia and thus more specifically in Prague.

83   This batch of sleevebands was never delivered to Wildflecken because the convoy did not stop. It is not known what happened to the sleevebands.

84   Witnessed by Soulat, letter to the author, 8/12/97. So was the Engineer Company the only unit of 'Charlemagne' to wear the sleeveband of the same name? To begin with, many former members of 'Charlemagne' still maintain to this day that the sleeveband was never worn, not even by the Engineer Company. Indeed, one former member of the Engineer Company cannot recall wearing the sleeveband.

with his chosen weapons of a Sauer pistol and an American M1 carbine. Surprised not to have a compass on him, he was shocked to learn that battalion headquarters only had one! Gren. Blanc of Company 5/58 was armed with a semi-automatic rifle, but it had no sight.

Fahrschwadron A went to Pomerania without much of its planned weapons and equipment. Uscha. Mercier would have left unarmed if it were not for his LVF comrade *Sergent* Labat, who had secretly given him a pistol at Greifenberg when trouble was expected in the wake of the attempt on Hitler's life on 20th July. Nevertheless, Hstuf. Schlisler confirmed to his men that they would be equipped anew on their arrival. They were led to believe that this situation was normal and that 'German organisation had everything in hand'.[88] The old hands of the LVF,

According to Angolia, "*Cloth Insignia of the SS*", page 491, 'some individuals from other units also acquired it'. Also, according to de la Mazière, "*Ashes of Honour*", page 72, he received a 'Charlemagne' sleeveband before attending Janowitz [Bohemia-Moravia], late December 1944. He wrote that Brigf. Krukenberg told him: 'we have just received supplies and you can sew the name of 'Charlemagne' on your uniform. Go and see Zimmermann on the way out. I want those at Yanowitz to know where you come from...' According to Roch, page 53, sleevebands were sent to Wildflecken and worn, but Krukenberg had them withdrawn. In response to this, according to Soulat, letter to the author, 20/2/98, sleevebands were never worn at Wildflecken. Roch also states that the 'Charlemagne' sleeveband was distributed to units on training courses in the region of Prague, although the Engineer Company was the only company of 'Charlemagne' to be fully kited out. Perhaps this explains how de la Mazière, who was at Janowitz near Prague from December to February 1945, actually came by his sleeveband, and how, in the words of Angolia, 'some individuals from other units also acquired it'.

85   Soulat, letter to the author, 20/2/98. But why was Krukenberg angered? According to Soulat, letter to the author of 20/2/98, Krukenberg objected to the wearing of the sleeveband until such time as the Division had seen battle. Mounine is also of the opinion (correspondence to the author, March 1999) that sleevebands were to be distributed once 'Charlemagne' had proved itself in battle, citing the examples of Waffen-SS divisions 'Frunsberg' and 'Götz von Berlichingen'. This, of course, would explain Krukenberg's anger at the Engineer Company for appropriating the sleevebands, but, by the same token, does not explain why he had honoured de la Mazière in such a way some two months before. Curiously, en route to Pomerania, Hstuf. Schlisler of Fahrschwadron A, who had the ear of General Puaud, confided to Uscha. Mercier that 'Charlemagne' was soon to receive the sleevebands. He assumed that this would take place at a parade. There was no mention of 'Charlemagne' proving itself in battle before the sleeveband could be worn.

86   Michel de Genouillac, correspondence throughout 1997. According to Rostaing, 'his' battalion, the III/58 (sic), had boarded the eleventh convoy on the 17th at 2200 hours. This date is incorrect.

87   Ibid. However, according to the article "*SS-Französische Flakbatterie*", the FLAK Company received the order to embark for the Eastern front on the 25th. Regarding this, elements of the FLAK Company, indeed it may have been the entire company, did arrive at Neustettin in Pomerania on the very same date as the bulk of the II/58. This suggests that elements of the FLAK Company were aboard this convoy.

88   Mercier, letter to the author, 9/10/2001.

who had made the same journey in 1941, were not so convinced. They had different memories.

The units, manpower and weaponry of 'Charlemagne' put at the disposal of Army Group Vistula was as follows:[89]

Units

Brigadestab	Headquarters
2 Gren. Rgt. mit je 2 Batl.	Two Grenadier Regiments with two Battalions
2 I.G. Kompanien	Two Infantry Gun companies
1 Abt. Art., 2 Battr. Je 4 I.F.H.	Artillery detachment
2 Pz.Schreck-Kompanien	Two Pz.Schreck companies
1 3.7 Flak-Kp.	Anti-Aircraft company
1 Pi.Kp.	Engineer company
1 (gem.) Nachrichten-Kompanie	(mixed) Signals company
1 Feldpoststelle	Field post office
1 Sanitätskomp.	Medical company
1 Krankenkraftwagenzug	MT ambulance platoon
1 Feldgend.-Kompanie	Military Police company
Werkstattzug[90]	Workshop platoon

Personnel

Offiziere	102
Unteroffiziere	886
Männer	5375
Total	6363

89   From a non-referenced report that Soulat found by chance in the archives of Army Group Vistula. Dated '15/2', the report would not have included the *bataillon de marche de reserve* which joined 'Charlemagne' at Körlin in the first days of March 1945. Of note is the absence of the *compagnie d'Honneur* and the PAK Company. Also, the reference to a Feldgend.-Kompanie is surprising and doubted. It was normal for a division to have no more than a Feldgend.-Trupp.

90   Soulat doubts that a Workshop platoon accompanied the Brigade to Pomerania (personal discussion).

Weaponry

Karabiner	3643	—
Pistolen	1030	—
M Pi	538	Machine pistol
L.MG 42	66	Light machine gun
S.MG	30	Heavy machine gun
MG 34	31	—
m PAK	3	—
s PAK	3	—
l.I.G.	12	Light infantry gun
s. I.G.	5	Heavy infantry gun
3.7 cm FLAK	9	—
1.F.H.	8	Light field howitzer
LKW	44	Trucks
Zgkw.	3	[Zugkraftwagen]
RSO	3	[Raupenschlepper Ost] Tracked tractor
Pferde	1082	Horses
Panzerfäuste	872	—
Panzerschreck	72	—
1 Veterinär-Kompanie	—	Veterinary company

This entry in the archives of Army Group Vistula is dated '15/2'. Two days later, in response to a note from Generaloberst Weiss commanding the 2nd Army, the headquarters of Army Group Vistula announced the imminent arrival of a 'strong französischen Brigade (Division)' of '2 Regimentern zu je 2 Bataillonen, 1 Artillerie-Abt., 1 Panther-Abt. 1 Sturmgesch. Abt. und Artillerie' [two regiments of two battalions, one artillery group, one battalion of Panther tanks and one battalion of Sturmgeschütze assault guns and artillery]. Needless to say, the strength of 'Charlemagne' is grossly exaggerated!! This response to Weiss was from RF-SS Himmler and signed by Ostubaf. Grothmann, his aide-de-camp.[91]

Marotin summed up his time at Wildflecken with the words: "I kept from Wildflecken the memory of the cold, the rain, the snow and the hunger … But also the memory of a warm camaraderie which helped us to endure the difficult moments and the rigours of our life … " Blanc was of the same opinion.

What now awaited the officers and men of 'Charlemagne' in Pomerania? They expected to receive further training before going into battle.[92] Also, they expected to receive new equipment and weapons. This was in line with current German Army practice, which was to equip new units at depots close to the front line. However, this is not what Oberjunker B. of the Panzerjäger Kompanie of Waffen-Gren. Regt. der SS 58 expected. News of the major Russian offensive had come to him from contacts made in the French POW camp near Wildflecken.[93] Because of this he became convinced that 'Charlemagne' would go straight into battle.

91   The question has to be asked: "Was Himmler deliberately attempting to mislead Weiss?" A serious accusation if true, but impossible to prove. However, there is little doubt in the mind of the author that Himmler was fully aware of the real strength of 'Charlemagne'. An accurate picture of the units, manpower and weaponry of 'Charlemagne' had been submitted to the headquarters of Army Group Vistula two days before its response to Weiss. Moreover, the author is convinced that Himmler would have paid particular attention to 'Charlemagne', for he was still the head of the SS, his 'private army', and the commander of the Army Group to which 'Charlemagne' was attached.

92   Correspondence with many veterans of 'Charlemagne'. In response to this, considering that Brigf. Krukenberg was pushing for the engagement of 'Charlemagne' without delay on the Eastern front then this would suggest that 'Charlemagne' was not scheduled to complete its training programme or receive further training before going up to the front. It should be remembered that there had been no battalion and regimental manoeuvres, nor manoeuvres in conjunction with the heavy units.

93   Generally, the French prisoners avoided the soldiers of 'Charlemagne'.

The command roster of the 33. Waffen-Grenadier-Division der Waffen SS 'Charlemagne' (französische Nr.1) mid to late February 1945 before the departure to Pomerania.

Note: Those names in italics are pseudonyms.

The German Inspection

General-Inspector	SS-Brigf. Krukenberg
1st Orderly Officer	SS-Ustuf. Patzak
2nd Orderly Officer	SS-Ostuf. Hegewald[94]
Orderly Officer	SS-Ostuf. Dally
Orderly Officer	SS-Ustuf. Gehring[95]
Office I/A (Operations)	SS-Hstuf. Jauss
Office I/B (Weapons, equipment, quarters)	SS-Ostuf. Meier
Office I/C (Intelligence)	SS-Hstuf. Schmidt
Office II/AB (Personnel)	SS-Hstuf. Pachur
Office III (Military justice)	SS-Ostuf. Dick
Office IV/A (Uniforms, clothing, rations)	SS-Hstuf. Hagen
Supply Office	SS-Hstuf. Dr. Gewecke
Supply Officer	SS-Hstuf. Reinholdt
Supply Officer	SS-Ostuf. Wahrlich
Office IV/B (Medical/sanitation)	SS-Stubaf. Schlegel
Office IV/C (Veterinarian)	SS-Hstuf. Scheiner
Office IV/D (Military chaplaincy)	?
Office V (Vehicle)	SS-Ostuf. Neubauer
Office VI (Political training and activities)	SS-Ostuf. Kopp
Training	SS-Staf. Zimmermann
Military Police	SS-Ostuf. Görr
Field Post	?
French Liaison Officer	W-Hstuf. Renault
?	SS-Ustuf. Friedrich
?	SS-Ustuf. Zander

94 Born on 14th July 1911, Rolf Hegewald was promoted to SS-Ostuf. on 1st January 1945.
95 Born on 10th February 1917 in Magdeburg, Heinze Gehring was transferred to the Inspection at the start of 1945. He was captured by the Soviets in March 1945 in Pomerania. His subsequent fate is not known.

| ? | SS-Ustuf. Engel |
| ? | SS-Stubaf. Katzian |

Divisional Staff

Commander	W-Obf. Puaud
Chief of Staff	W-Stubaf. de Vaugelas
1st Orderly Officer	W-Ostuf. Auphan
2nd Orderly Officer	W-Std.Ju. Platon
Office I/A (Operations)	?
Office I/B (Weapons, equipment, quarters)	?
Office I/C (Intelligence)	W-Ustuf. Delile
Office II/AB (Personnel)	W-Ostuf. Bénétoux
Office III (Military justice)	?
Office IV/A (Uniforms, clothing, rations)	?
Office IV/B (Medical/sanitation)	W-Stubaf. Dr. Lelongt
Office IV/C (Veterinarian)	W-Hstuf. Richert[96]
Office IV/D (Military chaplaincy)	W-Stubaf. de Mayol de Lupé
Orderly Officer	W-Ustuf. Cheveau
Office V (Vehicle)	?
Office VI (Political training and activities)	W-Ustuf. Dr. Büeler
Liaison Officer	SS-Stubaf. Dr. Lölhoffel then Major Roemheld
Military Police	W-Ostuf. Veyrieras
Civil Defence	W-Ostuf. Multrier

Divisional Units

Compagnie d'Honneur	SS-Ostuf. Weber
Staff Company	W-Hscha. Surrel
Signals Company	W-Ostuf. Dupuyau[97]

96 Born in 1904, Jean Richert studied veterinary medicine at the *Ecole vétérinaire de Lyon.* Obtaining the *brevet de PMS de service vétérinaire,* he gained admittance to the EOR. In 1934 came his appointment to *vétérinaire sous-lieutenant de réserve.*

97 Jean Dupuyau was a product of military school Saint-Maixent promoted from *sergent* to *sous-lieutenant d'active* in December 1939.

Engineer Company	W-Ostuf. Audibert de Vitrolles
Assistant	W-Ustuf. Mailhe
Medical Company	W-Hstuf. Dr. Bonnefoy[98]
Veterinary Company	W-Ustuf. Dr. Richter
Workshop Company	W-Ostuf. Maud'huit
Construction Company	W-Ostuf. de Moroge
Fahrschwadron A	W-Hstuf. Schlisler
Assistant (*Adjoint*)	W-Ostuf. Darrigade
Fahrschwadron B	W-Hstuf. Croisille
Assistant (*Adjoint*)	W-Ostuf. Huan[99]

Waffen-Grenadier-Regiment der Waffen SS 57

Commander	W-Hstuf. de Bourmont
Assistant (*Adjoint*)	W-Ustuf. Artus
Orderly Officer	W-Ustuf. Martret
?	W-Ostuf. de Londaiz
Office III (Military justice)	W-Ustuf. Stehli
Office IV/B (Medical/sanitation)	W-Hstuf.Dr. Leproux
Office IV/C (Veterinarian)	W-Ostuf. Vergnaud[100]
Staff Company	W-Ostuf. André
Reconnaissance platoon	W-Ustuf. Erdozain
Engineers platoon	W-Std.Ob.Ju. Lefevre
Signals platoon	W-Ustuf. *Brucard*
Infantry Gun Company (9/57)	W-Hstuf. Roy
Anti-tank Company (10/57)	W-Ostuf. Labuze

98   Hstuf. Bonnefoy probably received the command of the Medical Company from the aging Hstuf. Péribère before its departure to Pomerania. [Bonnefoy was not known to Cornu, a member of the Medical Company who left for a training course at Sbirow on 11th February 1945 and returned after 'Charlemagne' had left for the Eastern Front. Cornu made the acquaintance of Bonnefoy after the war.] Péribère stayed behind at Wildflecken. The reason for this may have been his age.

99   This former *Milicien* was a partially disfigured and severely disabled First World War ex-serviceman who was a holder of the prestigious *la Croix de Chevalier de la Légion d' Honneur.*

100 Born in Morocco, Jean Vergnaud studied veterinary medicine at the *Ecole vétérinaire de Toulouse.* Obtaining the *brevet de PMS de service vétérinaire,* he gained admittance to the EOR. In 1928, he was appointed *vétérinaire sous-lieutenant de réserve.* By 1945, he was probably in his forties.

1st Battalion (I/57)

Commander	W-Ostuf. Fenet
Assistant (*Adjoint*)	W-Ustuf. Hug
Orderly Officer	W-Std.Ob.Ju. Labourdette
Medical Officer	SS-Std.Ob.Ju. Anneshaensel[101]
1st Company	W-Ustuf. Brazier
2nd Company	W-Ostuf. Bartolomei
3rd Company	W-Ustuf. Counil
4th Company	W-Oscha. Couvreur

2nd Battalion (II/57)

Commander	W-Hstuf. Obitz
Assistant (*Adjoint*)	W-Ostuf. Roumegous
Orderly Officer	?
Medical Officer	W-Ustuf. Herpe and W-Hstuf. Duflos
5th Company	W-Oscha. Hennecart
6th Company	W-Ustuf. Albert
7th Company	W-Std.Ob.Ju. Million-Rousseau
8th Company	W-Ustuf. Colnion

Waffen-Grenadier-Regiment der Waffen SS 58

Commander	W-Stubaf. Raybaud
Assistant (*Adjoint*)	W-Ostuf. Baudouin
Orderly Officer	W-Std.Ju. de Vaugelas
Office III (Military justice)	W-Hstuf. Chautard
Office IV/B (Medical/sanitation)	W-Ostuf. Dr. Métais[102]
Office IV/C (Veterinarian)	?
German liaison officer	SS-Ustuf. Goliberzuch

---

101   Louis Anneshaense was born on 12th August 1915 in Strasbourg.
102   Pierre-Marie Métais was born on 15th July 1902 in Saint-Maixent.

Staff Company   W-Hstuf. de Perricot
  'Command' (Headquarters)
platoon   W-Ustuf. Daffas
    Reconnaissance platoon   W-Hscha. Gobion
    Engineers platoon   ?
    Signals platoon   W-Ostuf. Leune
Infantry Gun Company (9/58)   W-Ostuf. Français
Assistant   W-Ustuf. Pierre Werner?[103]
Anti-tank Company (10/58)   W-Oscha. Girard
Assistant   W-Std.Ob.Ju. B

1st Battalion (I/58)

Commander   W-Hstuf. Monneuse
Assistant (*Adjoint*)   W-Ostuf. Falcy[104]
Orderly Officer   W-Std.Ob.Ju. *de Brangelin*
Medical Officer   W-Ostuf. Dr. Thibaud
1st Company   W-Ostuf. Fatin
2nd Company   W-Ostuf. Géromini
3rd Company   W-Ustuf. Rigeade
4th Company   W-Ostuf. Tardan

2nd Battalion (II/58)

Commander   W-Hstuf. Berret
Assistant (*Adjoint*)   W-Ustuf. de Genouillac
Orderly Officer   W-Ustuf. *Rossigneux*
Medical Officer   W-Ostuf. Dr. Joubert
5th Company   W-Ostuf. Wagner
Assistant   W-Oscha. Rusco
6th Company   W-Ostuf. Saint-Magne
7th Company   W-Hscha. Walter
8th Company   W-Ostuf. Defever[105]

103 This position is unconfirmed, but possible because Werner, a former *officier de la franc-garde de la Milice de la région de Toulouse*, commanded Company 9/58 from time to time. He was born on 25th July 1905 in Charleville-Mezieres.
104 Unconfirmed, see Chapter 8.
105 Born in 1904, Paul Defever took the path of the PMS and the EOR. In 1926, he was commissioned *sous-lieutenant de réserve*.

Panzerjäger Battalion

Commander	W-Stubaf. Boudet-Gheusi
Assistant (*Adjoint*)	W-Std.Ob.Ju. Radici
Medical Officer	W-Ostuf. Dr. Durandy
Supplies Officer	W-Ostuf. Weiss
Anti-aircraft (FLAK) Company	W-Ustuf. Fayard
Anti-tank (PAK) Company	W-Ostuf. Krotoff
Assistant	W-Std.Ob.Ju. Vincenot
Assault Gun Company	W-Ostuf. Michel
Escort platoon	W-Oscha. Mongourd
German liaison officer	SS-Hstuf. Kroepsch

The Artillery Group[106]

Commander	W-Hstuf. Havette
Assistant (*Adjoint*)	W-Hstuf. Martin[107]
Medical Officer	W-Ostuf. Dr. Fraysse[108]
Officier d'Orientation	W-Ostuf. Chauffour
Supply Column	W-Oscha. Merméjean
1st Battery	Chillou?
2nd Battery	W-Ostuf. Salle[109]
3rd Battery	W-Std.O.Ju. Le Guichaoua[110]

106 Soulat, letter to the author, 16/7/98. This updates Mabire's command roster of the
     Artillery Group, page 525, "*La Division Charlemagne*", which was also based on
     information supplied by Soulat. Since then new information has come to light.
107 Born in Nancy in 1918, Jacques Martin was a product of the EOR, commissioned
     aspirant in 1939. He came to 'Charlemagne' from the LVF.
108 Born in 1900, René Fraysse studied medicine at the *Faculté de médecine de Paris*,
     before obtaining the *brevet de PMS* and gaining admittance to the EOR. In 1927,
     he received the rank of *médecin aide-major de 2° cl.*
109 Born in 1916, Louis Salle attended the *école militaire d'artillerie de Poitiers*. In
     1939, he graduated with the rank of *sous-lieutenant d'active d'artillerie.*
110 Born in 1918, Henri Le Guichaoua attended the *école militaire d'artillerie de Poitiers*
     during the years 1937-1938. On 15th September 1938, he was promoted to the
     rank of *sous-lieutenant d'active d'artillerie.*

Officers serving with 'Charlemagne' whose post or function is not known.

W-Ustuf. Pierre Alaux[111]

W-Ustuf. Gilles Imbaud

W-Ustuf. Labrousse[112]

W-Ostuf. Perrin[113]

W-Ostuf. Rimaud

W-Ostuf. Rouzaud

W-Ustuf. Dr. Seigneur[114]

W-Hstuf. Vincent[115]

111 He was a pharmacist at Nérac, a small city in le Lot-et-Garonne. Thus, the possibility exists that he served in a medical capacity, perhaps in the Medical Company. He was ex-*Milice*.

112 He was ex-*Milice*.

113 Perrin served with Waffen-Gren. Regt. der SS 57. His past included stints with the LVF and the *Milice* with the rank of *chef de centaine*, participating in the maintenance of order operation at Glieres. In October 1945, at Bourg-en-Bresse, he was sentenced to death. The author does not know if the sentence was carried out.

114 Born on 22nd January 1907 in the department of the Somme, Michel Seigneur studied medicine at the *Faculté de médecine d'Amiens*. Armed with the *brevet de PMS*, he gained admittance to the EOR, graduating in 1929. Four years later, he was commissioned *sous-lieutenant de réserve*. He came to 'Charlemagne' from the *Milice*.

115 Born on 6th July 1910 in Versailles, Roger Vincent became a reserve officer in 1931. Four years later, after graduating from the *école militaire et d'application de la cavalerie et du train de Saumur*, he became an *officier d'active* [a 'regular' officer]. His branch was the cavalry. He volunteered for the LVF and was serving with the 5th Company of its II. Battalion before its transfer to the Waffen-SS. He is known to have served with the 5/58 for a short time. This was probably in the capacity of company commander. His precise role within 'Charlemagne' *au moment du départ au front* is not known. He may have been serving as a staff officer at divisional headquarters. He was a holder of the KVK 2nd Class. He survived the war.

CHAPTER 9

The Hell of Pomerania, Part 1

A chance meeting

On 25th February 1945, in Berlin, Strmm. Vaxelaire of the Workshop Company, still on a training course, met Ostubaf. Gamory-Dubourdeau quite by chance in the street. To his great surprise, he learnt that 'Charlemagne' had been engaged in Pomerania. At that moment he knew that his place and that of his company was at the front supporting the combatant elements of the division. He went at once to his company commander, Ostuf. Maud'huit, and asked him if the company was leaving for Pomerania. The answer was 'No'. Strmm. Vaxelaire then asked if the company might go to Budapest. Again the answer was 'No'.

Two days later, the sixty-strong Workshop Company left Berlin for Wildflecken camp. On 1st March 1945, the Workshop Company arrived at Fulda, where it was employed in the aftermath of an air raid. Vaxelaire remembers bringing out bodies from a bombed house. One day later, the company was back at Wildflecken. Vaxelaire for one could not quite believe that he had been transferred away from the fighting on the Eastern front.

The military situation on the Eastern front from January to February 1945

On 12th January 1945, the Soviets broke out of the Baranów bridgehead. This was the start of a major Soviet offensive that would extend from the Baltic to the Carpathians by the 15th. To the north the 2nd White Russian Front under Marshal Rokossovsky had been given the task of striking north-west to the Baltic coast, cutting off East Prussia and clearing the line of the lower Vistula. On Rokossovsky's left, the 1st White Russian Front under Marshal Zhukov was to break-out of the Pulawy bridgehead towards Lodz, out of the Magnuszew bridgehead towards Kutno and encircle Warsaw on its right flank. Subsequently, the Front was to drive westwards to the river Oder.

On 14th January, the 2nd White Russian Front launched its attack against the German 2nd Army. The attack met with little initial success against stiff resistance and violent counterattacks from the 'Grossdeutschland' Panzer Corps. Even so, by the 18th, the 2nd White Russian Front had still covered forty kilometres and broken the front of the German 2nd Army. By the 20th, Mlawa and Dzialdowo (Soldau) had fallen and the East Prussian border had been crossed. The 2nd White Russian Front was now poised for the dash to the coast. Allenstein (Olsztyn) and Tannenberg (Stebauk) fell on the 22nd. Four days later, the Fifth Guards Tank Army reached the Baltic coast north-east of Elbing (Elblag), cutting off the 3rd Panzer Army and 4th Army in East Prussia from the rest of the Reich. The remnants of the 2nd Army fell back to the west.

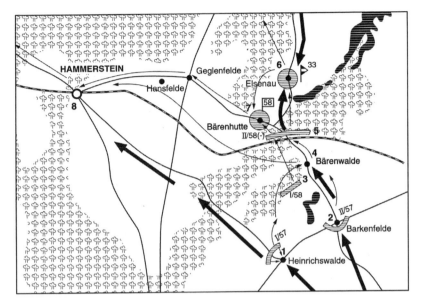

Map 3: The battle south-east of Hammerstein, 24-25 February 1945 (based on Mabire, page 260)

1. In the early evening of the 24th, battalion I/57 under Ostuf. Fenet attacks and penetrates into Heinrichswalde, but is repulsed. Facing superior enemy numbers, it disengages and retreats north-east.

2. Battalion II/57 under Hstuf. Obitz takes up position around Barkenfelde. Late on the 24th, it comes under attack. The fight is unequal. At nightfall, it retreats to a line of heights south of Barenwalde.

3. Battalion 1/58 under Hstuf. Monneuse takes up position between the I/57 and II/57. It too comes under attack.

4. Barenwalde falls to the Russians. The 1/58 and the remnants of the II/57 retreat to the Hammerstein-Barenwalde railway line.

5. By midday on the 25th, 'Charlemagne' is positioned along the Hammerstein-Barenwalde railway line. Fierce fighting erupts. After some four hours of fighting, the French defence line is pierced. The Russians advance to Elsenau.

6. Divisional headquarters is established at Elsenau. In the late afternoon of the 25th, elements of 'Charlemagne', including the Compagnie d'Honneur, fight to hold the village. They smash the armoured Soviet vanguard, but are forced once again to retreat. Some retreat west and some north.

7. The headquarters of Waffen-Gren. Regt. der SS 58 is established at Barenhutte. On the 25th, elements of Battalion 11/58, joined by those retreating from the railway line, take up defensive positions around the village. The Russians, however, do not attack in strength. At midnight, the French forces withdraw west to Hammerstein.

8. 'Charlemagne' evacuates Hammerstein by late afternoon of the 25th.

Also, on the 14th, the 1st White Russian Front exploded from the Pulawy and Magnuszew bridgeheads. By the end of the day it had smashed up five divisions of the German 9th Army. Modlin fell on the 15th, Radom on the 16th and Warsaw on the 17th. The 1st White Russian Front then proceeded to sweep west. The right flank of the front captured Kutno on the 19th and four days later, after having covered 150 kilometres, occupied Bydgoszcz (Bromberg) without a fight. That same day, the 23rd, the left flank of the front took Lodz. There was little resistance left before the Russians. On the 25th, the left flank of the 1st White Russian Front bypassed Poznan (Posen) and pushed on to the west and the Oder which was reached in the last days of January. Berlin was only 70 kilometres away.

The past three weeks had been disastrous for the Germans. The frontline, once deep in Poland, now ran along the line of the Oder and the Neisse. Losses in men and equipment had been heavy and irreplaceable. An enormous breach had been opened between the German 2nd Army, holding a front along the lower Vistula, and German forces on the Oder. The whole of Pomerania lay uncovered to the Soviet invader. To close this breach, Hitler put in the newly created Army Group Vistula (Weichsel in German) and gave its command to Himmler.

Help came to Himmler from a sudden thaw at the turn of the month that added to Zhukov's logistical problems and from the dissipating strength of the 1st White Russian Front. Zhukov had been forced to leave some of his forces to deal with the encircled garrisons at Poznan and Schneidemühl, and to divide his forces between the push into Pomerania and maintaining the bridgeheads over the Oder. By early February, Himmler had managed to erect a makeshift front.

To pinch off Zhukov's spearhead and gain time for the defence of Berlin, General Guderian, the chief of staff of the OKH,[1] approached Hitler about a two-pronged counterattack east of the Oder. The convergent counterattack hinged upon the employment of the 6th SS Panzer Army as one attack group, but Hitler refused to sanction its commitment on this front. Thus, through lack of resources, Guderian fell back on a single-pronged attack out of the area of Stargard (Stargard Szczecinski) against Zhukov's long right flank.

Divisions were amassed for the attack, code-named 'Sommersonnenwende' (Summer solstice), under the command of the newly created 11. SS-Panzer Armee. The III. (Germanic) SS Panzer Corps, comprising the 11. SS-Panzer-Grenadier-Freiw.-Division 'Nordland' and the 23. SS-Panzer-Grenadier-Freiw.-Division 'Nederland', was transferred from Courland to Pomerania for the attack.

But the divisions allocated to the attack had to be committed prematurely to hold the front and the assembly area in bitter fighting. Even so the attack commenced on 16th February 1945 and enjoyed initial success, lifting the siege of Arnswalde on the 17th. However, by the 21st, the attack had run its course and Hitler officially ended 'Sommersonnenwende'. The 11. SS-Panzer Armee began a general withdrawal to its jump-off positions.

In the meantime the Soviet High Command had abandoned its original plan to drive onto Berlin, considering its own forces too weak and extended and the German forces too strong. Seemingly it had become concerned about the build up of the new 11. SS-Panzer Armee and the danger it posed to Zhukov's right wing. To thwart the German's plans, the Soviet High Command came up with many measures. One such measure was the deployment of the 19th Army and the 3rd Guards Tank Corps on the left flank of the 2nd White Russian Front that would drive to the Baltic Sea

---

1   Oberkommando der Heeres or Army GHQ.

through Neustettin and Köslin. This would split the German forces concentrated in Pomerania. The attack was scheduled for no later than 24th February 1945.

The first convoys

On board the first convoy of 'Charlemagne' were elements of the divisional head-quarters under Obf. Puaud, Staf. Zimmermann of the German Inspection, the *Compagnie d'Honneur*, and a small advance party under Stubaf. Boudet-Gheusi charged with organising the equipping of the division.

Boudet-Gheusi was far from happy: his panzerjäger (or 'heavy') battalion was still not assembled. The FLAK Company, which had been participating in the defence of Fulda against Allied bombing since January, would be following later. The Assault Gun Company was still undergoing training in Bohemia. His command thus consisted of only the PAK company with its three platoons of four 75mm guns each. And the guns were training pieces of poor quality!

The journey of the first convoy to Pomerania did not pass without incident. Towards midday on the 20th, while held up in Altdamm (Dabie) railway station, the first convoy was attacked by the Soviet Air Force. Losses were taken: four (Soulat) or seven (Bayle) killed and some twelve wounded. These were the division's first losses in Pomerania.[2] Also of note is that when the convoy set off from Altdamm it left behind ten or so luckless men of the *Compagnie d'Honneur*.[3]

Five hours later, during a stop at Gollnow station, Obf. Puaud, Staf. Zimmer-mann, Hstuf. Renault and Oberjunker Platon, Puaud's orderly officer who was, remarkably, a former *Milicien*, left the convoy and continued on their way to Rummelsburg in a cross-country vehicle. Arriving at Rummelsburg station, they learnt that their convoy and all those of the division had just been diverted to the town of Hammerstein (Czarne), also in Pomerania.[4]

At 0200 hours on 22nd February 1945, the first convoy stopped at Hammerstein railway station. The large village of Hammerstein lies at the heart of Pomerania, approximately one hundred kilometres from the Baltic Sea and only twenty kilometres from Neustettin. The troops disembarked and took up residence in a nearby camp. It was a former Wehrmacht camp, converted into a Stalag for POWs, and of late evacu-ated and returned to its previous owner. Here the division was to be assembled, armed and equipped before going up to the front in a week or so.[5]

The camp was empty all except for some French prisoners in khaki uniforms. There was no sign of the promised equipment. This did not unduly worry Stubaf. Boudet-Gheusi as the front was still far off. However, as the day wore on, concern grew just like that of the continuous, muffled rumbling of guns that could be heard.

---

2   Soulat, page 17 and Mabire, page 265. However, according to Bayle, "*San et Persante*", page 152, the air attack that inflicted the division's first losses took place at Gollnow (Goleniów in Polish), north-east of Stettin (Szczecin in Polish). In response to this, Mabire also cites an air attack on the first convoy at Gollnow, but in contrast there is no mention of losses or damage.

3   Soulat would meet them later at Köslin.

4   Army Group Vistula probably issued the orders that diverted 'Charlemagne' to Hammerstein.

5   Soulat, page 17.

The next elements of 'Charlemagne' to arrive at Hammerstein were companies I/57, 3/57 and 4/57 of battalion I/57.[6] On the same convoy were Hstuf. de Bourmont and Ustuf. Martret.[7] After learning of the diversion to Hammerstein de Bourmont had held an officer's briefing on the train. It is not known what was said.

The XVIII. Gebirgs-Korps

That same day, the 33. Waffen-Grenadier-Division der SS 'Charlemagne' (französische Nr.1) was subordinated to the XVIII. Gebirgs-Korps of the 2nd Army.[8] General Hochbaum commanded the corps. The headquarters of the XVIII. Gebirgs-Korps, newly arrived from Lapland[9], was located at Stegers (Rzeczenica).

What was the situation of the XVIII. Gebirgs-Korps? In short, not good. To defend a front running from Landeck to Konitz, almost forty-five kilometres long, the Korps had two weakened divisions: the Pomeranian 32nd Infantry Division and the 15. Waffen-Grenadier-Division der SS (lettische Nr. 1).

Commanded by General Boeck, the 32nd Infantry Division held the sector west of Konitz. It had been transferred from Courland to Pomerania only weeks before. Although well tried, it continued to fight tooth and nail for its native land. Holding the left flank was Kampfgruppe Jutland, comprising Infantry Regiments 94 and 96. Holding the sector north of Preussische-Friedland was Infantry Regiment 4. It was badly depleted. Divisional headquarters was located at Stolzenfelde, north-west of Schlochau (Czluchow in Polish).

As for the 15. Waffen-Grenadier-Division der SS (lettische Nr. 1), Grenadier Regiments 33 and 34 were in defensive positions from Rosenfelde to Landeck along Brook Dobrinka and also in a northerly direction from Landeck along Brook Küddow. Although the tired Division had been in constant action over the past month, sustaining many casualties, its Latvian troops were still full of fight and now in well constructed trenches. Also, of late, SS-Obf. Burk had taken over the command of the division from temporary commander SS-Obf. Ax, who was too inexperienced to command a division. Divisional headquarters was located at Krummensee, north of Landeck.

---

6   The exact time of their arrival is unclear. According to Bayle, "*San et Persante*", page 153, the three companies of the I/57 spent the entire day of the 22nd at Hammerstein camp and were alerted around 2300 hours. Mabire is unspecific, but infers they did not arrive before midnight on the 22nd (page 271). According to Saint-Loup, page 175, 'SS Regiment 57' arrived in six echelons on the 22nd between the hours of 0200 and 1900. This seems very doubtful as both Mabire and Bayle record the arrival of elements of Waffen-Gren. Regt der SS 57 on the 23rd and even as late as the 24th.

7   Martret, personal conversation. Curiously, according to Mabire, page 272, regimental headquarters of the 57 was on the convoy carrying the 2/57 and the first elements of Hstuf. Obitz's II/57 that arrived the following day.

8   Soulat, letter to the author. However, according to the order of battle of Army Group Vistula on the date of 22nd February 1945, 'Charlemagne' was attached to the 2nd Army (see "*Russo-German war: 25th January to 8 May 1945*" page 35).

9   The headquarters of the XVIII. Gebirgs-Korps was transferred to Pomerania on 15th February 1945.

Shortly before midnight on 22nd/23rd February 1945, Stubaf. Boudet-Gheusi assembled all officers and NCOs at Hammerstein camp to inform them that the Russians had launched a massive tank attack in the region of Schlochau only twenty kilometres east of Hammerstein. This did not bode well. And still there was no sign of its promised equipment.

Alerted, by midday on 23rd February, the three companies of Fenet's I/57 had taken up a temporary position several kilometres to the south-east of Hammerstein to cover the other convoys due to arrive against a possible surprise enemy attack. A muffled rumbling could still be heard to the east and every so often the sound of tank tracks could be made out over this background noise.

The 23rd saw more convoys of 'Charlemagne' pull into Hammerstein railway station. They brought with them the 2/57, whose commander Ostuf. Bartolomei had already arrived, as well as elements of Hstuf. Obitz's II/57 [and perhaps the last elements of Hstuf. de Bourmont's regimental headquarters].[10]

That same day, in his daily report to O.K.H.[11], Colonel Eismann, the operations officer (Ia) of the headquarters of Army Group Vistula, indicated for 'Charlemagne' the following assembly area: Forstenau—Reichenwalde—Heinrichswalde—Klausfelde. He also signalled the arrival of the first five convoys of the Division.

That evening, in his message AOK 2/Ia 365/45 G.K.Chefs., General Weiss, the commander of the 2nd Army, remarked that the arrival of 'Charlemagne' would without doubt permit the reduction of the rather large front assigned to the 32nd Infantry Division of the XVIII. Gebirgs-Korps but would not permit the release of local reserves. The message was sent to the headquarters of Army Group Vistula at 0030 hours on 24th February 1945.

If General Weiss recognised that the front of the 32nd Infantry Division was overextended so had the Russians. At dawn on the 24th, literally hours after General Weiss sent message AOK 2/Ia 365/45, five Soviet divisions of the 19th Army, newly arrived from Finland, struck the 32nd Infantry Division between Marienfelde and north-west of Konitz. Under this crushing blow the Russians succeeded in ripping open the front of the 32nd Infantry Division between Marienfelde and Janznick. There were no reserves available. Thus, the German command could do nothing to seal the breach through which the enemy now poured. Unopposed, the Soviet divisions moved towards the river Haaken along which the 2nd Army now planned to establish a defence line.

The arrival of Stubaf. Raybaud and the I/58

Meanwhile, on the morning of 24th February 1945, two convoys, carrying elements of the I/58 and the regimental headquarters staff of Waffen-Gren. Regt. der

---

10   Again the exact time of their arrival is unclear. According to Mabire, page 272, Ostuf. Bartolomei's 2/57, the first elements of Hstuf. Obitz's II/57, as well as regimental headquarters arrived in Hammerstein railway station before midnight on the 23rd. René Forez, a waffengrenadier in Hennecart's 5/57 of the II/57, confirms that his company disembarked around 2130 hours (letter to the author). In contrast, Bayle, a Junker der Waffen SS in the 2/57, records his arrival at Hammerstein on the 24th around 1600 hours ("*De Marseille à Nowossibirsk*", page 158).

11   Reference I A/Br.Tgb.Nr.1842/45 geh.

SS 58, pulled into Hammerstein railway station.[12] Travelling with them was regimental commander Stubaf. Raybaud.[13]

At Hammerstein camp, Raybaud was alarmed by the same discovery made by all others before him: the military depot was, in a word, empty.[14]

In the evening of the 24th, two more convoys carrying elements of the I/58 arrived at Hammerstein.[15] The ninth convoy, carrying companies 1/58, 2/58 and 9/58 (IG), arrived towards 1700 hours.

Like its predecessors, the ninth convoy was attacked from the air en route to Pomerania. The first attack came soon after its departure on the 21st when two Allied fighters made a single pass and put the locomotive out of action and shot up the field kitchen, causing two casualties. On the following day, the 22nd, having just passed through Nordhausen station, the convoy was caught by six or seven fighters. This time the attack lasted about twenty minutes and was much more serious; the locomotive and three wagons of ammunition were destroyed, the line between Nordhausen and the next station of Halle was cut, and the dead totalled six and the wounded twenty. Thereupon, the convoy returned to Nordhausen where it spent the night. Also of interest to note is that at 1600 hours on the 25th, while stopped at Neustettin station, the ninth convoy was passed by another carrying (at least) the divisional Engineer Company.

Contact with the enemy!

During the morning of the 24th, Brigf. Krukenberg held a briefing at Hammerstein camp with Obf. Puaud, Stubaf. de Vaugelas, Stubaf. Raybaud and Hstuf. de Bourmont.[16] Staf. Zimmermann assisted Krukenberg. The

12   Raybaud, letter to Mabire, 3/11/74, and corrections to Soulat's *Historique de la Division Charlemagne*. This corrects Mabire who states (on page 296) that the four companies of Hstuf. Monneuse's I/58 arrived throughout the night of 24th/25th February. Incredibly the written interview with Raybaud in Landwehr's "*Charlemagne's Legionnaires*" details that 'his men' had actually disembarked from their trains at Bärenhutte. This is incorrect.

13   Raybaud, letter to Mabire, 3/11/74. This corrects Mabire's account of Raybaud disembarking at Hammerstein with Hstuf. Berret's II/58 after the engagement of the division in the sector of Heinrichswalde and Barkenfelde. In this same letter, Raybaud also wished to set the record straight that he had not fought 'for several days' with the Zalhmeisters (quartermasters) at Wildflecken while his first battalion was in action.

14   Mabire, page 332.

15   Raybaud, corrections to Soulat's "*Historique de la Division Charlemagne*". Rigeade, the company commander of the 3/58, also recalls that battalion I/58 arrived throughout the day of 24th February (letter to the author, 31/1/97).

16   A conclusion drawn by the author, although the exact time of this briefing and its participants remain unclear. According to Soulat, page 29, during the morning of the 24th, 'a meeting was held at Hammerstein camp which brought together' Krukenberg, Puaud, Raybaud and de Bourmont. According to Raybaud, letter to Mabire of 3/11/74, at some point after his arrival at Hammerstein on the 24th, Krukenberg summoned him to Hammerstein camp with de Vaugelas and perhaps de Bourmont. Although the simultaneous presence of Puaud and de Vaugelas is not

Brigadeführer told them that the front held by the Latvians had been ruptured[17] and that 'we will have to go and take up position immediately'.[18] Also reported was the intention of the 2nd Army to form a stop line, facing east, between Hammerstein and Schlochau. The following orders were given[19]:

The I/57 under Ostuf. Fenet was to deploy beyond the village of Heinrichswalde and take up defensive positions, facing south-east.[20]

The II/57 under Hstuf. Obitz was to deploy towards the village of Barkenfelde (Barkowo), some twenty kilometres south-east of Hammerstein. In addition, the headquarters of Waffen-Gren. Regt der SS 57 was to establish itself in Barkenfelde.

The I/58 under Hstuf. Monneuse and the headquarters of Waffen-Gren. Regt der SS 58 were to deploy to the village of Bärenhutte.

Furthermore, Stubaf. Raybaud was ordered to place the I/58 at the disposal of Waffen-Gren. Regt der SS 57[21] and to prepare the position of Bärenhutte while awaiting the arrival of Hstuf. Berret's II/58.

For tactical reasons, Waffen-Gren. Regt der SS 57 was subordinated to the 32nd Infantry Division whose right wing now extended to Bärenhutte railway station.[22]

By 1300 hours, both battalions of Waffen-Gren. Regt der SS 57 had set off to the front.[23] And thus began the engagement of 'Charlemagne' without artillery and tank support, without heavy weapons, and without radio equipment. Indeed, some soldiers were still without a steel helmet or a spade.

reported, the author believes that this briefing, which importantly led to the engagement of 'Charlemagne', would not have gone ahead without the presence of its commander and its Chief-of-Staff. Thus, the author has concluded that Soulat and Raybaud speak of the same briefing. Moreover, there is some agreement between Soulat and Raybaud on the content of this briefing.

17 Raybaud, letter to Mabire, 3/11/74. This is not strictly true. The Russians actually gained a breakthrough east of the 15. Waffen-Grenadier-Division der SS (lettische Nr. 1) in the sector of the 32nd Infantry Division.

18 Ibid.

19 Mabire records on pages 274-275 the issuing of these orders in different circumstances; on the morning of the 24th, Hstuf. de Bourmont and his regimental headquarters were making their way to Barkenfelde when German liaison officers informed him that the village was in danger of being captured by the Russians! He asked about the 32nd Infantry Division and was told that it had been dispersed which was then confirmed by the sight of retreating haggard, cold and frightened German soldiers. Thereupon he decided to deploy his regimental headquarters to the village of Bärenwalde and to 'push his two battalions forward to try and get a little clarity'. While it is true that de Bourmont learnt of the danger to or even the capture of Barkenfelde while making his way there after the briefing, it appears that Mabire, who does not record the briefing at which the orders were issued, has used this particular moment of 'high drama' to introduce the orders issued to the two battalions of Waffen-Gren. Regt der SS 57, but not those of the I/58, which, according to Mabire, had still not arrived.

20 Mabire, page 280. However, according to Soulat, page 29, Fenet's I/57 was also to deploy towards the village of Barkenfelde, to the east of Heinrichswalde.

Taking a route via Geglenfelde (Wyczechy), the headquarters of Waffen-Gren. Regt der SS 57 and Hstuf. Obitz's II/57 made their way to Barkenfelde. On learning that Barkenfelde was already occupied by the Russians, Hstuf. de Bourmont decided to establish his regimental headquarters at Bärenwalde, to the north of Barkenfelde.

The II/57 continued forward and made good time.

Around 1500 hours, the regimental reconnaissance platoon under Ustuf. Erdozain, a former cadet at the *École militaire de La Flèche*, unexpectedly engaged an enemy detachment near Barkenfelde. It was not a detachment of Soviets, but bizarrely a detachment of 'free Germans' in German uniforms!

At the end of the afternoon of the 24th, Obitz's II/57 cautiously entered a deserted Barkenfelde, but came under accurate sniper fire from a wood and lost a dozen dead and wounded before the Russians disappeared.[24] The companies then deployed; the 5/57 took up a position some four to five kilometres from Barkenfelde near a hamlet occupied by the Russians; the 6/57 occupied some farm(house)s at the southern edge of the village; and the 8/57, with its heavy weapons, set up some two kilometres north-west of Barkenfelde across the road running from Barkenfelde to Bärenwalde.[25] All now waited.

21   Raybaud, letter to Mabire, 3/11/74. This corrects Mabire, page 304, and Saint-Loup, page 192. For the record, Mabire recounts that at dawn on the 25th, during a meeting of senior officers at the command post of Waffen-Gren. Regt der SS 57 at Bärenwalde, Hstuf. de Bourmont requested and received from Obf. Puaud the subordination of battalion I/58 to Waffen-Gren. Regt der SS 57. This request was to realise the unity of command. Saint-Loup, for his part, recounts that late afternoon on the 25th, when Hstuf. Monneuse came for orders at the command post of Waffen-Gren. Regt der SS 57 near Bärenwalde, he was informed by Hstuf. de Bourmont that his battalion would 'march with the 57'.

22   Soulat, page 29. However, Mabire recounts, page 273, that as soon as de Bourmont disembarked from his train at Hammerstein he went to the 'headquarters of the German Division' (presumably the 32nd Infantry Division) for orders. Soon after, he returned to his headquarters with a furious air and the news that his Waffen-Gren. Regt der SS 57 was now 'integrated into' the 32nd Infantry Division. In response to this, if one takes into consideration that the headquarters of 'Charlemagne' had already arrived, that the headquarters of the 32nd Infantry Division was at Stolzenfelde, some twenty-five kilometres from Hammerstein, and that when de Bourmont arrived it was still not a question of a rupture of the nearby front, the question still remains would he still have gone to the headquarters of the German 32nd Infantry Division? The answer would have to be no.

23   According to Saint-Loup, page 176, the time was 1000 hours when the state of alert was issued to all those units which had disembarked, and 1300 hours when the two battalions of Waffen-Gren. Regt der SS 57 set off to the front, the II/57 following the I/57 after an interval of minutes. According to Mabire, pages 276-280, Fenet's I/57 set off at midday. Curiously, Mabire is unspecific about Obitz's II/57. Midday is also recorded by Soulat, page 29, for the I/57, and, on page 30, as the time the II/57 and the headquarters of Waffen-Gren. Regt der SS 57 arrived at Geglenfelde.

24   Saint-Loup, page 179. This is not recounted by Mabire.

25   De Misser of the 8/57, map to the author.

At twilight, the Russians attacked. 'With the energy of despair', Hstuf. Obitz's battalion fought them off against great odds.[26] The 5/57 withdrew to Barkenfelde, but what was left of the company was then separated between the other units of the battalion for the defence of the village.

At nightfall, Hstuf. Obitz decided to abandon Barkenfelde and take up a position on a line of heights to the north-east of the road that runs to Bärenwalde. Closely pursued by the Russians, his battalion conducted a fighting withdrawal to this defensive position and quickly dug in. Around 1900 hours, Obitz was reinforced by the timely arrival of the Panzerjäger (or Heavy) Battalion's PAK Company of twelve 75mm guns under Ostuf. Krotoff, as well as a battery of 105mm guns and two 88mm guns with German crews.

Heinrichswalde

Heinrichswalde is about twelve kilometres from Hammerstein and was connected by a direct dirt road, but after a recent thaw it had become nothing more than a muddy quagmire. It was along this road that Ostuf. Fenet's Battalion, the I/57, made its way to Heinrichswalde. Progress was not easy. The carts carrying the heavy weapons and ammunition sank up to their hubs which tens of men had to be detailed to get out and push along. Their horses waded about.[27] Sometimes the men suddenly sank up to their knees in muddy potholes. The battalion was then forced to advance in single file on each side of the road to allow the continuous passage of carts crowded with civilians fleeing from the Russians. That slowed its progress even more. As a result, the battalion stretched out.

Around 1700 hours (Mabire) or 1900 hours (Soulat), the 3/57 approached Heinrichswalde. Ustuf. Counil, the twenty-year-old company commander of the 3/57, despatched a patrol into the village, but it drew fire. The Russians were already occupying Heinrichswalde! Thereupon Fenet ordered Counil to attack with his company. This was repulsed. Counil reported back to Fenet that Heinrichswalde was strongly defended by the Russians who were perhaps in battalion strength. Fenet then decided to await the arrival of the other companies before proceeding with a battalion attack.[28]

Night fell, but Heinrichswalde was soon bathed in bright moonlight. Bartolomei's 2/57 would only arrive shortly before 1900 hours. Soon after Ostuf. Fenet deployed his companies: Ustuf. Brazier's I/57 to the right, Ostuf. Bartolomei's 2/57 to the left; Couvreur's 4/57, with its machine-guns and mortars, to a pit 800 metres from the village; and Counil's 3/57 to remain position at the western edge of the village. Fenet quickly drew up his attack plan: following a mortar barrage, Counil's 3/57 would attack through the village's entrance supported by converging flank attacks from the companies of Bartolomei and Brazier.[29] The attack was set for 1900 hours.

26   Mabire registers this unequal fight at one to ten (page 277).
27   Mabire, page 280. In contrast, Bayle of the 2/57, in a letter to the author, remarked that there were no horses at their disposal; they had simply not arrived yet.
28   Mabire, page 282. However, Saint-Loup does not document the attack of Counil's 3/57 and according to Soulat, page 29, Ustuf. Counil estimated Russian strength at a company.

Couvreur's mortar barrage was over in a matter minutes, his complete stock of mortar ammunition having been expended. The Russians replied with their own mortars. Supported by Couvreur's heavy machine-guns, companies I/57 and 3/57 stormed forward. Ustuf. Counil, the company commander of the 3/57, was not wearing a helmet; how could he when some of his men were without one? Among the first to be wounded was section commander Strm.-F.Bew Yvon Trémel[30]; he was hit in both arms. He was evacuated.

Brazier's I/57 advanced in successive dashes, but the supporting fire from Péléart's heavy machine-guns, perhaps of the company's organic heavy platoon, was too low and brought losses. Uscha. Darat was the first to be hit and wounded by friendly fire. Undeterred, the I/57 broke into Heinrichswalde. Uscha. Gillet's platoon dislodged the Russians from a large farmhouse with grenades and then entrenched itself. The Russians attacked and were shot up in a hail of bullets. They came again in greater numbers. To avoid encirclement, Brazier's I/57 was forced to fall back to its starting positions.[31]

After spending a long time in overcoming a machine gun nest, the 3/57 also managed to penetrate into Heinrichswalde. Advancing towards the cemetery, Ustuf. Counil, who was two or three metres in front of his company, was killed.[32] Suddenly, the Russians launched a massive counterattack. Although wavering from the loss of its commander, the company, reinforced by the headquarters of the I/57 and with fire support from other units, managed to stop the Russians dead. Again the Russians came. Again they were repulsed. Again they came. And again they were repulsed. Eventually the situation stabilised.

On learning of Counil's death, Fenet ordered Oscha. Quicampoix to take over the remnants of the severely tested 3/57 and hold Heinrichswalde at all costs. Wounded of the 3/57 taken to a first aid post in a house were killed or wounded again when enemy shells smashed into it.

29   Mabire, page 283. However, according to Saint-Loup, page 182, Ustuf. Brazier's I/57 was assigned to deliver the frontal attack and Ustuf. Counil's 3/57 to attack on the right wing.

30   Trémel was evacuated to a farm serving as a field hospital that came under air attack. Riddled with shrapnel, he was further wounded in the head, the throat, the left arm and the left knee.

31   Saint-Loup, pages 184-185. In contrast, Mabire recounts, pages 286-287, that the attack by Brazier's I/57 came to an untimely end when the company became pinned down and started to take heavy losses. Dead and wounded are described as littering the ground. In addition, there is no mention of the I/57 breaking into Heinrichswalde. According to Soulat, page 29, the I/57 was also quickly stopped by violent heavy weapons fire. However, Bayle is suspiciously quiet on the actions of Brazier's Company. Unfortunately, the author has not been able to explain these different accounts, but is it possible that only Uscha. Gillet's platoon broke into the village and that the other platoons were stopped dead?

32   Mabire, page 285, presumably based on the eyewitness account of Riberto (pseudonym). However, Saint-Loup recounts, pages 184-186, that Counil's 3/57, after breaking into the village, pushed on in hand-to-hand fighting and took the central crossroads that was held for over an hour. Losses mounted and, by the time the company fell back under great enemy pressure, its commander was dead.

Meanwhile, Ostuf. Bartolomei's Company, the 2/57, had become pinned down and unable to move from its starting positions in the village cemetery. Its line of attack was across a veritable glacis, but it was lit up like day by some burning hovels and swept by well placed Russian automatic weapons. Any attempt to cross would have been murderous and Bartolomei was not going to sacrifice his men needlessly. All the same his company started to take losses. Platoon commander Uscha. Mauclair, a former French Navy *second-maître* (Petty Officer second class), was one of the first killed. A second platoon commander, Oscha. Gastinel, a former *Milicien*, was also killed bringing orders from Bartolomei. Junker der Waffen SS Bayle took command of the platoon again.[33]

Enemy mortars zeroed in. Then, in turn, batteries of Katyusha rockets opened up. The men of the 2/57 took shelter as best they could. However, one platoon commanded by Uscha. Franchart, he was ex-Sturmbrigade, did actually attempt to attack and moved off across the fire-swept glacis. The platoon was made up of 'very young boys' and their reasons for trying to attack are not known as they were decimated in minutes. None of them would return.[34]

Bartolomei's position soon became untenable and he withdrew his company to a small height to his rear.

Despite the unsuccessful attack of his battalion, Ostuf. Fenet still believed he could take and hold Heinrichswalde. But reports from Brazier and then Bartolomei, which spoke of the Russians advancing unimpeded on the flanks, left him with the realisation that the battle was beginning to turn in the favour of the Russians. Moreover, contact had still not been made with the II/57 on his left flank nor with the 15. Waffen-Grenadier-Division der SS (lettische Nr. 1) on his right flank. Totally isolated, Fenet now abandoned any hope of recapturing Heinrichswalde. And although encirclement threatened he decided to hold on and 'await orders without yielding any ground'.[35] But he had no signalling equipment.

Ostuf. Fenet finally received orders from his regimental commander, Hstuf. de Bourmont, courtesy of liaison officer Ostuf. de Londaiz who arrived on horseback![36] Fenet was ordered to withdraw level to the lake midway between

33 Just before the departure of 'Charlemagne' from Wildflecken to Pomerania Oscha. Gastinel entered the 2/57. Outranked, Junker der Waffen-SS Bayle 'let Gastinel have his place'. Curiously, Bayle writes, "*San et Persante*", page 156, that Gastinel's former *Milice* rank gave him a superior Waffen-SS rank to his. This, however, might be incorrect. Officers and NCOs of the *Milice* were admitted into the Waffen-SS with the rank they held in the French Army and not that in the *Milice*. And any subsequent promotions came, undoubtedly, as a result of merit.

34 Saint-Loup, pages 185-186. However, Bayle, who was in the 2/57 and present at Heinrichswalde, cannot recall this suicidal attack or the existence of a certain *Zugführer* (platoon commander) by the name of Franchart. But Mounine, in a letter to the author, has confirmed the existence of Franchart, his rank as that of Uscha, his company as that of the 2/57, and his death at Heinrichswalde. The author has not been able to explain this discrepancy.

35 Mabire, page 288.

36 The time of Ostuf. de Londaiz's arrival remains unclear. According to Mabire, page 289-290, his first visit was nothing more than 'fact finding' and an information share. All the same, before midnight on the 24th, de Londaiz was back with the orders.

Barkenfelde and Bärenwalde, located two or three kilometres north-east of his current positions.[37] In turn, orders were sent to the companies, but the 2/57 had just withdrawn to avoid encirclement and could not be contacted. However, this did not unduly concern Fenet; Bartolomei was 'an old fox who knew how to avoid all the traps'.

After evacuating the wounded to the rear, Fenet withdrew.[38] There were no difficulties. By 0300 hours on the 25th, the I/57 was on its new positions, but contact could still not be made with the II/57.

Around 0715 hours on the 25th, a patrol from the 3/58 stumbled across the 2/57. An order signed by Hstuf. de Bourmont was passed onto Ostuf. Bartolomei. In this way, he learnt that 'the I/57 should have withdrawn at 0400 hours and, taking advantage of the darkness, withdrawn northwards in the direction of the level crossing situated 500 metres from Bärenwalde to receive new orders there'.[39] Alas, there was no way Bartolomei could pass on this order to Fenet, still in position north-east of Heinrichswalde, for he had lost all contact with the remainder of the battalion.

Around the same time as Bartolomei was handed de Bourmont's order, the Russian infantry hit the I/57 and punctured the company holding the centre of its disposition. To prevent being cut in two and to drive off the Russians, Ostuf. Fenet assembled all the forces of his right flank and immediately counter-attacked along the front line. This counterattack succeeded.

Ostuf. Fenet now decided to move his isolated battalion, less Bartolomei's Company, to Bärenwalde where he hoped to find Hstuf. de Bourmont and the regimental headquarters of Waffen-Gren. Regt der SS 57. Bartolomei's 2/57 was making for Hammerstein.

Bärenwalde

Let us now return to the II/57 occupying a line of heights before Bärenwalde. During the night, the 8/57 was deployed to Bärenwalde.

However, Saint-Loup is not in agreement and records, page 186, that de Londaiz finally found the headquarters of the I/57 at 0300 hours.

37 Soulat, page 30. Mabire, for his part, details, on page 290, that Fenet was to withdraw two or three kilometres to the rear.

38 According to Saint-Loup, page 186, when the time came for the 3/57 to withdraw from Heinrichswalde, Ustuf. Counil's body was brought along. However, this is contradicted by Mabire, pages 290-291.

39 Soulat, page 30. Curiously, according to Mabire, page 291, the order from de Bourmont that a patrol of Waffen-Gren. Regt der SS 57 handed to Bartolomei read as follows: "Order to the 1st Battalion [the I/57] to withdraw northwards to the lake situated between Barkenfelde and Bärenwalde where I have established my headquarters and where I will give new orders." In response to this, at no time was the regimental headquarters of Waffen-Gren. Regt der SS 57 established between Barkenfelde and Bärenwalde. Moreover, by the early hours of the 25th, Obitz's II/57 was in serious trouble and de Bourmont would not have issued orders to Fenet that would have moved his battalion into the direct path of the Russians and almost certain death. Thus, the orders to withdraw to the level crossing appear more befitting the circumstances.

Towards midnight, an enemy force of company strength appeared before the 6/57. Ustuf. Albert ordered his company to let the Russians approach to within twenty metres of its well-camouflaged and concealed positions before opening fire. The Frenchmen waited. Now the Russians were within twenty metres. Fire! Many of the attackers were felled. Surprised, the Russians immediately fled in total chaos. The Frenchmen rushed after them and brought back three prisoners, who were despatched to regimental headquarters.

A little later, the Russians started to pound violently Obitz's battalion with mortars, anti-tank guns, howitzers and Stalin Organs. Hell was let loose. The unimaginable barrage lasted more than an hour, inflicting heavy casualties and totally disrupting the battalion's disposition.

At 0500 hours, a fresh Siberian division, brought up by truck, charged the II/57. It was a savage and costly struggle, but the vast Russian flood could not be stemmed. Although ordered to hold on, Obitz could do little else than retreat. And as if his battalion was not in trouble enough, but the unexpected withdrawal of a Latvian SS unit exposed its left flank. Too dispersed, the II/57 now disintegrated. The commander of the 7/57, Oberjunker Million-Rousseau, suddenly found himself alone in the midst of an enemy horde and had to fight his way out.

Maurice Comte, serving in the 5/57, remembers:[40]

.... having been separated from my company, the 5th, I found myself withdrawing with my platoon and some stragglers in the direction of Bärenwalde where we arrived when Brigf. Krukenberg was preparing the defence. Questioned by Ostuf. Artus on what we knew of the Russian positions, I reported to him the closeness of a column of tanks. Brigf. Krukenberg gave Artus the job of a reconnaissance mission on this column; Artus took what was left of my platoon [and] some others (I think Uscha. Jacques), in all around twenty lightly armed (one or two MG 42 machine guns, personal weapons and perhaps panzerfäuste).

[We advanced] about twenty metres through a wood bordering and dominating the road along which the column was advancing [and made] contact, but without being spotted by the Russians. We waited for Artus' orders who, like us, was watching the column, made up of: two T–34s at the front, then one Stalin, then other T–34s, and escorting infantry in file on each side without apparent worry, with weapons lowered. [At this point Maurice Comte was the nearest to Ostuf. Artus, but still some ten to fifteen metres away from him. The Russian road column was about twenty to thirty metres away.]

Suddenly, [an] intense bombardment; the Russians took shelter; I looked at Artus, and saw him lifeless, hit in the neck, covered with blood; one of the men said: "The Lieutenant is dead."; I very clearly remember having said to the

40   Comte, letter to the author. This corrects Mabire's account, pages 326-327, of the death of Ostuf. Artus which, for the record, describes how Artus, on learning that Russian tanks had broken through their defensive line before the Hammerstein-Bärenwalde railway and were advancing on the railway station, dashed to its defence. Stalking a tank through the houses he managed to get within metres of the steel monster. Panzerfaust in hand, he took aim and fired, but nothing happened; the panzerfaust had not been primed. He was then cut down by the tank and died almost instantly.

Machine-gunner (Meunier I think): "Don't fire" before I was wounded by a piece of shrapnel in the top of my head. I passed out (perhaps some seconds or minutes) [and] was brought back by the men withdrawing to Bärenwalde. I was completely sleepy.

Thus, in all probability, Artus was killed and Comte wounded by friendly artillery fire attempting to stop the Russian column.[41]

All resistance was gradually submerged. The isolated companies fought a running battle at the cost of heavy losses. In desperation, 'to avoid a pointless massacre',[42] Hstuf. Obitz decided to withdraw the remnants of his battalion to the Hammerstein-Bärenwalde railway line north of his present positions. To cover the withdrawal, the 8/57 was deployed from Bärenwalde to the railway line.

The withdrawal of the II/57 exposed the headquarters of Waffen-Gren. Regt der SS 57, which had to evacuate Bärenwalde promptly, as well as the left flank of the I/58 which had moved up into action during the night of 24th/25th February 1945.

Enter the I/58

On the 24th, soon after the arrival of battalion I/58, Stubaf. Raybaud, Hstuf. Monneuse, the four company commanders of the I/58, Oberjunker de Brangelin, Monneuse's orderly officer, and (perhaps) Hstuf. de Bourmont went to a head-quarters briefing by Jauss of the German Inspection in a house quite close to Hammerstein railway station. The aim of the briefing was 'to engage the I/58 as re-inforcements to the I/57'.[43] After a rundown of the situation from Jauss, it was de-cided that companies 1/58 and the 3/58 would be committed as support behind the already engaged Waffen-Gren. Regt der SS 57. At the end, Monneuse received three maps for the whole battalion! He kept one for himself and gave another to de Brangelin who was ordered to accompany Fatin's 1/58 to its position.[44]

---

41   The 'artillery fire' put down on the Russian column could only have come from Hstuf. Roy's 9/57 which must have been unaware of the nearby presence of friendly troops. Moreover, to reinforce the point that the artillery fire was friendly, Comte reiterated in his letter to the author that the hidden French SS soldiers were watching the Russian tank column and waiting for Artus' orders, and also that the Russians did not open fire on their positions.

42   Mabire, page 294.

43   Rigeade, letter to the author, 18/8/97 and de Brangelin, correspondance to the author throughout 1997. The time of this briefing for the officers of the I/58 was probably late evening. Thus, the then desperate situation of Waffen-Gren. Regt der SS 57 would not have been known and the decisions reached at this briefing for the engagement of the I/58 reflect the picture known at that time. This role for the I/58 of support to Waffen-Gren. Regt der SS 57 is not, as such, confirmed by Mabire who recounts on page 303 that Puaud employed Monneuse's I/58 to try and plug the gap that existed between Fenet's I/57 and Obitz's II/57. But these roles were defined by Puaud on the morning of the 25th! Saint-Loup, for his part, records that Rigeade's 3/58 was 'to fill out' the left flank of the I/57 and that Monneuse was to plug the gap between Rigeade and the II/57.

44   De Brangelin remembers, letter to the author, 20/7/97, that the third map went to Rigeade. However, he did not receive one (Rigeade, letter to the author, 18/8/97).

Waffen-Gren. Regt. der SS 58 was to be committed even though it had no heavy weapons or radio equipment. The regimental reconnaissance platoon, like that of Waffen-Gren. Regt. der SS 57, had no motorcycles, just bicycles. Stubaf. Raybaud would later compare the engagement of his regiment without support to that on the Somme in June 1940.

Stubaf. Raybaud was in Bärenhutte before nightfall and here he spent the night with his regimental headquarters, receiving a visit from de Vaugelas and Puaud. Around 0400 hours on the 25th, Raybaud woke to the sound of a Russian bombardment on Bärenwalde to the south. Undoubtedly, his thoughts would have gone out to his troops of the I/58 over who he no longer had any authority.

During the night of the 24th/25th February, Monneuse's I/58 moved up to the front.[45]

Compass in hand, Ustuf. Rigeade took company 3/58 towards the front.[46] After marching a dozen or so kilometres during the night, he stopped his company at daybreak and dug in at the edge of a wood in front of a vast plaine. He was on his laid-down positions south-west of Bärenwalde.

Oscha. Blonet's platoon, which was positioned in a farmhouse, chanced upon some French POWs who advised the French SS to surrender to the Russians. The SS answered by asking the POWs to join them. They refused.

Unable to find Hill 105, the planned location for his headquarters, Hstuf. Monneuse set up instead at a forest road crossing. For the time being he kept in reserve Ostuf. Géromini's company 2/58 and the command platoon and mortar platoon(s) of Ostuf. Tardan's company 4/58; Fatin's 1/58 and Rigeade's 3/58 had each been reinforced by one MG platoon of Tardan's 4/58.[47]

As for de Brangelin, after accompanying Fatin's 1/58 to its positions, he reported back to Monneuse who then asked him to set off again and make contact with Rigeade's 3/58. He would march all night through the snow-covered woods without finding a living soul. So what then was the situation?

Although Rigeade's 3/58 was in contact with the Latvians of the 15. Waffen-Grenadier-Division der SS (lettische Nr. 1) on its right, contact could not be made with Fatin's 1/58 on its left. For its part, the 1/58 managed to establish contact with Obitz's II/57 to its left, but its right flank remained wide open. Thus, a solid defensive line had still not been formed.

Towards 0600 hours on the 25th, less than an hour after the arrival of the I/58 on the front line, the first enemy activity around the positions of company 1/58 was easily repulsed.

Three hours later, the first serious attack hit Fatin's 1/58 and was immediately repulsed, but at the cost of several dead and wounded. Around the same time, Rigeade found himself isolated; the Latvians on his right came under a ferocious

45   According to the written interview with Raybaud, the I/58 took up an unidentified position, 'facing east', and, at 1700 hours, was relieved by the II/58. Thereupon the I/58 was sent forward to Bärenwalde to reinforce the hard pressed 'SS Regiment 57'. This is incorrect; the II/58 had not arrived yet.

46   Mabire states, page 297, that each company of the I/58 was committed individually whereas Saint-Loup, page 192, pictures three of his four companies marching south-east towards the sound of the guns.

47   De Brangelin, letter to the author, 20/7/97 and Soulat, page 31.

artillery bombardment and quickly withdrew. In the belief that all resistance had been swept aside, the Russian infantry then advanced, but fled when the 3/58 opened up. Although better camouflaged than the Latvians, Rigeade's 3/58 had now given its position away. Their company commander knew the Russians would be back.

In the meantime, Monneuse had become increasingly concerned about his isolated situation. He still had no contact with Rigeade's 3/58, telephone lines to the command post of Waffen-Gren. Regt der SS 57 at Bärenwalde were continually cut, and runners sent in the direction of Bärenwalde never returned. To add to his despair, his command post was also coming under intense artillery fire and steadily taking casualties.

His right flank still wide open, Monneuse summoned Ostuf. Tardan and ordered him to establish contact with the 3/58. Tardan took with him his command platoon and the crews of a mortar 'group' (platoon?) under Uscha. Salmon, also a former *Milicien*.[48] After searching in vain for almost two hours, Tardan suddenly came across stragglers of Waffen-Gren. Regt der SS 57. For the most part, they were wounded and in a state of shock. Also, they were without weapons. Then more and more dazed Frenchmen and Latvians appeared.

Judging the situation perfectly, Ostuf. Tardan then sent his remaining mortars and crews to the level crossing between Bärenwalde and Bärenhutte where he believed resistance would be centred. He and his command platoon returned to Monneuse's command post.

As the hours passed, Fatin's 1/58 was subjected to further attacks, increasing in brutality each time, but for the moment his company held the Russians in check.

By now, Géromini's 2/58 may have been committed to the left of the 1/58.[49]

When Oberjunker de Brangelin, Monneuse's orderly officer, returned to the command post of the I/58 he found Ostuf. Falcy questioning a Latvian SS soldier who, after being captured by the Russians, had just escaped. Like most LVF legionnaires, Falcy spoke a little Russian. Notably he was wearing a W-SS camouflaged smock that few possessed.[50]

De Brangelin then reported back to Monneuse that the right of their disposition was totally 'in the air'. Soon after, Monneuse learnt from runners sent to Bärenwalde that the Russians were at the village. He immediately decided to withdraw and recalled his companies.[51]

By the time the orders to withdraw reached Ostuf. Fatin he was in trouble. Contact had been severed with Obitz's II/57 and the Russians had started to

---

48   Soulat, page 31 and Mabire page 300. Saint-Loup is incorrect on page 193 when he
       recounts that 'Tardan took the head of his company' for this mission.

49   Soulat's wartime drawing of the '*combat de la 3/58 (Ustuf. Rigeade) à Bärenwalde*'
       shows the 2/58 to the left of the 1/58. As such, no other source confirms the
       commitment of the 2/58 to the left of the 1/58. Nevertheless, according to
       Saint-Loup, pages 195-196, Hstuf. Monneuse despatched Géromini's 2/58 'to see
       what's happening' with Fatin's 1/58. In an enemy-infested area, Géromini found
       Fatin and then returned with nothing to report!

50   For example, nobody in the 1/58 possessed the camouflaged smock.

51   Saint-Loup, page 196. However, de Brangelin cannot remember if Monneuse had
       relayed or actually given the order to withdraw (letter to the author, 20/7/97).

infiltrate the resulting breach to his left in greater and greater numbers. In fact, faced with this deteriorating situation, he had already decided to withdraw his company with or without orders. His company was soon back with Monneuse at his command post.[52]

Hstuf. Monneuse laid down the battle plan and order: Ostuf. Géromini's company 2/58 was to be the battering ram which would open an 'escape route' and then provide flank cover for the battalion.[53] Then came Ostuf. Fatin's company 1/58 echeloned in platoons.[54] Oberjunker de Brangelin was to bring up the rear with the last elements of the 1/58.

It was then that de Brangelin saw Ostuf. Français and his company arrive whose infantry guns were now being pulled by hand as the horses had been cut down by machine-gun fire. To ensure a rapid with-drawal, Français requested permission from de Brangelin to destroy and abandon the infantry guns. A hand grenade in the gun barrel was sufficient to render them unusable. Seeing no other alternative, de Brangelin assented to his request. Besides the company had yet to receive ammunition for the guns!

And so began the withdrawal through the enemy-infested woods to the west of Bärenwalde. Despite enemy artillery fire, the assault of Ostuf. Géromini's 2/58 was irresistible. The battalion surged forward. Oberjunker de Brangelin assisted Ostuf. Falcy and soon witnessed his wounding by a mortar shell and immediate evacuation.[55]

52 Saint-Loup, page 196. However, according to Mabire, pages 309-310, when Ostuf. Fatin received orders from Hstuf. Monneuse to withdraw it was 'too late'. The 1/58 was already encircled. Géromini's 2/58, described as the last reinforcements, then had to be sent to free the 1/58. As such, this 'relief' operation conducted by the 2/58 is not confirmed by any other source. The possibility exists that Mabire has adapted the 'reconnaissance in force' conducted by the 2/58 as recounted by Saint-Loup, page 195.

53 Soulat, page 33. Although Saint-Loup confirms, page 196, that Géromini was to be 'on the flanks', there is no mention of spearheading the battalion's withdrawal.

54 De Brangelin, letter to the author, 20/7/97. This corrects Saint-Loup, page 196, which places Fatin's 1/58 as the vanguard.

55 De Brangelin, correspondence to the author throughout 1997. Curiously, according to Soulat, page 62 of his original manuscript, Ostuf. Falcy was wounded along the Hammerstein-Bärenwalde railway line. Also, the author has a brief sighting of Falcy behind Bärenwalde level crossing (Grenier, letter to the author, April 1998). And he did not appear to be carrying a wound, but then again the sighting was only brief. This sighting the author has not been able to explain.

Incorrectly, according to Saint-Loup, page 297, Falcy was killed along the Hammerstein-Bärenwalde railway line. Rigeade remembers meeting him in Paris shortly after the war. Moreover, de Genouillac met his good friend Falcy again at the start of 1947 at the camp of Carrère. He spent fifteen months in detention with Falcy. Curiously, they had often showered together and de Genouillac does not recall noticing any trace of injury on Falcy's body except two cut fingers on his left hand after being thrown onto a running circular saw by a prison warder 'anxious to prove his patriotism'.

As Oberjunker de Brangelin progressed in a northeasterly direction he continued to collect and rally stragglers from all manner of units. He soon had thirty men with him, but many were wounded and had to be carried on their backs. De Brangelin himself carried the wounded Hscha. Caténès on his back. Thus, the pace was not quick. Furthermore, they had few weapons.

Suddenly, the leading troops fell back onto de Brangelin; the Russians had outflanked and cut off the group from the rest of the battalion. In the hope that the Russians were still not too thick on the ground, and fully aware that if an immediate break through did not occur then all would be lost, de Brangelin gave the order to charge ahead. All bawled as loud as they could more to encourage themselves than to intimidate the Russians who took flight into the forest, leaving some corpses behind.[56]

Pushing on, de Brangelin and his group came to Bärenwalde level crossing, but Russian tanks soon caught up with them. They were only saved by the timely intervention of the anti-tank company which managed to hold off the Russian tanks long enough for them to take shelter behind the railway line. After evacuating the wounded, de Brangelin put himself at the disposal of Tardan.

And what of Ustuf. Rigeade and his 3/58? Still isolated, he and his company were oblivious of the fact that the rest of the I/58 had withdrawn. Around 1000 hours, he suddenly found himself in the path of the first brigades of enemy Russian tanks.[57] His company, having no anti-tank guns or panzerfäuste at its disposal, sought to fight off the tanks by depriving them of their escorting infantry and concentrated its fire on these 'soft targets'.

56   De Brangelin, correspondance to the author throughout 1997. However, Saint-Loup's description of the retreat of the I/58, pages 196-198, is, as you would expect, much more dramatic. To summarise, the battalion was making its way through the woods west of Bärenwalde when gunfire suddenly rang out 'with barbaric brutality'. This was followed by momentary silence and then shouts in Russian of 'Huré Stalin'. In terror, Fatin's men, the vanguard, fell back in disorder pursued by the Russians. The situation looked critical. Monneuse hesitated. A cry went up to outshout the Russians. It was repeated again and again. Fatin urged them to bawl anything. Instantly transformed 'into lions', Fatin's men, shouting at the top of their voices, charged back into action. Unsettled by these diabolic battle cries of rage, the superstitious Russians stopped in their tracks, turned around and hid under cover, 'refusing a hand-to-hand fight, which would have been terrible'! At an infernal pace, the Frenchmen continued on, but the Russians always seemed one step ahead and at each forest crossing they were raked by Russian machine-gun fire. Gashes were torn into them. Dead or wounded, they were left behind. Finally, 'like hunted animals', they emerged from the woods and before them was a road, the Hammerstein-Bärenwalde railway line, and men and equipment of the heavy battalion. Nevertheless, when questioned about the apparent similarities and discrepancies between the two versions, de Brangelin stated that the present version was that he had also supplied Saint-Loup. Clearly, Saint-Loup has dramatised this action, as well as inflating its participants to that of the whole battalion.

57   Cited Saint-Loup, page 199, and confirmed by Rigeade, letter to the author, 17/2/97. However, Mabire makes no reference to enemy tanks participating in the assault on Rigeade's 3/58.

Two Russian tanks made for Oscha. Blonet's platoon. The only anti-tank weapon Blonet had been provided with was a hollow charged anti-tank hand grenade, which he used without success. The tanks continued forward. Blonet could only look on helplessly as one of the tanks crushed some comrades who had taken refuge in the roadside ditch. Never would he forget the sight of the bloody body remains stuck to the tank tracks.

Unexpectedly, Rigeade's critical situation was helped by flanking fire from heavy machine-guns of arriving battalion I/57. Contact was made and only then did battalion commander Ostuf. Fenet realise that he had rendered service to a fellow unit of 'Charlemagne'.[58]

The I/57 pushed on towards Bärenwalde, leaving Ustuf. Rigeade to his own means once again.

Henceforth, Rigeade found himself isolated again. To stave off annihilation, he decided to withdraw his 3/58 towards Bärenwalde. But his hopes for an uninterrupted withdrawal suddenly ended with the clanking of tank treads; two Russian tanks and accompanying infantry appeared from the woods to the right of the road along which the company was withdrawing. Luckily his men now had panzerfäuste; although they had gone up to the front without anti-tank weapons, they had retrieved some abandoned by a routed unit. Panzerfaust in hand, several men of the command platoon hunted down the tanks while their compatriots with automatic weapons kept down the heads of the escorting infantry. A well-aimed panzerfaust struck home and blew apart one of the tanks.[59]

Rigeade hurried his company on towards Bärenwalde, but the Russian attack had separated him from his rearguard formed by Oscha. Blonet's 3rd platoon.[60] Without a map, Oscha. Blonet and his platoon would only rejoin the company at Neustettin days later.

By midday, Rigeade's 3/58 had reached the Hammerstein-Bärenwalde railway line.

---

58   Mabire, page 312 and Saint-Loup, page 199. Of interest to note is that, according to Soulat, page 32, when the I/57 regrouped near Bärenwalde and 'finally made contact with the I/58', Ostuf. Fenet learnt that orders had been issued at 0800 hours for his battalion to go to Bärenwalde. However, Rigeade had had no contact with Monneuse or indeed any unit of 'Charlemagne' since his arrival at the front, so Fenet could not have learnt of this order from Rigeade. So how did Fenet come to learn of this order? Perhaps from stragglers of Waffen-Gren. Regt der SS 58 which he is reported as encountering after leaving Rigeade and continuing his withdrawal to Bärenwalde. Also, the time was around 1100 hours when Fenet learnt of this order. That is around one hour after his battalion came to the timely assistance of Rigeade and would suggest that Fenet had already left him and pushed on.

59   Presumably, as no further fighting is remarked upon, the second tank thought better of continuing the attack and turned tail.

60   Blonet, letter to the author, 16/2/2002. This corrects Mabire, page 317, who recounts that Rigeade had ordered his company to separate into platoons for the withdrawal, Saint-Loup, page 203, that the company had split into three parts by the time it was behind the Hammerstein-Bärenwalde railway line, and Rigeade, who thought that the platoon had lost its way during the retreat through the woods (Rigeade, letter to the author, 17/2/97).

The Soviet forces facing 'Charlemagne'

Back at Hammerstein, Rttf. Sepchant of the Engineer platoon/Headquarters Company/58, which had not been engaged, met Oscha. Girard of the 10/58 (anti-tank). Sepchant knew him of old from the LVF. Then his conduct had always been exemplary, but now he was completely demoralised. Back from the front, he told Sepchant that they did not have the slightest chance of resisting the enemy tanks he had just observed, adding that he did not want to get himself killed.[61] Sepchant was stunned to silence. He did not ask Girard what he was doing at the rear.

So what was the size of the Soviet forces facing 'Charlemagne'? Saint-Loup claims, page 191, that the I/57 faced (elements of) ten Soviet Divisions and two Tank Corps whereas the II/57 was confronted by (elements of) no less than fifteen Divisions and three Tank Corps. Landwehr repeats the same Soviet concentrations against the two battalions of Waffen-Gren. Regt der SS 57.

So did the two battalions of Waffen-Gren. Regt der SS 57 face Soviet forces totalling some twenty-five (infantry) Divisions and five Tank Corps? The answer is no. Only the 19th Army and the 3rd Guards Tank Corps were tasked with the breakthrough and the drive to the Baltic coast by way of Neustettin. The organic units of the 19th Army were the 134th Guards Rifle Corps, the 40th Guards Rifle Corps and the 8th Guards Mechanised Corps. It was also reinforced with the 3rd Guards Cavalry Corps and a number of independent rocket and artillery divisions. The two rifle corps both had the strength of three rifle divisions. The Cavalry Corps had the strength of three cavalry divisions. Thus, the 19th Army could commit no more than nine divisions at any one time. Also, tactically speaking, it's quite inconceivable that the Russians could have concentrated so large a force on such a narrow frontage. That would have only invited chaos.

Nevertheless, Saint-Loup also claims, page 205, that on 25th February 1945 the Soviets employed all available forces against 'Charlemagne' and that they amounted to four infantry divisions, two tank brigades and several regiments of artillery and mortar.[62] This Soviet concentration is far removed from that previously claimed and thereby much more plausible.

Furthermore, Mabire estimates, pages 285 and 293, that the I/57 faced at least two Soviet regiments at Heinrichswalde and that on the morning of the 25th the

---

61 Despite much correspondence with Sephant the author is still not sure of the day of this meeting. Sepchant spent one day and one night at Hammerstein and evacuated Hammerstein the following morning. This suggests that he arrived on the 25th and meet Girard on the morning of the 26th before evacuating Hammerstein that same morning. In response to this, the author knows of no convoys that arrived on the 25th, but that is not to say that there were none. Moreover, the bulk of 'Charlemagne' evacuated Hammerstein in the early hours of the 26th and not on the morning of the 26th. Therefore, the author has dated this meeting to the 25th, suggesting that Sepchant arrived on the 24th along with the regimental staff of Waffen-Gren. Regt der SS 58 and the I/58.

62 The same concentration is repeated in the written interview with Raybaud in "Charlemagne's Legionnaires".

II/57 faced around 10,000 Russians, which equates to the strength of two weak infantry divisions. These estimates are not totally unreasonable.

Clearly, 'Charlemagne' was facing vastly superior forces supported by armour, artillery and aircraft.

Fenet's I/57

Around midday,[63] the vanguard of Fenet's battalion was in sight of Bärenwalde and Russian tanks could clearly be seen patrolling around the village. Unaware that a defensive line had or was forming along the Hammerstein-Bärenwalde railway line, Ostuf. Fenet then decided to make an about-turn so as to try and make contact again with the I/58. Soon after, his battalion encountered some isolated and demoralised men of Waffen-Gren. Regt der SS 58 who spoke of the latest Russian attack supported by flame-throwing tanks, described as the most violent yet, which had completely disrupted the defence. The survivors were incorporated into the battalion.

Ostuf. Fenet quickly reviewed his situation; with the Russians at Bärenwalde and advancing from Heinrichswalde to Hammerstein, encirclement was now a very real possibility. Perhaps he was already encircled. To extricate his battalion, he decided to return to Hammerstein through the woods.

The I/57 headed north-west. When the battalion came across the Hammerstein-Bärenwalde railway line in open ground, Soviet aircraft suddenly appeared at low level and machine-gunned its exposed ranks. However, no casualties are reported.

After passing Hansfelde, the I/57 entered a fir-tree plantation and was engaged by an enemy patrol. The engagement was unusual, brief and costly.[64] The battalion pressed on and joined the Hammerstein-Schlochau (Czluchow) road crowded with civilians desperately fleeing before the Russians. Following another air attack, the battalion arrived at Hammerstein camp around nightfall, specified as 2100 hours.

The battalion took stock. Both the I/57 and the 3/57 had suffered heavy losses.[65] The 4/57, although virtually intact, had lost much of its heavy equipment.

Although Fenet could find no sign of any headquarters at Hammerstein, yet who should he come across? Only Bartolomei and his 2/57. It was all present and correct save one platoon.

---

63   Soulat, page 33, and repeated by Mabire, page 313. However, according to Saint-Loup, page 199, at midday, the I/57 was at Hansfelde, some five kilometres east of Hammerstein. If correct then hours later the I/57 would have been in Hammerstein. Arguably, because of the desperate situation of 'Charlemagne', the I/57, although battered, would have been committed to the fighting once again. However, no such re-engagement is recorded in any of the sources. Therefore, the author has concluded that the I/57 was not at Hansfelde at midday.

64   See Saint-Loup, pages 200-202. This engagement is not confirmed by Mabire.

65   Indeed, according to Saint-Loup, page 199, Brazier's I/57 numbered 28 men!

The railway line

Having arrived at Hammerstein railway station, the divisional Engineer Company of 'Charlemagne' was immediately deployed along the Hammerstein-Bärenwalde railway line. Rottenführer Gonzales was still with his friend Juin. He recalls:

> We saw pass by from the other side of the line a whole 'armada' of cripples with barely human faces; many were wounded, they wore emergency field dressings [and] with wild eyes they shouted out to us: "Lads, we didn't half cop it! The Russians are behind us. They have tanks!" We had no artillery to oppose them apart from some panzerfäuste of limited range.

Also ordered up to the Hammerstein-Bärenwalde railway line was the one hundred and ten strong Panzerjäger Company of Waffen-Gren. Regt der SS 58, the 10/58, which had arrived at Hammerstein earlier that day. The orders came from Obf. Puaud in person, who seemed disorientated. The company was to occupy positions 'in front of the battalion [the I/58] in case of tanks attacking'.[66] Oberjunker B. took the company forward, which was without Kompanieführer Oscha. Girard as well as its three anti-tank guns. Oscha. Girard had left to see Stubaf. Raybaud before Puaud appeared[67] and the three anti-tank guns had been abandoned on the train at Hammerstein because the company had no tractors and no longer any horses, dead or not yet arrived, to move them.[68] Because of this, Oberjunker B. could not help thinking that all the training at Wildflecken was 'lost'.

The Panzerjäger Company of Waffen-Gren. Regt der SS 58 took up position north-east of the level crossing, approximately one kilometre from the railway line. As it started to dig in it came under mortar fire. Then the wounded and the survivors of the 57 started to arrive. They were in disorder. It was a sad sight.

Stretched out before the Panzerjäger Company of Waffen-Gren. Regt der SS 58 was a huge plain where Oberjunker B. sent two or three patrols. Oberjunker B. went with the patrols. He saw Russians.

By midday on the 25th, a makeshift defensive line was beginning to form around Bärenwalde railway station and its level crossing. The defensive line extended along the railway embankment for some two kilometres either side of the level crossing. To the left of the level crossing were the remnants of the II/57, and, to the right, Monneuse's arriving I/58. Woods enclosed the level crossing and closely lined the railway embankment. They would aid and hinder the Frenchmen.

Supporting the two badly hit grenadier battalions were the mortar platoons of the 8/57 under Uscha. Terret, positioned just behind the railway station, the two 150mm[69] and six 75mm guns of Hstuf. Roy's 9/57[70], and some 88s.[71] Also in

66   B., letter to the author, 16/10/99.
67   B. would not see Girard again until after the war.
68   Company commander Girard does not know what became of these guns.
69   Mabire, page 530. However, Saint-Loup records, on page 206, that Roy's batteries were made up of old 105mm guns. The article "*Mein Freund Georges*", based on the memoirs of a former soldier of Roy's 9/57, also talks of 105mm howitzers. But Soulat has confirmed that the Infantry guns of the 9/57 were 150mm howitzers. The author agrees; German Army Infantry guns were of two calibres, 75mm and 150mm. Thus,

support was Ostuf. Krotoff's PAK Company of the Panzerjäger Battalion, commanded by Oberjunker Radici in the absence of Stubaf. Boudet-Gheusi.[72]

The headquarters of Waffen-Gren. Regt der SS 57 had relocated behind the railway line.[73] Hstuf. de Bourmont had made Ustuf. Martret, who had no troops to command, responsible for liaison between the scattered units of the regiment.

Brigf. Krukenberg directed the battle from divisional headquarters, which had been established at the village of Elsenau (Olszanowo), north of Bärenwalde.[74] He paid several visits to Stubaf. Raybaud at Bärenhutte. He dismissed Hstuf. Obitz from command of the II/57.

The violent fighting that ensued along the defensive line took place in great confusion. Moreover, many French units were already appallingly mixed. As a result, few precise and conclusive details are readily available.[75]

Russian aircraft strafed the Panzerjäger Company of Waffen-Gren. Regt der SS 58. They were so low-flying that Oberjunker B. could see the heads of the airmen. Later, at the close of day, Oberjunker B. left his shelter to inspect the men, regain order, and position those of the 57 who were still armed and wanted to fight. He came under fire, but was not hit. He continued his work so as to encourage the men. A new wave of aircraft arrived. He came under fire once again.[76] This time he

---

a calibre of 150mm has been used.

70   The exact location of Hstuf. Roy's 9/57 remains unclear; according to Mabire, page 318, the 9/57 had deployed in the railway station's square, not far from the level crossing. However, Saint-Loup positions two of Hstuf. Roy's batteries to the right of the level crossing and one battery at the village of Bärenhutte, north-west of Bärenwalde (pages 203 and 209).

71   As seen by de Misser of the 8/57 (correspondence to the author).

72   Saint-Loup, page 204.

73   Raybaud, letter to Mabire, 3/11/74. This corrects Mabire who cites on page 326 that de Bourmont relocated the headquarters of Waffen-Gren. Regt der SS 57 to Bärenhutte.

74   By now, according to Mabire, page 315, and Saint-Loup, page 203, Brigf. Krukenberg had taken the command of 'Charlemagne'. However, in his letter to Mabire of 3/11/74, Raybaud wrote that he had no recollection of any note to this effect issued by divisional headquarters or of any verbal order to this effect. Moreover, de Vaugelas, with whom Raybaud had been in constant touch, had never reported to him any such takeover. Nevertheless, it would be true to say that Puaud's interest in command had waned progressively as his 'adventure' and that of his men took a greater and greater turn for the worse. Even so, it seems improbable that Krukenberg, who had proved himself a good diplomat thus far, would have publicly affronted Puaud by dismissing him from his command. Therefore, if Krukenberg was now in command, it appears to have been more of an understanding rather than in an official capacity.

75   For example, according to Mabire, page 324, the first serious Russian attack 'early in the morning' was broken up by the Frenchmen's howitzers, anti-tank guns and mortars. Indeed, Mabire pictures knocked out Russian tanks strewn in front of the French defensive line. However, no other source confirms this attack nor the losses inflicted on the Red armour.

76   B. does not know if he came under fire from the air or from Russian ground forces.

did not escape unscathed and was hit by two explosive bullets, which would have killed him outright if one had not been stopped by his holstered pistol and the other by his card wallet. Nevertheless, he was left seriously wounded and unconscious. Contrary to all expectations, he survived his terrible wounds. He owes his life to the LVF medical officer[77] who treated him and to two of his men who carried him, unconscious and bleeding, for more than ten kilometres to a medical convoy [presumably at Hammerstein]. He would remain in a coma for eleven or twelve days.[78]

Desperately, Ustuf. Martret of de Bourmont's headquarters staff tried to regain order, but this proved quite impossible. With him was Oberjunker Jean Ambroise of the 10/57 (anti-tank). He too was ex-Sturmbrigade. Martret escaped injury when he clumsily fell over a tree stump just as a shell landed nearby, but Ambroise was not so lucky. He was wounded in the thigh and evacuated.[79]

Around midday, a massive Russian attack supported by tanks, as many as twenty, smashed into the flimsy French positions around the railway station and the level crossing. The battle raged.

Ustuf.'s Albert's 6/57, which had not yet completed its withdrawal to the railway line, was caught out of position, but defended magnificently. The hard-pressed company was only able to disengage thanks to Hstuf. Roy and his 9/57 which stopped the enemy infantry with accurate and dense defensive fire.[80] Incredibly Albert's men managed to make it back to the railway line.

Doctor Métais and a medical team went out in search of abandoned wounded. Suddenly, an enemy tank spotted them. Strangely, the tank seemed hesitant to fire on them, choosing instead to chase them with the intention of crushing them under its tracks, but Métais and his medical orderlies, yelled on by a nearby platoon in its holes, made it to the safety of the woods. Shortly after, Métais set up a medical post in a group of farmhouses some five hundred metres west of Bärenhutte. Casualties poured in.

The PAK Company reduced two tanks to scrap. A third, losing its track, 'slipped from the top of the embankment, overturned in a ploughed field below and exploded'. In return, the Russians showered death and destruction on the French PAK which fell silent. Many guns were destroyed and the crews were almost all killed or wounded. Ostuf. Krotoff, the PAK Company commander, was hit by shrapnel, and his assistant, Oberjunker Vincenot, was seriously wounded in the ankle. They were evacuated.

Jean Gadeau of the PAK Company was killed. Although he ran away to join the Waffen-SS, he came to 'Charlemagne' via the Kriegsmarine. He attended Sennheim, but disappointment awaited him when he was transformed into a 'SS Frontarbeiter' and posted away to Mayence where he passed his time unloading wagons.[81] Wanting to serve in the German uniform, he 'escaped' and joined the

---

77   B. does not recall the name of the medical officer/doctor.

78   His wounds were such that three major operations and some five months in hospital awaited him.

79   His further fate is not known. Jean Ambroise was born on 7th November 1921.

80   Soulat, page 33. However, according to Mabire, page 325, Hstuf. Roy rescued the 6/57 when his 9/57 halted the Russian tanks making for the encircled company.

Kriegsmarine. No doubt his joy was great when he found himself transferred back to the Waffen-SS.

Patrice Rimbert was the sole survivor of his gun 'cleaned out' by a T–34. His conduct under fire was exemplary and he was later awarded the Iron Cross. He too was ex-Kriegsmarine.

Two more tanks were knocked out; the first exploded a mine laid by the regimental engineer platoon of Waffen-Gren. Regt der SS 57; and the second Oscha. Barclay[82] accounted for with a panzerfaust.

Roy's howitzers cut deep swathes in the waves of Red infantry. Undaunted by their unconscionable losses, the Russians continued to surge forward.[83]

Before long the whole defensive line was ablaze. The Frenchmen fought at one to ten in front of the positions of Monneuse's I/58 and at one to one hundred at the level crossing![84]

Machine gun in hand, accompanied by Staf. Zimmermann and Stubaf. de Vaugelas, Obf. Puaud went from position to position along the railway line to encourage the men. Occasionally he stopped to joke with former legionnaires of the LVF. He took so many unnecessary risks that it seemed as though he had a death wish, but he was not fated to meet his Maker quite yet.

Under tremendous pressure, the defensive line began to reel. It was now untenable. After an hour of combat, Hstuf. de Bourmont finally resigned himself to ordering general withdrawal when elements of Monneuse's I/58 started to pour back on the right.[85]

1500 hours came and went. Soon after, the French PAK and Hstuf. Roy's infantry guns spent their last ammunition.

Ordered to withdraw his infantry guns north-west to Bärenhutte, Hstuf. Roy managed to evacuate his lighter pieces by hand, but the heavier 150mm guns had to be abandoned because of the lack of tractors. They were spiked at 1515 hours.[86] The remaining PAK guns were also 'put out of action' for the same reason and the last gunners fought on as grenadiers.

At 1525 hours, the Russians forced their way across the level crossing. Through this breach swept its infantry and tanks like an irresistible tidal wave through a burst dam.[87] The French units withdrew. However, confusion soon overtook the withdrawal.[88] The seriously wounded had to be abandoned.

---

81 His transfer was probably as a result of a disciplinary offence (Soulat, letter to the author, 3/8/98).

82 Saint-Loup, page 206.

83 According to Saint-Loup, page 207, the Russians now attacked the railway station. Stubbornly, soldiers of the II/57 resisted the Russians every inch of the way, but were eventually dislodged in fierce hand-to-hand fighting. The defenders fell back and reformed behind the level crossing. In response to Saint-Loup, no other source confirms this fight for the railway station.

84 Saint-Loup, page 207.

85 Soulat, page 34. Curiously, according to de Misser of the 8/57, correspondence to the author, the order to withdraw was given around 0900 hours.

86 Saint-Loup, page 208-209. This is not confirmed by Mabire, who recounts instead, page 329, that Hstuf. Roy withdrew after nightfall.

Among the last to leave the railway station was Ustuf. Colnion and the 8/57. Setting off along the road to Hammerstein, they found the Russians in their path![89] Thereupon they made for Elsenau. Along a track shielded by forest, out of sight of the Soviet tanks, they managed to reach Elsenau, arriving about 1700 hours.[90]

Company 7/57 of Oberjunker Million-Rousseau, also on the left, conducted a fighting withdrawal every step of the way towards Elsenau.

Strmm. Marotin of Company 8/57 found himself integrated into a small group commanded by an Untersturmführer and fought near the level crossing. They made the Russians pay dear for its capture. Their Ustuf. then gave them the order to withdraw through the woods, following a main road, perhaps that to Bärenhutte. But Marotin soon lost sight of his comrades of the 8/57 after he went off to fetch his rucksack from the building where it had been stored. In fear of losing his way in the woods, he took the road and came across some lads of Waffen-Gren. Regt der SS 57 around an anti-tank barrier. They were armed with one or two panzerfäuste and some MGs. He joined them.

Soon after, an armoured Russian vanguard of three tanks with infantry support appeared before the anti-tank barrier. The first tank was destroyed by a panzerfaust and the infantry were scattered by MG fire. Fortunately for the Frenchmen the other two tanks did not press home their attack; the defenders had exhausted all their panzerfäuste and nearly all their MG ammunition. Other tanks and more infantry appeared hundreds of metres away. Wisely, the commanding officer gave the order to withdraw.

The 'last obstacle', an anti-tank barrier located at a road bend some three hundred metres from the level crossing, fell to the Russians 'at the end of the day'.[91] Manning the anti-tank barrier were elements of Fatin's 1/58 and Géromini's 2/58. Soviet tanks appeared. Two were soon blazing, victims of panzerfäuste. The first was probably the handiwork of Ostuf. Fatin and the second that of Uscha. Robert.[92]

Having now lost contact with the I/58, Fatin and Géromini followed de Bourmont who, with the remnants of the II/57, had withdrawn to Elsenau. In this way, Elsenau became an assembly point. The scenes at Elsenau were also repeated at Bärenhutte, to the north-west of the Bärenwalde level crossing, to which elements of 'Charlemagne' had also withdrawn.

---

87   Ibid. This rupture of the 'front' of 'Charlemagne' is possibly the same 'large breach' that Mabire recounts, page 328, as developing at the 'beginning of the afternoon'.

88   Soulat, page 34. However, according to Mabire, page 328, 'the retreat turned into a rout'. In response to Mabire, Saint-Loup does not confirm a rout.

89   Presumably the 8/57 was withdrawing westwards along the road from Bärenwalde to Hammerstein.

90   Curiously, according to Soulat, page 34, the 8/57, like the 7/57, conducted a fighting withdrawal every step of the way towards Elsenau.

91   Mabire, page 328.

92   By a strange coincidence, Grenier of company 1/58 recalls the presence of two NCOs with the surname of Robert. Thus, the tank-kill cannot be credited with any real certainty.

Bärenhutte

By early morning on the 25th, elements of the II/58 had arrived at Bärenhutte.[93] Later that morning, Brigf. Krukenberg ordered Stubaf. Raybaud to send one company 'midway between Bärenhutte and Elsenau'[94] to block off the road from Bärenwalde to Elsenau.[95] Raybaud was opposed to the order and protested; handicapped by a total lack of signalling equipment, he had no wish to isolate one of his companies in this way. His protests overruled, he went in person to Hscha. Saint-Magne, the company commander of the 6/58, and relayed the order. But Saint-Magne was without a map. This Raybaud took upon himself to sketch out.[96] Upon receipt of the map, Saint-Magne and his company left.

That same morning, Stubaf. Raybaud made contact with Hstuf. de Bourmont 'to the north-east of the Hammerstein-Bärenwalde railway line'. He also went to divisional headquarters at Elsenau. With him were his driver and his orderly officer Std.Ju. de Vaugelas. Returning from Elsenau, he abandoned his car to make direct contact with the 6/58 which he approached from the front and not from the rear, much to the surprise of Saint-Magne.

Now that elements of 'Charlemagne' were withdrawing to Bärenhutte, Raybaud set about fortifying the village into a hedgehog position. He immediately formed four kampfgruppen; two from the II/58 whose commanders remain unknown[97]; one from the I/58—companies 2/58,[98] 3/58 and 4/58—under Monneuse, and the last from the remnants of Waffen-Gren. Regt der SS 57 under Roy.[99] Raybaud may have carried out this reorganisation in conjunction with Obf. Puaud, also present at Bärenhutte.

The situation at Bärenhutte has been likened to that on an island surrounded on all sides by the rising flood tide.[100] Having no radio equipment, Raybaud soon lost contact with the Brigadeführer at Elsenau. Isolated and virtually helpless, his anxiety grew. Nevertheless, it soon became clear that the Bärenhutte to Hammerstein road was not a principal Soviet route of advance, although shadowy figures began to outflank the village. 'Luckily' for Raybaud, the enemy was bypassing Bärenhutte.

Elsenau

Having rolled up the French defensive line along the Hammerstein-Bärenwalde railway line, the mighty Soviet juggernaut turned north-east. The village of Elsenau and the divisional command post of 'Charlemagne' lay in its path. Without heavy weapons, without support, and without reserves, Brigf. Krukenberg faced a desperate situation and sent Staf. Zimmermann to the headquarters of the XVIII. Gebirgs-Korps at Stegers (Rzeczenica) to warn General Hochbaum that 'Charlemagne' would not be able to hold for more than several hours.[101] Ustuf. Patzak accompanied him on this mission.[102]

---

93   Saint-Loup recalls, page 204, that on the morning of the 26th the four companies of Hstuf. Berret's II/58 had arrived at Bärenhutte by forced march from Hammerstein.

    Mabire records, page 331, that the four companies of the II/58 disembarked at Hammerstein rail station. However, no exact date or time of arrival is provided which does seem rather suspicious. Mabire then details that the troops of the II/58 went up to the front 'without any support'.

Soulat also records, page 35, that on the morning of the 25th the intact and complete II/58 had arrived from Hammerstein. Of the battalion, while at Bärenhutte, there are specific references to the 8/58 and the 5/58, which formed the rearguard of the French forces when the time came to evacuate Bärenhutte.

However, Ustuf. de Genouillac, the assistant battalion commander of the II/58, recalls, in correspondence to the author throughout 1997, that the battalion only arrived at Neustettin railway station on the morning of the 27th. Although he cannot confirm that his convoy was carrying the four companies of the II/58, he still believes to this very day that it was the whole battalion. This would lead to the conclusion that the II/58 could not have been at Bärenhutte as the fighting around Bärenhutte was over by the early morning hours of the 26th and this conclusion de Genouillac has confirmed.

Hscha. Rostaing, also of the II/58, states, pages 160-161, that the troops of the II/58 had clambered out of their trains at the village of Neustettin (Szczecinek), west of Hammerstein, around 1600 hours on 24th February 1945. Rostaing continues that they had then spent the night in the barracks situated in the city centre and were sent forward to the village of Bärenhutte on the morning of the 25th. However, of importance to note is that Rostaing was an adjudant at the headquarters of the II/58 and, as such, should have arrived on the same convoy carrying the battalion commander, his assistant, his orderly officer, in fact all of the headquarters staff. This would suggest that he was on the same convoy as de Genouillac, also on the headquarters staff. In addition, Rostaing stated that on his arrival at Neustettin he learnt that 'the battalions, which had preceded his, had been engaged before Hammerstein and were in a desperate situation'. As such, this is impossible; Fenet's I/57 had not engaged, and although Obitz's II/57 may have engaged, its situation was not desperate yet. Moreover, during the course of the night 24th/25th that Rostaing spent in the barracks at Neustettin, he recalls that 'the first elements in retreat' joined him. While not impossible, it is extremely unlikely that divisional headquarters would have ordered any units to retreat when the situation at that time was more confused than desperate. To explain these anomalies, Rostaing, or the author of his book, may have been influenced by the previous written accounts of the actions of the II/58.

Ostuf. Wagner's 5/58 arrived at Neustettin, but was not sent forward to nor engaged at Bärenhutte. [See "*Stoi!*", pages 254-257, confirmed by Rusco, letters to the author, 2/98 and 5/3/98, and Blanc of the 5/58, correspondence to the author, 2001-2004.]

As for Raybaud himself, the commander of Waffen-Gren. Regt der SS 58, he recalls in his letter of 3/11/74 to Mabire that the II/58 had arrived at Bärenhutte during the night of the 24th/25th or early morning on the 25th. Of course this begs the question, why was the II/58 not committed to strengthen the hard-pressed defensive line on the 25th? It seems very doubtful that an entire battalion of around one thousand men would have been kept in reserve at Bärenhutte while their comrades were fighting for their lives along the Hammerstein-Bärenwalde railway line a matter of kilometres away. But Raybaud's precise memory of the detachment of the 6/58 on the morning of the 25th cannot be so readily dismissed.

In conclusion, despite the contradictory nature of the sources available, it appears that elements of the II/58, at least one company, perhaps two, did arrive at Bärenhutte on the morning of the 25th.

94   Raybaud, letter to Mabire, 3/11/74. Yet, according to the written interview with Raybaud in "*Charlemagne's Legionnaires*", the company was to be sent 'to the north of

When the two German officers of the Inspection arrived by car at the chateau that served as the headquarters of the XVIII. Gebirgs-Korps they found General Hochbaum looking exhausted and rather anxious. Grabbing Staf. Zimmermann by the arm as if an old friend, the General asked: "Well, are your Frenchmen going to hold?" Avoiding the question, Staf. Zimmermann chose to remind the general

Bärenhutte', and, according to Mabire, page 333, 'four kilometres to the north of his disposition [Bärenhutte]'. But this would place the company deep in woods well to the north-west of Elsenau and not even astride the road north from Elsenau to Flötenstein. In this position, the company would have served no purpose whatsoever.

95 The mission of the company has been defined as such; 'to cover Elsenau', Mabire page 333; 'to strengthen the defence of Elsenau', Saint-Loup, page 204; and 'to block off a possible route of advance for the Russians', the written interview with Raybaud in "*Charlemagne's Legionnaires*". Considering the deployment of the company, its mission could be defined as blocking off the road from Bärenwalde to Elsenau and thereby strengthening the defence of Elsenau. Remarkably Mabire described the mission as suicidal. This is far from the truth.

96 According to the written interview with Raybaud, "*Charlemagne's Legionnaires*", page 100, Raybaud derides his regimental staff as incompetent when they were unable to find a map. Mabire, for his part, provides another angle, page 333, which does not damn the regimental staff in quite the same way; Raybaud was obliged to copy his map because maps had only been supplied to battalion and regimental commanders!

97 According to Soulat, page 35, repeated by Saint-Loup, page 209, and Mabire, page 335, Berret commanded one of the two kampfgruppen of the II/58. However, Hstuf. Berret was not present. Ustuf. de Genouillac was by his side throughout the campaign in Pomerania and at no time was Hstuf. Berret at Bärenhutte. Indeed, Hstuf. Berret only arrived in Pomerania on 27th February 1945. (De Genouillac, letter to the author, 23/2/98). Also, in a strange twist, Stubaf. Raybaud, the commander of Waffen-Gren. Regt der SS 58, was of the opinion that Hstuf. Berret had stayed behind at Wildflecken camp because of sickness. Furthermore, according to Saint-Loup, page 200, Raybaud himself commanded a battlegroup. Raybaud has not denied or acknowledged any such temporary command. So this might well be true.

98 It should be recalled that elements, if not the bulk, of the 2/58 withdrew to Elsenau.

99 According to Saint-Loup, page 209, the forces at Bärenhutte totalled some 3,000 men which equates to one half of the strength of 'Charlemagne' deployed in Pomerania. This is extremely unlikely; few in number were the units of de Bourmont's Waffen-Gren. Regt der SS 57 which had withdrawn to Bärenhutte—the only complete unit may have been Hstuf. Roy and his 9/57; some units of the II/58 had still not arrived at the front; at least two convoys of 'Charlemagne' were still en route to Pomerania; and, finally, to say nothing of the holes already in the ranks of 'Charlemagne'.

100 Mabire, page 335.

101 Mabire, page 351. According to Soulat, page 35, Zimmermann went to the headquarters of the XVIII. Gebirgs-Korps at Stegers to examine the situation with General Hochbaum.

102 Zimmermann, letter to Saint-Loup, 10/8/65. This confirms Mabire's version, page 351, and corrects that of Saint-Loup, page 222, in which Brigf. Krukenberg and Hstuf. Jauss went to General Hochbaum's headquarters at Stegers on the fall of Elsenau.

that 'Charlemagne' was without anti-tank weapons, guns and tanks. Soberly, Zimmermann told the General that he was asking the impossible of them. The General would hear nothing of it and noted 'impossible is not a French word'.[103] At this, Zimmermann lost his temper and retorted that even the Pomeranians of the Wehrmacht were falling back. Again the General pressed him. Zimmermann could only conclude that they would get themselves killed, but still they would not stop the Russian onslaught.

Thereupon, General Hochbaum authorised the withdrawal of 'Charlemagne' to Stegers, where the division was to try and build a new defensive line. Divisional headquarters was to relocate to the town of Flötenstein, some fifteen kilometres north of Stegers. It was to this same location that the General had decided to re-establish corps headquarters.

As there was no time to lose, General Hochbaum hurried Zimmermann to set off back to Elsenau. Accompanied by Hochbaum, the German officers of the Inspection returned to their car parked up in the grounds. On the steps of the chateau they were horrified by the sudden appearance of a T–34 tens of metres away. The hard bark of its gun and the car burst into a ball of flames. The tank vanished as fast as it had appeared.[104]

Rather than return to Elsenau on foot, Zimmermann decided to accompany General Hochbaum and his staff officers to Flötenstein. As planned, they left at nightfall. During the night Zimmermann met by chance the Chief-of-Staff of the XVIII. Gebirgs-Korps. To the south, the sound of fighting could be heard. Zimmermann wondered how Krukenberg was still managing to hold onto Elsenau.

To defend Elsenau, Brigf. Krukenberg had at his disposal in total some four to five hundred men under Stubaf. Boudet-Gheusi, Hstuf. Renault, and Ostuf. Fatin,[105] as well as 'his guard', the *Compagnie d'Honneur*, which eagerly awaited the Russians with a point to prove that it was not a parade unit.

Commanded by Ostuf. Weber, the *Compagnie d'Honneur* arrived at Elsenau early on the 25th armed with panzerfäuste drawn at Hammerstein. As it made its way to Elsenau, the *Compagnie d'Honneur* encountered a stream of civilians mixed here and there with young, distraught-looking Latvian SS soldiers pouring back in disorder. At one point the *Compagnie d'Honneur* marched alongside the pitiful sight of a column of wounded from Waffen-Gren. Regt der SS 57. Leaning on one another, all wore blood-soaked bandages. Some were without limbs. Their eyes were widened with horror and fatigue. In similar circumstances this stark reality of battle would have totally demoralised many soldiers, but not those of the

103 Mabire, page 352.

104 Mabire, page 353. In contrast, according to Saint-Loup, page 223, a lieutenant of the headquarters staff, who had armed himself with a panzerfaust, blew apart the T-34.

105 According to Saint-Loup, page 210, Brigf. Krukenberg also had the troops and guns of *Capitaine* 'Marty' at his disposal at Elsenau. 'Marty' is undoubtedly a pseudonym for Martin, the assistant commander of the Division's artillery group. His presence at Elsenau is not recorded by any other source. Moreover, according to Mabire, page 362, Hstuf. Martin would only arrive at Schlawe in Pomerania on 3rd March 1945 with a one hundred strong detachment of the artillery group. This has been confirmed by Mounine, letter to the author.

Compagnie d'Honneur. Weber had repeatedly given them one single choice: the wooden cross or the Iron Cross. Of the two, all knew which one they wanted.

Once at Elsenau, the *Compagnie d'Honneur* was deployed as a 'stopper to permit their comrades to withdraw'.[106] But the *Compagnie d'Honneur* was greatly understrength as many of its trainees had not returned and only numbered eighty men.[107] Amid this chaos could eighty men make a difference? They did, dismantling the armoured Soviet vanguard that appeared before Elsenau.[108] It was a brave action of man against machine and one that cannot go untold, even if there is little or no agreement between the sources, those of Mabire and Saint-Loup.

According to Mabire[109], the *Compagnie d'Honneur* occupied positions just outside the village perimeter, covering the road from Elsenau to Bärenwalde. Combat emplacements were dug in ditches alongside the road. Most men were armed with panzerfäuste. Weber had sited company headquarters in a small wood on a slope. To the right of the wood, across the road, was the village cemetery, which was held by the company's *section des Jeunes* [literally youth platoon]. To his front was a wood, through which a road ran. It was cold, yet humid. Snow covered the fields and to camouflage themselves the men had made chasubles from sheets found in the abandoned houses of the village.

Supporting the *Compagnie d'Honneur* was a PAK gun that Ostuf. Weber had requisitioned from a Wehrmacht unit.[110]

In the early afternoon, Soviet aircraft suddenly swept overhead and machine-gunned the village. Their appearance was brief, but the spine-chilling shouts of 'Panzeralarm!' then rang out. The ground was vibrating.

---

106   Mabire, page 343. As such, the *Compagnie d'Honneur* was the only combatant unit at Elsenau before the arrival of those retreating from the Hammerstein-Bärenwalde railway line.

107   Soulat, page 34, repeated by Mabire, page 343. However, the NCO trainees from Paderborn were back with the *Compagnie d'Honneur*. In fact, when they returned to Wildflecken the company had already left for the front. One of the last convoys from Wildflecken took them to Pomerania and Hammerstein camp where they rejoined Weber. And yet, according to Saint-Loup, page 210, the *Compagnie d'Honneur* was at full strength, in total some two hundred to two hundred and fifty strong. Nevertheless, the question remains, if the company was greatly under strength, where else were its trainees?

108   The direction from which the armoured Soviet vanguard appeared remains unclear; according to Levast of the *Compagnie d'Honneur*, letter and maps to the author, dated 18/3/98, the Soviets came from the south, along the road from Bärenwalde. And yet, in contrast, according to de Brangelin, also present at Elsenau and in command of a group to the immediate left of the positions of the *Compagnie d'Honneur*, the Soviets attacked from the east (letter to the author dated 25/2/98).

109   Pages 343-350. His version was, undoubtedly, based on the eyewitness accounts of Boulau and Levast of the *Compagnie d'Honneur* (and perhaps even that of Weber himself). Note that the author has supplemented Mabire's version with additional material from Levast, correspondence to the author 1997-1998.

110   Mabire, page 346. Curiously, when the third platoon was moved up to reinforce those already in the front line, it passed a PAK gun described by the same author on page 345 as 'one of the last of the division'.

Towards 1400 hours, the platoon held in reserve was moved up to reinforce the two others already in the front line. Unterführeranwärter [potential NCO] Louis Levast commanded one of its sections. He had recently graduated from Paderborn and joined the *Compagnie d'Honneur* in the field. Upon leaving the village, the platoon came under fire from a T–34 that had suddenly emerged less than one kilometre away. Levast's section was practically annihilated. Only three or four survived, including Levast, who miraculously had only been hit in the ankle by a stone. His good friend Tissert was killed. The survivors then joined Weber at his headquarters.

Weber summoned NCO cadet Boulau and gave him orders. As soon as Boulau understood what was expected of him, he smiled and rushed off to the wood, followed by his section. In the wood he set up a tank booby trap which was quite simple, but effective. It consisted of a wire stretched across the road connected to the firing mechanisms of primed panzerfäuste, fixed firmly to tree trunks, aimed towards the middle of the road. The first tank to trigger the trip-wire would bring the hollow charges slamming into its sides.

Having completed the booby trap, Boulau and his men ran back to their positions alongside the road. It was not long before two explosions were heard. The Russian tanks responded by bombarding the wood before cautiously moving on. Fourteen tanks were counted.

The tanks approached. They were almost on top of the *Compagnie d'Honneur*'s positions before Ostuf. Weber ordered 'Fire!' The PAK gun fired first and hit the lead tank that came to a stop. The men sprang up. Tank after tank was knocked out by panzerfäuste, but the last two were still very much 'full of life' and began to shell the village. Weber himself dashed forward and knocked out one of them with grenade. The remaining tank continued to blast the French positions with its gun and machine-guns.

Ostuf. Weber had just devised a plan of attack to destroy this last troublesome tank when 'hundreds and hundreds' of Soviet infantrymen suddenly charged against the exposed positions of the *Compagnie d'Honneur*.[111] The German machine-guns started to rattle. Rifles cracked. The attackers fell as if mown down by a scythe. Their attack collapsed against a veritable curtain of fire. They flooded back. They came again. They were repulsed. Then again, jumping over the bodies of their comrades, they came on.

In the face of being overrun and annihilated, Weber decided to withdraw immediately and thus save his unit which had already suffered numerous dead and wounded.[112] A small ravine located to the left of the position held by his company

111 Levast recalls, in a letter to the author, 15/1/98, that the Soviet infantry hit the *Compagnie d'Honneur* from both sides of the road. However, de Brangelin is not in agreement (letter to the author, 25/2/98); positioned to the immediate left of the *Compagnie d'Honneur*, he and his group came under fire from Russian mortars and machine guns opposite, but were not on the receiving end of an infantry attack. Nevertheless, from his position, de Brangelin did see the Russian infantry attack the right flank of the *Compagnie d'Honneur* (on the other side of the road).

112 In contrast, according to Levast, letter to the author, 15/1/98, the company had to abandon its positions when T-34 tanks, pushing along the road, bypassed its positions and brought them under fire from the rear.

looked as though it would afford his 'boys' shelter, but the way there was across open ground swept by Russian gunfire. Although the *Compagnie d'Honneur* had repeated this manoeuvre tens and tens of times before at Wildflecken, this time it was for real. The *Compagnie d'Honneur* emerged and dashed to the ravine. This position, however, soon became as untenable as the first and Weber ordered withdrawal again.

In the meantime, now supported by infantry, the remaining enemy tank had advanced. Armed with panzerfäuste, Weber and three volunteers rushed forward to confront the steel monster. Crash. A direct hit. On fire, smoke poured from the T–34.

Having destroyed the last enemy tank, Ostuf. Weber returned to his men. Disheartened, the Russians broke off their attack and dug in. The fighting fell away. Elated, Weber and his *Compagnie d'Honneur* returned to Elsenau.

Saint-Loup approaches the engagement with much more of an individual touch. There is very little preamble other than it was a question of destroying the tanks that appeared or being crushed by them. The positions of the *Compagnie d'Honneur* in the passageways between the dunes, marshes and ponds were good strategically, but poor tactically as the enemy tanks could only be engaged from the front rather than from the less armoured sides. Needless to say, this demanded composure and bravery. Were the grenadiers of the *Compagnie d'Honneur* equal to the challenge? That was soon answered.

Soviet tanks appeared. Panzerfäuste flew towards them. Crash. Crash. T–34s burst into flames. One tank got through, but was destroyed by Soulier with a T-mine. At 1615 hours, he destroyed his second by a panzerfaust and his third a few minutes later. When Soulier returned to the command post to collect more panzerfäuste, Weber took off his Iron Cross 1st Class and pinned it on him. Soulier went back to the fighting. The twenty-four-year-old Appolot 'helped himself' to two T–34s in quick succession and the nineteen-year-old Sturmmann Fontenay also bagged two. Twenty-year-old Oudin, a former student at *lycée Charlemagne*, was wounded attacking 'his' tank but refused evacuation. He was killed when he missed a second tank. Eugène Vaulot got one. Weber himself destroyed three T–34s.

Then a heavy 'Josef Stalin' tank was spotted. Stationary, it had broken down, but had infantry cover. Soulier and Vaulot crawled towards it and shot up the infantry with their Sturmgewehrs.[113] Those that were not dead or wounded fled. Attracted by the sound of fighting, their comrades Dupuis, Garrot and Schenitz appeared. Encircled, the tank tried to keep them at bay with its machine-guns, but it was in vain as Vaulot got within panzerfaust range and fired. A direct hit and it was soon blazing like a torch.

The assault group withdrew, dragging along Schenitz seriously wounded by a friendly bullet which had ricocheted off the armour plating of the Stalin. He died minutes later at the first aid post.

There was no decoration for Vaulot from Weber, but a shot down German fighter pilot presented Vaulot with his own Iron Cross. Fighting side by side with the French, this downed German airmen even notched up two tanks himself one after the other.

113 The author, however, doubts that they were armed with Sturmgewehr.

By 1700 hours, eleven tanks had been knocked out. That figure had risen to nineteen by 1730 hours of which seventeen were credited to the *Compagnie d'Honneur*.

But the success of the *Compagnie d'Honneur* in halting the Soviet tank vanguard had been brought at a terrible cost. Soulier was killed attacking his fifth tank. Rouvrier was killed destroying his third. Fontenay was killed on his fourth. Appolot was wounded again and evacuated. Of note is that many of the principal 'tank destroyers' were ex-Kriegsmarine.

Halted, the Russian armour then proceeded to bypass Elsenau to the east and to the west, whereas their infantry, in close line abreast, charged in turn against the village. It was literally a forest of men. The machine-guns barked out. Then began the battle for Elsenau cemetery.

Elsenau cemetery

Holding Elsenau cemetery were elements of Colnion's 8/57, Million-Rousseau's 7/57 and Fatin's 1/58.[114] They stood firm and repelled attack after attack. The Russians brought up tanks.[115] Company commander Oberjunker Millon-Rousseau failed to halt the first tank when he hurriedly fired a panzerfäust and missed. The tank continued to advance. A volunteer dashed forward and managed to stop the steel mass with a rifle-grenade.

Marotin of the 8/57 found himself in Elsenau cemetery. From Bärenhutte, he had left with a group for Elsenau where he had been told he would find comrades of his battalion. He came to the cemetery and to one or two lads of his company. He commented that this cemetery 'soon became a small annex of hell'.

Armed with a French MAS 38 submachine-gun which he had brought along with him from his days with the *Milice*, Marotin fired short bursts at fleeting silhouettes in the darkness and smoke. Emptying another magazine, he suddenly realised that he would soon be out of ammunition. During a brief lull in the fighting, he picked up a Mauser 98k rifle complete with bayonet. It was not a moment too soon as a 'giant devil' suddenly appeared before him. He thrust his bayonet into the Russian; he had repeated this manoeuvre many times before, but this time it was for real. He tried to withdraw the bayonet but could not; the Russian soldier was doubled up on his weapon, which he had grabbed with both hands. In the end he had to use a foot to pull out the bayonet. He called it 'not very elegant'. All this had only lasted a matter of seconds. He then watched silhouettes of Russian soldiers pass him on his right and left …

Rifle in hand, a French POW fought stubbornly for Elsenau cemetery before succumbing in turn. His name is not known.

From Polish 'regulars' or liberated French POWs serving with the Russians came insults in perfect French.

For hours the pattern of attack, defence, and renewed attack repeated itself without let up.[116] The fury of the Russian attacks grew with each passing hour. Eventually, at enormous cost, the Russians did succeed in gaining the cemetery

---

114   Saint-Loup, page 215, confirmed by Grenier, letter to the author, 12/4/98. However, the presence of Ostuf. Fatin and his 1/58 in Elsenau cemetery is not recorded by Soulat or Mabire.

115   Mabire, page 356.

with their fifth attack. Enraged, the Russians put to death the helpless French wounded lying between the gravestones.

As for Marotin, he was fortunate to get out of the cemetery alive. Suddenly, he had found himself before a T–34, but moments later the tank was a ball of flames, undoubtedly the work of a panzerfaust. Then, from behind him, he heard his name shouted out. At one bound he rejoined his comrades who disengaged, abandoning the cemetery. They ran off chased by tracer bullets. To this day, he still does not know who had actually called out to him.

With the loss of the cemetery, Elsenau became untenable. Greatly outnumbered, its last defenders were outflanked, disorganised and overwhelmed. Also, they had no anti-tank weapons left. Any further resistance would serve no purpose. Should they surrender? Should they break-out? Most choose the latter. Ostuf. Weber and some twenty men of his *Compagnie d'Honneur*, including Levast, withdrew in good order along the road to the town of Flötenstein. The losses of the *Compagnie d'Honneur* were heavy.[117]

Eighty totally exhausted survivors, without ammunition and supplies, withdrew to the north under Ostuf. Fatin. By the time they had reached the comparative shelter of the woods, they had been joined by other individuals and groups, notably that led by Oberjunker de Brangelin, swelling their number to one hundred and twenty.

Ostuf. Fatin immediately formed three platoons whose command went to Oberjunken de Brangelin and Lapart, and Oscha. Bonnafous. He decided to return to Hammerstein, to the west, but his patrollers immediately ran into enemy infantry. Tormented by a lack of ammunition, Fatin had to avoid a pitched battle and keep moving. He now opted for the east. Thanks to the night, they made good their escape and came to a place of rest. Only then did de Brangelin realise that he had been awake, and almost in constant action, for some thirty-six hours.

Also withdrawing eastward were men from Albert's 6/57 and Million-Rousseau's 7/57. They formed a sizeable group.[118]

As for Krukenberg, he broke out of Elsenau with a group of French SS men.[119] Arriving at the town of Flötenstein on the 26th, he met Zimmermann and Patzak who had arrived before dawn that same day with General Hochbaum and his staff officers.

After abandoning its equipment, the Signals Company, whose commander was Ostuf. Dupuyau, also managed to make good its escape from Elsenau. It was still virtually intact, numbering a good one hundred men, but many were now without a rifle. It retreated westwards.

At Elsenau, 'Charlemagne' fought bravely and tenaciously against superior odds. Moreover, it gave the Soviets a 'bloody nose'. As previously stated,

116 According to Mabire, page 357, Brigf. Krukenberg also ordered Weber and the *Compagnie d'Honneur* into the fiercely escalating maelstrom. However, at no time did Levast, a member of the *Compagnie d'Honneur*, find himself in Elsenau cemetery.

117 According to Saint-Loup, page 215, the *Compagnie d'Honneur* lost one half of its strength, thus all told some one hundred men. However, according to Soulat, page 34, its losses were one quarter of its strength of eighty, thus some twenty men.

118 Hstuf. Renault may have been with group.

119 Mabire, pages 367-368.

Saint-Loup cites nineteen tanks destroyed by 1730 hours, of which the *Compagnie d'Honneur* had accounted for seventeen, and a further fourteen tanks by artillery. Landwehr cites that Weber's company 'had halted the Soviet tank attack on the divisional H.Q. at Elsenau by destroying the entire vanguard of 18 tanks, the greater portion of which were Stalin models'. Levast of the *Compagnie d'Honneur* puts the number of tanks destroyed by his company at 'fourteen T–34s'[120]. Mabire cites this same figure destroyed by the *Compagnie d'Honneur*. Presumably this figure does not include the one tank destroyed in the fighting for the cemetery. Soulat cites that the *Compagnie d'Honneur* destroyed three tanks and that four PAK guns destroyed several more.

So what are the true figures? Unfortunately, they will probably never be known, but Saint-Loup's claim that artillery destroyed fourteen tanks is either doubtful or very inflated. No other source records the presence of artillery, French or otherwise, at Elsenau. In addition, former divisional soldiers present at Elsenau do not recall any such artillery support. Moreover, the Russians would have been quick to suppress any artillery support the defenders might well have enjoyed. Such was their superior firepower at Elsenau.

Bärenhutte and the retreat to Hammerstein

Meanwhile, the isolated French garrison at Bärenhutte could only make a nuisance of itself by firing on the bumper to bumper Soviet motorised columns making for Elsenau. In this way, the last infantry and anti-tank guns under Roy, and the mortars of Tardan's 4/58 and Defever's 8/58[121] registered direct hit after direct hit. There was little reply from the Russians other than a reconnaissance force which its outposts stopped, destroying a motorcar and an armoured car, as well as the occasional foray by an armoured car which Roy's guns chased off.

However, of increasing concern to the garrison were the Russian snipers that kept the village under fire. They did not give the Frenchmen a moment's peace. The German liaison officer to Waffen-Gren. Regt der SS 57[122] was hit by two explosive bullets in the arm and evacuated.

Then came the first Russian attack against Bärenhutte. It was contained.[123]

Around 2000 hours, the infantry guns fell silent. All ammunition had been exhausted. As there were no tractors or horses available to move his guns Hstuf. Roy had them destroyed. By now, Bärenhutte was totally encircled.

120   Letter to the author, dated 15/1/98.
121   Soulat, page 36, repeated by Mabire, page 337. However, if Ostuf. Defever's 8/58 was one of the companies of the II/58 to have arrived at Neustettin on the 27th, then it could not have been present at Bärenhutte.
122   According to Soulat, page 46, the German liaison officer to Waffen-Gren. Regt der SS 57 was an unidentified Ustuf. with the initial of H. However, according to Mabire, page 526, the same German liaison officer was SS-Ustuf. Goliberzuch, in fact an Austrian. But Soulat positions SS-Ustuf. Goliberzuch as the German liaison officer to Waffen-Gren. Regt der SS 58.
123   The first Russian attack against Bärenhutte materialised in day time and not night time (a correction penned by Raybaud to Soulat's original manuscript which, for the record, details that the Russians first launched an attack around 2300 hours.)

One hour later, Ostuf. Labuze, assigned a liaison mission between Bärenhutte and Hammerstein[124], led a patrol from the PAK Company of Waffen-Gren. Regt der SS 57 into the village of Geglenfelde on the road westwards from Bärenhutte to Hammerstein.

The village was not as empty as it first seemed. An LVF veteran suddenly appeared and handed the patrol a Russian he had just taken prisoner in the village. When interrogated the prisoner indicated that several of his comrades were at an isolated farmhouse not far from the village.

Led by the prisoner, a small group of Frenchmen made their way to the farmhouse. Covered by his men, Ostuf. Labuze curiously planted himself in front of the farmhouse and shouted out to those inside to surrender. The reply was a submachine-gun burst that killed him outright.[125]

A firefight started. The Russian prisoner was seriously wounded. Several Frenchmen also received wounds. They withdrew hurriedly. Under a NCO, the patrol made it back to Bärenhutte and reported the 'capture' of Geglenfelde by the Russians.

By now, Stubaf. Raybaud had preparations to break-out and retreat to Hammerstein well underway. He was acting on orders received from Brigf. Krukenberg.[126] The break-out plan was simple. The French forces were to take the quickest and the most direct route to Hammerstein through Geglenfelde. Hscha. Walter's 7/58 would form the rearguard. H-hour was set for midnight.

As there was no motorised transport available, all ammunition caches were destroyed and each man received a panzerfaust.

Noisily, the break-out began at midnight, but the Russians did not intervene. What was the reason for this? Such was the din that perhaps the Soviets were convinced that the exhausted French SS units were far stronger and better equipped than they really were! Perhaps the Soviets were also exhausted and had momentarily lost their vigour. Indeed, if they had opened up on the compact and disorganised column it would have been a slaughter.

At Geglenfelde, there was a skirmish. The reconnaissance platoon of Waffen-Gren. Regt der SS 57, led by Obf. Puaud himself, immediately moved into action and neutralised the Russians blocking the way forward. The response from the French side had been so quick that the progress of the column had not been impeded.[127] Without any further incident the French SS men arrived at Hammerstein towards 0300 hours on the 26th.[128]

Hammerstein was now unrecognisable. It was a picture of panic, disorder and despair. The roads were swarming with terror-stricken civilians. POWs of numerous nationalities were wandering about and mocked the arriving columns of

---

124 Soulat, page 36.
125 Mabire, pages 339-340, and Saint-Loup page 219. However, according to Raybaud, his letter to Mabire dated 3/11/74, Ostuf. Labuze was killed later that night in the skirmish at Geglenfelde during the retreat from Bärenhutte to Hammerstein. In response to this, Mabire's account of the death of Ostuf. Labuze appears to be eyewitness based and, for that reason, has been chosen over Raybaud's recollection.
126 Raybaud, letter to Mabire dated 3/11/74. This corrects Mabire, page 337, that Raybaud and de Vaugelas decided among themselves to break out and withdraw to Hammerstein.

French SS troops. Latvian Waffen-SS troops and Germans of the Wehrmacht were looting military warehouses. Uniforms and brand new weapons littered the ground.[129]

At the camp white flags abounded. There was the smell of schnapps in the air from the hundreds of bottles broken by the looters who could not carry them off.

Some, like Marotin and his comrades of the 8/57, had arrived at Hammerstein from Elsenau. He does not recall how he found himself on the road from Elsenau to Hammerstein and in the company of some comrades, but they made haste, fearful that the Russians might cut their line of retreat.

Hammerstein

In the early evening of 25th February 1945, 'Charlemagne' received orders to assemble at Neustettin (Szczecinek), twenty kilometres to the west.[130] By 1900 hours, the first elements of 'Charlemagne', the motor and horse-drawn columns, were already on the road to Neustettin. Fahrschwadron A had arrived at Hammerstein earlier that same day, after a quiet journey.[131] It was still without much of its equipment and weapons. Indeed, not all of the grooms had a rifle. And few had a steel helmet.[132]

The I/58 and the Engineer Company set off in turn. As the Engineer Company crossed Hammerstein its inhabitants looked on in total silence. They seemed lifeless. They knew what now awaited them.

Making his way westwards on foot to Neustettin with the Engineer Company was Rttf. Gonzales. He was upset about having to leave behind his pack at Hammerstein railway station. For his pack contained not only his changes of clothes, but also at least two hundred photographs of his time with the LVF and the two cameras, one German and one French, with which he had taken them.

No sooner had the French W-SS troops that had made good their escape from Bärenhutte arrived at Hammerstein than they set off again to Neustettin. By 0300

127   Raybaud, letter to Mabire dated 3/11/74. Furthermore, according to Saint-Loup, page 219, a medical orderly, on hearing the sound of shooting went for news and reported back to Dr. Métais that the skirmish was 'nothing'. This corrects Mabire's account, pages 340-341, of the same incident, which appears to be over-dramatised.

128   Soulat, page 36. But Saint-Loup is not in agreement; on page 220, he states that their arrival at Hammerstein was at daybreak.

129   Saint-Loup, page 220. However, this would seem to dispute the idea that the military depots were empty.

130   Mabire, page 341. However, it is not recorded who or what headquarters actually issued 'Charlemagne' orders to withdraw to Neustettin, but it was not the headquarters of the XVIII. Gebirgs-Korps. Therefore, they may have come from the 2nd Army or Army Group Vistula.

131   The only incident Mercier of Fahrschwadron A recalls is of a brief stop in the suburbs of Berlin, during which kids came begging for bread. He had to refuse them. Grenadier Harnu said to Mercier that it was very sad to have to refuse them a single piece of bread in their own country.

132   Regarding this, Uscha. Mercier of Fahrschwadron A said: "At Wildflecken, I had heard Hstuf. Croisille proudly say that an SS officer does not wear a helmet. On this point, we could have all been officers." (Letter to the author, 6/11/2001.)

hours, all had left. Behind them they left a rather unique rearguard formed at the camp on the evening of the 25th from all available personnel of the divisional Headquarters Company and the Supply Corps.

Hurriedly armed, this French kampfgruppe of 'penpushers' moved up to the front during the night of 25th/26th February. In accordance with its orders to protect the flank of the French SS units withdrawing from Bärenhütte to Hammerstein, the kampfgruppe took up position in woods to the north of the road from Hammerstein to Geglenfelde.[133]

Under Stubaf. Katzian, an old Austrian officer, the kampfgruppe was made up of three platoons: the first platoon assembled German personnel of the Inspection; the second platoon consisted of tailors, orderlies, secretaries, quartermasters, interpreters and messengers of the Headquarters Company; and the third was the escort (combat) platoon of Fahrschwadron A under Ostuf. Darrigade, which had even been given one panzerfaust.

The night passed in peace. Towards 0500 hours on the 26th, Stubaf. Katzian finally issued orders to withdraw. During the withdrawal one of their number, Rttf. Soulat, became lost and, after first ending up at a Latvian SS artillery position, he returned to Hammerstein towards 1400 hours. At the camp, he came across some Germans whose field kitchen was still functioning. He took the time to eat and was amazed to see the service records of 'Charlemagne' personnel littering the corridor floors of a hut!

Rttf. Soulat then set off by foot to Neustettin. Catching up with some stragglers of 'Charlemagne', he was invited aboard the field kitchen of the divisional Signals Company by its *chef-cuisinier* [head cook]. Being exhausted, he gladly accepted this kind invitation.

The platoon under Ostuf. Darrigade rejoined Fahrschwadron A the following day.

At 1700 hours, the first Soviet armoured columns entered Hammerstein.[134] At that same time arrived the bulk of the divisional Signals Company. This was not its first brush with enemy armour that day.

Withdrawing westwards from Elsenau, the Signals Company was stopped by a German officer of the Inspection. First he praised the fighting qualities of the Frenchmen and then ordered Dupuyau to deploy his company on a hillock as 'a sort of roadblock' against Russian forces advancing from Bärenhütte and Elsenau. Russian tanks were soon on the scene. The signalsmen tried to stop them with rifles and sub-machine-guns. It was hopeless. The enemy armour did not even bother to

---

133   Soulat, letter to the author, 14/11/97. Curiously, according to Mabire, page 375, this
      French kampfgruppe took up position after a march of some ten kilometres. But the
      distance from Hammerstein to Geglenfelde is barely five kilometres. Thus, Mabire
      must be mistaken.

134   Soulat, page 36, repeated by Saint-Loup, page 223. According to Silgailis, "*Latvian
      Legion*", elements of the 15. Waffen-Grenadier-Division der SS (lettische Nr.1)
      occupied positions around the town of Hammerstein on the morning of the 26th.
      Despite beating off Russian attacks in the morning, the flanks of the Latvians were
      turned in the forenoon. By noon, the Russians had broken into Hammerstein. In
      response to this, as previously stated, Soulat left Hammerstein sometime after 1400
      hours and he saw no sight of the Russians!

engage them. The Frenchmen ran off. They continued westwards. In this way, they came to Hammerstein and Soviet tanks once again! It was a slaughter. A group of telephonists was cornered and crushed by a T–34. The rest scattered and fled from Hammerstein.

By midday on 26th February 1945, the bulk of 'Charlemagne' had reached Neustettin. The survivors were totally exhausted. Units were completely disorganised. The bulk of the division was quartered in one large barracks. If the Russians had intervened the consequences would have been disastrous, but fortunately they remained quiet.

The losses

Thus ended the 'battle of Hammerstein'[135], a battle that had lasted no more than forty-eight hours for the 33. Waffen-Gren.-Division der SS 'Charlemagne' (französische Nr.1). And yet its casualty balance sheet was terrible.

According to Soulat, at Neustettin, 'out of the 4,500 men who had left Wildflecken, 3,000 replied at the roll call'. Of the difference, Soulat details that 1,000, including 15 officers, were missing and, that 500, including 5 officers, were killed. Sources Mabire, Bayle and Landwehr repeat the same figures. However, Saint-Loup cites a total of 3,000 dead, wounded and missing while de la Mazière cites 1,000 dead and another 1,000 missing. In response to Saint-Loup and de la Mazière, it is important to note that the figures Soulat cites are derived from the roll calls 'officially fed back to us [the staff of the Headquarters Company] by our chefs'[136] and reproduced from memory. Thus, of the three, his figures are perhaps the most accurate and 'official'.

Of the 1,000 generally accepted as 'missing', up to 300 were now withdrawing from Elsenau to the north. The balance was thus made up of those who had been wounded and evacuated, of those who had been captured, of those who were missing, of those who had taken advantage of the chaotic situation to desert,[137] and perhaps of those who had joined German units. To be sure, the greater portion of the balance was those who had been wounded and evacuated. The number of deserters was probably small.

Went the battle well?

At Hammerstein, 'Charlemagne' found itself in an impossible situation. It was not combat-ready. It went straight into battle off the trains. It went into battle with no knowledge of enemy strength. It went into battle without radio equipment and few maps. It went into battle without its artillery battalion, which had not yet arrived. It received no armour or air support. And yes, the battle went badly, but it went down fighting. It knocked out between forty and fifty tanks, destroyed a consider-

135 Saint-Loup, page 223.
136 Soulat, letter to the author, dated 20/2/1998.
137 For example, during the retreat from Elsenau, Levast and the *Compagnie d'Honneur* came across two soldiers who had deserted from 'Charlemagne'. Also, during the retreat from Neustettin to Belgard, Std.Ju. Bayle of the 2/57 was approached by two former *Miliciens* who asked him about 'leaving' his platoon. He agreed to this, but not to them taking their weapons. At a roll call, he reported the disappearance of the two to Kompanieführer Ostuf. Bartolomei.

able quantity of motorised equipment and inflicted casualties that far outweighed its own. Deeds of self-sacrifice and bravery were many. Indeed, at Neustettin, thirty Iron Crosses were awarded for various feats of arms.[138] Overall, 'Charlemagne' performed well under very adverse combat conditions. Realistically speaking, little more could have been expected of it.

138 Undoubtedly, the number of Iron Cross and other decorations awarded at Neustettin would have been greater if it was not for the absence of part of the division.

CHAPTER 10

The Hell of Pomerania, Part 2

Neustettin

According to the situation maps of Army Group Vistula, the bulk of 'Charlemagne' was south-east of Flötenstein. In reality, the bulk of the division was some thirty-five kilometres away at Neustettin!

On 27th February 1945, two convoys of 'Charlemagne' pulled into Neustettin station.[1] Aboard the first convoy, the sixteenth, arriving in the morning, were the headquarters staff of the II/58 and elements of the II/58, including Company 5/58. The day before, at Stargard (Stargard Szczecinski), the journey had been interrupted when an armoured Soviet spearhead cut the railway line.[2]

As the troops of the II/58 disembarked, the Soviet Air Force attacked,[3] but guns of Ustuf. Fayard's FLAK Company[4] in position on flat wagons returned fire and shot down one of the attackers.

Men of Oscha. Rusco's platoon of the 5/58 were busy unloading a small car when 'a hail of shells' suddenly rained down on the railway station. Shaken by the blast of the explosions, they let go of the car, which rolled off the wagon and onto their platoon commander. Thrown to the ground, Rusco was badly hurt in the right knee. Although in great pain, he could still get around.

---

1   Message Ia/Tgb.Nr.2143/45 geh. of the 27/2/45 reported the arrival of two convoys of 'Charlemagne'. Although the message does not specify their arrival at Neustettin, there can be little doubt it does refer to the two convoys of 'Charlemagne' that arrived at Neustettin on the 27th.

2   According to de Genouillac of the headquarters staff of battalion II/58, the convoy lost a day at Stargard, whereas it was only several hours according to Blanc, Castrillo and L.G. of Company 5/58 travelling on the same convoy (Blanc, letter to the author, 11/4/2001).

3   De Genouillac, letter to the author, 27/6/1997. Curiously, Blanc, Castrillo and L.G. of Company 5/58 travelling on the same convoy do not recall this air attack (Blanc, letter to the author, 11/4/2001). Furthermore, Blanc makes the suggestion that it was another convoy, arriving before that of the II/58 and carrying elements of 'Regiment 57', which was attacked. In response to this, the author knows of no convoy carrying elements of 'Regiment 57' that arrived at Neustettin.

4   According to de Genouillac, the FLAK Company was dispersed on several of the last convoys to provide some form of protection to all (letter to the author, 15/7/97). However, Mabire and Saint-Loup imply that the entire FLAK Company arrived later on the convoy of Bassompierre. Soulat is of the same opinion (letter to the author).

Gren. Castrillo of the 5/58 hurried off for news. He saw a train of wounded. They too were from 'Charlemagne'. In this way, Castrillo and the men of the 5/58 were shocked to learn of the 'setback' at Hammerstein.

The troops of the II/58 were then sent to a barracks in the city where they met some survivors from the earlier fighting. 'The greatest confusion reigned among these troops'. Anxious to have news of his friends of the I/58, Ustuf. de Genouillac went from shed to shed, making inquiries, and came across Hstuf. Monneuse who was busy sawing up a telegraph post for the stove in his bedroom. He revealed to de Genouillac that he had no idea of the fate of his orderly officer, Oberjunker de Brangelin, nor of the overall situation, other than his battalion had 'exploded' in every sense of the word.

That afternoon arrived the second convoy under convoy commander Hstuf. Bassompierre.[5] He had been ordered to stay behind at Wildflecken, but refused. The convoy was also carrying elements of the FLAK Company, as well as eight 105mm howitzers of the Artillery Group[6] under Ustuf. Daffas, the commander of the command platoon of the Headquarters Company of Waffen-Gren. Regt der SS 58.[7] But there were no crews with the artillery guns; they were still en route to the division from Bohemia-Moravia where they had just finished their training course. In total, around one hundred and fifty men were abroad this convoy.

Shortly after arriving at the station, this convoy was 'warmly' greeted by the Soviet land forces and Air Force. It was violently attacked by a Russian advance

5   This is a conclusion drawn by the author. According to Soulat, page 41, and repeated by Mabire, page 382, the convoy of Bassompierre arrived on 26th February 1945. In response to this, de la Mazière, present on this convoy, implies twice ("*Ashes of Honour*", page 105 and page 107) that its arrival was on the 27th. Moreover, message Ia/Tgb.Nr.2143/45 geh. of the 27/2/45 reports the arrival of two convoys of 'Charlemagne' carrying one company and 'Artillery elements'; the convoy of Bassompierre was carrying the FLAK Company, as well as guns of the Brigade Artillery Group. Thus, this message appears to refer to the arrival of the convoy of Bassompierre. For this reason, the author has concluded that the convoy of Bassompierre arrived on the 27th and not the day before. As for its time of arrival, Saint-Loup cites, page 256, the afternoon. (Presumably Saint-Loup's account was based on that of Soulat, who cites the same time, but with the 'incorrect' date of the 26th.) In addition, as previously stated, the convoy of Berret arrived in the morning. From this, the author has concluded that the convoy of Bassompierre arrived in the afternoon and was thus the second of the two convoys to arrive. However, in correspondence to the author, Oscha. Rusco of the 5/58, undoubtedly on the convoy of Berret and the II/58, wrote that 'we were the last to arrive in Pomerania'. This the author has not been able to explain. Lastly, according to Mabire, page 382, the convoy of Bassompierre was the fifteenth and last convoy of 'Charlemagne' from Wildflecken. This convoy was, in all likelihood, the last from Wildflecken, but the fifteenth? This has proved impossible to confirm.

6   Soulat, letter to the author, 9/11/97. These guns are described by Saint-Loup on page 256 as 'part of the guns of the artillery group' and by Mabire on page 384 as some infantry guns brought along from Wildflecken.

7   According to Mabire, page 384, Ustuf. Daffas was the commander of '*la section de commandement du régiment 58*' which can only refer to the command platoon of the Headquarters Company of Waffen-Gren. Regt der SS 58.

party of armour and infantry. Jumping down from the train, Uscha. de la Mazière[8] was immediately captured by two Russians who made him put up his hands! He was shoved towards a shed, the station lamp-room, but his comrades, who saw his plight, came to his assistance, killing his two captors. He then watched as the FLAK guns went into action and knocked out a T–34, setting it on fire. The others quickly made off.[9]

At that same moment a Soviet aircraft bombed the station 'with incredibly bad aim'. On its second pass the FLAK hit and brought down the twin-engine plane, which crashed just outside the town. The others did not return. All this had lasted a matter of minutes.

No sooner was the train empty than it was occupied again by German units that were withdrawing.

Darkness fell. That night of 27th/28th February 1945, Obf. Puaud called together the officers for a meeting. Because the Russians were already threatening Neustettin a decision was made to evacuate the town[10] and reform 'Charlemagne' at the town of Belgard (Bialogard). This meant a withdrawal of eighty kilometres northwards. The withdrawal was scheduled for 0700 hours.

Towards 0100 hours on the 28th, the order was issued to reload the artillery and the Flak guns[11] on a train bound for Belgard. Shortly after, an officer woke Ustuf. Daffas with the order. Accompanied by the station master, Daffas went in search of wagons and soon located some. The loading began.

At 0300 hours, the alarm was given. The clanking of tank treads could already be heard. Under the protection of an armoured train, which had gone and taken up a position outside the railway station, the loading continued.

Towards 0700 hours, the enemy launched an attack. Because of a lack of loco-motives the armoured train due to leave for Kolberg coupled the wagons of artillery and departed.[12] It was not a minute too soon. Ustuf. Fayard's FLAK Company had

---

8   Contrary to what is written in "*Ashes of Honour*", page 95 and in the article "*Le Rêveur Casqué*", de la Mazière was not an officer with the rank of Untersturmführer. For whatever reason, he chose to rewrite his rank.

9   De la Mazière, "*Ashes of Honour*", pages 106-107. Suspiciously, neither Soulat, Mabire nor Saint-Loup confirm this brief and violent land engagement. Moreover, in correspondence to the author, de Genouillac considers as unlikely the appearance of Russian tanks at that moment.

10   According to Mabire, page 386, Stubaf. de Vaugelas announced during this meeting that the 'Latvian Division', which he called their rearguard, had been swept aside by a strong Soviet attack. As such, this role of rearguard to 'Charlemagne' or indeed to any other unit is not found in Arthur Sigailis' "*Latvian Legion*".

11   "*Pommern-1945*" and Soulat, letter to the author, 6/3/98. Curiously, de la Mazière wrote of the Flak guns, page 109: "It [the withdrawal] was to be covered by a dozen anti-aircraft guns, the ones we had brought on our convoy. Failing tractors to tow them, they were left on their railway trucks and the whole train with the empty wagons, moved off again to a position north of the town." This the author has not been able to explain.

12   Soulat, page 41. However, according to Mabire, page 385, Ustuf. Daffas could not locate at first a locomotive to pull the wagons. Then he spotted an armoured train which 'had moved several hundreds of metres away to cover the railway station with

just finished the re-embarkation of its 'equipment'[13] when it was surprised by a Russian attack. Indeed, the FLAK gunners were actually in the wagons waiting to depart when the Russians suddenly appeared on the platform![14] They had to extricate themselves in hand-to-hand fighting. So instead of following their equipment, they now found themselves engaged as grenadier.

Eventually, via Bublitz (Bobolice) and Köslin (Koszalin), the armoured train reached the city port of Kolberg on the Baltic coast where the artillery pieces were subsequently employed in its defence.

At 0700 hours, as planned, the first elements of 'Charlemagne' left the barracks situated to the north of the town and set out towards Belgard.

A mood of sudden alarm was produced by the report of Russian tanks encircling Neustettin to the north, cutting the railway line to Kolberg. This changed the situation. Disaster now threatened, but the enemy was not aggressive and did not follow up.

Shortly before 0800 hours, the troops of the II/58 left the town. This was the last battalion to leave. A little later, Oberst Kopp,[15] the 'Festungskommandant' [fortress commandant] of Neustettin, who was in command of the defence of the town with elements of the Division 'Pommern', came and asked Obf. Puaud to provide him with a battalion to help him hold the town till evening and also to hold the enemy at bay so as to permit the withdrawal of the civilian population and those units not yet engaged.

Obf. Puaud reflected: if Neustettin fell too soon, the withdrawing division would be overtaken by disaster and crushed. The division desperately needed breathing space, but the last of its battalions had already left. Nevertheless, to buy the necessary time, Puaud agreed to supply a *bataillon de marche*.

Turning to the divisional headquarters staff around him, Obf. Puaud ordered Ostuf. Auphan, his orderly officer, to form a *bataillon de marche* with those units which had not already left the town. In this way, he formed a weak battalion, which comprised the following companies:

The FLAK Company under Ustuf. Fayard

The 4/58 under Ostuf. Tardan

The 10/58 (Panzerjäger Company of Waffen-Gren. Regt der SS 58) under Oscha. Girard

In total, some 250 men, but the companies commanded by Tardan and Girard had participated in the recent fighting and were completely exhausted.

---

the fire of its guns and to check a possible Russian tank spearhead'. He spoke to the commander of the armoured train who had just received orders to leave Neustettin for Kolberg on the Baltic coast. Because Belgard was en route the commander of the armoured train agreed to couple the flat tractors to his train.

13   Soulat, page 42, repeated by Mabire, pages 389-390. The word 'equipment' presumably refers to its Flak guns.

14   Mabire, page 398.

15   "*Pommern 1945*", page 189.

The French *bataillon* was assigned a sector, 1,200 metres long, between two Wehrmacht battalions. After acquainting himself with the situation of the FLAK Company, Auphan went to inspect the sector assigned to the *bataillon*. To defend the sector, he decided to deploy the FLAK Company to the north and the 4/58 to the south. His third company, the 10/58, was to provide a 'group', perhaps a platoon, of 'tank-hunters' armed with panzerfäuste to each of the two line companies. In this way, he would have at his disposal a small reserve of around one and a half platoons.

But first the heavily engaged FLAK Company had to be pulled back to the defensive positions. And Auphan was all too aware that a withdrawal conducted before an aggressive and overwhelming enemy presence was not only difficult, but dangerous.

To collect the FLAK Company, Ostuf. Auphan sent forward Ostuf. Tardan and his 4/58. Joined by the 4/58, the FLAK Company withdrew. Despite the fire support of the 4/58, the FLAK Company still encountered difficulties, but managed to extricate itself. The two companies then occupied their laid-down position in the centre of the disposition.

Marotin of the 8/57 awoke to the shrill rent of the MGs and the din of the artillery. Around him men were running out of the barracks. Was this the start of their offensive? ... But nobody had thought to wake him from his deep sleep. He hastily equipped himself and dashed out in turn. Outside there were crowds of people around; soldiers trying to find their *gradés* and the *gradés* their men, and dazed civilians roused from sleep. The town was being evacuated.

He left the town in search of his comrades. He was stopped by a German officer who was looking for volunteers to slow down the enemy and buy enough time for the retreating columns of soldiers and civilians to put some distance between themselves and the Russian spearheads. The officer was quite insistent. Marotin joined a fifty-strong group armed with four PAK guns and some MGs for which there was little ammunition.

Two Soviet tanks appeared. Behind them followed their infantry support. The defenders stood firm and one tank fell victim to their PAK. The other tank withdrew in great haste. Their MGs shot up the exposed enemy infantry. The Russians flung themselves against this post a further two times and were repelled, but the defenders were now out of ammunition for their PAK guns and MGs. Once again the same old story!

The Russians now seized their opportunity to crush this post and reappeared with tanks from two directions. There was nothing the defenders could do this time and they withdrew in a mad rush. The Russian infantry were soon on top of them. Marotin wrote: "A large guy was tossing grenades just anyhow ... I threw myself on the ground but my mouth and eyes were full of earth and I was groggy ... A German grenadier on my right cut in two this 'uncouth individual' with a precise burst."

After sharing out the last ammunition, the survivors set off on their long march to Belgard.

And meanwhile, back in Neustettin, how were its French SS defenders faring? Quite simply they were in the thick of battle. The Soviet armour had been halted 400 metres from the town after making no headway against anti-tank roadblocks manned by the Frenchmen and the Germans.

Preceded by an air strike at 1030 hours,[16] the Russians attempted to punch their way into the town again. Supported by artillery and mortar, tanks approached. Alongside them charged the infantry.

The troops of the improvised French *bataillon de marche* and the Wehrmacht stood fast. Again the enemy tanks got no further than the roadblocks. The enemy infantry, slipping through the gardens, was halted by a devastating hail of fire from the defenders posted on the roofs, at the windows and at the basement windows.

Having failed frontally, the Russians launched encircling attacks to the north and the south against the two German battalions. In this way, the French *bataillon de marche* enjoyed a relative calm until 1600 hours. By that time, in the southern sector, Soviet tanks had battled their way up to the barricade on Tempelburg Road, but were being contained in savage battle. In the end the Germans came out on top, destroying two tanks and throwing back the enemy infantry with heavy losses. On the other hand, in the northern sector, the German battalion of territorials holding the area around the railway station had fought without ardour and given way. As a result, the flank of the French FLAK Company now lay exposed. The full weight of the Soviet infantry fell onto Fayard whose men withdrew, contesting every building in fierce hand-to-hand fighting.[17]

The end at Neustettin

An hour later at 1700 hours, the end was clearly in sight for the defenders. In the northern sector, the enemy had managed to get across the railway bridge and capture the railway station. In the southern sector, enemy cavalry was skirting around the lake alongside Neustettin. Encirclement now threatened. It was now only a question of time.

Faced with encirclement and a crumbling defence, Colonel Kopp was forced to give up Neustettin to the enemy. He decided to withdraw all his units, starting with the battalion on the left flank, then the French 'alarm' battalion[18] and, lastly, the battalion on the right flank in echelons, to the fortified line of 'Pommern-Stellung' ten kilometres west of Neustettin. He issued orders to this effect.

Two different versions exist of what followed next.[19] The first is according to Ostuf. Auphan.

Watching the right-hand battalion assigned to protect the disengagement and withdrawal scattering before his eyes, Ostuf. Auphan decided to leave the town last. And the *bataillon de marche* did and in good order at that.

The *bataillon de marche* came to the rallying point, the command post of the German regiment five kilometres from the town on the road to Bad-Polzin (Polczyn Zdrój) where Colonel Kopp was to have awaited the units, but the command post was now empty. Auphan noted the obvious signs of a hurried

---

16 Soulat, page 42, repeated by Mabire, 391. According to Saint-Loup, page 257, the Soviet air strike against Neustettin began at 1200 hours and also marked the beginning of their assault against the town which would continue into the evening.
17 Saint-Loup, page 257. However, this withdrawal by the FLAK Company is not recorded by Soulat or Mabire.
18 Soulat, page 44.
19 Ibid.

departure; abandoned maps, papers and field telephone. He did not hang around and left. Shortly after, the command post was hit repeatedly by enemy mortars and brought under fire by automatic weapons from the direction of the lake. He raced back to hurry the withdrawal to Bärwalde.

The *bataillon de marche* retreated westwards, but two sections sent ahead on reconnaissance were quick to report back that the way forward had been cut and that the Russians were firmly holding the first village (possibly Streitzig).[20] In no position to give battle, Ostuf. Auphan decided to follow the railway line, which still seemed clear. It was not. The battalion only just managed to get through. It then split into two detachments; Fayard left on a locomotive[21]; Auphan and Tardan continued on foot.

With the remnants of their respective commands, Auphan, Fayard and Tardan rejoined the Division at Körlin. With the approval of Puaud, Auphan proposed Fayard, Tardan and five other ranks for the Iron Cross 2nd Class.

The second version is that of Ostuf. Tardan.

When the fighting flared up at the barricade on Tempelburg Road Ostuf. Tardan left his command post to go there. Half an hour later, after the fighting had died down, he returned. And it was then that he discovered that both the heavy machine-gun platoon and the mortar group held in reserve had simply disappeared.[22]

Ostuf. Tardan then went to see Ostuf. Auphan at his command post. Nobody was there! They too had disappeared. Undaunted, he continued on his way to see

20 According to Mabire, page 395, after sending ahead the two sections to reconnoitre the village, Ostuf. Auphan 'heard bursts from automatic weapons, grenade explosions and shouting'.

21 According to Saint-Loup, page 258, Fayard and his FLAK Company left the town last on a locomotive, which they got moving under fire from Russian infantry. Mabire repeats this, page 396, but in a much more dramatic style. According to Mabire, the last defenders of Neustettin rushed over to the rail line but were soon spotted by the Russians and fired upon. The Russians closed in for the kill. Suddenly out of the darkness arose their possible saviour: a locomotive with steam up. To cover their retreating comrades, Ustuf. Fayard and a handful of his men immediately transformed the locomotive into an 'armoured train' bristling with guns. The first Russians to appear were warmly greeted. Slowly the train pulled away. By now, the track was swept by enemy fire, but there was no halting the locomotive, which left behind it a trail of tracer bullets. In this way, they escaped into the night. However, realistically speaking, this particular episode appears questionable. Furthermore, the primary source, Soulat's "*Histoire de la Charlemagne*", from which Saint-Loup and Mabire wrote their accounts of the battle of Neustettin, does not include this dramatic 'escape' by train. Unable to trace any eyewitnesses, the author has reluctantly concluded that the whole truth will possibly never be known.

22 According to Mabire, page 393, on 'thinking that they had been abandoned', the men of the heavy machine-gun platoon and the mortar group [of the Panzerjäger Company] decided to withdraw westwards along the road to Bad Polzin. In response to this, when Tardan went to the German Colonel's command post he was told that the FLAK Company and the 'Tank Hunters' Company 'had left their positions to withdraw to Bad Polzin' (Soulat, page 44). This implies that the heavy machine-gun platoon and the mortar group were acting on orders when they withdrew.

Colonel Kopp in command of the defence of the town. He was not at his command post. Tardan questioned the other officers present and learnt that the other two French companies had left their positions to withdraw to Bad Polzin.[23] Thereupon, he returned to his men.

Ostuf. Tardan reviewed his situation; by now sounds of battle could be heard southwest and west of the town; the road to Bad Polzin had been cut five kilometres from Neustettin; both Colonel Kopp and Ostuf. Auphan were nowhere to be found—perhaps they had already withdrawn? He did not know; the Russian advance had been held up all day; and lastly Obf. Puaud had made it clear to him 'that it was only a matter of a retarding action and not an all-out resistance'. In light of this, he did not hesitate to give his 4/58 the order to withdraw to Bad Polzin (Połczyn Zdrój).

The time was around 1800 hours when Ostuf. Tardan and the seventy men of the 4/58 still with him pulled back and made off on foot along the railway line, which was under artillery fire.

The 4/58 managed to make it through the Soviet ring of steel around Neustettin, but only just!

To avoid the Russian vanguards, the 4/58 was forced to detour time and time again.[24] In this way, by the time it reached Bad Polzin at 1100 hours on 1st March 1945 it had covered sixty-three kilometres. Here the 4/58, resupplied with supplies and ammunition, rested.

At 0600 hours on 3rd March 1945, Tardan's 4/58, which had been joined by Ostuf. Auphan, pushed on to Belgard. Ten hours later, at 1600 hours, the 4/58 rejoined 'Charlemagne' at Körlin.

At Neustettin, the *bataillon de marche* was in action for some twelve hours. And what of its losses? Of its complement of 130, the FLAK Company lost some 40 or 50 men.[25] While no casualty figures are available for the other two French companies of 'Charlemagne' engaged at Neustettin it does not seem unreasonable to suggest that they were on a par with those of the FLAK Company. A sacrificial mission indeed, but their sacrifice, along with that of the Wehrmacht battalions, had halted the Russian advance for twelve hours and in so doing saved the bulk of 'Charlemagne' threatened by disaster, as well as hundreds, perhaps thousands, of civilians.

One cannot conclude the battle of the French *bataillon de marche* for Neustettin without reflecting on the two different versions of its last moments. That of Auphan appears to flatter himself and his unit, which was last to leave the town after the German units had fled back in disorder without respecting the orders issued to them. This, however, is disputed by one source, that of

---

23   Although according to Mabire, page 393, Tardan was told that the two French companies 'had had to leave their positions to rejoin the Division at Belgard'.

24   In contrast, according to Saint-Loup, page 258, to cover the withdrawal of the inextricably intermingled columns of civilians and soldiers, Ostuf. Tardan imaginatively plagued the advancing Soviet tanks with groups of cyclists armed with panzerfäuste. Again and again his men successfully ambushed and halted the pursuing enemy armour. Making the most of the great confusion they had sown among the leading Russians, they jumped on their bikes and hurriedly cycled off.

25   Soulat cites 40 and Bayle 50.

Lindenblatt.[26] Indeed, according to Lindenblatt, because the Frenchmen of 'Charlemagne' were not up to the task and 'to avoid pointless losses', Major Sann, charged with the defence of Neustettin, 'released them from their mission with orders to join the closest formed unit'. Regarding this, would officers and men of a unit not quite up to the task have received a number of decorations? Surely, the answer is no. Also, even if the *bataillon de marche* was among the first to withdraw, one cannot but help reflect that by then it had actually fulfilled the mission as defined by Obf. Puaud.

As for that of Tardan, it is much more matter of fact and not self-praising.

In conclusion, both versions are plausible, although that of Tardan is perhaps the more plausible of the two. What happened for certain will probably never be known.

Belgard

'Charlemagne' would cover the seventy-two kilometres from Neustettin to Belgard in a little less than twenty-four hours. Through a snowstorm, the exhausted and frozen men withdrew first to the west and then turned to the north at Bad Polzin (Polczyn Zdrój). Most were on foot. So was Obf. Puaud, who had handed over his car to the wounded. Hstuf. de Perricot was on horse-back. He went up and down the column like 'a good guard dog'.

At the head of the division was Hscha. Walter's 7/58 and at the rear Wagner's 5/58.

The men were loaded with munitions. Puaud was seen to shoulder for several kilometres a machine-gun or an ammunition box that was too heavy for an exhausted gunner. But bit by bit equipment was discarded along the way. Indeed, Waffen-Gren. Regt der SS 34 of the 15. Waffen-Grenadier-Division der SS (lettische Nr.1) was able to replenish its heavily depleted weapons with those discarded.[27]

Since Neustettin the morale of many ex-LVF *légionnaires* had collapsed with the news of Doriot's death on 22nd February 1945. 'It was the end of their dream'.[28]

Towards 1400 hours, in the vicinity of Bärwalde, the exhausted survivors were strafed and bombed by Soviet aircraft[29], which dropped darts and glass grenades dating from the First World War![30] Losses were light; the Russians had attacked from the sides and not down the line of the column, and the road was well protected by trees.[31]

26   "*Pommern-1945*", page 189.
27   Arthur Silgailis, "*Latvian Legion*", page 176.
28   Mabire, page 400.
29   The written interview with Raybaud and Soulat, letter to the author dated 9/11/97. According to Saint-Loup, the column was attacked some time later after leaving Bad Polzin. Of course, the possibility exists that the column was attacked more than once which would explain this.
30   Saint-Loup, page 261.
31   Soulat, page 47 (repeated by Mabire, page 397, and Saint-Loup, page 261). However, the written interview with Raybaud in "*Charlemagne's Legionnaires*" is the only source to claim that losses were heavy.

Having no real anti-aircraft weapons with them, the soldiers struck back with machine guns, sub-machine guns and rifles. Oscha. Rusco's platoon of Wagner's 5/58 even managed to shoot down a low-flying aircraft, which had been met by a fusillade of machine-gun fire.

Night fell. An hour's rest was granted at or near the town of Bad Polzin. Belgard was now thirty kilometres away. The men fell out and collapsed onto the frozen ground. There was no shelter. The icy wind got up. Puaud tried to raise their spirits, saying to each: "I led you into this but I'll lead you out again, be sure of that". The hour was over all too soon. Wearily they picked themselves up, but some had to be kicked hard to be woken. Teeth clenched, they set off again and trudged on.

Puaud seemed everywhere. While trying to sort out a bad traffic jam he was heard to say: "Ah! If only I had gendarmes!"

None of the survivors would have cared if they had been told that their division was now under the higher formation of the 3rd Panzer Army whose headquarters was far away at Plathe (Ploty).[32]

The march continued all night. The column lengthened. Blanc of the 5/58 recalls:

> Towards three in the morning, Wagner ordered a halt, we collapsed in a farmyard beside the road. I still often have a thought for little Denamps[33] who, [as] a perfect comrade, found the strength to collect the platoon's flasks, for to go and fill them and redistribute them, before stretching out himself. He would be killed some days later … We set off again.

Dawn came up. Around 0600 hours, German motorised and armoured units overtook the retreating columns of 'Charlemagne'. The march continued.

Hours later[34], the vanguard of the column received the order to halt and bivouac several kilometres south-east of Belgard.[35] Throughout the day more and

32 The attachment of 'Charlemagne' to the higher formation of the 3rd Panzer Army probably coincided with its simultaneous attachment to ad hoc *Korps Gruppe* [Corps Group] Tettau.

33 He was one of three brothers serving with 'Charlemagne'; two were in the 5/58 and the third with the engineers.

34 According to the written interview with Raybaud in "*Charlemagne's Legionnaires*", page 102, the tired soldiers were finally allowed to stop at approximately 1200 hours.

35 The exact location of this bivouac is not known. According to Saint-Loup, page 263, it was in the forest locality of Spring-Krug. However, Spring-Krug is about one kilometre east of the main road from Bad Polzin to Belgard and is across the Neustettin-Belgard railway line. Blanc of Company 5/58 does not recall leaving the main road at the end of the march from Neustettin. Also of note is that Saint-Loup states that the officers continued on for some time and arrived at the small chateau of Boissin (see page 263). This is contradictory because Boissin is some two kilometres south of Spring-Krug. There are three possible locations for the bivouac: the crossroads east of Ristow, which would enable the officers to continue on, the crossroads east of Boissin, and, lastly, the hamlet of Sternkrug, some four kilometres from Belgard. Blanc favours Sternkrug, the main reason being that when 'Charlemagne' left for Körlin it seemed to him that 'we only had three or four

more units joined those already there. Soldiers who still had tents pitched them. Completely numbed by the cold, all tried to keep warm and fight off the hunger gnawing them. They had few supplies with them.

With great energy, the officers attempted to find their men and reform their commands once again. The German Inspection installed itself in a small chateau in Boissin (Byszyno) nine kilometres south-east of Belgard. Puaud established his headquarters in a chateau in Kowanz,[36] some two kilometres due west of Körlin.

During the march from Neustettin to Belgard, horse-drawn Fahrschwadron A stopped three times. Uscha. Mercier of Fahrschwadron A recalls[37]:

> One of the stops was in a village where we received a visit from a Wehrmacht Lieutenant commanding a group of infantrymen in retreat. He gave us information on the Russians following him. As we had a panzerfaust at our disposal (and only one), he was so kind as to give us some advice on the efficient use of this weapon and did not linger more, being rather pressed. He wished us good luck.
>
> I recall another stop in a XVIII century chateau where the lady of the house and her butler welcomed us. *Capitaine* Schlisler, still very old-world, presented his men to this lady who put her hall at our disposal. When our *chef* protested that such luxury could only be suitable for the NCOs the butler made us realise that future customers would not have the same restraint.
>
> Another stop, probably the last, was in the house of a village burgomaster who was saddened at having his house requisitioned by several carts with horses and drivers, who spent a day waiting for orders that never came. His wife listened, incredulous, to the advice I gave her to make for the left bank of the Oder so as to be certain to see final victory.
>
> It was at this last stop that we received supplies, which I went and got.

Much to the surprise of all Brigf. Krukenberg soon joined the exhausted men at the bivouac. He had come from Flötenstein via Köslin.[38] It was at Köslin (Koszalin) near the coast that it had been planned to assemble and reform the scattered 'Charlemagne', but this had come to nothing as the Russians were already threatening the city. Nevertheless, some did make the journey to Köslin. One of those who did make the journey was Rttf. Soulat of the Headquarters Company, but no sooner had he arrived than he was ordered by the German Feldgendarmerie of the Inspection to turn around the lorry and return to Belgard.[39] And yet, for several days, the situation maps of Army Group Vistula reported 'Charlemagne' in the vicinity of Köslin!

kilometres to cover before reaching Belgard' (letter to the author, 29/3/2002).

36 Soulat, letter to the author, 9/11/97.

37 Mercier, letter to the author, 6/11/2001. However, Mercier is not sure of the location of the stops, although the last may have been before Belgard or Körlin.

38 Saint-Loup paints a rather dramatic picture of Krukenberg standing up in his car, surrounded by tank fire, as he slipped between the Russian spearheads. Undoubtedly this is apocryphal.

39 In addition to the German Feldgendarmerie of the Inspection, only some stragglers were present at Köslin.

The very first volunteer that Brigf. Krukenberg came across at the bivouac was a Sturmmann of Bartolomei's Company who had bagged a doe, which he was carrying across his shoulders. Hunting, of course, was 'Verboten'. Krukenberg had him arrested and ordered him to be shot. The execution was carried out but a dummy was substituted. Once Krukenberg had gone the executed man miraculously rose from the dead and devoured the doe with his executioners!

Brigf. Krukenberg had come with the intention of completely reorganising 'Charlemagne'. For him, there was only one solution and that was to form the best elements of the division into a *Régiment de Marche* (RM) and all others into a *Régiment de Reserve* (RR).

Because the situation was becoming more and more critical by the hour he ordered Stubaf. Raybaud to form the *Régiment de Marche* in three hours.[40] It took him ten hours.[41] In view of the circumstances, this was a remarkable achievement of which he remained rightly proud.

Two battalions were formed. Each battalion was made up of two grenadier companies and a support company.

The first battalion of the Régiment de Marche, the I/RM, comprised the best elements of Waffen-Gren. Regt der SS 57 and its command went to the battle-proven Ostuf. Henri Fenet. The order of battle of the I/RM was as follows:

Commander:	W-Ostuf. Fenet
Adjoint (Assistant):	W-Std.Ob.Ju. Labourdette
1st Company:	W-Ostuf. Roumegous
2nd Company:	W-Oscha. Hennecart
4th Company:	W-Oscha. Couvreur

Both Oscha. Hennecart and Oscha. Couvreur were veterans of the Sturmbrigade who had fought in Galicia. Ostuf. Roumegous was a former *Milicien* who would never completely assimilate himself into the ways of the former Sturmbrigade perpetuated by this battalion.

Because the second battalion of the *Régiment de Marche*, the II/RM, was mainly made up of former Legionnaires of the LVF or young *Miliciens* of Waffen-Gren. Regt der SS 58, Stubaf. Raybaud picked Hstuf. Bassompierre as its commander. He was the perfect choice, having fought with both the LVF and the *Milice*, although he did not find favour with Krukenberg because of his 'Maurrasian nationalism and lack of SS spirit'.[42]

The order of battle of the II/RM was as follows:

Commander:	W-Hstuf. Bassompierre
Adjoint (Assistant):	W-Ostuf. Wagner

40   According to Mabire, pages 405-406, Stubaf. Raybaud protested that such a task would normally require at least forty-eight hours to carry out. Conceding the point, Brigf. Krukenberg granted him ten hours and not one more! However, no other source confirms such a conversation. Also, Raybaud wrote, letter to Bayle dated 22/2/92, that Mabire's account, reporting a criticism from Krukenberg, is 'simply imaginary'.

41   Soulat, page 47.

42   Saint-Loup, page 267.

1st Company:	W-Hscha. Walter
2nd Company:	W-Ustuf. Rigeade
4th Company:	W-Ostuf. Français

Wagner and the three company commanders were capable former Legionnaires. Ustuf. Rigeade was satisfied to see himself and his whole company incorporated into the *Régiment de Marche*.

The platoon of Company 5/58 trained by Walter was now attached to his command, the 1st Company of the II/RM. There can be little doubt as to the reason for this. Moreover, the platoon was still in good shape and well armed. The platoon commander was still Oscha. Blaise.

At this point, the *Régiment de Marche* totalled around 1,200 men. Its units were equipped with the division's last heavy weapons and panzerfäuste.

To the command of the *Régiment de Reserve* Brigf. Krukenberg appointed Hstuf. de Bourmont. To perpetuate the spirit of the Waffen SS, Hstuf. de Bourmont choose former SS-Sturmbrigade veteran Hstuf. Pleyber as his assistant. His orderly officer remained Ustuf. Martret.

As though a mirror image of the *Régiment de Marche*, the *Régiment de Reserve* was made up of two battalions[43] of four companies each[44] and its first battalion, the I/RR, was built around former members of Waffen-Gren. Regt der SS 57 and its second battalion, the II/RR, around those of Waffen-Gren. Regt der SS 58.

Hstuf. Monneuse, a former *Milicien*, was appointed the commander of the I/RR. The order of battle of the I/RR was as follows:

Commander:	W-Hstuf. Monneuse
Adjoint (Assistant):	?
Orderly officer:	W-Ustuf. Brazier
1st Company:	W-Ustuf. Erdozain
2nd Company:	W-Ostuf. Bartolomei
3rd Company:	W-Ustuf. Hug
4th Company:	W-Hscha. Terret

43   Mabire, page 409, and Soulat, pages 47-48. However, de la Mazière, page 115, and the written interview with Raybaud, page 102, depict Hstuf. de Bourmont's command as a battalion. The author believes this to be incorrect, although its strength may have only been that of battalion.

44   According to Mabire, page 409, the two battalions consisted of four grenadier companies each. Traditionally, each abteilung (battalion) within an Infantry Regiment had three infantry companies and one 'heavy' company (or machine-gun company) which was numbered the fourth. This, of course, does not prove that each battalion of the RR had a heavy company, but the appointment of Hscha. Terret to the fourth company of the I/RR, theoretically the heavy company, could suggest that his past skills as a platoon commander in heavy company 8/57 were still very much in demand. Nevertheless, his new command may not have been equipped with the necessary weaponry and thus a heavy company in name only. Also, in correspondence to the author, de Genouillac believes that Ostuf. Devefer and his 8/58 became the heavy company of the II/RR. Again the possibility exists that the heavy company was in name only.

Hstuf. Berret, a former Legionnaire, took the head of the II/RR. Its four company commanders still remain unclear.[45]

During the reorganisation, about three hundred men may have been evacuated to Kolberg.[46] Mercier of Fahrschwadron A witnessed one soldier, whose unit was unknown to him, feign sickness in the hope of evacuation. The doctor who examined the soldier sent him packing with an almighty kick.[47]

This reorganisation took place throughout the day of 1st March 1945 (and may have only concluded in the morning hours of the 2nd). By now, 'Charlemagne' was attached to ad hoc Korps Gruppe [Corps Group] Tettau, named after its commander General Hans von Tettau. As of 1st March 1945, the Corps Group consisted of Wehrmacht divisions 'Pommernland'[48] and 'Bärwalde', the remnants of 15. Waffen Gren.-Division der SS (lettische Nr. 1), and a kampfgruppe of 'Charlemagne'.[49] But what now for the Corps Group and 'Charlemagne'?

On 2nd March 1945,[50] towards 1800 hours, Brigf. Krukenberg received orders from 'headquarters'[51] to move 'Charlemagne' immediately to the town of Körlin (Karlino). Its mission was to fortify the town and to contain the Soviet offensive as best it could, thereby protecting the retreat of the German forces towards Kolberg.[52] Some still saw and voiced the division's mission as sacrificial and by all accounts that included Krukenberg himself.[53]

Körlin

The market town of Körlin was of great strategic importance and something of a natural strongpoint.

---

45   According to de Genouillac, correspondence to the author throughout 1997, the intact II/58 was transferred en bloc to the *Régiment de Reserve* and constituted the II/RR. Nevertheless, although he cannot substantiate that the four companies of the II/58 did end up in the II/RR, to this day, 'no doubt has crossed his mind on this subject'. If true, then Hscha. Walter and his company, that of the 7/58, were not transferred to the II/RM.

46   According to Saint-Loup, page 266, during the reorganisation, Obf. Puaud proposed that those who wished to give up the fight would be evacuated, along with the wounded, to Kolberg. About three hundred, described as sick or malingerers, took up his offer. In this way, Obf. Puaud, whom Saint-Loup describes as 'a poor strategist but an exceptional leader of men', won a risky gamble whose repercussions could have been more serious. In response to this, Obf. Puaud's proposal is not confirmed by any other source. However, during the march of 'Charlemagne' from Neustettin to Belgard, de la Mazière makes mention of the selfsame number of 'disabled', sick and those of broken morale who would have to be evacuated (page 113).

47   Mercier, letter to the author, 6/11/2001.

48   "*Russo-German War, 25 January to 8 May 1945*", page 35. This division can also be found with the title of 'Pommern' (see, for example, Lindenblatt, "*Pommern 1945*").

49   Ibid. Curiously, 33SS 'Charlemagne' is also shown to the rear of the 3rd Panzer Army/11th SS Panzer Army.

50   Soulat, page 48. However, according to Mabire, page 411, the date of this order was 1st March 1945.

51   Ibid. Unfortunately no specific headquarters is detailed.

Situated eight kilometres north-west of Belgard, Körlin commands the road to Kolberg and also the highway from Köslin to Stettin (Szczecin). Körlin is virtually enclosed by the river Persante (Parseta) that flows into the Baltic Sea, and by its tributary the Radüe (Radew). Thus, access into the town was only by way of several bridges.

Throughout the night of 2nd/3rd March, the French SS companies set off on foot to Körlin. The RM was to be centred on Körlin whereas the RR was to guard the crossing points over the river Persante that winds serpent-like north-west of Körlin.

When elements of the RM entered Körlin they found the town empty.[54] Thereupon, the companies were sent onto their designated positions. The staff of the *Régiment de Marche* entered the town with the rearguard. Stubaf. Raybaud was most disturbed by the apathy shown by his officers, and, to improve their efficiency, he dismissed his Chief-of-Staff[55] and replaced him with Hstuf. de Perricot. By the side of de Perricot as an interpreter was Rttf. Sepchant.

Once at their positions, the Frenchmen quickly dug combat emplacements, sited machine guns and erected anti-tank barriers. German sappers mined the bridges.[56] By dawn, the *Régiment de Marche* was in position; Fenet's I/RM had

52   Ibid. However, according to Saint-Loup, page 265, Brigf. Krukenberg came to Obf. Puaud's headquarters armed with similar orders—headquarters had asked him to hold Körlin for a period of twenty-four hours to 'facilitate' the withdrawal of the 32nd Infantry Division. Responding, Puaud protested that the men were exhausted. But late on the 2nd when the time came to reorganise the division and 'sell' its new mission, Puaud announced to the survivors that he had spoken to the Führer in person and, in their name, had promised him that Körlin would be defended. In response to this, while some parts may well be true, the part about Puaud speaking to the Führer is, undoubtedly, apocryphal.

53   Mabire, page 411.

54   Saint-Loup and confirmed by Sepchant, correspondence to the author. However, according to de la Mazière, page 116, the RM found Körlin almost empty except for the main street, which was crowded with refugees.

55   The written interview with Raybaud in *"Charlemagne's Legionnaires"*, page 104. Presumably Raybaud was referring to his *adjoint* Ostuf. Baudouin whose age and lack of combat experience may have contributed to a less than active role in these most demanding of circumstances and hence his dismissal.

56   According to Landwehr, the defences of both Körlin and Belgard had been laid out somewhat in advance by Staf. Zimmermann and an ad hoc construction battalion made up of French SS volunteers from various dispersed units. In response to this, there was no such ad hoc construction battalion and the division did not prepare Körlin or Belgard in advance for defence. To begin with, no other source makes reference to this advanced preparation of Körlin and Belgard for defence or to the existence of an ad hoc construction battalion. [Moreover, Soulat has confirmed, letter to the author, that there was no such ad hoc construction battalion and that no defensive positions were prepared in advance at Körlin or at Belgard.] Secondly, it was planned to reorganise 'Charlemagne' at the city of Köslin, some thirty kilometres north-east of Belgard, and this had only been dropped at the last moment. Thus there would have been very little reason for 'Charlemagne' to prepare Körlin or Belgard for defence. Thirdly, the first elements of 'Charlemagne' arrived in the town of Körlin

been deployed to the south-east, straddling the main road from Belgard, and Bassompierre's II/RM to the north-east, straddling the road from Köslin. Regimental commander Stubaf. Raybaud, appointed 'Kampfkommandant' [battle commandant] of Körlin, had established his headquarters in a house on the main square. At 0800 hours, the order was issued to evacuate the civilian population.

'German stragglers were stopped, interrogated, and if possible, made use of'.[57] In this way, a Tiger tank that turned up at Körlin was also pressed into its defence. The morale of the tank crew was at a low ebb, but discipline remained. This was in contrast to a Wehrmacht Infantry company Stubaf. Raybaud also had at his disposal. Its morale was poor.

Rttf. Sepchant was hungry. He entered a grocery that was still open. Yes, it was stocked. And yet, because he had no coupons, the shopkeeper would not sell him anything! The shopkeeper was blissfully unaware of the tragedy of the situation.

And what of the *Régiment de Reserve*? To carry out his orders of securing the crossing points from Körlin to Gross Jestin over the river Persante, Hstuf. de Bourmont was again forced to disperse widely his command. In this way, the two battalions of the *Régiment de Reserve*[58] had to hold a front that was twenty-two kilometres long. The I/RR was deployed at crossing points over the Persante in the triangle of villages Bartin—Mechentin—Peterfitz. The 2nd Company, commanded by Ostuf. Bartolomei, held Peterfitz ten kilometres north-west of Körlin. One small consolation for the widely dispersed *Régiment de Reserve* was the Persante itself; normally a small and unimpressive river, it was swollen by a thaw.

Divisional headquarters relocated from Kowanz château to one at Kerstin, a village some four to five kilometres north-west of Körlin. This same château also became the location of the headquarters of the German Inspection.[59]

The remaining 75mm guns of Roy's 9/57 were also located to Kerstin[60] and then moved to Körlin.[61] Establishing his headquarters in the house of the level crossing keeper, Roy slept on the first floor. A renowned womaniser, he soon seduced the widow of the level crossing keeper, but 'remained more reserved as regards the daughter'.[62]

hours after the receipt of orders to move there. Consequently, this would have allowed little or no time to prepare its defence in advance, yet alone mobilise an ad hoc construction battalion. Lastly, after the fighting south-east of Hammerstein, Staf. Zimmermann was ordered to Greifenberg to mobilise a *Bataillon de Marche*. He probably rejoined the division at Körlin with the *Bataillon de Marche*, which arrived on 3rd March. And even if he did rejoin the division earlier than the 3rd he would have had little time to do anything.

57   De la Mazière, page 116.
58   By now, according to Mabire, page 417, the RR was ten companies strong. This has to be a mistake.
59   Soulat, letter to the author, 9/11/97. According to Rostaing, page 163, the German Inspection had established its own headquarters in a chateau two kilometres due west of Körlin (undoubtedly Kowanz) while that of Puaud's was in a chateau north-west of the town (undoubtedly Kerstin). Thus, the possibility exists that the headquarters of the German Inspection was also at Kowanz before it too transferred to Kerstin.

The *Bataillon de Marche de Greifenberg*

On 3rd March, 'Charlemagne' was joined at Körlin by a *Bataillon de Marche*. The battalion had only been activated days earlier at Greifenberg.

On 26th February 1945, at Flötenstein, to fill the depleted ranks of 'Charlemagne' after the 'battle of Hammerstein', Brigf. Krukenberg ordered Staf. Zimmermann to Greifenberg, where, from the ranks of the Franz. SS-Gren. A.u.E. Btl., he was to mobilise and organise the departure of a *Bataillon de Marche* (or *Bataillon de Reserve*).[63] Ustuf. Patzak, Krukenberg's orderly officer, went with him. They made it to Greifenberg. Feverishly, they mobilised a *Bataillon de Marche* of some five hundred men organised into three grenadier companies and an engineer platoon. The order of battle of the *Bataillon de Marche* was as follows:

Commander:	W-Hstuf. Bisiau[64]
Assistant:	SS-Ostuf. Ludwig
1. Kompanie:	W-Ustuf. Pignard-Berthet
2. Kompanie:	W-Hstuf. Flamand
3. Kompanie:	W-Ostuf. de Bregeot
Pionierzug:	SS-?

Born on 20th July 1914, Michel Bisiau was ex-LVF.

Ustuf. Pignard-Berthet was ex-Sturmbrigade. His company was that trained by Ostuf. Michel whose command he had received three days before the departure of the *Bataillon de Marche* from Greifenberg. Pignard-Berthet recalls two of his platoon commanders: Breuvet and Uscha. Jacquet. He knew Jacquet from the Sturmbrigade. Then Jacquet had commanded the 2nd section of his 1st platoon in the 1st Company. The two of them had been wounded on the first day of combat in Galicia.

Hstuf. Georges Flamand was also ex-LVF.[65] He was in his forties.[66]

60   A conclusion drawn by the author from the relevant sections of the article "*Mein Freund Georges*" which, in the opinion of the author, contains 'a lapse of memory'. According to the article, the 75mm guns of Roy's 9/57 set up at Fritzow where 'divisional headquarters went into quarters in the chateau'. While it is true that 'Charlemagne' divisional headquarters did relocate to Fritzow chateau for no more than one day the author is convinced that the 9/57 first set up at Kerstin. To explain: when 'Charlemagne' took up position around Körlin Russian attacks were expected initially and solely from the east. Thus, would the unsupported 9/57 have been set up at Fritzow on the east bank of the Persante when no other unit of 'Charlemagne' was? The possibility of any such situation is indeed very remote. Of course the possibility exists that the company was at Kerstin and followed divisional headquarters to Fritzow, but this would not have represented a sound tactical move; Fritzow is a good eight kilometres north of Körlin, thus the company would not have been in as good a position to move and respond to fire support missions as at Kerstin.

61   According to the article "*Mein Freund Georges*", the 9/57 moved to Belgard and dug in. However, the author is convinced that the 9/57 moved to Körlin. To explain: throughout 4th March 1945, the Wehrmacht forces holding Belgard were engaged in heavy defensive fighting, but in the end could not prevent the Russians from taking the city later that night. Curiously, the article "*Mein Freund Georges*" makes no

Ostuf. Cyrille de Bregeot was a former cavalryman and, of late, a prisoner of war in Stalag III/B. His company was that trained by Ostuf. Ludwig.

A German officer commanded the engineer platoon, but his name is not known.[67]

The *Bataillon de Marche* left Greifenberg on 27th February 1945.[68] It came up by train, travelling through Treptow (Trzebiatów) and Kolberg.[69] While stopped at Gross Jestin (Goscino) railway station a French POW volunteered his services. He was welcomed aboard. On again.

Close to Körlin, the *Bataillon de Marche* disembarked. It continued on foot, arriving in the evening.

Pignard-Berthet's Company was sent straight to divisional headquarters. Deprived of the *Compagnie d'Honneur* since the battle at Elsenau, Brigf. Krukenberg was in need of a new 'guard'. The company was divided into two.

On Krukenberg's orders, the *Bataillon de Marche* was broken up and shared out.[70] Ostuf. Ludwig, the German liaison officer to the *Bataillon de Marche*, went across to Krukenberg's headquarters staff. Hstuf. Flamand's 2nd Company was placed at the disposal of Bassompierre's II/RM and Ostuf. de Bregeot's 3rd Company at Fenet's I/RM.

As the day wore on liaison had become an increasing problem for both regiments. Telephone lines were being constantly cut by saboteurs and since radios were not always available couriers had to be employed and relied upon.

mention of the company being drawn into this fierce fighting neither on that date or on any other. Also, the same article alleges that while the 9/57 was at Belgard Staf. Zimmermann went about distributing the contents of a tobacco shop to his grenadiers. Regarding this, neither Staf. Zimmermann or elements of 'Charlemagne' were at Belgard at a time when the Russians were 'close', as stated by the article. Arguably, Zimmermann 'played the supply officer' at Körlin.

62   Cited in the article *"Mein Freund Georges"*.

63   Mabire, page 368.

64   Curiously, the texts of Bayle and Mabire cite Hstuf. Rémy as the commander of the *Bataillon de Marche* and yet their respective command rosters cite Hstuf. Bisiau. In fact, it was Hstuf. Bisiau who was the commander.

65   Flamand held various posts in the LVF. For example, in 1942, as a *lieutenant*, he served with the 11th Company of the III. Battalion, acting first as a platoon commander and then company commander.

66   Possibly, he was a veteran of the Great War.

67   SS-Ustuf. Hegewald may have commanded the Engineer platoon at Körlin.

68   Saint-Loup, page 253.

69   Saint-Loup, page 253. However, according to Mabire, page 413, the *Bataillon de Marche* came up from the depot of Greifenberg by forced march. This is incorrect (letter to the author from Pignard-Berthet).

70   It is not known to which command Hstuf. Bisiau was transferred. Also of note is that, according to Mabire, page 413, when Brigf. Krukenberg broke up the *bataillon de marche* he put Hstuf. Rémy at the disposal of Obf. Puaud because he doubted Rémy's capability, which stemmed undoubtedly from Rémy's aborted mission to Greifenberg.

A concerned Ostuf. Fenet complained to his regimental commander, Stubaf. Raybaud, that he could no longer command his battalion because he had been forced by orders to disperse it over too wide an area. As a result, having no means of communication, some of his platoons had now become isolated. Overruling Krukenberg's orders, Raybaud authorised him to tighten his disposition. Fenet established his command post in the village of Redlin[71] and then, as a priority, gave himself over to maintaining contact with his companies and his platoons.

By late afternoon on 3rd March 1945, the four thousand men of 'Charlemagne' were in position and awaiting the Russians, but over the past few days its headquarters had viewed the deteriorating situation in Pomerania with great anxiety.[72]

On the 1st, the Russians crossed the road and railroad east of Köslin, cutting the German 2nd Army's last land communications with the rest of the Reich.

That same day, Zhukov launched an offensive into western Pomerania. His 1st White Russian Front ripped open the German front at Reetz (Recz) and the 1st Guards Tank Army raced due north towards Kolberg. The Russian momentum could not be halted.

On the following day, the Russians struck the German forces of the X. SS Corps and adjacent Corps Group Tettau to the east of the breakthrough.

Now back to the 3rd. The Russians continued to press forward. The situation map at the headquarters of Army Group Vistula looked terrible. Breakthroughs everywhere. Henceforth, 'Charlemagne' could expect the Russians from the north-east, as well as from the south-east. And then, around 1800 hours, divisional headquarters was informed of a strong concentration of Russian mechanised and motor forces in the region of Stolzenberg (Slawoborze) only twenty kilometres south-west of Körlin! Two hours later, a Soviet armoured column of ninety tanks and two motorised regiments was reported on the move northwards from Stolzenberg in the direction of Kolberg. This was danger; if the Russians could not be halted then 'Charlemagne' would soon find itself in the grip of the Soviet pincers.

Gross Jestin

With each passing hour of the night 3rd/4th March 1945 the fate of 'Charlemagne' was sealed tighter and tighter. Shortly after 0200 hours on 4th March 1945, Soviet tanks of the 45th Guards Tank Brigade crashed into the village of Gross Jestin (Goscino), fifteen kilometres west of Körlin. Stationed there were various rear and support elements of 'Charlemagne' under the overall command of Stubaf. Katzian. These elements comprised the *automobile train* with its last motor vehicles, divisional service units, the Headquarters Company and the engineer platoon of the *Bataillon de Marche* that had arrived from Greifenberg.

71   Mistakenly, Mabire records (page 419) that Fenet established his command post in the small village of Denzin, which is several kilometres due south of Belgard.

72   By now, 'Charlemagne' may have been under 'Corps Group Munzel' (Soulat, page 53, and Arthur Silgailis, "*Latvian Legion*", page 171). 'Corps Group Munzel' was part of 'Corps Group von Tettau' (Soulat, page 53). On 4th March 1945, both 'Corps Group Munzel' and 'Corps Group von Tettau' were subordinated to the X. SS Corps. The higher headquarters remained that of the 3rd Panzer Army.

The Soviet armoured column swept through Gross Jestin, easily overrunning the French units and, after pausing outside the village, continued on its way to Kolberg, only fifteen kilometres away. Even though the Soviets were literally in and out of Gross Jestin like a shot, leaving a trail of death and destruction in their wake, many Frenchmen were captured. Ostuf. Bénétoux, in charge of headquarters Department II A/B (Personnel), was actually taken prisoner by Polish partisans and then handed over to a Soviet officer. After a brief interrogation, Bénétoux was placed in charge of a convoy of captured Frenchmen which was made up of French Waffen-SS volunteers of 'Charlemagne', as well as French 1939/1940 POWs and French STO labour conscripts! However, the Frenchmen in civilian clothes and khaki uniforms were furious at being associated with their compatriots in field-grey. Not wishing to remain a prisoner, Bénétoux slipped away and miraculously managed to make it through to German lines two days later.

Soviet infantry did not immediately follow up the armour to secure the village. This at least gave the many Frenchmen left in the village a chance to get out of there and make it to safety. Hurriedly the last trucks were loaded. A motor column, carrying some two hundred men, left Gross Jestin sometime after 0200 hours and made for Treptow. Bringing up the rear in a Kübelwagen was Ostuf. Meier, in charge of headquarters Department I/B (equipment). His fellow passengers sprayed the roads of Gross Jestin behind them so as to keep down the heads of possible Polish partisans or Russians disguised in civilian clothing.

At 0500 hours on 4th March 1945, the Russians reached the south-west suburb of Kolberg. Short of fuel, ammunition and above all infantry support, the Red armour stopped. By now, 'Charlemagne' had been turned and was in mortal danger.

The Battle of Körlin

Meanwhile, during the night of 3rd/4th March 1945, the command of the II/RR had changed hands. A French POW employed on the farm used by the II/RR as headquarters came and informed the French SS officers present that a *pauvre monsieur* was lying on the steps of the perron. It proved to be none other than battalion commander Hstuf. Berret. At first, many, like Ustuf. de Genouillac, thought Berret had been assassinated, but he carried no visible sign of an injury. A doctor examined him and had him evacuated on account of exhaustion. Informed, Hstuf. de Bourmont appointed Ustuf. de Genouillac the battalion commander of the II/RR. Obf. Puaud confirmed this appointment on the following day.[73]

73 Correspondence with de Genouillac throughout 1997. This corrects Soulat, page 54, repeated by Mabire and Saint-Loup, that Ostuf. Defever, the former commander of heavy company 8/58 (and perhaps of the 4th company of the II/RR), succeeded Berret. But there is also Rostaing's account of Berret's evacuation. Called to the chateau of the German Inspection, Rostaing was met by Stubaf. Katzian who told him that Hstuf. Berret had been found on the steps unconscious with a wound to the head. However, Rostaing did not get to speak to Berret before the latter was hurriedly evacuated from the spot to 'the rear'. Thus, he was not to know that what he had been told was, in fact, incorrect. Curiously, according to Rostaing, Ostuf. Leune, who up to then 'had been commanding the heavy company', succeeded Berret. In response to this, Leune did not succeed Berret and nor was he the heavy company commander.

The night of 3rd/4th March 1945 also saw Brigf. Krukenberg alert Obf. Puaud's headquarters. Henceforth, their headquarters at Kerstin, north-west of Körlin, could be taken any moment by Soviet tanks which had smashed through Gross Jestin. Puaud decided to up and move to the centre of Körlin, but Krukenberg, for the meantime, chose to remain where he was.[74]

Nevertheless, it was not long before Krukenberg changed his mind and, on the morning of the 4th, he abandoned Kerstin and established 'divisional headquarters' at Fritzow (Wrzosowo) chateau, a good eight kilometres north of Körlin.[75]

Taking stock of the deteriorating military situation, Krukenberg decided to draw 'Charlemagne' tighter around Körlin which would become the centre of resistance. Orders were sent out to this effect.

A courier on horseback from Gross Jestin brought Ostuf. Bartolomei news of what had happened there during the night. Realising that he could now be attacked from the west, Bartolomei relocated his company to the village of Bartin on the east bank of the Persante. To the west the flat rumbling sound of tanks could be heard. Monneuse, his battalion commander, was still in contact and ordered him to withdraw to Körlin. The village of Mechenthin was given as the first stop.[76]

Reacting in turn, Bartolomei despatched runners who discovered that many combat emplacements were already deserted. Due to a total breakdown in liaison, many platoon and section commanders had felt abandoned and thus under no obligation to await orders that might never come. So they had simply decided to try their luck and make for Kolberg under their own steam.

Back at Körlin, in the early morning, Rttf. Gonzales, now of the *Régiment de marche*, was awoken by the cannonade which was getting closer and closer. He joined Hstuf. Bassompierre at his command post, a great building in the centre of town, which was probably that of the mayor. Bassompierre was in the company of Stubaf. de Vaugelas. Both were leant over a military map of the area. Bassompierre was very happy to see his former orderly from his LVF days; they had not seen each other for over a year.

Gonzales asked 'his *Capitaine*'if he could use the small amphibious car parked outside in the road. The keys were immediately handed over to him. He would spend the whole day driving around. He soon realised that the bulk of the Russian forces were bypassing the city.

Around mid-morning on the 4th, a most extraordinary incident happened at Körlin. A Leutnant of the Wehrmacht Company assembled his platoon. He put it to his men that they had nothing in common with 'these strangers' [the Frenchmen] who wanted to fight it out at Körlin, and proposed that they should withdraw to Kolberg. One NCO protested and this carried the others. They remained.

---

74   Mabire, page 422. However, Saint-Loup does not agree; on page 285, he records that when dawn broke on the 4th Obf. Puaud and his headquarters staff were still at Kerstin.

75   Mabire, page 432.

76   Ibid. However, according to Saint-Loup, page 287, Hstuf. Monneuse moved Ostuf. Bartolomei's Company to Mechertin (sic) because it was a safer position to spend the night, that of 4th/5th March 1945.

Although that was the end of the matter for the time being, it came back to haunt the Heer Leutnant when his conduct was reported to the SS Führungshauptamt.[77] At the beginning of April 1945, RF-SS Himmler stripped the Leutnant of his rank and then posted him as a simple grenadier to 'Charlemagne' at Carpin. But that was a month away.

Around midday, Stubaf. Raybaud made his way towards the bridge over the Persante to the west of Körlin. He intended to remind the German engineers charged with its destruction not to proceed without a formal order from him; this bridge was necessary for the withdrawal of the division's outposts of around company strength on the other side of the river, and also for the imminent entry into Körlin of the promised reinforcements of German armour.

When Stubaf. Raybaud arrived at the bridge the only enemy activity he noted was heavy small-arms fire against a building surmounted by a bell-turret some eighty to one hundred metres to his left. With the naked eye no enemy tanks were visible on the horizon. Besides, the outposts had not given the alarm. However, with binoculars, he spotted about one kilometre away a tank under cover, but could not make out if it was Russian or German. Suddenly, at that same moment, a shell exploded near him and he crumpled to the ground, badly wounded. His right knee was crushed and his left tibia fractured in two places.[78]

Hstuf. de Perricot rushed over to Stubaf. Raybaud. Although in great pain, Raybaud ordered that the command of the *Régiment de Marche* be passed to Hstuf. Bassompierre. While awaiting the arrival of Bassompierre, de Perricot took command temporarily.[79]

Because there was little that could be done for Stubaf. Raybaud, Ostuf. Dr. Durandy decided to have him evacuated.[80] That night, Oberjunker Platon drove Raybaud to Kolberg.[81] Days later, Raybaud was evacuated by boat.[82]

---

77   The SS-FHA was the SS main operational office which controlled the organisation of field units of the SS and which was also responsible for the training and replacement units of the Waffen SS as well as its schools. It should be noted that before the creation of the SS-FHA in 1940, the SS-Hauptamt (Main office) controlled all training in the SS.

78   Based on Raybaud's memoirs written in 1946, supplemented by additional material from Soulat, page 54. This corrects the accounts by Saint-Loup and Mabire of Raybaud's wounding. For the record, Saint-Loup records that Hscha. Gobion brought Raybaud word of a developing attack from the south-west and then added that German engineers were preparing to blow the bridges over the Persante. Aghast, Raybaud dashed out of his headquarters. He had to stop those engineers blowing the bridges; the outposts on the other side of the river had not been withdrawn. Accompanied by de Perricot, Gobion and several others, Raybaud walked swiftly to the bridge that carries the main road from Plathe (Platy) over the Persante. The southern suburb of the town was now being pounded by the enemy tanks. The church steeple was hit again and again and collapsed. They finally emerged in sight of the bridge. Just at that same moment a T-34 on the other side of the Persante fired. The shell exploded in front of the small group, seriously wounding Raybaud. As for Mabire, there are only a few minor differences from that version already recounted by Saint-Loup; Raybaud was actually watching the approaching Russians from an observation post 'in the area of a bridge' when he spotted German engineers bustling

Soon after the wounding of Stubaf. Raybaud, around 1230 hours, the Soviets launched an attack on Körlin from the south-west with a force estimated at twenty-five tanks and two companies of infantry.[83] The bridge was blown. A Tiger tank immobilised through lack of petrol set ablaze three or four Russian tanks within a short period. This brought the Soviet attack to a halt, albeit momentarily.

The Soviet armour then responded by laying down intensive fire on the southern sector of Körlin that prevented any movement in the roads or across the bridge to Belgard. Rttf. Sepchant was present when the bridge over the Radüe was blown. He recalls:

> When the German officer told him that the bridge over the river at the far end of the fairground was to be blown, Hstuf. de Perriot turned towards me: "Tell him that I will blow his brains out if one single man is left on the other bank when the bridge is blown." I could not bring myself to translate it all and contented myself with pointing out that nobody should be on the other bank when the bridge is blown. The Heer [Army] Oberleutnant replied to me by quoting the maxim: "Difficulties are made to be overcome." The strength of a company crossed the bridge at the double. There were no latecomers. The bridge was blown. Very proud of the result, the Heer Oberleutnant could not stop himself (from) proclaiming: "Pionierarbeit!" [Engineer's work].

And what about the *Régiment de Reserve*? By the afternoon, the RR had taken up improvised and flimsy positions on the other bank of the Persante and was now facing westwards. Hstuf. Monneuse's I/RR still remained widely dispersed along the Persante while Ustuf. de Genouillac's II/RR was either side of a railway bridge over the Persante.[84] The headquarters of the II/RR was in a level-crossing

around the bridge, which is not specified. Lastly, it is not known whether tank or artillery fire actually wounded Raybaud.

79   Incorrectly, the written interview with Raybaud in "*Charlemagne's Legionnaires*" states that Hstuf. de Perricot took command of the *Régiment de Marche*.

80   Soulat, page 54. However, according to Saint-Loup, page 291, Stubaf. Raybaud was evacuated to the medical post north of Körlin where Dr. Métais gave him the best medical attention he could.

81   Fronteau recorded in his *Journal de marche*: "Towards midnight, I meet *commandant* Raybaud who is being taken to Kolberg by *aspirant* Platon. He is seriously wounded". Fronteau was at Klaptow. This corrects Mabire, page 435, and Saint-Loup, page 291, who both record that Raybaud was evacuated by ambulance soon after his wounding.

82   The *souvenirs* of René M. (as told to Mounine). Indeed, it could be said that Raybaud saved the life of René M.; recognising René M. among the wounded, Raybaud had him evacuated from the encircled port along with him.

83   Saint-Loup, page 290, and Mabire, page 433. However, Rttf. Sepchant, who was still at the disposal of Hstuf. de Perricot, does not recall any such attack from the south-west (letter to the author). Indeed, while at Körlin, he saw only one single Russian tank and that approached from Belgard. A German tank destroyed it. So is this attack of 25 tanks and two companies of infantry nothing more than fiction?

84   Soulat cites, page 54, that the II/RR under Ostuf. Defever 'came to reinforce the defences to the west of Körlin where the danger was urgent'. According to Mabire, page 439, the four ill-equipped and understrength companies of the II/RR were rushed to the west of Körlin to meet an attack developing from the south-west. They

maisonette some two hundred metres from the bridge. The headquarters of the *Régiment de Reserve* had relocated from the chateau of Fritzow to the village of Alt-Marcin (Mierzyn).

To shore up the defences to the west of Körlin, Brigf. Krukenberg fed in Flamand's Company and de Bregeot's Company which had both arrived with the *bataillon de reserve* from Greifenberg and been assigned as reinforcements to the two battalions of the RM.[85]

Then, around 1430 hours, the Russian infantry came en masse. Machine guns raked their ranks. The battlefield was covered with dead and wounded Russians, but they came on and on.[86] No matter how many Russians were killed others instantly took their place. The supply of attacking troops seemed totally inexhaustible. Several platoons got across the Persante and established a bridgehead on the right bank. This spelt great danger for the defenders of Körlin; not only were the Russians now in the rear of Fenet's I/RM around the village of Redlin, but also behind the south-east defences of the town.

Galvanised into action, Fenet immediately improvised a counterattack with Hennecart's Company and all the stragglers he could round up.[87] Even the slightly wounded and 'those who had lost morale and reason' were recruited, assembled and engaged by Fenet.[88] Supported by Couvreur's machine guns and mortars, the French SS troops brutally and efficiently repulsed the Russians who fell back and took refuge in the woods on the other side of the Persante. Indeed, Fenet had to hold back his men from pursuing the beaten Russians.[89] In this way, for the time being, the danger had been averted. Thereupon, Fenet's I/RM returned to its positions around Redlin.

The counterattack also permitted the withdrawal behind the Persante of the advanced French units that had found it impossible to disengage and pull back.

Around 1600 hours, part of the horse-drawn train was sent to Kolberg. The road from Körlin to the city port was open, although nobody knew for how long. This news had been brought back to Fritzow by a mounted patrol from the

arrived, of course, just in the nick of time. In response to this, the battalion commander of the II/RR, Ustuf. de Genouillac, does not concur. And although he cannot substantiate that none of his companies were engaged, to this day he is convinced that none saw action at Körlin as he would have been informed of this and then gone to their positions. This alone is sufficient to cast serious doubt on the redeployment of the II/RR to the west of Körlin as cited by Soulat and repeated by Mabire.

85 Soulat, page 54. According to Mabire, page 439, these companies were formed into an improvised battalion. In response to this, no other source cites the formation of such a battalion. Militarily speaking, the formation of such a battalion (or kampfgruppe) at this point would have made good sense, but could it have been formed so quickly and provided with the necessary support and staff structure? This is extremely doubtful. In addition, Mabire does not cite the name of the battalion commander. To the author, this is suspicious.

86 Saint-Loup, page 292.

87 Mabire, page 437.

88 Saint-Loup, page 292.

89 Mabire, page 438.

Artillery Group which had reached the very gates of Kolberg two hours earlier
where weak Russian elements were already holding the mill and the bridge over the
first branch of the Persante. Proudly, the patrol also reported the destruction of a
Russian tank with panzerfäuste. The 'tank destroyers' were Oscha. Ranc and
gunners Blaise and Hoinard.

1800 hours. A meeting at divisional headquarters brought together Brigf.
Krukenberg, Obf. Puaud, Stubaf. de Vaugelas, Hstuf. Schlisler, Hstuf. de Perricot
and other German and French officers, which included Ostuf. Tardan and Ostuf.
Huan. It was decided to hold Körlin at all costs. Undoubtedly, this decision had
been influenced by the order received at divisional headquarters earlier that afternoon from Reichsführer-SS Himmler. The order had simply read: "The town must
be held at all costs!" There was probably little or no consideration given to withdrawal.[90]

At the meeting the question may have been asked of the whereabouts of the
10. SS-Panzer-Division 'Frundsberg'. Was it still coming to the rescue?

To the rescue?

Towards 2100 hours on the 3rd, Brigf. Krukenberg had personally ordered Ustuf.
Pignard-Berthet[91] to take two platoons of his company to the hamlet of Neuland,
south-west of Körlin at the junction of roads Körlin-Plathe and
Kolberg-Schivelbein, and there to make contact with a pioneer company and ele-
ments of the III. (Germanisches) SS-Panzer Korps. Together, they were to stop the
Soviet vanguards and, in this way, keep open a line of communication to the rear.
The two platoons[92] had set out on foot and not in lorries as planned.

Towards 0900 hours on the 4th, when Ustuf. Pignard-Berthet and the two
platoons of his company approached Neuland crossroads there was no sign of the
pioneers, only the Russians whose units were advancing north to Kolberg.
However, east of the crossroads, they came across a friendly motorised reconnaissance detachment of three armoured cars from the III. (Germanisches)
SS-Pz.-Korps.[93] The commanding officer with the rank of Obersturmführer and
the crews were Dutch. They passed on yet more bad news to their French comrades
of the Waffen-SS. The III. (Germanisches) SS-Pz.-Korps. was without fuel and
would not be coming to the aid of 'Charlemagne' nor to the other encircled forces.

90   It is interesting to note that the road to Kolberg was still not totally closed by 1800
      hours. Thus, a withdrawal to Kolberg was still a genuine possibility for
      'Charlemagne'. And even if the road was closed 'Charlemagne' could still have got
      through because the Russians were still not around Kolberg in any great strength.

91   Saint-Loup's account of Pignard-Berthet's mission to Neuland, page 285, is riddled
      with inaccuracy; to begin with, he incorrectly identifies the company ordered to
      Neuland as that of Million-Rousseau and then lists Pignard-Berthet as a platoon
      commander. He also incorrectly records that Puaud gave Pignard-Berthet the orders.

92   According to Saint-Loup, page 285, and Mabire, page 443, the two platoons were
      fifty-strong whereas Soulat cites, page 56, eighty men.

93   Mabire, page 442, and Pignard-Berthet, letter to the author. However, according to
      Soulat, page 56, repeated by Saint-Loup, page 285, the reconnaissance detachment
      was somewhat larger and also included one radio car and two *voitures-canon*
      [presumably armoured cars equipped with a cannon].

The Frenchmen and Dutchmen teamed up. Across the road along which Pignard-Berthet had come they built a roadblock.

Suddenly, a Russian column of lorries loaded with troops appeared. The armoured cars immediately engaged the enemy, destroying two lorries. The others about-turned, but Russian tanks soon joined the fight. Their appearance changed the odds drastically. Thereupon, Ustuf. Pignard-Berthet ordered his men to with-draw eastwards, back to Körlin, but half of his command had disappeared in the confusion of the engagement. The Dutchmen then decided to take on board their remaining comrades-in-arms and together they raced off. In vain they repeatedly tried to call the headquarters of the III. (Germanisches) SS-Pz.-Korps. and Brigf. Krukenberg at Körlin.

At a crossroads three kilometres from Körlin, they came face to face with Russian tanks coming from Stolzenberg by way of an adjacent road and lost one armoured car in a brief, one-sided firefight. After picking up those who had dismounted from the destroyed armoured car, the other two made off across country to a nearby wood situated to the north.[94] They took shelter.

Accepting that the road to Körlin was now cut by the Russians,[95] Ustuf. Pignard-Berthet and the Dutch Obersturmführer decided to try their luck north-wards. So they belted towards Kolberg, but their luck was short-lived as one armoured car after another ran out of petrol. After blowing up the armoured cars, they continued on foot and, at nightfall, bivouacked in a wood. By then, the group was about forty-strong, half Dutch and half French.

Hours later, the group was 'joined' by a Soviet patrol. Both sides soon realised that they were not alone. Because the situation was so confused nobody dare fire. They fought hand-to-hand.

Like all in that wood, Ustuf. Pignard-Berthet was completely lost. On hearing the Dutch SS officer shout *Sammlung* he started out towards him. Suddenly, in front of him, he saw the shadow of a man appear. In the belief that it was one of his men, he grabbed hold of him by the belt and tapped him on the shoulder only to discover that it was a Soviet soldier! He wrestled himself free from the clutches of his adversary and ran off in the direction of the Dutch SS officer. Along with ten others he hid away and tried to keep silent. Shots rang out, but they became less and less frequent.

At nightfall, the group set off. Kolberg was only fifteen kilometres away. When the group dispersed Ustuf. Pignard-Berthet found himself in the company of three others, two Frenchmen and one Dutchman, who wanted to make for Cammin,

---

94   Pignard-Berthet, letter to the author, 1997. However, Mabire recounts, page 60 of "*Mourir pour Dantzig*", that after this engagement Uscha. Jacquet had found himself isolated with ten or so men. This would seem to suggest that all the men were not picked up. Subsequently these men were hunted down.

95   Saint-Loup cites that the reason for this decision was that all the bridges over the Persante had been blown. This is impossible. When Ustuf. Pignard-Berthet and the two platoons of his company left Körlin on this mission the bridges over the Persante would still have been standing because the Russians at that time were not a direct threat. Besides, as previously recounted, the bridge over the Persante to the west of Körlin was blown shortly after 1230 hours on the 4th. Having no radio contact, the mixed detachment could not have known this.

but he still favoured Kolberg. So Kolberg it was. Well he was their superior. Besides, Kolberg was the nearer of the two.

Avoiding contact with the Russians, they continued northwards and were joined, much later, by some Latvian SS troops. On one occasion they could not refuse combat when they suddenly came face to face with a Soviet armoured reconnaissance detachment. In a matter of minutes, they managed to knock out three tanks with panzerfäuste and kill ten or so Russians before quickly disappearing into nature, chased by gunfire.

In the evening, they slipped into a village held by the Russians. While they slept German peasants mounted guard, but their presence was detected and they took to the fields and woods again. Finding their way north barred by an increasing concentration of Soviet artillery, they took cover and decided to turn westwards and to the Oder. They waited for nightfall before making their move.

Progress was slow, but each day brought the 'fugitives' closer to the Oder. At dawn on 10th March[96], near the banks of the Oder, they were facing danger once more; a regiment of Cossacks started to pass tens of metres away from the edge of the wood where they were hiding. They 'flattened themselves and tried to make themselves invisible'. Squadron followed squadron. At the end of the column came some stragglers. They seemed half-asleep. Suddenly, one stopped his horse, dismounted and walked over towards their hideout. He was on the point of urinating when he spotted them only metres away. The shots that killed him also awoke the other Russians to their presence. So this was the beginning of the end. And yet capture did not bring death.

The prisoners were marched towards Greifenberg. Night started to fall when Pignard-Berthet made good his escape by slipping into a copse.

After another night in the open, Pignard-Berthet was making his way towards Plathe (Ploty) when he was stopped by some Poles who took him on as a cook. Changing into civilian clothes, he made good his escape once again only to be stopped by a Russian patrol. Revelling in victory, the happy Russians actually handed him a pass! However, several kilometres later, this pass did not get him through Polish partisans.

Eventually, Ustuf. Pignard-Berthet was taken to a POW repatriation camp and, soon after his arrival, denounced as an officer of the SS and *chef* of the *Milice* by one of his compatriots from 'Charlemagne'. He was handed over to the Russians. Would his fate await all those still entrenched at Körlin?

The break-out

On the evening of the 4th, Ustuf. de Genouillac was visited by Obf. Puaud. The battalion commander of the II/RR complained to him that he had no means of blowing up the bridge or even of securing the approach road. He also mentioned that he had not eaten since the day before. Puaud was soon back with a Tellermine and a smoked herring. As soon as the herring was consumed, de Genouillac left and, by the light of a torch, mined the bridge himself.

---

96   Pignard-Berthet, letter to the author. This corrects Saint-Loup, page 287, who cites his capture on the 7th, and Mabire ("*Mourir pour Dantzig*", pages 62-68), who implies the 7th.

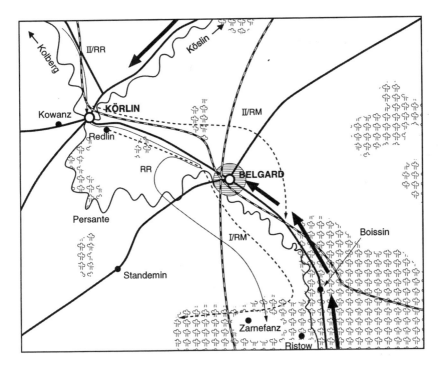

Map 4: The break-out from Körlin, 5-7 March 1945
(based on Saint-Loup, page 296, and Mabire, page 366)
On the night of the 5th, 'Charlemagne' broke out in echelons from Körlin. The first
echelon, the I/RM under Fenet, made it to the woods south of Belgard undetected. The
second eschelon, the bulk of 'Charlemagne' composed of the RR under de Bourmont,
was caught by the Russians in a clearing south-west of Belgard and massacred. The third
echelon, the II/RM under Bassompierre, although scheduled to break out on the 5th, did
not until late on the 6th. It went east of Belgard. It starts to disintegrate.

A little later, following a radio conversation with Reichsführer-SS Himmler at
the headquarters of Army Group Vistula, Brigf. Krukenberg and Obf. Puaud
'decided to break-out to the west in several echelons'.[97]

Now that the route to Kolberg seemed cut and with Russian forces holding
positions to the west of Körlin, the break-out would be attempted via Belgard still
held by the Wehrmacht. From Belgard, the division was to bear west, reach the

97   Soulat, page 56. However, the time and the contents of this conversation remain
      unknown. According to Mabire, page 444, RF-SS Himmler authorised the
      break-out. Curiously, at 1820 and then again at 1840, General Krebs, the chief of
      operations of the O.K.H., signalled to Lieutenant-General Kienzel at the
      headquarters of Army Group Vistula that, by order of the Führer, Group von Tettau
      was to hold its position. Undoubtedly, Himmler would have known or been made
      aware of this order. So did Himmler openly disobey the order? The answer is not
      known.

river Rega, traverse it and then make for the river Oder via Plathe or Greifenberg. If the dangerous withdrawal was to have any chance of success the Frenchmen would have to avoid the main roads criss-crossed by enemy columns, go across country, hide in the woods, live off the land, march at night and travel light. This was most important. Nothing should be carried to slow the withdrawal down.

The order of march was laid down at once: Ostuf. Fenet's I/RM and divisional headquarters was to be the vanguard. Then came de Hstuf. Bourmont's *Régiment de Reserve*. Hstuf. Bassompierre's II/RM was to be the rearguard. The assembly area was Körlin. The break-out was scheduled for 2300 hours.

After finalising the details, Brigf. Krukenberg, Staf. Zimmermann and Hstuf. Jauss drove to Redlin to join Fenet. Obf. Puaud was not with them; he had refused to join the vanguard because he wished to remain at Körlin 'until the departure of his last elements'.[98] The time was now around 1900 hours.[99]

Fahrschwadron A, which was already on the road to Kolberg, was ordered to turn around and return to Körlin.

Obf. Puaud and Hstuf. de Bourmont visited the headquarters of the II/RR. They told Ustuf. de Genouillac that, at 0200 hours on the 5th, the *Régiment de Reserve* was to set off 'to break through the encirclement'.[100] The battalion commander's hunger suddenly disappeared. After explaining the details of the plan his visitors left.

For de Bourmont, problems arose well before the hour of the break-out. Very few of his runners had returned and some units of Monneuse's I/RR were still far from Körlin. At 2100 hours, he decided to fetch the battalion himself. He came across Bartolomei's company, which had just reached Mechentin and was beginning to dig in. Ostuf. Bartolomei was ordered to withdraw to Körlin and to abandon all heavy equipment on the spot. However, horses were to be kept to transport the wounded. Bartolomei then assembled all the French SS troops around him. Only twenty were from his own company. Most were stragglers or those who had become detached from their parent units. Hurried by Bartolomei, they arrived at Körlin shortly before midnight.

Bartolomei wasted precious time before he found headquarters. He was greeted by Obf. Puaud who informed him that they would not be leaving straight away![101] And yet the break-out depended upon time and speed. In one corner Bartolomei saw Monneuse. He looked aged and exhausted.

As planned, the vanguard consisting of Ostuf. Fenet's I/RM and divisional headquarters left Redlin noiselessly at 2300 hours. As per orders, all heavy

<hr/>

98   Soulat, page 56. Curiously, according to Mabire, page 446, Obf. Puaud came to see Brigf. Krukenberg and told him that he would be leaving with the *Régiment de Reserve,* for the most part *légionnaire,* and not with the true 'SS' of the RM. Today, this has been impossible to verify.

99   Mabire, page 447.

100 The memoirs of de Genouillac. Yet, according to Mabire, page 447, by midnight of 4th/5th March 1945, Brigf. Krukenberg expected no French SS troops to be left in Körlin. Undoubtedly Krukenberg would have consulted and agreed this timetable with Puaud. From this, one can conclude that Puaud was quick to change his mind about the timetable of the break-out. Furthermore, it appears that Puaud did not convey his decision to Krukenberg who would have overruled him.

equipment had been abandoned. By 0200 hours, the vanguard was in sight of Belgard, ablaze from end to end.[102] The Wehrmacht was still holding the town and stubbornly resisting the Russians. The vanguard crossed the cemetery on the northern outskirts, then skirted round the town and proceeded south-east. The thick woods swallowed them up.

Towards 0100 hours on the 5th, Obf. Puaud had a sudden change of heart and took off by car with de Vaugelas and Renault to 'catch up' the vanguard. But the car broke down and they returned on foot to Körlin and the assembling *Régiment de Reserve*.[103]

Towards 0200 hours, the II/RR left its position along the Persante, joined the rest of the regiment[104] at Körlin and took the road to Belgard.[105] At the head of the column marched Hstuf. de Bourmont, the commander of the RR, and, beside

101   Mabire, page 448-449, presumably based on the eyewitness account of Bartolomei. The delay brought about by Obf. Puaud to the withdrawal of the *Régiment de Reserve* has never been fully explained and will forever remain a mystery. Saint-Loup explains, page 295, that Puaud had wanted to hold Körlin twenty-four hours longer than that asked of him by the Germans.

102   Some doubt that 'Belgard was ablaze'. As a prisoner Sepchant happened to cross Belgard along the railway line from north to south shortly after the capitulation. He saw no visible trace of fire. Moreover, he spent the best part of a day (and perhaps the following night) in one of the two rail stations and it was completely intact. (Letter to the author, 14/6/99.)

103   Soulat, page 57, repeated by Mabire, page 453. However, Ustuf. de Genouillac was to meet Obf. Puaud, Stubaf. de Vaugelas, Hstuf. Renault, and Ustuf. Delile later that same night near the Persante. And this is what he learnt from them. To join the retreating troops, the four of them had left Körlin in a Volkswagen car driven by Delile. Travelling without lights, Delile had crashed into an abandoned vehicle, throwing Puaud into the windscreen. After abandoning their wreck, they had set off across country in search of de Bourmont's column and this is how they came upon Ustuf. de Genouillac and the two men with him. Delile was the only one of the four to be armed. The group would cross the Persante and find de Bourmont's column. Regarding this, undoubtedly, Soulat and de Genouillac are referring to the same departure of Puaud by car from Körlin. But importantly, the memoirs of de Genouillac suggest that at no time was Puaud with de Bourmont's column on the east bank of the Persante. This contrasts with the presence of Puaud with de Bourmont's regiment before Belgard (cited by Mabire, pages 453-455) or his presence in Belgard cemetery (cited by Saint-Loup, pages 297-298.) In response to Mabire and Saint-Loup, if Puaud was with de Bourmont's column he did not march beside de Bourmont; de Genouillac was beside de Bourmont and does not recall the presence of Puaud. Also, would Puaud and the three staff officers separated from de Bourmont's column without an armed escort? This is doubtful, but considering the great confusion of that night just about anything could have happened. In conclusion, the author has reservations about the presence of Puaud and the command group with de Bourmont's column on the east bank, but has not been able to substantiate that they were not.

104   The *Régiment de Reserve* had a strength of more than 2,000 men (Mabire, page 453) or 3,000 men (Soulat, page 57).

105   De Genouillac, letter to the author, 29/4/1997.

him, Ustuf. de Genouillac, the battalion commander of the II/RR. Confusion overtook the *Régiment de Reserve*, which had disregarded Krukenberg's orders and marched with horse-drawn wagons and much of its unnecessary heavy equipment. All units were completely disorganised.

Belgard was not far off when Hstuf. de Bourmont called the *Régiment de Reserve* to a halt. The city was still ablaze from end to end and the continuing sounds of battle could be heard. He told Ustuf. de Genouillac to take a patrol into Belgard and find a bridge over the Persante.

Accompanied by the first two soldiers he met, Ustuf. de Genouillac penetrated into the city centre as far as a large bridge over the river Persante and came under heavy fire. 'Convinced that the din they had unleashed was every bit as good as a progress report', they hurried out of the city. Skirting round the city, they came again to the Persante that they followed westwards in search of a bridge. It was dark and snowing lightly. They were alone; de Bourmont had not waited for their return.

In the cold, the *Régiment de Reserve*, halted two kilometres before Belgard, had waited and waited. Small groups started to leave the column and push on. Others bunched around their best hope: former NCOs of the LVF. Some others even tried to get their heads down. Officers tried to get some order into their companies, but officers and men alike were totally spent. Then the order to about-turn went down the column.[106]

In ever increasing confusion the disintegrating column backtracked to Körlin. Carts overturned. Horses bolted. Then another order was received. The *Régiment de Reserve* was to cross the Persante between Körlin and Belgard and continue its march south-east on the left bank. Men hurried off in search of crossing points. Like many, Hstuf. de Bourmont, the regimental commander, was overcome by despair.

---

106   And yet, according to Saint-Loup, page 295, towards 0400 hours, the men of the *Régiment de Reserve* appeared before Belgard cemetery, where they were greeted by Russian machine-gun fire. By now, Belgard had fallen to the Russians. The Frenchmen rushed into the cemetery and sheltered behind the tombstones. The enemy infiltrated. Machine guns rattled out and rifles cracked from all sides. It soon became impossible to distinguish who was firing on who. Suddenly a shout was heard. It was: "French SS forward". This was repeated by a thousand voices. The Frenchmen responded and dashed forwards. Grenades exploded here and there. Their attack was irresistible and the Russians fled. Advancing among his men, Puaud was hit in the calf and dropped to his knees. It was not a serious wound and he got back on his feet and limped off. The cemetery was taken, but casualties had been heavy.

Saint-Loup continues that the Frenchmen resumed their march. They split up and went in different directions. The bulk went to the west of Belgard and continued southwards. Some also ventured into Belgard itself. At the central square they came upon an indescribable scene. It was 'entirely covered with corpses of women, old men and children. All women, whatever their age, had been disembowelled'. Terrified and haggard Wehrmacht soldiers who had taken refuge in cellars came up one by one. They were handed arms and incorporated into French SS units.

In response to this, no other source confirms this action in the cemetery. Also, the notion that elements of the RR entered and actually captured Belgard from the Russians is disputed by de Genouillac (letter to the author, 26/5/97). Moreover, Mabire suggests that the RR gave wide berth to Belgard.

For over an hour, de Genouillac and his two companions walked alongside the Persante searching for a way to cross. Suddenly, to his right, de Genouillac saw some silhouettes running towards them. Fearing that they were Russians, he called out to them in a combination of Russian and French dialects: "*Stoi Halte*". When the silhouettes revealed themselves he saw the faces of Obf. Puaud, Stubaf. de Vaugelas, Hstuf. Renault and Ustuf. Delile. Embarrassed about scaring them to death, he offered Puaud his apologies. Nevertheless, the newcomers were not altogether displeased to come across some armed individuals because Delile was the only one of them carrying a weapon.

The group continued along the Persante for some time without finding a bridge. Suddenly Ustuf. de Genouillac spotted an iron boat aground in the rushes less than two metres away from the bank. Their luck had changed or had it? Unfortunately, de Genouillac could not reach the boat with the end of his rifle. It was just too far away. As he tried desperately to reach out he let go of the person holding him and plunged headfirst into the river. He collected the boat. Using their rifle butts as oars, they managed to get the heavy skiff moving and across to the other bank. As they were disembarking it stopped snowing and the fog lifted, revealing in the early morning light a long column crossing the river four or five hundred metres away. It was de Bourmont! They had found him.

De Bourmont and the *Régiment de Reserve* pressed on. For the time being there was no question of stopping to rest. Only the woods far off offered the dead tired men relative security.

The going got more and more difficult and very time consuming. All kinds of obstacles had to be crossed: streams, hedges, barbed wire fences and water holes. Progress was slow, much too slow.

By daybreak, the *Régiment de Reserve* was only in the woods near Zarnefanz to the south-west of Belgard which was still burning. Thick fog had come down, affording the regiment some protection.

Among those to make it out of Körlin and into the woods was Uscha. Mercier of Fahrschwadron A. As per orders, Fahrschwadron A had abandoned all heavy equipment. Mercier travelled light. He had distributed the few provisions he had (tins of food and sausage) and gave to those who wished them the things that up to now he had guarded jealously, but kept in his pockets the unit's records. A little later, one of his comrades, a *Milicien* NCO, exploded with anger when he noted that he had lost his camera 'because of those bloody records'.

Mercier followed his *chef*, Hstuf. Schlisler. Along with some comrades, he 'played the sheep dog', encouraging those of his column to keep grouped and moving. The route that his column took was first along a main road and then through a wood.[107]

107   Mercier, letter to the author, 6/11/2001. Mercier does not know to which column he belonged but curiously he cannot recall crossing the Persante. In this same column was Rttf. Sepchant of the Headquarters Company/RM. He recalls an advance solely through woods (letter to the author, 12/1/2001). He can neither recall the about-turn on the road to Belgard, nor the search for a bridge over the river Persante, nor the presence of streams, hedges, and holes of water to get round or cross. Because of this he is now convinced that his column had followed a totally different route to that of the bulk of the division. Thus, the possibility exists that a third column evacuated Körlin during the night of 4-5 March 1945. The composition of this third

The horses slowed the progress of the column. Despite his perfect ignorance of matters equestrian, Mercier gave advice to the former drivers on the subtle manoeuvre required to get the horses to cross the ditches. Day broke. There was thick fog. Those leading the horses by the bridle were repeatedly told that on no account were they to mount them, but they could not be stopped from leaving the wood to walk more easily.[108]

The massacre

Towards 0800 hours, under the cover of the fog, the *Régiment de Reserve* started to move across a vast and bare plain. The troops were dangerously crowded together.

Marching within earshot of Obf. Puaud was Ostuf. Dr. Métais. He heard Obf. Puaud ask: "What's happening? It's crazy! Who is in front?" The reply was "De Bourmont." Puaud then turned to Stubaf. de Vaugelas and ordered: "Take a horse. Tell him to find an unoccupied wood immediately, stop there and organise protection."

As Stubaf. de Vaugelas galloped off towards the head of the column, Obf. Puaud exclaimed: "It's crazy. And yet I had recommended hiding away in the woods during the day. If this continues, we're heading for a massacre!"[109]

Moments later, the thick fog suddenly lifted, exposing the regiment to daylight and presenting a perfect target for nearby Russian columns of armour and motorised artillery on the move.[110]

There was no cover for the Frenchmen. Russian mortars and machine guns poured murderous fire onto the Frenchmen and in minutes hundreds were dead and wounded. Tanks rumbled towards them. Bayle, a witness to the massacre, speaks of at least fifty T–34/85s with all guns blazing in an unbroken line. Anti-tank weapons might have turned the tables, but the *Régiment de Reserve* had handed theirs over to the rearguard at Körlin. Nothing could now stop them. The tanks crushed into pulp everything in their path. It was a massacre. The Frenchmen fled and made for the shelter of the woods.

The few dramatic and terrible accounts that exist of the massacre are worth recording here. Jacques C., a former *Milicien*, had this to say of the massacre[111]:

> We didn't know where we were going and I think our *chefs* no longer knew. With this fog and the snow it was difficult to find our way. We heard the sound that the tank tracks were making. When the fog lifted, we noticed that we were advancing right in the middle of T–34 columns. Immediately shells started to

column is not known, but when the column was sighted and overrun by the Russians Sepchant was captured and taken to a barn where prisoners from various units were assembled. There were medical and supply personnel, engineers, and German 'support' personnel, who were known to Sepchant from his LVF days. This suggests that the column comprised the support services.

108   Mercier still regrets that they had kept the horses, which 'loaded us down, delayed us and, later, got us spotted' (letter to the author, 6/11/2001).

109   Cited by Soulat, page 57. Saint-Loup also repeats, page 299, the same eyewitness account of Métais, although there are one or two minor changes of words.

110   Some have questioned the site of the massacre. In a letter to Mounine, dated 29/7/99, Sepchant suggests further west near Natztow. This is far from Belgard and Zarnefanz.

111   Delperrié de Bayac, page 606.

rain down on us. There was no organised resistance. We simply tried not to be caught. I was taken prisoner around 1100 hours or midday.

As for Hscha. Rostaing, he was stretched out on the ground under a fir sharing the last piece of black bread he had with his orderly, Martinet, when the silence was broken by an explosion. He scrambled to his feet, machine pistol in hand. Unsure of what was happening, he went to the edge of the wood. There was a second explosion in the exact spot he had just left. The fir he had been under moments earlier had been uprooted.

Rostaing was convinced that they had been spotted and decided to make for a small village in the distance. Followed by his men, he raced across the vast glacis between the hamlet and the wood. When the fog suddenly lifted Russian tanks were only four hundred metres behind them. An unequal battle began. Shells crashed murderously into the French troops who had no cover at all on the flat ground. Rostaing tried to run faster. He was out of breath. His orderly was hit by a machine-gun burst and went down. Rostaing did not stop. His fear of capture by the Russians drove him forward. He kept running and running. Shells were exploding around him. Some even ricocheted off the frozen ground. He could not help thinking that the next was for him. It seemed impossible for anybody to survive. All that mattered was getting out of this hell.

Finally he reached the village. It was occupied by the Russians! The battalion was following on his heels. Firing to his right and left, he crossed the village. Bullets mewed all around him, but his luck held. Some were less fortunate. He climbed up a slope, crossed its crest, hurtled down the other side and rushed into the woods.

Rostaing then records that Puaud, de Vaugelas, Renault and other officers 'did the same' to his left. He estimates that some one hundred and twenty men managed to finish this 'race of hope'. Turning round, Rostaing saw thirty of his comrades, who could not follow, stop and raise their arms.

Ustuf. de Genouillac was also a witness to the massacre. He was sat at the foot of a fir tree, trying to empty his boots of water, when an explosion rang out nearby. This was followed by the crack, then the din of a large fir tree smashing its way to the ground through the branches of its neighbours. This caused great panic among the troops who fled in all directions and de Genouillac found himself swept along in the middle of a terrorised crowd. Almost immediately the true nature of the danger facing them revealed itself in all its horror: hell was unleashed.

Going in what seemed the opposite direction to this inferno, de Genouillac then found himself outside of the wood on a ploughed field covered with snow. His boots became ice-blocks that make it difficult to run. Regardless, he continued to press on. It started to snow again. Now and then he was passed by silhouettes that were going in every direction, except his.

The snow then stopped 'as if raising the curtain on a theatre scene': hundreds of grey silhouettes made their appearance on a vast plain. Up to then the Russians had been firing blind, but now they could choose their targets. Transfixed, de Genouillac came under fire and watched the earth and snow dance around him. It did not occur to him to fall to the ground and feign death. Somehow he made it to the first trees of the forest bordering Belgard plain. He was out of breath and at the end of his strength. He saw some buildings. As he moved towards them he encountered once again the command group of Puaud, de Vaugelas, Renault and Delile.

Offering to walk point, Ustuf. de Genouillac led the command group deeper into the forest and to a narrow track which he surveyed through binoculars. To his left about two hundred metres away there was a suspicious looking object that brought him to shout: "Tank to the left!" Nevertheless, the tank was stationary and relatively blind in such surroundings. He cleared the track at one jump and then yelled to the others that they could cross. Nothing stirred. After waiting several minutes he pressed on.

Uscha. Mercier of Fahrschwadron A was in a wood when the fog lifted. He recalls what happened next:[112]

We heard a fusillade in the plain on our right. With *Capitaine* Schlisler, we observed what was happening in the plain and saw many Russian tanks approach.

We were not armed to face them and the only solution was to take advantage of the thickness of the bush to conceal us and wait for the Russians to go away.

At first, there was some panic. Men ran in every direction. Some shouted 'Les Soldbuch! Les Soldbuch!' and started to tear them up. *Capitaine* Schlisler was against this, saying to them: "You have nothing to hide!"

And he restored calm [by] promising them that he would get them out of this spot, which was perhaps a bit optimistic.

Lieutenant Darrigade left with one member of the escort (combat) platoon and tried his luck at another end of the wood.

Some were killed or captured in the plain stretching out on our right.

Two steps from me, a man of Fahrschwadron A committed suicide by firing a Mauser bullet into his mouth. I knew him by sight since 1941. He belonged to the *train de combat* of the 3rd Company of the I. Battalion of the LVF. In 'Charlemagne', he was a driver. I think he was a Sturmmann. He was rather silent, but I believe that, if before his desperate gesture, I had spoken to him with one of our ritual gibes, such as 'Well, old man! It's always the same', I may have influenced his fate. I still regret this. He was called Roche.

The Russians undertook to clean up the plain and started to take care of the forest, but the vegetation was dense enough to enable us to camouflage ourselves.

It is difficult for me to estimate how long we remained hidden in the bushes. Nothing was happening. And then, a Russian, who could not have been any older than fifteen, entered the wood yelling 'Komm! Komm!' He saw nobody and, when he passed beside me, I had the ludicrous idea to shoot him down, without imagining that the slightest gunfire would have alerted the Russians outside the wood and caused a massacre. Luckily, my pistol jammed.

My LVF comrade *Sergent* Godard, one of the old brigade [LVF veteran of 1941], applied the partisans' method and climbed a tree. He was to be flushed out shortly after and was shot in the leg to help him down. Most fortunately, the wound was slight, but made him suffer at the start of his captivity.

And then other Russian soldiers entered the wood. We could no longer remain (where we were) and *Capitaine* Schlisler took us (off) in a breakthrough attempt across the plain.

Suddenly, we found ourselves facing about thirty tanks.

112   Mercier, letter to the author, 12/10/2001.

Capitaine Schlisler gave the signal for surrender and angrily threw down his submachine gun.

I expected to be shot in the nape of the neck and wished to die with dignity.

I was greatly surprised to note that the Krasnoïarmist who took charge of me did not experience an immediate need to make me pass from life to death, but was concerned above all with getting my watch …

I had much to learn.

Unbeknown to Mercier, Uscha. Jean-Pierre Lefèvre, who became a good friend after the war, was beside him when Sturmmann Roche committed suicide.

After serving first with the 10/58, Lefèvre came to Pomerania as the *chef* of the command section of the 8/58. Made de Bourmont's bodyguard for the retreat from Körlin, he lost him in the chaos following a Soviet bombardment with mortars and Stalin's organs. He searched for de Bourmont, but it was as though he had vanished into thin air. On Belgard plain when the Russian tanks emerged he took to the woods and hid away.

Russian tanks and infantry approached. Lefèvre destroyed his Soldbuch and his papers, only keeping a photo of his parents and a picture of La Sainte Vierge.

The Russians started to comb the woods. A soldier near Lefèvre fired a bullet into his mouth. [This was Sturmmann Roche.] With no means of escape, he surrendered.[113]

Capture was also the fate of Rttf. Sepchant. He said this of how his adventure came to an end:

> Suddenly, as day was breaking, we discovered that we were in contact with the enemy. Immediately, an officer on horseback that I did not know ordered: "Direction due north". I followed another in the direction of the south-east. This was to throw myself into the lion's jaw. I soon heard pleas of "Friend! Friend!" And had as neighbours only a young Feldwebel, smoking a cigarette peacefully and, a little further, a Major, who seemed as relaxed.
>
> A Russian soldier appeared and disappeared. I brought him to the attention of the Major who advised me not to bother him: "I'm a doctor." A Russian tank approached and went away. I noticed a sheet of water and immersed myself in it up to my nostrils. For whole hours I heard bursts from submachine guns. One of them had 'my number on.' I felt nothing and only saw the leggings and boots of the gunner, but later I counted a good half-dozen small tears on the collar of my greatcoat.
>
> When the calm returned, interested by the faraway rumbling of the cannonade, I got out of my bath with the intention of approaching it. I did not get far. Suddenly, behind me, I heard cries of rage. A patrol—two men and a twelve-year-old kid—had caught me. I was presented to an officer who interrogated me in perfect German.

---

113   For accounts of Lefèvre's capture see Mabire, pages 465-466, and Delperrié de Bayac, pages 605-606. There are, however, differences between the two sources, of which one is noteworthy. According to Mabire, Lefèvre was on Belgard plain when disaster overtook the *Régiment de Reserve* whereas Delperrié de Bayac suggests that 'Jean-Pierre L.' was not with the main body. In response to this, de Bourmont was with the *Régiment de Reserve*, which was the main body of 'Charlemagne'.

Stubaf. de Vaugelas and several other divisional officers were also taken prisoner. Although beaten up, de Vaugelas was not put to death.

So what fate awaited those who went undetected? Invariably death or capture which came days if not weeks later. In small groups, sometimes in pairs or even singly, they tried to make their way westwards to the Oder through enemy territory. Few would rejoin the German front. Not only were the survivors of the massacre pursued by the Russians, and later by their Polish allies of the 1st Polish Army, the cold, the snow and the wind were also on Stalin's side. Weakened by dysentery and a lack of food, wounds and fatigue took their toll. Little help was forthcoming from the terrorised local population. Danger lurked everywhere. The fate of many is just not known.

Ostuf. de Londaiz, the cavalryman and former *Milicien*, who had made himself the commander of the remnants of the 'regimental engineer platoon', was marching at the head of the *Régiment de Reserve* when the fog lifted. He was so close to the Russians that it proved relatively easy to burst through their thin 'cordon' and slip undetected into the woods.

Around him Ostuf. de Londaiz formed a small group which was determined to wage war. As luck would have it, they came upon an isolated farmhouse and food. They ate and drank in peace. Suddenly there was a shout from the lookout posted outside the farmhouse. The Russians were coming. In fact they turned out to be Polish regulars.[114] They had an armoured car with them. Strangely, de Londaiz, machine pistol in hand, went alone to confront them and was killed outright by a machine gun burst. His men returned fire. The Poles replied. Abandoning the farmhouse, the French SS men made off through the woods. Some of the group would later make it back to the Oder.

Ustuf. de Genouillac came so near to freedom; on or around 13th March 1945, he was captured at Cammin on the shores of the Oder. After the massacre on Belgard plain he came across isolated groups which followed him for several days. In this way, his group may have grown to around forty, but he lost them all crossing a road along which enemy convoys were travelling. Fortunately, on that same day, two Wehrmacht soldiers joined him and followed him until their capture by Polish troops. He was not ill-treated by them or by the Russians to whom he was handed over.

Two Waffengrenadier, one from Hstuf. Roy's 9/57, were captured after spending four days 'on the run'. Fearing the worse because of their Spiegel collar insignia, they were dragged before two Russian officers who, as luck would have it, had studied in Paris and spoke French! The officers integrated the two of them into their unit as cooks. However, one month later, the officers warned them that their unit was leaving for the front and that, consequently, they could no longer keep them. Thus, the two French prisoners found themselves handed over to NKVD troops.[115]

The ultimate fate of the commander of 'Charlemagne' still remains a mystery. Nevertheless, Puaud did not meet his death on Belgard plain; he was seen on horseback by some soldiers around 1400 hours on that tragic day of the 5th. Wounded

114   Saint-Loup, page 325. However, according to Mabire, page 468, the Russians turned out to be Polish partisans.
115   Cited in the article "*Mein Freund Georges*".

in the shoulder, he ordered them to try and reach the west.[116] Of Puaud's subsequent movements, Ostuf. Multrier has stated the following:[117]

> General Puaud, wounded in the leg, was dragging himself along a road. A French NCO met him and sat him on the rear seat of a motorcycle. But they were attacked by Russian snipers. General Puaud was wounded again. Too serious to continue on. Approaching Greifenberg, the NCO left his commander in a hotel and placed him in a ground floor room where other wounded were already. Then he went off on foot. This NCO would return the following day in civilian clothes, although the Russians had seized the town. He then saw that the ground floor room where he left General Puaud was empty. But the ground and the walls were bloodstained.

This version of Puaud's disappearance was recounted by the NCO, a former *Milicien*, to Multrier, also a former *Milicien*, at Prague in the last days of the war. Multrier then wrote down the story exactly as he heard it from the mouth of the NCO whose identity still remains unknown.[118] There are no reasons to discount this version, even if fifty kilometres separate Greifenberg from Belgard. Thus, along with the other non-transportable wounded at the hotel, Puaud may have been murdered by the Russians who were probably unaware that he was a General. Because it is fair to say that even at this late stage of the war the Russians still prized the capture of a General. But the possibility also exists that Puaud died of his wounds while in captivity.

After the war there were many reported sightings of Puaud. Marcel H. of *La Milice d'Angers* claims that he saw Puaud alive and well in a POW camp at the start of May 1945 and, then later, in Russia in the uniform of a Red Army officer.[119] Puaud was also sighted in the uniform of a NKVD officer in East Berlin![120] Indeed, it was even claimed that Puaud became the head of the Russian police in Berlin![121] Undoubtedly all such sightings were rumours or wishful thinking. And although Puaud's ultimate fate has never been substantiated the only conclusion that can be reached is that he lost his life somewhere in Pomerania.

Although a doctor, Hstuf. Bonnefoy realised that his life was in the balance when he was captured with a group of German policemen and Ukrainians of the 'Vlasov army' who could expect no mercy from the Soviets. They were loaded onto an American lorry and driven away. As expected, retribution followed swiftly. Now

---

116 Soulat, page 58.
117 "*Histoire #32*", page 135.
118 This same testimony is retold by Mabire, page 473-474, and by Saint-Loup, page 518, as that of '*commandant* M.' However, there are differences between all three versions, although they are of little significance: according to Mabire, the NCO returned to Greifenberg in the company of a comrade from 'Charlemagne', whereas Saint-Loup has the NCO returning to Greifenberg days later and as a prisoner. In addition, Saint-Loup states that after the NCO saw the hospital empty and covered with blood he came to the conclusion that all the wounded there had been put to death.
119 Delperrié de Bayac, page 606.
120 Saint-Loup, page 518.
121 Giolitto, page 143.

and then the lorry stopped and each time two prisoners were made to kneel at the roadside and summarily executed. It was now only a matter of time before it was his turn. It came all too soon when he was lined up with nine others near a forest.

Suddenly, a staff car drew up and out stepped a high-ranking officer. An argument ensued between him and the officer in charge of the transport. While this was going on, a female soldier, who was with the high-ranking officer, came over to the prisoners. Bonnefoy did not know why she appeared to be especially interested in him and him alone. She then pointed Bonnefoy out to the other Russians and told them that he was a doctor and was not to be executed. It was only then that he understood that the female soldier was a doctor too. He was saved.

Bonnefoy was taken before the high-ranking Soviet officer who, on noticing his French armshield, tried to converse with him in broken French. Bonnefoy had much to say, but the Soviet officer seemed to understand little, if anything, of the replies he gave. As the Soviet officer returned to his car the nine other prisoners were put to death. Indeed life had become a lottery! Spared, Bonnefoy got back on the lorry, which continued eastwards.

Out of hell

Against all the odds, Ostuf. Fenet brought his entire battalion to Meseritz.

As dawn was breaking on 5th March, Brigf. Krukenberg had the men of Ostuf. Fenet's I/RM hide in the woods, but they could not rest because it was that cold and still snowing continuously. There was, of course, no question of lighting a fire or even a cigarette.

Hours later, Brigf. Krukenberg held a *petit conseil de guerre* with Staf. Zimmermann, Hstuf. Jauss and Ostuf. Fenet. Concerned that his men would be frozen stiff by a whole day of keeping still and thus in no condition to set off again, Fenet insisted that they should not wait till night to push on. Besides, there was no time to lose. He proposed that they conduct a daytime march by taking advantage of the vast forest extending westwards and the disorder in the wake of the Russian advance. Krukenberg was won over by reason. His overriding desire was to save the men to fight for another day.

Suddenly, all could hear the sounds of battle from the region of Zarnefanz, Ristow and Boissin. They had no inkling that it was the main body of the division.

Towards 0900 hours, the men of the I/RM started out again. Ostuf. Fenet himself was at their head. Silently they marched on and on. In this way, they came to the Rambin (Rabino)-Belgard road and also danger; the Russians had lined the road with watch posts. There was no way forward without being spotted and being drawn into a fight. They detoured and crossed at a point out of sight of the Russian watch posts.

As night fell they suddenly lost the cover of the woods. They took a chance on the cover of darkness and marched on. After skirting round the village of Stolzenberg from the south, they came to the main Schievelbein-Kolberg road. From roadside ditches, they watched a continual stream of Russian tanks and trucks pass by. Between convoys, small groups of Frenchmen dashed across the road, hid away on the other side and waited for others to cross. All made it safely across. They continued on.

Unseen, the French column crossed a village occupied by the headquarters of a Russian regiment. But when several men of the rearguard under Hstuf. Jauss entered a house in search of something to drink they woke the Russians there. Shots were fired. The Frenchmen made off. Fortunately, casualties were not heavy.

The column then came to the village of Falkenberg which was strewn with the debris of war: burnt out tanks, disfigured corpses, and abandoned rifles, tent sheets, equipment and ammunition. The smell of death hung in the air. Hurried by their officers, they quickly crossed the village. On they went.

At 0400 hours, the column reached the village of Schlenzig. By now, the men were totally spent and Brigf. Krukenberg finally granted a three-hour rest. It was over all too soon and the I/RM continued on its way again. At this point Greifenberg was still its destination.

In the morning, Krukenberg and Zimmermann learnt from German peasants that the Russians were at Plathe (Ploty), fifteen kilometres south-east of Greifenberg, and that Greifenberg itself was totally encircled. This was worrying. Fenet and Jauss were immediately informed, but it was thought better not to let the men know this bad news just yet. Undaunted, they pushed on, keeping to the forests and the woods. The snow was still falling and the temperature was still well below zero centigrade.

Brigf. Krukenberg then decided to head north to the village of Petersfelde (Poradz). They arrived in the afternoon. Unoccupied, the village now awaited the Russians with white flags from every window. Some Frenchmen were angered by this sight and wanted to tear them down, but their NCOs pushed them on.

Once again, the civilians were the best source of information. From them, the Frenchmen learnt that a Wehrmacht Army Corps was regrouping at Meseritz, some ten kilometres away.

At nightfall, the I/RM arrived at Meseritz. The remnants of General Munzel's Corps Group were camped in the village and around the grounds of the chateau in which the General had established his headquarters.

For bringing the I/RM out of hell, Brigf. Krukenberg decided to award Ostuf. Fenet with the Iron Cross 1st Class.[122] Unable to obtain the relevant decoration for Fenet, Krukenberg went to General Munzel with his predicament to which the General replied by unhooking his and handing it over. Some moments later, in a brief ceremony, the Brigadeführer decorated Fenet.

However, not all those with Fenet had made it out. The day of the 5th had presented Ustuf. Fayard and his FLAK Company with few problems, but then, on the morning of the 6th, he and his men had suddenly found themselves encircled in a wood. It was each for his own. Some were captured. Others escaped and managed to dress in civilian clothes thanks to the help of German refugees. This was how Stabsscharführer Hscha. Lenoir, Uscha. Lhomme, Gefechtsschreiber Uscha. Trinqenaux, Schirmeister Uscha. Deschamps, tailor Ob.Schutz Chomy, telephonist Cardet and the young Russian Samassoudov, the company mascot, escaped.

122 Mabire, page 17. However, according to Saint-Loup, page 327, it was General Munzel who, on the basis of a report submitted by Krukenberg, conferred on Fenet his own Iron Cross.

Ustuf. Fayard was captured but he too, with some others, managed to escape.[123] Days later, they came across Lenoir and the others with him. One by one they went their own way.

At Meseritz or near to Greifenberg, a group of survivors from the massacre on Belgard plain led by Ustuf. Leune joined Fenet.

The odyssey of the group led by Ustuf. Leune began in a small wood some hours after the massacre on Belgard plain. The group was some sixty or one hundred strong.[124] Among them were officers Ostuf. Métais, Ustuf. Herpe, Ostuf. Tardan and Ustuf. Leune. Of them, it was Ustuf. Leune who immediately took the group in hand. And from that moment on the eyes of the former Merchant Navy petty officer remained glued to a compass as he led the group westwards.

Three different accounts exist of how Leune guided these men to safety.[125]

The first two sources, Saint-Loup and Rostaing, are not dissimilar in their coverage of the first few days. They recount that for three days the cold and hungry survivors 'advanced' without making a stop or eating. They detoured tens of times to avoid concentrations of Red Army troops and tanks. Even so there were a few close shaves. None more so than when they were caught by two T–34s whilst crossing a strip of bare ground between woods. They ran for their lives and somehow managed to lose them. Remarkably there were no losses.

On the second day, they came to the main Belgard-Stolzenberg road and, without waiting for night-fall, dashed across one by one. There were no losses. They were so tired that they imagined tanks everywhere. These tanks often turned out to be nothing more than abandoned cars or bundles of firewood! They plodded on.

Rostaing continues that to quicken the pace the wounded were abandoned at a farm(house) in the knowledge that they would be well cared for and then dressed in civilian clothes. The others carried on. They came across a terror-stricken peasant, but their uniforms seemed to reassure him. With a smile on his face, he now approached them. He was a Pole who, days before, with his family, had fled from his village occupied by the Russians.

The Pole had an abundance of provisions with him, which he shared with them. He also gave them information on enemy emplacements. Finally the survivors rested. They slept all night.

On the following morning, they set off again and, hours later, were lucky enough to meet a German couple who knew the region like the back of their hand. On a map Leune was carrying, the couple drew the route the Frenchmen should take to reach Greifenberg. In fact, to make sure the Frenchmen were on the right route, the couple accompanied them part of the way. Greifenberg was now no

123 Cited in the article "*La SS-Französische Flakbatterie*". According to Soulat, page 58, repeated by Bayle, "*San et Persante*", page 179, a detachment under Ustuf. Fayard (presumably his weakened FLAK Company) had joined a Volkssturm Company and were captured on the 7th by Russian tanks. This could be possible.
124 Soulat cites sixty (page 58) and Saint-Loup cites one hundred (page 321).
125 There is a fourth account which is that of Mabire ("*Mourir à Berlin*", page 9), but his source, undoubtedly page 67 of Soulat's "*Histoire de la Charlemagne*", was later amended because it was inaccurate. For this reason, the author has not included Mabire's account.

more than forty kilometres away. Elated, the hardships of the previous days were almost forgotten.

Next morning, after covering twenty kilometres, they suddenly came upon a village. It was a picture of peace and quiet. Its occupants were coming and going about their daily business. But could this be? Rostaing took a patrol into the village. It was not occupied by the Russians.

In 'this small corner of paradise' they took the opportunity to shave, eat and sleep off their tiredness before pushing on to Greifenberg. To honour the uniform they were wearing, they wanted to make a dignified entry into the town which was now only twenty kilometres away. The column stretched out along the road. From flasks they drank the milk they had acquired earlier that same morning. 'It was a fantastic energiser'.

At the edge of a wood appeared some German soldiers. Nearby was Ostuf. Fenet's I/RM and Brigf. Krukenberg's headquarters staff.

According to Soulat,[126] on the morning of 7th March 1945, Ustuf. Leune and some sixty men joined Ostuf. Fenet's I/RM at Meseritz. Their guardian angel was a French prisoner of war they met quite by chance; he fed them and dissuaded them from staying on the same route, a route which would have led them straight into the Russians. And then, finally, he showed them a pathway through the under-growth, which enabled them that same evening to find Brigf. Krukenberg and *bataillon* Fenet.

In contrast, Saint-Loup recounts that on the third day despair set in after they had been going round in circles for hours on end. Totally exhausted, they sank into the snow. At that point Tardan suggested splitting up the men into two groups to give them a better chance of getting through. However, no decision appears to have been made. For the first time Leune hesitated. They settled down for the night, which was rent by the nearby sound of a tank battle around midnight. Next morning, two groups, one under Leune and the other under Tardan, set out. 'To conform to the inexorable law of the retreat', the wounded German warrant officer, transported thus far on horseback, was abandoned.

Ustuf. Leune is next pictured arriving at Meseritz chateau where General Munzel had established his headquarters. Camped around the chateau were the survivors of Munzel's battered Corps Group as well as Ostuf. Fenet's virtually intact I/RM.

In conclusion, while there is some agreement between the accounts, there is little or none between all three. As such, no account can be readily dismissed. However, what can be said is that some days after the massacre on Belgard plain a group of survivors led by Leune joined Fenet's battalion at Meseritz or near to Greifenberg.

Unlike Fenet, Leune was not decorated for the feat of bringing 'his' group of survivors out of hell.

Hstuf. Roy and Ustuf. Martret joined Fenet at Meseritz. After the massacre they had started out with a group that was one hundred-strong and led by a French Haupsturmführer.[127] As the group made its way westwards through a gauntlet of hell it lost men in ambushes and to wounds and exhaustion. Before long Roy and

---

126   Soulat, pages 58 and 89.
127   Martret cannot recall the name of the French Haupsturmführer.

Martret were alone. As luck would have it, they met a platoon of Sturmgeschütze that took them all the way to Meseritz.

Another group did make it 'out of hell'. On the morning of 5th March[128], some one hundred and fifty French and German stragglers assembled around three assault guns at Fritzow and struck north to Kolberg. Halfway there, in a small village, the group was engaged by Soviet tanks, but still managed to pass and then break through the enemy investment of the city.

Bartolomei's Company

The fate of the *Régiment de Reserve* on Belgard plain was not shared by its rearguard, the ninety or two hundred[129] men of Ostuf. Bartolomei's 2nd Company of the II/RR. Two kilometres before Belgard, Bartolomei's Company was ordered to halt and cover the retreat of the *Régiment de Reserve*. Hstuf. de Perricot's parting words were: "Only set off again on a new order. *Général* Puaud will not forget about you."[130]

From Belgard came the noise of battle. Hours passed and still no new orders. Towards 0700 hours, feeling abandoned and sensing the growing anxiety of his men, Bartolomei gave the order to start out to Belgard. Suddenly they came under mortar fire. The fog lifted. A Russian tank emerged some tens of metres away and opened up. Panic-stricken, they scattered. They too were without anti-tank weapons. To escape the Russians, many ran back towards Körlin.

Ostuf. Bartolomei managed to assemble several men around him and set off back to Körlin where the II/RM should still be. Approaching Körlin, they came under violent fire again; by now, the Russians had completely invested the town. They turned around and took refuge in a copse.

Following the Persante, they went back up to Belgard in the hope of rejoining de Bourmont and the *Régiment de Reserve*. By means of a footbridge, they got across onto the left bank. Trying to avoid the open fields, they slipped from wood to wood.

The time was around midday when, in a wood, Bartolomei's group met up with three officers and 100 or 150[131] men who had escaped the morning massacre on Belgard plain. They were led by Hstuf. de Bourmont. Thereupon, they decided to make for the region of Stettin by night marches. To march by day in a region filled by the rumbling of Russian tanks would be suicide.

A snowstorm set in and Bartolomei found himself separated from the other group. He continued on. As for de Bourmont, Bartolomei was the last person to see him alive. And although de Bourmont was never heard of again, there is little doubt that he met his death in Pomerania.[132]

Bartolomei's group, now of platoon strength,[133] spent the whole of the following night, the 5th/6th, marching to the south-west. At dawn on the 6th, Bartolomei took shelter in the loft of a farmhouse. He was disturbed by the farm owner fetching hay for his livestock with a pitchfork! Almost immediately a Russian submachine-gun barked and bullets passed near him. He desperately tried

---

128   The date is unconfirmed (Soulat, page 58).
129   Soulat cites ninety (page 57) and Mabire that of two hundred (page 463).
130   Mabire, page 463.
131   Saint-Loup, page 299, cites 100 and Soulat, page 57, 150.

to get his boots on, but one fell through the hay trap door into the cowshed. He retrieved it and dashed off to the woods. It would have been useless, no suicidal, to continue on without boots.

With a small number of comrades, Bartolomei waited until nightfall before starting out on the way again. Direction: Greifenberg. Towards midnight, they came across a forest chalet and settled down for the night. At 0500 hours on the 7th, fifty men led by Ustuf. Rigeade suddenly joined them. Nearly all were LVF veterans who did not seem to be unduly concerned by their present situation. The chalet, on their way, seemed the ideal place to treat a soldier, named Clabots, who had been wounded during an engagement.[134]

Bartolomei and his men continued on through the woods. They encountered others.[135] They too were half-starved and cold. Many no longer had weapons.

On the morning of the 8th, they came to a farm[house]. Was it deserted? Bartolomei and two men, named as Guillemert and Derbaeke, went off to investigate. They spoke to a Ukrainian prisoner of war-cum-labourer and the German farmer who gave them some supplies, biscuits, pots of conserve, and milk. The latter invited them back in the afternoon for hot milk. The small group of Frenchmen would not get to enjoy his hospitality because he denounced them to the Russians. Surrounded by a Russian company, the group surrendered.[136]

To the victors went the spoils of war: Bartolomei's group was robbed of wedding rings, watches, compasses, in fact all manner of personal possessions.

132 According to Landwehr, de Bourmont was one of the first to be killed on this tragic day. This is incorrect.
133 Saint-Loup, page 312.
134 According to Saint-Loup, page 312, the newcomers noisily made themselves at home and their noise was such that Bartolomei eventually gave the place over to them! Saint-Loup goes on to imply that Bartolomei's decision resulted from the infighting between the different factions within 'Charlemagne'. However, Rigeade, in a letter to the author, 17/2/97, said of this implication: "It's sheer lunacy!" Yes, while it's true that some were unhappy about being woken up, there was definitely no factional squabbling.
135 According to Soulat, page 127, by the morning of the 8th, Bartolomei had four men with him, named as Jullian, Guillemert, Verlecoq and Carrier. Mabire repeats that Bartolomei found himself with three or four men. And yet, according to Saint-Loup, page 313, Bartolomei and his small group were joined by others, including 'Brochart and two *caporaux*' from column Bassompierre 'wheeling about' not far from there.
136 Soulat, page 127. According to Saint-Loup, in the evening, the Ukrainian came and collected the small group of Frenchmen. He brought them back to the farmhouse. Just as they arrived so did a company of Cossacks! Had the Ukrainian betrayed them and led them into a trap? The Frenchmen did not have the time to contemplate this question and ran back to the woods, chased by bullets. Bartolomei fell into a pond, hauled himself out, ran off again and finally reached cover. Although he had managed to evade capture, one of their number by the name of Julian (pseudonym) was not so fortunate. The Cossacks then put those hiding in the woods in a terrible situation; unless they surrendered, their compatriot would be put to death. They came out. In response to Saint–Loup, again he writes with a sense of drama, but this might be how the adventure of Bartolomei and the men with him came to an end.

Suddenly, not far away, gunfire was heard. It did not last long.[137] Soon after, part of the Russian company reappeared with two dead and one wounded. They were furious. The Ukrainian farmhand was shot in cold blood and the prisoners were asked to present their soldbuchs. The SS insignia on them provoked a fit of rage and a political commissar struck two of the prisoners in the face with a pistol.

The Cossacks then had their prisoners kneel alongside a ditch. The Frenchmen thought death was at hand, but they were 'only' struck across the back of their heads with a pistol. Blood flowed. Yet they were still alive!

The prisoners were then sent to the village of Zarnefanx.[138] On their arrival they were hit and spat at by Soviet rearward personnel. The female soldiers proved more aggressive than their male counterparts and gashed the prisoners' faces with their nails.

Bartolomei was then brought before a Soviet Colonel whose questions an interpreter put to him in German. Wishing 'to be more French than ever', the French officer left the questions unanswered. As the interpreter could not speak French, the Colonel did not insist and dismissed him. Nevertheless, the Colonel had food and glasses of schnapps brought to the prisoners. He toasted them all one after the other. Guillemert did not drink fast enough and was struck around the head again!

Again the prisoners were robbed. This time it was their soap, razors, belts and wallets. They were left with absolutely nothing of value.

On joining a column of prisoners, mostly from 'Charlemagne', Bartolomei and his men noticed that 'many had swollen faces'.

The rearguard

And what of the rearguard at Körlin under Hstuf. Bassompierre? Brigf. Krukenberg had 'suggested' to Hstuf. Bassompierre that Körlin be held for twenty-four hours after the withdrawal of the *Régiment de Reserve*, but Puaud had 'outbid' him with forty-eight hours.[139] It may have been this conversation that pinned the 500 to 750 men[140] of the II/RM to Körlin[141] and which greatly reduced their already slim chances of making it to the Oder and safety. Indeed, it could be said that after 0200 hours on the 5th, by which time the bulk of 'Charlemagne' had evacuated Körlin, the presence of Bassompierre and the rearguard at Körlin served little or no meaningful purpose. Surely, it would have been better to break-out there and then, but orders are orders.

---

137   It is believed by Soulat, page 127, repeated by Mabire and Saint-Loup, that the Russians had engaged elements of 'Charlemagne', perhaps those of Bassompierre's battalion.

138   Soulat, page 127, repeated by Mabire, page 471. The same location is identified by Saint-Loup, page 314, as a big market town.

139   De la Mazière, page 128.

140   Saint-Loup, page 300, cites 500, Soulat, page 74, cites 600 and de la Mazière, page 128, cites 750.

141   If Brigf. Krukenberg had expected no French SS troops to be left in Körlin by midnight of the 4th/5th, then it seems doubtful that he would have suggested to Hstuf. Bassompierre that he hold Körlin for twenty-four hours.

Bassompierre positioned his forces; Walter's Company to the north and Rigeade's Company to the east. The men dug in. Now and then there was enemy artillery and mortar fire. Otherwise things were quiet.[142]

During the night, Castrillo of Walter's Company found himself in action when his company was outflanked by Russian armoured cars. He hit the first armoured car with a panzerfaust, which stopped it dead. As he ran to the rear he turned to see the armoured car ablaze.

As night turned to day, the Russians increased the pressure on Körlin. They seized the cemetery to the north of Körlin, but were immediately chased out by elements of Walter's Company.[143] Uscha. René Maixandeau and another young NCO by the name of Guillarme were killed.

Gnabel's section of Walter's Company was positioned along the pathway leading to the cemetery. By now, Blanc of Gnabel's section had been awake for two days. Utterly exhausted, he fell into a deep sleep. The section came under fire, but he slept on.

Suddenly, Castrillo of Gnabel's section saw a gigantic Russian descending upon him. Castrillo had in his hand a P38 pistol, which he had got from a wounded NCO. He raised his weapon and, turning his head away, fired without taking aim. The Russian fired at the same time. When Castrillo looked back he saw the Russian lying dead. He reflected that he had had a lucky break.

In the morning, troops under Uscha. de la Mazière, defending one of the few intact bridges over the Persante, set ablaze two tanks. Finally they blew the bridge itself.[144]

With artillery, tanks and mortars, the Russians began to reduce Körlin to rubble. Shells and rockets tore into buildings. Fires broke out and blazed. Forced to abandon their positions, the French SS troops pulled back to the inner suburbs.[145] They came under sniper fire from all directions; Russian infantry and Polish partisans were infiltrating along the rooftops. The Frenchmen fought back and shot down the enemy where and when they appeared. By now, 'their fighting strength had suffered bloody losses'[146] but 'Russian corpses piled up'.[147]

142 If there were engagements they were not very serious.

143 The battle for the cemetery may have raged throughout the day. According to Mabire, page 490, shortly after dawn on the 6th, Russian infantry supported by armour retook the cemetery. Walter counterattacked à la baïonnette and in savage hand-to-hand fighting managed to recapture the cemetery for a second time. A few minutes later, hell was let loose. Multiple rockets rained in and massive explosions ripped gravestones and crosses into pieces. In the face of this hellish barrage, Walter ordered a withdrawal. As rockets continued to explode all around, the company returned to its starting positions. The time was now 1100 hours. Indeed, according to Saint-Loup, page 300, by nightfall, Walter had retaken the cemetery four times.

144 The author believes that this Russian attack was launched on the morning of the second day at Körlin and not the first stated by de la Mazière (page 128).

145 According to Mabire, page 493, Ustuf. Rigeade's Company of the II/RM, to the east of the town, 'hung on to the ground fiercely' as Walter's Company. This is incorrect. While at Körlin Ustuf. Rigeade's Company was not attacked. (Rigeade, letter to the author, 10/4/97).

After almost two days of battle, the French defenders of Körlin were running out of ammunition and supplies. As evening approached, all knew that the end was near. Around 1600 hours,[148] Bassompierre called together several officers; finally he had decided to try and break-out, but it would be a break-out into uncertainty. Nobody knew where the German lines were. His plan was to leave Körlin to the east, follow the Körlin-Belgard railway line to the south-east, cross the Persante between Körlin and Belgard, and then march westwards.

Ustuf. Rigeade asked why weren't they breaking out towards Kolberg. This seemed the most logical direction, but Bassompierre replied that the port had already fallen to the Russians. This was tragically inaccurate. Rigeade's Company was assigned the role of vanguard and Walter's Company that of rearguard. H hour was set for nightfall.

Towards late afternoon, the companies silently abandoned their positions and hurriedly assembled east of Körlin near the railway line. The less seriously wounded, basically those who stood a chance of surviving the journey, were fastened to horses whose shoes were covered with rags to prevent them making a noise. The more seriously wounded and the non-transportable were stripped of their military uniforms and papers, and left in the care of the civilian representative of the German Red Cross.[149] Several medical orderlies volunteered to stay behind with them. Nevertheless, for all concerned, it was still a painful decision to leave the non-transportable wounded behind.

Orders to destroy all heavy equipment were carried out to the letter. The men would march light. Indeed, no provisions were to be carried. Some men volunteered to stay behind and man the combat posts to keep the Russians guessing about their intentions. They were to disengage in turn.

In the evening of 6th March[150], the break-out began. Many, like Blanc of Walter's Company, knew nothing of their destination, but assumed it was Kolberg, where they could embark for safety.

146   According to de la Mazière, page 130, of the 750 men of the II/RM, only about 350 remained, but Soulat cites, page 74, that Bassompierre still had 500 men with him when the II/RM broke out of Körlin later that day.

147   De la Mazière, page 129.

148   Mabire, page 494. However, according to Soulat, page 75, it was around 1800 hours when Hstuf. Bassompierre 'decided to try and carry out the order to rejoin the main body of the Division'.

149   Soulat, page 75.

150   Different authors, however, have cited various times and dates. Mabire cites, page 498, that the II/RM left the town during the night of the 5th/6th, but started before 1900 hours. Rigeade, in a letter to the author, 17/2/97, cites the date of the 6th and the time of evening. Delperrié de Bayac cites, page 607, the early hours of 6th March. Saint-Loup writes, page 301, that at midnight of the 5th/6th, 'they abandoned their positions'. Saint-Loup continues that, two hours later, 'a column of ghosts' was passing along the railway line southwards. Landwehr cites, page 86, the night of the 5th/6th. De la Mazière implies the evening of the 6th and night of the 6th/7th. Soulat cites, pages 74-75, 1900 hours on the 6th. Regarding this, swayed in particular by the eyewitness accounts of Rigeade and also that of de la Mazière, the author has used the 6th as the date and 'evening' as the time of the break-out.

Following the Körlin-Belgard railway line in a south-easterly direction, the battalion's vanguard, Rigeade's Company, passed the railway station and crossed the tributary Radüe over the railway bridge. Its movement went unnoticed thanks to the night and a diversion in the west sector, a barrage laid down by all remaining heavy weapons to expend the last of the ammunition. Besides, the movement had been quite noiseless. But it could be said that luck was with the battalion as it now filed out of Körlin; the town was lit up like the middle of the day by a bright moon and by burning buildings. At 2200 hours, the last elements left Körlin. Now and then the Russians sent a shell into the town at random. There was no reply.

Luck was still very much with Bassompierre's battalion when Rigeade's Company overran sleeping Soviet infantry and armour in its path.[151]

Bassompierre forced the pace. There was a brief engagement with a Russian patrol, which brought about casualties on both sides. The battalion marched on. Later, it was joined by those who had stayed behind at Körlin to cover the break-out. While evacuating Körlin one group had inadvertently walked into a minefield sown by engineers of 'Charlemagne'. Roger Wyckaert of Walter's Company was gashed in the leg by shrapnel. Hastily dressed, he had limped on.

After following the railway line towards Belgard for some four kilometres, Bassompierre's battalion then went across country. The going was tough. Between each field there was barbed-wire fencing and no wire cutters were to be had.

The men were so exhausted that they started to hallucinate. Blanc of Walter's Company thought he saw ship masts, which convinced him that they had reached the port of Kolberg. Only later did he learn that Kolberg was not their destination.

When dawn came up the battalion took to the woods and hid away. The battalion's hiding place may have been the forest of Nassow, north of Belgard.[152]

The men rested. In the afternoon, a German plane flew over at low level. Some got up to cheer it, but it did not have German markings. And so they wondered if the plane was really German or 'under new management', that of the Russians.

Walter, who had somehow managed to find a civilian coat, went on reconnaissance. On his return he assembled his company, which was still some one hundred strong. He announced that at nightfall they would 'set off again the direction of the coast'.[153] He finished with a few words of encouragement. They still had hope.

---

151   In a letter to the author, Rigeade recalls a very quick engagement which is far removed from de la Mazière's account, pages 132-133, of a 'pitched battle' which lasted almost half an hour.

152   Blanc, letter to the author, 6/6/2002, and personal conversation. According to de la Mazière, page 133, progress during the first night was good. He goes on to imply that the battalion reached and crossed the Persante south of Belgard. If true, then the progress of Bassompierre's battalion during that first night was truly remarkable; the men were exhausted and cold; the route was to the east of Belgard; the route was through forests; and the last units of the battalion did not leave Körlin until around 2200. For these reasons, the author has concluded that the battalion was still on the 'wrong' bank of the Persante (Mabire, page 504) after its first night 'on the run'. Also, according to Mabire, page 503, during that first night the battalion went round and round in circles.

153   Blanc, personal conversation. This is surprising given that Kolberg and the coast were not the destination.

The break-out had succeeded, but it was not a break-out to freedom. The ensuing days and weeks were a confusing succession of marches, detours, and violent engagements, perhaps fifteen in total.[154] Death or capture awaited all. As a result of the battalion's fate, it has been difficult, at times impossible, to reconcile the different accounts. What follows is the tragedy of Bassompierre's battalion presented in the form of 'snapshots' (although they may not appear in strictly chronological order).

On the evening of 7th March, the battalion set out again single file. The rearguard was formed by Oscha. Blaise's platoon of Walter's Company.

All went well for the first hour, but then, while crossing open ground, the battalion was suddenly exposed by flares. Mortars immediately opened up and crashed down on the frozen ground. The troops dived for cover. Darkness returned when the flares burnt out. The firing stopped.

It was then that the men of the rearguard realised they were alone. As they raced back to the woods several others joined them. They too were lost. They numbered thirty or so.

Overcome by fatigue, they immediately fell asleep in the woods. Next morning, they awoke to find themselves buried under snow. Oscha. Blaise and Uscha. Le Cavelé went on reconnaissance. The two of them were never heard from again. This left them without an officer or a NCO.

Their objective remained Kolberg, but they had neither map nor compass. They would walk round and round for days.

They were cold, thirsty and hungry. Such was their hunger that they risked detection when they shot a doe. One of them drank the warm blood from the wound and felt better for it.

They encountered the Russians and lived to fight another day. They were walking in single file along a forest track when a lorry loaded with Russian soldiers suddenly appeared. Those at the head of the file shouted 'Russians, Russians' and fell back. But those following them misheard 'hives'[155] for the shouts of 'Russians' and rushed forward screaming: "We're going to eat honey!" Curiously, the Russians did not give battle and drove off.

To reach Kolberg, they had to cross the Persante, which was in spate, but the bridges were guarded and they were too few to overcome the guards. They built a raft but they were so weak from not having eaten for three or four days that they could not carry it to the water's edge. Moreover, a Russian patrol arrived on the opposite bank.

They pushed further east. They came to a road and watched a stream of Russian vehicles pass before crossing at one bound.

They were still cold, thirsty and hungry. Gunfire could still be heard in all directions. This gave them hope. Thus, nothing was finished. There was no talk of surrender. Besides, they had grave doubts about the fate that the Russians had reserved for the SS that they captured.

By now, they numbered eight or nine. They had started with thirty or so, but one by one they had disappeared. In this way, good friends Blanc and Castrillo were separated.

154   Soulat, page 75.
155   The French word for hives is ruches.

Finally, one evening, they came across a deserted forest cabin and here they stayed. After some days of rest two or three men went their own way. They were never heard from again. Some, however, were in no condition to continue. Two brothers by the name of Hovelacque left. The youngest one, who was barely seventeen, had got frostbite in some toes, but was convinced that they should push on. They were now five. There was Jean P. and Jacques R., who were still able, and Blanc, Rimbert, and Désigot, who were not. Blanc was suffering from frostbite in his feet.

The cabin was known locally. A group of German women courageously came to feed them and look after them a number of times. Then, one evening, they heard women shouting and bursts from automatic weapons not far away. They never saw the women again.

The three *invalides* survived on the food foraged nightly by Jean P. and Jacques R., but as the weeks passed they weakened.[156] They dreamt of food and, when awake, they talked of little else but food.

On 18th April 1945, after five weeks in the cabin, the Russians discovered them. Jean P. and Jacques R., who were outside, shouted a warning and disappeared[157], but there was no escape for the *invalides*. They saw two young Russian soldiers push open the door and aim their submachine guns at them. Blanc said of what happened next[158]:

> We did not move (how could we?), them neither. I waited for the small flame to appear suddenly from the gun since I was certain that they were going to kill us; I thought about my parents with sadness because they would never know where, how and when I died, nor that I had so much sadness for them. That was all that was in my mind, but the curious thing is that I had absolutely no fear.
>
> The small flame did not come.
>
> They were joined by an officer, who looked at us with a sort of pity, perhaps contempt, but also disgust (we smelt bad and he saw that we had lice, which the Russians fear because of typhus). He murmured in German 'Kindersoldaten', then in Russian 'Fransouski'.

The Russians left, convinced that the Frenchmen were not going to escape. They returned one or two hours later with a horse and cart driven by a civilian. The Frenchmen were brought out. The civilian lit a fire, helped them undress and burnt their rags. Then he shaved them all over. Disgusted, the Russians looked on from a distance. To warm himself up, Blanc crawled to the edge of the fire but got too close, badly burning his knees. In the following months, this would cause him more trouble than the frostbite and amputations.

Placed onto the cart, the Frenchmen were taken to a medical post, where they were treated. Each of them had a bed and a guard. 'Perhaps they are frightened that we might escape', Rimbert commented. They remained feverish.

---

156   Jean P. recalls 'visiting' the neighbouring villages of Pustchow and Buchhorst. This would place the cabin in the forest of Nassow, north of Belgard.

157   Jean P. and Jacques R. were captured one week later.

158   Personal conversation with the author, 2001.

They had time to reflect. They had survived. And it was because of Jean P. and Jacques R. that they had survived. Bonded by camaraderie, Jean P. and Jacques R. had not deserted them in their hour of need.

As for Blanc's good friend Castrillo, he found himself in the company of a comrade from the town of Mirepoix.[159] Castrillo was in bad shape; hit by shrapnel in the groin, he was losing much blood. And yet he continued to press on in the hope of evading capture. He did not. The Russians caught the two of them on a railway track motorcar. He ended up in the city of Koslin with German and Russian wounded and it was here that a Soviet Major operated on him in a quite rustic field hospital.

Death could strike at any time. Robert Lacoste of Ostuf. Français' Kompanie recalls:[160]

> We were marching in column at the edge of a wood; the Russians had occupied the main roads. Ostuf. Français was bringing up the rear of the column. A shot [rang out]. A Russian sniper hiding in the trees shot him in the back. He gave a squall and collapsed. I turned to give him help, but alas he was already dead. I took his identity disc and pistol and set off on my way again with the column, abandoning the body beside the path.

Français was his friend.

Hstuf. Rémy was also killed. Hstuf. Bassompierre had known him from his LVF days and held him in great respect. Thus, at Körlin, Rémy had found himself back under Bassompierre and serving in the II/RM. And when the time came for the II/RM to evacuate Körlin and retreat westwards, Bassompierre entrusted Rémy with the command of the rearguard. Oscha. Duchène wrote of Rémy's death:[161]

> At the beginning of the morning we were a handful of men, hidden in a forest closely watching the movements of the enemy tanks. Beside me were *Capitaine* Bassompierre, *Adjudants-Chefs* Gaubion [Gobion—the author] and Cabannes (the latter from Lyon I think) and men that I did not know from disparate units.
>
> Over one hundred metres in front of us a big copse in which were two men, *Capitaine* Rémy and his orderly.
>
> I got the information from a runner that this *Capitaine* Rémy, on an order from *Capitaine* Bassompierre, had advanced up to there in order to observe better the Russian armour.
>
> Personally I disapproved of his presence in the copse.
>
> Actually some moments later, I saw get out of a Russian tank, imprudently as only Russians can be, a member of the crew, submachine-gun in hand.

159   His name may have been Cabirol.

160   Lacoste, letter to the author, 3/12/2002. This corrects Mabire who implies that Ostuf. Français was killed when the battalion crossed the Körlin-Belgard road (see Mabire, page 502).

161   Duchène, letter to Nadine Rémy, the wife of Henri, 28/8/50. According to Mabire, page 503, Bassompierre learnt of the death of Rémy after the road crossing which had cost Hstuf. Monneuse his life. This may be true, but it should be clarified that Rémy was not killed during this very same road crossing.

He looked intently towards the place occupied by your husband while I aimed at the man a rifle that I borrowed from a man hidden beside me.

The Russian ran forward bent double, submachine-gun ready to fire. I took aim at my man, and when he went down on his knees, behind and against a slight mound, his gun went off and I pressed the trigger some tens of seconds slower than him. The delay, pardon me Nadaine, cost the *Capitaine* his life. If it can come as a consolation, I'll have you know that the Russian was also dead on the spot.

After the Russian's burst, we saw the *Capitaine*'s orderly leave the grove and return in our direction under the fire of the tanks, running until he was out of breath.

I sent for him to ask him for information: the *Capitaine* was realising with binoculars the encirclement of which we were victims when, suddenly, a sub-machine-gun burst coming from their right, struck down the officer.

The thirty-four-year-old Henri Rémy left behind a wife and three children.

Oscha. Robert, who had come to the W-SS from the LVF,[162] saved the battalion, pursued by Soviet tanks, when he knocked out two of them with panzerfäuste.[163]

Lacoste of Ostuf. Français' Kompanie could march no more. His feet were frostbitten. He was with a group, which had become separated from the battalion. He recounts:

I asked *mon adjudant* Marcel Duchène, who commanded the group, to abandon me. He refused. With incredible courage for several days he carried me on his shoulders. We were in the vicinity of Belgard when we were made prisoner by the Russians in a beetroot silo, where we were hiding. We were on our knees and going to be shot when a Russian woman officer arrived, shouting not to fire. Then we joined the great column of prisoners.

Lacoste was to witness the unbelievable group rape of a small girl by some ten Russians, after which the victim was disembowelled.

Unable to face his battalion disintegrating around him, Hstuf. Bassompierre sent his assistant, Hstuf. de Perricot, in search of two lost detachments.[164] Off he went with two liaison officers. They did not find those they were looking for and eventually became lost in turn. They marched westwards, hoping to find the Persante. The Russians seemed everywhere.

162 In 'Charlemagne', his unit may have been the 3/58.

163 According to Saint-Loup, page 311, Bassompierre's battalion was being tracked down by a Soviet armoured brigade when Oscha. Robert saved the day. Realistically speaking, it seems inconceivable that the Soviets would employ and tie up a whole brigade pursuing a battalion that numbered no more than three hundred at this stage unless the Soviets believed the French SS troops were far stronger than they really were.

164 While there is great similarity between Mabire's and Delperrie de Bayac's accounts of Hstuf. de Perricot's (mis)adventure, they do not agree on the date and the time of these events; Mabire is unspecific and Delperrie de Bayac details the dawn of 6th March 1945.

Near the Persante, de Perricot was seriously wounded; a bullet entered through his hip and lodged itself under his breastbone. Convinced that he was near to death, de Perricot told, then ordered, the two liaison officers to try and rejoin the column. They left. Much to his surprise, he did not draw his last breath. After tearing up his Soldbuch and his *carte de chef Milicien* and burying the pieces in the snow, he got to his feet and headed to the Persante, one of the few landmarks in the snow-covered region. He suddenly came upon a Russian soldier and fled as fast as his legs would carry him. When he stopped, out of breath, he suddenly realised that for a man in agony he had run quickly and for a good length of time!

Like many, Hstuf. de Perricot walked round in circles, but was lucky enough to come across his two liaison officers who were as lost as him. They tried in vain to find Bassompierre's column. However, they did discover a forest house where 'Charlemagne' had sited a small supplies depot. Here they spent four or five days and were only spotted and captured by the Soviets after one of the liaison officers had foolishly lit a fire to get warm; the smoke from the fire had given them away. They surrendered without a fight.

After skirting around Belgard to the east, Bassompierre suddenly changed direction to the west. In this way, the battalion came to the Persante and a footbridge, which was still intact, but guarded. Even so, the Frenchmen were wary. 'For safety's sake', half of the men took to the river and swam across to the other bank. As for the others, they used the footbridge after dispatching the Russians guarding it. They too made it across. So it was not a trap after all. Again they took to the forests which should have meant security.[165]

Tragedy over took the battalion on attempting to cross a major road.[166] Quietly, the Frenchmen had crept up to within fifty yards of the road. From roadside ditches they waited for an opportune moment to cross. They watched two or three light convoys pass. And then a column of T–34s, 'Joseph' Stalin tanks and truck-borne infantry appeared. Their lights blazed. Gripped by the fear of being spotted, they waited and watched. The minutes passed agonisingly. Ten. Twenty. Thirty. Those who were crushed by fatigue fell off to sleep, but for most the waiting became harder by the minute. However, it now seemed as though the convoy

165 The date of this crossing remains unclear; de la Mazière's account implies the same night as the break-out from Körlin. However, Mabire records, pages 504-505, that when the first dawn 'on the run' came up the battalion was still on the 'wrong' bank of the Persante.

166 The date and location of this tragic road crossing varies. First, according to Mabire, page 501, the tragedy over took the battalion during the night of the break-out when it attempted to cross the Körlin-Belgard road clogged by a constant stream of Soviet convoys. Second, according to Saint-Loup, page 311, and Delpierré de Bayac, page 607, the location was the Belgard-Stolzenberg road, on the other bank of the Persante, and days later. Third, de la Mazière, an eyewitness, describes the road on page 137 as 'an important artery with three carriageways leading to Stettin and Frankfurt-on-the-Oder', possibly the Körlin-Plathe highway, and times this tragic road crossing days after the break-out from Körlin. Fourth, Rigeade, also an eyewitness, in his letter to the author of 5/3/97, suggests a road south of Belgard or further west, dating the road crossing to the night of the break-out from Körlin, noting it was much later than that recounted by Mabire.

might pass without spotting them. Suddenly, a 'Joseph' Stalin tank came to a stop and its turret started to turn towards them

Panzerfaust in hand, Hscha. Walter jumped up and ran forward through the bursts of machine gun fire around him. He fired and destroyed the tank. The Russians responded with flares to illuminate the night. And so began the battle. Those with panzerfäuste raced towards the enemy tanks. Moments later, two more were ablaze. These 'kills' are credited to Gabin and Krebs.[167] Gabin survived, but Krebs was killed. Many trucks and other kinds of vehicles were also destroyed.[168]

The fighting became hand-to-hand. Some Russians turned out to be women who were 'as furious as the men'. They were shot down without a second thought.[169]

There was total confusion among the Russians, enabling the Frenchmen to cross the road and reach the forests again. Indeed, a picket of Russians deployed on the plain between the road and the forests melted away.[170] Under the false impression that the few Frenchmen who had got through thus far were just a small 'advance-guard', an insignificant number not worth bothering about, the Russians went off for the 'rich pickings' among the larger force which had to be to the rear.

But the Frenchmen paid a terrible price to forge this road crossing: around one hundred men. Hstuf. Monneuse was hit by a large calibre bullet and died almost instantly. His last words were "*Mon Dieu*". Std.Ju. Maurice Comte, Oscha. Pierre Meric, the former *adjoint* of the 2/58, and four others carried his body several hundred metres and buried him at the foot of a tree.

Among those who disappeared during this violent engagement was Ostuf. Dr. Philippe Joubert of the II/58. A former *chef* of the *Avant-Garde de la Milice*, Joubert had led into the ranks of the Waffen-SS many very young students from the *École des cadres* at Chapelle-en-Serval.

After dressing the wounded and regrouping, Bassompierre's battalion, if such it could be termed, marched on. Its numbers continued to dwindle. Spotted by Russian patrols again and again, the worn out survivors were forced to hold their ground, fight it out and then disengage as fast as their legs would take them. It was kill or be killed. A wound meant almost certain death. And then there were the enemy tanks that fired directly at them, one shell per man.[171] Where possible they kept to the forests. They were also against the elements. They were dying of thirst and many took to sucking snow, which burnt certain parts of the system and increased their thirst. All were hungry and they raided farms and hamlets in search of food. Infested with lice, it could be said that many were more dead than alive,

---

167 Saint-Loup, page 312.

168 De la Mazière, page 139. Soulat specifies, page 75, that ten or so trucks and other vehicles were destroyed with panzerfäuste. These same figures are repeated by Saint-Loup, page 312.

169 De la Mazière, page 138. Curiously, Mabire also writes, pages 510-511, of an engagement in which three tanks were destroyed and Russian women soldiers appear, but this engagement postdates that of de la Mazière and was not the result of a 'failed' road crossing. So do de la Mazière and Mabire write of the same engagement? Perhaps, both versions do have remarkably similar details.

170 De la Mazière, page 139.

171 De la Mazière, page 140.

but there was no question of surrender after they came across a pile of SS corpses; the Soviets had killed all of these wounded prisoners with a bullet in the back of the neck.

The wounded had to be abandoned.[172] One soldier, wounded in the leg, said to Bassompierre with a smile: "*Au revoir, mon capitaine*, don't forget to tell my family that I did my duty to the end and that I fought so that they would not know it [Bolshevism]. *Vive la France!*" Bassompierre would not forget him or his words.[173]

Some of the wounded took their own lives, but many could not bring themselves to pull the trigger. They lived in the hope that the Russians would attend to them, honouring their promises broadcasted at Körlin, but others, physically unable to kill themselves, pitifully begged their comrades to put them out of their misery. On the whole this wish was fulfilled.

The 'battalion' continued to disintegrate. One such group to become separated from Bassompierre counted Rttf. Gonzales and six others—Robert Maurel, Favier (a *sergent* originating from Marseille), Robert (whose brother, an officer in the *Milice*, was shot at liberation), Micha (a small Russian who had served with the 1st Battalion of the LVF) and two other comrades not known to Gonzales.

Gonzales was lightly wounded, carrying a piece of mortar shrapnel in the calf of his left leg, but he could still run. He and the others made their way westwards. He recounts:

> We tried to cross a bridge over the Rega[174] (a small river in the neighbourhood of Greifenberg) because we still had a mind to pass through the Russian lines to find the Oder; the bridge was guarded by a platoon of Russian soldiers … thus impossible to cross.
>
> We went along the river and we arrived in sight of a forest house (numerous in the region). Nobody in sight, apart from a horse all on its own, abandoned in a place adjoining the house. We were starving, having not eaten anything for several days. Thus we decided to kill the animal. I fired a bullet from my P38 between its eyes first. It was still standing looking at me! I fired a second bullet and it was still looking at me … Thus I decided to use a third bullet; this time behind the head, level with the cerebellum. It fell down in a heap … I still regret having killed it.
>
> A little later we arrived near a great farm. After many precautions, assuring us that there were no enemy soldiers, we were welcomed by several women, most of whom were young and of Russian and Polish origin. They gave us some eggs and milk. The invaders had still not passed through there because there wasn't a main road nearby.
>
> A little further, as we neared a small house, we heard a bizarre noise certainly coming from the said house. Cautiously we approached. When we arrived in front of the door, we heard a significant grunting; it was a pig that had been shut up there! I killed this one this time with no regrets because in Russia we were in the habit of appropriating a pig from time to time. This one was

172   De la Mazière explains that it became necessary to abandon the seriously wounded when the remaining horses were shot for food.

173   Bassompierre, "*Frères ennemis*", page 157.

174   In his memoirs Gonzales names the river as the Persante. The author believes that Gonzales is mistaken and has corrected the name of the river to the Rega.

quickly jointed. We took the two rear legs and liver because we could not carry everything, still having some horsemeat steaks.

That same day, at nightfall, after perhaps fifteen or twenty days spent behind Russian lines, I started to limp. My wound started to become seriously infected. All the more because an abscess formed inside my thigh. And to crown it all, I fell in a ditch full of water. I could not go on any more and I felt that I was becoming a 'heavy weight' for my comrades, delaying our march.

During the night we saw a light coming from a small maisonette, some one hundred metres away. We approached, still with caution, and through the glass window we saw that some women and children, as well as a man in civilian clothes who was missing an arm occupied this dwelling place. Exhausted, we decided to go inside. We were made very welcome because we had an abundance of food that we hastened to cook on the cooker. We shared all that with the occupants, after which, exhausted, we were ready to sleep. The civilian [man], certainly a Pole, left to go and 'spend a penny'.

Unbeknown to Gonzales and his comrades, the Pole went and denounced them to the Russians. At dawn, Russian soldiers surrounded the house. Machine-guns covered the only exit out of the house. The Russians put to the Frenchmen inside that if they did not surrender then they would have to massacre the women and children also inside. They could do nothing else but surrender. Fearing the worst, they were surprised when the Sergeant commanding the Russians pulled out a bottle of Vodka and asked them to drink with him. In reply, Gonzales offered him a box of cigars that he had acquired at Körlin. To him, this was no great loss as he could have taken it anyway. They talked. It was very cordial. The Russian Sergeant was from Smolensk, also the birthplace of Micha who was still with his comrades of 'Charlemagne'. The Russian Sergeant advised them to burn their *Soldbuch* and tear off their SS collar insignia. They did. They were then sent to Greifenberg, which was only some three kilometres away.

Hstuf. Bassompierre called together the eighty men with him and told them to split up into groups of ten and make their way back to the German lines as best they could. So they separated.

At sunrise on 17th March 1945, the twenty or thirty survivors, including Std.Ju. Comte and Marcel Carlier, now commanded by Hstuf. Bassompierre, found themselves surrounded by Polish cavalry in a farmhouse where they were resting. Exhausted and without munitions, they surrendered.[175] They were treated correctly. Hstuf. Bassompierre was taken to a camp at Arnswalde (Choszczno).

Marching with Hscha. Walter's Company was Uscha. Pierre Briault[176] of the Veterinary Company. He had 'changed employment' at Körlin when the last of the horses in his care were slaughtered for food. However, after a brief and violent engagement with the Russians, he now suddenly found himself alone in a forest and on the receiving end of an enemy artillery bombardment. He took shelter under several tree trunks. For around half an hour, shrapnel whistled all around him, but his mind was taken off the bombardment and the cold when he

175 In his book "*Frères ennemis*", Bassompierre does not mention the location of his capture, however, according to Saint-Loup, page 312, Bassompierre and the men left around him were captured in the region of Schivelbein.
176 Pseudonym.

discovered nearby a comrade, like him a former *franc-garde* of the *Milice*, with whom he exchanged words about bullfighting.

And then the shelling ceased and the Russian infantry came on. At least two platoons. Advancing from fold to fold, they approached the two Frenchmen. Their situation looked black and minutes later a wounded Briault was captured. However, this was not the end of his odyssey. He managed to escape, but was recaptured. This happened again and again, perhaps five or six times in total. In this way, he drew nearer and nearer to the Oder and was only about a dozen kilometres away when he was found 'half dead' on a dung heap by Polish partisans. By now, he was in terrible physical shape—his feet were bleeding, he was suffering from exposure, hunger and exhaustion, and he was carrying a serious wound to his shoulder.

The partisans took Briault to their commander who spoke French well. 'Struck by the Frenchmen's courage', the Polish officer asked him if he wished to fight under his command. The former *milicien* hailing from Nîmes declined his offer.[177]

As for Hscha. Walter, he met his death bravely attacking a tank.[178] Rumour has it that a NCO by the name of Verschtichel, a *lillois*, who had served with Walter in Company 5/58 and greatly admired him, committed suicide when Walter was killed.

Ustuf. Rigeade's Company broke up when it attempted to cross a road along which Soviet convoys of tanks and trucks were moving. It had been decided to cross this road in groups of roughly ten men each during the breaks in the traffic and then regroup on the other side, but the crossing did not go as planned. Rigeade's group made it across and entered the forest, but no other

---

177   Mabire, pages 511-513. However, there is a certain similarity between the odyssey of Briault and that of 'Alain D...' which appears in *"Historia #32"*, page 180. Both individuals were from Nîmes, both have a passion for bullfighting, both were captured five times and both escaped five times, both were 'finally' captured by Polish partisans, both were brought before a Polish officer, both were asked by the Polish officer to fight under him, and both replied with the same words which declined the offer. Notwithstanding the numerous similarities, there are a host of insignificant differences between the two accounts, but the account of 'Alain D...' contains two 'extra' episodes of note that do not appear in that of Briault. Firstly, Alain D... was captured in the evening of 'the hell of Belgard', briefly interrogated by a Russian officer and when he confirmed that he was French he was allowed to go free! And yet the German SS prisoners with him were shot on the spot. Secondly, after speaking with the Polish officer, he was again allowed to go free! He set off again. On foot and alone, he made his way through Germany and then France, before crossing into Spain where he took refuge in the Baleares to await the end of the political 'storm'. Alain D... is described as twenty-five, a specialist in the use of the bayonet and 'a hero of Charlemagne'. Also of note is that Alain D... could not have been with Walter's Company if he was captured in the evening of 'the hell of Belgard'; as part of the II/RM, Walter's Company had remained at Körlin after the departure of the I/RM and the RR. Thus, Walter's Company was not with the RR on Belgard plain when disaster overtook it.

178   Mabire, page 516.

groups followed. Rigeade believes that the group following his must have moved away from the road and in this way lost contact with his group as well as the following group. One of the groups was never heard from again, although it is easy to imagine the ultimate fate of its men.[179] Among the group were Hscha. Perrigault, Prevost, Scheyder and Ferrer. All were LVF veterans of 1941 and very dear to Rigeade who now found himself with just six of his men (Armani, Leonard, Reynier, Sage, Seurre? and one other). They continued westwards.

Separated from Rigeade when the company had attempted to cross the road carrying Soviet convoys, Oscha. Blonet and his platoon, joined by French, German and Latvian escapers, tried to make for the Oder. They marched by night and tried to rest by day. They were not only cold, but also hungry. There was no escape from the frost, which struck at limbs. Fingers and toes froze. But they too continued to push westwards. Day after day passed. They neared Stolzenberg. Blonet said of his capture:

> On the morning of 17th March 1945, [suffering from] frostbitten feet for the second time (the first time was in 1941 before Moscow), I could march no more. I asked Ostuf. Veyrieras who was with me to take command of the group, which he did, deciding to leave the wood in broad daylight. A hill hid a road along which a Polish convoy was passing. Spotted, the group surrendered, signalling my presence in the wood, thanks to which I was saved.
>
> A medical officer, a Polish Jew, had me transported on a cart pulled by German prisoners. Speaking French, he told me that his regiment was composed of compatriots deported to Siberia following the Soviet occupation of part of Poland under the German-Soviet Pact of 1939, which partitioned Poland. They had to enlist in the Red Army so that they could return to their country.
>
> I was sent to Greifenberg and then to a field hospital in Pulawy, Poland, where a German medical officer amputated the toes of my left foot.

Tracked by a large group of Polish troops, Rigeade's group could not shake them off. And then, at dawn one morning, it was surrounded in a small wood. As there was little point in fighting it out, Ustuf. Rigeade ordered his men to surrender. They had covered some fifty kilometres on foot and reached Greifenberg, but in the end it had all been in vain.

Much to the surprise of Rigeade, he and the men with him were treated well. Other prisoners arrived. Separated into small groups, all were herded eastwards. The Frenchmen soon found themselves among thousands of German prisoners which the Russians 'goaded' on.

Rigeade was to witness the roadside summary execution of a young German SS soldier walking near him. He only escaped this same end because he was no longer wearing his distinctive SS collar patches, which he had torn off as a precaution against retribution.

---

179   Rigeade, letter to the author, 17/2/97. This corrects Mabire's account, page 515, that the group disappeared from a column of prisoners Rigeade had joined after his capture.

Eventually Rigeade would join the group of captured officers of 'Charlemagne' and share their fate.

Separated from Rigeade when the company had attempted to cross the road carrying Soviet convoys, Oscha. Girard managed to lead twenty men, mostly from the PAK Company of Waffen-Gren. Regt der SS 58, all the way back to the Oder, but they were unable to cross over and all were captured.

Hscha. Gobion, perhaps the most decorated former NCO of the LVF, also managed to reach the Oder. He had ten men with him. However, no boats could be found. On the night of 23rd/24th March 1945, the group attempted to cross a partly destroyed bridge at Wollin (Wolin), but was spotted by the Russians. Three men were hit. Two of them had to be abandoned when the group gave up the idea of crossing and withdrew under fire.

From the west bank, German soldiers, attracted by the fusillade, pointed to rubber dinghies hidden on a river island. An LVF veteran then tried to swim across and reach them, but he got cramp in the icy water and had to give up. Hope faded.

At dawn on the 24th, after an artillery duel, the Reds attacked and Polish soldiers captured the nine survivors of 'Charlemagne' in a potato silo.

And yet the trek still continued for some. According to former *Milicien* Marcel H.:[180]

We marched all night. During the day we hid in the woods. We tried to eat in abandoned farms. Tanks and Russian and Polish cavalry tracked us down. I had lost my Company. We were thirty Frenchmen commanded by a former lieutenant of the Sturmbrigade, Bergeat [arguably Ostuf. de Bregeot, the author]. We wanted to reach the Baltic and try and go over to Sweden from there. In fact we went through Stettin, in flames, and we had continued westwards, still on foot, still pursued. We were captured by Polish cavalry just at the end on 2nd May 1945 in a village beyond the Sprée.

---

180   Delperrié de Bayac, page 607.

CHAPTER 11

The Hell of Pomerania, Part 3

'Corsair' Gagneron[1]

In the fierce fighting at Bärenwalde and Elsenau on 25th February 1945 'Charlemagne' splintered. A number of groups withdrew to the north-east and into the forming Danzig defensive pocket. Some of the groups were no longer composed of soldiers from one specific unit. Some teamed up with German units. One such group was that led by Oscha. Jacques Gagneron, who was ex-LVF and a recipient of the KVK II.[2] It consisted of the forty or so men of his almost intact platoon of the 1/58.

After the fighting in Elsenau cemetery, the platoon suddenly found itself separated from Ostuf. Fatin and the company, and withdrew northward, passing through Flötenstein on 28th February. The following day, at the village of Falkenhagen (Milocice), the Frenchmen chanced upon an intact German unit of eight assault guns, which was operating independently. The crews were young, their morale was high, and the commanding officer, a young Hauptmann, was in need of infantry support. Thereupon, Oscha. Gagneron offered the services of the French platoon. Besides, the German unit was well equipped with provisions! The platoon had not eaten properly for three days. Together they set off to the north. The Frenchmen, now elevated to the role of Panzergrenadiere, were sat on the superstructure of the assault guns.

Gagneron was a legionnaire of old who knew well the partisan war of 'hit and run' and it was the same tactics the armoured group was to employ. After nightfall, they came to the town of Rummelsburg (Miastko) which was occupied by nearly forty Russian tanks. Within gun range, they took up positions around the town and awaited dawn to attack. All night long they listened to the screams of women being raped and the muffled shouts of wounded being finished off. This, of course, enraged them. And it was only the first gun shot that released their pent-up rage. In minutes, one third of the Soviet armour was knocked out. The other tanks fled, leaving its infantry support to its own devices. Gagneron's men then efficiently cleaned out the town of drunken Russians. By midday, the town was in their hands.

The smell of death hung in the air. Dozens and dozens of disembowelled women lay in the middle of the roads. Clearly, some, after being raped, had been thrown out of windows to their death. Brutally, this brought home to them what they were fighting for.

---

1   See Saint-Loup, pages 270-277.
2   Saint-Loup, page 271. However, his rank appears as Ustuf. in *Der Freiwillige* 10/97. This is unlikely. In the LVF he served as a NCO, not an officer.

Adhering to the tactics of 'hit and run', the German armour and Gagneron's men evacuated the town before the arrival of considerable Soviet forces from the direction of Baldenburg (Bialy Bor). They went east towards Radensfelde, arriving at 1700 hours. Here they rested.

Whilst on sentry duty Gagneron stopped a column of twenty-four French POWs making their way to the Russians and liberation. He advised them to think again and not to set foot in Rummelsburg but they did not heed his advice, replying that they had nothing to fear from the Russians. He let them pass.

Later that night, the German unit received orders to retake Rummelsburg and hold it for twenty-four hours to allow the passage of an armoured train. A German company of infantry was detailed to support the attack. The 'illegal' presence of the Frenchmen was not disclosed in case they would have to part ways.

As to be expected, the reception was considerably 'hotter' this time. Although two assault guns were lost, one to tank fire and the other to a mine, Rummelsburg was retaken. Again they discovered in the town what the Russians were capable of: the twenty-four French POWs that Gagneron had spoken to earlier that day had all been killed, either bayoneted in the stomach or shot in the head.

After seeing through the armoured train, the mixed force moved to Bütow (Bytów), but their time together was now over. With the 'illegal' presence of the Frenchmen reported, the *kommandantur* of Bütow forced them to go their separate ways.

Singing in full voice, Gagneron's platoon set off on foot to the north and was picked up by a convoy of German lorries that conveyed it all the way to Schlawe (Slawno).

The *Compagnie d'Honneur*

After the fighting at Elsenau which had been costly for the *Compagnie d'Honneur*, Ostuf. Weber had assembled his command and led it to the village of Flötenstein, where it spent the best part of a day, time enough to rest and find something to eat, before pushing on to Kolberg in the evening. It now had orders to make for Greifenberg, orders that Brigf. Krukenberg had left in his wake.

At dawn next morning, the *Compagnie d'Honneur* was crossing a village when refugees suddenly appeared from all sides, repeating the same warning: "The Russians are coming". This was not their imagination at play as minutes later Russian tanks materialised. Two Sturmgeschütze moved into action and fought off the T–34s. Relieved, the *Compagnie d'Honneur* continued on its way to the Baltic Sea.

Refugees and their baggage crowded the road. Crushing everything in their path, Russian tanks soon caught up with the *Compagnie d'Honneur* again. Taking a calculated risk that the tanks would not follow him across country, dotted with frozen ponds and marshes that might give way, Weber ordered his men to continue their withdrawal parallel to the road. At a distance of several hundred metres from the road, the retreating *compagnie* was only inconvenienced by the occasional short burst of machine gun fire. Even so Weber hurried his exhausted and frozen men; the Russian infantry might not be that far behind.

And then, some fifteen kilometres from Flötenstein, the *Compagnie d'Honneur* came to a village and, unbelievably, a train bound for Kolberg sitting in its railway station. It boarded and found itself in the presence of other elements of 'Charlemagne'. They numbered a good one hundred.

That same evening, the *Compagnie d'Honneur* was installed in a lavish officers' casino in Kolberg. The following day, a train took the *Compagnie d'Honneur* along the coast to Greifenberg.[3]

Greifenberg

Before the Soviet advance through Pomerania, the *französischen Ausbildungs-und-Ersatz-Bataillon* [Franz. A.-u.-E. Btl.] evacuated Greifenberg and relocated to Wildflecken camp.[4] However, elements may have seen action in the defence of Greifenberg.

The motor convoy

The motor convoy of the divisional staff company and divisional service units under Stubaf. Katzian also made good their escape from Pomerania. Leaving Gross Jestin at 0200 hours on the 4th, it made good time and, at daybreak, entered the town of Treptow-an-der-Rega (Trzebiatów), where it stopped.

From the back of a truck an armed Russian suddenly appeared; he must have jumped aboard in the belief that the truck was friendly. There was great surprise, even panic. A driver shot the Russian dead as he was about to fire. The other trucks were immediately searched. No more unwelcome passengers were found. But the rumbling of enemy tanks could be heard distinctly. At 0600 hours, the convoy left Treptow. Destination: Swinemünde (Swinoujscie) at the mouth of the Oder.

Around 1000 hours, in the region west of Treptow, a Russian tank column appeared and gave chase to the convoy. The drivers put their foot down, leaving behind the enemy tanks which fired wildly at the convoy. Thankfully rain covered the convoy from air attack. Its progress often slowed to walking pace as the roads became more and more congested with refugees and littered with wreckage. Crossing the island of Wollin (Wolin), the convoy finally came to Swinemünde at 1100 hours on the 6th. And it was here that Rttf. Soulat rejoined his French and German comrades of the divisional *Stabskompanie* with the motor convoy. He was overjoyed. He had come from Kolberg, via Cammin and Wollin, and on foot most of the way! He was not the only one to join the motor convoy, which was now ferried across the city to the island of Uznam.

On the 7th, the survivors, now numbering two hundred, left Swinemünde for Jargelin, near Anklam in Western Pomerania. However, they were minus all their equipment. They had been required to hand it over. Also Ustuf. Sarrailhé was missing. Stubaf. Boudet-Gheusi was absolutely furious. However, the recalcitrant was found hiding away in a barracks and brought along. Sarrailhé explained he preferred to stay behind and participate in the defence of Swinemünde rather than leave with them. The following day, at 1600 hours, they arrived at Jargelin and

---

3   According to Mabire, page 374, the *Compagnie d'Honneur* left Kolberg singing the SS *marschiert.*

4   At Wollin station, Rttf. Soulat of the Headquarters Company saw some wagons full of French volunteers. He went to investigate. They were from Greifenberg and, according to the officer in charge, bound for Wildflecken. Soulat noted that all had new equipment.

found themselves billeted in a barn full of holes. Their straw litter was vermin infested.

They passed the time delousing themselves. To relieve the monotony, some of the NCOs put the exhausted and demoralised survivors through the joys of close order drill again. There was little else to do.

On the 14th, they were moved to Menzlin, three kilometres from Jargelin. Their thoughts went out to their comrades still trapped in the 'hell of Pomerania'.

The Danzig pocket

Forced to withdraw to the north-east and into the forming Danzig pocket were the groups led by Ostuf. Fatin and Oberjunker de Brangelin. Many of the men under Fatin belonged to his own company, the 1/58, which, despite many MIAs, was one of the few units to have retained some form of cohesion. Following Fatin's group was that under de Brangelin of which only a few were still armed and able-bodied. While continuing to reassemble his men de Brangelin strove to maintain contact with Fatin.

At 0500 hours on 3rd March, after an exhausting night march, the group under Ostuf. Fatin arrived in Schlawe (Slawno). He was surprised to learn that other French SS troops, some three hundred in total, were already there. For the most part, they were from the II/57 under Hstuf. Obitz.

Oberjunker de Brangelin and his group arrived soon after Fatin.

That same day also saw the arrival by train of a one hundred strong detachment of the division's artillery group under Hstuf. Martin, which had just completed its training at artillery school Beneschau in Bohemia-Moravia.

At 1600 hours, Hstuf. Obitz, the senior officer, took command of the various isolated elements of 'Charlemagne' at Schlawe. All told, he had the command of some five hundred men. Wishing to move the men and equipment by train, he requisitioned railway wagons, but the lack of a locomotive thwarted that idea. Nevertheless, the ever-resourceful Frenchmen used the wagons as sleeping accommodation.

The following day at dawn, Hstuf. Obitz assembled all officers and passed on to them the news that the last railway links with the main force of Army Group Vistula had just been broken to the east of Köslin. In fact, this news was days old. They were cut off. Henceforth, there was no longer any hope of reaching Greifenberg as per orders. Obitz could do little else for the time being other than order the officers to take their men in hand again. Thus, the day was made over to cleaning weapons, repairing equipment, and searching for food, but mainly the latter.

That same day, Uscha. de Misser and the twelve men of his section of the 8/57 arrived at Stolp, east of Schlawe. They had walked there all the way from Elsenau.

As the day of the 4th passed Hstuf. Obitz grew more and more restless. Night fell. Dawn broke. By now, Obitz could bear it no more and placed his detachment at the disposal of the headquarters of the 4. SS-Polizei-Panzer-Grenadier Division, which enjoined him to take his command to Neustadt a.d. Rheda (Wejherowo),[5] some one hundred kilometres to the east.

As if by a miracle, an old locomotive was found and, at midday, Hstuf. Obitz and his detachment left Schlawe. Towards midnight, the train pulled into Stolp

(Slupsk) station. Progress had been slow, taking the best part of twelve hours to cover the twenty-five kilometres between the two major towns.

While sat in Stolp station disaster suddenly struck: a single Russian fighter-bomber swept overhead and dropped three or four bombs. All were direct hits. The effect in the packed railway cars was devastating: fifty men were killed[6] and sixty were wounded. Among the dead was Ustuf. Colnion, the commander of company 8/57. He was the youngest officer in 'Charlemagne'. Among the wounded were Hstuf. Obitz[7] and Ostuf. Salle who had only arrived at the front with the artillery group days before.

Command of the detachment now went to Hstuf. Martin. He formed a *bataillon de marche* of three combat companies of some one hundred and twenty men each.[8] As his assistant he chose Ostuf. Fatin. It was Fatin who would prove to be the real commander of the battalion.

The command of the companies went to Oberjunker de Brangelin, Oberjunker Lapart, and Oscha. Bonnafous.

Oberjunker de Brangelin was the former orderly officer of Hstuf. Monneuse. Oberjunker Lapart was ex-LVF and had attended the same Lehrgang as de Brangelin at Wildflecken. Oscha. Bonnafous was also ex-LVF and had served on the Eastern front since the first winter. In 'Charlemagne', he became the commander of the 3rd platoon of the 1/58.

In the evening of the 6th, the French SS troops continued their journey by train and finally arrived at Neustadt. The three companies were then sent to billets in three separate villages north of Neustadt. Even so the companies were no more than three kilometres apart.

On the 6th, thanks to the personal leadership of Uscha. Racine, a small group of French SS soldiers also arrived at Neustadt. Racine first served France in the ranks of the Air Force and then, from 1941, in the LVF. A very capable and resourceful NCO, Racine was appointed the commander of the 1st platoon of the 1/58 after the departure of Oscha. Girard to command the 10/58.

After Elsenau some twenty men assembled around Racine. He hoped to join another Waffen-SS unit and go back up to the front again, but this proved impossible! When they tried to integrate themselves into a company of the 4.

---

5   Soulat, page 80. However, according to Mabire, page 106, Hstuf. Obitz went off to find someone who would give him orders and when he came across an officer of the 4. SS-Polizei-Panzer-Grenadier Division he put his command at his disposal. Naturally this officer had no specific orders for Obitz, but decided to send him and his command to the depot of the 4. SS-Polizei-Panzer-Grenadier Division at Neustadt a.d. Rheda (Wejherowo). The officer was sure that the Division could make use of them.

6   Mabire, page 107, and de Misser of the 8/57 who was present at Stolp at the time of the attack (correspondence to the author). However, according to Soulat, page 80, eight men were killed.

7   On 12th March 1945, Hstuf. Obitz was evacuated by sea from the port of Gotenhafen, but his ship was torpedoed by a Russian submarine and went down with all hands.

8   De Brangelin, letter to the author, 31/8/97. This corrects Mabire who details the formation of this same *bataillon de marche* at Neustadt one day later.

SS-Polizei-Panzer-Grenadier Division they were told that all French stragglers had to be sent to collection stations at either Stolp or Neustadt. As they marched eastward their number grew. In this way, they became forty-strong. Finally, the group led by Racine managed to board a train bound for Danzig.

The journey was brought to a sudden halt when the train came under fire. All out! Officers of the 4. SS-Polizei-Panzer-Grenadier Division appeared and formed a *unité de marche* made up of Latvian SS troops also on the train. Racine offered the services of the Frenchmen, but this was declined as the only orders they had for them stated that they were to be sent to Neustadt to be regrouped. And the orders were definite. They felt all the more redundant on learning that their train journey was suspended temporarily. Thus, they took up residence in the cinema of a small village to while away the hours of waiting. Exhausted, some soon fell off to sleep.

In the evening, a Waffen-SS NCO informed the Frenchmen that the Germans were pulling back and that they had best leave on foot as the train was now out of the question. So at nightfall they set out. Some 'clever dicks' were even on bicycles. Finally they came to the city of Lauenburg between Stolp and Neustadt. And as luck would have it another train took them the rest of the way to Neustadt, which they reached hours later.

Uscha. Racine went straight to the headquarters of the 4. SS-Polizei-Panzer-Grenadier Division and was told of the whereabouts of other French SS troops in villages north of Neustadt. It was added that he should really go and get some sleep before joining his compatriots the next day.

The group was sent to a barracks where warm soup and clean bedsteads awaited.

In the early morning hours of 7th March, Hstuf. Martin and Ostuf. Fatin went by car to Danzig to make contact with a Waffen-SS headquarters. During their absence the Russians unexpectedly attacked Neustadt, but met stiff resistance from German tanks of the 7th Panzer Division, which had been dug in through lack of petrol. So rather than continue this investment which had already cost them several tanks and numerous other vehicles, they decided to skirt around the city to the north. In their path lay the weak French SS companies of the *bataillon de marche.*

On learning from a German motorcyclist that the Russians were turning north after being repulsed at Neustadt, Oberjunker de Brangelin came to the conclusion that the only way of reaching Danzig and of finding Ostuf. Fatin was to march due east. Oberjunker Lapart and Oscha. Bonnafous converged with de Brangelin to go in this direction. They decided to await nightfall before setting out.[9]

---

9   According to Mabire, *"Mourir pour Dantzig"*, page 115, the French SS companies
     quartered north of Neustadt repulsed Soviet spearheads with rifle and machine gun
     fire. Thereupon, the three French SS company commanders 'improvised a resistance
     to delay the enemy and give their men time to withdraw to the east'. However, the
     notion that the three French SS companies fought north of Neustadt is disputed by
     de Brangelin (letter to the author, 3/8/97). Also, if there was no fighting, then it is
     doubtful that Oscha. Bonnafous 'disappeared in the fighting' (as cited by Mabire,
     page 115). Furthermore, de Brangelin has confirmed that Bonnafous, Lapart and
     himself were in contact during this period and during the retreat later that night.
     Curiously, according to Saint-Loup, page 277, detachments *Chartrons* and *Labart*

Aided by night, the three companies set off and marched eastwards. By now, whether they realised it or not, they were, in fact, encircled.[10] Compass in hand, Oberjunker de Brangelin guided them to within sight of the sea whereupon the lights of a powerful lighthouse became their new guide to the south.

And then, quite suddenly, they found themselves in front of positions held by a German armoured unit and were greeted by gunfire.[11] Making themselves known, they came forward. The Germans were full of apologies and explained to de Brangelin that they had been expecting to see the Russians appear at any moment. This misunderstanding was soon forgotten about when a lift was secured for the whole *bataillon* on a lorry convoy of a bridging unit en route to Danzig. Upon arrival to Danzig, the *bataillon* was billeted in a school and it was here that Fatin rejoined the *bataillon*.

When tallied the *bataillon* was still some 250–300 strong[12] and, despite the very difficult night march, it had retained its cohesion. But the *bataillon* had a great many wounded and was without much of its weaponry[13]

As for the French SS troops led by Uscha. Racine, they were thrown into the battle at Neustadt. Requisitioned at Neustadt barracks with other stranded French SS soldiers, Sturmmann André Bourreau of the 7/57[14] found himself sent up to the front and guarding a sort of public garden from a hole he had hastily dug in the frozen ground. Several metres from him Bourreau thought he recognised a comrade from the *Compagnie d'Honneur*. The situation was so confused that he watched the Russians arrive by lorry barely one hundred metres away and disembark without attempting to camouflage themselves.

It was around six in the evening when Bourreau heard, then caught sight of German troops slipping from tree to tree. Were they changing position or withdrawing? Soon after, he heard the sound of foot-steps on dead leaves just in front of

were 'set up as a rearguard'. And to whom were they a rearguard? Because the French SS companies were alone and without orders. Needless to say, the role of rearguard remains unconfirmed.

10   Saint-Loup, page 277. Although encircled, there was no such break through as cited by Mabire, page 115. (De Brangelin, correspondence to the author.)

11   In correspondence to the author, de Brangelin positions the German armoured unit 'on the main road connecting Danzig to Hela'. This 'main road', now multilane highway 6, runs the whole length of Gotenhafen and exits the city to the north-west. Thus, the German armoured unit and the French *bataillon*, which had not yet reached the city of Gotenhafen, were somewhere north-west of Gotenhafen when they 'met'.

12   A figure of 'approximately three hundred' is cited by Mabire, page 116, whereas that of two hundred and fifty is cited by de Brangelin, letter to the author, 22/9/97.

13   Soulat cites, page 80, one third of the *bataillon* as able-bodied and armed, another third as able-bodied, but not armed, and the last third as wounded. Mabire, page 116, and Saint-Loup, page 277, repeat one third of the *bataillon* as able-bodied and armed, but cite the wounded respectively as over half and two-thirds of the *bataillon*.

14   Cited in the article 'André Bourreau' and Mabire, "*La Division Charlemagne*", page 536. And yet, according to Mabire, "*Mourir pour Dantzig*", page 109, Bourreau was of the 8/57.

him. He cocked his machine pistol. This time it was the Russians who were coming!

Bourreau then spotted a Russian well beyond his position. The young *Milicien*[15] thought that he was done for; the Russians seemed everywhere. Firing a short burst, he brought down the Russian. He let off another burst somewhat at random, and, out of fear, began to shout. Thereupon, he became convinced that the more he shouted, the more he would instil fear in the Russians. In response, he heard shouts and explosions. Then, some one hundred metres away, he recognised the unmistakable sound of a German machine gun joining in. 'Surprised by this unexpected resistance', the Russians fell back. Silence returned.

In the early morning hours, Bourreau and his comrade from the *Compagnie d'Honneur* cleared off and crossed Neustadt. Stopped by a German NCO of the 'Polizei' who wanted to send them back to the front, they 'played dumb'. Baffled by their reply, the German NCO spoke sternly and then let the matter drop. Besides, he had to stop others now arriving from Neustadt.

Bourreau and his compatriot then found themselves with a mixed unit composed of Wehrmacht troops and Russian volunteers of the Vlasov Army who had no desire to fall into the hands of the Red Army. Soon after, they met up with the other Frenchmen that Uscha. Racine had brought to Neustadt the day before. Uscha. Racine was still at their head. Of the forty men with him the day before, he now had twenty. He pushed them along the road to Gotenhafen where they would eventually join the other French SS volunteers trapped in the Danzig pocket.

The 'Waffen-SS Headquarters at Danzig' decided to rest and rearm those Frenchmen still capable of continuing the fight. Deloused, they were quartered in accommodation that overlooked port Gotenhafen and the Baltic Sea. While waiting to go back up to the front line, the Frenchmen were employed digging combat emplacements and taking prisoner shot down Soviet airmen, about ten a day. Old reflexes soon reappeared.

A small group of four French SS soldiers arrived at Gotenhafen from the Hela (Hel) peninsula. Led by Uscha. Vasseur, this small group was the perfect cross section of the diverse elements that had gone to make up 'Charlemagne'; there was René Forez of the 5/57, a former *franc-garde*; Chauvin, a former LVF *légionnaire*; and a former volunteer of the N.S.K.K. The group came to Hela by train via Stolp.[16] From Hela, a motor launch brought the Frenchmen across the bay of Danzig to Gotenhafen.

Inseparable, the four Frenchmen would participate in the heavy defensive fighting for the port city of Gotenhafen. They would remain totally independent of the other French Waffen-SS personnel in the 'Danzig pocket'.

The small group led by Uscha. Vasseur was not the only one to make it to Gotenhafen under its own steam. Another such group was that led by Uscha. Grenier of the 1/58. He had fifteen men with him. And he knew not one. He found himself in their company after the fierce fighting in Elsenau cemetery which

---

15   Cited in the article 'André Bourreau'. However, according to Mabire, page 113, "*Mourir pour Dantzig*", Strmm. Bourreau was a *Franciste*.

16   While at Stolp railway station the group witnessed a violent Soviet air strike. Presumably this was the very same air strike that had inflicted terrible losses on those French SS troops making their way to Neustadt by train.

had seen his platoon, the 1st, shatter. It was to a small hamlet beside Rummelsburg that the group withdrew.

At the end of several days without orders and supplies, Grenier sent a grenadier to Rummelsburg for news. He reported back that there was no one left in the city. Thereupon, the group left to the north and Stolp. Its stay in the small hamlet had lasted between eight to ten days. At this moment Grenier still did not know that he and his group were in a great 'pocket'. From Stolp, he hoped to withdraw to the west.

Arriving at Stolp, Grenier learnt that a withdrawal to the west was now out of the question; the German Second Army, holding Eastern Pomerania, had been cut off in its entirety, and was falling back east towards Danzig and Gotenhafen. The group went east too, following the coast as though a handrail. At Danzig, feldgendarmen sent the group onto Gotenhafen.

At the *Kommandantur* of Gotenhafen, Grenier met Uscha. Racine, his platoon commander. They fell into each other's arms. The two of them were on the verge of tears. They had not seen each other since becoming separated in Elsenau cemetery.

Racine told Grenier that Fatin, their company commander, and others of the 1st platoon were two kilometres from here in a villa beside the Baltic Sea. The others with Grenier, of various units, did not share his joy or that of Racine. With a joyous heart, the two of them made their way to the villa and Fatin. At an open door there Fatin stood. For the first time, looking him straight in the eyes, Fatin shook his hand. Grenier was overjoyed. He had found his family again. Uscha. Guilcher, a Breton and also of the 1st platoon of the 1/58, then came towards him. Grenier was now back home. He felt a sort of relief, although his thoughts were still very much with those he would never see again: the missing and the fallen.

Uscha. de Misser arrived at Danzig from Hela and was incorporated into the 4. SS-Polizei-Panzer-Grenadier Division. Forty-eight hours after his arrival, he was sent to Praust (Pruszcz Gdanski) some ten kilometres south of Danzig. He would fight under a German officer.

On 11th March 1945, the seventeen men of a platoon under Uscha. Combin,[17] all from Fatin's 1/58, lost their way while on reconnaissance south-east of Gotenhafen. The frozen corpses of deserters and civilian looters hung from the branches of trees along the road and swayed in the wind. This was the work of the merciless Feldgendarmerie. To avoid a similar fatal meeting with the military police, the French platoon integrated itself into a column of German pioneers.

The French platoon was assigned a mill to defend. Later, the Frenchmen noticed that the Germans had pulled back without informing them. Faced with little other choice, Uscha. Combin decided to try and make it back to Gotenhafen. First their route lay through large woods deep in snow and sometimes under foot were the frozen bodies of women or peasants. Then they came to a vast plain. Alarm bells started to ring. Cautiously they advanced across, observing the terrain. Convoys could be seen far off, but whose were they? They approached the road. And then it happened. A machine gun opened up and only missed them by a fraction. The convoys were Russian! Two tanks came straight for them. It was the end. They had gambled and they had lost. Now they were prisoners. A Soviet gestured to the Frenchmen to climb aboard. They obeyed.

17   Might be a pseudonym.

The eight prisoners aboard one tank expected the worst when the tank stopped in the remote corner of a wood. The Soviet tank commander, pistol in hand, called the first down. Uscha. Combin complied. The pistol was brought down on his nape and then his valuables were stolen: wedding ring, watch and pen. The next was called down and he too was hit and robbed. This was repeated a further six times. It was only then that Ivan concerned himself with the weapons the prisoners were still carrying! They set off again. The Frenchmen could not believe that they were still alive.

As for the other nine prisoners who had clambered aboard the second Soviet tank, they were never heard from again. Undoubtedly, the fate of the nine was the same as that of many other French Waffen-SS personnel captured by the Soviets, that of death by execution.

On 20th March 1945, all combat worthy French SS troops within the Danzig pocket were reformed into a W-SS Ersatz (Replacement) Battalion[18] and deployed to the front north-west of Gotenhafen.[19] It was in the third line of defence behind German and Latvian troops. Trenches were built.

'Ersatzbataillon Martin'[20] was no more than three hundred-strong and remained subordinated to the 4. SS-Polizei-Panzer-Grenadier Division. Attached to the French battalion were three German NCOs who had served in the Foreign Legion, spoke perfect French and were veterans of the Eastern front.[21] But Ostuf. Fatin resented this 'outside' interference.

From the 21st to the 30th, the front was rather calm.[22]

On the 31st, the Russians broke through the first two defensive lines. Would the Frenchmen fare any better? The battle began with infernal artillery and mortar bombardments and it was during one such mortar shower that Oberjunker de Brangelin was wounded in the heel by a piece of shrapnel measuring 2cms by 1cm. He was evacuated.

And then, in the early morning hours of 1st April 1945, the Russians attacked.[23] The number of T–34 tanks could not even be counted! Nevertheless,

---

18   The battalion may have only counted two companies (memoirs of Grenier) or three companies (Mabire).

19   According to Soulat, page 87, its positions may have been the villages of Kielau, Ciessau and Sagorsch. One member of Battalion Martin recalls that its positions were between Oxhöft and Rewa. According to Mabire, page 119, the French *bataillon de marche* took up positions along an airfield whose runways and hangars had been destroyed by heavy bombardments, and then deployed to new positions, not far from the sea, overlooking a sort of plateau, possibly Oxhöfter Kämpe. However, Mabire does not date the movement of the *bataillon* into these two positions.

20   Mabire, "*Mourir pour Dantzig*", page 120.

21   De Brangelin had one of the German NCOs attached to his company (correspondence to the author throughout 1997).

22   Soulat, page 82, and the *souvenirs* of a French SS-grenadier of 'Battalion Martin' (as told to Mounine). This corrects Landwehr, page 126, who states that the battalion 'soon' faced a powerful Communist assault.

23   Mabire, "*Mourir pour Dantzig*", page 120. However, one French SS-grenadier of 'Battalion Martin' recalls that the tank attack took place during the night of 31st March/1st April 1945.

the tank attack collapsed under the watchful eye of three Tiger tanks whose long-barrel 88mm guns knocked out the T–34s one after the other. Eleven Russian tanks were soon blazing before the Tigers were called to another sector. Calm returned. And although 'SS-Ersatzbataillon Martin' had managed to hold its ground and halt the Russians with 'a bloody nose', its own losses had been heavy, in fact crippling.

The Russians then turned to a war of words. By means of leaflets and powerful (loud)speakers, they invited the Frenchmen to surrender or face the attack of several divisions. Nobody went over. Again the Russians unleashed a violent hurricane of steel on their positions. Shells and rockets churned up the ground. Positions caved in.

Finally, 'SS-Ersatzbataillon Martin' received orders to prepare for a night-time embarkation.[24] Night came and the remaining Frenchmen withdrew to the Baltic shoreline. From a small creek offering some protection from Russian fire, they were evacuated by all manner of boats and transported across the bay to the sandy Hela peninsula where the defenders of the Danzig pocket were now being assembled for sea evacuation.

Late on 2nd April 1945, the Frenchmen boarded a former British cargo ship, converted of late by the Kriegsmarine into a troop ship.[25] Bound for Denmark, the ship was crowded with civilian refugees of all ages and wounded soldiers.[26]

Three days later, on 5th April 1945, the ship docked at Copenhagen. At 1600 hours, the Frenchmen disembarked. Granted several hours leave, they went off sightseeing. The Danish capital seemed to have been spared the ravages of war. Indeed, people were bathing in the sea!

Entering a cake shop, the Frenchmen could not believe their eyes: cream cakes! Hungry for so long, they gorged themselves.

As soon as they were full up, the Frenchmen continued their sightseeing. The sun had even come out. The contrast between the hell of Pomerania and this paradise of Denmark was just too great and left many feeling totally disorientated.

Later that evening, the Frenchmen caught a train to Germany. Orders had been received to rejoin 'Charlemagne' grouped near Neustrelitz. They arrived on 10th April 1945.

Of the five hundred French SS men assembled at Schlawe one month earlier, only one hundred rejoined 'Charlemagne' at Neustrelitz. Thus, the losses of Martin's battalion amounted to around eighty per cent, and while many had been wounded or were missing, many had indeed 'died for Danzig'.

Among the wounded was Oberjunker de Brangelin. From Copenhagen, he was conveyed by hospital train to a hospital at Halle. En route, the hospital train, which was clearly marked with the Red Cross, was machine-gunned by the Allied Air Force. After only two days in hospital, he was sent on his way to Austria of all

---

24   The memories of a French SS-grenadier of 'Battalion Martin'. However, according to Mabire, page 121, orders were received around midday 'to withdraw and reach the shore'. And although it is suggested that there was little or no delay between the receipt of the orders and the embarkation it should be noted that the time and the date of the embarkation are not specified.

25   Ibid and Soulat, page 82.

26   In all likelihood the wounded de Brangelin was aboard this same ship.

places. It was explained to him that nobody knew where 'Charlemagne' was and that the Russians were closing in from the East and the Allies from the West. From Austria, he went on to Italy, arriving on 3rd May 1945. The day after, he 'vanished into thin air'.

And what of those Frenchmen who 'fought for Danzig' independent of Ersatzbataillon Martin?

On 26th March 1945, Uscha. de Misser, fighting at Praust with 'SS-Polizei', was wounded in the head by mortar shrapnel. It could be said that he was 'lucky' because the other two men with him were killed. Evacuated to the peninsula of Hela, he was shipped on the General Sankt Martin to Copenhagen, Denmark, arriving on 1st April 1945. He was then taken by hospital train to Saxony and hospitalised in a converted school at Ernsthal, some twelve kilometres south-west of Chemnitz. At the end of April, he left hospital and set out for home.

On 28th March 1945, after several days of hard and violent defensive fighting for Gotenhafen, the three-man group led by Uscha. Vasseur was evacuated from the city to the collection point of Hela.[27] In turn, the group was shipped westwards. Before docking at the port of Stralsund, Germany, the ship had had to wait out to sea for a decision where to disembark. It was now early April 1945.

After spending five days at Stralsund, the group was issued a travel warrant to return to Wildflecken. By train, the four Frenchmen journeyed back through a devastated Germany; first, Stettin; then Berlin; Leipzig; Munchen; Ulm; and, finally, by the end of April 1945, Sigmaringen. The war was soon over.

Still as a group, they headed south and, after destroying their weapons, separated at Konstanz near the Swiss border. Thanks to some French POWs, they were now in civilian clothes. As for René Forez, he crossed into France via Bale. To this day, he does not know what became of his comrades.

The Siege of Kolberg

It is estimated that some six hundred Frenchmen of 'Charlemagne' managed to reach Kolberg before the Baltic Sea port was completely encircled on 7th March 1945. All were billeted on the ground floor of the Casino Municipal. Many were from the divisional staff and support units, but there was also a sprinkling of those from the elite *Compagnie d'Honneur* and the *Régiment de Marche*. Nevertheless, a good number of them were totally demoralised and unfit for combat duty.

At the head of the Frenchmen was ageing Hstuf. Havette, the commander of Waffen-Artillerie-Abteilung der SS 57. His assistant was the sixty-three-year-old Ostuf. Multrier, a veteran of World War One, who had been responsible for civil defence at Wildflecken. But the two officers were as exhausted and demoralised as the troops. However, two 'Charlemagne' officers, Ostuf. Ludwig and Ustuf. Büeler, not of French origin but German and Swiss respectively, were still very much full of fight. They had arrived at Kolberg on 5th March 1945. Of late, Ludwig had been attached to Krukenberg's headquarters and Büeler to that of Puaud.

At first the Frenchmen were gainfully employed on constructing anti-tank obstructions. When Oberst [Colonel] Fritz Fullriede, the town commander, asked Havette and Multrier to man these same defences with Frenchmen they replied

---

27   Most sources record that the Soviets took Gotenhafen on this day.

that they could not with so many men that were non-combatant. Hence, it came down to Ludwig and Büeler to assemble those French volunteers determined to fight on. Between two and three hundred men came forward to fight.[28] In this way, a reinforced *compagnie de marche* of three platoons was raised and added to the defence of the city.[29] At the head of the company was Ostuf. Ludwig. His *adjoint* was Ustuf. Büeler. The French *compagnie de marche* was attached to Battalion 'Hempel'.[30]

Among those to come forward to fight was Oberjunker Claude Platon, Puaud's orderly officer. A *Milicien*, he joined 'Charlemagne' at Wildflecken. Of note is that his father was Admiral Jean Platon.[31]

As for those Frenchmen who stayed put at the Casino, they were disarmed. All the same, they agreed to continue building fortifications and assist in the evacuation of civilians and soldiers.

To defend the city packed with refugees, Oberst Fullriede had at his disposal a motley force from all branches of service. Total military personnel amounted to some 3,300 men, of whom one third were Volkssturm organised into two battalions. Heavy weapons were scarce: eight 105mm howitzers, whose previous owner was 'Charlemagne'[32]; seven heavy and eight light FLAK cannons; eight tanks of Panzer Division 'Holstein' sent to Kolberg for repair, supplemented on the 5th by the arrival of a further seven[33]; one armoured train which arrived on the 4th; and one Volkssturm rocket battery with 800 rounds. However, his trump card was the Kriegsmarine. From the 7th, the defenders could call upon destroyers Z–34 and Z–43 and their 150mm guns. Their fire support would smash up tank attacks and knock out artillery batteries.

At first fortress Kolberg and its 'garrison' faced the Soviet 45th Guards Tank Brigade and the 272nd Infantry Division of the First Guards Tank Army. When these two units were withdrawn the 6th and 3rd Infantry Divisions of the First Polish Army took their place.

---

28 Mabire cites, page 85, two hundred and Saint-Loup cites, page 302, three hundred.

29 Soulat, page 61, Saint-Loup, page 302, and Mabire, page 86. However, in Bayle's book "*San et Persante*", page 180, an eyewitness with the initials of 'AA' gives a very brief account of the fighting at Kolberg and talks of two French companies taking up positions facing the enemy.

30 The *compagnie de marche* was probably raised on the 5th and attached to Battalion 'Hempel' that same day. It should be recalled that Ostuf. Ludwig and Ustuf. Büeler only arrived at Kolberg on the 5th (Saint-Loup, page 301).

31 Considered 'ultracollaborationist', Admiral Platon was the former Vichy minister for the Colonies, before Pétain dismissed him from the government for his views. Arrested by the Resistance, he was brought before a military tribunal of the F.F.I. at Limoges. Condemned to death on 24th July 1944, he was shot or barbarically quartered on 18th August 1944.

32 These were the same howitzers that 'Charlemagne' sent by train from Neustettin to Belgard. See chapter 10.

33 Soulat, page 61. However, according to Saint-Loup, page 302, Oberst Fullriede had at his disposal six damaged Tiger tanks that had to towed about and employed in a fixed position.

The French *compagnie de marche* was soon in action. Accounts of its first actions differ.

First, according to Saint-Loup,[34] battalion Hempel and the French *compagnie de marche* launched a counterattack at 0600 hours on the 6th to redress a dangerous situation that had arisen along the road to Treptow during the night. The counterattack was irresistible and Neugeldern, beyond the city perimeter to the south-west, was regained, but the German and French forces were now in open country and exposed, which the Russians were quick to exploit. And although the Frenchmen fought tooth and nail, they could not hold and withdrew to crossroads Köslinerstrasse-Körlinerstrasse, behind the church of Saint-Georges. Losses were considerable.[35]

Oberst Fullriede pulled the *compagnie de marche* back along Köslinerstrasse, east of the Persante, to a position around Saint-Georges crossroads and along the railway line that led to the city centre. The Frenchmen fortified themselves in cellars from which they could cover the roads with their weapons. Anything that moved was shot up. Above them the city burned. In bitter fighting, they held their ground till the 9th.

Second, according to Mabire,[36] the French *compagnie de marche* was deployed on the left flank of the sector held by battalion Hempel. Fierce street fighting ensued. The Russians attacked with flame-throwers. The French answered back with machine guns and panzerfäuste. Making use of the cellars connected by a series of underground passages and with the support of dug-in tanks and small calibre guns manned by Luftwaffe crews, the defenders were able to throw back the Russians.

Blocked overground, the Russians now attempted to advance through the cellars. Furious hand-to-hand fighting erupted in the darkness. 'They slit each others throats'.[37]

During lulls in the fighting, the Russians turned to a war of words. In French, loudspeaker broadcasts invited the Frenchmen to stop fighting and surrender. Nobody is reported as having been persuaded into going over.

On 9th March, the Kolberg garrison counterattacked in the sector of the gas works. Battalion Hempel struck along the road to Treptow and captured twenty-four heavy weapons. For its part, the *compagnie de marche* also went over to the attack.[38] Two sections of its 2nd platoon[39] had received orders to retake Saint-George cemetery, not far from the gas works, alongside the railway line. Their mission was to hold a salient in the Russian lines so that reinforcements of German armour could get through to the besieged defenders. Bayonets fixed, the sections of SS-Oscha. Francke and W-Uscha. Aimée-Blanc[40] charged forward.

---

34   Pages 303-306.
35   Saint-Loup, page 303. This is not confirmed by Soulat or Mabire.
36   Mabire, "*Mourir pour Dantzig*", page 86.
37   Ibid.
38   Soulat, page 62. However, Mabire cites, page 87, the date of the counter-attack one day later.
39   Ibid. Mabire is at variance and cites, page 87, that the 1st and 2nd platoons of the *compagnie de marche* took part in the attack.

They swept aside the Russians and retook the cemetery. Support arrived. Now began the battle for the cemetery.

Strmm. Marotin of the 8/57 also fought in Kolberg cemetery, but not in the ranks of the '*compagnie de marche* Ludwig'. Arriving at Kolberg, he was sent to the casino where he met up with two comrades. Like many, he was suffering from dysentery but still wished to remain a soldier. The spectacle of defeat and rancour prevailing at the casino disgusted him all the more. They left. And then by chance the three Frenchmen met a patrol from a *demie compagnie* of the 4. SS-Polizei-Panzer-Grenadier Division. Taking to each other, the Frenchmen incorporated themselves. At this point Marotin still did not know that there were other Frenchmen at Kolberg besides the sick and wounded at the casino.

Sixty-strong, the 'SS-Polizei' half-company was commanded by a very young Untersturmführer 'in a warm ambience of camaraderie' and was a sort of 'fire-brigade' put in by the headquarters wherever the need was greatest. The half-company was committed to the fighting in the cemetery, where Marotin now met Frenchmen of the *compagnie de marche*. To find other Frenchmen who still wanted to fight pleased him. Two of them even had news of his brother.

Soviet artillery sprayed the cemetery with shellfire. Marotin wrote that 'the bombardment mixed dead and alive in a great fraternal dance'.

Furiously, the Frenchmen of the *compagnie de marche* and their German comrades in arms fought for the cemetery, but the enemy pressure was too great and the defenders were forced to give ground step after step. Yet they managed to hold the cemetery for twenty-four hours before being thrown out.

The *compagnie de marche* then withdrew to a new defence line which ran along Köslinerstrasse from the gasometer.[41]

The losses of the *compagnie de marche* numbered five killed and three wounded. Again they were losses it could ill-afford. For this action, three men received the Iron Cross, of which one was 1st Class and awarded posthumously.

Elsewhere the fighting continued unabated. Volkssturm battalion Pfeiffer, to the west of the city, and battalion Hempel, to the south-west, were offering stubborn resistance and succeeded in throwing back the constant tank attacks. On this day, Hempel was proposed for the Knight's Cross.

Day after day the defenders fought desperately to buy the time to complete the sea evacuation of all civilians within the city. The Polish forces were heavily

40   Ibid. Once again Mabire is at variance and cites, "*Mourir pour Dantzig*", page 87, that Ustuf. Büeler and Oscha. Francke were in command of those units which went over to the attack. However, of interest to note is that Mabire cites the names of *Franc* and *Ayme-Blot* (pseudonyms) in his earlier work "*Mourir à Berlin*". So why the different names? This the author has not been able to answer unless Mabire was in receipt of new information following the publication of "*Mourir à Berlin*". Nevertheless, as *adjoint* of the *compagnie de marche*, Ustuf. Büeler may well have co-ordinated and overseen the attack. Of course, the possibility exists that Ustuf. Büeler was the commander of the 2nd platoon or acting as a temporary platoon commander for the attack. In both cases, he would have almost certainly been with the troops conducting the attack.

41   Saint-Loup, page 306.

reinforced with an additional infantry division, the 4th, and with the 4th Heavy Tank Regiment to bring about the swift capture of Kolberg.

On the morning of the 13th, the Poles mounted another attack. For the first time they sent in all their forces. The attack was opened with a violent bombardment from all guns. The defenders yielded. Events took a dangerous turn; the Poles captured the gasworks and penetrated towards the harbour on both sides of the Persante.

On the 14th, after heavy fighting in the morning, the Polish commander used the open radio at 1530 hours and again at 1600 hours to demand the surrender of Kolberg. The 'invitations' went unanswered. The fighting began again in all its fury. By now, it was impossible for the defenders to dig trenches because the water table was so high.

On the 15th, the Poles continued to gain ground despite the defenders contesting every single yard. Shielded from view by thick fog, two companies of Festungs-regiment 5 [Fortress regiment 5] were landed without opposition from the Polish artillery. The newcomers immediately counterattacked in the sector of the railway station. They suffered heavy losses.[42]

That same day, a communiqué[43] from the headquarters of Army Group Vistula laudatory cited the elements of the 33. SS-Waffen-Gren.Div (franz.) 'Charlemagne' fighting at Kolberg. According to the communiqué, they had fought in a remarkable manner.

During the night of the 15th/16th the last of the women and children were evacuated. Their suffering would have been made worse, if that was possible, by the arrival that day of the 6th Rocket Artillery Brigade whose Katyushas pounded the small perimeter now held by the defenders.

To Marotin, still with his 'newlyweds' of the 'SS-Polizei', the days became indistinguishable; a succession of patrols, missions and violent engagements. One such mission was to protect the armourers and the explosive experts ordered to blow up a munitions depot of large calibre naval shells. Just as they were completing the demolition preparations the Soviets appeared. The engineers and their escort withdrew in haste. The depot was blown. It was like a crash of thunder. The ground opened beneath the Soviets. The Germans were thrown to the ground. They had been a bit too close!

Marotin had a brush with death. Coming back from patrol, he stopped to talk to some Feldgendarmen. His comrades went on without him. A brief conversation later, he hurried off to rejoin them. In front of him marched two lads of the Wehrmacht. Suddenly a mortar shell landed in the street, throwing him high into the air. He blacked out. The very next thing he remembered was his comrades, who had returned for him when he did not rejoin them, 'shaking him like a plum tree to see if he had anything broken'.[44] Although covered in blood, remarkably he was not wounded, only dazed. He looked around; the two soldiers of the Wehrmacht lay

42   Soulat, page 62. This is possibly the same fortress infantry unit that, according to Saint-Loup, page 306, became lost in the maze of roads and 'disappeared, decimated by enemy fire'. And according to Duffy, "*Red Storm on the Reich*", page 234, the low-grade newcomers proved 'useless' in the intense fighting.

43   Ia/Nr. 3191/45 geh.v. 15.3.45.

44   Marotin, "*La longue marche*", pages 74-75.

flat on the ground, dead. Pieces of shrapnel were everywhere; his greatcoat had taken the blast. All the same he continued to fight on.[45] Only later, when back in France, did he learn that several ribs had, in fact, been broken.

During the night of 16th/17th the embarkation began of male civilians, railwaymen, those of the para-military organisations, and soldiers without arms. In this way, the first Frenchmen from those residing at the Casino may have been evacuated. By now, conditions there were terrible. Their straw bedding was filthy. Water was in such short supply that they had to drink the foul water of the Persante polluted upstream by human and animal corpses.

On the morning of the 17th, the French *compagnie de marche* took up defensive positions in front of the railway station. It was now under a certain '*lieutenant*' Erdmann[46] or Ustuf. Büeler[47] and its strength stood at between fifty and sixty men.[48] By the time the company received orders to withdraw to the port and make ready for embarkation, it totalled thirty-three men.[49]

At 1700 hours, redoubt Waldenfels fell. This was a disaster. From there, the Poles could bring fire to bear on the whole of the east bank of the Persante, the port entrance and the remaining artillery positions. The end was clearly in sight; the defenders were now left holding a strip of land 1,800 metres long and 400 metres deep on the East bank of the Persante. The only heavy weapons they still had with them were three light FLAK cannons, two mortars and one gun.

The pressure was such that the *compagnie de marche* had to be committed to the fighting once more. In hand-to-hand fighting it retook some houses next to the wood bordering the beach.

To reinforce the engaged *compagnie de marche*, Ostuf. Ludwig formed a platoon from those still at the casino who were now willing to fight. Moments later, while making its way to the positions held by their compatriots, the platoon was caught in a 'Stalin Organ' barrage and totally annihilated. All but four were killed.

The *compagnie de marche* continued to counterattack till nightfall. Receiving orders to embark, the company was relieved by German troops. It now counted no more than twenty men![50]

At midnight, Ostuf. Ludwig guided the survivors to the port. From there, they were evacuated.

At 0630 hours on the 18th, after beating off a final attack, lieutenant Hempel and the small rearguard were evacuated.[51]

---

45   Ibid. However, according to Mabire, page 88, Marotin played no further part in the fighting and lapsed in and out of consciousness over the next few days before being evacuated.

46   Saint-Loup, page 308. However, it is not known if Erdmann was an officer of 'Charlemagne'.

47   Mabire, page 89 and Soulat, letter to the author, 17/4/98. It appears that Ostuf. Ludwig had burnt himself out and 'could not take it any longer' (Mabire, page 89). Nevertheless, Ludwig joined Fullriede's command staff at the town hall.

48   Saint-Loup, page 308.

49   Mabire, page 92.

50   Saint-Loup, page 309.

Later, while on the bridge of a destroyer, Büeler was approached by Fullriede, Hempel and Ludwig. Full of praise, Hempel congratulated him on the performance of 'his' Frenchmen.

On the 19th, the survivors disembarked at Swinemünde. They were sent back to Wildflecken.

As for Marotin, he said of the last days at Kolberg:

> It was time we evacuated this main road which leads to the harbour station from the north-east and withdraw towards the mouth of the Persante, commanded by the tower of fort 'Münde' which raised its red bricks over the Baltic.
>
> Ivan broke through along the Persante where the avenue is very large and where the railway lines of the harbour station converge. Two times the Soviets would attack the barricades at the end of the avenue, they would take them once which would be retaken from them … I found some Frenchmen again on the beach … with them we would participate in the holding of this avenue … Our strength melted like snow in the sun … But, we were still there … There were old men of the Volkssturm with us … I had lost several comrades I knew … The demi-compagnie of the 'SS-Polizei' no longer had twenty able-bodied men fit for combat duty … Our Ustuf. and about ten of them were still going to disappear in this avenue and on the beach.
>
> At night, on the night of the 17th to the 18th I believe, we withdrew to the beach, facing the fort. The Volkssturm were holding the last barricades … The boats approached but they could not come to the beach and we had to take a sort of long footbridge made of shaky planks. Without panic the men ran … arched … In front of me, an unknown soldier fell into the water without (letting out) a shout!

He embarked on a sort of troop transporter armed with a captured French 75mm gun and was taken out to sea.

Once sixty-strong, the *demi-compagnie* of 'SS-Polizei' could now be counted on the fingers of one hand! As for the *compagnie de marche* of 'Charlemagne', its losses amounted to ninety per cent.[52] But the contribution made by the *compagnie de marche* of 'Charlemagne' and also by the *demi-compagnie* of 'SS-Polizei' to the defence of Kolberg brought about the successful evacuation of some 35,000 local residents, more than 50,000 refugees, numerous wounded and nearly all of the surviving soldiers. Thus their sacrifice had not been in vain. Indeed, it could be said that the impossible had been pulled off.

In addition, the defenders of Kolberg had killed and wounded thousands and thousands of Russians and Poles, and destroyed as many as thirty tanks, some of which were credited to the French *compagnie de marche*.[53]

---

51   Duffy, "*Red Storm on the Reich*", page 235. However, according to Saint-Loup, page 309, Fullriede was among the last group to leave at 0430 hours. Incorrectly, according to Mabire, the company received orders to withdraw on the morning of the 18th and was later evacuated in the early hours of the 19th.

52   Saint-Loup, page 310. It should be noted that the losses of the defenders as a whole amounted to fifty per cent.

53   At least three different figures exist of the number of tanks the enemy lost. Saint-Loup cites, p. 310, twenty-four. Soulat cites, p. 62, twenty-eight, and Mabire cites, p. 93, thirty. Additionally, Saint-Loup credits four tank kills to the *compagnie de marche*, whereas Mabire credits three tank kills to Oberjunker Platon alone.

Escape

Not all of the Frenchmen at Kolberg received the order to evacuate. Among those left behind was eighteen-year-old François de Lannurien. Of note is that his father was *général* Barazer de Lannurien, a prominent figure in the M.S.R., who worked out of Rennes recruiting French volunteers for the struggle against Bolshevism. François was the youngest of three sons. Following in his father's footsteps, he too rallied to the cause of Deloncle. His oldest brother donned the uniform of the LVF whereas his was that of the Waffen-SS. In fact, he enlisted under his father's first name.

Arriving at the depot of Greifenberg, François de Lannurien was assigned to Ostuf. Michel's training company. The company became that of Ustuf. Pignard-Berthet and was sent to the front as part of the *bataillon de reserve de* Greifenberg. Losing his unit during one of the first engagements near Neuland crossroads, he joined a group of German panzerjägers. Evacuated to Cammin, then onto Kolberg, he was among those Frenchmen who came forward as combatants for '*compagnie de marche* Ludwig'.

In a hole three or four kilometres from the city centre, de Lannurien was over-whelmed by the sudden silence that reigned. The guns of the Kriegsmarine covering the embarkation could no longer be heard and those of the Russians had fallen silent in turn. Suddenly, enemy tanks and thousands of infantry approached. Escape was out of the question. It was all over. The young Breton put his hands up. To his great surprise, he was not shot dead.

Brought to a forest, de Lannurien joined several hundred other prisoners held there. It was twelve degrees below zero and all were cold. The wakeful nights and days of savage fighting had also left the vanquished hungry and exhausted.

Although guarded, the prisoners were able to come and go as they pleased in this forest. In this way, de Lannurien came across one of the panzerjäger with whom he had fought in the sector of Neuland.

The two of them had escape on the mind. The panzerjäger explained his plan: since the Russians had not counted their prisoners all they would have to do was to hide themselves away and then wait for the guards and the other prisoners to leave the forest. A simple plan, but was it good enough to succeed?

A group of four, including de Lannurien, took to a shell hole which comrades covered over with branches and snow. Moments earlier, he had asked some of his compatriots to accompany him, but all had replied that he was mad.

All day long the four hid away in their hideout. They remained undetected when the other prisoners were assembled at nightfall and marched away. The plan had worked like a dream. Nevertheless, to be on the safe side, they only emerged from their hideout four or five hours after their comrades had left.

Luckily one of the group, a Kriegsmarine officer, had managed to keep hold of a compass. He took his three companions to the west. For fifteen nights they trav-elled and for fifteen days they camouflaged themselves in groves and ricks. Villages were avoided as all were Russian occupied. Still in jackets and shirts, they suffered horribly from the cold. They had no food on them and had to suck on frozen snow that resulted in raging dysentery. But on they went. In this way, they eventually reached the banks of the Oder at Stepenitz (Stepnica). The western bank was still in German hands. There lay salvation.

The small group encountered hundreds of soldiers who, like them, had managed to escape from the enemy, but could not cross the final obstacle of the Oder. The Russians had yet to clean out its banks and had taken up position on cliffs from where they could watch over the river and intervene against all crossings. However, one lifeline for those stranded on the 'wrong' bank was the small boats, skippered by civilians, that slipped across from the western bank each night. Indeed, the small boats had kept coming to their help night after night, but this lifeline was, of course, full of danger. To reach a boat, the escapers had to dash across several hundred metres of sand lit up by enemy flares and swept by mortars and gunfire. And then and only then, in the full view of an alert enemy, could the crossing begin.

Nights later, the four, with many others, tried their luck. Under fire, all dashed towards a boat. Those who still had weapons tried to cover them. The young de Lannurien, who against orders had removed his boots, outran the others with him, dived into the river, swam to the boat and hauled himself abroad. Was he saved now? No. Unfortunately, the boat was hit and started to sink. There he was in the water again. He could have quite easily given up and returned to the east bank, but he swam off to the west bank.

The Oder is more than two kilometres wide, but dotted with numerous islands and sandbanks. It was these that de Lannurien used to rest and get his breath back before swimming on. Finally he came to the west bank where he was joined by two Germans who had also managed to swim across. All were rudely welcomed by gunfire. They dived for cover and started shouting to persuade this welcoming committee of their identity. Eventually, their shouts were understood and their saviours approached. His strength failing him, de Lannurien fainted.

The young Breton was admitted to hospital. He was in need of treatment for a bullet he now carried in his back, as well as for a piece of shrapnel in his foot, and for frostbite, but he had escaped from the hell of Pomerania. Two or three weeks later, after regaining his strength, he asked to rejoin his French comrades of 'Charlemagne'.

No less dramatic was the escape of Fenet's I/RM.

Fenet's Battalion

As many as eight hundred men of 'Charlemagne' managed to reach Meseritz. Ostuf. Fenet had them assembled into four *compagnies de marche* of nearly two hundred men each.[54] What now? This was the same difficult question that General von Tettau was asking himself. For in his hands was the fate of those units of his Army Corps and of the X. SS-Armee-Korps encircled in Pomerania. He had intended to make for Schmalentin (Smolecin) and, from there, onto the island of Wollin via the city of Cammin (Kamien Pomorski), but on the 6th he learnt that Cammin had fallen to the Soviets. As a result, he now inclined north towards the coast and the small port of Horst from where he hoped to be evacuated by sea.

Towards midnight on the night of 6th/7th, after several hours' sleep, the Frenchmen of 'Charlemagne' set off again. In the early morning hours, they arrived at Pinnow. Continuing on, they came to Nabelfitz, about ten kilometres from Greifenberg, where it was learnt that forces of Corps Group von Tettau were to

54   Saint-Loup, page 330, and Mabire, page 29.

launch an attack to free the encircled garrison of Greifenberg. The attack went ahead without the French battalion which was completely exhausted. From its starting point of Nabelfitz, the attack gained three kilometres before grinding to a standstill.

'Battalion Fenet' then set off again to reach the new rallying point of Cammin[55] on the east bank of the Oder. In the evening of the 7th, the French column arrived at Wendisch-Pribbernow, where it rested for the night.

At dawn, the battalion continued its march to the north-west. Soon after, civilians supplied the news that the Russians were already at Cammin. Its direction of march remained the same.

The battalion came to the river Rega. A bridge was found intact, but guarded by two T–34s. Because the enemy tank crews were playing cards on the riverbank, the Frenchmen could have quite easily dealt with them and then passed, but they still remained under strict orders to avoid any contact with the enemy.[56] Thus, they steered well clear of this bridge. Ten kilometres upstream, south of Treptow, they found another bridge and crossed over without incident.

Then, on the road from Treptow to Greifenberg, a vehicle exploded a mine and wounded seven men.

In the afternoon, battle raged around the villages of Görke (Górzyca) and Woedlke. The latter was recaptured from the Soviets who had already given themselves over to pillage and violence.[57]

During the day, Staf. Zimmermann assembled the men to wish Brigf. Krukenberg a happy birthday. He was fifty-seven-years-old. Krukenberg seemed touched and gave a brief speech, congratulating them on their discipline and performance, and then gave the order to march on.

In the early evening, the battalion arrived at Gross-Zapplin[58] and settled down for the night.

Throughout the 9th the battalion continued its march northwards, arriving at the small fishing port of Horst (Niechorze) late into the night. Exhausted, the men collapsed on bare shopfloors and fell off to sleep.[59]

In the afternoon of the 10th, the battalion left Horst for Rewahl (Rewal) along the coast, arriving around 1700 hours.

---

55   Soulat, page 70, and repeated by Mabire, page 29.

56   Saint-Loup, page 332.

57   Soulat, page 70. Of note is that there is no mention of 'Battalion Fenet'. However, according to Mabire, pages 20-21, 'Battalion Fenet' did sweep aside the Russians in *both* villages. In response to this, Soulat mentions the recapture of one village, but not both. In addition, what of Saint-Loup and Rostaing who claim that the battalion was under strict orders to avoid any engagement? Thus far, these orders appear to have been carefully followed, although, in this particular instance, combat may have been unavoidable. Unfortunately, the author has not been able to confirm if 'Battalion Fenet' did see combat at either village or both.

58   According to Mabire, page 22, the battalion rested at the village of Zappten.

59   Soulat, page 70. However, according to Saint-Loup, page 334, part of the battalion, not finding sufficient space available at Horst, continued on its way to the seaside resort of Rewahl.

Ostuf. Perrin, Ostuf. Rozède and Oscha. Charles Pantalacci[60] joined the battalion with an amazing story to tell. On the 4th, between Körlin and Kolberg, the three of them and nine others were cut off from the bulk of 'Charlemagne'. Taking up the role of rearguard, the three became separated in turn.

For days, the three of them wandered across country. In search of food and shelter, they were chased away from farm after farm by peasants frightened by the prospect of brutal Russian reprisals. On the point of giving up, they came to another farm where they expected the same response. Miraculously they were welcomed with open arms and fed hot food, meat and milk. Their saviour was surprised to learn that his guests were French. To convince him, they gave him a brief history of 'Charlemagne' and showed him their Soldbuch. Eventually, with tears in his eyes, their host went on to explain that his son had served in France and been treated well before his death. In return, he now wanted to do something for the French.

According to their host, the Germans were still holding Deep (Mrzezyno). The town, although not that far away, lay beyond a lagoon several kilometres wide. Perrin answered that they no longer had the strength to swim across. Their host then revealed to them a route straight across the lagoon to Deep. He spoke of a walkway, running just under the water, which followed and was marked out by an overhead electrical line. The Russians were unaware of this route.

The Frenchmen covered the two kilometres to the lagoon and entered the water that came up to their chest. Cautiously, they waded across. Eventually, they reached the other bank and liberty. But this was not the end of their story. To their great surprise, they discovered that Deep was only defended by weak elements of the Waffen SS, an anti-tank platoon and the Volkssturm. In the face of a Russian attack, the defenders could not offer resistance for long. Indeed, it might only be a matter of hours before the town fell. Thus, the three Frenchmen did not linger in Deep where chaos reigned.

Perrin, Rozède and Pantalacci set off westwards and were swept along by the tidal wave of terror-stricken civilians fleeing 'the horror' coming from the east. Their feet were a bloody pulp, but they had to keep putting one foot in front of the other. They were racked by hunger, but they had to concentrate on one step at a time. With the last of his strength, Perrin jumped onto a toe-bar between a tractor and trailer, and there he stayed, with the help of two young girls, all the way to Horst. Rozède and Pantalacci also managed to reach friendly lines: the former on a lorry bumper and the latter on a bicycle.

Others managed to rejoin Fenet's battalion, but they were few in number. Among them was Uscha. Fronteau of the 10/58. He wrote in the notebook he had on him:

5th March: At Belgard, it's a scattering! The last elements disperse around 0700 hours. In the evening, I make my way towards the Russian lines with a group of three men (including *sergent* COMTE) to try and break through them.

---

60   Saint-Loup, pages 334-335. Rozède might be a pseudonym for Rouzaud. Pantalacci served with the LVF on the Eastern front where he was wounded. Notably, he went on to become one of the three bodyguards to Henriot. And yet, politically, he was member of the P.P.F.

6th March: After having marched all night in the direction of Greifenberg with my compass as the only means of orientation, we stop in a small wood beside a village occupied by the Russians. Exhausted.

7th March: numb with cold, we go up and install ourselves in a mirador to spend here our second day. At night, we enter a house where a small, old man, happy to see Frenchmen, all the more reason if they are wearing the field-grey uniform, literally filled us to bursting. We had eaten nothing for three days!
Around midnight, we come upon a German column withdrawing from Greifenberg (about fifteen kilometres from here) which, they announce to us, has just fallen into the hands of the Russians.

8th March: after having spent some hours in a stable, we wander through the Russian lines. We cross the Rega around 1500 hours. In the evening, we halt in a village.

9th March: departure around 0700 hours. We are surrounded by the Russians. We break through thanks to the flak (20mm and 88mm pieces). For an hour and a half, I come within a hair's breath of death under machine-gun and mortar fire.

Avoiding Horst, I make my way to Rewahl and Hoff where I meet friends again. We spend the night in a stable. At 2100 hours, alert! Withdrawal to Rewahl and Horst.

The breakthrough to Dievenow (Dziwnów)[61]

And what now for the encircled forces under General von Tettau pinned against the Baltic Sea in the area around the coastal resorts of Hoff and Horst? Disappointed in his hopes of being evacuated by sea, he had decided to break through by land to a bridgehead still held around Dievenow (Dziwnów).
At 2200 hours on the 10th, the breakthrough to the west began. The spearhead of the forces breaking out was composed of the Fusilier battalion of Panzer Division 'Holstein' and regiment 'Buchenau'. At 0200 hours on the 11th, after piercing the Soviet ring, the first German elements arrived at Dievenow, but in their wake the Russians penetrated into the escape corridor.
For 'Battalion Fenet' the day of the 11th was spent resting and preparing for its all-important mission. Through Staf. Zimmermann's personal friendship with von Tettau, the mission of the French battalion was upgraded from covering the retreat to spearheading 'the last breakthrough, along the shore, so as to clear the way for five thousand refugees'.[62] H-hour was set for midnight.

61   Soulat and Mabire record that the breakthrough was from Rewahl to Dievenow. This is confirmed, for example, by "*Russo-German war: 25 January to 8 May 1945*", page 22, and "*Red Storm over the Reich*", Duffy, pages 197-198. However, Saint-Loup details, page 339, that the journey from Rewahl to Dievenow had presented few problems for 'Battalion Fenet' and that the breakthrough was from Dievenow to Swinemünde (Swinoujscie). This would suggest that the Russians had got across the river Oder and onto the island of Wollin in sufficient strength to encircle the German forces holding the bridgehead around Dievenow. This is not true. With that said, it should be noted that there is great similarity between the accounts of the breakthrough recounted by Saint-Loup and Mabire.

Would they break through? Few dare ask themselves this question. The Russians were applying great pressure and all knew that fierce fighting lay ahead.

Sporadic shelling caused casualties among the hapless refugees crowded in Rewahl.

For the breakthrough, 'Battalion Fenet' was split into two. The first group, under Ostuf. Fenet, was to pass along the beach at the water's edge. The second group, smaller than the first, with Hstuf. Roy, Ustuf. Leune and Ostuf. Darrigarde, was to escort the convoy of civilians and wounded along the coastal road at the top of the cliffs. Armour was to precede this convoy. Warships of the Kriegsmarine were to support the breakthrough.[63]

Towards H-Hour, the refugees and their French escort under Ostuf. Fenet lined up on the beach. The battalion was now to escort some ten thousand refugees, double the number than that first planned. At midnight, all set off along the beach.[64]

At their head, pistol in hand, marched Hstuf. Jauss.[65] Also among the twenty-strong vanguard armed with panzerfäuste was Staf. Zimmermann. An engineer of old, he was on the lookout for mines.

With the rearguard that also comprised troops of the 4. SS-Polizei-Panzer-Grenadier Division was Ustuf. Martret.

The vanguard came to and easily overwhelmed the first Soviet outpost. Prisoners were taken. Staf. Zimmermann was slightly wounded in the foot by a piece of grenade shrapnel, but marched on in a pair of slippers. The element of surprise was now lost.

The beach was so narrow in places that the troops and refugees could only advance in single file. Sometimes they even had to take to the water. Hence, the advance slowed. This gave the alerted Soviets time to intervene. From the cliffs, they harassed the column with machine-gun fire and grenades that exploded with devastating effect. The French soldiers urged the civilians on.

Suddenly, Kreigsmarine heavy cruiser *Admiral Scheer* and torpedo boat T–33, out to sea, opened up and shells now started to rain down on those on the beach; the naval support had mistaken them for Russians. Some were wounded. Jauss reacted immediately and fired multi-coloured flares skywards that silenced the guns. They hurried on.

Three times they found their route barred and three times they had to smash their way through. Every now and then they stumbled across dead and wounded

62   Soulat, page 70.
63   In the afternoon, according to Saint-Loup, page 340, a young SS General arrived by Fieseler Storch on Dievenow beach to discuss the details of the breakthrough with Brigf. Krukenberg. This might be possible.
64   According to Rostaing, page 176, a five-hour artillery and naval barrage preceded the breakthrough. However, this seems rather doubtful as, firstly, no such barrage is recorded by either Mabire or Saint-Loup and, secondly, the element of surprise, a key precondition to the breakthrough, would have been sacrificed. Indeed, Krukenberg had dispensed with the idea of a covering detachment at the top of the high dunes running along the beach 'in order to avoid alerting the suspicions of enemy patrols and look-outs' (Soulat, page 70).
65   Saint-Loup, page 341.

from the fighting of the day before. At the approach of the column the wounded woke and cried out pitifully to be taken along, but that was quite impossible.

All of a sudden the cliffs levelled off and gave way to beaches lined with villas. This spelled danger. Were the Russians holding them? The answer was not long in coming. Enemy machine guns barked out. They threw themselves onto the sand. Minutes later, mortars showered death on the Frenchmen. There was no escape from the shrapnel on this flat beach. Jauss signalled for the naval support. With deadly accuracy, it crashed down among the Soviet-held positions. Galvanised by this, the Frenchmen went over to the attack. Led by Jauss, they dashed towards a Russian Maxim heavy machine gun positioned in the middle of the beach. It was destroyed by rifle grenade launchers. Casualties mounted on both sides, but the attack continued. They knew what was at stake if the attack bogged down.

Hstuf. Jauss charged towards another Maxim in a villa. With a grenade, he put an end to the enemy machine gun and its crew. Moments later, Uscha. Gilles of company I/57 saved Jauss' life; he killed a wounded Russian taking aim at him.

In close quarter fighting, the Frenchmen proceeded to clean out the villas. Then and only then could the column continue on its way. Again the cost was dear. Yet more dead and wounded. Among the wounded was Gilles who had been hit by a piece of mortar shrapnel.[66] He was brought to an improvised first aid post, also shelled, and then evacuated by sea on a patrol boat.

The fighting was not over yet. There were countless more skirmishes and losses.

Std.Ob.Ju. Dr. Anneshaensel was last seen alive treating the wounded. It is said that he was, in turn, seriously wounded and would succumb to his wounds while being transferred to a field hospital in the rear.[67] Brigf. Krukenberg subsequently awarded him a posthumous Iron Cross 1st Class.

At 0400 hours, 'Battalion Fenet' effected a junction with German forces.[68] Ustuf. Martret could not, and even today still cannot, understand how the battalion had managed to break through. He and the battalion pushed onto Dievenow. There was no sign of the column that had attempted to break through along the coastal road. The hours rolled by and still no sign of it. So what had happened to the column? Unfortunately, there is little agreement between the sources on the answer to that question.

According to Mabire,[69] the column made good initial progress thanks, in the main, to the escorting Tiger and Panther tanks that had opened up the coastal

66   Saint-Loup, page 343.
67   Mabire, page 32. However, according to Saint-Loup, page 346, Dr. Louis Anneshaensel went 'missing' during the breakthrough along the coastal road and not along the beach. (Presumably this was based on the eyewitness account of Dr. Métais.) This might be possible. According to "*Siegrunen VIII. Nos 5 and 6*", Dr. Anneshaensel was listed as MIA at Heinrichswalde. This has to be incorrect.
68   Saint-Loup, page 343. According to Soulat, page 74, it was around 0800 hours when 'Battalion Fenet' arrived at Dievenow. This is possible. It should be recalled that German forces were holding a bridgehead around Dievenow that extended for up to five kilometres. However, Mabire recalls, page 33, that the time of 0800 hours was when the battalion effected a junction with 'German Waffen-SS troops who were coming from Dievenow to meet their French comrades.' This has to be incorrect.
69   See Mabire, page 35.

road. But the escorting armour proved a double-edged sword: they also awoke the Russians to their presence. By 0500 hours, the column had a fight on its hands against Soviet motorised elements and took to the wood for refuge. However, the fighting continued in the undergrowth. It was savage. Finally, around 1000 hours, with the support of German paratroopers, the Luftwaffe and the Kriegsmarine out to sea, the column swept aside the enemy and got moving again. It was around 1400 hours when 'detachment Roy' rejoined the battalion at Dievenow.

According to Saint-Loup,[70] columns under Hstuf. Roy and Ustuf. Leune set off at 0200 hours in an indescribable disorder. (Of note is that there is no mention of escorting tanks.) The column under Ustuf. Leune comprised seriously wounded on carts. Cover was provided by French SS troops and a German company. The night was still except for the cries of the wounded. Progress was good for the first three kilometres, but then the scenery changed theme. Now in its path lay broken telegraph poles that slowed progress. The ruins of a village could be seen in the distance and on the horizon flames danced briefly. The rumbling of enemy guns could be heard. Many of the escorting German and French SS troops got jumpy and dashed off.

Suddenly shots rang out. The column came to a halt. More of the escort disappeared. Night started to draw to a close. Uncertainty heightened. Ustuf. Leune ordered the column to a wood ahead, but when it entered gunfire erupted from all directions. The Russians were already there. The French and German troops panicked and fled. Many of them were battle-hardened veterans, but they could not take it any more. Their nerves had finally gone to pieces. Leune and Dr. Métais were carried along by this rout.

Then German officers suddenly appeared, pistol in hand, shouting: "Forward! Forward!" The fleeing troops hesitated, stopped, about-turned, reassembled and went back to the battle. The fusillade stopped as suddenly as it had broken out. The column continued forward, straight over the dead and wounded lying across the road. The important thing was to keep going. The escape route might only remain open for hours, perhaps even for a matter of minutes.

The column came to two T–34s on fire. Smoke poured from them. Further on was a gutted Russian lorry which Ustuf. Leune stopped beside. He was approached by Oscha. Boucret, who offered him rich foodstuffs all the way from America! A Russian convoy, unbelievably full of American goodies, had just been intercepted. After stuffing themselves, they set off again. They marched on and on. Towards 1500 hours, the survivors finally re-established contact with the German front line.

Dr. Métais was stopped by Brigf. Krukenberg who admonished him for being improperly dressed; he had bandages stuffed in his tunic pockets! Krukenberg then questioned him about his gloves. What had he done with them? Métais replied that he had left them behind at Körlin. By way of conclusion, Krukenberg remarked that an officer of the Waffen-SS had to remain impeccably turned out at all times whatever the circumstances.

---

70   See Saint-Loup, pages 343-348. It should be noted that this account is similar to that
      of Rostaing, pages 176-178. There are, of course, many possible explanations for this,
      but the most obvious is that Saint-Loup had the eyewitness testimony of Rostaing as a
      source for his book. (His testimony was as yet unpublished.) With that said, there are
      differences, although minor, between the two accounts.

Regrouped, 'Battalion Fenet' set off towards Kolzow (Kolczewo). At its head marched Fenet and an impeccably dressed Krukenberg complete with gloves. Despite a foot wound, Zimmermann was still with them. He had refused to be evacuated. Crossing the pontoon bridge at Dievenow over the Oder, the survivors now set foot on the island of Wollin, which confirmed their final deliverance from the hell of Pomerania.

By the evening of the 12th, the last units of Group von Tettau had reached Dievenow. The seashore behind them presented an appalling sight. The coast was littered with corpses—civilian, German and Russian soldiers—abandoned and destroyed military vehicles, overturned carts of the refugees and dead horses.

'Battalion Fenet' made its way across the island of Wollin. Staf. Zimmermann came into possession of a bicycle and pedalled along.

Late on the 13th, the battalion reached Swinemünde. Along the way, Staf. Zimmermann went to the headquarters of General Aiching at Misdroy where his Chief-of-Staff congratulated him on the spirit and the fine appearance of the battalion. The General had seen the battalion on the road withdrawing in good order and singing.[71] Indeed, the conduct of the battalion was in such sharp contrast to the general ambience that the General decided to let it retain its weapons rather than hand them over.[72] This was exceptional.

This was not the only recognition that the Frenchmen of 'Charlemagne' received. A communiqué from 'General Headquarters'[73] was to recognise the important part they had played in the breakthrough to Dievenow.

From Swinemünde, the battalion left for Jargelin in the vicinity of Anklam where the other survivors of 'Charlemagne' were assembling. It arrived around midday on the 16th.

71   Soulat, page 74, and Mabire, page 37. According to Saint-Loup, page 349, it was General Aiching himself who congratulated Staf. Zimmermann on the spirit and appearance of the battalion. Indeed, the General said that it had been a long time since he had last seen men march past who still resembled soldiers! Mabire repeats this same comment, but attributes it to the General's Chief-of-Staff.

72   Soulat, page 74. In contrast, according to Mabire, page 37, the French battalion did obey the order to hand over its weapons, although some *gradés* [officers and NCOs] were permitted to retain their personal sidearm. This order is said to have exasperated the survivors who, during the past weeks of battle and march, had carried their weapons to safeguard them.

73   Saint-Loup, page 348. The headquarters referred to is possibly OKH, which was responsible for directing Eastern Front operations.

CHAPTER 12

Reformation of 'Charlemagne'

Anklam

The survivors were sent to Jargelin, north-west of Anklam, where they were to assemble. On the 8th arrived some two hundred men of the divisional Head-quarters Company, divisional service units and the *Compagnie d'Honneur*. Every day saw the arrival of more and more survivors.

Headquarters was established in a vestibule of a large country residence crowded with civilians. The clerical staff worked from two tables in front of the window. Because it was necessary for the clerical staff and runners to be there night and day, they decided to make themselves a bed of straw under the gigantic billiard table cluttering the vestibule. When Rttf. Soulat went for straw the German owner of the property confronted him. Soulat was furious. Had he not fought to defend Germany and Europe? He shouted as much to the German who shouted back, but then turned on his heels and left. As he did so Soulat warned him that the Russians would not ask his permission first before helping themselves.

On the 16th arrived Brigf. Krukenberg and the 23 Führer and 701 Mann of 'Battalion Fenet'. With them was Ostuf. Bénétoux, who had managed to escape from Soviet captivity.

Two days later, the 18th, Krukenberg visited the field headquarters of Reichsführer-SS Himmler near Prenzlau to give him a report on the performance of 'Charlemagne' in Pomerania. On his return, later that day, Brigf. Krukenberg bestowed a number of promotions and decorations on the survivors. For the first time, Rttf. Soulat noticed that Krukenberg was wearing the *tricolore écusson* (badge). At an awards ceremony, for his exceptional bravery, Fenet was promoted to Waffen-Hauptsturmführer.[1] Labourdette, his assistant, was promoted from W-Standartenoberjunker to W-Untersturmführer.[2]

Krukenberg then presented the Iron Cross 1st class (EKI) to newly promoted Ustuf. Labourdette, and the Iron Cross 2nd class (EKII) to Ustuf. Martret and some fifteen men. Also awarded were a far greater number of posthumous decorations. Thereupon, Krukenberg spoke briefly and passed on a message of congratulations from the Reichsführer-SS.[3] These awards were not final. In the following weeks, more awards were issued.

---

1   Fenet was actually promoted to Hauptsturmführer on 1st March 1945. (Message Tgb.Nr.1380/45 and SS-Soldbuch of Fenet.) Possibly, his promotion was backdated or news of his promotion did not get through to the division at the time.

2   Mabire, page 41. Labourdette was not appointed to Obersturmführer as stated by Landwehr.

3   Soulat, page 72, and Mabire, page 40. In contrast, according to Saint-Loup, page 370, the awards ceremony took place at Carpin on 27th March 1945.

That same day, SS-Stubaf. Katzian left for Wildflecken. He had orders to return from there with the French Ausbilungs-und-Ersatz-Bataillon. Also, Staf. Zimmermann[4] finally went into hospital at Anklam to receive treatment for his foot wound suffered in Pomerania.[5]

On the 19th, RF-SS Himmler spoke to his private physician, Dr. Felix Kersten, about his Waffen-SS and its losses. The Reichsführer informed Kersten that of the 6,000 Danes, 10,000 Norwegians, 75,000 Dutch, 25,000 Flemings, 15,000 Walloons and 22,000 French in the Waffen-SS, one in three was killed in action. He added that the losses of the volunteers hailing from the Baltic States, the Ukrainians and the Galicians were higher. Praise indeed, but his figure of 22,000 Frenchmen in the Waffen-SS is pure fantasy.

On 21st March 1945, the survivors gathered at Anklam town railway station to await transportation to their new billets in Mecklenburg. Because no trains were running they set off on foot. Marching in quick time, they sung out loudly.

Passing Anklam airfield, they saw lines of impeccably camouflaged German fighter planes. All were grounded through lack of fuel. They marched on, the first stop was the village of Schwerinsburg, where they were quartered in the great room of a requisitioned inn whose previous occupants were prisoners of war.

The following day, they set off at dawn. They passed through the villages of Sarnow, where supplies of foul-tasting biscuits were received, and then Friedland before being split up for the night in various locations. The divisional Headquarters Company spent the night in Schönbeck school.

The day of the 23rd was good to them. It started with milk in the morning. Towards 1600 hours, they arrived at the village of Bredenfelde, where they rested. Suddenly two enemy aircraft flew overhead, but did not interfere with them. In the evening, having covered over twenty kilometres, they came to Stolpe and a 'feast of potatoes'. Indeed, the day had been good to them.

On the 24th, they arrived in the region of Neustrelitz and were billeted in surrounding villages. The headquarters staff went to the village of Carpin. Brigf. Krukenberg established divisional headquarters in castle Carpin, a rather grandiose title for nothing more than a rather large farmhouse, but it was one of the few to have electricity.

Reorganisation

The day of the 25th, a Sunday, was given over to delousing.

Also, on this day, the SS-FHA ordered[6] the 33. Waffen-Grenadier Division der SS 'Charlemagne' to reorganise into a Grenadier Regiment with a structure based on the 'Type 45' (1945) Infantry Division of 2 Grenadier Battalions and 1 Heavy Battalion of:

1 Panz.Jäg. Kp.   (Anti-tank company)

---

4   Curiously, according to Mabire, page 39, and Landwehr, page 108, Zimmermann was now at the head of Waffen-Grenadier Regiment der SS 'Charlemagne'. However, according to official documentation, 'Charlemagne' was not ordered to convert to a regiment until 25th March 1945.

5   Mabire, page 79. Curiously, according to Soulat, page 96, Zimmermann was hospitalised at Neustrelitz.

1 Jagdpanzer-Kp.   (Assault gun company)
1 Fla-Kp. of 1–2 batteries   (Flak company)

In addition, the division was to have the support elements of:

1 Nachr.Zg.   (Signals platoon)
1 Pi.Zg.   (Engineers platoon)
1 Verpfl.Kol.   (Supply 'train')
1 Werkst.Zg.   (Workshop platoon)

This order was to be executed by 15th April 1945.

As such, the division was not officially disbanded. It remained subordinated to the 3rd Panzer Army of Army Group Vistula.

Brigf. Krukenberg responded by naming Staf. Zimmermann as the commander of Waffen-Grenadier Regiment der SS 'Charlemagne' and also by forming three battalions for the Regiment:

SS-Bataillon 57 under Hstuf. Fenet

SS-Bataillon 58 under Ostuf. Géromini

Heavy Battalion under Stubaf. Boudet-Gheusi

The nucleus of SS-Bataillon 57 was the former regiment of the same number. Hence SS-Bataillon 57 was the direct heir of the French SS-Sturmbrigade. Fenet, of course, retained its command. In its ranks remained many men who had enlisted in the Waffen-SS during the summer of 1943 and who, one year later, went on to fight in Galicia.

For the time being, SS-Bataillon 57 remained at Bergfeld with its command post in the five-building 'Familie Kunitz-Gusthof Kunitz' and its three assigned grenadier (infantry) companies in nearby farms.

At the head of the 1st Company was Ostuf. Roumegous. However, he was so demoralised that, in the end, Hstuf. Fenet had him relieved of his command. He was put at 'the disposal of the division'. Ustuf. Labourdette took over.

SS-Bataillon 58 was born of the former regiment of the same number. The morale of its former LVF legionnaires and *Miliciens* was not as high as that of their counterparts in SS-Bataillon 57. The baptism of fire in Pomerania had been particular hard on those from the *Milice*. The difficult job of commanding SS-Bataillon 58 went to Ostuf. Géromini, himself a former *Milicien*. Although regarded as outspoken and temperamental, this Corsican had proved himself a courageous and popular company commander in Pomerania. He was still full of fight, but all was not well with him, which culminated in a scene with Brigf. Krukenberg who abruptly cut him short and asked him to leave his office. Even so Géromini remained at the head of SS-Bataillon–58 billeted around the village of Grünow, five kilometres west of Carpin.

6   SS-FHA Amt II Org. Abt.Ia/II Tgb.Nr.2?54/45 gkdos. Curiously, according to Landwehr, page 108, on 15th March 1945, the Division was reorganised as Waffen-Grenadier Regiment der SS 'Charlemagne' at Anklam. In response to this, the author believes that Landwehr may have misinterpreted Mabire. (See page 39 of "*Mourir à Berlin*".)

The fifty-strong *Compagnie d'Honneur* was quartered at first in the village of Ollendorf, some four kilometres north-east of Carpin, but was quickly moved to Georgenhof, due north of Carpin.[7] It was still under the command of Ostuf. Weber who immediately resumed his harsh training programme.[8]

Uscha. Puechlong rejoined Weber and the *Compagnie d'Honneur*. Much to his disappointment, he had missed Pomerania. Towards the end of February 1945, he was hospitalised following a training accident at Paderborn. During an exercise to occupy and leave a Tiger tank with great speed he fell and dislocated his right hip. He called himself clumsy and stupid, all the more so when his fellow countrymen at the training school were recalled to Wildflecken and from there sent on to Pomerania.

After three weeks in hospital, Puechlong was discharged. He returned to Wildflecken. Assigned to Kreis' Company, he was entrusted with the task of accompanying to Sigmaringen a convoy of some one hundred *Miliciens* who had refused to serve in the Waffen-SS. This he performed. From Sigmaringen, he then journeyed northwards to Carpin where 'Charlemagne' was reforming. It proved a most difficult journey, taking days to complete, but it mattered not because he was back with Weber and his beloved *Compagnie d'Honneur*.

At Carpin, Puechlong was again the victim of bad luck. A candle with which he was reading fell into straw and set fire to a barn in which some of his compatriots were sleeping. On Weber's orders, he was transferred to Labourdette's 1st Company. He found it impossible to hide the humiliation of the transfer.

More French volunteers continued to arrive at Carpin. Among them were returning wounded and various trainees and specialists who had been away on courses while the division had been engaged in Pomerania. Yet there were also new recruits from the French community in exile. Many believed that the front could not be any worse than life in the German cities under air raids. Also, some were under the rather naive impression that they would eat better as members of the Waffen-SS than they would as civilians. Their illusions were soon shattered.[9]

However, inexplicably, the survivors of Kolberg, who had disembarked at Swinemünde, were sent straight to the French Ausbildungs-und-Ersatz-Bataillon at Wildflecken.

As the strength of 'Charlemagne' grew, its billets, which had not been very conducive to training in the first place, became more and more overcrowded. As a result, SS-Bataillon 57 was relocated from Bergfeld to a former training camp at

---

7   Soulat, page 83, and repeated by Mabire, page 51. And yet, according to Levast of the *Compagnie d'Honneur*, the company was stationed for three or four days at Georgenhof then at Ollendorf.

8   According to Levast, 'general headquarters' [OKH?] mentioned the *Compagnie d'Honneur* in dispatches for its success at Elsenau, awarding it the War Merit Cross. That same day, the PK (propaganda-kompanie) photographed the assembled company for the magazine *Signal*. This, however, Soulat does not recall (letter to the author).

9   According to Delperrié de Bayac, "*Histoire de la Milice*", page 610, six to seven hundred German SS soldiers were 'added' to 'Charlemagne'. This remains unconfirmed.

Fürstensee, eight kilometres south-west of Carpin, whereas SS-Bataillon 58 went
to the village of Wokuhl, eight kilometres due south of Carpin.

Military training was accelerated, but the morale of some continued to fluc-
tuate and cause problems. Disheartened former *franc-gardes* vented their bitterness
against the Germans. Former members of the SS-Sturmbrigade confronted them
and accusations were angrily traded.

In early April 1945, a Wehrmacht staff group commanded by Oberst von
Massow reconnoitred the region of Neustrelitz with a view to preparing secondary
defensive positions. The French SS soldiers were ordered to begin work on fortifications and anti-tank obstructions. However, the demeaning order was met with
little enthusiasm. Hstuf. Fenet, who regarded such work as demoralising, was well
aware that he had been given an order and that it was an order he would have to
carry out like any other.

To win his men over to the order, Fenet successfully employed the approach of
'actions speak louder than words'. On the morning the work was to begin, he
appeared in front of his assembled men, took off his shirt, asked for a shovel and
started to dig. He laboured in silence for hours and one by one all of his men joined
him.

A question of discipline

Breaches of discipline remained an ongoing problem even though the smallest
breach inevitably resulted in harsh punishment. An order circulated from the
Führer himself set out the penalty of death for deserters, looters and thieves. To ensure that all his men had read this order, Hstuf. Fenet had them sign it.

Days later, a worried Ustuf. Labourdette reported an incident of petty theft to
Hstuf. Fenet. A farmer had complained that the NCOs billeted with him had
stolen some light bulbs. An investigation was conducted and the culprits were
brought before Fenet. Well aware of the Führer's order, they expected to be shot,
but a lenient Fenet only scolded them.

Not all would be so lucky. After refusing to obey his platoon commander
during the construction of the anti-tank ditches, Uscha. Emile Gérard, a former
franc-garde de Nice born on 14th September 1920, found himself on a charge of
deserting his post at Elsenau even though it had passed off in silence at the time.
Court-martialled, Gérard was found guilty and sentenced to death. The
Compagnie d'Honneur supplied the firing squad and at the head of the firing squad
was Oscha. Apollot. During the night of the 19th/20th April, Gérard was executed
by firing squad in Carpin cemetery.

Two deserters arrested in Berlin wearing civilian clothes were brought to
Carpin for court-martial. They had been encouraged to desert by some Belgian
women with whom they had set up house.[10] The names and rank of the deserters
were Sturmmann Turco and Grenadier Harel. The former was a veteran of the
French SS-Sturmbrigade and had fought in the ranks of its 1st Battalion in Galicia.
In the eyes of Fenet, this made him all the more guilty. Harel was
ex-Kriegsmarine.[11]

10   Mabire, page 68.
11   Harel was known to Soulat.

The two deserters were brought before a court martial over which Stubaf. Boudet-Gheusi presided. The court martial found them guilty of desertion, but did not sentence them to death as ordered of late by the Führer.

Brigf. Krukenberg was furious. In his opinion the deserters were either guilty and should be shot. Or they were innocent and should be acquitted. No other outcome was acceptable.

The two sentences were quashed. The two deserters were judged again before another court martial over which Ustuf. Labourdette of SS-Bataillon 57 presided.[12] This time, on 12th April 1945, the court martial sentenced them to death by firing squad. The execution was set for the following morning.

The two spent the night drinking, smoking and eating as they pleased. At 0430 hours, all assembled to witness the execution. It had been made compulsory for all. The firing squad, made up of volunteers, escorted the condemned to stakes erected in a grove some five hundred metres north of Carpin. Ustuf. Verney administered the last rites to the condemned. At 0500 hours, as the firing squad took aim almost at point-blank range, the condemned shouted "Vive la France!" The salvo of the firing squad resounded. SS-Ostuf. Görr of the Feldgendarmerie administered the coup de grâce. Germans and Frenchmen alike acknowledged the courageous attitude of the two before the firing squad.

One night, a Luftwaffe supply depot near to Fürstensee, guarded by French SS troops from Bataillon 57, was looted. 'A weeks ration for a whole battalion' was taken. In response, Ustuf. Labourdette was ordered to conduct an investigation, which he entrusted to his *adjudant de compagnie*, a certain Uscha. Girald.[13] His investigation proved damning: not only were pots of margarine from the Luftwaffe depot found in the battalion's billets, but the four-man guard on duty that night was in fact responsible for the looting. Indeed, the *chef de poste* [post commander], a certain Uscha. Gastinel[14], had broken open the warehouse door and then actively encouraged the looting. Furthermore, he had even let his accomplices call four of their comrades to share the 'loot'.

The culprits were arrested, but Uscha. Gastinel had flown. A former Std.Ju., he had been broken by Oscha. Hennecart for bad conduct during the retreat through Pomerania.

The accused were brought to Carpin. Two versions of the court proceedings exist, although the final sentences meted out are the same.

According to Mabire,[15] Brigf. Krukenberg insisted that the accused must be judged by their unit, that of SS-Bataillon 57. An order laid down the make-up of the court: Fenet would preside, and Labourdette and a private would assist. The three men on guard duty and their four accomplices appeared before the court. The Führer's order countersigned by the three men on guard duty was produced. From that moment on there was only one possible sentence for them and all three were sentenced to death.

---

12 Mabire, page 68. Presumably Krukenberg, who would have had the final say, quashed the court's sentences and ordered a 'retrial'.

13 Might be a pseudonym.

14 Saint-Loup, page 377. Mabire cites, page 71, a name of Gatiniol, but footnotes that it is a pseudonym. However, Soulat cites, page 96, a name of Benet.

15 See Mabire, pages 71-72.

Hours after sentence was passed on the three, Gastinel was brought back to the camp and placed in the 'dock'. Also charged with desertion, he was found guilty on both counts. He too was sentenced to death by firing squad, but 'higher authorities of the division' requested that his sentence be changed to death by hanging. This Fenet rejected outright. In reply, Fenet requested that one of the condemned, an officer's son who was 'crushed by having failed to keep honour', be sent to a 'special unit' [penal unit?] to meet a soldier's death. This was rejected by 'Division'. As for the four accomplices, they were not sentenced.

According to Saint-Loup,[16] Brigf. Krukenberg immediately brought the four accused before a court martial over which Stubaf. Boudet-Gheusi presided. Assisting him was *officier de justice* Ustuf. Stehli and defending the accused was *lieutenant* Sabatieri.[17] Boudet-Gheusi employed all his skills as a lawyer to save Gastinel and the three sentries on duty, named as Labarret, Dreveau and Beynac,[18] from the death sentence, although Gastinel, the instigator, was sentenced alone to twenty years hard labour. However, Krukenberg immediately quashed the sentence and replaced Boudet-Gheusi with Fenet as the presiding judge for a new court martial. Subsequently the four accused were found guilty and sentenced to death.

Chaplain Verney came to comfort and administer the last rites to the four condemned men. Shortly before sunrise, the condemned were brought before a firing squad of twelve volunteers picked from the more than fifty who had come forward. Waiting to witness the execution at Fürstensee was the entire Bataillon 57. The condemned were not tied to posts and stood in front of trees. A shout of: "Aim! Fire!" Once again the salvo of the firing squad resounded. They fell without crying out. An Oberscharführer administered the coups de grâce. It was a needless formality. All four were dead. Lost in thought, the companies silently returned to their barracks.

Three others went to the firing squad for looting.[19]

Ostuf. Audibert of the Engineer Company also found himself before a court martial. He was charged with having abandoned on Bärenwalde platform station the equipment of the Engineer Company, in particular its most recent model flame-throwers, which fell into the hands of the Russians. Vigorously, he contested the charge. Covered by an order from Obf. Puaud, he managed to exonerate himself. He was acquitted.

The rebuilding of 'Charlemagne'

By early April 1945, the strength of 'Charlemagne' had grown to around one thousand men. RF-SS Himmler and Brigf. Krukenberg now decided to reorganise 'Charlemagne' by culling those who did not want to continue the fight to the very end. They would be formed into a Construction Battalion (Bau-bataillon). Krukenberg assembled the survivors and told them:[20]

16   See Saint-Loup, pages 377-378.
17   Might be a pseudonym.
18   All three names might be pseudonyms.
19   Saint-Loup, page 377, confirmed by Soulat, page 96.
20   "*Entretien avec le général Krukenberg*", "*Historia #32*", page 136.

I only want volunteers. You may abandon the armed fight. You will remain in the SS, but as workers. I only want to have combatants with me now.

To a man, the *Compagnie d'Honneur* chose to fight on. For Uscha. Puechlong, he had sworn an oath of loyalty and he for one was going to remain faithful to it. Moreover, he could not demean himself in this way. Levast, also of the *Compagnie d'Honneur*, said:[21]

> Although we knew full well that the war was lost we choose to continue the fight so as not to fall into the hands of the Russians alive. In spite of everything we believed in the new weapons.

75% of the men of Fenet's SS-Bataillon 57 and 50% of those of Géromini's SS-Bataillon 58 chose the rifle rather than the pick and shovel.

As for Soulat, although he realised the war was nearing its end, the choice of 'keeping out of things' appeared to him shameful when so many of his comrades had disappeared in Pomerania.

In total, one officer and around four hundred[22] men opted for the Construction Battalion. Many were former *Miliciens*. Uscha. Fronteau of the 10/58, ex-LVF, went across to the Construction Battalion. His adventure in Pomerania had annihilated him both physically and morally.

To the command of the Construction Battalion Brigf. Krukenberg appointed Hstuf. Roy. This Roy greatly resented. Nevertheless, Krukenberg was not 'punishing' him; he had need of solid officers for the battalion. And in Pomerania Roy had fought with tenacity, skill and courage.

Krukenberg also transferred Ustuf. Martret to the Construction Battalion. This he too resented, but orders are orders.

When the Construction Battalion was activated on 10th April 1945 its order of battle was as follows:

Commander:	W-Hstuf. Roy
Assistant:	W-Ustuf. Martret[23]
1 Kompanie:	W-Ostuf. Roumégous
2 Kompanie:	W-Ostuf. Géromini
3 Kompanie:	W-Ostuf. Darrigade

Notably the three company commanders were former *Miliciens*.

Different accounts exist of how Géromini ended up as a company commander in the Construction Battalion.

According to Mabire,[24] Ostuf. Géromini actually volunteered to continue the fight at the head of Btl. 58, but found himself instead demoted to a company

---

21   Letter to the author.

22   Mabire, page 78. This figure has been confirmed by Soulat, letter to the author 9/11/97. According to Saint-Loup, the figure was three hundred.

23   According to Soulat, page 96, Martret held the position of Orderly Officer and Hstuf. Martin that of *adjoint*. In response to this, Martret does not recall Hstuf. Martin serving with the Bau-Bataillon and his position was not that of the O.O. (letter to the author, 12/7/99).

24   See Mabire, page 80.

commander in the Construction Battalion. Mabire explains that Géromini had finally paid the price of his all too regular outspoken views in the presence of Krukenberg. In contrast, according to Landwehr,[25] Géromini actually resigned his command to take up that of a Construction Company. Then there is the account written by Delperrié de Bayac[26] which begins when Brigf. Krukenberg called together the officers at Carpin late March and declared:

> I only want volunteers in the 'Charlemagne' Regiment, real volunteers, and people who want to fight. Some came to Wildflecken against their will. I no longer want them. They may go.

Krukenberg continued by slandering the former P.P.F. militants, the former *Miliciens* and Darnand. After this outburst, he told the officers: "Those who want to fight, to the right; those who do not want to fight, to the left." Only Ostuf. Géromini went to the left. A lively tête-à-tête followed between Géromini and Krukenberg that confirmed yet again Krukenberg's view of Géromini as a trouble-maker.[27]

In keeping with his temperament, Ostuf. Géromini would prove as trouble-some to Hstuf. Roy as he was to Brigf. Krukenberg.

The Construction Battalion was quartered in the vicinity of the village of Drewin. Its morale was, at best, low. Throughout its short existence the Construc-tion Battalion had little, or no, contact with the 'fighting' elements of 'Charlemagne'.

Ustuf. Martret had at his disposal a section of ten soldiers. Notably, they were the only men in the whole battalion to carry arms. This, of course, was unofficial.

Finally, on that same day of the 10th, 'Bataillon Martin', which had fought in the area of Gotenhafen, joined Regiment 'Charlemagne' in the region of Neustrelitz. Many of its survivors reinforced Bataillon 57 and Bataillon 58, even though some were still suffering from severe frostbite to the hands and feet, and were carrying wounds. But they were determined to fight on and 'follow the pace of the training'.

As for those who volunteered to fight on, they were required to sign an 'oath form' which pledged unconditional loyalty to the Führer till death. For some, it was the third oath they had sworn to Hitler. One such volunteer was Hscha. Rostaing who commented that he was not even a National Socialist. He was driven by one desire alone: to fight Communism, 'the enemy of every civilisation'.[28]

Following the cull, the already high morale of SS-Bataillon 57, still stationed at Fürstensee, rose. The order of battle of SS-Bataillon 57 was as follows:[29]

| Commander: | W-Hstuf. Fenet |
| Assistant: | ? |

25   See Landwehr, page 114.
26   See Delperrié de Bayac, pages 609-610.
27   The details of this lively *tête-à-tête* supplied by Delperrié de Bayac seem repeated and expanded by Mabire, page 58, in a similar confrontation. Unfortunately Mabire does not date the confrontation.
28   Rostaing, page 180.
29   Unconfirmed.

1 Kompanie:	W-Ustuf. Labourdette
2 Kompanie:	W-Hscha. Hennecart
3 Kompanie:	?
4 Kompanie:	W-Oscha. Ollivier

The three company commanders were battle-proven.

Little is known about Ollivier other than he served with the 9/57 in Pomerania before going on to serve with the 6/58.

The cull left SS-Bataillon 58 seriously depleted, but it had its desired effect. The battalion was now made up of a hardcore of battle-proven LVF veterans who were still full of drive and fight. Many of them had served on the Eastern front since the first winter of 1941/1942.

The order of battle of SS-Bataillon 58 was as follows:

Commander:	SS-Hstuf. Jauss
5 Kompanie:	W-Std.Ju. Aumon
6 Kompanie:	W-Hscha. Rostaing
7 Kompanie:	W-Ostuf. Fatin
8 Kompanie:	W-Ustuf. Sarrailhé

However, the new commander of the battalion, Hstuf. Jauss, was not the same courageous individual who had acted alternately with Fenet as a guide for the I/RM across Pomerania or who had been at the forefront during the break through to Dievenow. He had become disenchanted, silent for long periods of time, and had let his appearance go.

Two of the company commanders had similar credentials to their men, namely Ostuf. Fatin and Hscha. Rostaing. Both had served and made their mark in the LVF. Of late, Fatin had been promoted to the rank of Obersturmführer and won the Iron Cross 1st Class for his part in the defence of Gotenhafen.

Pierre Rostaing[30]

As for Pierre Rostaing, he was born on 8th January 1909 in Gavet in the department of l'Isere. At the age of eighteen, he enlisted in the French Army. By the time war broke out, he had completed twelve years service including tours of duty overseas in the French colonies of Indochina, Morocco, Algeria and Tunisia. The *2e bureau de l'Armée* sent him as a technical advisor to the Finnish Army then at war with Russia. On his return to France, he fought, in vain, against the Germans. A career soldier, he went on to serve in the Armistice Army.

30   According to Rostaing, "*Le prix d'un serment*", pages 1-40, he engaged in *La Légion Tricolore* on 13th October 1941, went over to the LVF in early January 1942, left Versailles, the base of the LVF, for the training camp at Kruszyna, Poland, late March 1942, spent more than eight months training at Kruszyna, and joined the LVF in the field in April 1943. However, this schedule is questionable; *La Légion Tricolore* was not created until April 1942. Also of note is that he may have only spent three months at Kruszyna (see page 36 of the same book). Arguably, he engaged in *La Légion Tricolore* on 13th October 1942, went over to the LVF in early January 1943 after the *La Légion Tricolore* was disbanded, left Versailles for Kruszyna, where he received three months training, and joined the LVF in the field in April 1943.

A fervent patriot, Rostaing joined *La Légion Tricolore*, where he wished to continue serving France and its legal government under Pétain. Months later, when the Germans disbanded *La Légion Tricolore*, he hesitated to join the LVF. He detested politics and saw the LVF as an overtly political 'army'. Also, he felt no great enthusiasm to don the uniform of the enemy of yesterday. But being called a coward by his comrades who had already joined the LVF rudely jolted him to sign up. He was no coward. And yet he still had doubts. But the fact that Marshal Pétain, the legal head of State, had given his backing to the LVF eased his patriotic conscience. For Rostaing, the word 'legal' was all-important. His visceral anti-communism and his love of France also won him over to the crusade of the LVF.

With the *6e renfort*, Rostaing left Versailles, the base of the LVF, for the training camp at Kruszyna, Poland. On the completion of his training, he was sent to the Eastern front and there assigned to the 9th Company of the III. Battalion. In January 1944, after the departure of the sick and elderly *sergent-chef* Froidevaux, he became Lieutenant Seveau's *adjoint* in the battalion's *section de chasse* [which roughly translates as 'hunting platoon'].[31] In the months that followed, he was always to be found in the thick of battle. He was tireless. On 20th April 1944, he received the Iron Cross 2nd Class.

In August 1944, Rostaing was transferred from the LVF to the Franz. Brigade der SS. He served on the headquarters staff of the II/58. Attending SS-Unterführerschule Lauenberg, Pomerania, he regained the enthusiasm of his youth. He wanted to prove to his German comrades that he was their worthy equal. Thus, it was no surprise that he graduated. He retained his former rank. His time at Wildflecken camp had few memories.[32] In February 1945, Rostaing found himself in the 'hell of Pomerania', but he was one of the few to return.

Rostaing was, undoubtedly, one of the most decorated French soldiers serving in the German Army: *la Croix de Guerre Légionnaire* with twelve citations, the wounded badge and the Iron Cross 2nd Class.

In the wake of the creation of the Construction Battalion, Hstuf. Jauss appointed Hscha. Rostaing to the head of the 6th Company. In this way, Rostaing replaced Ustuf. Leune who was posted to the signals detachment.

The *Compagnie d'Honneur*, by now some eighty-strong[33] and renamed the Kampfschule (Combat School), was unaffected by the reorganisation. Weber's boys had literally laughed at the order offering them the option to become rear area construction troops. They were proud and fanatical. Indeed, they had been first to receive the camouflaged uniforms.

The reputation of the Kampfschule continued to grow when one morning the men paraded without belt buckles for a German officer of the Inspection. Calmly, Weber explained to the staff officer that the Kampfschule had only received

31   Rusco, letter to the author, 21/3/2001. This corrects the date of 24th December 1943 on which Rostaing became Seveau's *adjoint* ("*Le prix d'un serment*", page 90) and thus also the notion that Rostaing was Seveau's *adjoint* from the outset of the *chasse*, which was formed on 26th October 1943.

32   See "*Le prix d'un serment*", pages 151-158. There are so few personal details of his time at Wildflecken camp.

33   Levast, letter to the author, 1998.

Wehrmacht belt buckles with the inscription "Gott mit uns" (God is with us) which, of course, were not suitable for members of the Waffen-SS! He then added that they had no need of God! The staff officer was stunned to silence. Shortly after, the appropriate belt buckles bearing the Waffen SS motto were received.

Theoretically speaking, the Kampfschule was directly answerable only to the German Inspection, but Brigf. Krukenberg had become more and more distant for these French troops of the Waffen-SS, who now only obeyed Weber and him alone.[34]

Also reassembled were the support elements of Regiment 'Charlemagne', which comprised one engineer platoon, one signals platoon, one horse-drawn supply column, one motor column, and a repair workshop. All were understrength and desperately short of equipment. The engineer platoon had no equipment to its name. The signals platoon was without radio sets and had to make do with some poor field telephones. All were stationed at the village of Zinow, some five kilometres due west of Carpin.

The so-called Heavy Battalion, located in Goldenbaum, had the strength of a reinforced company. Many of its men had gone across to the Construction Battalion. The 'Battalion' was armed with light machine-guns, mortars, panzerfäuste and panzerschreck, but no PAK guns.

The medical and veterinary staff were merged together under a German doctor transferred from the 3. SS-Panzer-Division 'Totenkopf'.

Headquarters still awaited impatiently the arrival of the 1,200 French SS troops under SS-Ostubaf. Hersche who had set out on foot from Wildflecken camp during the night of 30th/31st March 1945. There was no news of their progress. Also expected was the Assault Gun Company of the Panzerjäger Battalion that was away training in Bohemia-Moravia.

More awards were issued. Ostuf. Dupuyau and Std.Ju.Ob. Radici received the Iron Cross 2nd Class. Many individuals were also awarded the Wounded Badge and nominated for the Assault Badge and the Close Combat Clasp.

Shortly after, Radici was promoted to Untersturmführer.

Toward mid-April, the headquarters staff of 'Charlemagne' underwent a number of changes to look as follows:

Commander:	SS-Brigf. Krukenberg
Assistant and Office IA:	SS-Hstuf. Pachur
Orderly officer:	SS-Ustuf. Hegewald
Kommandant Stabsquartier:	SS-Ostuf. Ruhnow
Office IB:	SS-Ostuf. Meier
Office IC:	SS-Ostuf. von Wallenrodt
Office IIA/B:	SS-Hstuf. Pachur
Office IVA:	SS-Hstuf. Hagen
Office IVB:	SS-Stubaf.Dr. Schlegel
Office IVD:	W-Ustuf. Abbé Verney
Office V:	SS-Ustuf. Datum
Felgendarmerie:	SS-Ostuf. Görr

34   Mabire, page 84.

Even though the Regiment had its own commander, namely Staf. Zimmermann and in his absence Hstuf. Kroepsch, it was Brigf. Krukenberg and 'his' headquarters that exercised control, perhaps total control, over its subordinate units. It appears that at no time was Kroepsch opposed to Krukenberg.[35]

Krukenberg's new assistant, Hstuf. Pachur, a Berliner, was very much after his own heart.

The headquarters staff company under Ostuf. Ruhnow was stationed at Carpin. Ostuf. Görr and his Military Police were at the village of Thurow, about six kilometres north-west of Carpin.

On 14th April 1945, some twenty French officer candidates rejoined Regiment 'Charlemagne' at Carpin. They had just completed their training course at annex Neweklau of SS-Panzergrenadierschule Kienschlag. The course had moulded their minds and bodies, and they now burned with fanaticism and idealism. The arrival of these Oberjunker would contribute greatly to bringing the regiment to a state of combat readiness and to strenthening the regiment's spirit of determination by moulding their troops in their own image. Indeed, their impatience to fight had to be quelled.

The officer candidates came from no one particular origin. The majority of the new officers who had served with the LVF were assigned to Bataillon 58. Oberjunker Baumgartner,[36] Chavant, Dumoulin and Ginot were assigned to Rostaing's 6th Company. Gaston Baumgartner and Jean Dumoulin were known to Rostaing from the days of the LVF. Baumgartner had served with the 9th Company of III/638.

SS-Bataillon 57 also benefited from the influx of new officers. Assigned to Labourdette's company were Oberjunker Boulmier,[37] Cossard, Croisille, de Lacaze and Le Maignan de Kérangat. Boulmier and Jean Cossard were ex-LVF. The twenty-one-year-old Maxime de Lacaze was ex-*Milice*. In the summer of 1943, he and his brother, Jean, had received officer candidate training at the *École des cadres de la Milice* at Uriage. One of their instructors was Pignard-Berthet. In November 1944, the brothers entered 'Charlemagne'. Jacques Le Maignan de Kérangat had 'deserted' the cause of the French N.S.K.K. for that of the French Waffen-SS, arriving at Sennheim on 3rd April 1944.

Ollivier's 4th (heavy) Company received Oberjunken Bellier and Protopopoff. In late 1943, 'Prince' Protopopoff attended the *École des cadres* of the LVF at Montargis near Orleans.[38] Transferred to the W-SS and 'Charlemagne', he served in Pomerania with Hstuf. Roy's 9/57.

Fenet took Oberjunker Douroux as an orderly officer. Born in 1920, Alfred Douroux volunteered for the LVF at the start of 1943. He too attended the *École des cadres* of the LVF at Montargis. At the end of the year, he was posted to the Eastern front and incorporated with NCO rank into the 6th Company of II/638. He too was transferred from the LVF to the W-SS and 'Charlemagne'.

---

35   But Krukenberg outranked Kroepsch. Arguably, a French regimental commander, whatever his rank, may have had 'much more to say'.
36   Mabire employs a pseudonym of Gardinier for the same individual.
37   His brother was also serving in 'Charlemagne'.
38   Incorrectly, Landwehr states that Protopopoff served with the *Milice*. (Page 148.)

Other Oberjunker to arrive at Carpin included Coste, Frantz, Garrabos, Lebrun, Maisse, Piffeteau, and Poupon, a *franciste*. All were ex-LVF with the exception of Jacques Frantz, born on 7th March 1925, who volunteered for the Waffen-SS, attending Sennheim late 1944. Their appointments are not known.

Also out of Kienschlag was Jean Malardier who had been promoted to the rank of Unterscharführer. Ex-LVF, he was assigned to Rostaing's 6th Company. He served as the *adjoint* to a section commander of the 1st platoon now commanded by Oberjunker Ginot.

Former *chef de bataillon* Fortis left Kienschlag with the rank of Oberscharführer. Born in 1892, he fought in the trenches of 1914–1918, winning 17 citations and the *Légion d'Honneur*, and suffering 7 wounds. France applauded him as a hero. Becoming a *Commandant de bataillon* in the 139° *Régiment d'Infanterie*, he fought the Germans for a second time in 1940 and was taken prisoner.[39] In March 1944, he enlisted in the Waffen-SS.[40]

April also saw the return of the Assault Gun Company from its course at Votice, Bohemia-Moravia. It had been equipped with Jagdpanzer 38(t) Hetzers[41], but en route the assault guns were 'confiscated' by Army Group Schoerner.[42] Because of this, the men of the Assault Gun Company would now have to fight as grenadier.

Shortly after the integration of the new Oberjunker into Regiment 'Charlemagne', Ostuf. Michel, one of their former instructors, arrived at Neustrelitz.[43] Assigned to SS-Bataillon 57, he received from Hstuf. Fenet the command of the 2nd Company, displacing Hscha. Hennecart who was transferred to battalion headquarters.

The 2nd Company had a solid core of leadership in platoon commanders Oberjunker Neroni, Oscha. Mongourd and Oscha. Lardy. Neroni, a *pied-noir*, had left his native Algeria to enlist in the Waffen-SS.[44] Mongourd, a native of Lyon, was a former *chef de centaine de la Milice* who had participated in the maintenance of order operations in the Limousin. Of late, he had received assault gun training in Bohemia-Moravia. Oscha. Lardy, who was seriously wounded in the spring of 1944 while training with the Sturmbrigade in Bohemia-Moravia, is described as an 'excellent instructor'.[45]

39   According to Mabire, page 86, Fortis was a *chef de bataillon* in the Foreign Legion.
40   On 14th November 1945, the *tribunal* [court] of Marseille sentenced Fortis to five years hard labour. He died in 1952.
41   Soulat, letter to the author, 11/1/99, and Mabire, page 90.
42   Soulat, letter to the author, 19/2/99.
43   Different sources provide various dates as to when Michel was an instructor at Kienschlag. According to his SS file, Michel was transferred as a 'Inspektionschef' to SS-Grenadierschule Kienschlag on 1st March 1945. However, according to Soulat, page 87, Michel was an instructor at Kienschlag until December 1944. Also of note is that Michel was with the Assault Gun Company for training at Votice. Thus, he may have joined his company in either December 1944 or in early April 1945 after the closure of Kienschlag. If true then Michel was at the head of the Assault Gun Company when it rejoined 'Charlemagne' at Neustrelitz.
44   Neroni may have been among those Oberjunker to have returned of late from the training course at Neweklau.

And yet Brigf. Krukenberg's problems were still not at an end. Hstuf. Jauss, the young commander of SS-Bataillon 58, had become more and more disillusioned.[46] This, of course, Krukenberg could tolerate no longer. He had to protect the exceptional spirit of the seven hundred combatants from corruption and erosion. In a report addressed to the SS-Führungshauptamt (or SS-FHA), he said:[47]

> Hstuf. Jauss is perhaps perfect to supervise a Junkerschaft of officer cadets but his place is not with the French volunteers.

This was tantamount to requesting his transfer. And, in due course, Jauss was transferred.

The calm before the storm

On the morning of 16th April 1945, the Soviets launched a massive offensive against the German 9th Army and 4th Panzer Army along the river Oder. The Germans fought back with stubborn resistance. However, by the 19th, the Soviets had broken through the German lines and were racing to encircle Berlin. And yet for 'Charlemagne' this period was one full of almost comic moments.

To supplement the poor rations of his company employed on building anti-tank obstructions, Hscha. Rostaing had a doe shot daily. This he had continued even after a rebuke from battalion commander Hstuf. Jauss; hunting was forbidden by law on Reich property. And then one day the forest warden of Wokuhl confronted him.

Wild with anger, the forest warden kicked in the door to Rostaing's office. He then blurted out that he had caught one of Rostaing's men, an LVF veteran by the name of Minot, killing a doe. And when he had approached the soldier he had fired over his head.

In an attempt to cover up the incident, Rostaing angrily retorted to the forest warden that he must be mistaken, adding that he reigned over his men with an iron discipline. Unconvinced, the forest warden kept on. Rostaing, whose patience was short, abruptly jumped up, grabbed hold of the forest warden's rifle and violently threw it on the ground. It smashed. At this, the forest warden's anger suddenly died away and his eyes filled with tears. He retreated. The following day, in a gesture of friendship, he sent Rostaing a stag he had just killed.[48]

And then it was the turn of Ostuf. Fatin to be confronted by a forest warden!

Angrily, the forest warden complained to Fatin: "Your men are cutting down trees in the forest." Yes they were, but Fatin explained that they needed them for anti-tank obstructions. Remarkably, the forest warden reacted with the words: "But they're felling without authorisation and that is a crime against the Greater Reich!" Fatin went red, then pale. However, as a compromise, the forest warden suggested that Fatin could fell only those trees that were 'administratively

---

45   Mabire, page 91.

46   Indeed, according to Saint-Loup, page 376, Jauss was now going round 'making the worst accusations against Krukenberg'. Moreover, it appears that Krukenberg and Jauss had never quite seen eye to eye.

47   Memoirs of Soulat. Mabire has slightly different wording.

48   As told by Rostaing, page 182. However, according to Saint-Loup, page 372, the ending was more civil.

designated'. At this, Fatin exploded. Seizing the forest warden by the collar, Fatin ejected him.[49]

And then one day two volunteers of the Indische Freiwilligen-Legion der Waffen-SS (Indian Legion of the Waffen-SS) arrived at 'Charlemagne' headquarters. It turned out that they had actually been sent there by mistake! Soulat of the headquarters staff got talking to one of them who knew some German. He was surprised to learn that they were in fact English soldiers captured in Egypt by the Africa Korps!

The 20th of April 1945 was a memorable day for many reasons. In the first place, it was Hitler's fifty-sixth birthday. At 1700 hours, a simple ceremony was held at the anti-tank ditch at Georgenhof. Ustuf. Bender gave a short speech in French and then in German. This was followed by a rendition of the 'Treuelied'. Krukenberg was next to speak. After hinting at the coming final battle, he evoked the fallen. By now, Soulat of the headquarters staff was so lost in thought that he did not hear the rest of the speech that brought the ceremony to a close.

When the Frenchmen returned to their billets each received a modest present 'containing objects of use': a razor and blades, a comb, a mirror, a notebook, a small phial of schnapps and a small piece of marzipan. Those of office IIA/B also received from Hstuf. Pachur a modern German novel inscribed by him.

In the second place, new weaponry arrived for the seven hundred men of 'Charlemagne' determined to continue the fight. They received MG 42 heavy calibre machine guns, the redoubtable Sturmgewehr 44 assault rifles and panzerfäuste. In this way, their training was finally enriched with weapons.

Also, that same day, Rttf. Soulat was proposed for the KVK II. Klasse because he was only one at headquarters without it. The course of events was such that he would never receive this award.

In the late morning of 21st April 1945, on hearing of the murder of the forest warden[50] of Serahn, a small hamlet in the woods five kilometres from Carpin, Brigf. Krukenberg immediately ordered Subaf. Boudet-Gheusi to lead a manhunt for the killers, said to be two deserters from the Stettin front, one of whom spoke no German and the other only badly. The story went that the two deserters had called on a neighbour of the forest warden, begging for bread, and that he had urged them to follow him and the warden to the Feldgendarmerie at Carpin. The deserters agreed, but on the way they pulled out a gun they had hidden, killed the warden and disappeared.

All available units of 'Charlemagne' were alerted and despatched on a concentric sweep. During the sweep the headquarters staff of SS-Bataillon 57 visited the warden's house to pass on their condolences to the family. Admitted, they were greeted by a sombre scene. They felt ill at ease. Fenet spoke with the daughter of the family. She was touched by his sympathy and wished him well before returning to her grieving mother.

---

49   Saint-Loup page 375. Rostaing also recollects a similar 'visit' from a forest warden
      with the selfsame complaint. And although Rostaing treated his visitor with more
      respect than Fatin, the forest warden threatened to make him pay for his crime! His
      words of warning would come to nothing.
50   Or game warden.

After a sweep of five kilometres through the woods, the French W-SS units returned to their billets empty-handed.[51] Later, from a reliable source, Soulat was to learn that the two deserters were, in fact, a Polish paratrooper (or parachutist) and a soldier of the 3/57, who had met him by chance in the woods. It was the Pole who had pulled the trigger. Frightened, the Frenchman had cleared off and returned to his billets without saying anything to anybody.

On 22nd April 1945, 'Charlemagne' Headquarters at Carpin received reports of enemy paratroopers in the sector. As proof, a peasant from Goldenbaum brought along with him a parachute that he claimed he had discovered in his fields.[52]

And now to the 23rd of April 1945 and remarkably the arrival of a new French recruit! Hstuf. Fenet received him. A former prisoner of war, he had grown to love Germany and, now that Germany was in her hour of need, he wanted to come to her defence. So he had enlisted in the Waffen-SS. Told to report to the nearest unit, instead he went in search of 'Charlemagne'. And one month later here he was.

Although Fenet was convinced that the new recruit was genuine, he decided that he could not accept his sacrifice. So he turned him down gently. After pointing out that they were busy at the moment and that the enlistment office was not open, he told him to go home and wait to be called, which would be in a matter of days. The recruit clicked his heels, saluted and left.[53]

The mission

During the night of 23rd/24th April 1945, Brigf. Krukenberg was ordered to Berlin to assume a new command. He would be accompanied by a French battlegroup from 'Charlemagne'.

Much has been written of what transpired that night, but what is the truth?

According to Krukenberg[54], he received two telephone calls one after the other around 0400 hours on 24th April 1945. The first was from the Personalamt [the Personnel Office] der Waffen-SS [of the SS-FHA] near Fürstenberg and the second from the headquarters of Army Group Vistula near Prenzlau.

51   The *souvenirs* of Soulat. However, according to Mabire, page 105, it was on the evening of 23rd April that the headquarters staff of SS-Bataillon 57 visited the warden's house. This is possible, but realistically speaking the most opportune moment would have been during the sweep.

52   According to Mabire, page 102, and [repeated by?] Landwehr, page 117, reports of enemy paratroopers trigged the employment of companies of SS-Bataillon 57 and SS-Bataillon 58 in search of them.

53   Saint-Loup, pages 375-376. However, according to Mabire, page 99, and repeated by Landwehr, page 117, Hstuf. Fenet told the new recruit that he was too late because he had no military training and 'Charlemagne' no longer had [any] training units. The new recruit asked: "You really don't have any place for me?" The answer was no. Thereupon he left.

54   In 1964, Krukenberg wrote his account of the battle of Berlin under the title 'Battle for Berlin'. Since then, his account has been faithfully reproduced by Soulat, pages 100-116, by Mabire, and by Landwehr under the chapter heading of "*Fighting for Berlin: A Battle Memoir*".

Both calls transmitted the order of the O.K.W.[55] to proceed rapidly to Berlin where he would receive the command of a division whose commander had fallen ill. Also, upon his arrival in Berlin, he was to report to Colonel-General Krebs, the Army Chief-of-Staff, and to Ogruf. Fegelein, the liaison officer of the Waffen-SS to the headquarters of the Führer, who were both at the Reichs Chancellery.

Krukenberg asked about the situation in Berlin. He was told that the Russians had broken through the defensive front along the river Oder and were advancing in two columns on Berlin. It might only be a matter of hours before Berlin was encircled. A Panzer Corps [the LVI Panzer-Korps], to the east of the city, had been thrown back into the suburbs and was now engaged in hard defensive fighting.

However, the situation was not without hope. It was explained to Krukenberg that 'our commander' had made contact with the 'commander of our enemies in the West'. The Americans were already on the river Elbe and all resistance had been ceased against them so that they could continue to advance and occupy Berlin first or at the same time as the Soviets. Also, in the region of Rathenow-Genthin, a Panzer Corps [the XXXXI Panzer-Korps[56]] with General Wenck [the commander of the 12th Army] had received orders to advance in the direction of Potsdam. It was to open a passage for the Americans into West Berlin so that they could occupy from there the other quarters of the city.

Momentarily, Krukenberg became lost in thought. He asked himself the question: how was the defence of a city with several million inhabitants possible? In June 1940, France had declared Paris an 'open city', sparing its inhabitants the horrors of street battle. But the Red Army had raped, pillaged and looted its way through West Prussia and Pomerania. If Berlin fell to the Red Army, then the same excesses awaited its inhabitants. But the capital city had been declared a *Festung* [fortress] on 1st February 1945 and ever since work had been continuing on its defence. So perhaps the city could be defended.

Because the situation awaiting him in Berlin appeared so very unclear, Krukenberg, also prompted by past experiences, asked for permission to take with him to his new posting 'one part of his usual headquarters and an escort detachment of about ninety men'. The headquarters of Army Group Vistula agreed to his requests and added that the route to Berlin via Oranienburg and Frohnau, 'still clear of the enemy', was the most suitable.

According to Soulat[57], at 0030 hours, Brigf. Krukenberg received a telegram ordering him to 'form a Sturmbataillon [Assault Battalion] with the remnants of 'Charlemagne' on receipt of this order, equip it ready for action and take it immediately and via the shortest routes to Berlin' where he was to report to the Chancellery for orders.[58]

A Sturmbataillon was immediately formed. It comprised the entire SS-Bataillon 57,[59] one company of SS-Bataillon 58[60] and the Kampfschule.

55   Oberkommando-der-Wehrmacht (OKW-Armed Forces GHQ).

56   It was a panzer corps in name only.

57   Page 100 and *souvenirs*, repeated by Saint-Loup, page 381.

58   Of note is that Soulat actually laid eyes on the telegram. He remembers it well because it was so extraordinary.

59   According to Soulat, page 100, and also letter to the author, 19/2/99, on its departure from Carpin, SS-Bataillon 57 counted four companies; company 3/57 had been

Rostaing and his company felt proud to be the only company of SS-Bataillon 58 chosen to leave for Berlin. All other combatant units of 'Charlemagne' were readied to follow in a second echelon the very next day.[61]

So did Brigf. Krukenberg receive a telegram ordering Division 'Charlemagne' to Berlin? And was his escort ninety-strong or of battalion strength?

Ostuf. Weber also saw a telegram ordering Division 'Charlemagne' to Berlin.[62] The telegram was from the *Führerhauptquartier* and signed by Adolf Hitler. Its existence was confirmed after the war by Stubaf. Günsche, an SS officer in Adolf Hitler's immediate entourage, who also declared to Weber that he himself dispatched the telegram. Therefore, it appears that a telegram was sent and received by Brigf. Krukenberg ordering 'Charlemagne' to Berlin.

According to many French and German survivors of all ranks, the so-called escort that accompanied Brigf. Krukenberg to Berlin was of battalion strength.[63] Furthermore, to settle the debate once and for all, a report from Pz.AOK 3 [3rd Panzer Army] dated 24th April 1945, states that, from its rear zone, the headquarters and '1 Batl. 33. SS-WGD. 'Charlemagne' have set out direction Berlin'. Therefore, it appears that the 'escort' Brigf. Krukenberg took to Berlin was of battalion strength.

Brigf. Krukenberg assembled all officers at his headquarters in Castle Carpin. Hstuf. Fenet was the first to arrive. A 'smiling' Krukenberg greeted him. He was briefed about Berlin.[64] His reaction was one of joy.

The officers assembled one by one and were conversing in hushed tones when Krukenberg made his entrance.[65] Without preamble, he started by telling them that the Russians would soon invest Berlin. Continuing, he told them that he had been called to Berlin to receive a new command and that they were coming along with him to defend the capital. He concluded by detailing the proposed route to Berlin: via the city of Oranienburg, north of Berlin.

Open-mouthed, the French W-SS officers had listened to him in total silence. Suddenly it dawned on them what destiny had in store for them: Berlin, the Chancellery, the last battle. However, that was not to be the destiny of all those present.

placed under the command of Ostuf. Fatin.

60   According to Soulat, letter to the author, 19/2/1999, Hennecart was with the 6/58.

61   It appears that sufficient transport could not be made available to move the whole of 'Charlemagne' as one. According to Mabire, page 111, the first echelon was to comprise the three companies of SS-Bataillon 57, its staff, and Weber's Kampfschule, but space could be found for a further one hundred men. Thereupon, headquarters decided to include one company from SS-Bataillon 58. The 6th Company, that of Rostaing, deemed the most solid and combat ready, was chosen. However, for his part, Rostaing recalls that he was not just an 'afterthought'.

62   See Saint-Loup, page 382 and Mabire, page 110. Curiously, each author reproduces the text of the telegram, but the wording differs.

63   For example, Puechlong of Labourdette's Company recalls that the same Company went to Berlin eighty-five to ninety strong including officers and NCOs. (Letter to the author, 24/11/97.)

64   Mabire, page 110.

65   According to Saint-Loup, page 381, Zimmermann was present. This is not correct. Zimmermann was still in a hospital at Anklam. (Zimmermann, letter to Saint-Loup, 10/9/65.)

Ustuf. Chaplain Verney and Ostuf. Dr. Métais were left unsure whether or not
they would be leaving for Berlin. Verney went straight up to Krukenberg and asked
him outright. He would be leaving. Métais tried his luck but was not so fortunate;
Krukenberg had no need of his services because the German doctor from 'Division'
[presumably Schlegel] and Ostuf. Dr. Herpe of SS-Bataillon 57 were already
leaving, and this he considered sufficient.

The news of the mission to Berlin spread like wildfire through the billets. The
men may have had the choice of leaving for Berlin or remaining behind.[66]

Ammunition and weaponry were distributed. Nearly all grenadier of
SS-Bataillon 57 were armed with a Sturmgewehr. Those of Rostaing's company
were not quite so fortunate; 'only' one in three held a Sturmgewehr in their hands.
Every section was equipped with at least one MG 42 machine-gun, some with two.
The redoubtable Panzerfaust was not forgotten. For the first and last time, rations
were issued generously, but many troops preferred to draw ammunition.

The Sturmbataillon assembled. To Soulat, his comrades had never looked in
such fine form. Indeed, their enthusiasm reminded him of 'those victorious
German soldiers of the first years of the war'. Their morale was excellent. He saw,
for the first time, a strange flame burn in their eyes.

At 0530 hours, the French Sturmbataillon left Carpin for Alt-Strelitz. It was
from here at 0830 hours that Brigf. Krukenberg had decided to leave for Berlin.
The column consisted of several private cars and seven or eight trucks.[67]

66 According to Saint-Loup, page 382, at the briefing, Brigf. Krukenberg ordered Fenet,
company commanders Labourdette, Michel, Ollivier, Rostaing and Weber to
assemble their commands immediately and explain to their men what awaited them
and offer them the choice of leaving for Berlin or remaining behind with the Heavy
Company (sic). The reason given for this decision was that not enough weapons were
available to arm everyone. Krukenberg's orders were carried out, although the way in
which the company commanders went about were quite different. Weber simply
ordered his men to assemble at 0745 hours to leave for Berlin. Labourdette and
Michel carried out Krukenberg's orders to the letter, explaining the mission entrusted
to them. A single command was put to the assembled company: "Volunteers for
Berlin, one step forward!" Each of the two companies advanced to a man. Rostaing
said to his company: "Lads, we're leaving to defend Berlin! I hope that nobody of the
6th Company will chicken out. Volunteers, one step forward." Without a moment's
hesitation, the 125 soldiers of his company all advanced as one.

In addition, according to a certain Oberjunker of Rostaing's Company [possibly
Ginot], the choice was given of leaving for Berlin or remaining behind. Brigf.
Krukenberg assembled the companies of the *bataillon de marche* going to Berlin and
told them that the 'supreme moment had come [and] the Führer had called the French
units to him'. Continuing, he spelled out that 'he wanted only volunteers for this
mission' and that they should take one step forward. All did. (See Roch, page 130.)

This choice, however, is not confirmed by any other source. And, curiously,
according to Levast, a member of the *Kampfschule*, Krukenberg told the company
that it had the distinguished honour of participating in the defence of Berlin with the
other companies of 'Charlemagne'

67 Soulat, page 100. However, the exact number of vehicles will probably never be
known; for example, according to Krukenberg, the column consisted of two saloon
cars and three trucks; Mabire, page 110, cites 'ten Luftwaffe trucks with several

While the French SS volunteers were assembling at the Marktplatz of Alt-Strelitz,[68] they saw a black Mercedes approaching the column at great speed. At the wheel of the car was Reichsführer-SS Himmler himself. Krukenberg, his assistant Pachur and his orderly officer Patzak threw themselves to attention. Passing the column, the Mercedes did briefly slow down but did not stop. In fact, Himmler did not even look their way. The Mercedes disappeared. There was great surprise and obvious disappointment; the Reichsführer had not stopped, even though he had not inspected members of 'Charlemagne' before. Then they went back to the job in hand.

Krukenberg commented after the war:

> Later I discovered that Himmler had just met Bernadotte in Lubeck. As he knew all about our orders, and seeing that he had been trying to negotiate a surrender, he ought, in all conscience, to have stopped us from going on to Berlin or at least have informed me about the situation. I have no doubt that, by driving straight past us, Himmler was trying to avoid this painful necessity.

At 0830 or 0900 hours[69] on 24th April 1945, the column of trucks and private cars carrying some 400 to 500[70] French volunteers of the Waffen-SS set off southwards to Berlin, around 100 kilometres away as the crow flies. Also with the convoy was Ostuf. Fatin.[71]

Would the convoy make it through to Berlin?

private cars'; Georgen cites at least two cars and nine trucks that carried up to 45 men each; and according to an Oberjunker of Rostaing's Company (see Roch, page 131), each truck carried one platoon packed tight. Assuming that each of the five companies leaving for Berlin had [a minimum of] three platoons each, then the column counted fifteen trucks.

68   Mounine, correspondence to the author, 1998. Incorrectly, Rostaing states that the French *bataillon de marche* boarded at the *grand-place* [main square] of Neustrelitz (see page 186). 'South of Neustrelitz' and 'the southern road out of Alt-Strelitz' have also appeared as the embarkation point.

69   Mabire and Krukenberg cite 0830 hours and Saint-Loup cites 0900 hours.

70   Different authors have cited various figures. Georgen, part 1 page 19, cites no more than 410 to 420, Mabire, page 110, cites around 350, Landwehr, page 118, cites 350, Roch, page 131, cites 400, and Soulat, page 100, cites 500.

71   Was Ostuf. Fatin alone or at the head of company 3/57? If alone, then why did he accompany the Sturmbataillon to Berlin? There are two very real possibilities. First, he went to Berlin as Fenet's assistant. Two months before, at Gotenhafen, he had proved himself admirably in such a capacity. Second, he was brought along to 'support' three company commanders of the Sturmbataillon, namely Labourdette, Ollivier and Rostaing, who, although able, had only been company commanders for little more than one month and had yet to lead their commands in combat. He was more than 'qualified' for such a role; his military record made excellent reading and his credentials as a battle proven company commander were second to none.

CHAPTER 13

The First Days at Berlin

To Berlin

The convoy carrying the French *bataillon de marche* made its way southwards. Encountering more and more refugee convoys heading north, its pace often slowed to a crawl. It also passed prisoners from concentration camps Oranienburg and Ravensbrück. Civilians and soldiers alike were surprised to see a convoy heading in the opposite direction to them.

Brigf. Krukenberg stopped one vehicle of soldiers and questioned them on the whereabouts of the Russians. He was told that Russian armour had already been sighted not far from Oranienburg. Thus the route to Berlin via Frohnau was now out of the question. Thereupon Krukenberg decided to try another route via Neuruppin.

Near Löwenberg, Krukenberg gave the order to proceed westwards in the hope of reaching Fehrbellin and from there Friesack where the convoy would pick up the highway[1] from Hamburg that leads straight into Berlin.

As they continued, fighting against traffic jams in every village and at every cross-roads, they passed all manner of troops. From the Waffen-SS, they saw only the signals battalion from the Scandinavian 11. SS-Freiwilligen-Panzer-Grenadier-Division 'Nordland' which, according to its commander, had been ordered to Holstein. Its morale and discipline were still intact. They encountered Police battalions. And although they looked rested, their vehicle convoys were in the greatest disorder. Several times, they also ran into groups of dishevelled, but joyous German soldiers singing at the top of their voices. Why? They now believed they were saved. Because of agreements made between the Allies, the Soviets could not follow them any further and the western powers would immediately demobilise them!

At Friesack, the convoy came upon a police battalion manoeuvring in impeccable order and singing 'as if it had reached the gates of Moscow'.[2]

While crossing the town of Nauen the column was strafed by a Soviet aircraft, but escaped without damage. It proceeded on to Wustermark. Finding the route blocked at Wustermark by enemy artillery fire, Krukenberg searched his memory of the outskirts of Berlin and then decided to turn back and take the country road to Ketzin. From there, they would proceed to Marquart. The time was around midday.

The convoy covered six kilometres without problem. Suddenly Soviet troops were spotted cautiously converging on the road from the south-west, from the region of Paretz, and also from the north-east, from the region of Priort. They were small in number and without heavy weapons. Undoubtedly they were just patrols from the spearheads of the Soviet formations encircling Berlin, but once they linked up, Berlin would be cut off from the outside world.

---

1   Now Durchgangsstrabe 5.
2   Saint-Loup, page 387.

In turn, the Soviet troops spotted the convoy. They halted and took cover in small copses.

Krukenberg thought over his next move. Should they turn back? There was absolutely no question of this until every available option had been expended. Orders are orders. Should they go on? There was much to consider. Firstly, as the Russians had not effected a link-up, the route ahead was their last chance to get into Berlin. But what if they continued? They would have to face the Russians, growing in number by the minute, and cross the canal near the farms of Falkenrehde. Was the canal bridge still standing? This he did not know. What if they continued and the canal bridge was down? They might not be able to continue to Berlin or turn back. And the Russians were not far away. Then again, what of the telephone conversations earlier that day? He was convinced that the Americans and the English would never abandon Berlin to their Communist allies, but 'we', its defenders, would have to hold out until such time as they arrived. His decision was to keep going forward.

The convoy continued on quietly. By holding fire, Krukenberg hoped to mislead the Russians into believing that the convoy was one of theirs. His ruse worked. And the road ahead was clear.

Henceforth, the convoy was dogged by all kinds of misfortune. It was as though it had expended all of its good luck. To the rear of the convoy, the truck carrying Oberjunker Ginot's platoon of Rostaing's Company suddenly broke down. Luckily, Ginot managed to convey his plight to the truck in front. A towrope was attached and he was soon on his way again. Window down, leaning out the door, he kept a constant watch on the towrope, his lifeline to the battalion and Berlin.

Two other trucks were no longer with the convoy. Remarkably, they would make it back to Carpin. On board were Ostuf. Fatin [and perhaps a weak company under him[3]], Ostuf. Herpe, Ustuf. Verney, and Oberjunker Chavant's 3rd platoon of Hscha. Rostaing's 6th Company.[4]

Around 1500 hours, the convoy reached Falkenrehde canal bridge. It was still intact! Krukenberg's gamble had paid off and in less than an hour the convoy would be in Berlin. But first a flimsy anti-tank obstruction thrown across the entrance to the bridge had to be dismantled. Troops were detailed to clear this 'slight inconvenience'. Some headquarters staff of SS-Bataillon 57 also ventured onto the bridge.

Suddenly the bridge blew up in their faces! The force of the explosion literally picked men up and threw them in all directions. Some landed in the canal. Although nobody was killed, one grenadier, standing near Krukenberg, was seriously wounded in the legs and several others were lightly wounded, including Krukenberg. Also, the explosion immobilised his saloon car.

Eighteen-year-old Uscha. Roberto[5], one of 'Fenet's gang', whom the explosion had thrown into the canal, swam to the bank and was pulled out by two men. Although temporary blinded and deafened, he refused to be evacuated.

Badly damaged, the canal bridge was now impassable to vehicles but not to pedestrians. Quickly recovering from the shock of the explosion, Krukenberg ordered all supplies and equipment unloaded from the trucks. They would continue on foot. The trucks and the badly wounded man were sent back to

3   See *chapter* 11.
4   Rostaing would only see Chavant again in 1946 in Fresnes prison.
5   Pseudonym.

Neustrelitz via the same route they had come between the two Soviet spearheads. Some hours later and without incident they arrived back.

The troops started to cross the damaged bridge and several trips had to be made to bring across all the ammunition. On the other bank, three old men of the Volkssturm (Home Guard) approached Brigf. Krukenberg and confessed to blowing up the bridge. Ordered to destroy the bridge at the approach of the enemy, they had acted accordingly in the belief that the convoy was Russian. They were blameless. Strangely enough, in the space of hours, troops from both sides had mistaken the French SS troops for Russians!

Berlin was still twenty kilometres away. Rapidly assembled, the column, loaded down by weapons and ammunition, now set off at a brisk pace. At its head marched Brigf. Krukenberg, Hstuf. Fenet and the 'runners'. Krukenberg marched with a limp; he had leg problems. Millet and Bicou guided Roberto along by the arm. Behind them came Weber's Kampfschule, then the companies of Michel, Rostaing, and Ollivier. Labourdette brought up the rear, picking up the stragglers.

They went east. They covered kilometre after kilometre. The ammunition and weapons grew heavy. They became drenched in sweat and white with dust. To subdue their impatience at not having reached Berlin yet, they sang. They passed columns of civilians evacuating the capital. At one stop, Krukenberg called together the platoon commanders and ordered them to stop singing because it was having an adverse effect on the civilians! All the same they continued to sing.

They came to the unfinished Ringbahn, which they were able to make use of for several kilometres. On and on they marched.

Remarkably, a Supply Corps officer approached Brigf. Krukenberg and tried to persuade him to let the Frenchmen 'plunder' his dump. Krukenberg refused point-blank and gave as a pretext that they were pressed for time. Even so Rostaing sent some of his men to stock up. A wise precaution!

In the opposite direction fled more and more columns of civilians and servicemen who wore the face of the vanquished. And then a group of French 39–40 prisoners of war. They actually applauded their compatriots and wished them luck! Some young lads even threw them chocolate and American chewing gum.

Night started to fall. Berlin was still far off or so it seemed. They passed through Gross Glienicke, Gatow and Pichelsdorf. Along the way they came across no defenders except for three Hitler Jugend boys on bicycles each armed with a panzerfaust.

Finally they came to the Freybrücke which carries the Heerstrasse (East-West Axis) over the river Havel. The bridge was closed by roadblocks, but unguarded. They crossed.

Towards 2200 hours, they arrived at the Reichssportfeld [Olympic stadium]. It had been a long and very exhausting march of more than twenty kilometres there.

Nearby was an unguarded, but full Luftwaffe supply depot. Brigf. Krukenberg ordered his men to go and help themselves but their reaction was one of horror: that was tantamount to looting! To ease their conscience, he requisitioned the depot! It was full of chocolate and those who ate too much would remain awake all night.

Staff of various services occupied the houses lining the road. Judging by the noise and the music that could be heard, they seemed untroubled by the situation.

Krukenberg confiscated one of the many civilian cars parked up in front of the houses. Only then did he order his 'escort' to rest under trees to avoid being spotted by enemy aircraft. They bivouacked for the night on the slopes of Grunewald forest overlooking the river Havel. The Freybrücke was about one hundred metres away.

Brigadeführer Krukenberg and his first night in Berlin

Just before midnight or at 0030 hours,[6] Brigf. Krukenberg and his adjutant, Hstuf. Pachur, jumped into the requisitioned car. At its wheel was Ustuf. Patzak. They drove off to the Reichs Chancellery. Their journey took them across Adolf Hitler Platz, down Bismarckstrasse, under the Brandenburg Gate, across Pariser Platz, down Wilhelmstrasse and into Vossstrasse, where they pulled up on the footpath at the entrance to the Chancellery Bunker. Surprisingly, the journey had only taken half an hour. Indeed they had not been stopped once along the way. Berlin was literally deserted. An uneasy silence hung over the city, occasionally broken by the distant rumbling of Russian artillery.

Furthermore, the city was devoid of any defensive works and yet at the beginning of February 1945 Hitler had declared Berlin a 'Festung' (Fortress). Where were the troops? Where were the guns? Where were the defensive works? Where was this so-called fortress?

Krukenberg and Pachur now made their way down the few steps to the Bunker guarded by sentries. Krukenberg asked to meet with General Krebs, and although completely unknown to the sentries, he was admitted. Nevertheless, the General was absent for the time being and they were asked to sit down in a communications room. And here they waited for the General. The minutes ticked by. Krukenberg called his old Army Group Headquarters at Prenzlau to report his safe arrival in Berlin. The minutes became hours.

In the oppressive and warm atmosphere of the signals room they reflected on Berlin's apparent lack of preparedness to receive the Russian onslaught. Indeed, a Soviet commando team could easily have captured the bunker and the Führer himself in a surprise attack!

Finally, towards 0330 hours, some three hours after arriving at the Bunker, Krukenberg was shown in to see General Krebs who he knew from 1943 when he himself was serving in the Wehrmacht with von Kluge's Army Group Centre. With General Krebs was General Burgdorf, Hitler's Chief Adjutant and a committed National Socialist. The two generals were very surprised to see him. Krebs explained that forty-eight hours ago they had ordered a whole string of officers and units positioned around Berlin to come to the defence of the capital immediately. And so far he was the only one to have arrived!

Krebs then briefed him on the situation. And it was a briefing all too similar to that he had received before his departure. Krebs talked of little else other than the future help of the western powers and the approach of Army Wenck.

When Krukenberg described his experiences near Ketzin, Krebs answered that the Soviet spearheads were certainly weak in strength and added that Wenck's Army, coming to the rescue of Berlin, would easily brush them aside.

Krebs then ordered Krukenberg to report in the morning to General Weidling who had become the overall Commandant of the Berlin Defence Area the day before, 24th April 1945. Krebs let it be known that it was Weidling who had

6   Mabire cites 'Just before night', page 133, whereas Saint-Loup cites '0030 hours', page 409.

personally asked for him and that he would explain why. His command post was to be found on Fehrbelliner Platz on the Hohenzollerndamm in the former Headquarters of the peacetime III Corps and the wartime Deputy III Corps. Krukenberg knew it well.

Before leaving, Krukenberg asked as to the whereabouts of SS-Ogruf. Fegelein, Himmler's liaison officer to the Führer, to whom he was also supposed to report. When Fegelein could not be found he was told to return to the Chancellery in the next couple of days.

Shortly after 0400 hours on 25th April 1945, Krukenberg and Pachur left the Chancellery. The roads proved just as empty on the return journey. Again there was no sign of defensive troops. Towards 0500 hours, they arrived back at the Reichssportfeld. The sun was coming up. The sky was clear.

The Frenchmen were still asleep. Most had enjoyed an unbroken night's sleep despite the sound of concentrated Russian artillery fire pouring down on the nearby Freybrücke.

Krukenberg was welcomed back by Fenet who was impatient for orders. Krukenberg told him that he was to see General Weildling that morning and that as soon as he knew in what sector they were to be engaged he would send Ustuf. Patzak to collect them. Fenet would have to wait.

Krukenberg and Pachur now rested.

One by one, the men of the French SS-Sturmbataillon were pulled from their slumber by officers and NCOs going from group to group. A roll call was taken. Not a single Frenchman was missing. The last of the stragglers had rejoined their comrades during the night. They now prepared themselves for the coming battle; after washing in the Havel, they shaved, brushed down their uniforms and polished their equipment. To pass the time and take heart, they sang.

Hstuf. Fenet reorganised the Franz. SS-Sturmbataillon.[7] This reorganisation may have amounted to nothing more than the designation of numbers to the four companies that had got through to Berlin. The resultant formation looked as follows:

Battalion commander	W-Hstuf. Fenet
Assistant and V.O.	SS-Ostuf. von Wallenrodt
Orderly officer 1	W-Std.Ob.Ju. Frantz
Orderly officer 2	W-Std.Ob.Ju. Douroux
1st Company	
Commander	W-Ustuf. Labourdette
Assistant	W-Std.Ob.Ju. Cossard

---

7   The designation of the French unit of the Waffen-SS that fought in Berlin has often been supplemented with the title of 'Charlemagne'. For example, Landwehr repeats the use of SS-Sturmbatallion 'Charlemagne' and Le Tissier cites that of SS 'Charlemagne' Battalion. Curiously, Fenet, its commander, makes no reference to a designation that includes the title of 'Charlemagne' in his account of the battle for Berlin, '*A Berlin Jusqu'au Bout*'.

Assistant	W-Std.Ob.Ju. Croisille
Platoon commander	W-Std.Ob.Ju. Boulmier
Platoon commander	W-Std.Ob.Ju. de Lacaze
Platoon commander?	W-Std.Ob.Ju. Le Maignan de Kérangat

2nd Company

Commander	W-Ostuf. Michel
Platoon commander	W-Oscha. *Lardy*[8]
Platoon commander	W-Std.Ob.Ju. Neroni
Platoon commander	W-Oscha. Mongourd

3rd Company

Commander	W-Hscha. Rostaing
Assistant	W-Std.Ob.Ju. Dumoulin
1st platoon: commander	W-Std.Ob.Ju. Ginot
Platoon commander	W-Std.Ob.Ju. Baumgartner

4th Company[9]

Commander	W-Oscha. Ollivier
Assistant	W-Std.Ob.Ju. Protopopoff
Platoon commander	W-Uscha. Fieselbrand
Platoon commander	W-Std.Ob.Ju. Bellier
Platoon commander	Sauvageot[10]

Kampfschule

Commander	SS-Ostuf. Weber
Platoon commander	W-Oscha. Pierre Bousquet
Platoon commander	W-Uscha. Aimé-Blanc
Platoon commander	W-Uscha. Fontenay

Also serving with the French Sturmbataillon in Berlin were the following W-Std.Ob.Ju.: Garrabos, Maisse and Poupon.[11] Notably many platoons were still commanded by non-commissioned officers. This was true of the Kampfschule.

8   Pseudonym.
9   Of interest to note is that Saint-Loup and Fenet make no mention of a Company commanded by Ollivier.
10 Sauvageot was ex-LVF. Transferred to the W-SS, he served with the 9/58.
11 W-Std.Ob.Ju. Lebrun may have also been with the French SS-Sturmbataillon in Berlin.

Twenty-four-year-old Uscha. Aimé-Blanc had fought with the French Marschkompanie at Kolberg. Uscha. Fontenay was nineteen years old.[12] Oscha. Klein was still with the Kampfschule as *Spiess*.

Throughout the coming battle, Krukenberg would have a number of German headquarters staff with him as well as a small French Begleitkommando. The composition and strength of the escort has been impossible to determine, although some were from the Kampfschule.[13]

SS-Uscha. Max Walter of the Staff Company also came to Berlin with the Sturmbataillon.[14]

After a few hours rest, Brigf. Krukenberg journeyed through the city to Weidling's command post on Hohenzollerndamm. With him were Pachur and Patzak. By now, a few patrols and barricades had appeared in the streets, but there was still no sign of any defensive troops. A closed Soldbuch got them through the sentries and into corridors full of officers, as well as civilians and secretaries.

Krukenberg was taken to Oberst [Colonel] von Dufving first. He was the Chief-of-Staff of the LVI Panzer Corps. Krukenberg was then introduced to General Weidling who struck him as a man totally without confidence. They were left alone to talk.

Weidling told Krukenberg that he had been brought to Berlin two days previously and, despite his conflicting ideas for its defence, appointed the 'battle commandant' of the city.

The forces General Weidling had at his disposal to defend Berlin were wholly inadequate. Besides his old command, the LVI Panzer Corps, which had suffered greatly in the recent fighting,[15] there were the badly armed units of the Volkssturm and the hurriedly formed alarm units from the administrative services, Luftwaffe auxiliaries and the Hitler Jugend. Although they showed a great willingness to fight and die, they were of dubious military value.[16]

Weidling spoke of his predecessor, General Reymann, whom the Party had removed from post. Lines of command were confused. His request to have sole authority for the issue of orders for its defence had been ignored![17]

---

12 Fontenay would survive the 'holocaust' of Berlin.

13 One such Frenchman of the Begleitkommando was Levast of the *Kampfschule*.

14 A translator, he was, undoubtedly, attached to Fenet or Krukenberg. Seriously wounded in the fighting, he died on 15th September 1945 in Halle hospital.

15 The strength of the LVI Panzer Corps was around 13-15,000 men. Its component forces were the relatively intact 18th Panzergrenadier Division, the severely reduced 20th Panzergrenadier Division, the 'Müncheberg' Panzer Division, of which only one-third would participate in the fighting, the badly battered and reduced 9th Parachute Division and the 11.SS-Freiwilligen-Panzer-Grenadier-Division 'Nordland' under Brigf. Ziegler.

16 Weidling also had at his disposal the Waffen SS units under SS-Brigf. Mohnke that amounted to the strength of half a division. They included the Berlin-based regiment of the 1. SS-Panzer-Division 'Leibstandarte Adolf Hitler' which provided Hitler's ceremonial bodyguard. The regiment consisted of some 1,200 troops. All told, Weidling had under his command some 60,000 men with only some 50-60 tanks. The LVI Panzer Corps and the Waffen SS units were the only forces that could be considered cohesive and reasonably equipped.

In the presence of his Chief-of-Staff who had joined them, Weidling told Krukenberg that the south-east of the city, designated Defence Sector C, had been assigned to the 11. SS-Freiwilligen-Panzer-Grenadier-Division 'Nordland' under Brigf. Ziegler. As of late, Ziegler had become very troublesome and seemed to have lost control of his division. He himself had met members of the division throughout the various western districts of Berlin. He wanted Ziegler removed from command and he had brought Krukenberg to Berlin to replace him.

Concerned that his orders were verbal, Krukenberg asked Weidling for a written order to present to Ziegler. This Weidling penned and signed. Furthermore, Ziegler was instructed, as soon as he handed over command to Krukenberg, to report to the Reichs Chancellery.[18]

Although all telephone contact with the divisional headquarters of 'Nordland' had been lost for some time, its location was thought to be on Hasenheide, between the suburbs of Neukölln and Kreuzberg. Krukenberg proceeded there immediately.

'Nordland'

When Krukenberg came to Hasenheide he found the divisional headquarters of 'Nordland' without difficulty from the many vehicles quite openly parked around it. Unfortunately, the Soviet Air Force had also spotted the same telltale signs and just bombed it.

Clouds of dust were still pouring out of the building. Its upper floors had been destroyed. Disorder reigned on the ground floor where the command post was. Wounded were lying about everywhere and among them, in a corner, was Ziegler.

The two Generals knew each other. Their paths had crossed in the second half of 1944 in the Baltic States. Krukenberg informed Ziegler that he was here to replace him. This Ziegler was expecting. As a comrade, he warned Krukenberg that he too would not be in post more than twenty-four hours.

According to Ziegler, the defence of Berlin was an impossible mission and that is why those 'at the top' were out for scapegoats.

Krukenberg asked him what forces he had deployed in the front line and was shocked when Ziegler quoted him a figure of seventy men! The rest were too exhausted and resting. Indeed, the two grenadier regiments of 'Nordland' each had the strength of a strong company or, at best, that of a weak battalion! 'Nordland' still had some tanks and assault guns at its disposal, but was desperately short of petrol. The Artillery Regiment was also a shadow of its former shelf. On orders from Corps, its few guns had been sited in the Tiergarten. In addition, 'Nordland' had no contact with the Volkssturm or the neighbouring sectors.

Krukenberg sent Ustuf. Patzak and trucks back to collect 'his detachment' from the Reichssportfeld complex. Meanwhile, Pachur set about reorganising the command post.

17   Weidling was further handicapped by poor communications. It could take a runner hours just to cover a few hundred metres as the roads were now under shellfire and choked by debris.

18   According to Mabire, page 140, Krukenberg then asked about his French Waffen-SS troops. To which Weidling replied that they could constitute an 'independent assault battalion within the 'Nordland' Division'. Curiously, the memoirs of Krukenberg do not substantiate this attachment.

At midday, Ziegler took his leave and left by car for the Reichs Chancellery.[19]

Still very much 'in the dark', Krukenberg walked towards the front to learn more of the situation. By now, the Hasenheide was under light artillery fire. Guarding the Hasenheide and the neighbouring terrain from possible surprise attack were small alarm units of 'Nordland'. Surprisingly, in the foremost positions, Brigf. Krukenberg only found members of the Volkssturm. Sent into battle armed with a wide selection of captured French, Belgian, Czech or Italian rifles, and already short of ammunition, 'they seemed lost and confused'.[20] Krukenberg said of them: "These men cut rather poor figures." He went in search of their commander.

Krukenberg found the local Volkssturm commander, a Kreisleiter [NSDAP District Leader], in a large building on Hermannplatz at the corner of Hasenheide and Kottbuser Damm. From the first floor, the Kreisleiter had an excellent view of the whole south-eastern suburb of the city.

The Kreisleiter complained that the Volkssturm had been engaged 'alone' and without contact with regular troops.

And what of the situation? According to the Kreisleiter, the Soviets were advancing from the east and the district of Treptow had already fallen the day before. He had posted weak elements on Urbandam and Sonnenallee but, with only a few machine-guns and very little ammunition at their disposal, they were expected to offer little resistance.

And what of the neighbouring sectors? The Kreisleiter was in telephone contact with the sector of Görlitzer Bahnof (railway station) on his left and had just learnt that Reichsleiter Hilgenfeld had fallen in combat two hours previously. His only news of Tempelhof airfield on his right came from refugees, who told him a violent tank battle was raging.

While they were talking two Soviet tanks suddenly appeared on the opposite side of Hermannplatz and opened fire. As the tanks were not supported and alone, Krukenberg thought the chances of fighting them in close combat were good.

After telling the Kreisleiter that 'he was going to do something' to relieve his men, Krukenberg returned to the Hasenheide and 'Nordland' divisional command post. On the way back, he was nicked in the face by shrapnel. Back at the command post, Pachur greeted him with the good news that the French SS-Sturmbataillon had just arrived safely from the Reichssportfeld.

Tightly packed together in lorries, the French W-SS volunteers of the Sturmbataillon had crossed the city of Berlin in the direction of Tempelhof. By now, Berlin had awoken. The S-Bahn was running. In squares sat office workers eating their sandwiches. Policemen were directing traffic at crossroads. The Frenchmen started to sing:

SS marschiert im Feindesland
Und singt ein Teufeslied

Surprised, the Berliners cheered and applauded them from their windows, from their doors and from the pavements. Many may have assumed this convoy to be the vanguard of Army Wenck, ordered by Hitler to march to the relief of Berlin whose

---

19   On his arrival, Ziegler was placed under arrest on a charge of failing to hold the defence line along the Spree and then the Teltow canal.

20   "*Battle Memoir*", page 155.

anticipated arrival had been the theme for many newspaper articles. A spirit of optimism, false though it was, animated the Berliners. With tears welling up in their eyes, the Frenchmen responded in kind to their warm reception. They gave the Nazi salute, brandished their weapons and blew kisses to the girls. When the lorries came to a momentary stop groups of all ages gathered round them. The Frenchmen offered cigarettes to which the Berliners could only reply with a smile. That was all they had left to give. The Frenchmen were soon on their way again, not before the Berliners had shaken the hands outstretched towards them and said thank you.

In the late afternoon,[21] the French SS-Sturmbataillon arrived in the sector of Neukölln and found 'lodgings' in the quarter to the north of the Hasenheide between Hermannplatz and the church on Gardepionierplatz. Rostaing's Company took up residence in a pub cellar, which, fortunately, was stocked with beer. The Kampfschule went to a pub on Hermannplatz, but theirs was dry. The men of Michel's Company accommodated themselves on the ground floor of a carpet warehouse and made themselves comfortable among precious oriental carpets and rugs.

No sooner had Weber's Kampfschule arrived than it was employed at a road barricade alongside the Feldgendarmerie checking the papers of soldiers and civilians alike. The Frenchmen were relieved in the evening and returned to the pub on Hermannplatz.

All companies were ordered to send out patrols. Oscha. Ollivier, the commander of the 4th Company, insisted on taking out a patrol himself. The patrol, consisting of Sauvageot's platoon, ventured towards Tempelhof airport across the Hasenheide. The noise of battle drew closer. The patrol came across an old Berliner sitting on a bench who seemed to have died peacefully from a heart attack. The dead man was found to be carrying some provisions on him. This find would go some way to subduing their pangs of hunger, for no rations had been made available to them yet. A little later, and without further incident, the patrol returned to its billets.

Oscha. Mongourd led one of the patrols conducted by Ostuf. Michel's 2nd Company. He took his twenty-strong platoon out on patrol with him. And although many of the platoon were young and had never been in action, they seemed eager for battle.

At the head of the patrol marched Grenadier Jean-François Lapland, who was not yet eighteen, and his section commander, Uscha. Fodot. Both were from the Limousin. The light was fading and the roads seemed strangely deserted. Lapland heard machine-gun fire and explosions whose location he could not pinpoint, but the Russians were thought to be near. Suddenly shots rang out. The troops closely hugged the walls. Mongourd shouted out orders. Fire was returned at random. Suddenly it dawned on Lapland and Fodot that they were alone. Footsteps were heard close by and they called out in hushed voices. The reply was in Russian! The two Frenchmen hid themselves behind a fence and, through gaps, watched the Russians pass by and then return to a tank which was 'waiting in ambush' not far away. Minutes later, they spotted a second tank near to the first. As the Russian tanks were off their guard, they decided to 'deal' with them after nightfall; the two of them were armed with the redoubtable panzerfäuste. It was a nerve-racking ordeal to wait quietly.

---

21   Mabire, page 151. In contrast, according to Krukenberg, page 8, the French
      detachment was found quarters in Gneisenau barracks.

Sometime after 0300 hours, Lapland and Fodot crept out of their hiding place and along the houses towards the two Russian tanks. All was silent except for the sound of a crackling tank radio set. The Russians seemed to be either asleep or dead drunk. They fired, threw away the empty tubes and dashed off. Behind them they left two tanks consumed in flames. Minutes later, they ran into a patrol from their platoon. Oscha. Mongourd informed them that they were going to counterattack at dawn which was now only hours away.

Lapland and Fodot were not the first French volunteers of the Waffen-SS to knock out a Russian tank in Berlin.[22] That honour went to Grenadier Ronzier, also of the 2nd Company.

Krukenberg and the afternoon of the 25th

The immediate priority for Krukenberg was to relocate the divisional headquarters of 'Nordland' from the Hasenheide. The aerial bombardment had so devastated the building that it was no longer usable. He decided to relocate to Gneisenau barracks, reported to him as a possible place of refuge by elements of his headquarters already 'in residence'. This police barracks was nearby, completely intact and, importantly, had excellent communication facilities, because the absence of its Signals battalion, sent to Holstein, was being sorely felt.

At Gneisenau barracks, Krukenberg sought and received from the headquarters of the LVI Panzer Corps authorisation for the relocation. He also requested to be freed from the responsibility for Sector 'C' and to be assigned a more central district for the regrouping of 'Nordland'. This was granted when he reported the presence of two well-equipped, fresh police battalions at Gneisenau barracks that could handle the 'Nordland' sector. The two police battalions appeared to have been forgotten about!

'Nordland' was assigned the district around Gendarmenmarkt in the city centre. Thereupon Brigf. Krukenberg chose the cellars of the Opera house as his temporary headquarters.

Summoned to the headquarters of the LVI Panzer Corps, now sited more centrally on Bendlerstrasse, Krukenberg arrived at the appointed time of 2000 hours. The Chief-of-Staff of the LVI Panzer Corps ordered him to engage 'Nordland' in Defence Sector 'Z'[23] by midday next day. The commander of this defence sector was a certain Oberstleutnant [Lieutenant Colonel] Seifert of the Luftwaffe whose headquarters was located in the Air Ministry building.[24] Krukenberg went at once to report to him.

The corridors of the Air Ministry were full of Luftwaffe soldiers, but Krukenberg noted that none were officers. Seifert received Krukenberg in the

22 According to Krukenberg, page 8, he immediately deployed half of the 'French anti-tank group' under Hstuf. Fenet against the Soviet armour sighted on Hermannplatz. Also, he attached Weber to Fenet. And in the course of the evening and the night the Frenchmen managed to shoot up 14 Soviet tanks in close combat, 'forcing the enemy to abandon its pressure in this sector'.

23 According to Krukenberg, the 'Z' stood for Zentrum [Centre] whereas, according to Le Tissier, the 'Z' was for 'Zitadelle' [Citadel].

24 According to Mabire, page 147, Krukenberg complained of finding himself subordinated to a Luftwaffe officer who was not even a Colonel!

presence of an orderly officer who, incredibly, was the sum total of the headquarters staff for his Defence Sector!

Oberstleutenant Seifert proved extremely hostile towards Krukenberg, 'Nordland' and the Waffen-SS in general. Bluntly, he told Krukenberg that he had no need of his regimental commanders or their headquarters staff because he had been told that the fighting strength of each regiment was no more than that of a battalion. Krukenberg defended 'Nordland'. He argued that sector 'Z' would become the centre of resistance and that greater the number of proven officers available greater the resistance. This fell on deaf ears.

In reply, Seifert stated that the defence of the district had already been organised and that, as such, he had no need of support. Pulling out a map, he showed Krukenberg the machine-gun posts and the other combat positions.

Krukenberg offered Seifert the services of one or two of those with him to reinforce his headquarters staff. This he refused. Curtly, he also refused Krukenberg's next offer to place himself at his disposal to advice him on the defence plan. Seifert wanted to hear nothing of it. Such was his prejudice against the Waffen-SS that nothing could shake. Krukenberg pointed out that he had transferred to the Waffen-SS about a year previously and that he had been on the Army General staff during both world wars. But Seifert was still not won over. His distrust of the Waffen-SS was too deep-rooted.

Towards 2300 hours, Krukenberg returned to his new command post in the Berlin Opera House. The meeting with Seifert had left him with a 'very bad feeling'. Before getting some sleep he relayed the orders from Corps to the commanders of regiments 'Danmark' and 'Norge'. Also, such was his concern about Seifert that he informed them of his hostile attitude.

The night of 25th/26th April Krukenberg remembers as calm.

The battle for Neukölln[25]

On the 26th, well before daybreak, the companies of the French SS-Sturmbataillon set off from their billets north of the Hasenheide and silently made their way towards Neukölln town hall. At 0500 hours, from Neukölln town hall, the French SS-Sturmbataillon was to counterattack along Berlinerstrasse. 'Nordland' was to advance on its left along the Landwehr canal and provide tank support.

As they neared their starting positions, the French W-SS troops passed the promised tank support. Waiting were a massive Königstiger (King Tiger) tank with its long 88mm gun, two 'slim' Panther tanks at crossroads Donau-Fuldastrasse, and several low-slung Sturmgeschütze (assault guns) with the short 75mm gun near Neukölln town hall. The crews were calmly smoking and joking 'as if they were leaving for a worthy outing in the country'.[26]

---

25   Curiously, Krukenberg's memoirs of the battle of Berlin make no mention of the counterattacks launched into Neukölln on 26th April 1945 by 'Nordland' and the French SS-Sturmbataillon. And yet, according to Saint-Loup, page 418, Krukenberg told Fenet in person of the planned counterattack. Regarding this, the author cannot believe that 'Nordland' planned a counterattack, in which it was to commit tanks, without the involvement of its divisional commander. Indeed, such was the desperate shortage of tanks in Berlin that Division probably had to go to Corps for approval to employ them.

26   Saint-Loup, page 420.

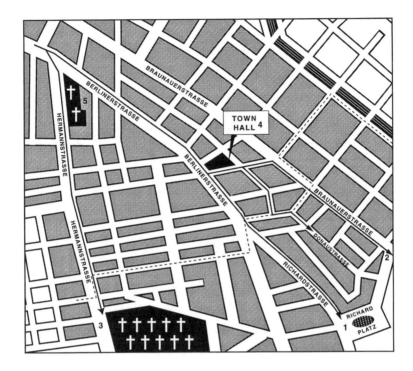

Map 5: The battle of Neukölln, 26th April 1945 (based on Saint-Loup, page 419)
The attack of the French Sturmbataillon, supported by armour of 'Nordland', starts well but bogs down as resistance increases.
1. The 2nd Company under Ostuf. Michel attacks along Berlinerstrasse/Richardstrasse.
2. The 3rd Company under Hscha. Rostaing attacks along Braunauerstrasse. It works its way forward to Richard Platz.
3. The Kampfschule under Ostuf. Weber, held in reserve at Hermannplatz, is commited along Hermannstrasse.
4. The Russians go over to the attack and the French forces turn the town hall into the *centre de résistance.* They hold out until retreat becomes inevitable.
5. The platoon (of the 4th Company?) held in reserve in the cemetery at the corner of crossroads Berliner-Hermannstrasse is hit by Russian artillery and suffers losses.

Shortly before 0500 hours, the French SS-Sturmbataillon was in position. Fenet planned to attack with Rostaing's 3rd Company and Michel's 2nd Company. The battalion's 4th Company, commanded by Ollivier, was to be held in reserve. Battalion headquarters was to be established in Neukölln town hall. The 1st Company was not available to Fenet. It had been placed at the disposal of the Tempelhof sector.

Day was ushered in by the roar of Russian artillery. The platoon held in reserve in the cemetery at the corner of crossroads Berliner-Hermannstrasse was hit and suffered some losses.[27]

27   Ibid.

Time fast approached H Hour, but the order to attack had still not been received. 0500 hours came and went … nothing. The district was still wrapped in silence. The minutes ticked by. And still nothing at 0530 hours. The troops grew impatient. The day brought promise of good weather. The blue sky was cloudless. Finally, shortly before 0600 hours, the order to attack arrived.

The columns of waiting French SS troops rushed forward, closely followed by the tanks. Opposite nothing stirred. This, however, was short-lived. Maxim heavy machine guns were the first to wake. And then the anti-tank guns with their raucous bark. As if on exercise, the French SS troops dashed from doorway to doorway, jumping over walls and debris, and flushing out Red snipers.

The attack of the 3rd Company

Rostaing's 3rd Company advanced along Braunauerstrasse.[28] It had the support of the Königstiger. However, due to a lack of petrol, the tank could not accompany the advance. Thus, from afar, it would cover the advance.

Advancing on the left was Oberjunker Baumgartner's platoon. And on the right Hscha. Rostaing, his assistant Oberjunker Dumoulin, liaison officer Pilsin and Oberjunker Ginot with his 1st platoon.

Suddenly a burst of gunfire rang out and Oberjunker Dumoulin, standing beside Rostaing, crumpled to the ground. He was dead. Rostaing immediately ordered the 1st platoon forward, but had to replace Oberjunker Ginot, its commander, who was paralysed by fear. The troops pushed forward.

Ahead, in the middle of the avenue, stood a German anti-tank barricade that was now held by the Russians. Some fifty metres from the barricade Rostaing came to a transverse road. Before crossing, he glanced down the road on his right. He drew back. A T–34 was parked up about ten metres away. And its dismounted crew had caught sight of him. He opened fire with his Sturmgewehr, killing two, but the other three managed to find shelter in the porchway of a block of flats.

Rostaing then gestured to his *pourvoyeur* to pass him a panzerfaust. Taking aim at the tank, he fired, hitting it just below the turret. A massive explosion blew apart the tank; the panzerfaust round had struck the tank's ammunition. Debris and metal fragments were scattered in every direction. Rostaing's *pourvoyeur,* who was leaning out to watch him, was decapitated by a piece of sheet metal. Rostaing was hit in the right temple by metal fragments and collapsed.

Rostaing soon came round. Wearily, he got up and brushed himself down. He turned round and, to his horror, he saw the dead bodies of twelve of his men sprawled on the pavement. A survivor, seriously wounded, was crying out for his mother. He wondered how this had happened. The other platoons had seen and heard nothing.

Rostaing looked around closely. Suddenly, only metres away, he noticed the doors of a portal slowly open and then the barrel of a Maxim machine gun appear. He threw himself forward, rolled into the road and opened fire, killing the three Russians around the Maxim. Waiting in ambush, the Russians had opened up as each of his men had passed the porch. They had gone unnoticed because the terrible din coming up from the city had drowned out the noise of the machine gun.

Carefully, Rostaing's 3rd Company now pressed on along the road, but already, in less than an hour, it had lost more than one quarter of its strength.

28   Now Sonnen Allee.

Casualties continued to mount. One man crumpled to the ground every five minutes. All were victims of snipers. Platoon commander Oberjunker Baumgartner and his assistant, Oscha. Verfaillie[29], were both hit in the ankle. Oberjunker Ginot was wounded in the elbow, but refused orders to be evacuated. He had regained his spirit and his sangfroid [30]

A bullet tore through Rostaing's trousers above his right knee. His good luck had not deserted him. Two of his four runners became casualties. One of the surviving two had also been hit in the ankle but continued to carry orders and messages. Purposely, Rostaing entrusted him with a message to battalion HQ at Neukölln town hall in the hope that he would get himself attended to and evacuated if need be. Rostaing never saw him again.

Rostaing now felt alone. In his book, he commented that the other company[31] that should have been covering him had been decimated at the start of the attack. His only support came from the immobilised 'Nordland' Tiger that had knocked out two T–34s in his path.

At one point Rostaing found himself outflanked and was forced to withdraw. However, it was only a temporary setback. His troops reorganised and pushed forward once again, clearing out room after room, apartment after apartment, and building after building in brutal hand-to-hand fighting. A young soldier beside Rostaing was hit right between the eyes and crumpled to the ground face down. Believing he was dead, Rostaing turned him over to collect his Soldbuch, but the soldier smiled at him, sat up and asked for a cigarette. He was evacuated to the rear for treatment. Rostaing thought that was the last he would see of him. He was wrong. For most of the following day, Rostaing saw him glued to the turret of a tank. His head was bandaged and he was still smoking!

Mortar bombs rained down in the avenue. Against all the odds, the counterattack was vigorously pressed home. The barricade fell to the Frenchmen.

Rostaing ordered grenadier Tillier, a strapping Norman, and one of his comrades to clear the ground floor of a house where he wanted to take up position. They entered a room that looked out onto a square not far from the spot where the Russian machine gun nest had inflicted such a grievous 'body blow' on the Company. His comrade left the room. Tillier made himself comfortable. Suddenly he noticed about six Russians in the square only metres away. Without hesitation he fired his rifle grenade at them. The Russians scattered and withdrew. Informed of this incident, Rostaing decided to change buildings and make for another across the road.

To distract the Russians while they crossed, Rostaing had a panzerfaust fired in their direction. But, as the Frenchmen crossed, they received sniper fire from across the road. Oscha. Dedieu was killed by a bullet in the middle of the head. Alert, Rostaing spotted the sniper. Pointing to a window, he shouted to Tillier to place a grenade inside. It took him three attempts. The Russian sniper fell silent. When

29 Of Belgian nationality, Roland Verfaillie was 'one of the old brigade' [LVF veteran of 1941]. In 1942, he joined the 2nd Company of the I. Battalion. After the war, he too went on trial in France. When asked by the chairman of the court why he had enlisted in the LVF he 'disarmed' him by replying that it was to gain French nationality.

30 Unable to fire his Sturmgewehr, Ginot was eventually persuaded to go and get himself attended to.

31 Presumably Michel's 2nd Company.

they entered the building Tillier came face to face with a Russian, a very small Mongol, who disappeared 'like through a trap door'.[32]

Rostaing's Company worked its way forward to Richard Platz but could not debouch because a Russian anti-tank gun had the square covered. An assault gun was brought up. A shot on target and the enemy anti-tank gun 'barked' no more. However, a Maxim heavy machine gun continued to hold up Rostaing's troops, now sheltering in porches.

Stealthy, Rostaing made his way towards the Russian machine gun nest. A grenade tossed by him put an end to it. Triumphantly, his company followed him onto the square. Even though he had lost contact with battalion headquarters, he now decided to press on with the attack towards the Tempelhof-Treptow 'S-Bahn' line.

Suddenly one of the men with Rostaing called Arbonnel started to sob heavily. He was convinced he had been wounded in the stomach. Rostaing examined him. He had been hit, but in the belt buckle! The impact had led him to believe that he was done for. Rostaing slapped him several times which brought him back to his senses. Arbonnel set off again.

The attack of the 2nd Company

Company commander Ostuf. Michel was missing one of his platoons. Contact had been lost with Oscha. Lardy's platoon of fifteen or so men while on patrol in an enemy infested district.

On hearing a curious loud sound of hammering Lardy took his platoon to investigate. They came to an immobilised Russian tank, which the crew was hurriedly trying to repair. Lardy called upon a certain grenadier by the name of Daspins[33] to deal with the sitting target.

A former *chef* of the *Jeunesse catholique de* Seine-et-Oise, Daspins had enlisted in the Waffen-SS at the age of eighteen. He saw action at Kolberg in the ranks of Ludwig's *compagnie de marche* and now desperately wanted to open his 'account'.

Approaching the tank, Daspins was suddenly disturbed by a Russian soldier. He had to silence him and quietly or else the alarm would be raised. Daspins launched himself at the Russian and eventually overcame him, not before the Russian had almost bitten off a thumb. He had nearly howled out in pain, but that would have 'given the game away'. Excited, he rushed back to his comrades to tell them loudly of his victory in this most primeval of contests: hand-to-hand combat. Lardy told Daspins to keep quiet and get back to the task in hand. Daspins took up position within panzerfaust range, carefully took aim and fired, 'scoring a hit'.

Lardy and his platoon quickly made off, but the Russians seemed everywhere now. They took to a house. From the attic, they were amazed to see hundreds of Russians sitting on a waste piece of ground who were all armed with a mortar! Their situation looked hopeless and clearly it was. Hours later, they were taken prisoner. Daspins talked himself and his comrades out of a bullet in the back of the neck by claiming that they had been deported for work and then mobilised by the Germans. They were sent to the rear.

The 2nd Company attacked along Berlinerstrasse[34] that runs parallel to Braunauerstrasse.

32   Mabire, pages 163-164.
33   Pseudonym.

At the head of the 2nd Company advanced Oscha. Mongourd's platoon. The Russians were quick to lay down a curtain of defensive fire. Bullets whistled all around. Hell had supplanted peace. Among the first to fall was Company commander Ostuf. Michel. Seriously wounded in the face, he was evacuated to a cellar.[35]

The curtain of fire brought the advance to a halt. Pinned down, the attackers took shelter. They could not emerge. In this way, platoons became cut off from the Company and the sections from the platoons.

Some men of Mongourd's platoon, including Uscha. Fodot and Gren. Lapland, found themselves in a 'sort of hangar' cut off from the rest of the platoon. A liaison officer went off to the rear, but was back minutes later. Several houses away, he had come face to face with a Russian. They had fought with their bare hands. And then, strangely, each had let go of the other and run off to their respective sides.

Again the Russians seemed to be everywhere. The men around Fodot came to realise that they were isolated, perhaps even encircled. Fodot quickly organised them into defensive positions. Tanks, which they presumed Russian, could already be heard.

Tiredness overcame Lapland and he fell asleep; he had been on his feet three days and two nights. When he woke, just moments later, Fodot had gone. Henceforth he felt alone.

The 4th Company

Although held in reserve, the 4th Company of the Sturmbataillon commanded by Osha. Ollivier, was struck by disaster when it came under fire from either an enemy anti-tank gun or a captured 'Nordland' tank.[36] Fifteen (Saint-Loup and Fenet) or seventeen (Mabire and Soulat) corpses were now stretched out or hunched up on the blood-soaked pavement and roadway. It was a devastating blow. All were under twenty. There were also many wounded. And among them was platoon commander Uscha. Fieselbrand whose right leg had almost been severed above the ankle. While waiting for an ambulance his comrades had to

---

34   Now Karl Marx Strasse.

35   Although the ultimate fate of Michel is unknown, the severity of his wounds leaves little doubt that he would die of them. Even so some have claimed that Michel survived the war and later served in the *Sécurité militaire*, but the physical description of a certain '*Capitaine* Michel' does not agree at all with that of Ostuf. Michel.

36   According to Fenet, page 158, a salvo of anti-tank shells massacred a reserve platoon that, thinking itself safe, had carelessly assembled. According to Saint-Loup, page 425, the reserve platoon, which carelessly assembled in the middle of crossroads Donaustrasse-Schönstedt, was hit by four anti-tank shells. According to Soulat, page 103, Oscha. Ollivier was giving orders to his platoon commanders around him when the company was 'taken to task' by a Russian anti-tank gun. In contrast, according to Mabire, page 160, Oscha. Ollivier was giving orders to his *adjoint* and his three platoon commanders when a 'Nordland' tank, parked up nearby, suddenly opened fire with all guns on his company. Men of Bellier's platoon attacked without hesitation, silencing the tank with panzerfäuste, but it had already wrought carnage. Had the Russians captured the tank? Or, tragically, had the tank mistaken the Frenchmen for Russians and opened up? Ollivier was convinced that the Russians had captured the tank and without a sound. And although this seems improbable, it cannot be dismissed because Mabire interviewed Ollivier for "*Mourir à Berlin*".

complete the amputation with a knife. Also among the wounded was Oscha. Ollivier. He had a piece of shrapnel lodged in the chest between two vertebras. Also shrapnel had gashed his right hand. All told, the 4th Company lost over one third of its strength.

Ollivier passed command of the 4th Company to Oberjunker Protopopoff. An ambulance evacuated him and three other seriously wounded men.

When informed of the massacre Hstuf. Fenet hastened to the scene. Joined by a 'Nordland' officer, there was little they could say. Lost in thought, Fenet returned to his headquarters.

At some point the 4th Company was called upon to shore up the advancing companies experiencing more and more difficulties.

Ollivier's travels

Evacuated to one of Berlin's many medical posts, Jean Ollivier, the commander of the 4th Company, had his hand wound bandaged up and the shrapnel in his chest removed. Impatient to return to his unit, he left as soon as the doctors had finished with him. He found himself in the sector of the Tiergarten. He decided to report to a nearby Waffen-SS artillery unit in the hope that it would give him a helping hand back to the Sturmbataillon in Neukölln. Unexpectedly, on entering the command post, he came face to face with SS-Hstuf. Heller who he knew. Their paths had crossed at the Waffen-SS Infantry Gun school at Breslau. Then Heller was an instructor and Ollivier his pupil.

Far from giving Ollivier a helping hand, Heller immediately put him in command of a battery of two 150mm infantry guns served by recruits of the 2. SS-Panzer-Division 'Das Reich' who had no artillery training. Nevertheless, they were very willing. Two Rottenführer served as both gun commander and gun-layer. The battery was motorised; two converted private cars towed the guns and a Citröen P.45 van was the ammunition carrier!

Ollivier and his battery were immediately sent into action. He was to secure an important crossroads. After much difficulty, the two guns were eventually unlimbered and positioned in an avenue some 500 metres from the crossroads.

Ollivier only had to wait fifteen minutes for the first Russian tank to appear. This was destroyed. The young Germans rejoiced. Needless to say, this tank was not alone. A further eight tanks would appear and all were destroyed one after the other, but it was impossible to keep the guns camouflaged. The Russians unleashed 'Stalin's Organs'. One gun was destroyed and the crew killed. The Citröen van was blown to bits in turn. Even so Ollivier decided to fight on.

Ollivier managed to knock out three more tanks by constantly changing the position of his second gun. This was as much as he could do. Not only had the last rounds been expended due to the loss of the ammunition carrier, but also the gun had become a sitting target; by now, the ground was so churned up that the gun could not be moved.

After rendering the second gun useless, Ollivier assembled the few survivors and led them back to the command post of the Waffen-SS artillery unit. Although Heller was still not prepared to let Ollivier go just yet, sending him on patrol in the sector of the Reichs Chancellery, he did promise him that he would eventually rejoin his compatriots.

Confusion

Back at Neukölln town hall, Hstuf. Fenet had become more and more concerned about the growing isolation of his battalion. Friendly troops should have been on their flanks, but the Russians were infiltrating almost at will, making life extremely hazardous.

Suddenly a strange order arrived from Division: "If the attack has not already begun, stop and come and get new orders; if it has, then do your best!" Perplexed, Hstuf. Fenet immediately sent his assistant, Ostuf. von Wallenrodt, to 'Nordland' divisional headquarters to seek clarification. He returned 'much later'.[37] He was the bearer of grave news.

The situation was black. Earlier that morning, just as the French SS-Sturmbataillon and 'Nordland' had started to counterattack into Neukölln, the Reds had resumed their drive to the centre of Berlin with overwhelming forces. The main defensive ring had already started to crack. Fenet was infuriated. History was repeating itself. It was like Heinrichswalde two months before. Then his I/57 had been three hours into a successful assault when he had to fall back because there was no liaison on either flank or to the rear.

Phlegmatically, von Wallenrodt asked: "What are we going to do?" In the hope that the situation on their flanks could be restored, Fenet sent orders to the three companies to hold where they were and not to let themselves be encircled. It was a forlorn hope.

Shortly after midday, Ostuf. Weber's *Kampfschule*, held in reserve at Hermannplatz, was committed on the right flank of Fenet's positions, not far from Tempelhof airport. Supported by a Sturmgeschütz assault gun, Weber's men, now mixed with 'other units', moved down Hermannstrasse and then along the wall of one of the many cemeteries around the airport. They received intense mortar fire but pressed on, running from doorway to doorway to shelter from the lethal razor-sharp shrapnel. They came to two Tiger tanks, presumably of 'Nordland', that were keeping the Russians at bay down the road. The tanks supported the grenadier as best they could, but one tank was soon out of shells.

Weber's men now took cover from the heavy and continuos fire through which there was no way forward. Casualties were suffered. Levast was sent back to the pub on Hermannplatz to get orders. He managed to find the pub where he had spent the night, but it was empty. He went back to the fighting.

Worse still, the Kampfschule lost the support of the two 'Tigers' when they were called to another sector. Henceforth, the men of the Kampfschule would have to fend for themselves.

Later the Kampfschule withdrew or was ordered back to the pub on Hermannplatz.

The Sturmbataillon now formed a salient in Russian lines. Contact with friendly units to the left and the right was broken. From those patrols and runners who managed to return to battalion headquarters all reported that the Russians were everywhere. The situation now demanded that troops be withdrawn from the 'nose' of the advance to reinforce the threatened flanks. The city hall was made into the *centre de résistance*.

---

37 Fenet, page 6.

Reinforcements arrived. They were from the Hitler Jugend and all were aged between fourteen and seventeen. They numbered several hundred and burned with an indescribable enthusiasm to emulate the exploits of their elders, even though the panzerfäuste and Mauser rifles they carried were sometimes as big as they were. They seemed wholly impervious to danger and would pay the price for their youthful naivety.

The Sturmbataillon continued to hold its ground.

Thanks to its runners, battalion headquarters managed to keep up communication with the attacking companies. Since dawn, Rottenführer Millet, the section commander of the runners, had run the most important and dangerous assignments himself. Each time Millet entered the ruins for a run Fenet feared that would be the last he would ever see of him, but the cheerful Millet had always returned, cool and calm, to report: "Mission carried out!"

In the afternoon, accompanied by Rttf. Millet, Hstuf. Fenet toured the companies. The situation had not improved. They returned to the town hall. As they were crossing the road to enter the headquarters they suddenly came under fire. Millet folded in two then collapsed face down. One final twitch and he remained still, dead. Millet was only twenty years old and had fought in Galicia and Pomerania.

At the very same moment Fenet felt a burning sensation in his left foot. He too had been hit. Carried inside the town hall, he was treated by a German doctor. A bullet had gone straight through his left foot without hitting bone. Like Rostaing, luck had not abandoned him.

Firing continued outside. So the Reds were much nearer than first thought, perhaps some fifty metres to the rear of the town hall. With the Reds now so close to the town hall and behind their positions, the battle had taken a dramatic turn. There was no time to lose.

To avert encirclement, Fenet ordered Oberjunker Douroux, his orderly officer who still carried an injury, to clear the Russians from the immediate vicinity. To make matters worse, French SS and some bewildered Germans were 'surging back' in disorder.[38] The situation had to be redressed immediately or else disaster would be inescapable.

Pistol in hand, Douroux assembled all those around him and set about freeing the immediate vicinity from Russian possession. In vicious hand-to-hand fighting with hand grenades and bayonet they cleared out house after house. In less than quarter of an hour, the Russians attempting to take the Frenchmen from the rear were either dead or had turned tail. But this failure seemed to make the Russians all the more determined to capture the town hall and they now made a frontal attack, sparing on neither men nor ammunition.

The Frenchmen and the boys of the Hitler Jugend defended like devils. When the Russians seemed to hesitate, the defenders, led by Oberjunker Douroux, launched a counterattack in force and drove the Russians out of the immediate vicinity.

The Russians replied with tanks along Berlinerstrasse. Up to now the face of the fighting had been inside blocks of houses between infantry, but that all changed when the T–34 tanks arrived in single file. Panzerfäuste accounted for one or two, but the others rolled on unchecked.

The Königstiger was alerted. Taking up position in Jägerstrasse, perpendicular to Berlinerstrasse, it waited in ambush. Not far from the tank, Fenet and Douroux

38   Mabire, page 184.

could hear the 'march of the red armour'. The sound of the tank tracks approached. And then there they were.

When the leading T–34 showed its turret to the Königstiger the German tank fired. The T–34 stopped in its tracks. With weapons raised, the Frenchmen watched and waited for the Russian crew to emerge from the hatches, but nobody left the 'iron coffin'.

Close by lay Millet's body in his brown and green spotted camouflaged uniform, his fair hair caked with dust, and his red face already drained of colour by death. Some of his comrades carried his corpse under cover. Millet was the first of his group [or section] to fall. The tall nineteen-year-old black-haired Roger Roberto took the place of Millet.

In his memoirs of Berlin, Fenet described Roberto as being fanatical to the core. One year earlier, aged seventeen, he had enlisted at Nantes. When an officer commented mockingly: "Our kind of life is far too hard for Frenchmen", Roberto immediately retorted: "That's precisely why I'm enlisting!" In the coming days at Berlin, this Corsican would display extraordinary courage time and time again. Indeed, 'his prodigious contempt for anything that might smack of half-heartedness, mediocrity, or weakness, his worship of loyalty and camaraderie, [and] the nobility and purity of his ideals', made him, in the opinion of Fenet, the 'SS type'.

As the afternoon wore on the situation at the town hall became more and more critical. The front to the left and to the right had completely given way and the Russians were pouring through. Unstable on his legs, Fenet continued to direct the defence of the town hall from a chair. In the opinion of Douroux, Fenet 'embodied the very soul of the resistance'. For his part, Fenet commented that he managed to hold this breakwater thanks only to the drive and exceptional fighting spirit of his troops.

One such example, among many, was Uscha. Cap, a small Fleming, who had traded his secretary's desk pad for a machine gun and was holding a road all by himself. He fired on everything that moved opposite with a precision and a rapidity that clearly disconcerted the Russians. Each and every time the Russians spotted him and tried to silence him, he seemed to change position 'just in the nick of time'. It was as though he was one step ahead of them.

Fink joined Cap. He too was a secretary at battalion headquarters. He had been helping Fenet to get about until he grabbed a passing teenager from the Hitler Jugend to take his place.

Taking turns, Cap and Fink would hold the road until evening without letting the Russians advance a single step.

By 1700 hours, the French Sturmbataillon was all alone and jutting out from the main line. Those 'Nordland' tanks short of ammunition and fuel had withdrawn. Cut off from Division, Fenet decided to stay put at the town hall as long as there still remained a withdrawal route to friendly lines. Besides, he had not received orders to withdraw.

At 1700 hours, Fenet sent word to Rostaing of the 3rd Company to fight on a little longer and then withdraw to his headquarters at Neukölln town hall. Rostaing was mad with rage. Because of the other companies he now had to stop his successful 'offensive'.[39]

---

39   Rostaing, page 193.

The Reds desperately and obstinately continued to attack frontally and from the flanks, even though a small determined number, say fifty, could have easily outflanked the defenders and cut off their line of retreat. This time the Reds employed combined arms, but their attacks still came to nothing: as soon as their infantry appeared they found themselves targeted by a deadly hail of bullets and were cut to pieces. As for their 'big brothers', there was no hiding from the panzerfäuste.

The Russians then unleashed a hurricane of fire over Neukölln, which grew in intensity. It deafened and stretched the nerves of the defenders towards breaking point. For some, it was all too much.[40] They were either too young or too old.

Suddenly, Oberjunker Douroux saw about one hundred men appear from roads near to the town hall. They were in flight and throwing away their weapons. Pistol in hand, he rushed among them. He knew that he had to check their stampede or else they would spread panic before them. However, a gigantic blond German, standing in the middle of the road, legs apart, firing on the enemy with an MG 42 held at hip level, also saw the flight. He turned around and fired a long burst just over their heads. When this had no effect he did not hesitate to fire lower and shorter, which stopped them dead. Panic over, he then went back to firing on the enemy along Berlinerstrasse. Douroux rounded the men up and pushed them forward.

Then a 'Nordland' Tiger tank commander approached Oberjunker Douroux and presented him with his Iron Cross 1st Class. Taken aback and touched, Douroux thanked him vaguely. Impractical to wear the decoration on his battle dress, he shoved it into his pocket with great respect.[41]

Towards 1900 hours, runners reported that Soviet tanks were approaching Hermannplatz, some nine hundred metres to the rear! That left only two roads, Hermannstrasse and Berlinerstrasse, open for a withdrawal. And they would not remain open for long. The fate of the Sturmbataillon and its comrades in arms from the Hitler Jugend now hung in the balance: if the Russians managed to take Hermannplatz then there was no way out for them. It was the law of numbers making itself felt again. This time there was really only one decision Fenet could make and, reluctantly, he ordered the general withdrawal back to Hermannplatz. Any delay now could lead to disaster.

During a lull in the fighting Fenet quickly regrouped the SS and HJ for the withdrawal. Rostaing's 3rd Company would bring up the rear. Covered by 'Nordland' Panther and Tiger tanks, they withdrew to Hermannplatz. The withdrawal was orderly and did not meet with any interference along the way. It took them quarter of an hour to reach Hermannplatz. By then, darkness had set in.

Feverishly, the French Sturmbataillon and the HJ organised defensive positions behind barricades of paving stones. It was not a moment too soon; Soviet tanks were held at bay barely one hundred metres from the square and, minutes after the arrival of the Sturmbataillon, all roads east of the square fell into enemy hands.

Time and time again Soviet tanks attempted to emerge onto Hermannplatz from Brauerstrasse and Weserstrasse. Sturmgeschütze beat them back, scoring a bull's-eye with each and every shot. The night was lit up like day from all these burning tanks which noisily exploded one after the other. Fenet called the battle 'a

40   Saint-Loup, page 430.
41   See Saint-Loup, page 431.

veritable massacre of Red tanks'. Indeed, in less than an hour, some forty Soviet tanks were destroyed on the approaches to Hermannplatz.[42]

The Frenchmen also had their hands full: there was the Russian infantry to contain. Hennecart took the sorely tried 2nd Company in hand. Finding himself quite by chance under the 88mm barrel of a Tiger tank just as a round was loosed off, he was left deaf for twenty-four hours.

When the Reds submerged the barricade on Weserstrasse the French SS, together with 'Nordland', the Hitler Jugend, the Volkssturm and the Kriegsmarine, counterattacked. Shouting like madmen, they stormed the strongly defended barricade and overwhelmed the Russians, but casualties were appalling, especially among the Hitler Jugend.

The 1st Company

Late in the evening, Ustuf. Labourdette's 1st Company finally rejoined Fenet at Hermannplatz. Since early morning the fifty-strong Company had been at the disposal of the German commander of sector Tempelhof. And yet most of its day was spent in reserve. This inaction gave rise to a growing sense of impatience among the officers to do battle.

Finally, 'towards the end of the day', the 1st Company was deployed, occupying a defensive line between Tempelhof airport and one of the many neighbouring cemeteries. Individual holes were dug and machine guns were sited. Nobody knew quite where the Russians were until they started to appear and establish themselves in position hundreds of metres away. The Frenchmen fired on them. This was to make their presence known as well as their intention to hold the ground.

Labourdette dispatched Uscha. Puechlong to find and make contact with Fenet at Neukölln town hall. Unfortunately, Labourdette had no map of Berlin to give Puechlong. In fact, he only had a sketch map of the city himself! Thus it is no wonder that Puechlong soon became lost in the labyrinth of roads. Fired on by friend and foe alike, he made his way across a cemetery. For once, as luck would have it, he met some comrades who pointed him in the right direction of the town hall. There he reported to Fenet who seemed pleased to have news of Labourdette and the 1st Company. Fenet then briefed him on his unfavourable situation and gave him a message to pass on to Labourdette: if he has to break off the action then he could rejoin the Sturmbataillon at Hermannplatz.

Puechlong immediately set off. He came to the same cemetery and got lost again. Everything looked the same. He wandered round the deserted cemetery for ages before finding his way again. He reported back to Labourdette. In his absence, the situation of the 1st Company had deteriorated. Labourdette left him in no doubt about its seriousness. He had no contact to the left or to the right and the Russians were infiltrating. Encirclement was looming.

Suddenly, the roar of guns and the crump of mortars interrupted the conversation. Shells crashed down all around. The intensity of the Soviet bombardment grew and grew. It was hell. Shrapnel filled the air. Uscha. Gérard was badly wounded in the buttocks and evacuated to the rear by a group led by Puechlong.

42   Saint-Loup, page 432.

Quite unexpectedly the group chanced upon an ambulance but the German medical orderlies did not want to know. After making all kind of feeble excuses, they concluded by pointing out that the doors of the ambulance were locked.

Seeing red, Puechlong blasted the lock with his Sturmgewehr. Turning to the medical orderlies, he told them to evacuate his wounded comrade to a first aid post. And threatened that if they refused then he would kill them. That did the trick. As soon as the ambulance was on its way, the group returned to the defensive positions of the 1st Company. The Soviets were still bombarding Tempelhof airport.

The Soviet bombardment would only abate in the late evening. Then came the Russian infantry. They infiltrated houses to the north-east of the positions held by the 1st Company. From there, the Russians now overlooked the airfield. This gave the Russians a distinct tactical advantage that they were quick to exploit. Labourdette saw disaster coming and withdrew his Company to the cemetery.

Once in the cemetery the 1st Company was immediately set upon by hordes of Russians screaming 'Urra!' There was great confusion. Desperately the Frenchmen fought back. Russian pressure mounted by the minute. Death swept over that cemetery again and again. With an enormous effort the Frenchmen extricated themselves and sought out new positions easier to defend. The survivors received an order to assemble and take up position at the corner of Hermannstrasse and Flughafenstrasse.

Labourdette now decided to occupy and fortify a block of houses. He then set about assembling his disorganised Company, which had lost many men.

Finally, in the late evening, Labourdette and his 1st Company rendezvoused with Fenet. There was considerable joy at their return.

Towards midnight on 26th/27th April 1945, Fenet received the order to withdraw. Along the way, the 1st Company was once again stripped from the Sturmbataillon to seal a new breach in the front. Fenet went to the sector commander to protest. He asked him to let the last survivors of the French Division fight together, but the sector commander was insistent about requisitioning the 1st Company. Because the situation was disastrous Fenet agreed to the limited employment of the 1st Company.

Before the 1st Company parted from the Sturmbataillon, Fenet had a quiet word with Labourdette. He told him to return at all costs at the agreed time. He replied: "You can count on me." And yet Fenet was suddenly gripped by a terrible premonition that he would never see the courageous Labourdette again. Shaking him by the shoulder, Fenet said: "You must return with the blokes, you must return, do you hear me?" Silence descended. This was but for a brief moment. In a distant and somewhat hesitant voice, Labourdette replied that he would return. They then exchanged a few last words and shook hands for a long time. It was as though Fenet was reluctant to let him go.

Labourdette left with his men of the 1st Company and disappeared into the night. His attitude worried Fenet. His attitude was that of a man leaving for battle knowing that he would not be coming back.

Fenet reflected. He was being stupid. No, Labourdette would return. He was furious with himself for giving way to such black thoughts. He put this down to his strained nerves and his 'ridiculous' wound that had transformed him into a *béquillard*.

Roberto interrupted Fenet's thoughts. He had a chair with him and urged him to rest. Fenet replied: "Not now, Roger!" A place had to be found where the exhausted men of the Sturmbataillon could sleep. Leaning on Roberto's arm, Fenet hobbled along.

Out of the darkness appeared von Wallenrodt. He had found sleeping accommodation for part of the Sturmbataillon in the Thomas Keller brewery opposite Anhalter Bahnhof. The others would lodge with Weber and the *Kampfschule* at the Opera house.

Deciding to leave for 'Nordland' divisional headquarters, Fenet told his German assistant to take the weary French SS troops to their accommodation and to join him in the late morning.

And what of those Frenchmen of the Sturmbataillon who, for whatever reason, had not been able to make it out of Neukölln? Death or capture was their only certainty. In such a predicament were the ten men of Mongourd's platoon of the 2nd Company.

Bypassed by Russian troops, the ten French men had remained holed up in a big factory in Neukölln. Food was the least of their worries; German civilians came and fed them. Night fell and they were still there. Also hiding out in the same cellar was a French POW who they had immediately adopted, calling him 'old man' because he was at least thirty! He had ended up as a 'free' worker in Berlin, which he knew quite well now. Like the SS, he too was in no hurry to surrender. Some of his friends had warned him about the Russians.

The Frenchmen discussed their situation. It was hopeless. They had no heavy weapons and very little ammunition. Their best chance of escape was through the labyrinth of interconnected cellars that now existed underground. Several months before, as a precaution against being buried alive in the event of air raids or artillery bombardments, the inhabitants of Berlin had been ordered to connect cellars. The prisoner offered to act as a guide, but this he would only do if they stripped to pass themselves off as foreign workers.

Only Lapland removed his tunic, all of the others hesitated. They seemed too exhausted and afraid to try and escape. Lapland stayed close to the prisoner as they made their way from cellar to cellar. Just in case, Lapland kept a pistol in his pocket. They became covered in dust and plaster. This combination masked the prisoner's khaki and Lapland's field-grey uniform trousers.

When the two of them emerged from the cellars and went out into a road they sighted Russian tanks fifteen to twenty metres away. The crews glanced at the newcomers and, after reassuring themselves that the newcomers were not armed, they seemed to pay them no further attention. Lapland then saw German prisoners of war being escorted to the rear. Among them he recognised some of his comrades who had stayed behind at the factory not so long ago. In turn they saw Lapland and the prisoner, but did not give them away with any show of emotion. Lapland would never see any of them again.

Together they hurried on, but a Russian, who had spotted Lapland's field-grey trousers, approached them. To his question of whether or not they were Germans, they replied they were French. He let them continue.

The two merged into the grey throng of civilians beginning to emerge from the cellars of Neukölln. The fighting was definitely over.

It was now time to reflect and count the cost. For the Sturmbataillon, the outcome of the battle must have been a bitter disappointment. Not only had its counterattack, which had started so promisingly, been forced to a halt, but its attempt to hold onto Neukölln had ultimately been in vain. And yet its counterattack was one of the few during the battle of Berlin that had actually pushed the Russians back. This achievement in the face of greater enemy numbers and power was a source of pride to many, but pride tinged with deep sadness at their losses.

Rostaing's 3rd Company, which had started the day with some eighty men, now only counted thirty. Ollivier's 4th Company now counted twenty. As for the 2nd Company, hit as hard as the 4th Company, it would be reasonable to assume that it suffered the same high percentage of casualties. The 1st Company was some forty-strong when requisitioned for the second time. All told, the French SS-Sturmbataillon may have numbered no more than one hundred and fifty 'effectives' after the battle for Neukölln. Thus, the casualty balance sheet of Neukölln was between 150 and 200 men.

The cost to the Sturmbataillon was high, in fact very high, but it had dealt out death and destruction upon the Russians out of proportion to its limited resources fielded. The Frenchmen 'scrapped' fourteen T–34s.[43] Gren. Aubin is credited with one, Uscha. Bicou with one, Oscha. Apollot with one, and Uscha. Vaulot with two. The number of Russian dead and wounded was untold. However, it seemed as though the Russians had a never-ending supply of men and material to replace their losses.

Taking their leave of von Wallenrodt and the Sturmbataillon, Fenet and Douroux went in search of a car to take them to the city centre. Supporting himself on Douroux, Fenet was still limping badly. They came to the command post of Regiment 'Danmark' and were warmly welcomed by the Scandinavian and German staff. Unfortunately, they could not oblige the two French SS officers with transport to the city centre: yes, they had vehicles but not a single drop of fuel. Fenet asked about the whereabouts of Brigf. Krukenberg and was informed 'Nordland' divisional command post had just moved again, but its new location was not known.

Accepting an invitation to get some rest, the two French SS officers were put up on mattresses in the medical post. A badly burned Panzer crewman was brought in and laid beside them. In terrible pain, he called out for his mother and begged them to finish him off.

Meanwhile, north-east of Neukölln, some five hundred metres from the French SS-Sturmbataillon, a Frenchman, dressed in the uniform of the LVF, continued to fight his own war. His name was Pierre Soulé. This was the same individual who, some eight months earlier, had refused to pass to the Waffen-SS and, as a result of his protest, been sent to Danzig-Matzkau.

On his release, Soulé was sent to Berlin and demobilised as a free worker. However, he was not prepared to stop fighting for Europe and, in November 1944, decided to join a commando unit under the control of Otto Skorzeny.[44] He was wounded. His hands were so badly burnt that he had to spend some six weeks in hospital. At the end of March 1945, he was released. Thereupon he left for Berlin in search of another combat post. With difficulty, he got through to the German capital.

---

43   Saint-Loup, page 430.
44   Presumably Soulé joined one of the SS Jagdverband.

It was then that the Russians unleashed their great offensive on Berlin. Soulé joined a makeshift group of Hitler Jugend and Volkssturm organised by a SS-Sturmbannführer of 'Nibelungen' who had released himself from hospital in order to fight. Soulé commanded fourteen boys of the Hitler Jugend. One by one he lost twelve of them in the fighting, but they destroyed seven tanks. The Stubaf. awarded the Iron Cross 2nd class to Soulé and to the last two kids with him who were both wounded, but fighting on.

Krukenberg and the day of the 26th April 1945

Towards midday, the commanders of SS-Panzer-Grenadier-Regiment 23 'Norge' and SS-Panzer-Grenadier-Regiment 24 'Danmark' reported to Brigf. Krukenberg that they each had about six to seven hundred combat troops at their disposal. Krukenberg ordered them to place one-third of these troops at the disposal of Defence Sector 'Z' and continue equipping and preparing the rest for combat. As such the Scandinavian Waffen-SS troops of 'Nordland' should now have passed to the direct control of the Wehrmacht and the obdurate Seifert, but Krukenberg also ordered the two regimental commanders to remain responsible for their commands even if the Sector 'did not wish to hear of them'.

Towards 1900 hours that evening, the two regimental commanders reported back that they had found nobody at the front apart from their panzergrenadiers. They were alone. Moreover, Defence Sector 'Z' was totally devoid of the prepared defensive positions that Seifert had shown Krukenberg on a map. Krukenberg was now convinced that all the defence plans for Sector 'Z' only existed on paper. He then understood why Seifert had refused all his offers of help. Because of this he decided not to put off any longer his introduction to Ogruf. Fegelein. And although he did not know Fegelein he believed that he could interest him 'in the peculiarities of our engagement'.[45]

Later that evening, Brigf. Krukenberg went to the Führerbunker. Once again, on entering, he was not challenged. Escorted through the busy rooms and corridors of the Bunker, he noticed officers as well as NSDAP party members of various ranks. One stocky individual in the uniform of the Party attracted his attention: as he passed him, he was dictating to his secretary the following words: " … and relieved of his duties with immediate effect … " He asked his guide who this person was. Surprised at the question, his guide replied: "What, you don't know Reichsleiter Martin Bormann?"[46] No, he did not.

Krukenberg was shown to a long room and it was here that Ogruf. Fegelein came to meet him.

Krukenberg urged Fegelein to support him in his efforts to prevent the scattered employment of the only Waffen-SS division in the defensive zone of Berlin. He complained that Defence Sector 'Z', where 'Nordland' was to be engaged, was 'only ready on paper'. He warned Fegelein that the removal of the regimental commanders from 'Nordland', coming after the dismissal of Ziegler, might be fraught with consequences. Worse still, he foresaw the Waffen-SS blamed for the failure of the defence in Sector 'Z'!

---

45   Krukenberg, page 10.
46   Mabire, page 202.

At that same moment General Weidling entered the room. Krukenberg repeated to him what he had told Fegelein. Krukenberg appealed to Weidling to engage 'Nordland', the only unit he stressed in the city centre with combat experience, under its own officers. Weidling did not look pleased. This gave Krukenberg the impression that Weidling wanted 'Nordland' engaged without its officers.

Nevertheless, Weidling eventually gave in, assigning the command of Defence Sector 'Z' to Brigf. Mohnke of the Waffen-SS and announcing the creation of two Sub-Sectors. Oberstleutant Seifert, located in the Air Ministry building, would command the Western Sub-Sector and Brigf. Krukenberg the Eastern Sub-Sector. The demarcation line was Wilhelmstrasse. And it was in the Eastern Sub-Sector that 'Nordland' was now to be engaged and also under its own officers.

Krukenberg was allocated Stadtmitte U-Bahn station as his command post.

Lastly, those units of 'Nordland' already under Seifert were to remain in his sector until such time as they could be relieved and handed back to Krukenberg.

Then General Weidling left. That was the last contact Krukenberg had with him, verbal or otherwise.

Just as Krukenberg was about to leave, Dr. Goebbels, the Reich Minister of Public Enlightenment and Propaganda, arrived. Krukenberg had worked with Goebbels in the Propaganda Ministry, but in the spring of 1933 they had clashed and Krukenberg had resigned his post. Now, as Gauleiter of Berlin and Reichs Commissar for Defence, Goebbels had a direct responsibility for the defence of the capital and it was a task he had gone about with the same drive and efficiency he applied to his Ministry.

Goebbels asked Krukenberg for his unvarnished view of the morale of the troops placed under him. In his reply, he talked of their origin, of their fighting qualities, of their resolve to fight on, and of their recent battles, concluding that they would hold the sector assigned to them until the arrival of western troops.

Goebbels responded that negotiations with the West were well under way and that Army Wenck was fast approaching the Havel. Thus, the garrison of Berlin would only have to hold out for several more days. Krukenberg had no reason to doubt him. Later, he was to find out it was all propaganda.

By 0100 hours on Friday 27th April 1945, Krukenberg was back at his command post in the Opera House. The rest of the night passed quietly.

CHAPTER 14

To the Death

Krukenberg and the day of 27th April 1945

Friday 27th April proved relatively quiet. In the early morning, Brigf. Krukenberg held a briefing of 'Nordland' officers at his command post in the Opera House. Hstuf. Fenet arrived late.

Earlier that morning, a German officer came to collect Hstuf. Fenet from the 'Nordland' regimental medical post where he had spent the night. The German officer had a car with him, but rubble-strewn roads cut short their journey. The three officers then continued on foot.

The German officer, an elderly Berliner twice the age of Fenet, continually lamented at the sight of the city's ruins. To him, this was the end of the world. He considered himself too old to ever see better days again, but foresaw them for the youth. The Reds interrupted him with a violent artillery barrage. Caught out in the open, the officers found temporary shelter in the basement of the Imperial Castle.

Shells rained down on the entire quarter. It was a veritable hurricane of steel. The ground trembled under the explosions. Walls collapsed. Fenet reflected, 'if we had only half the ammunition that these savages waste shelling deserted squares and ruined monuments'. Eventually, he made it to the briefing.

At the briefing, Krukenberg reviewed the situation. He declared himself satisfied with the operations that 'Nordland' and the French Sturmbataillon had conducted yesterday. He seemed more relaxed, even jovial, which was in sharp contrast to the austere face he normally wore. He granted the Sturmbataillon a day of rest. It would then be engaged as an 'anti-tank Kommando'.[1]

Leaving his subordinates to continue preparing 'Nordland' for its engagement at midday, Brigf. Krukenberg went to report to Brigf. Mohnke at the Chancellery. Krukenberg did not know him.

Not far from the entrance to the Chancellery, Krukenberg ran into General Krebs. They talked. Krebs told him that the leading elements of Army Wenck had just reached Werder, west of Potsdam. When Krukenberg questioned him about the negotiations with the West he could tell him nothing new. Krebs turned to the subject of the troops' morale just as a Police General passed them, who he named as Gestapo chief Heinrich Muller. They parted.[2] Krukenberg reported to Mohnke.

---

1   Fenet, page 12. According to Saint-Loup, page 442, Brigf. Krukenberg also spoke of a counterattack planned for the night of 27th/28th April 1945 to relieve the great pressure on the city centre from the direction of the Spittalmarkt to the east. This counterattack did not materialise for several reasons: the Reds blew the bridges over the river Spree to cover themselves, Russian strength tripled during the course of the day, and there was a lack of operational co-operation between the Party-sponsored Volkssturm and the Army.

Mohnke promised Krukenberg all possible support for his 'difficult mission'. Krukenberg expanded on his difficulties. 'Nordland' was new to him, their paths having not crossed before. He knew nobody. He was a total stranger. On the other hand, he had the advantage of being extremely familiar with his defence sector as well as the roads and squares of Berlin, but the air raids had changed the face of the city and to find one's bearings, even for him, was not easy.

Mohnke surprised Krukenberg by placing at his disposal a company of naval infantrymen that had been airlifted into Berlin during the past night. Its commander was summoned. He made an excellent impression.

And then what of SS schwere Panzer Abteilung 503 presently attached to 'Nordland'? Mohnke left it under the command of Krukenberg. It still had eight 'runners'.

Krukenberg left.

That morning, 'Nordland' occupied its new defensive sector without any problems. Outposts were established along the Landwehr Kanal. Brigf. Krukenberg divided his command into three. One third he assigned to the foremost lines in the ruins south of Hollmannstrasse. It was to observe the enemy and contain its patrols, but in the event of an enemy attack in force, it was under orders to fall back slowly to the main line of defence along Besselstrasse and Ritterstrasse. The second third, his shock troops, held in ready reserve near regimental and battalion command posts, was to seal off enemy penetrations. The last third, still needing rest and recuperation, was to remain houses along Leipzigerstrasse.[3]

The few remaining tanks, short of petrol, were concentrated on Leipzigerstrasse, which offered them some degree of movement other than in single file. They were to have the support of groups of French tank hunters.[4]

Concerned that the artillery of 'Nordland' was poorly positioned, Krukenberg had it moved from the Tiergarten to the rear of his sector. The guns were now deployed in such a way that they could deal with enemy tanks arriving from the North, the Reichstag and Schlossplatz. Despite repeated demands, he still knew little of the situation in these areas.

Krukenberg was still missing part of his command; Seifert was proving slow in returning those forces put at his disposal. Indeed, some he would keep hold of.[5] Nevertheless, Krukenberg continued to receive reinforcements, who were for the most part volunteers of the Waffen-SS. In time the whole of Europe was represented.

The enemy was quiet along the 'Nordland' front. Some isolated soldiers were reported approaching the canal at Hallesche Tor. Krukenberg decided, with the support of the naval infantrymen, to launch a counterattack against them. The

---

2   Krukenberg, page 12. Curiously, according to Saint-Loup, page 443, Krukenberg struck up a conversation with Krebs in the presence of Mohnke.

3   According to the "*Battle Memoir*", page 161, the last third was to be held in emergency reserve. However, this is unconfirmed.

4   The "*Battle Memoir*" recounts that the French SS troops found themselves heavily engaged in the northern sector of Zitadelle under Seifert (see page 161). This too is unconfirmed.

5   Curiously, according to Krukenberg, page 13, one part of the French volunteers would remain under Seifert to the end.

counterattack, he hoped, would 'reawaken the feeling of superiority' in a unit that over the past few days had conducted one retreat after another. Orders were given. However, when the Russians were first sighted approaching the 'bridge over the canal', presumably the Hallesche Tor bridge, Volkssturm personnel, still operating independently, blew it. In this way, the counterattack had to be scrapped.

All morning the Soviet bombardment on the Opera House, the Imperial Castle and the surrounding area continued unabated. Reaching a punishing intensity, the bombardment forced Krukenberg to move the divisional command post. During the first lull in the shelling, the headquarters staff left the Opera House and made for the Schauspielhaus, a theatre, on Schillerplatz between the 'French' and 'German' cathedrals.

On the way, Dr. Zimmermann, a 'Nordland' doctor, informed Fenet that they were on Französichestrasse (French Street), named after the Huguenot émigrés who had settled in this quarter two hundred and fifty years earlier. Fenet thought to himself: "We're fighting in the ruins of this capital that they helped to build." Zimmermann added: "Henceforth, this road will also be in your honour."

During the afternoon, 'Nordland' division headquarters relocated from the Schauspielhaus to Stadtmitte underground station.

That afternoon, Krukenberg went to his newly designated command post in Stadtmitte underground station. He was shocked to discover that the so-called headquarters of the central sector of 'fortress' Berlin was nothing more than an underground car that was without both electric and telephones. [Then again this was all too typical of the lack of preparations which he would complain about after the war.] However, his assistant, Pachur, 'worked miracles' to bring organisation to the command post.

The ceiling of the underground station was so thin that a Soviet artillery shell pierced it, exploded and wounded some fifteen men. Dr. Zimmermann, now working out of a railway car crudely converted into a first-aid post, promptly treated them. Some were evacuated by ambulance to the medical post in the air-raid shelter of Hotel Adlon.

Food supplies were readily available from grocery shops in the nearby Gendarmenmarkt. To prevent pillaging, all were put under guard. And in the interest of discipline, the drinking of alcohol remained banned. Ammunition had to be fetched from far-off police barracks and the lack of panzerfäuste was a cause for concern until a supply was 'found' at the Reichs Chancellery.[6]

That same afternoon, von Wallenrodt brought the French Sturmbataillon from the Opera House and the Thomas Keller brewery to Stadtmitte underground station.[7] Not far from the Reichs Chancellery, von Wallenrodt was caught in a violent bombardment and forced to take shelter. Entering a launderette, he came to a group of thirty German and Scandinavian SS troops, who were resting. An officer dashed towards him. It was none other than Oscha. Ollivier of the French Sturmbataillon. The launderette was the headquarters of 'Group Heller'.[8]

---

6 Krukenberg was convinced that without this find of panzerfäuste his troops would have gone without (see page 14).

7 Fenet, "*Historia #32*", page 161. And yet, according to Rostaing, page 195, he and his company spent the entire day at the Opera House. Also, according to Georgen, part 1, page 25, the Sturmbataillon assembled in the cellars of the Schauspielhaus.

Quite naturally Ollivier expressed a wish to return to his former command. Von Wallenrodt spoke to the commanding officer, who agreed to 'release' Ollivier. Von Wallenrodt returned Ollivier to his 4th Company sheltering and resting in the machinery cellar of a theatre. Ollivier was shocked and dismayed to find the 4th Company no more than twenty strong.

Irritated by two Soviet observation aircraft circling the district in search of targets, Ollivier had two machine-guns set up in an anti-aircraft role. Flying at roof level, the Soviet aircraft returned. Oberjunker Protopopoff immediately ordered one of the machine-gunners out of his seat, sat down and, when one of the slow moving aircraft came well within range, loosed off burst after burst, hitting it. The aircraft nose-dived and crashed down behind a block of houses with a muffled explosion. The second aircraft disappeared.

Towards the end of the afternoon, Krukenberg held an awards ceremony on the station platform for the French SS troops and bestowed the Iron Cross again and again.[9] In this way, the courage they had displayed during the battle for Neukölln was recognised and rewarded. Among the recipients were W-Oscha. Hennecart, decorated with the Iron Cross 1st Class, and SS-Uscha. Claude Cap, decorated with the Iron Cross 2nd Class.

After the brief ceremony came bonbons, chocolate and cigarettes. There was an air of general elation. Everybody was singing. A little later, when Hstuf. Fenet appeared his men rushed over to him and crammed his pockets full of goodies. The festive mood, however, was marred by a single shadow: Ustuf. Labourdette and his 1st Company were still not back.

The 1st Company

First back was a small group led by Oberjunker Robelin, followed that evening by the bulk of the 1st Company under the command of Oberjunker de Lacaze. But where were Oberjunker Croisille and his platoon? And where was Ustuf. Labourdette?

Requisitioned, the 1st Company, which was down to some forty men, was deployed by platoon. The platoon under Oberjunker de Lacaze was assigned to the defence of a barricade that formed part of the 'second line of defence around Belle-Alliance-Platz', while the platoon under Oberjunker Croisille, twenty-strong, was sent towards the quarter of Schöneberg, to the south-west. Taking up positions in the tunnels of the underground, 'platoon Croisille' was to 'parry' possible Soviet underground penetrations.

When 'platoon Croisille' reappeared from the underground the sector was empty and 'platoon de Lacaze' had disappeared, but it did meet up with a small group under Oberjunker Robelin. Some losses were taken from the shelling that had resumed.

Towards midday, near S-Bahn station Yorkstrasse, the company was requisitioned by a Major of the Wehrmacht. The Frenchmen were to mount a counterattack.

---

8   Soulat, page 104. In contrast, according to Mabire, page 230, Ollivier had found himself at the launderette by pure chance, being as good as any other place to rest.

9   The exact number is not known.

Labourdette sent Oberjunker Robelin and his small group to keep Fenet updated about the situation of the company.[10]

By now, 'platoon Croisile' counted no more than fourteen men, plus one soldier of the Wehrmacht, one airman, and one member of the Volkssturm.

Towards 1400 hours, the company participated in a limited counterattack that permitted the Major to evacuate his wounded. Seven Russian tanks then appeared along Yorkstrasse and with them were large numbers of infantry, but they seemed hesitant. The Russians sent forward five or six men pulling a cart disguised as civilians. Fired on, they fled.

An old gentleman then came and asked Labourdette to remove the boxes of munitions cluttering up his flat on the fifth floor. When opened they contained panzerfäuste. A godsend because the first T–34 was approaching. Oberjunker Croisille missed the tank, but the Wehrmacht soldier with his platoon hit it. The Russians pulled back.

That evening, Oberjunker de Lacaze returned more of the 1st Company to Fenet. Labourdette was not with them either; he had taken a few men out to an advanced post in an underground tunnel and lost contact.[11] True to his orders, de Lacaze had not worried about Labourdette and returned the company to Fenet at the required time. For the time being, Fenet too was not worried about him because a few hours delay in the confusion of this kind of fighting was nothing out of the ordinary.

It was only later that the fate of Labourdette became known.[12] Sturmgewehr in hand, covering the withdrawal of his men through the underground, he was cut down by a burst.[13] He was only twenty-two years old and prided himself on being the third volunteer for the French unit of the Waffen SS.

Still 'missing' was the platoon under Oberjunker Croisille. It was never to rejoin the battalion.[14]

News came through to Fenet that Army Wenck had reached the area around Potsdam. On the other hand, the Russians had launched a great offensive across the river Oder south of Stettin and had already reached Prenzlau. Fenet thought of his comrades at Neustrelitz waiting to join those already at Berlin. Convinced that they were now in the middle of a battle, he knew that they would not be coming. He overheard one of his men say: "What a pity for them. They'll have missed a fine occasion."

---

10   According to Soulat, page 124, they were never heard from again and yet, according to Georgen, part 3, page 25, they did make it back to Fenet and the battalion. The author has used Georgen's version.

11   Ustuf. Labourdette was either covering the withdrawal (Fenet, "*Historia*" #32, page 161), or on reconnaissance (Fenet, "*Die letzte Runde…*", page 13, and Mabire, page 232), or had gone out to 'bring in some grenadiers from an exposed position' (Landwehr, page 136).

12   According to Saint-Loup, page 449, Fenet only received news of Labourdette on 30th April.

13   According to the article "*The defeat in the ruins*", page 136, as Labourdette turned to follow the last of his men, a high explosive shell hit, spraying shrapnel in all directions and ripping him to shreds.

14   The author does not know what became of this platoon.

Uscha. Malardier was now at the disposal of Hscha. Rostaing. Notably, he knew the local area well, having spent over two months (April 1944 to 6th June 1944) hospitalised at Berlin Lazaret Wilmersdorf for bronchial-pneumonia. In the days that followed, Malardier stuck close to Rostaing as though he was his shadow, except for the times Rostaing sent him on secondment as a runner to Brigf. Krukenberg.

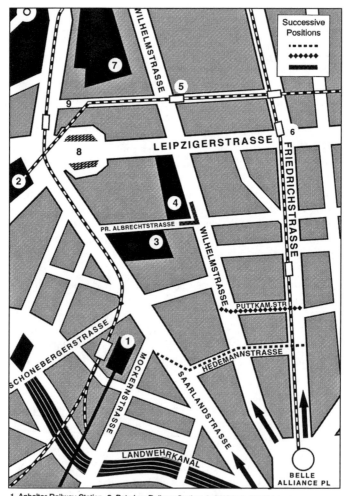

1. Anhalter Railway Station 2. Potsdam Railway Station 3. RHSA 4. Air Ministry
5. Kaiserhof U-Bahn 6. Stadtmitte U-Bahn 7. Führerbunker 8. Potsdam Plaz 9. Vossstrasse

Map 6: Götterdämmerung, Berlin, 28 April - 2 May 1945 (based on Saint-Loup, page 438). The Frenchmen of the Sturmbataillon fight for every yard of ground as the Russians approach the Führerbunker.

Saturday 28th April 1945

In the early morning hours of 28th April 1945, the Russians managed to throw pontoon bridges across the Landwehr kanal near the Hallesches Tor and then proceeded to send over a large number of tanks. In their path was Belle-Alliance-Platz. From this square emanated three key roads that led to the Reichs Chancellery.

During the night the Sturmbataillon sent two anti-tank commandos to Belle-Alliance-Platz. The first commando, assembled and on its way within quarter of an hour of the request from 'Nordland', was commanded by Ostuf. von Wallenrodt.[15] Oscha Hennecart commanded the second, requested one hour after the first.[16] Aged thirty-eight, Lucien Hennecart was like an old man to the youngsters around him. Hands in pockets, he was celebrated for coming through storms of bullets and shrapnel without picking up a scratch.

After repeating his orders back to Fenet, Hennecart took his leave and disappeared into the night. The hours passed by. Nobody returned.

A direct order from 'Nordland' also brought Weber's Kampfschule to Belle-Alliance-Platz.

When dawn came up 'Nordland' requested more reinforcements for the same sector. The last of the Sturmbataillon was now to be engaged. Douroux took Fenet to Krukenberg who explained the situation to him in detail. The whole battalion was to be engaged near Belle-Alliance-Platz in an effort to block access to the Reichs Chancellery via Wilhelmstrasse and Friedrichstrasse. The Sturmbataillon would be engaged without its commander; as Fenet raised himself to leave, Brigf. Krukenberg asked: "Where are you going?" Fenet replied that he was going to get the rest of the battalion ready to march. Mindful of Fenet's foot wound, Krukenberg then ordered: "Do not move from here, you can't stand up; get your orders carried and keep quiet at headquarters!" When Fenet protested Krukenberg curtly reminded him to execute the orders given to him. Furious, Fenet went and sat in a corner where he quickly scribbled out orders for von Wallenrodt and handed them to Douroux to take to him.[17]

With panzerfäuste, the French SS troops shot up one tank attack after another. Each time they broke up an attack the Russians would instantly renew a punishing artillery bombardment. Their ammunition stocks seemed inexhaustible. Time and time again the defenders were buried when roofs caved in, when floors gave way, and when buildings collapsed, but they seemed spirited as ever.

When Uscha. Puechlong of the 1st Company met his comrade de Lannurien, who he knew from the 'old' days of the *Compagnie d'Honneur*, he decided to rejoin Weber. Liaison had become a serious problem again. To redress this, Weber ordered a patrol to reconnoitre Wilhelmstrasse in the direction of the Chancellery.

---

15   Fenet, page 14. However, according to Georgen, part 1, page 26, von Wallenrodt led a patrol in the direction of Wilhelmstrasse to establish a picture of the situation.

16   Fenet, page 14 (and repeated by Mabire, page 234). However, in contrast, according to Saint-Loup, page 450, Rostaing commanded the second (anti-tank) commando despatched to Belle-Alliance-Platz, but Rostaing makes no mention of this assignment in his book.

17   Ibid. For the record, both Mabire and Saint-Loup have slightly different wording for the conversation.

Volunteers immediately came forward and one of them was Puechlong, who wanted to 'stretch his legs a bit'. A German NCO, who knew the capital well, led the patrol.

In single file, the patrol left. Suddenly it came under fire from a Soviet anti-tank gun only eighty to one hundred metres away. Caught in the open, the patrol was decimated: of the eight men, only two escaped death and they were seriously wounded.

Puechlong was one of the 'lucky' two. When he came round he was lying in the middle of the road and so he tried to make for cover under a porch, but crumpled to the ground again. It was only then that he realised the extent of his injuries. Shrapnel had lacerated his leg and his foot was virtually hanging off. Blood was pouring along his leg. Calmly, he took a leather lace from his belt and tied it around his leg as a tourniquet.

Puechlong was joined by another French SS soldier, whose chest had been ripped open by shrapnel. They called out to their comrades, perhaps some 200 to 300 metres away, to come and collect them, but they could not make themselves heard over the din of battle. The sound of explosions and gunfire were their only company.

Still out in the open, Puechlong tried to drag himself to shelter, but the fear of losing his foot was too great and he stopped. A boy suddenly appeared, looked at them and ran off.

Then an old, fragile women showed her face. Although Puechlong could not make himself understood she dragged the two of them into the corridor of a house and then fetched a blanket, but that was as much as she could do for them.

Puechlong gave the old woman his Soldbuch and that of his compatriot, identifying them as SS; they were as good as dead if the Russians found such documents on them. With a puzzled air, she looked at the papers. Puechlong could not explain to her what to do with them. Like his badly wounded comrade, he lost consciousness.

Puechlong awoke to the sound of battle drawing closer. He saw Russian soldiers suddenly appear and as they passed they kicked him to make sure he was dead. Holding his breath, he made no sound. The Russians quickly checked the house and moved on. By now, Puechlong had lost all hope and made up his mind to commit suicide. He searched for his pistol and came across instead the rosary from his first communion that his mother had asked him to keep with him at all times. Hope flooded back and he decided to wait. He was in more and more pain. By now, his comrade beside him was awake. Again the sound of battle could be heard getting louder and louder.

More shadows appeared in the corridor. This time they were Rumanian or Hungarian SS troops. As one, Puechlong and his compatriot cried out to them. Saved, they were carried out to a tank in the road and set down on the ground beneath its gun barrel. Their suffering was still not at an end; the fighting was continuing and the infernal noise of the gun firing to cover the withdrawal burst their eardrums.

Finally, the two wounded were lifted onto the tank. Puechlong desperately tried to convince himself that he was not going to lose his foot. The tank set off and so began a long journey of confusion, noise and fear. They were left at a medical post. Eventually, a nurse attended to Puechlong. She did what she could for him: his leg was put in an iron splint and fastened by paper.

Several days later, Puechlong underwent an operation to save his leg. Anaesthetic was in such short supply that he only received a reduced dosage. As a result, Puechlong came round too early and heard the doctor amputating his leg with a saw.

Back at Stadtmitte underground station, Fenet and Krukenberg continued to monitor the course of the battle north of Belle-Alliance-Platz by means of runners who bravely risked their lives time again and again in their work of liaison. A veil of thick smoke hanging over the city did not help matters. It was all too easy to end up lost.

Time hung heavy for Fenet impatient to rejoin his troops. Nevertheless, he now felt better for the rest. He finally made up his mind to try his luck with Krukenberg. This time Krukenberg seemed much more congenial and allowed him to leave. After saluting, he turned and quickly made off just in case Krukenberg changed his mind.

Before setting forth to the front line Fenet and Douroux visited Oscha. Hennecart who had just been wounded and evacuated. Hit in the leg and knee, he could no longer stand and was disappointed to be out of action. They promised to keep him some Russians for when he returned!

By now, the French SS troops were in position along Hedemannstrasse. Their right flank extended to Mockernstrasse. Thus, they closed off the three key roads from Belle-Alliance-Platz to the Chancellery, those of Friedrichstrasse, Wilhelmstrasse and Saarlandstrasse.[18]

Led by Fink, Fenet and Douroux made their way through the underground to Kochstrasse station. Surfacing, they cut across blocks of houses in ruins and then down a ladder to a yard below. Here Ostuf. Weber warmly welcomed them. He showed Fenet into a low-roofed room overlooking Wilhelmstrasse.

Putting a finger to his lips, Weber took Fenet by the arm and led him towards a hole in the wall. He said: "Look!" Three metres away stood a knocked out Soviet T–34. The turret bore the fatal hole of the panzerfaust. Flames suddenly appeared from the underside and slowly licked away at the steel carcass. Weber quietly asked: "Is it not beautiful?" This tank was his handiwork.

Weber reported that so far today five or six Soviet tanks had been destroyed with panzerfäuste and that numerous infantry attacks had been repelled with heavy losses. And all this had been achieved with only Sturmgewehr, panzerfäuste and some MG 42s. The Frenchmen no longer had at their disposal a single tank, a single anti-tank gun, a single howitzer, a single mortar or even a single grenade-launching rifle. It was so different for the Russians opposite: they had never-ending squadrons of tanks, and a very large number of anti-tank guns and 120mm mortars, the deadliest enemy of infantry in the field. To say nothing of their considerable and formidable artillery arm upon which they could always call. On the other hand, their infantry, although great in number, had been rather timid

18   According to Saint-Loup, page 452, 'Weber, Rostaing and de Lacaze' clashed with small enemy units coming up Wilhelmstrasse and drove them back to Belle-Alliance-Platz, but the square was teeming with Russian tanks, guns and troops. Because an attack on the square was out of the question, Hedemannstrasse was then made into a 'line of resistance'.

up to now. And yet, before this overwhelming superiority in weaponry and manpower, the Frenchmen were still holding fast.

Fenet found battalion headquarters in a neighbouring room, where he was greeted with cries of joy from the couriers under Roberto who dashed over, surrounded him and started to recount their latest exploits. Since dawn they had been busy.

Roberto's actions that day once again proved the extraordinary talent he had for close combat. He was soon off. He and his acolytes had spotted a large building occupied by the Russians in numbers. Entering a sewer in Hedemannstrasse, they slipped undetected through a series of interconnecting cellars into the basement of the building, where they started a fire. After which they retired and took up position. Patiently, with Sturmgewehrs trained on the exits, they waited for the building to go up in flames. Minutes later, the building was engulfed in flames and the Russians hurriedly evacuated, but they had reckoned without the waiting Sturmgewehrs that now barked from all sides. Tens of Russians were cut down. It was a veritable slaughter. Grenades 'encouraged' the remainder out who were trying to hide in the building. They too were greeted by Sturmgewehr. All fell one after the other. Over fifty corpses were now scattered all around the building and in its entrance. All at battalion headquarters were jubilant. They embraced each other and slapped each other on the back. On his return, Roberto declared: "It's better than the cinema." Fenet called life fine.

A few minutes later, the fifty or so corpses strewn over the road were crushed under the tracks of T–34s launched in another attack that would be 'as furious as it was in vain'.

Reinforcements arrived.[19] Some one hundred strong, they were Ministry of Security officials. Most were between the ages of fifty and sixty and yet they were not found wanting in willingness, discipline or courage. This was in sharp contrast to the officers with them, three or four Sturmbannführer, two Hauptsturmführer and five or six other officers, who seemed only fit for traffic control rather than the command of men in street fighting.[20] The reinforcements, although armed with outdated rifles, were a most welcome sight and permitted the French battalion to flesh out its disposition noticeably.

Enemy snipers continued to exact their deadly toll. Appearances at windows and porches, however fleeting, immediately drew fire. The slightest careless movement brought death or serious injury. Oberjunker de Lacaze, from South-west France, who had replaced the missing Labourdette at the head of the 1st Company, fought with reckless abandon and broke up the attacks of the Russian infantry time and time again. He put all his energy into this fight, but was stopped by a sniper's bullet that seriously wounded him. Dragged under cover, he was evacuated to a medical post.[21]

19   According to Saint-Loup, page 463, the reinforcements arrived at 1700 hours. This
      conflicts with Fenet.
20   Mabire, page 251.
21   Fenet, page 19, [repeated by Mabire, page 252]. However, the manner of de Lacaze's
      wounding may have been quite different. Saint-Loup records, see page 465, that de
      Lacaze was riddled by hundreds of grenade fragments while attempting to clear the
      Russians from the first floor of a house whose ground floor the French were holding.

Uscha. Roberto and his inseparable 'accomplice' Bicou, who was eighteen and hence the youngest NCO in the Sturmbataillon, ventured onto the roofs to do battle with the Reds. Armed with pistol and grenade, they engaged Red snipers overlooking their position. After flushing some out, they returned to battalion headquarters to stock up on grenades. Here they were greeted with cries of joy. As the two of them spoke to Fenet of their rooftop action, they stuffed egg-shaped grenades into their pockets, hung stick grenades from their tunic buttons and slipped them under their belts. The two NCOs then rushed back to the roofs where they took on a group of Reds hiding behind a line of small chimneys. The Reds gave in first and withdrew, covering themselves with grenades. One exploded near Roberto, wounding him. Blood poured from the grenade splinter he had 'taken' just under his right eyelid. He could barely see. The roof seemed to sway beneath him and he thought he was going to fall into the street below.

Bicou brought Roberto back to battalion headquarters and sat him down in an armchair. Fenet noted that Roberto looked more pale than normal. Although in pain, Roberto soon dozed off. A little later, Bicou took Roberto to the first-aid post with a convoy of wounded. The doctor told Bicou that the right eye was lost and that he did not know if he could save the other. Bicou vowed to make the Reds pay for this. For Roger Roberto, the war was now over.

After returning from the first-aid post, Bicou took up position behind a barricade of rubble. With his finger wrapped around the trigger of a Sturmgewehr, he kept watch. Suddenly, a Soviet anti-tank shell smashed into the barricade and he was knocked unconscious. His section of runners thought it had just lost its third commander after Millet and Roberto, but Bicou soon came round. After resting for an hour, he was back on watch over a night that proved rather quiet towards its end.

The road outside battalion headquarters was deserted[22] except for the T–34 destroyed by Weber, which continued to burn. Long flames were now dancing around the steel carcass.

Flames, leaping from the burning buildings, reddened the sky in the form of a halo above the roofs.

Sometimes the quiet of the night was pierced by the heart-rending screams from women being raped and tortured by the 'men of the steppe'. The screams were not human. The Frenchmen could only clench their fists and reflect that if they had a few tanks they would have quickly cleared the whole quarter of 'these hirsute and foul-smelling brutes'. They thought of the men and women who had cheered them on as they crossed Berlin and of those who still courageously risked

---

Before passing out, he found the strength to pull from his finger the emblazoned signet ring he wore and throw it into the rubble around him to conceal it from the Russians.

22   Fenet, page 19. In contrast, according to Rostaing, page 196, Berlin came to life after the Russian offensive stopped at 2100 hours. Civilians came out of cellars and shelters 'like rats abandoning a ship in distress'. Mindful of the Russians using any guise or means to fall on their positions, Rostaing fired a few bursts into the air to clear the civilians from the road. This would prevent the Russians from mingling with them and turning their positions when they were least expecting it.

life and limb to bring them food and water under enemy fire. Henceforth, they fought with anger in their hearts.

Sunday 29th April 1945

The onset of daylight brought the Soviet tanks again. The noise from the engines gave them away. Well-placed panzerfäuste quickly brought the first wave to a bloody halt. The success of the Frenchmen was also due in part to the Russians themselves; they continued to commit tanks spaced well apart and this gave the Frenchmen time enough to see them coming and prepare a 'warm' reception for each of them.

After the failure of the first wave, the Russians reverted to blasting at point-blank range those houses occupied by the Frenchmen. Walls collapsed, roofs caved in on the stalwart defenders and, sometimes, a well placed shot through a window or entrance showered them with earth and debris, and plunged them into dusty darkness for minutes. The curtain was now going up on the last act as the Russians attacked all-out. The defenders, pounded non-stop by mortars, tanks and anti-tank guns, had to face several tank attacks per hour. There was no respite as the fighting flared to new heights of ferocity. Nevertheless, the Frenchmen did not lose morale. Defeatism did not exist for them, although they were well aware of how desperate their situation was becoming.

Weber and the men of the Kampfschule struck back at the tank columns again and again. Weber presented Uscha. Vaulot to Fenet. Vaulot already had four tank kills to his name.[23] On a score of three was Uscha. Albert-Brunet.

A native of Dauphiné, Roger Albert-Brunet joined the *Milice française* in early 1943 and went on to attend its national *École des cadres* at Uriage. In the autumn of the same year, he volunteered for the Waffen-SS. He came to Berlin with the *groupe des liaisons* ['runners' section] of the Sturmbataillon.

Loudly, Albert-Brunet insisted on laying claim to the next tank to appear. A score of four would equal that of his friend Vaulot.

Each wanted his own tank but there were no longer enough panzerfäuste to go round and arguments ensued. The never-ending anxiety over the lack of panzerfäuste necessitated costly sorties to the Reichs Chancellery to replenish their supply.

Audry, an LVF veteran getting on for forty, was mortally wounded attacking his third tank towards the end of the afternoon. He died during his evacuation to the medical post at Stadtmitte underground station.

The harder the Frenchmen resisted the greater the firepower the Russians visited upon them. Fenet's command post became the main bastion of the defence and its walls were expected to fall in on their heads at any moment. The whole house seemed to sway under the impact of each shell. Fenet bowed to the inevitable and the inevitable was that sooner or later they would have to evacuate this increasingly untenable building before they were all crushed or buried. But he delayed the withdrawal for as long as possible because it would have serious consequences; the configuration of the quarter was such that the whole front would have to be pulled back fifty metres and that brought the Russians fifty metres nearer to the Chancellery. And the Chancellery was now only some hundreds of metres away.

---

23   His score of four included the two T-34s he had destroyed at Neukölln.

Thinking that the Frenchmen were dead, the Russians came with tanks again, but this time without a preparatory artillery barrage. Tens and tens of tanks converged on Hedemannstrasse at the same time. The Russians realised their mistake when two tanks went up in flames and a third was badly damaged. They about-turned and, as soon as they were sat out of panzerfäuste range, they began to blast the French positions. Also brought to bear were all their barrels in the sector. Under this avalanche of fire floors disintegrated and caved in. The rooms of Fenet's command post filled with thick dust that gave rise to breathing problems and reduced visibility to fifty centimetres! Parts of the ceiling collapsed, wounding several men.

By now, a gaping hole had appeared in a wall that was right in the Russian tanks' line of fire. This was the end. Moreover, the Reds were infiltrating on the left flank and the command post was already under fire from snipers in a large building opposite. Fenet could delay his withdrawal no more, but had he left it too late?

A Russian oversight answered that question. The Frenchmen discovered that 'Ivan' had neglected to occupy the basement of the building opposite where huge quantities of paper were stored. Couturin, a former Parisian fireman, set fire to the paper with hand grenades. The fire soon caught hold of the building and while the Russians 'played the fireman' the Frenchmen made off.

Although greeted by gunfire and grenades from the Russians in the burning building, the Frenchmen made it across the strip of ruins separating them from their new positions without suffering any losses. Clearly, as hoped, the fire had distracted the Russians.

The Frenchmen dug in along Puttkamerstrasse. In this quarter, one house in three remained standing.

Fenet told grenadier Levast of the Kampfschule to take a badly wounded man to Stadtmitte U-Bahn station and while there to ask Krukenberg for reinforcements and ammunition. Levast made it over to the underground station, confided his wounded comrade to 'Nordland' medics and passed on Fenet's request to the Brigadeführer. He promised the few resources he still had available and that included a Tiger tank. Levast smiled. It had been a dream of his to go up to the front on the track guard of one of these giant tanks.

Levast and some comrades boarded the tank loaded with boxes of ammunition and panzerfäuste. The tank rumbled off towards the buildings occupied by Fenet and the Sturmbataillon. The roads were deserted. Suddenly, the tank rocked violently; a large calibre mortar shell had just fallen close by. The blast shredded the Frenchmen at the rear of the tank. Levast was hit in the small of his back. Getting up, he accidentally put his hand on the exhaust pipe, horribly burning himself. Then he noticed that he was covered in blood; one of his comrades whose face had been blown off had fallen on him. He jumped to the ground and saw another dying comrade. He did not know him. Alas, there was nothing that could be done for this very young volunteer.

When Levast tried to move away and take cover from the continuing bombardment he fell. He was in pain and could not walk. A comrade picked him up, helped him to a house and took him down steps to a cellar where he fainted. When he came round this comrade had disappeared, but he was not alone; he was now in the company of a young Belgian of the Luftschutz.[24] The Belgian commented that they should not stay where they were and offered to help him.

The two of them left the cellar and crossed the road, leaping from shell hole to shell hole. They came to the corner of Kochstrasse and Wilhelmstrasse and were about to make their way to shelter behind a destroyed machine-gun carrier when a shell crashed down and exploded on that very spot. Instead they took to the underground passages. Moments later, Levast was lucky enough to be receiving treatment from a medic. Along with six other seriously wounded, he was loaded onto an ambulance, driven by an Italian SS soldier, and taken to a medical post, a cellar. More medics. Further injections. He lapsed into sleep.

In haste, the Frenchmen organised combat positions. The new front along Puttkamerstrasse would be easier to defend because a network of inner courtyards provided the Frenchmen with an excellent means of communication that was under cover from the enemy. However, there was one weak spot and that was a house in ruins at the corner of Friedrichsstrasse. It was difficult to watch over and thus quite open to infiltration.

To straighten the front, Fenet counterattacked with the elderly officials of the Sichereitshauptamt. Supported by fire from the Frenchmen, they drove back the Red infantry infiltrating through the ruins. In the total absence of heavy weapons support, they suffered very heavy losses.

While this furious infantry battle was going on the Russians unleashed another massive tank attack. This time the Russians employed a new tactic. Having realised their error of the previous days, they attacked no longer in staggered single file but in packs of seven or eight abreast, almost track to track. It was a veritable wall of steel. Fortunately for the Frenchmen the rubble strewn on the road reduced the thoroughfare to two tanks at a time and it was at this very spot that Weber's men, panzerfäuste in hand, awaited their arrival. And when the time came his bleary-eyed tank hunters were not found wanting, destroying first time the two lead tanks and so blocking the way to the others following which about-turned. However, the Russians were not done. Moments later, they tried to tow the wrecks to the rear in order to clear the road for the next attack. The shelling resumed. It was heavier than ever. The fighting continued.

Ill at ease, Oscha. Ollivier decided to take up a more advantageous position in a building on the other side of the road. With Strmm. Coulomb and six or so men from his 4th Company, he attempted to cross, but was caught in a violent bombardment. Ollivier and Coulomb found themselves buried under a pile of bricks. Nevertheless, Ollivier managed to pull himself partly out of the rubble, but he was in a bad way: his nose was fractured and his knees crushed. He warned those who rushed over to help him to proceed with great care; he and Coulomb were 'live bombs'. They had on them a primed panzerfaust and grenades that any false movement might explode.

Anxiously, the rescuers started to clear away the bricks one by one. They expected, at any moment, to be blown to bits. After what seemed an eternity to all, the trapped men were free. Coulomb was also in a great deal of pain; his legs had been mutilated. They were evacuated to a medical post located in a hospital basement. Ollivier was operated on. Conducting the operation was a British doctor

---

24   Either the Luftschutzdienst, the Air-raid Protection Service, or the Luftschutz Warndienst, the Air-raid Warning Service

serving in the Wehrmacht. He did what he could for Ollivier, but this time Ollivier would not be returning to take the head of his company again.

Rostaing uses another of his nine lives

Again there was that distinctive rattle of tank tracks. This time it was a heavy 'Iosef Stalin' tank coming up Friedrichstrasse. From his observation post on the second floor of the building serving as the battalion's command post, Hscha. Rostaing watched this approaching steel monster. He shuddered with fear: only the 88mm gun could penetrate its heavy armour and the Frenchmen only had panzerfäuste. The enemy tank closed rapidly and was only thirty metres away when four pear-shaped panzerfäuste cones crashed simultaneously into its tracks. The very next moment the building 'caved in'. Hit on the head by a large beam, he collapsed and was buried, buried alive by the falling rubble. He passed out not before he heard the characteristic sound of the Sturmgewehr.

Because there was no sign of life from Rostaing he was believed to be dead. Rostaing's comrades reported to Fenet that their company commander had just been killed. It was a blow to Fenet who went in person to the scene. He too was now convinced that Rostaing was dead, but he too was wrong.

When Rostaing came round he tried to move his arms and legs. All responded. Thankfully nothing seemed broken. With his hands and feet, he dug himself out of the rubble, emerging to darkness and a sky full of stars. Nobody was about, yet he could still hear the sounds of battle. He wandered around for minutes trying to work out what had happened. He started by thinking that when the tank had exploded it had brought down the building, but concluded that the tank had fired at the same moment as it was hit by the panzerfäuste. And the tank shell had smashed into the facade and totally demolished the floor, burying him. Luck, his faithful companion, had not deserted him. It never would.

Rostaing glanced into the road. It was empty and calm. He was at a loss what to do next, but there was no question of surrender. He made out voices coming from the basement and, on recognising that of his old LVF comrade Protopopoff, he hurtled down the stairway and into the battalion's command post.[25] In a rare show of affection, Fenet embraced him. Fenet expressed the surprise of all present and offered him a cup of coffee to 'get him back on his feet again before the harsh

25   Rostaing, "*Le Prix d'un Serment*", pages 199-201. Mabire, Fenet and Saint-Loup also recount the 'death' of Rostaing, but all differ. Firstly, according to Mabire, page 271, both Rostaing and the young Breton de Lannurien were buried 'alive'. In fact, after freeing himself from the rubble, Rostaing dug out his companion. He too was more stunned than wounded. Since Mabire interviewed de Lannurien for "*Mourir à Berlin*" there is no reason to disbelieve his version of events. Also, Saint-Loup confirms that both Rostaing and de Lannurien were buried, although the circumstances of the burying differ and no awards ceremony followed their reappearance at battalion headquarters (see Saint-Loup, page 474). And yet, curiously, according to Malardier of the Sturmbataillon, letter to the author of 11/10/98, he met Rostaing shortly after his 'wakening' and Rostaing was quite alone. Also, Rostaing was in the company of Malardier when he rejoined his comrades and de Lannurien was not present.

Secondly, Saint-Loup and Rostaing record this episode taking place on 30th April 1945 rather than the 29th as stated by Mabire and Fenet.

fighting awaiting them'. Fenet then arranged a brief ceremony to award Rostaing the Iron Cross 1st Class.[26]

Rostaing said of this ceremony: "Even today when I think about these moments I get a lump in my throat and my eyes fill with tears. It was marvellous … I will never forget it and I will carry the memory of it to my grave."

Before his comrades, standing to attention impeccably, Rostaing received from Fenet the Iron Cross 1st Class. Fenet, taking three paces back, saluted. Rostaing returned his salute. His comrades responded in kind and then struck up the *Horst Wessel Lied* in French.[27]

Before they parted another tornado hit the building, raising clouds of dust so thick that all were left blind and suffocating, and unable to speak or move. Dazed, they were unsure of where they were. It was minutes before they regained the use of their senses.

By now, the Frenchmen had taken on a new appearance. It was not human. Their eyes, deep-set, were bright with fever and their faces, hollowed with tiredness, were caked with dirt and dust.

Water was in short supply. There was little enough for drinking, yet alone for washing or shaving. Supplies from division had been few and far between. Thus, 'they ate what they found, when they found it and when they could'. Nevertheless, because of their feverish state, hunger did not torment them.

The past few days of hell had turned them into automatons. All what they now did seemed as natural to them as any action in everyday life. They snatched sleep when they could and minutes of 'shut eye' seemed like hours to them. Nevertheless, their aggressiveness survived the exhaustion, the hunger and the thirst.

By now, they had lost all notion of time. Dust and clouds of smoke had blanketed the sky. Since the early morning hours of 28th April 1945 they had fought non-stop. Their world was one of endless alerts, bombardments, explosions, fires and ruins. For them, the problem of the future no longer arose. They saw no other future than that to destroy tanks, fire on the Red infantry, and throw hand grenades … All their energy and all their strength was channelled into holding out and not letting the enemy pass. That was their reason to both live and die.

---

26   According to Rostaing, "*Le Prix d'un Serment*", page 200, Fenet asked him: "Tell me, do you not have the Iron Cross?" His answer was yes, explaining that although he had the certificates for both classes of the Iron Cross he still did not have the medals themselves. However, according to Mabire, page 271, after his 'wakening', Fenet told him that he had just been awarded the Iron Cross 1st Class.

27   According to Rostaing, page 200, the awards ceremony was held in a library and that Fenet was wearing around his neck the Knight's Cross which Brigf. Krukenberg had presented to him. This is unconfirmed.

    Also, Rostaing does not appear to have been the only French volunteer of the Waffen-SS decorated during this brief ceremony: Uscha. Albert-Brunet, who had just destroyed his fourth tank, was decorated with the Iron Cross 1st Class (Fenet and Mabire, page 271); Oberjunker Douroux had the Iron Cross confirmed the 'Nordland' officer had presented to him; Oberjunker Protopopoff was posthumously awarded the Iron Cross (Saint-Loup, page 476); and SS-Ostuf. von Wallenrodt may have received the Iron Cross 1st Class (Georgen).

The French holders of the Knight's Cross

Back at Stadtmitte underground station, Krukenberg felt a growing sense of unease and loneliness: neither he nor Brigf. Mohnke had been summoned to any briefings at Weidling's Headquarters. He did not even have a radio set. His only outside communication and intelligence came from Fenet and Weber who kept him in the picture about the 'front' along Puttkamerstrasse. On learning that Uscha. Vaulot of the Kampfschule had just shot up his eighth tank within twenty-four hours, Krukenberg recommended him for the Knight's Cross.

Born in Paris on 1st June 1923,[28] Eugène Vaulot was a plumber-heating engineer by trade.[29] Among the first to volunteer for the LVF in late 1941, he served with the 1st Company (1942–1943), gaining NCO rank,[30] and winning the Iron Cross 2nd Class. Declared unfit for service, he was invalided out of the LVF.[31] However, in 1944, he volunteered for the Kriegsmarine and was accepted.[32] He trained with the 6th Company of Schiffsstammabteilung 28.

Transferred to the forming Franz. Brigade der SS in the autumn of 1944, Vaulot was assigned to the *Compagnie d'Honneur*. He held the rank of Unterscharführer. He went to Pomerania and saw action at Elsenau and Kolberg. Distinguishing himself, he was decorated with the Iron Cross 1st Class. He came to Berlin as the 6th Truppführer [section commander] of the *Kampfschule*.

During the afternoon of 29th April 1945 Krukenberg bestowed the Knight's Cross upon Vaulot. He conducted the awards ceremony in the presence of his staff and some of Vaulot's comrades assembled in his candle-lit command post at Stadtmitte underground station. In a short address in French, he said that 'the bearing of this young volunteer was what we had come to expect of French soldiers, men who had won their spurs on the battlefields throughout the world'.

After the ceremony, Vaulot said to Rostaing: "I fought with a single desire: to get this decoration. Now it's done. I can die."[33]

The newly decorated Vaulot was ordered to lead a patrol to Kaiserhof Hotel in search of table linen for Krukenberg's command post! The Russians were still bombarding the area when the patrol emerged from the underground station and set off to the ruins of the Hotel. On the way, a Sturmmann was hit by shrapnel and taken to a cellar, where the Russians would capture him three days later. The mission went on. The patrol reached the Hotel from where it returned with dozens

28 The *Journal officiel* of 2/3/48 and birth certificate. Incorrectly, according to Landwehr, page 192, Vaulot was born in 1921.

29 Georgen and Mabire, page 272. However, according to Landwehr, Vaulot was an electrician by trade.

30 Vaulot gained the NCO rank of Obergefreiter (Landwehr) or Sergeant (Mabire).

31 Vaulot was invalided out as a result of sickness or war wounds (see Mabire, page 272, and Landwehr).

32 According to Landwehr, page 192, Vaulot had been 'unsatisfied with civilian life while the fate of Europe hung in the balance'.

33 Rostaing, page 194. However, Rostaing is mistaken about Vaulot's name, rank and the circumstances of his death. Also, according to Saint-Loup, Rostaing was full of bitterness at not receiving the same decoration.

of serviettes for Krukenberg, as well as several good bottles of wine that were kept from him.

Krukenberg also said of 29th April: "The commander of SS-Panzer Abteilung 503, 'Major' [Stubaf.] Herzig, also received the Knight's Cross from the hands of 'Major-General' [Brigf.] Mohnke. These were the last two such decorations in this war."

However, according to Krätschmer,[34] on that same day of 29th April 1945, three other awards of the Knight's Cross also went to members of the French SS-Sturmbataillon, namely Hstuf. Fenet, Ostuf. Weber and Oscha. Appolot. In the post-war years, Krukenberg has questioned the authenticity of these awards, awards for which no official wartime documentation exists. So what else has been said of the disputed awards of the Knight's Cross to Fenet, Weber and Appolot? Can the awards be confirmed?

According to Georgen,[35] Weber was wounded on the 29th and evacuated to the field hospital beneath the Reichs Chancellery. 'Like the majority of officers coming down from the front', he too gave a brief description of the situation along the front to Brigf. Mohnke, the commander of Sector 'Z', whose headquarters was in the next room. After hearing Weber's report, Mohnke went to General of infantry Burgdorf, the chief of the Heerespersonalamt (HPA), and proposed the awarding of the Knight's Cross to several officers and NCOs of the French Sturmbataillon. That same day, General Burgdorf signed off the appropriate 'paperwork' and handed Brigf. Mohnke the certificates and medals. In this way, no more than a few hours after the nominations had gone forward to the chief of the HPA, Brigf. Mohnke decorated Weber with the Knight's Cross.[36]

According to Saint-Loup,[37] Weber was wounded in the early morning of the 30th and evacuated to the 'bunker of the Reichsführer SS' and from there onto the Führerbunker itself. This was his sixth wound of the war. Mohnke came to visit him and told him that Vaulot had received the Knight's Cross and that he, along with Fenet and Appolot, had been awarded the Knight's Cross. Mohnke added that Krukenberg would receive 'the papers' the following day. He did not.[38]

Mabire, for his part, recounts that on the afternoon of the 29th, a Scandinavian Obersturmführer from 'Nordland' [possibly Ostuf. Christensen] visited the command post of the French SS-Sturmbataillon. Full of praise for his 'singular neighbours', the 'Nordland' Obersturmführer handed round some bottles of wine he had brought along as a present. He then whispered to Oberjunker Douroux that Hstuf. Fenet had been proposed for the Knight's Cross, but cautioned him not to tell Fenet because it was not yet official. However, Douroux did tell him [presumably before the end of the war]. Fenet would hear no more of a Knight's Cross until years after the war.[39]

34   See "*Die Ritterkreuzträger der Waffen-SS*".
35   See part 3. Based on the eyewitness accounts of Brigf. Mohnke, Hstuf. Pachur and Ostuf. Weber.
36   Curiously, according to Krukenberg, page 15, on one of the last days of battle, Weber received 'The German Cross in Gold' for destroying his fifth enemy tank in this war.
37   See Saint-Loup, pages 477 to 478. Arguably his source was Ostuf. Weber.
38   Saint-Loup explains that the papers were lost en route or never sent (see page 478).

Reportedly, Appolot was awarded the Knight's Cross for knocking out six Russian tanks. His story starts some five years before. In that infamous month of June 1940, *Sergent-chef* François Appolot of the *28e régiment d'infanterie de forteresse* went into German captivity. Towards the end of 1942, he became a *Freiarbeiter* (free-worker). He worked at Pillau and Königsberg, but one afternoon his Schichtmeister (literally shift master) caught him with his wife when he came home one hour earlier than normal. Thereupon, Appolot was offered the choice of either joining the Wehrmacht or being sent to a concentration camp. Instead he opted for the Kriegsmarine.[40]

Assigned to the 6th Company of Schiffsstammabteilung 28, Appolot underwent basic training at Sennheim from May to June 1944 and then at Duisberg where the company was renumbered 2/28.[41]

In September 1944, Appolot was transferred to the forming Franz. Brigade der SS and assigned to the Wach-und-Ausb.Kp. He received the rank of Oberscharführer and the command of a platoon. He went to Pomerania, where he ably demonstrated his skills as a soldier and as a leader of men, and also proved himself in battle as a man of great personal courage. He came to Berlin as the 2nd Truppführer of the Kampfschule.[42]

Although most commentators have him meeting his death in Berlin, Appolot did, in fact, survive the war. Ever since, he has kept a low profile.

Remarkably, Appolot was and still is a card-carrying member of the *Parti Communiste Français*.

This now brings us back to the question, can the awards be confirmed? With only verbal evidence to prove that the awards were made, the answer would have to be a resounding no. Nevertheless, today, it's generally accepted that Fenet, Weber and Appolot were awarded the Knight's Cross.

The fighting continues

The defensive line either side of the positions held by the Frenchmen had now disintegrated or been withdrawn, leaving them in a salient in the shape of a clenched fist. The Russians stepped up their attacks against the defenders in frequency, ferocity and strength. It would be no exaggeration to say that the French Sturmbataillon was now fighting for its very life.

39   Notably, Fenet was silent about the award of the Knight's Cross in his memoirs of the battle for Berlin and later in the article "*A Berlin Jusqu'au Bout*".

40   Gaulois, "*Der Freiwillige*", issue of 3/97 [confirmed by Lefèvre]. However, according to Landwehr, page 184, Appolot's background was somewhat different: a former member of the French Navy, Appolot had his ship, the cruiser *Provence*, sunk from beneath him at Mers-el-Kebir on 3rd July 1940 by the British Navy. Like many French sailors, he was left permanently embittered against the British. Soon after, he left the French Navy and volunteered his services to the Kriegsmarine.

41   According to Landwehr, page 184, Appolot was a platoon commander. In reply, Landwehr is incorrect. While at Duisburg no Frenchman of the 2/28 was promoted (Soulat, corrections to the author, 2006).

42   According to Landwehr, Appolot came to Berlin as a platoon commander in the *Kampfschule*. This is incorrect. Puechlong, letter to the author, 24/11/97.

Although dropping with fatigue, the Frenchmen stemmed the northward surge of the Russians time and time again. But after the failure of their constant frontal attacks, the Russians attempted to dislodge the defenders by infiltration. As support, they brought up the fearsome flame-thrower.

By now, all of the Frenchmen had lost friends and companions to death. If Russian losses were heavy, so were those of the French. Only the seriously wounded were evacuated for good: 'the others made do with a makeshift dressing and continued to fight on, or would rest several hours at the medical post before returning to take their place'.[43]

The officers of the French Sturmbataillon, for the most part very young, had paid a particularly heavy tribute. Labourdette, Le Maignan, Cossard, Dumoulin, Billot and Robelin had been killed. Among the wounded were Michel, de Lacaze, Ginot, Ollivier, Baumgartner, Hennecart, Bert or Bertant, Croisille, Fieselbrand, Frantz, Boulmier and François. Douroux and Protopopoff may have been the only French officers to come this far without a scratch. There was also von Wallenrodt, of late a war correspondent, who, in the words of Fenet, 'remained very calm and very at ease in all this din'.[44] His Iron Cross 1st Class was well deserved.

The fighting did not abate. That evening, Fenet relocated his command post once more, this time to the basement of a library that held magnificent art books.[45] One of the runners discovered a colour book dedicated to Spain, which became the main source of entertainment for those who came, in turn, to rest awhile. They would leaf through its pages of sunny landscapes as if in search of an antidote to their 'visions of hell'. As a former *Khâgneux*, Fenet was furious at the thought of all these books ending up consumed by fire or, worse still, ripped to shreds by a group of drunken Mongols. For Rostaing, the rare Reiner Dietrich editions housed in the library, were a 'symbol of our western civilisation for which we were fighting'.

The battle continued to rage throughout the night, but what was night? Darkness had been chased away by this huge inferno that Berlin had become. The burning houses and tanks were their torches. The fires devouring Berlin lit it up as bright as day. Fenet noted that a 'sinister light', with a reddish halo, had spread over the whole city.[46] 'In this lighting of a tragic spectacular, the ruins, standing out against the incandescent sky, took on unreal and twisted outlines'.

Fenet poetically recounts that the Frenchmen had become actors starring in a cosmic drama. The enemy opposite them were no longer men, but dancing silhouettes with gigantic shadows that the dry crack of their bullets spun round before crashing to the ground, while all around rumbled the noise of battle. The setting of this drama was not the earth they had once known; ruins collapsed into heaps of rubble with a deafening crash, the ground trembled beneath their feet and tragic colours 'exploded like grenades'. Sometimes they had the impression that the ground was going to open up and that everything was going to return to chaos ...

With greater and greater fierceness, the Frenchmen fought on in this duel to the death. The Russians brought up more and more tanks and more and more men, and fired more and more shells. The air was thick with exploding shells from

43   Fenet, page 23.
44   Ibid.
45   Ibid.
46   See page 24.

mortar and artillery bombardments. Although death, injury or captivity seemed the only certainties for the Frenchmen, an almost superhuman determination to hold drove them on. Hold. HOLD. That was the only thought in their minds and on their lips. Hold. Hold until when? That question did not arise as long as they still had cartridges, grenades and panzerfäuste! They would fight to the bitter end.

Monday 30th April 1945

Although sleep weighed heavy on the most exhausted, those at the library had remained awake and alert all night thanks to the endless hot drinks prepared by the two women they had come across on their arrival at the library.

The Russians started early again. They came with tanks. Panzerfaust in hand, standing in windows, the Frenchmen awaited them. A Russian T–34 charged up Friedrichstrasse. One well-aimed panzerfaust tore the tank apart. It went up in a ball of flame. Then came the next tank. It too exploded into a flaming pyre. By the end of the day, Rostaing counted no less than twenty-one burning hulks around the library. Moreover, this cemetery of Russian armour, a barrier of steel and flames, now protected the Frenchmen better than if they were entrenched in a blockhouse.

This victory gave the Frenchmen heart and a victory it was. The Russians had lost twenty-one tanks to a group of men that numbered no more than 25 or 26[47], but it was to a group of men that, as Rostaing remembers, had defended 'with an energy that I can barely imagine today'.

The Russians also had troubles of their own. In the evening, a Russian prisoner, a strapping NCO, was brought to headquarters. He had let himself be captured without putting up a fight. He was given cigarettes in exchange for the cob loaves he was carrying. The last bread the Frenchmen had seen was days before. Oberjunker Protopopoff[48] questioned the prisoner who proved very talkative and explained that he was Ukrainian and not Russian, and that he was not a communist, having been drafted into the Red Army. All, of course, doubted the prisoner's sincerity, but continued to listen with interest to what he had to say. Put at ease, the prisoner replied at great length to the questions of military interest the young Oberjunker casually slipped in during the course of their conversation.

The information gleaned from the Ukrainian prisoner was of great interest: earlier that day, the Red Army had issued a communiqué announcing imminent victory as there was no more than one square kilometre of Berlin left to conquer. And this last bastion was to be taken the following day, the first of May, as a May Day celebration. All greeted with wild laughter the translation of these last words. Uscha. Bicou commented: "Tomorrow, we'll still be here, my friend, and your buddies will be received as usual when they try to pass!" Protopopoff translated Bicou's words for the prisoner. The Frenchmen could not believe their ears when the prisoner suddenly announced that the Russian tank crews had to be forced at gunpoint to mount their armoured vehicles, adding: "Those in the lead tanks know that they will not be coming back!"

47   Rostaing, page 198. His own command, around eighty-strong six days earlier, now counted six men.
48   Mabire, page 281. According to Saint-Loup, Pachur interrogated the prisoner.

The Soviet offensive to conquer the last square kilometre of Berlin began in earnest and continued throughout the night and into the morning of 1st May.[49] So the Ukrainian prisoner had not been lying!

The Soviets came with tanks and infantry. The French SS troops let the T–34s approach, they would engage them at point-blank range, but poured fire from their Sturmgewehr on the infantry, pinning them down. The Soviet soldiers tried to advance further, but did not get far.

Helpless, the unshaven and grimy defenders observed the Russians concentrate their tanks barely three hundres metres away. Peacefully, in the shelter of this steel barrier, their infantry now assembled. The defenders bemoaned the lack of guns, mortars and MGs with which they could have broken up the Russians positioning themselves for the kill. All knew what was at stake if they were overwhelmed and crushed: the Reichs Chancellery, the very heart of Berlin. And even though more and more of their comrades were dead or dying their will to resist remained unshaken. For some, however, like *sergent* G. and his friend P., the time had now come to 'demobilise themselves'.[50]

During a particularly violent assault a T–34 managed to break through. Was this the beginning of the end? For seconds, a terrible anguish gripped them, 'as if a chasm had opened at their feet', but the tank was stopped some thirty metres behind their 'line' by a volunteer with a well-aimed panzerfaust shot.

Tuesday 1st May 1945

At 0700 hours on Tuesday 1st May 1945, Brigf. Krukenberg received a call on his recently installed field telephone at 'Stadtmitte' underground station. On the other end was Brigf. Mohnke. He opened with the news that during the night Colonel-General Krebs, Oberst von Dufving and Lieutenant-Colonel Seifert had crossed the front lines in the sector of Seifert with a view to opening negotiations with the Soviets, but could not be more precise about their mission.[51] This, of course, came as a great surprise to Krukenberg.

Mohnke had more bad news: Army Wenck had ceased its attack towards Berlin in face of superior enemy forces and was withdrawing to the river Elbe in very heavy defensive fighting. Also, Krebs and his companions, given a free pass to come and go by the Russians, were not back yet. Mohnke thought that they might be under interrogation in which case the Russians now knew of the weak spots in

49   Fenet and Mabire, page 282. However, not all sources are in agreement. Krukenberg's "*Battle Memoir*" and Le Tissier's "*The Battle For Berlin*" speak of the battle suddenly quietening down at midnight on the 30th April and then continuing in a desultory fashion, 'sometimes building up briefly and then dying down again'.

50   "*Historia #32*", page 175. *Sergent* G. was a former LVF legionnaire transferred to the Waffen SS.

51   Krukenberg, page 17, repeated by Mabire, page 284. However, according to Le Tissier, page 207, with Krebs was von Dufving and an interpreter by the name of Neilands. Also, according to the "*Battle Memoir*", page 164, Krebs had gone to the Soviet command centre to discuss the surrender of the city. In fact, 'Krebs was to give the Soviet High Command the following information: the Führer's suicide, the contents of his will, a request for an armistice, and the government's wishes to open negotiations with the Russians for the surrender of Germany' (Weidling, page 174).

the city's defence. One such weak spot was 'Potsdamer Platz' underground station. Still not closed off, it offered an approach to the Reichs Chancellery via Vossstrasse. This subway route Mohnke ordered Krukenberg to bar. In addition to this, Krukenberg was ordered to go to the Air Ministry and assume command of 'sub-sector Seifert' that was now without its *chef*.[52]

During a quiet moment Rostaing and his friend Protopopoff went out for a breath of fresh air in the ground to the rear of the library. Walking side by side, they chatted away and agreed that they were the last two from the LVF still fighting in the Waffen-SS. Suddenly, Rostaing heard the distinct whistling of an incoming mortar shell. As he took cover he yelled to Protopopoff to flatten himself. The shell fell in the courtyard and exploded. The barrel, behind which Rostaing had taken shelter, was riddled with shrapnel. Unhurt, he got up and saw that his friend was lying on his side, motionless. Rostaing knelt beside him. Protopopoff muttered: "You're the last left." And then died.[53]

Told of Protopopoff's death, Fenet went at once to the scene of his death where he performed a brief 'funeral' ceremony: he broke in half Protopopoff's identity disc, took his *Soldbuch* and saluted. That was all. Fenet returned to the battle. 'Prince' Protopopoff, this 'last representative of old Russia',[54] is credited with the destruction of five tanks at Berlin.

As the afternoon wore on the situation of the French SS troops deteriorated. The large building, almost intact when first occupied, was now falling in ruins. Long floorboards hung from the floors into the road, presenting a perfect target for the Russian flame-thrower teams infiltrating through the ruins. Weak on the ground, the French had not been able to stop them nor keep them at distance. After several unfruitful attempts, the Russians finally managed to set fire to this pyre 'so kindly offered to them'. The building was tinder-dry. The flames spread.

Georges, the radio operator and a former Paris fireman, tried to fight the flames as best he could, but without a drop of water he never had a chance. The flames seared through the building. Fenet bowed to the inevitable later rather than sooner: the flames were approaching the last exit when, reluctantly, he gave the order to withdraw. It was 1800 hours.

The French SS volunteers took up position some tens of metres away in the Sicherheitshauptamt (the Ministry of Security) at the corner of Wilhelmstrasse and Prinz-Albrechtstrasse. Although this large building was in ruins, its cellars, opening out onto Prinz-Albrechtstrasse, were still very much intact and useable as shelters and gun positions. Soon after, the sounds of a violent infantry battle could be heard from the direction of Saarlandstrasse and Anhalter railway station on their right. The battle ebbed back and forth, but there was only ever going to be one outcome.

Nightfall found the French SS troops still ensconced in the Ministry of Security building. Fenet had installed himself in a vault that served as both a shelter and a place of rest.

---

52   Curiously, according to Mabire, page 284, on drawing his telephone call to a close, Brigf. Mohnke commanded that you must hold out, stating that they were the Führer's orders. This Krukenberg does not confirm.

53   Rostaing, pages 201 and 202.

54   Saint-Loup, page 476.

In the light of a candle burning on a *Julleuchter*, a Jul Candlestick,[55] symbolising the never dying sunlight,[56] Fenet decorated a number of comrades with the Iron Cross.[57] Although simple, the ceremony that evening seemed all the more extraordinary.

Death had been the constant companion of the Frenchmen for the past week. The day of 1st May was costly: Protopopoff, the *Milicien* Dedieu[58], Mazoué, the son of a Sorbonne professor, Jacquier, Funel, Duchot … all dead.[59] Few were now left.[60] Would this night be their last?

Meanwhile, Krukenberg had been busy. After his early morning conversation with Mohnke, he set about securing his rear area, sending a section of 'Nordland' engineers to block the underground tunnel running from Potsdamer Platz which had been left wide open. Then he left for the Air Ministry. With him was an escort of German and French SS troops. The journey was one fraught with danger.

As Krukenberg and his small escort crossed Wilhelmplatz they were caught in a violent artillery bombardment, but still managed to make it across. Continuing along Wilhelmstrasse, they drew fire, but again passed unscathed. They came to the Ministry. Outside stood some wagons of infantry munitions, which were not camouflaged. Hit by enemy fire, two of them exploded, showering their contents in all directions.

To the great surprise of Krukenberg, the Air Ministry was not guarded. The entrance was wide open. They entered. It was empty. They went down into the cellars and found asleep more than one hundred soldiers of the Luftwaffe under the command of an old general, who was also asleep. Woken, he stated that he obeyed only Luftgau-Kommando Berlin and not the Army Corps of Weidling.

Krukenberg asked the general where the Luftgau-Kommando was. He replied: "At Neustadt-an-der-Dosse." [Neustadt-an-der-Dosse is some seventy kilometres northwest of Berlin!] Krukenberg made him aware of the situation and the immediate Russian threat on his doorstep. Only then did the general post guards.

55   The *Julleuchter* was a traditional folklore candlestick used throughout the year to mark celebrations, such as New Year's Eve and the Summer Solstice, and commemorations. For more information about the *Julleuchter* as an essential symbol of the SS, see "*The SS family*", which is an English translation of the book "*The Celebration of Special Festivities in the life of the SS-family*" written just after the outbreak of war.

56   "*The SS family*", page 34. For Fenet, the flame of the *Julleuchter* symbolised the victory of light over darkness as well as hope over death (see Mabire, "*La Brigade Frankreich*", page 27).

57   According to Mabire, page 287, the awards came from Krukenberg via a runner. This, however, Krukenberg does not confirm.

58   Possibly a pseudonym for SS-Mann Guy Jacques Dediev, born on 29th June 1918 in Toulose (sic), although he is officially listed as MIA (*Siegrunen* 49).

59   Saint-Loup, page 479. However, Billot and Cossard also appear among this list, but Fenet and Mabire have already registered the death of these two officers earlier in the fighting.

60   No more than twenty according to Rostaing, page 203, or as many as fifty according to Saint-Loup, page 493.

Krukenberg continued on. There was still no sign of Oberstleutnant Seifert. He came across a young Hauptmann [Captain] of the Wehrmacht who told him that he had been attached the day before to the headquarters of the Sub-Sector at the Air Ministry. And yet Seifert had told him that he had no need of anybody! Anyway, from the Heer Captain, Krukenberg learnt that Seifert had locked himself away in an office with his orderly officer and was probably busy destroying papers and documents. Together they went to Seifert's office, where they could only locate a Luftwaffe Leutnant, the same one Krukenberg had met on the evening of April 25th. They entered into a lively discussion. The Leutnant still refused to give Krukenberg the exact whereabouts of his commander even after Krukenberg explained his mission to him. Just then Oberstleutnant Seifert, flanked by two French NCOs of Krukenberg's escort, entered the room; they had found him in another part of the building.

Seifert was 'saved' by a telephone call from Mohnke's headquarters, revoking the order Krukenberg had received earlier that morning.[61] It was all a misunderstanding! Such was the confusion in those last days.

Before leaving, Krukenberg wrote up a short report and asked Seifert once again for the return of the 'Nordland' troops and the French detachment still under his command. In reply, Seifert gestured his helplessness.

Contrary to all expectations, 1st May remained quiet in the sector of 'Nordland'.

Towards midday, Brigf. Mohnke commandeered the last 'Nordland' Tiger tank.[62]

Lying in ambush, de Lannurien of the Kampfschule watched a number of Russian tanks approach. They stopped. And before continuing they shelled the ruins of buildings that could conceal the enemy tank hunters. Rounds screamed in. A wall collapsed on de Lannurien and once again he found himself covered with rubble. He could not pull himself free. The rubble was just too heavy. Entombed, he could not breathe nor cough. He was sure he was going to die. He blacked out.

When de Lannurien came round the first person he recognised was his company commander, Ostuf. Weber, and it was Weber he had to thank for pulling him from the rubble. However, against his wishes, Weber had him evacuated to the medical post at Stadtmitte. He was the sole survivor of his section.

From Krukenberg, de Lannurien received the Iron Cross 1st Class. One of his friends, Jean-Claude Dautot, was also brought to the medical post. He had a serious leg wound.[63]

---

61   Krukenberg, page 17. Curiously, according to Mabire, page 295 [and repeated in the "*Battle Memoir*", page 165], the telephone call was from Mohnke himself.

62   Krukenberg, page 18, Mabire page 296 and the "*Battle Memoir*", page 166. However, according to Saint-Loup, page 490, the call came earlier at 1000 hours, and the Tiger tank was not the last.

63   Mabire, pages 296-297. Curiously, it should be recalled that Saint-Loup and Fenet have already spoken of the (serious) wounding of Weber. Thus, had Weber recovered sufficiently from his wounds to enable him to return to the battle and his French comrades-in-arms? Or was François de Lannurien, through Mabire, mistaken about the date of his wounding and his subsequent decoration?

At 1900 hours, Krukenberg attended the Führerbunker for a real briefing, the word 'real' stressed by the order that summoned him. He took with him the Ia of 'Nordland' and his assistant, Pachur. In the antechamber of Mohnke's headquarters, Brigf. Ziegler, still under 'house arrest', came to meet him. Taking Krukenberg to one side, he brought him up to date about the latest developments. The Führer was dead. He had committed suicide yesterday afternoon. Before his suicide he had married Eva Braun, the sister-in-law of Ogruf. Fegelein, who had been shot on the Führer's orders. Also, Joseph Goebbels and his family had committed suicide. This shocked Krukenberg. Worse still, Army Wenck had stalled days before and the negotiations with the Western allies had ended in total failure. Clearly, this was the end. Krukenberg felt deceived. He was to write years later: "All the sacrifices of the troops had been in vain. The idealism of the volunteers had been abused in the worst way."

After a long wait, Brigf. Mohnke entered the room. With him were Reichsjugendführer Axmann and several others who were not known to Krukenberg. In several short sentences, he confirmed what Brigf. Ziegler had just told him. Then he spoke of General Kreb's night-time attempt to obtain an immediate cease fire in Berlin. This proposal the Soviets had refused, demanding unconditional surrender.

Turning to Krukenberg, Mohnke asked him, as the senior officer present, if he was willing to take command of the defence of the city centre with all available forces placed under his command. He was not, calling it a 'mad idea'.[64]

Mohnke raised no objection. Continuing, he explained that there was nothing else to do other than follow an order from Weildling that the Berlin garrison was, in small groups, to try and break through the Soviet encirclement.[65] Each unit would be on its own, moving in the general direction of Neuruppin to the north-west. There would be no rearguard. To prevent chaos, the news of Hitler's death was not to be made public before 2100 hours that evening. Lastly, 'in accordance with General Weidling's order communicated to all sectors', the fighting was to cease at 2300 hours.[66]

64   Krukenberg, page 18. According to Saint-Loup, page 491, Krukenberg refused because he was still very bitter at being excluded from the briefings by Mohnke and Weidling over the past few days. Curiously, a different reason appears in the "*Battle Memoir*": 'he was in no mood for any more useless sacrifices'.

65   Ibid. And yet, the "*Battle Memoir*", page 166, credits Krukenberg with suggesting the break-out in small groups to which Mohnke and Ziegler agreed. However, this claim does not concur with other sources consulted (for example, Le Tissier and Trevor-Roper). In fact, Hitler had given his formal approval for a break-out on the night of 29th/30th April. Indeed, Brigf. Mohnke was ready to break-out from the Reichs Chancellery the following night, that of 30th April/1st May, but had delayed the attempt by twenty-four hours when the Russians cut the East-West axis on the 30th.

66   Ibid. However, such an order would clearly have placed those attempting to break out in an impossible situation. So did Weidling issue such an order? It appears not. Weidling held back his surrender negotiations until after midnight in order to give the cover of darkness to those attempting to break out (Weidling, page 173-174). Perhaps Krukenberg is mistaken about the author of the order. (According to the

Deciding to break-out with his old command, Ziegler returned with Krukenberg to Stadtmitte.

Noting the preparations to evacuate Stadtmitte, François de Lannurien and Jean-Claude Dautot, two French volunteers of the Sturmbataillon, grew worried; both were wounded.

The night of 1st/2nd May 1945 and the break-out[67]

Assembling his officers in his underground command post for one last briefing, Brigf. Krukenberg told them that even if they had to split up into small groups to facilitate their break-out then each officer was to remain with his unit. Now that the situation was so critical comradeship was more important than ever.

The break-out was to follow such a plan: from 2300 hours the division was to start assembling. A number of frontline posts were to remain manned until midnight so as to mask from the enemy the total evacuation of its positions. At midnight, regiments 'Danmark' and 'Norge' were to strike northwards via Charlottenstrasse and Friedrichstrasse. Although Krukenberg regarded the underground system as a 'man-trap', its use was not ruled out.[68] However, a solid grille prevented passage under the river Spree.[69] Once across the Spree, the troops were to pause near the *grand* Opera in order to regroup and decide the next move. Krukenberg himself, in the company of officers who knew the area well, was to scout out the route.

A little before midnight, Krukenberg set off.[70] With him were his headquarters staff and his French escort. He sent Ustuf. Patzak to the Air Ministry in order to

"*Battle Memoir*", it was General Krebs who had made the decision to declare a cease fire at 2300 hours. This is unconfirmed.) Perhaps such an order was issued and later cancelled. Needless to say, confusion did exist. Simply stated, whether or not such an order was issued will probably never be known.

67   The events that transpired during the night of 1st/2nd May 1945 differ in every source. Needless to say, this will come as no great surprise. Those who attempted to break out were desperate and worn out. It was a question of survival, not of putting pen to paper. Moreover, many of those attempting to break out did not know Berlin and probably did not have maps of the city. Communications, as well, were non-existent. Consequently, to reconstruct a definitive account of that night is now impossible. What follows is Krukenberg's account of that night, which is 'unblemished'. As noted earlier, some sources differ and their version of events can be found in the footnotes.

68   Krukenberg, page 19. However, according to the '*Battle Memoir*', page 167, Brigf. Krukenberg 'ruled against its use [the subway] because he was fearful his men might be totally entrapped therein'. In response to this, such a decision to avoid the underground tunnels would seem rather ironic considering that those breaking out of the Chancellery planned to make full use of the U-Bahn and S-Bahn tunnels.

69   Ibid. Of interest to note is that when the first group to break out of the Chancellery, led by Mohnke, came to pass under the Spree through the very same S-Bahn tunnel it found itself stopped by two transport authority watchmen guarding a bulkhead that they refused to unlock. And although armed, Mohnke's group accepted the situation and returned to Friedrichstrasse station to seek another route across the Spree. So was Krukenberg actually referring to this bulkhead when he spoke of a 'solid grill'? This will probably never be known.

bring back the soldiers of 'Nordland' and the Frenchmen still in this sector. Patzak knew Berlin well. It was his native city. However, Fenet did not receive Krukenberg's orders to break off the battle and attempt to break-out northwards. Patzak disappeared en route from Stadtmitte U-Bahn station to the Air Ministry. His ultimate fate is not known.

The roads were choked off with rubble and debris. Vehicles could not pass. Without noise and in good order, 'Nordland' withdrew northwards.

Once across the Spree,[71] Krukenberg sent two officers, both born locally, to make a reconnaissance. Neither of them returned.

Around 0300 hours, Krukenberg decided to go on reconnaissance himself with his French escort. He met up with elements of 'Nordland' led by Brigf. Ziegler, which joined him. In this group were no fewer than four or five holders of the Knight's Cross, including Uscha. Vaulot.

In the meantime, day started to break, exposing the column to enemy artillery. Drawing intense fire, it about-turned in the hope of breaking out via Gesundbrunnen, towards Pankow and from there towards Wittenau.

The column followed Brunnenstrasse. By Lortzingstrasse, it again received a barrage of well-aimed mortar fire, but sought refuge in the backyard of a block of flats only to come under still more violent fire. Brigf. Ziegler, who was beside Krukenberg, was mortally wounded by shrapnel and died almost immediately.[72] Others were wounded.

Concerned that they would endanger the inhabitants hiding away in the cellars if they stayed here long, the Scandinavian and French SS volunteers set out again. Suddenly, they came under sniper fire. Faced with no way forward, they made their way back towards the city centre in order to get away from the enemy fire and consider their options.[73]

---

70   According to Tieke, Krukenberg was extremely furious at Mohnke who had attempted his break-out before he had been able to fully assemble and brief his troops. Krukenberg's decision not to issue orders to break out before 2200 hours might have resulted in the delayed assembly of his command. Now that the Russians had been alerted, Krukenberg opted to break out with those troops on hand. Also, according to the article "*Berlin 1945: Sur les traces de la division Charlemagne*", Krukenberg and an advance party moved off very promptly at 2300 hours.

71   According to the article "*Sur les traces de la division Charlemagne*", Brigf. Krukenberg and the advance party reached Weidendamm Bridge, crossed, turned left along the bank of the Spree and then turned up a side street (Elbrechtstrasse?) to await the scouts [undoubtedly the Berlin-born officers] sent out on reconnaissance. The main body of 'Nordland', some 1,500 men, now gathered at Friedrichstrasse station, attracted Russian attention and decided to get underway at 2330 hours. This was before 'Krukenberg had had a chance to report back'.

72   Le Tissier and Mabire ("*La Division Nordland*") do not agree; Ziegler is placed with Mohnke's group and his death on either Invalidenstrasse (Le Tissier) or Albrechtstrasse when advancing behind an assault gun (Mabire).

73   Le Tissier is the only source to recount that Krukenberg and the survivors of his group actually joined Mohnke's group in a disused goods yard by Stettiner Railway station sometime in the morning (before 0700 hours).

By Ziegelstrasse, Krukenberg came upon the burnt out carcass of the 'Nordland' Tiger tank he had despatched to Mohnke the day before.[74]

To greatly improve their chances of escape, Krukenberg and his men slipped into civilian clothes. It was now 1000 hours.[75] They went north via Schönhauser-Allee. And as they made their way out of the city centre they passed one Soviet patrol after another. Wearing identical clothes, they fully expected to arouse the suspicions of the Soviets, but the Soviets took no notice of them; all eyes were fixed on the fronts of the houses from where they seemed to fear some surprise.

In Pankow, Krukenberg entered the house of a railwayman to exchange clothing. Minutes later, after finding something suitable, he went back outside only to discover that his companions were not there. A woman was who told him that the Russians had taken all of them away. And, on the other side of the road, were two Soviets waiting for him. Krukenberg went straight up to them and dangled before them a gold bracelet-watch. They could not resist it. And while they argued over possession as he hoped they would he took off, disappearing in the direction of Schönholzer Park, where, for more than an hour, he searched, in vain, for his men. This convinced him that they had been taken prisoner.

Alone, Krukenberg continued on in the direction of Wilhelmsruhe. Towards 1300 hours, he was arrested by Soviet artillerymen. A Soviet NCO took hold of his Soldbuch and ripped it up, saying: "Not good!"

After crossing the Spree, those with Krukenberg were divided into groups of platoon strength.[76] One such group comprised Weber, twelve or so Frenchmen, including Appolot, Vaulot, and Rttf. Evrard of the 3rd Company, as well as German and Scandinavian SS troops. They went west. Accompanying them were two Tiger tanks.[77] They crossed the Tiergarten, but ran into strong Russian resistance along the main road through Charlottenburg. The tanks smashed through, but Vaulot was killed.[78] The survivors dispersed.

Evrard clung to Weber. He had joined him in the belief that his chances of escape would be better with a German commander than a French commander, who would not know his way about Berlin. Weber now ordered those still with him to take to the ruined buildings. They soon found themselves encircled. Their situation was hopeless. After holding off the Russians for several hours, they made their bid to escape. Some got through the Russian net and out of Berlin. Others were not so lucky. As for Evrard, he dashed across the road, rushed into a house, went down a corridor and opened a door only to find a Russian seated peacefully. Surprise was total and mutual. By the time the Russian reacted and fired a burst in his direction, he was already back across the road and running towards the house where he had been holed up since dawn.

---

74 Both Mabire and Saint-Loup record that this tank was indeed the one behind which Reichsleiter Bormann and his companions took shelter during their attempted break-out.

75 According to Saint-Loup, page 465, Krukenberg 'changed identity' at 0800 hours.

76 Saint-Loup, page 494.

77 Saint-Loup, page 495.

78 Ibid. According to the "*Battle Memoir*", Vaulot fell victim to a sniper's bullet.

In the course of the afternoon a Soviet tank took up position in front of the house defended by the German and French SS troops. The tank brought its gun to bear, but inexplicably seemed hesitant to fire.[79] German civilians suddenly appeared from the cellars, surrounded the SS soldiers and beseeched them to cease fighting. Rather than fight on, they choose to lay down their weapons. Evrard had thought of changing into civilian clothes, but dismissed the idea in favour of remaining together with his fellow compatriots in uniform. After destroying arms and ammunition, they went out to surrender.

The strange case of Reichsleiter Bormann[80]

Grenadiers François de Lannurien and Jean-Claude Dautot were the only French SS volunteers left at Stadtmitte U-Bahn station after the departure of Brigf. Krukenberg and 'Nordland' headquarters for the Chancellery. Both of them were wounded. Dautot was in such great pain that de Lannurien decided to take his comrade to a medical post for attention.

Told that there would be an SS nurse at the Chancellery, the two wounded men made their way there. Finally, after overcoming many difficulties, they reached the entrance to the Führerbunker on Vossstrasse. Admitted, they received medical care: the seriously wounded Dautot was taken away on a stretcher and de Lannurien was bandaged up. Nobody was available at present to remove the grenade splinters from his hand that were causing him more and more pain.

Two nurses brought in a stocky man who had just been seriously wounded in the face, near an eye, and who was bleeding profusely. De Lannurien noted that this newcomer was given precedence over the other wounded. So who was the newcomer? That de Lannurien did not know, but a soldier beside him told him that the newcomer was Reichsleiter Bormann. He was none the wiser!

Loneliness suddenly gripped de Lannurien. Quite convinced that some of his comrades would still be 'roaming about in the vicinity of Stadtmitte station', the rallying point, he left the Führerbunker and went in search of them. Shortly after, he joined a small group of men advancing behind a Tiger tank. In the group he thought he recognised Reichsleiter Bormann.

Combat experience had taught de Lannurien not to stay too close to a tank in battle, an obvious and irresistible target for enemy gunners and tanks. Thus, he followed the Tiger tank at a distance of some twenty metres.

Suddenly, the Tiger tank took a direct hit and exploded. De Lannurien was thrown to the ground, but those nearer the tank were killed, including the individual he believed to be Reichsleiter Bormann. His throat had been ripped wide open by a piece of shrapnel, practically severing the head from the body. De Lannurien hurried on to Stadtmitte.

Disappointment awaited de Lannurien at Stadtmitte. The only person he could find was a young, distraught looking German SS soldier behind a heavy machine gun firing off belt after belt with little concern about expending his last

79   Arguably the Russian tank crew, aware that the Berlin garrison had been formally ordered by Weidling to cease all resistance earlier in the day, were offering these obstinate defenders an opportunity to stop fighting first.

80   See Mabire, "*Mourir à Berlin*", pages 308-310, and personal conversation with de Lannurien.

ammunition. The Frenchman served him as a loader. After firing off their last round, they took to a cellar to await their inescapable fate. Minutes later, they were captured by a Russian patrol.

Fenet and the 2nd of May 1945

The night of 1st May/2nd May 1945 proved relatively quiet for Fenet and the surviving French SS troops ensconced in the Ministry of Security building. They had occupied the sector of a neighbouring company, presumably of 'Nordland', which 'had gone on an assignment' for the Chancellery.

Towards the end of the night, the Frenchmen found themselves out on their own again. Patrols were sent out. They confirmed beyond all doubt that nobody was to their left or their right.

A little later, another patrol brought back the alarming news that the front line was now running level with the Luftfahrministerium (Air Ministry) at the corner of Wilhelmstrasse and Leipzigerstrasse behind them. Exposed, Fenet took the decision to pull back to the Air Ministry, 'the last defendable position before the Chancellery'.[81]

Carrying what arms and ammunition they could, the Frenchmen pulled back to the Air Ministry. No problems were encountered. Contact was made with the forces of the Luftwaffe holding the building. No sooner had they taken up position than cars appeared from enemy lines flying white flags. Sat side by side in the cars were German and Soviet officers. They spoke of capitulation. Then came unarmed Red Army soldiers, offering cigarettes. Some Luftwaffe soldiers even started to fraternise. Other Reds appeared from behind German lines.[82]

The Luftwaffe Major commanding the soldiers in the Air Ministry approached Fenet. He announced his intentions to surrender. "It's all over", he added. "The capitulation has been signed." Fenet could not believe that it was all over. That was impossible. Nevertheless, despite a quite magnificent display of dedication and bravery, they had lost.

Fenet decided to go and see at first hand what was happening at the Reichs Chancellery. Defiantly, he thought to himself: "And if there is one last square to form, it's there that we will form it." Besides, to remain at the Air Ministry would be to foolishly invite capture.

Again they picked up their weapons and boxes of ammunition. Each carried a panzerfaust across his shoulder. They left the building without responding to the

81   Saint-Loup, page 493.

82   Fenet, page 29, [and repeated by Mabire, page 315]. However, according to Saint-Loup, pages 499-501, when Fenet arrived at the Air Ministry, it was packed full of military, paramilitary and party personnel in a rainbow of uniform colours, but all seemed to be without fight. Told that the Führer was dead, Fenet answered haughtily that he did not believe a word of it. Then he went off to speak to the commanding officer, a Colonel, about organising the fight. He found him busy getting a white flag sewn together. The Colonel told him the war was over, adding they would capitulate at 0800 hours. Overwhelmed, Fenet returned to his men. Behind a pillar he surprised two of them burning their papers. He said nothing. Day broke. The roads started to fill with civilians. Then came the Red Army soldiers, offering cigarettes.

Russians warmly calling out to them to lay down their weapons. An unnerving silence had descended over the city. The road was swarming with civilians and unarmed German soldiers. Fenet took to the ruins to avoid contact with marauding Russian patrols.

Bringing up the rear was Rostaing. Suddenly a Russian appeared beside him. Lost in thought, he had not seen or heard him approach. The Russian ordered him to throw down his weapon. His response was to run off in the direction taken by his comrades.[83] There was no shot. He rejoined Fenet and continued on through the silent ruins.

Via an air vent, they entered the underground system that offered them their best chances of survival and also of reaching the Reichs Chancellery undetected. In this way, they came to Stadtmitte U-Bahn station, of late Krukenberg's command post. There was not a living soul to be seen. They continued on to Kaiserhof U-Bahn station, across from the Chancellery.

Arriving at the station, they noted an iron ladder that went all the way up to a ventilation grill at road level. Fenet went up. His injured foot was still hurting him. As he climbed, he listened for the noise of battle, but only heard a heavy rumbling of motor vehicles. This puzzled him. Just a few more rungs to go now. Finally he could see.

Fenet could not believe the sight before him: Russian troops and vehicles as far as the eye could see. The Chancellery was in ruins and holed by artillery and small weapons fire. Also, there was not a single German field-grey uniform to be seen. So it was all over. He came back down without saying a word.

For those below, it had been an agonising wait for news. They surrounded Fenet. He announced that the Russians were everywhere and that the Führer was certainly dead. Their heads lowered silently.

Despair gripped some. A young Uscha. asked Rostaing if they should don civilian clothes. His reply was typical of the professional soldier he was: "We did not come here to disguise ourselves." Even so, the realisation of defeat had brought him to tears. Nevertheless, he added: "We will continue."

For Fenet, the only solution was to get out of here and then to try and break-out in the direction of Potsdam where Army Wenck should be. He intended to make use of the underground system for as long as he possibly could and then take advantage of night to complete the rest of the journey. All agreed with him. They still lived in hope: the distance from the Chancellery to Potsdam was less than that from Körlin to the river Oder.[84]

Without making the slightest noise, they now made for Potsdamer Platz. They had to climb over fallen debris and sometimes dig their way through collapsed sections with hand or bayonet, but they kept going. At Potsdamer Platz, a 'cruel

83   Rostaing, page 205. Also, according to Saint-Loup, page 502, Rostaing lost his revolver to the Russian. It was a magnificent American colt which he had 'spirited away' from a *Milicien* at Wildflecken.

84   Fenet, page 28. However, according to Rostaing, page 206, the Russians had invested the underground system and were firing on them. This left the French survivors with no other choice than to disappear into the underground tunnels. Also, Rostaing writes that they were pursued part of the way.

deception' awaited them: scouts reported that the underground continued over ground.

It would soon be midday. This, of course, made it impossible to continue following the railway lines in the open air. And so it was decided to hide out in this underground maze and wait for nightfall before trying their luck again. They split into small groups and vanished from sight one after another. One of the tunnels opening under a bridge arch cluttered with fallen debris and assorted objects offered them excellent hiding places.

Some old men of the Volkssturm arrived. They too had the same idea as the French SS survivors. Slow to hide, they attracted the attention of a Soviet patrol that arrived unexpectedly moments later. The first to be captured cried out: "Don't shoot! Don't shoot!" The Russians then proceeded to search the whole area and small groups of Frenchmen were discovered one after another.

The search, however, was not thorough. Fenet, von Wallenrodt, Douroux, Georges and Bicou went undiscovered: cleverly, they had hidden themselves behind a pile of wicker baskets. From there, with their heart in their mouth, they had witnessed the capture of their comrades. All of a sudden the wicker baskets parted and Albert-Brunet slipped in beside them, murmuring: "I want to stay with you. This is not the time to leave!" He stayed. The search was continuing. They held their breath each time the Russians passed by. Their hearts were racing. On several occasions the Russians actually stopped before this pile of wicker baskets, but looked no further. Fink was captured in turn some ten metres from them and was heard to shout out to his comrades: "Surrender as National Socialists."

The prisoners were assembled, counted and recounted by a Russian officer and then marched off. Fenet looked at his watch: only one hour had passed. Would night never come?

Suddenly, the sound of footsteps and voices: yet more Russians. The enemy was returning. This time the search was much more thorough. Nonetheless, twice they passed the hideout of Fenet and the other survivors. Squeezed up against one another, the six Frenchmen felt like hunted animals. However, they did not give up hope.

The end was all very sudden. With rifle butts and boots, the Russians smashed their way through the shield of wicker baskets and 'pounced' on the six Frenchmen. They were searched and stripped of their possessions: watches first, then weapons! The time was after 1500 hours.[85]

The prisoners were dragged outside. Lorries full of Russian troops, who were singing and playing the accordion, were criss-crossing Potsdamer Platz. Groups were staggering about blind drunk. One Russian called out to the French SS prisoners as they passed by: "Hitler kaputt!" With a bitter grin, von Wallenrodt replied: "Ja, Hitler kaputt!" Another promised them the charms of Siberia. Others pretended to shoot them down with invisible rifles, yelling: "SS ... Puk! Puk! Kaputt!" Yet another, who noticed that Fenet was limping, deplored his comrade who had only managed to wound Fenet in the foot instead of blowing his head off. 'The dance of the scalping began'.[86]

85   Saint-Loup, page 508.
86   Fenet, page 30.

The guards marched the prisoners away. Marching beside Fenet was Albert-Brunet. A drunken Red grabbed him by the arm and dragged him off towards a neighbouring house, but one of the guards was quick to intervene and brought his prisoner back to the column.[87] Albert-Brunet said to Fenet: "I had a narrow escape."

The drunken Russian, however, was not to be denied his revenge: he came running back, grabbed hold of the young Frenchmen once again, drew his pistol and, screaming: "SS! SS!", fired point-blank. Albert-Brunet fell at Fenet's feet with a hole in his temple. Noting that the prisoners were slowing, the guards hurriedly pushed them forward. The prisoners continued on their way.

The prisoners were marched past the Chancellery, 'their last hope', which was being looted by Red Army soldiers. Hundreds and hundreds of tanks flying Red flags were parading from the Tiergarten to the Brandenburg Gate whose disfigured silhouette defiantly reared up towards the grey sky.

Rostaing and sixteen other French survivors were captured at Potsdamer Platz around midnight. A voice woke them with an ultimatum: either they surrender or the station would be blown up. When they did not reply the ultimatum was repeated in French. They looked at each other. What else could they do? With arms raised, they came out of hiding. This was not the time to antagonise the battle-happy Russian soldiers.

Their watches were taken first, followed by everything in their pockets: papers, photos, money, and jewellery. Their captors repeatedly asked if they were SS or had destroyed tanks. They gave no reply. Hours before, they had ripped off their collar insignia and arm badges, but one of them had forgotten to remove two silver 'tank destruction' emblems on his sleeve. A Soviet NCO saw them and flew into a towering rage, screaming at him, and then punching and kicking him. Suddenly, he drew his pistol and executed him with a bullet in the head. Was this to be the fate of all?

As for the other prisoners, they were lined up against a wall, convinced that their last hour had come. Rostaing was strangely calm. To his right was an eighteen-year-old volunteer by the name of Kapar. He was crying. He had shown exceptional courage throughout the battle for Berlin, but now his nerves had gone to pieces. Rostaing tried to reassure him.

Just then a drunken Russian officer entered the courtyard, holding a bottle at arms length. Staggering across, he finally stopped before Rostaing and started to question him in Russian. Thankfully, Rostaing knew the language and explained that they were Frenchmen who had been forced to serve alongside the Germans. Rostaing must have been convincing as the officer ordered those with raised weapons to lower them and move away. The officer then told Rostaing to get his men into a column and follow him. He was only too happy to oblige.[88]

87   According to Saint-Loup, page 509, Albert-Brunet had drawn attention to himself because he was wearing on his (right upper) sleeve four silver emblems each denoting the single-handed destruction of an enemy tank [or other armoured fighting vehicle]. So frightful had been the Russian losses in tanks and crews during the Battle of Berlin that the sight of these emblems would have incensed their comrades.

88   Rostaing, pages 211 to 213.

By way of a conclusion, years later, Krukenberg summed up the contribution of the French Waffen SS volunteers to the defense of Berlin:[89]

"Without the Frenchmen, the Russians would have taken Berlin eight days sooner ... "

Praise indeed, but they are credited with knocking out some fifty Red Army tanks.[90]

---

89   "*Historia #32*", page 137.
90   Krukenberg, page 15. This number, however, does not include those knocked out after 29th April. Thus, the final tally was undoubtedly higher. Indeed, according to Mabire, page 321, in one week of battle for Berlin, troops of the Waffen-SS knocked out some 800 Russian tanks and armoured vehicles.

CHAPTER 15

'Charlemagne' and Its End in Mecklenburg

On the morning of 24th April 1945, with the return of two lorries that had not made it through from the Berlin-bound convoy, 'Charlemagne' totalled some 700 men[1] garrisoned in and around Neustrelitz. Of this number, 300 were combatants of SS-Bataillon 58 and headquarters and support staff. The other 400 were workers of the Baubataillon [Construction battalion]. The revised structure and command of 'Charlemagne' was as follows:[2]

Commander:	SS-Staf. Zimmermann
Adjoint:	W-Stubaf. Boudet-Gheusi
V.O. and office I/C:	SS-Ustuf. Bender
Office II/AB:	W-Ostuf. Bénétoux
?	W-Ostuf. Audibert
?	W-Ustuf. Radici (orderly officer of Boudet-Gheusi)

SS-Bataillon 58

Commander:	SS-Hstuf. Kroepsch
Assistant:	Haensel
Kompanie 5/58:	W-Std.Ju. Aumon
Kompanie 7/58:	W-Ostuf. Fatin
Kompanie 8/58:	W-Ustuf. Sarrailhé

Baubataillon (unchanged since its formation)

Commander:	W-Hstuf. Roy
Assistant:	W-Ustuf. Martret
1 Kompanie:	W-Ostuf. Roumégous
2 Kompanie:	W-Ostuf. Géromini
3 Kompanie:	W-Ostuf. Darrigade
San-und Vet-Staffel	
Office IV/B:	W-Ostuf.Dr. Métais
Office IV/D:	W-Ustuf. Verney
Fahrkolonne	
Office IV/A:	SS-Hstuf. Hagen

1 According to Halard, letter to the author of 26/9/98, he left in a second small convoy to Berlin, but got no further than Oranienburg. Thereupon the Frenchmen formed a kampfgruppe with comrades from 'Nordland'. In response to this, curiously, no authors or any other veterans questioned by the author have made mention of a second convoy to Berlin. However, if true, then the figure would be less than that quoted.

2 Soulat, page 118.

Office I/B: SS-Ostuf. Meier

With SS-Staf. Zimmermann still hospitalised, Stubaf. Boudet-Gheusi commanded 'Charlemagne'.

Regiment 'Charlemagne' remained subordinated to the 3rd Panzer Army of Army Group Vistula.

Orders were received to man the anti-tank positions around Carpin and Fürstensee. One company of SS-Bataillon 58 was deployed to Carpin and the two others across the Berlin-Neustrelitz road, south of Neustrelitz.[3]

On the morning of 25th April, at anti-tank positions around Drewin, Oberjunker Decongnck and twenty men of the Baubataillon were working away when up drew a convoy of some twenty trucks and out of a car stepped RF-SS Himmler in person. Decongnck presented his men to Himmler who gave him some words of support and encouragement.[4]

On the evening of the 26th, the 3rd Panzer Army radioed 'Charlemagne' that the Soviets had reached the line Prenzlau-Pasewalk.

On the 27th, the front was pierced at Prenzlau. At 1000 hours, Soviet armour was reported in the region of Woldeck, thirty kilometres north-east of Carpin, and Feldberg, fifteen kilometres east of Carpin.

In the late afternoon, Stubaf. Boudet-Gheusi relocated 'Charlemagne' headquarters five kilometres westwards to Zinow, behind the anti-tank positions.

On the morning of the 28th, Rttf. Soulat of the headquarters staff was heartened by the appearance of a Heer panzer division moving forward to Carpin. However, its counterattack towards Woldeck came to nothing. The Soviets continued to advance. That evening at 1800 hours, they occupied the former 'Charlemagne' garrison town of Bergfeld.

At 2100 hours, Stubaf. Boudet-Gheusi withdrew 'Charlemagne' headquarters by truck to Neustrelitz and sent the company manning the anti-tank positions around Carpin, now relieved by the Wehrmacht, to rejoin the main body of Bataillon 58 around Drewin and Fürstensee.

The situation was critical. The Soviets were closing in on Neustrelitz from the south-east and the north.

Bataillon 58 or Bataillon Kroepsch started the day of Sunday the 29th positioned as follows:

Kompanie 5/58:	facing south manning the anti-tank barricades on the Berlin-Neustrelitz main road
Kompanie 7/58:	to the left of Kompanie 5/58
Kompanie 8/58:	facing east astride the road from Fürstensee to Wokuhl

Kompanie 8/58 saw action, destroying 2 or 3 Soviet tanks.[5]

---

3   The date of deployment is not known. It may have been as late as the 27th.

4   Cited in the *souvenirs* of Soulat.

5   Soulat, page 118. Of note is that Marotin of an unidentified 'combatant' company [presumably of Bataillon 58 because he was armed] and a small group of artillerymen still with artillery guns did brief battle with the Russians at nightfall on the 28th and managed to immobilise a tank before withdrawing. (See "*La longue*

Stubaf. Boudet-Gheusi went to speak with the Kampfkommandant of Neustrelitz. He took along Rttf. Soulat of the headquarters staff as an interpreter. However, his services were not required. To their great surprise, the Kampfkommandant was, in fact, Oberst von Massow who spoke French. He authorised the withdrawal of Bataillon Kroepsch, but insisted that Boudet-Gheusi also obtain the prior agreement of the Kommandeur of the German division holding the sector. However, his whereabouts was not known. So off went Boudet-Gheusi in search of him and this phantom division! He was back one hour later. The withdrawal could now go ahead.

Bataillon Kroepsch was relieved and, at 1400 hours, left Neustrelitz along the road to Wesenberg. This was the only 'escape route' left open to it. Westwards it retreated, with the Russians in pursuit. Air attacks were also the 'constant companion' of Bataillon Kroepsch.

Also 'on the road' were the headquarters staff and the *train auto*. The plan was to reach the region of Schwerin and from there continue onto Lübeck and perhaps even Denmark.

The roads were full of soldiers wearing all manner of uniform. It seemed as though every organisation of the Third Reich, be they military or paramilitary, was represented. They too were retreating westwards away from the Russians.

By the evening of Tuesday 1st May 1945, 'Charlemagne' headquarters staff, the *train auto* and Bataillon Kroepsch had reached the region of Schwerin. In a village east of lake Schwerin, the headquarters staff were approached by 'POWs of 1939–40'. Wearing a mocking smile across their face, the POWs were quick to inform the headquarters staff that the English had launched an offensive across the river Elbe and that 'the English radio' [arguably the BBC world service] now reported them some thirty kilometres away. After thanking them for the information, the headquarters staff responded that the Russians were only ten kilometres away. This news wiped the smile off their face. They too did not want to fall into Russian hands! They ran off to warn their colleagues.

At nightfall, the headquarters staff continued on. Two hours later, the convoy stopped for the night in a village near Bad Kleinen, north of Schwerin.

Early next morning, a German Oberscharführer of the Inspection brought Stubaf. Boudet-Gheusi the news that the English had occupied Bobitz which was only three kilometres away. If true, Lübeck was now of the question. It was. This meant that 'Charlemagne' was completely encircled in a vast pocket between the English and the Russians. And the pocket was contracting by the hour.

Then, via radio, came the OKW announcement that the Führer had just died in Berlin during the fighting for the Chancellery. For Soulat, with the Führer dead, the war was definitely lost. He no longer wished to fight on.

At 0900 hours, Stubaf. Boudet-Gheusi assembled the fifty Germans and Frenchmen of the headquarters staff still with him. He ordered the Germans to 'try and join any formation of the Wehrmacht' or alternately to try and reach German lines. Soulat wondered to himself where they were going to find German lines. As for the Frenchmen, Stubaf. Boudet-Gheusi gave them the option of surrendering

marche", page 79.) However, it is not known if these engagements are one and the same.

to the English with him or of putting on civilian clothes and trying to pass themselves off as prisoners or repatriated workers.

With emotion, Soulat shook hands with the *Spiess* of the Stabsquartier, he had always been decent, and with several other loyal comrades. He chose to surrender in uniform whereas nearly all of the Frenchmen put on civilian clothes. Besides, he bore the 'SS tattoo' which would be discovered sooner or later.

Arms and ammunition that the Germans could not take with them was disposed of in a marsh. Off went the Germans in the direction of nearby woods. At their head was Swiss Ustuf. Bender. They were swallowed up.

In turn, 'the civilians' dispersed. Eight Frenchmen in uniform remained behind in the village to await the enemy. They were Stubaf. Boudet-Gheusi, Ostuf. Bénétoux and Métais, Ustuf. Radici, Hscha. Sergant, Rttf. Mignol and Soulat, and the orderly of Boudet-Gheusi.

The hours passed. Turning to all, Stubaf. Boudet-Gheusi said: "Be sure to say that you are not SS but *légionnaires*." Soulat, for one, did not have the heart to reply to him but was quite determined to do nothing of the sort. He was SS.

In the early afternoon, Boudet-Gheusi decided to make haste to Bobitz and surrender to the English. The Russians were just too close to comfort and he had no wish to fall into their hands.

The eight Frenchmen followed the railway line to Bobitz. At 1500 hours, they came to Bobitz railway station and a motorcyclist of the English Army who did not even look at them until Boudet-Gheusi called out to him in English. The motorcyclist told them to continue along the same way. Soulat noted to himself that for the second time in five years he was on the side of the defeated.

At the level crossing, they came upon a column of tanks. Presenting himself to an English tank officer as the *chef* of the *Légion des Volontaires Français contre le Bolchevisme*, Boudet-Gheusi asked to be taken to an English General. He wished to defend the interests of his men held as prisoners. He and Radici, a good friend whom he chose to accompany him, were actually taken before a Major who exploded, saying: "Since you are the *commandant* of the *légion française antibolcheviste*, we're going to take you to Wismar [and] to the Russians who have just occupied the city and you will sort it out with them."

In disbelief, Boudet-Gheusi even asked himself if this was a joke. However, it seemed all too real when he found himself aboard the superstructure of a tank taking him and Radici to the Communist lines.

It was dark now. Needless to say, the two French SS officers decided to escape. Boudet-Gheusi was the first to make a move. He jumped and ran off into the night. Radici was about to follow him, but held back after noticing that the following tank had seen Boudet-Gheusi make his escape. The column came to a stop and went in search of Boudet-Gheusi, but he was long gone. As for Radici, reasoning that he was only a simple second Lieutenant and thus of little or no interest, the English released him. Thereafter the two officers joined the mass of anonymous prisoners of war.

And what became of the other elements of 'Charlemagne' on the run from the Russians? Kompanie 5/58 was still some sixty-strong when it arrived south of Schwerin. By now, it was literally sandwiched between the Americans and the Soviets. On 1st or 2nd May, after firing off its last bullets at the Soviets, it turned and surrendered to the Americans.

On 1st May 1945, two inhabitants of Neustrelitz came across the lifeless corpses of two W-SS soldiers. Their throats had been cut which suggests that they had been killed after their capture by the Soviets. Sadly the two W-SS soldiers were undoubtedly Frenchmen of 'Charlemagne'.[6]

The end of the Construction Battalion

For W-Ustuf. Martret, life at Drewin with the Construction Battalion was like a prison sentence. He had wanted to go to Berlin, but orders are orders. However, later on, if it were not for his personal intervention then the name of 'Charlemagne' could have been tainted with war crimes. This situation arose when a train from the Swedish Red Cross stopped quite unexpectedly beside the camp of the Construction Battalion and down stepped SS auxiliaries and female deportees from concentration camp Ravensbrück. They started to look around. Martret looked on from the camp. The deportees, wearing blue and white striped suits, seemed in good health. Even so, their arrival disturbed him, for he had no wish to leave himself open to prosecution as a war criminal. He took action. Gun in hand, he led his armed guard of ten men out to confront the SS auxiliaries. He told them that there was nothing for them here and that if they did not move on he would fire. And yes, he meant it. They did not argue. The train whistled. All boarded. The train continued to the north.

During the night of 27–28 April 1945, the Construction Battalion withdrew to Waren, north-west of Neustrelitz. From Waren, it retreated westwards through Güstrow. Air attacks inflicted losses. With the Americans and Russians closing in, Hstuf. Roy, on the advice of Ostuf. Géromini, decided to disband the battalion.[7] At that same moment, American tanks appeared. The battalion scattered. It suffered yet more losses. Another group was surprised and overrun by a Russian vanguard. Such was the ironic end of those who had chosen to continue with the pick and shovel in their hands rather than weapons.

In the evening of 1st May 1945, Uscha. Fronteau of the Construction Battalion arrived at Schwerin, where he spent the night in a bunker. The following day, he learnt of the Führer's death. Continuing west, he was captured by the Americans ten kilometres west of Schwerin. At the end of May, he was handed over to the British at the former concentration camp of Neuengamme.

Unable to make it through a cordon of sentries, Hstuf. Roy and Ustuf. Martret went into British captivity at Bad Kleinen, north of Schwerin. This, however, was not the end of their adventure. Handed a change of clothes and identity papers by German prisoners of war who knew of their situation, they managed to make good their escape. They tried to make it back to France, but four or five days later they were recaptured by French forces. This time it was the end. Martret was to reflect,

6   Research provided by Soulat, letters to the author, 5/2/98 and 12/2/98.
7   Soulat was to meet in prison members of the *Baubataillon* who assured him that Roy had already started to negotiate the embarkation of his unit for Sweden with the Swedish consul at Schwerin, but the Russian advance had put paid to its realisation (*souvenirs* of Soulat.) In response to this, Martret, who was with Roy throughout the retreat and when the *Baubataillon* was disbanded, has no recollection of Roy entering into any such negotiations. Undoubtedly, this was nothing more than rumour or wishful thinking.

years later, that he should have stayed and hid out in Germany until such time as the 'coast was clear' to return home.

To the end with 'Horst Wessel'?

On 20th April 1945, a group of French volunteers of the W-SS joined a kampfgruppe of 'Horst Wessel' commanded by SS-Hstuf. Heinz Dittmann.[8] Unfortunately, no other information has surfaced about this group.

8   See volume 1 of "*Im letzten Aufgebot 1944-45*". Dittmann died on 15th June 1998.

CHAPTER 16

The French Waffen-SS in the West

Wildflecken

Having supplied a *battalion de marche* (or in German a Feldersatz-Btl) to fill the depleted ranks of 'Charlemagne', the resultant order of battle of the französischen Ausbildungs-und-Ersatz-Bataillon [Franz. A.-u.-E. Btl.] garrisoned at Greifenberg was as follows:

Commander:	SS-Ostubaf. Hersche
1. Ausbildungskompanie:	SS-Ustuf. Schueler
Stammkompanie:	SS-Ostuf. Allgeier
Rekrutenkompanie:	W-Ostuf. Crespin

Before the Soviet advance through Pomerania, the französischen Ausbildungs-und-Ersatz-Bataillon evacuated Greifenberg and relocated to Wildflecken camp.

At Wildflecken, the battalion joined other various elements of 'Charlemagne' that had not been sent to Pomerania or were still in training. After purging itself of some 250 'undesirable and doubtful'[1] men, the battalion was still some 400 strong.

On 18th March 1945, Reichsführer-SS Himmler ordered the französischen Ausbildungs-und-Ersatz-Bataillon to rejoin the *33. Waffen-Grenadier-Division der SS 'Charlemagne' (franz. Nr. 1)*. This order was not executed immediately.[2]

On 20th March 1945, the forty-strong Workshop Company was sent to Fulda railway station, where it was employed to keep the heavily bombed railway system operational. It worked alongside Hungarian soldiers and French POWs. Then, on the 22nd, the Frenchmen in field-grey and also in khaki attended to a bombed train carrying cheese. There was cheese everywhere. Of course, all helped themselves; they were hungry and they were French! However, the scene turned ugly when, for whatever reason, a French SS officer shot dead a French POW. The officer then phoned Wildflecken camp and attempted to justify his shooting of the POW by stating that all his soldiers were stealing cheese. Thus, on the return of the Company to Wildflecken late that night, all were searched. And all, with the exception of one or two men who had come to learn of the officer's phone call and rightly feared repercussions, were found with cheese on them. In this way, almost to a man, the entire Workshop Company was transferred to the Penal Company.

French SS Regiment 59?

Ostubaf. Hersche organised the estimated 1,200 French volunteers of the Waffen-SS at Wildflecken into the following units:

---

1   Soulat, page 49.
2   The reason for this is not known to the author.

Marschbataillon (in French *Bataillon de Marche*) under SS-Stubaf. Katzian of three battle-ready companies.

Sonderbataillon (in French *Bataillon spécial*) under SS-Stubaf. von Lölhöffel of two *compagnies de travailleurs* (Construction companies) and the Penal Company.[4]

Train de combat and the Workshop Company still under Ostuf. Maudhuit.[5]

Counted among the three battle-ready companies of the *bataillon de marche* were the two depot and education companies which had been based at Greifenberg and relocated to Wildflecken late February 1945. Ustuf. Kreis commanded one of the three companies.

The 'Special' Battalion was some 400 strong, but only equipped with two spades and four picks![6] Its morale was low. SS-Stubaf. von Lölhöffel had at his disposal French officers (in alphabetical order) Ostuf. Dupeyron, Ostuf. Dupuyau, possibly Ostuf. Perrin, Ustuf. Raillard, born in 1911, and possibly Ostuf. de Rose.

Ostuf. Dupuyau was the former commander of the divisional Signals Company of 'Charlemagne'. He counted himself among those who had managed to make it out of the 'hell of Pomerania' unscathed. His military background was the same as that of Gaston Raillard; both had attended and graduated from the *Ecole militaire d'infanterie de Saint-Maixent* with the rank of *sous-lieutenant d'active*. [Their roles within the 'Special' Battalion are not known.]

As for Henri Dupeyron, in 1936, he was commissioned *sous-lieutenant* in the reserves.[7] He is known to have served briefly with the FLAK Company. However, for whatever reason, he did not accompany this unit to the front.[8]

W-Ostuf. Henri Victor Louis-Paul,[9] born on 5th February 1898 in the Lot-et-Garonne, commanded the Penal Company. Of late, the company had shed itself of fifty men by lorry to Dachau.

The two battalions and 'odds and ends' have appeared under different titles; Soulat cites *régiment No 59*;[10] Saint-Loup cites *59e régiment d'infanterie*; Mabire cites a regiment without a number; and Landwehr cites SS March Regiment 'Charlemagne'. In response to this, none of the titles are supported by official wartime documentation. However, as previously noted, on 18th March 1945, RF-SS Himmler ordered the franz. Ausbildungs-und-Ersatz-Bataillon to rejoin the Division. Thus, the possibility exists that all French Waffen-SS units present at

3   Soulat, page 112. However, different authors have cited different titles for this battalion; according to Saint-Loup, page 393, its title was "*Bataillon de travailleurs*" [Construction Battalion] and according to Landwehr, its title was 'Special Use'.
4   According to Oertle, page 308, the Sonderbataillon also comprised a Divisions-Kampfzug (or in French *section de combat divisionnaire*).
5   Maud'huit may now have held the rank of Hauptsturmführer.
6   Saint-Loup, page 394.
7   Dupeyron was probably ex-*Milice*.
8   One should not read too much into this. Perhaps he was sick or away on a training course.
9   Louis-Paul was probably of *Milice* origin.
10   While based at Carpin Soulat recalls (letter to the author of 8/9/98) having heard this designation during a telephone conversation he had with Wildflecken.

Wildflecken were subordinated to the Franz. A.-u.-E. Btl. and should appear as such under this title.[11]

In late March, advancing American forces of General Patton's Third Army neared Wildflecken camp. During the night of 28th/29th March 1945, the Workshop Company evacuated Wildflecken.[12] The march of the Workshop Company was as follows:[13]

Night of the 28th to 29th March: depart Wildflecken camp. Cross the communities of Oberbach, Bad Kissingen and Schweinfurt.

3rd April: stop at Bamberg.

4th to 12th April: stationed at Bayreuth.

Evening of 12th April: stop in a village situated 10 kilometres from Truppenübungsplatz Grafenwohr.

13th April: continue retreating-direction Weiden, stop at Schwandorf.

16th April: Regensburg.

17th April: Egmuhl.

18th to 23rd April: stop in a village close to Ergolsbach.

Evening of 23rd April: continue retreating-direction Landshut.

24th April: arrive at Landshut. Company is transferred to 38. SS-Grenadier-Division 'Nibelungen'.

During the night of 30th/31st March 1945, the 'Regiment' left Wildflecken for Neustrelitz where 'Chalemagne' was reforming. The 'Regiment' was on foot. American armour was now less than twenty kilometres away.

The 'Regiment' went Bischofsheim, Mellrichstadt, Rttschenhausen and Meiningen.[14] Enemy aerial activity was intense. Halting for the first time, the column was attacked by some ten planes. On 1st April 1945, the 'Regiment' quartered in a small village some seventy kilometres from Wildflecken, but had to withdraw that night before advancing American armour, only to enter another village at dawn on the 2nd at the same time as American tanks!

By forced march day and night, and by evading the main roads interdicted by enemy air attacks, the 'Regiment' managed to stay ahead of the American armour. From Meiningen, it marched eastward to Schleusingen, and then Eisfeld, Sonneberg and Kronach before reaching Hof on 13th April, but Hersche now had

---

11   Of course, the regiment could have been formed after the 18th.
12   According to Soulat, page 112, Mabire, page 333, Landwehr, page 170, and Saint-Loup, page 393, the decision to begin the evacuation of Wildflecken was made on the 29th. Curiously, this does not explain how the Workshop Company came to evacuate the camp the night before.
13   Courtesy of Henri Mounine.
14   Oertle, page 308. However, according to Soulat, letter to the author of 29/7/99, after Rttschenhausen, the French column went to Römhild.

problems. The column had started to disintegrate and troops desert. First to break up was the Penal Company, whose morale was non-existent. Next to decompose was the 'Special' Battalion, whose morale was no better than that of the Penal Company. 400 strong at Meiningen, there were 300 left at Eisfeld and 200 at Sonneberg.

On 13th April 1945, at Hof, Ogruf. Berger, chief of the SS Hauptamt, spoke in person to the French SS troops. He announced that they would not be going to Mecklenburg, but instead to Bavaria, to the 'Alpine Redoubt', where the Reich would conduct its last-ditch stand.[15]

On the following day, the 14th, the 'Regiment' took a train journey from Marktredwitz[16] to the town of Regensburg on the Danube. By now, its strength had dwindled to around six hundred men. It would be unfair to contribute this reduction solely to desertions. The general confusion and the arduous march would have also taken their toll. Indeed, many might have felt no longer bound to their oath which, to them, was to fight Bolshevism and only Bolshevism.

That same day at Regensburg, the Marschbataillon of the 'Regiment' split into two when Ostubaf. Hersche attached part to the 38. SS-Grenadier-Division 'Nibelungen'.[17]

On foot, the 'Regiment' continued south.

On the 18th, near Wartenberg, elements of the 'Regiment'[18] fought a delaying action and were swept aside. That same day, the Penal Company was disbanded. Strmm. Vaxelaire now marched with the 1st Company.

The 'Regiment' continued south.[19]

On the 28th, before advancing American forces, the main body of the 'Regiment',[20] now re-equipped, crossed Landshut and came to the small town of Moosburg at the confluence of rivers Isar and Amper.

On 29th April 1945, elements of the 'Regiment' went into the front line. With Dutch SS troops of 'Nibelungen', Dupeyron's Company (probably of the Sonderbataillon) and the 5th Company (or 5th *Compagnie de marche*) under Ostuf. Kreis guarded a bridge over the Amper.[21]

At 1100 hours, the first American tank appeared. SS-Ostuf. Burkhardt of 'Nibelungen' knocked it out with a panzerfaust. The defenders, however, were hampered by a lack of ammunition. Kreis then resorted to a ruse: in a meadow

15 Mabire, page 333. However, according to Saint-Loup, page 402, the attempt to reach Krukenberg at Neustrelitz failed because of the breakdown of the railway network.

16 Mabire, page 332. However, the column may have boarded a train at Bayreuth (see Saint-Loup, page 399).

17 Saint-Loup, page 402.

18 According to Soulat, page 91, the elements were from those attached to 'Nibelungen'. However, according to Oertle, page 309, the elements were from the Sonderbataillon (Special bataillon).

19 According to Oertle, page 308, on the 18th, the first column of the *Marschbataillon* with the headquarters staff arrived at Lindkirchen. From Lindkirchen, it went Mainburg and Pfaffenhofen.

20 Probably, the elements of the Marschbataillon attached to 'Nibelungen' and those of the Sonderbataillon.

21 Soulat, page 92.

bordering the river he placed hundreds of uniforms and helmets found in a depot. The Americans fell for it and, in the afternoon, three large waves of bombers pounded the meadow![22]

On the following day, the 30th, the Americans forced their way across the Amper to find both French SS companies in position along the Isar and with ammunition for their machine-guns.[23] They held for twenty-four hours before being forced to withdraw.

Strmm. Vaxelaire remembers the 30th well. He was in Moosburg. Exhausted, he and a good friend took a rest in a farm. His feet were a bloody pulp. The farmer brought him warm water for them. And it was here that the Americans overran them. Vaxelaire noted that the Americans were sympathetic. One of them even told Vaxelaire of his sorrow at what they had done to the German cities, adding that he did not understand why.

Elements of the 'Regiment' now went their own way.

One group, comprising elements of the Marschbataillon and the headquarters staff, went Traunstein, Salzburg, Hallein, Bad Reichenhall, Lofer and Reit im Winkel.[24] And it was here that on the night of 8–9 May 1945 Staf. Hersche[25] and this group went into American captivity.

A splinter group, including Ostuf. Kreis, made for Italy. Ostubaf. Gamory-Dubourdeau, attached of late to the SS Hauptamt in Berlin, joined the group at Innsbruck. Together Gamory-Dubourdeau and the group travelled through the Brenner Pass and onto Bolzano in the South Tyrol where they surrendered to the Americans, having first obtained a concession that none of them would be handed over to their compatriots for one year.[26]

Another group, comprising the remnants of the Sonderbataillon—Ostuf. Maudit, Ostuf. de Rose and some fifty men—made for Innsbruck. On 5th May 1945, they were captured by the Americans on the east bank of the Chiemsee.[27]

Specifically, the march of the Medical unit from Wildflecken was as follows:[28]

Night of the 30th to 31st March: depart Wildflecken. Stop at Nordheim.

Night of the 31st March to 1st April (Sunday): stop at Bauerbach.

Night of the 1st to 2nd April: Closter-Vestra.

Night of the 2nd to 3rd April: Crock (Brünn).

Evening of the 3rd April: embark at Eisfel-then Sonneberg, Pressig, Aïla.

---

22   Saint-Loup, page 402, presumably as told to Saint-Loup by Kreis.
23   Ibid. However, Soulat states that the Americans managed to get across the Amper around midday on 29th April (see page 92).
24   Oertle, page 309. However, according to Mabire, page 334, the French SS men 'continued towards Rosenheim' where word of Hitler's death was received.
25   Hersche was promoted to Standartenführer on 1st May 1945. On this same day, he was awarded the EK II and also the KVK II.
26   Landwehr implies that the Americans were as good as their word.
27   Soulat, page 92.
28   Courtesy of Henri Mounine.

Night of the 4th to 5th April: Aïla, Langenbach. Here to Sunday 8th April.

Night of the 8th to 9th April: Bad Steben, then Bug on Bruck.

Night of the 11th to 12th April: Hof. Depart in the afternoon of the 12th.

13th April: embark at Kirchenlamitz, south of Hof, then Weiden, Schwandorf, Regensburg. That same evening arrive at Obertraubling.

Night of the 13th to 14th April: Obertraubling.

14th April to the evening: depart, arrive at Alteglossheim.

15th April: Alteglossheim.

Night of the 15th to 16th April: stop unknown.

Night of the 16th to 17th April: Sandelzhausen.

Night of the 24th to 25th April: depart Sandelzhausen, arrive to the north of Mainburg.

Night of the 27th to 28th April: depart. Cross Moosburg.

Sunday 29th April: disengage: depart, direction Dorfen, then Haaz.

30th April: arrive at Wasserburg.

1st May: in the vicinity of Rosenheim. Dispersion.

Not all of the Frenchmen at Wildflecken went with Hersche and the 'Regiment'. One of those 'left behind' was André Doulard. He remembers:

> Towards 15th or 16th April 1945, I ended up isolated with two other comrades as a rear echelon at Wildflecken. There was nothing to do. We then decided to don the tracksuit after having of course unstitched the SS runes.
>
> The American troops approached. We thus left due west hoping to slip through the net and get back to France. One early afternoon, from afar I hear a radio from which was coming the music of Benny Goldmann. Being a great lover of Jazz, I had immediately recognised [him]. I approach and see that it is a jeep with 2 or 3 G.I.s. My comrades remain hidden and I go up to the Americans. They are the first who are surprised to 'see' a European speak to them of Benny Goldmann and others. So at once he gave me a pass in due form.

And thanks to this pass Doulard managed to make it back to Paris.

The Black Forest

In late April 1945, French SS soldiers may have also seen action against the 1st French Army in the Black Forest. The *Journal de Marche* [unit war diary] of the *1e Régiment de Cuirassiers* reads:[29]

29   This entry was probably based on the report from the *2e escadron du 1e Régiment de Cuirassiers* which reads: "Entering Brotzingen, numerous sniper fire: it is French SS soldiers or French *Miliciens*. The fire is remarkably accurate and the losses of our infantry are enormous".

... entering Brotzingen, it is French SS soldiers or French *Miliciens* who 'set up' *Capitaine* Dorance's tanks, the *Légionnaires* and the infantrymen of the *Bataillon de Choc*. The fire is accurate and the infantry losses are heavy. Leaving Brotzingen, the situation gets worse: the infantry can no longer keep level with the first tanks. At 1500 hours, *Capitaine* Dorance is killed by a sniper, a bullet right in the head, [while] in his turret ... The losses are heavy: twenty or so killed, including *Capitaine* Dorance (commanding the *2e escadron*), eighty wounded ...

The possibility exists that the 'French SS soldiers' were Frenchmen of the Brandenburg Division or of SS-Jagdverband Süd-West.

Also, several French SS soldiers fought with SS-Kampfgruppe Schleuter in Montreux-Chateau and Brébotte against the 1st French Army.

Bad Reichenhall[30]

On the morning of 8th May 1945, around 1000 hours, twelve French SS troops surrendered without a fight to American troops in Bavaria, who immediately handed them over to the *2ème Division Blindée de les Forces Françaises Libres* (2nd Free French Armoured Division) under General Leclerc.[31] The *2e D.B.* was attached to the XXI US corps under General Milburn.

Among the twelve were Ostuf. Serge Krotoff, Ustuf. Robert Daffas, Ustuf. Paul Briffaut and Gren. Raymond Payras.[32] Some, such as Krotoff, were members of the Franz. A.u.E. Bataillon and had undergone the long march from

30   Much has been written about Bad Reichenhall, but what follows is solely based on eyewitness accounts. Of note is the inclusion of three such eyewitness accounts not cited before. The first is a letter written in 1985 from former Second Lieutenant Florent, a platoon commander in the 4th Company/1st Battalion/*Régiment de marche du Tchad* of the *2e D.B.* who witnessed the execution of the prisoners. The second is the transcript of an interview conducted in 1984 with Serge des B., a former serviceman of the *compagnie de commandement* of the *2e D.B.* who guarded the prisoners, albeit briefly, witnessing General Leclerc's interrogation of the prisoners. The third is from a civilian who witnessed the execution of the prisoners.

31   Letter of 7/2/1946 from *Père* Gaume, former chaplain of the *2e D.B.*, to a country priest in which he forwarded the last letter from Serge Krotoff, one of those murdered at Bad Reichenhall, to his wife. However, according to the article "*Fusillés sans jugement*", "*Historia #32*", page 182, the Americans held the Frenchmen with German prisoners in Gebirgsjäger Kaserne (Mountain Troops Barracks) Bad Reichenhall, but on hearing that their guards were to be relieved by the Gaullists, the Frenchmen decided to escape. Crossing the barracks' fence, they made it to a nearby wood, but their escape was quickly discovered. Two companies of the *2e D.B.* surrounded the wood and recaptured them. In response, this version of events is unconfirmed.

32   Some sources state thirteen men surrendered and were subsequently handed over to the *2e D.B.*, but one of them was spared execution. The son of a senior French Army officer who counted General Leclerc among his friends, he was spirited away by Leclerc in the greatest secrecy and sent back to his father. However, all eyewitness accounts speak of twelve prisoners (Florent, Serge des B. and Gaume). Therefore, there was no thirteenth prisoner.

Wildflecken. Likewise, Briffaut had 'marched' with the medical unit from Wildflecken.[33] Others were outpatients from Bad Reichenhall military hospital and carried evacuation cards on their uniform.[34]

The prisoners were brought to General Leclerc's advanced headquarters,[35] which had been set up in a villa in Bad Reichenhall. Serge des B. of the Headquarters Company of the *2e D.B.* managed to talk to two or three of the prisoners, most notably Krotoff. He said to Krotoff: "You are mad to surrender to Frenchmen. Anything might happen! You should put on civilian clothes and try and return to France!" With extraordinary dignity, Krotoff replied: "We are soldiers fighting for their ideals and we will not put on civilian clothes." Indeed, with the exception of perhaps one or two, the prisoners made the best impression on Serge des B. And it was with dignity that all of them faced up to things.

General Leclerc turned up in person to speak to the twelve French prisoners and reproached them for wearing the German uniform. Words were exchanged.[36]

A Sergeant and Serge des B. were then made responsible for guarding the prisoners and ordered not to speak to them. They would guard them for about two hours. By now the time was around 1400 hours.

The order was given to have them shot, but it is not known who gave the order.[37] Undoubtedly, the order was given in the full knowledge that the capitulation had been signed at Reims the day before and hostilities were due to cease later that day at 2300 hours. There was no trial before a military court. The prisoners, however, were granted the succour of a Catholic priest.

On hearing of the decision to shoot the prisoners, Serge des B. of the Headquarters Company went with some others to the *2e Bureau* to get them to think it

33 Letters from Mme. Wüthensohn to Mme. Briffaut, January and February 1948, in which she specifies that Paul Briffaut arrived at Sandelzhausen with some one hundred men on 17th April, that he 'lodged' with her, and that he departed for Moosburg during the night of 27th/28 April. Therefore, he had not 'retired' to the headquarters of the P.P.F. on the banks of lake Constance (as stated by Mabire, page 335).

34 Mabire, page 335, and Soulat, page 124, however the evacuation cards are not visible on the photographs that exist of the twelve prisoners.

35 Of interest to note is that *Père* Gaume of the *2e D.B.* and an eyewitness to the execution, wrote to doctor Lelongt who served with the LVF and 'Charlemagne' (letter of 19/4/1958): "Your comrades surrendered to the Americans who 'found' nothing better than to hand them over to the French... who were, believe it, greatly embarrassed."

36 Various versions exist of what was said. However, two are important. The first is by Serge des B. serving with the Headquarters Company of the *2e D.B.*, an eyewitness, who states that 'the interrogation by Leclerc went off as correctly as possible'. The second is by Father Fouquet also of the *2e D.B.*, the divisional Chaplain, who may have been 'in the know' because of his position and his later involvement. (See the article which appeared in *Deutsche Wochenzeitung*, No 47, November 1981.) He stated that 'the French SS men had a particularly arrogant air. To a French officer, who had reproached them for having put on the *boche* uniform, they had replied that he himself seemed to be very comfortable in an American uniform.'

through. The decision was not reversed. Serge des B. was later rebuked for his action.

It proved 'one hell of a job' forming a firing squad.[38] Even veterans of the International Brigades[39] refused. Nevertheless, the 4th Company of the 1st Battalion of the *Régiment de marche du Tchad* under Lieutenant Ferrano supplied the firing squad.[40] In the ranks of the 4th Company were many Spaniards of the defeated Republican Army.[41] The 1st platoon of the 4th Company under Second Lieutenant Florent was put in charge of guarding and transporting the prisoners to the place chosen for the execution, a clearing in the locality of Kugelbach.

And so, in the late afternoon, the prisoners were trucked the short distance from Bad Reichenhall to the village of Karlstein and then taken on foot to the clearing. Second Lieutenant Florent got talking to a *petit gradé* [NCO] and asked him what had prompted him to enlist in the LVF. He replied: "My father was killed during the 1914–1918 war on the Belgian front and my mother abandoned me. Taken in by an elderly person living in Lyon, I enlisted in the LVF to help her out financially as best as possible. What I can tell you is that I fought against the Reds but I did not fire on Frenchmen." This *petit gradé* asked Florent if he had English cigarettes on him, because he had never smoked them before, and 'if he wished to give him one'. Florent handed him one.

The prisoners were shot about 1700 hours. According to Serge des B.,[42] the execution was 'rotten, very rotten'. The prisoners protested vehemently.[43] One officer shouted: "You do not have the right to shoot me. I am married. I am not

---

37   Many sources claim that General Leclerc gave the order to have the prisoners shot when he met them, but there are no eyewitness accounts to substantiate this claim. However, regarding the order, three accounts from former servicemen of the *2e D.B.* do exist and are worth recording. First, according to Serge des B. of the Headquarters Company of the *2e D.B.*, General Leclerc contacted Paris for orders and received an evasive response. Second, *Père* Fouquet, the divisional Chaplain, told one of the families of the executed that the 'decision was taken at Headquarters by an officer, whose name was not known to him, and after a telephone conversation with General Leclerc' (Soulat, page 124). Third, according to Boch, also a veteran of the *2e D.B.*, de Gaulle phoned Leclerc to order him to have the prisoners shot for political reasons (see "*Le guet-apens de Bad Reichenhall*").

38   Interview conducted with Serge des B. of the Headquarters Company of the *2e D.B.*, 13/12/1984.

39   Composed of volunteers from around the world, the multinational International Brigades fought on the side of the Republicans in the Spanish Civil War.

40   Florent wrote in his letter of 27/5/1985: "*Sur ordre du Lieutenant Ferrano des groupes de quatre furent constitués et les chefs de section désignés.*" Unfortunately, this sentence is ambiguous, but one suggestion is that the firing squad was formed from 'groups of four' soldiers from each of the three platoons of the 4th Company and that each 'group of four' was commanded by its respective *chef de section* [platoon commander]. The three *chefs de section* of the 4th Company were *Sous-Lietenant* Florent of the 1st platoon, *Aspirant* Morvan of the 2nd platoon and *Aspirant* Beyle of the 3rd platoon.

41   Bayle, "*de Marseille à Novossibirsk*", page 240, although unconfirmed.

42   Interview conducted with Serge des B. of the Headquarters Company of the *2e D.B.*, 13/12/1984.

even French … " Another officer questioned Lieutenant Ferrano on what right they were to be shoot, adding that 'being an officer and responsible for these men he should be shot first'. Second Lieutenant Florent said of this officer [possibly Krotoff]: "He was an example of courage for all". And later as this same officer stood before the execution squad he encouraged his men to sing loudly with him the *Marseillaise*.[44]

Of the 'shooting', Catholic priest Maxime Gaume, the chaplain of the XI/64e R.A. of the *2e D.B.*, later declared to one of the families of the executed:[45]

> After the decision was made at divisional headquarters to shoot the prisoners without trial, Father Fouquet, the divisional Chaplain, gave me the order to comfort them in their last moments. The young Lieutenant who received the order to command the firing squad did not come from my unit and was completely panic-stricken at having to carry out such an order, even wondering if he wasn't going to refuse to obey. He then made up his mind to do at least all in his power to comfort the last moments of the victims and even received communion with them before the execution.
>
> The eleven [twelve—the author] men were taken by truck from Bad Reichenhall, where the headquarters of the *2e D.B.* was, to Karlstein. Only one refused the help of religion; three of them declared that they had no message to pass on to their family.
>
> The shooting was carried out three times: by groups of four in such a way that the last living fell on their comrades under their (very) eyes. All refused to be blindfolded and bravely fell with cries of "*Vive la France*". Among the last four were lieutenant Briffaut and, probably, soldier Payras. Following the orders received, I left the corpses there, but I spoke to American soldiers billeted in the vicinity, recommending them to bury the corpses which was done some days later.

Gaume would later write:[46] "They were executed simply, without hate, by respectful and distressed soldiers."

Gaume also provided writer René Bail with more details of the execution.[47] One of the twelve men refused 'the help of religion', explaining to Gaume that although he was a believer he had lived his life as a non-believer and that he intended to die as he lived. Also, of the three who had no message to pass on to their family, one stated that he had no parents or friends to write to while another said that he preferred that his family did not know what became of him.

Lastly, 'on the day before his departure from Bad Reichenhall, Gaume contacted the local mayor to have the corpses buried, but the mayor wanted to do

43 Indeed, according to Soulat, page 124, when the prisoners were told that they were to be shot in the back they protested violently and were allowed to face their executioners. However, the original source of this information is not known. It may well have been Gaume.
44 Letter from Florent, 27/5/1985.
45 From the article "*Fusillés sans jugement*", "*Historia #32*", page 183. An abridged version of this testimony also appears in Mabire's "*Mourir à Berlin*", page 336.
46 Gaume, letter to doctor Lelongt of 18/4/1958.

nothing and sent the *père* back to the American authorities. The US liaison officer to the *2e D.B.* would 'sort out the matter'.'

The execution was witnessed by a local woman who later testified:

> They arrived with two cars and I thought, my God, what are they going to do? I was with soldiers that I had hidden in my house; they said to me: don't go. But me, I thought why not go and see what's happening ...
>
> While hiding, I slipped into the ditch ... Two young men asked for [some] water and wood to make a cross. One of them did not want to be blindfolded, the others yes; then they fired. It was terrible. I cried out; fortunately they did not hear me because of the shots, otherwise they may have also killed me ...

Notably this testimony contradicts that of Gaume, who testified that all of the prisoners refused to be blindfolded. Today, such contradictions remain irreconcilable.

By the evening of 10th May, the last units of the *2e D.B.* had left Bad Reichenhall. American forces replaced them. Finally,[48] in the presence of an American military chaplain, American soldiers buried the bodies of the twelve. The names of the executed were inscribed on wooden crosses.

Rumours circulating among the civilian population of Bad Reichenhall that a dozen or so French SS soldiers had been shot in the region of Karlstein prompted the local German police to investigate, who confirmed the rumours, naming those responsible as the Gaullist troops of the *2e D.B.* Nevertheless, the police file was closed.

Soon after the shooting, Mgr de Mayol de Lupé and his orderly Henri Cheveau, who were in hiding at Bad Reichenhall, came to Kugelbach and blessed the burial places.[49]

During the winter of 1945/1946, the crosses 'disappeared'. The circumstances are not sinister. The forest around the clearing was the site of considerable felling of trees and unfortunately the trunks were rolled over the graves, crushing or burying the crosses that nobody at the time bothered to replace.

In February 1946, some nine months after the 'shooting', Maxime Gaume contacted the families of the executed direct or through an intermediary to pass on their last letters.[50]

---

47   See Roch, pages 162-164. There are, however, doubts about the validity of some of the 'new' details. According to Bail, while Father Gaume heard the confession of one prisoner the others chatted with the soldiers of the firing squad 'in an atmosphere of quasi camaraderie'. This is not true. As stated by Second Lieutenant Florent, the prisoners protested vehemently. Also, according to Bail, a lorry full of troops of the *2e D.B.* appeared during the executions and when one prisoner of the third group cried out: "*Vive la France!*" one of the occupants of the lorry thought it good to retort: "Ours is not the same." Others considered this remark out of place. Again this is not true, confirmed by Bail to Paul Briffaut junior in 2004.

48   According to Soulat, page 124, the bodies went unattended and unburied for three days. If true, this would date the burial to the 11th, the day after the Americans replaced the French at Bad Reichenhall.

49   Article "*Monseigneur*", "*Historia #32*", page 143, and Roch, pages 164-165.

On 6th December 1948, an inquest opened at the demand of Mme Briffaut who was advised by Mme Wüthensohn, with whom her son Paul Briffaut had 'lodged' briefly at Sandelzhausen during the march from Wildflecken. The outcome was inconclusive; nothing precise was obtained concerning the capture and the interrogation of the victims, nor the circumstances preceding and accompanying their deaths.

Finally, on 2nd June 1949, the bodies were exhumed from the clearing at Karlstein and transferred to a common grave [with plot number Grupp 11, Reihe 3, Nr. 81 und 82] at Sankt Zeno cemetery, Bad Reichenhall. Inscribed on the graveside cross were four names: Lt Paul Briffault, Lt Robert Stoffart, Sd Raymond Payras and Sd Sergey Krotoff. Notably, only one name is correct, that of Raymond Payras. Personal belongings found on the exhumed bodies were handed over to the local police.

On 6th July 1963, the bodies were exhumed again and buried this time in front of a wall close to the monument commemorating the dead of the First World War. A commemorative plaque was fixed to the monument and carries the five names of Paul Briffaut, Robert Doffat, Serge Krotoff, Jean Robert, and Raymond Payras. This time, the names of Briffaut, Krotoff and Payras are correct, Doffat is incorrect, whereas Jean Robert was added by mistake. In fact, Jean and Robert are the first names of Daffas, one of the twelve executed.

On 25th October 1981, a commemorative cross was erected at the site of the execution.

Of those executed, only four have been positively identified.[51] They are:

W-Ostuf. Serge Krotoff

W-Ustuf. Paul Briffaut

W-Ustuf. Robert Daffas

W-Gren. Raymond Payras

Paul Briffaut was born on 8th August 1918 in Hanoi, Vietnam. He attended Saint-Maixent and in October 1939 was commissioned *aspirant de réserve de infanterie* and posted to the 16° RTT in the Levant. In 1941, he fought for Vichy France against the British and Gaullists and was cited *à l'ordre de la division*. In 1943, he volunteered for the LVF. Graduating from its *école des cadres* at Montargis, he left for the Eastern front that October. He served with the 1st Company and, in February 1944, during Operation Morocco, was seriously wounded. He was still in hospital when the LVF was transferred en bloc to the Waffen-SS. He went on to command the Infantry-Gun Kompanie of

50 Gaume contacted families Briffaut and Krotoff through the intermediary of a local clergyman. Also, according to the article "*Fusillés sans jugement*", "*Historia #32*", page 183, the Catholic priest gave to Mme. Briffaut two small photographs of *général* Leclerc in the presence of the twelve Frenchmen. This is not true. In fact, she received two photographs from Serge des B., which, curiously, were dated 7th May 1945 on the reverse.

51 One of the others executed is known by sight to Mercier, but alas not by name. He too had served with the LVF.

Waffen-Gren. Regt. der SS 58, which may have been in the absence of Français, but in December 1944, due to his war wounds, he was demobilised. When executed he was still in the uniform of the Wehrmacht worn by the LVF. He was a holder of the Iron Cross 2nd Class.

Serge Krotoff was born on 11th October 1911 in Tananarive, Madagascar.[52] Paris was his home. By the time he volunteered for the Waffen-SS, he had behind him years of service at sea as an officer in the Merchant Navy. He underwent basic training at Sennheim and then officer training at Kienschlag, graduating in September 1944. He went to Pomerania with 'Charlemagne' at the head of the Anti-tank (PAK) Company of the 'Heavy Weapons' Battalion.

Born on 13th April 1908 in Auch, Robert Daffas served with the NCO rank of *adjudant-chef* in the III. Battalion of the LVF. Transferred to the Waffen-SS and 'Charlemagne', he served with the rank of Untersturmführer in the Headquarters (Staff) Company of Waffen-Gren. Regt der SS 58. He too saw action in Pomerania.

Raymond Payras was born on 16th December 1922 in Colombo, Sri Lanka. He passed from the S.T.O. to the Waffen-SS and 'Charlemagne'. His rank was Grenadier. His parents formally identified him.

In 1979, Jacques Ponnau was tentatively identified from a photo of the victims prior to their killing. His rank is not known.[53]

In conclusion, the facts are that on 8th May 1945 the *2e D.B.* under General Leclerc did commit a war crime at Bad Reichenhall, however there are a number of unanswered questions, including:

Who gave the order to have the prisoners shot?

Why were the prisoners not judged before any form of military court?

Did the fact that hostilities were due to stop on 8th May 1945 at 2300 hours actually hasten the decision to have the prisoners shot?

What did the Americans know of the shooting?

It is deplorable to think that some sixty years after the events at Bad Reichenhall such questions still remain unanswered. Moreover, today, the truth will never be known.

52   As such, Krotoff was not of Russian origin, as stated by most sources. One of his ancestors, attached to the court of the Emperor, acquired French nationality in 1805.

53   Brooks, article "*Death at Bad Reichenhall*", page 178.

CHAPTER 17

Prisoners

In the East

On the morning of 5th March 1945, in Pomerania, Uscha. Mercier of Fahrschwadron A followed his *Capitaine* into captivity. They were joined in captivity by the men hiding with them in the woods and sent to a village where the victors were quartered.

Mercier was like in a dream. He had but one thought in his mind and that was his uniform. He was convinced, and he does not know why, that the Soviets would liquidate the officers, but keep the men who would make excellent slaves for their camps. So, if he was going to be shot, at least he would stand upright. And the survivors would bear witness to it.

The prisoners then arrived in a sort of farmyard. Mercier thought he was going to be shot in the nape of the neck, but to his great amazement the prisoners were greeted with jibes from a group of kids and women in uniform. A Soviet NCO restored a little order by saying to the prisoners: "Franzous-Pétain-Laval" and made *Capitaine* Schlisler, who was at the head of the prisoners, leave the ranks.

At Schlisler's request, Mercier accompanied him as a French-German translator. His knowledge of Russian, like that of the majority of his comrades from the LVF, was very broken.

Schlisler's appearance was such that the Soviet NCO realised that he was dealing with an important person who should be forwarded to a higher echelon. They were taken to a Colonel, who was relatively young. The Colonel was with two or three officers and a private who was an interpreter.

To the great surprise of Mercier, the Colonel said that it was lunchtime and that they could continue the conversation over the table. The Soviet interpreter remained standing, but Mercier was invited to sit beside Schlisler.

The Soviet Colonel, who had gone into raptures over Schlisler's decorations, asked for their names and origins. He only moved on after getting it confirmed that the originals were still in France. Mercier expected a classic military interrogation, but not a society conversation. Above all the Colonel wanted to know how they had ended up as French soldiers dressed in German uniforms. Schlisler answered: "Order from our government."

The Colonel said: "But you fought against the Germans in 1939, since you have a decoration."

To which Schlisler replied: "Yes, we prepared for years to fight against the Germans and during this time the French Communists were anti-militarist. In 1939, the French Communists were against our war and in 1940 our English allies abandoned us."

The Colonel did not seem to understand until he had spoken in private with one of his assistants. The conversation then turned for a rather long time on the details of European and American diplomacy.

477

Mercier was very careful to be as faithful as possible to the subtleties of the words of Schlisler, who broadly claimed total obedience to the orders of the legal government of France.

At one point, with the Russians surprised at Franco-German rapprochement, Schlisler said that the alliance of the Soviets with American capitalism was as abnormal. For the first time, this triggered off a movement of irritation from the Soviet Colonel who energetically asserted that the Americans did not command in the Soviet Union.

Having come to the end of the meal, the Colonel said to them that the war was almost finished and he suggested to Schlisler that he finish it at his side as an advisor. Still very much 'old France', Schlisler replied that he appreciated this offer, but that military honour made it his duty to remain with his men. Then, turning towards Mercier, the Colonel said to him: "And you?" Mercier replied that his duty was to remain with his *Capitaine*.

At the end of the conversation, the Frenchmen asked what had become of their soldiers. There must have been some confusion in the translation because the Colonel replied: "None of today's prisoners have been shot." They pressed the Colonel for more information. He became very evasive. Evidently he knew nothing. However, he said to Mercier that they had been following his unit for the past week and they were the first prisoners they had taken.

Schlisler told Mercier to thank the Colonel for his courtesy. The interpreter replied to Mercier: "Das Oberst sagt: ich bin Graf." [The Colonel says: I am a count.] Schlisler added: "Je suis cavalier."

Schlisler and Mercier rejoined their comrades. Now real captivity began.

Days later, they were marched off to Arnswalde. It was a march of several days. To lighten his load and deprive the Russians of booty, Mercier followed the sound words of advice from his friend Henri Bellanger to throw away everything. Mercier thought about escape, which was a real possibility, but the total absence of a civilian population augured ill.

At Arnswalde, the men were separated from the officers. Mercier saw for the first time Germans of Freies Deutschland. He was horrified. And yet, despite everything, he kept faith in the cause and never lost hope.

Days after arriving at Arnswalde, Mercier was on the move again. First to Landsberg, then by train to Posen (Poznan), where he learnt of the Roosevelt's death, and finally by train to Voronèje and work camp 82/4. Put to work under the supervision of Latvians and Bessarabians, he was kicked, beaten, and starved. Voronèje was hell. He is convinced that he would have 'thrown in the sponge' if it were not for the friendship of a veritable saint, Uscha. Jean Fauconnier, who was ex-*Milice*.[1] Weeks later, he hit rock bottom when Fauconnier was struck down with dementia. The Soviets had cared for him by putting him in the dungeon next to the morgue. He would have died but for the Russian doctor who took an interest in his case and cured him … by feeding him normally. Mercier would later reflect such was the Russia of contrasts. The country of Ilya Ehrenbourg and Ivan the Terrible, but also of Tolstoî and Soljenitsine.

---

1   Jean Fauconnier is not to be confused with Le Fauconnier, the hero of Saint-Loup's *Les Volontaires*.

Curiously, Mercier was paid at Voronèje. One night, he saw some comrades waiting for something in front of a door. One comrade told him to be quiet and wait. Shortly after, he was shown into an office where an officer asked him for his name and handed him some roubles *contre signature*. This was quite by chance and never happened to him again.

In August 1945,[2] Mercier left Voronèje for camp 188, that of Rada, near Tambov, commonly called camp Tambov.

Taken prisoner, Ustuf. de Genouillac was sent to a POW camp at Arnswalde, where he was nearly strung up. To gain the favour of the victors, a French soldier had made totally unfounded accusations against each and every officer present in the camp. The French soldier responsible was undoubtedly a *Milicien* because he had made a particular point of accusing the *chefs miliciens* who had participated in the *opérations du maintien de l'ordre* in France and notably against the Communist maquis, but these events had left the Soviets completely indifferent. On the other hand, they were very interested by the account of a massacre of Russian prisoners at Hammerstein whose responsibility the informer laid at the feet of de Genouillac. The Soviets interrogated him and then, thankfully, took the time to confirm his statement. When they were convinced that he was not present at the scene of the crime, they very kindly provided him with the identity of the one 'who had wasted their time just in case he came across him in the future'!

At Arnswalde, de Genouillac joined a group of 'Charlemagne' officers captured in Pomerania. On 14th April 1945, the group was moved to Landsberg (Gorzow Wlkp) and then, on the 24th, to Posen.

The French SS officers at Posen that May were Alaux, André, Bartolomei, Bassompierre, Baudouin, Bonnefoy, Defever, Delile, de Genouillac, Labrousse, de Perricot, Renault, Rigeade, Rossigneux, Rouzaud, Schlisler, Tardan, de Vaugelas, Vergniaud and Veyrieras.

Also with the group of French SS officers were a Luxembourg national by the name of Ambrosini, as well as four *malgré-nous*[3] of the Wehrmacht: Jules Vilbois, a native of Lorraine, Alsatians Schottlé and Würfel, and Müller.

While the group was at Posen there were two departures; seriously ill, Labrousse was transferred to a hospital as a patient whereas Bonnefoy, a doctor, was transferred to a hospital to ply his trade.

On 12th August 1945, the group left Posen and headed east, arriving five days later at Walka in Lithuania. Held at Walka until 23rd December 1945, the group was then moved to Tapa, Estonia.

On 27th January 1946, the group of French SS officers boarded a goods wagon which was to return them to France. Each had been handed a *certificat de libération*. For the journey, Stubaf. de Vaugelas was made to sign a receipt for various items: a 100 litre can which was quickly converted into a stove; a large pile of yellow stones which actually turned out to be oil shale; a barrel of herrings pickled in brine; and two or three potato sacks filled with slices of dry bread.

The goods wagon was to be their 'palace' for the next twenty-two days. To combat the cold, they burned the 'yellow stones'. At one point the wagon was

2   Unconfirmed.
3   Literally 'against-our-wills', this expression was used to signify those Frenchmen forced into German service.

attached to a convoy which went east. This was not reassuring. They journeyed via
Dortpat, Vitebsk, Mogilev, Zhitomir, Tarnopol, Lemberg, Stanislav, Voronenka
and Bacicoi. Finally, on 17th February 1946, they came to Sighet in Transylvania
and one more POW camp.

In exchange for the remnants of their military dress, the French SS officers
were given disparate and faded civilian clothes. Only the headdress was uniform:
caps with earflaps still displaying the metallic insignia of the Feldgendarmerie.

On 27th March 1946, the French SS officers found themselves again aboard a
train. After travelling through Satumare, Debrecen, Cegled, Budapest, Veszprem,
Szombathely, Vienna, and Saint-Polten, they arrived at Saint-Valentin, Austria,
where they entered yet one more POW camp. It was 2nd April 1946.

At Saint-Valentin, the officers were joined by some one thousand Frenchmen
who, for the most part, came from a POW camp at Kursk. Of the one thousand,
some one hundred were former 'Charlemagne', the others were Alsatians or
Lorrains.

The Russian commander of the camp, a jovial giant of a man, had a liking for
military music and had formed a military orchestra from Russian nationals in
transit through his camp to forced labour in Siberia. Each and every day, the
Frenchmen were invited to march past a platform where the orchestra was
standing. And each and every day, because of the lamentable spectacle they gave,
the Frenchmen were subjected to the vehement reproaches of the camp
commander who went as far as to say that it was appropriate that soldiers who
paraded so bad had lost the war. For their part, the Frenchmen, tired of hearing
about the wrongdoings of Prussian militarism, had no wish to fall back into its
ways.

On 2nd May 1946, a detachment of French soldiers came to the camp to take
charge of the French nationals present. Before boarding the goods wagons, the
camp commander had the French prisoners assembled in front of the 'band stand'
for a farewell ceremony. He spoke for a long time, but only the most gifted among
the prisoners could understand him. His speech was cordial. After wishing them
well on their return, he invited the prisoners to parade one last time, in his words,
'as a slap in the face to your fellow citizens who have just come to collect you and
who certainly do not know how to parade'.[4]

The orchestra then struck up the 'Friedrich-der-Grosse-Marsch'. Moved by
the camp commander's speech, the prisoners responded by executing a left turn
perfectly and then proceeded to parade in a manner as to give the camp
commander the fright of his life! Indeed, a few would have attempted the 'Parade
Marsch' if they had not feared losing their clogs in doing so.

With his hand on the peak of his cap, the joyful-looking camp commander
shouted to the prisoners: "Karacho, karacho, dos vidania" [It's good, goodbye!].

The prisoners were then made to board the wagons. Thereupon the French
servicemen disappeared to the front car, and Russian sentries came and sat on the
edge of the sliding doors left open.

Pushed slowly by a locomotive, the convoy headed west, towards the demarcation line of the river Enns. When the lead car entered the American zone of Occupation the locomotive retired with the Russian sentries, leaving the convoy

4   *Souvenirs* of de Genouillac.

unguarded on the railway bridge. And there it stood for nearly an hour before a locomotive from the American side appeared. By then Bassompierre and de Vaugelas had taken advantage of this unexpected opportunity and made good their escape. No other officer followed the example of Bassompierre and de Vaugelas.

After passing through Linz, Salzburg, Innsbruck, Bregenz, and Donaueschingen, the prisoners came to Strasbourg and again a POW camp. It was 5th May 1946. Two days later, they were sent on to Paris. Prison awaited them.[5]

However, not all captured 'Charlemagne' officers were with this group. One such officer was Ustuf. Pignard-Berthet. Sent to Woldenberg, then on to Posen, he ended up in the POW camp at Kissilowka, Russia, with a small group of French SS volunteers also captured in Pomerania:[6] Ostuf. Auphan, Oscha. Meric, Std.Ju. Comte, Marchese, Carlier, de Perricot,[7] Aymar, Salmon, and Oberjunker Pasquet. Also with this group were Alsatians Amman and Guichard, as well as Oberleutnant Jentgen, a Luxembourg national.

From Kissilowka, they were transferred to camp Rada, near Tambov. In mid-October 1945, Pignard-Berthet was put on a train to the west. On 3rd or 4th November 1945, at Wolfsburg, he was arrested by the French *Sécuritée militaire* and taken to Niemberg. He was questioned about the Red Army. In June 1946, he was repatriated to France.

Captured three kilometres from Greifenberg, Rttf. Gonzales was first moved to Plathe, then on to Arnswalde, where he managed to get some much needed days of rest, and finally to Posen. He was still in the company of Robert Maurel. Because they had met no other Frenchmen they thought they were the only ones to have been captured! In great pain from his knees, Gonzales was admitted into the camp infirmary, which was basic, but then again he did receive some sort of herbal tea twice a day. Days later he was discharged, but in the meantime his friend Robert Maurel was sent on to Odessa, leaving him all by himself. Not long after came his transfer.

Along with fifty others, Gonzales was crammed into a railway horse wagon with a single opening for air and another in a corner for their needs. Thankfully, he found himself once more in the company of a fellow countryman. His name was Labonne.

The convoy departed Posen. For the prisoners, not told of their destination, it was a journey into the unknown. Gonzales tried to follow the route of the convoy from the place names of the stations. Those of Minsk, Borisov, Orscha and Smolensk were well known to him from his LVF days. By now, he was of the opinion that the convoy was making for Moscow. It was, but Moscow was not its destination. The convoy continued eastwards. Siberia beckoned.

Fed one piece of bread daily, hunger became the constant companion of the prisoners.

5   The *malgré-nous* officers were not repatriated because the Russians had decided that they were Germans. They were repatriated in July 1946 (de Genouillac, telephone conversation with Vilbois, 18/2/2000).

6   This corrects Landwehr, "*Charlemagne's Legionnaires*", page 256, who states that the French SS volunteers had been captured during the battle for Berlin.

7   One of the sons of Hstuf. de Perricot, the commander of the Headquarters Company of Waffen-Gren. Regt der SS 58.

Finally, after a journey that had lasted one month, the convoy shed its cargo of prisoners at Asbest. Thankfully, the camp was nearby. Exhausted and unsteady on their feet, few of the prisoners could have gone far. The prisoners were counted. Of those in the same wagon as Gonzales, three or four had died along the way. [Perhaps of exhaustion or starvation.] A shower was next, but it too had its price as the prisoners were stripped of the last personal objects they could not hide. In this way, Gonzales came to part with a small *bossu* [a coin of Napoleon I], a memento given to him by his maternal grandfather that had been with him through the 14/18 war.

After the shower, the prisoners were shaved all over. The blunt razors cut the skin again and again. There was literally blood everywhere. Because Gonzales could speak Russian well he was assigned to the kitchens. On the other hand, his friend Labonne was sent to work in the asbestos mines, where he would work without the protection of a facemask.[8]

Gonzales spent two months in the camp and, because he was working in the kitchens, not once did he go hungry. He also made use of his situation to steal pieces of bread for his comrade. For two months he had no news of the outside world, which he found hard to bear, but that was until the day a Russian woman doctor turned up at the camp to examine the prisoners. She told them that they were going to be repatriated to their respective countries of origin. Good news indeed, but alas this did not happen immediately.

Finally, Gonzales and Labonne were moved to another camp, not far from the first, where they found themselves among the likes of Bulgarians, Hungarians and Rumanians. Days later, in the company of a Russian NCO, the two of them started out by train to Tambov, some 400 kilometres south of Moscow.

At Moscow, they had to change trains, but their connection was not due for hours. To kill the time, the Russian NCO, along with his two prisoners, went to visit his parents in the suburbs! During the journey Gonzales had the chance to speak to a Russian woman of Jewish origin. She spoke good French and deeply regretted that she did not have the freedom to go to France. At that she embraced him. Her eyes then filled with tears.

That same evening, they continued on to Tambov. Many were the stops that presented Labonne with opportunity after opportunity to improve their lot by plying his former occupation of circus showman. Before an audience of peasants who had come to sell or trade their goods to passing travellers he would eat glass or razor blades. For his show he was given eggs, glasses of milk or black bread.

It took two days to reach 'camp Tambov'. Called the 'camp of the Frenchmen', its inmates were, for the most part, Alsatians. Once more Gonzales felt quite alone, especially when Labonne entered the infirmary. Conditions at Tambov were terrible. Typhus was rampant. Gonzales had no need to fear this sickness, having contracted it some months beforehand. However, there was no escape whatsoever from the terrible black-coloured parasites called *Gimelanke*. More vicious than any lice or bugs Gonzales had known before, one of these irritants would prevent sleep. Also of nuisance at night-time were the fleas living in the bark of the logs used as beds. Not wanting to become a host for them, he was forever shaking his shirt outside his hut. And then there was the hunger.

8   Labonne would later die of tuberculosis.

Weeks, perhaps months later, Gonzales, along with a group of Alsatians, numbering twenty or so, was moved a matter of kilometres to another camp, much smaller, situated in the middle of a huge peat bog.[9] Notably two Alsatians ran the camp. Gonzales likened them to comedians 'Laurel and Hardy', but Laurel was without joy. In fact, he was rather hard-hearted. In contrast, the Russian guards were rather friendly.

Coming forward as a carpenter, Gonzales was assigned to the construction of a small guard post at the entrance to the camp. Yes, this work, of course, was less tiring than the digging of the peat, but for Gonzales, he also got to go out to the forest with the other prisoners to cut wood for the proposed guard post. Generally a guard who had lost an arm in the war accompanied them. On more than one occasion, he had an opportunity to talk to him freely. To the great surprise of Gonzales, the guard confessed to him that he was not in agreement with the Communist regime, explaining that after his discharge from his regiment he had requested a patch of land and a cow, but this had been refused.

Gonzales was at this camp for some two months. In all that time, he never once received a meal that varied from cabbage soup, a handful of small fish and a piece of black bread. The monotony of camp life was broken once by a visiting troop of comedians and performers. A light tenor brought tears to the eyes of the prisoners at the end of a quite beautiful song entitled 'The return of the prisoner'.

Then came the day Gonzales was moved back to 'Tambov' to prepare for his repatriation to France. He was shocked to lay eyes on a deserter from his former LVF unit, the 2nd Company, in the uniform of a Red Army sergeant.[10] Nevertheless, as he counted down the days to repatriation he got to meet more and more French POWs, including Jean Pierre Lefèvre.

Days before the prisoners left Tambov for France their rations suddenly improved. Obviously Russia was desperate to show the world that it fed its prisoners well.

And so, in October 1945, began the train journey back 'home'. Mercier of Fahrschwadron A was on the same train. The stops were frequent. The train had to make way for those bound for Russia. At each stop, the prisoners were free to descend and walk about. In this way, unbelievably, Gonzales actually missed his train that suddenly departed. He went to a smaller station nearby where he caught another westwards. He was soon back on the 'right' train.

At each stop, Gonzales found himself opposite, more often than not, a convoy of Russian prisoners who had fought under the German sponsored General Vlasov. The Allies were exchanging them for their own nationals. Apprehension was written all over their faces. [And with good reason.]

While stopped at Radom, Poland, the train was visited by a detachment of the French Red Cross. Three or four ladies distributed cigarettes. One French prisoner was pacing up and down the platform smoking away when, passing by the ladies, he heard one of them say to the others: "If we had known that they were volunteers

---

9   Gonzales called this camp 'Raja'. Presumably he was referring to Rada. Arguably, this 'new' camp was part of or an annex of camp Rada.

10   This LVF deserter was also well known to Mercier, who in 1942 had served with him in the same platoon of the 2nd Company.

… " Without hesitating, the prisoner held out his half smoked cigarette with the words: "Take it, it's not finished!"

At Berlin, during one more stop, Gonzales assisted in the burial of a Russian General. The coffin was open. The face of the deceased was completely swollen and scarlet. It appeared as though excessive eating and drinking had struck him down.

The very next day, the train crossed into Holland, but it was the British Army to which the prisoners were handed over. First they were deloused. Then they were fed. However, the food proved too rich for many and they were sick, including Gonzales.

Soon after, the prisoners were sent on to Bruxelles where the Belgium Red Cross gave them a warm welcome. This was in contrast to the French Red Cross that received them 'like dogs'.

Finally, in early November 1945, they crossed into France, arriving at Valenciennes. The French 'authorities' were somewhat confused when they realised that the convoy comprised not only martyrs from Alsace-Lorraine and Luxembourg, but also suspects. Ironically, from a loudspeaker welcoming the repatriates came the *Marche Consulaire*.[11]

The newly arrived were screened in a hasty manner and 'those comrades not from Alsace-Lorraine' isolated. Next they heard an appeal for volunteers to take the repatriates to 'village nègre'.[12] The escort appeared and asked if there was an officer among them. In this way, Pierre Million-Rousseau, probably the 'most senior officer with the highest rank', took command of the manoeuvre. And it was as soldiers that the veterans of the LVF, SS, and *Milice* went from the station to the barracks, despite their rags and their skeletal appearance.

Many other French POWs passed through 'camp Tambov'. For some, it was their final resting place.

In contrast, Robert Blanc of Walter's Company, who spent some five and a half months in Russian captivity, was well treated. In terrible physical condition and suffering from frostbite when captured, he was taken to a hospital in Köslin. He went to the operating table. Under local anaesthetic, the dead parts of his feet were amputated.

Blanc went back to the operating table a further two times. During one operation another Frenchman was brought in. His name was Nöel V. and he was from the same origin as Blanc, who could now hear the sound of the saw amputating his countryman's legs below the knees.

Blanc and his comrade Patrice Rimbert shared the same hospital room. A good drawer, Rimbert was popular as a portraitist with the nurses. When one of the nurses brought them a collection of post cards of Paris Blanc gave them all a talk and for this he drew a sort of map of Paris to position the different views. He had a great deal of trouble getting them to accept that the Sacré-Coeur was not a mosque!

Blanc was moved to a ward mainly of Soviet nationals. Not once was he made an object of hostility.

11   When Jacques Benoist-Méchin conceived the *Légion Tricolore* he decided that its
      official anthem would be the *Marche Consulaire*, which he considered as 'the most
      beautiful anthem after the *Marseillaise*'.
12   'Village nègre' translates as 'Negro village' and in this instance appears to have been
      used as a code name.

One day, the surgeon, who also spoke a little French, asked Blanc what would please him. Modest in his demands, Blanc requested a drink weaker than the daily vodka ration, which he then replaced with Dubonnet. Also, there was no reading material to be had. The surgeon brought him *Nouvelle Héloïse* by Jean-Jacques Rousseau, of which he read twenty pages out of courtesy.

At the end of about a month, Blanc, Désigot, Rimbert, and Nöel V. were moved to a field hospital in Bromberg. Separated from his comrades, Blanc found himself in a hut with some French 'POWs of 40', who soon learnt that he was SS. The atmosphere took a turn for the worse. The following morning, the French POWs denounced Blanc to the medical officer and asked him to rid them of him. The medical officer, who spoke a little French, put them in their place: "You, you let yourself be captured. At least, he fought." Blanc was not troubled again.

More surprises awaited Blanc at Bromberg. One morning, a giant of a man, whom Blanc believed to be of high rank judging by the size of his epaulettes, accompanied the medical officer on his round. At the foot of each bed the giant acquainted himself with the case and the situation of the occupant. Then he came to Blanc, who distinctly heard "Fransouski SS", but understood little of what else was said. Nevertheless, he still thought to himself that the good life was now over and that he was going to find himself God knows where. When the dialogue ended, to the great surprise of Blanc, the *haut gradé* took him by the hand, squeezed it and shook it vigorously, and said to him in French these few simple words: "*Maréchal Pétain, grand soldat!*", after which he passed to the next bed.

Désigot died suddenly. His family would have no news of him; his compatriots had not thought of asking him for his address when he was still in possession of his mind.

One month later, Blanc was transferred to a third and last hospital in Thorn. The hospital, which adjoined a huge POW camp, had some one thousand patients. In the same room as Blanc were two Italian soldiers and five Frenchmen, of whom three were 'POWs of 40' and two were S.T.O. Again Blanc was well cared for. Each day he was taken to the treatment room, where his feet were examined by a doctor and bandaged by a nurse. The food was adequate. He regained his strength and started to walk.

Blanc, who made no secret that he was SS, soon discovered that the two S.T.O. were in fact also SS. They were Truchet, who was in his forties, and Jacques A., who was the same age as Blanc and also ex-*Milice*; he had followed his father and elder brother into the *Milice*, the latter being killed in a terrorist ambush. The *Milice* led him to the Waffen-SS. He served with the Artillery Battalion of 'Charlemagne'. Seriously wounded at Danzig, he was evacuated to the city's military hospital, where he witnessed some horrifying scenes when the Russians arrived. From the top floor, all the SS patients were systematically defenestrated.[13] He had escaped a similar fate quite by chance; he had not responded to the call of his name, which the Russians, trapped by their Cyrillic alphabet, had mispronounced.

With nothing to do and nothing to read at Thorn, the days were long. Blanc tried to learn Russian. He gleaned very many words, but his request for more formal learning was politely but firmly refused. Perhaps the Russians feared that it would make a spy of him.

---

13   One of Blanc's comrades witnessed similar scenes at Swinemünde.

In September 1945, along with Jacques A., Truchet, Nöel V. and two or three other comrades, Blanc was repatriated.[14] Blanc would later reflect that he had fought Bolchevism, but not the Russians who had cared for him with such kindness and concern.

In the West

Rttf. Soulat was held first in a camp at Gadebusch. Joined by others of 'Charlemagne', they soon counted 20. Of the 20, whose average age was 27, 3 were married (2 with children) and 17 were single. As for their background, 3 came from the LVF, 3 from the Kriegsmarine, 2 from the SS, and 12 from the *Milice*. Notably, twenty-one-year-old *milicien* Andre D. was in fact a 'converted' maquisard. The professions of the twenty was split; 6 were students, 4 were farmers, 2 were mechanics, 2 were bakers, 2 were 'employees', 1 was a driver, 1 was a typographer and 2 had no profession.

On 25th May 1945, Soulat and the other French POWs of 'Charlemagne' were moved to SS-POW-Camp 357 at Fallingbostel, Hanover.[15] They remained 20 in number until the arrival of a second group of 150 with *aspirant* de Vaugelas junior and 4 or 5 *adjudants*. Also with this second group was Uscha. Fronteau.

Days after their arrival, a list was circulated calling for volunteers to fight with the American Army of the Far East against the Japanese.[16] Soulat signed up. However, nothing came of his gesture, a gesture he was to later call low and ill-timed because he would have ended up serving against a courageous people one hundred times better than the Americans. This he regretted.

There was much talk of the Americans shooting Ostuf. Herpe and Ustuf. Sarraillé at Schwerin on 2nd May in 'strange circumstances', but this proved to be nothing more than hearsay.

On 20th September, Soulat and the third and last detachment of French W-SS POWs left the camp by truck for France. Two days later, they arrived at Lille. All out! As they got out one of them hummed:

SS Marschiert
In Feindesland ....

On 16th May 1945, at concentration camp Neuengamme, Staf. Zimmermann symbolically dissolved 'Charlemagne' in the presence of Martin, Roumegous, Platon, another French officer, 'some lads from the Brigade', and about a dozen German officers. His Tricolore badge, respectfully kept, served as a miniature flag in the middle of the worn-out circle on the grass. Martin gave a resumé, presumably of the history of 'Charlemagne', while Zimmermann pronounced his acknowledgements. Hail to Franco-German camaraderie.[17]

---

14   There was a French Waffen-SS nurse by the name of Truchet, who was born in 1924, but the two of them were not related.

15   SS-POW-Camp 357 was later renamed Civilian Internment Camp (C.I.C.) 3.

16   Of interest to note is that a rumour at the time had it that the survivors were going to be sent to fight side by side with the Americans against the Japanese.

17   Zimmermann, letter to Saint-Loup, 10/8/65.

CHAPTER 18

Le Bataillon d'Infanterie légère d'Outre-Mer

As the war in Indo-China dragged on France became desperate more than ever for fresh manpower. The politicians came to consider the many thousands of prisoners the country was then holding as an acceptable and accessible source of manpower.

On 27th May 1948, André Marie, the Minister of Justice, issued a circular to the regional directors of the Prison service asking for the number of prisoners who wished to enlist in Far East combat units in order to 'make amends vis-à-vis the nation'.

The politicians then went to the military, which drew up proposals to raise a *demi-brigade* of three battalions of political prisoners. So as not to alarm the public unduly it was decided to raise one battalion first. Thus, on 6th July 1948, the Minister of the Armed Forces communicated the decision to create the *1er Bataillon d'Infanterie légère d'Outre-Mer* (BILOM) to the general headquarters of the Armed forces.

The BILOM was to be composed exclusively of political prisoners capable of military service overseas. For those volunteering, there would be no question of amnesty, but merely of a suspensive pardon. They would wear no insignia and have no pennant. They were not eligible for promotion; all leadership positions were to be filled by Colonial Troops.

So who were these political prisoners that France was to recruit for the BILOM? They were veterans of the LVF and the Waffen-SS who had survived the fighting on the Eastern front. And they were those who had advocated a New Order and who had survived the court martials and summary sentences that came with 'Liberation'.

Among those accepted was the apolitical Giorgio Lave[2] born of Italian and Austrian parents. Life had been hard for him. Throughout his youth he had dreamt of being French, the country which had given him security and bread. When he was eighteen he opted for French nationality, but the civil servants attempted to dissuade him. Convinced that there was no better way of being French than by fighting bolshevism, he enlisted in the LVF in May 1944. Besides, he craved adventure and the idea of a Europe of united nations in the same battle appealed to him. He enjoyed soldiering and wanted to be among the best. Thus, his transfer to 'Charlemagne' in August 1944 did not trouble him. He was proud to fight in the Waffen-SS that had the reputation of being an elite unit.

At Wildflecken, Lave was assigned to 'the heavy company of Waffen-Gren. Regt der SS 58'[3] and tattooed. Seriously wounded in Pomerania, he was evacuated

---

1   See Muelle, "*Le Bataillon des réprouvés*".
2   Pseudonym.

by ship to Bremerhaven via Copenhagen. Although his wounds were far from healed he was sent to the depot of 'Charlemagne'.[4] When the Russians launched their 'Berlin' offensive he fled west and surrendered to the British in May 1945.

Lave was sentenced to ten years hard labour. He often thought of escape, but he knew that he could go nowhere without money and a 'network'. For him, volunteering for Indo-China was an escape. Besides, he was a *homme de guerre*.

Some volunteers were from military families. Indeed, Jean de Marivalle's[5] father was a hero of the Great War. As a Nationalist and royalist, reserve Captain de Marivalle did not welcome favourably the idea of his son Jean donning the uniform of the *Légion Tricolore* to fight bolshevism. It was this refusal that incited him to action. Aged seventeen, he enlisted in the Waffen-SS.

Arriving at Sennheim in the spring of 1943, Jean de Marivalle drew attention to himself through his knowledge of the German language and also his enthusiasm, but his individualism was of concern. After recruit training, he attended the Signals training school in the Tyrol, then the Interpreters school at Oranienburg near Berlin.

Transferred from the French SS-Sturmbrigade to Waffen-Gren. Regt der SS 57 of 'Charlemagne', Strmm. de Marivalle saw action in Pomerania. He was made a liaison officer to Artus, Bassompierre, and de Bourmont. Captured by Polish partisans, he was hid by French POWs, but handed over to the Russians by STO 'volunteers'. He was sent to a camp at Poltava. To embarrass the Soviet authorities into releasing him, he bombarded them with complaint after complaint and request after request. Some were ludicrous. He even requested asylum, claiming that his life would be in danger if he was returned to France. This received no reply, but one day he was set free. Making his way through Germany, he was denounced to the British by a catholic priest of whom he had asked hospitality. In turn, the British handed him over to the French authorities.

In early 1946, when brought before the *tribunal militaire* of Landau, de Marivalle was acquitted, because 'he had not come of age at the time of the events', and invited to engage for Indo-China. But then the *justice civile* of Bordeaux sentenced him in his absence to death for enlisting in the Waffen-SS. He was brought to Bordeaux. The court reiterated his punishment, that of death. In May 1947, his sentence was commuted to twenty years imprisonment. To get out of prison, he volunteered for the BILOM. He managed to get himself accepted even though he was medically unfit: he had lost several toes to frostbite in Pomerania.

Cottelowe and Forrez were inseparable. Their journey to the BILOM began together with the rank of *quartiers-maître* [leading seaman] aboard the *Bretagne* at the time of the English attacks at Mers-el-Kebir. They survived, but many of their comrades were killed. Soon after, they enlisted in the LVF. The Russian winters and combat did not diminish their memories of their comrades who had fallen one summer's day at the foot of the mountain of Santa-Cruz. Their transfer to 'Charlemagne' did not pose them problems, nor did it weaken their determination to fight the Soviets allied with the English, the hereditary enemy.[6] They both became

3   Muelle, page 19, possibly the 4/58 or 8/58.
4   Ibid, page 22, possibly Neusterlitz.
5   Pseudonym.
6   Muelle, 126.

model NCOs. They remained inseparable; they were decorated at the same time, and judged and sentenced together. They decided to continue their brotherly crusade in the BILOM.

Pierre Littrey was one of the oldest. A romantic adventurer and convinced anti-Communist, he had fought on the side of Franco. The nationalists made him an officer and decorated him for his courage under fire. In September 1939, when storm clouds gathered over Europe, he returned to France. In May 1940, with the rank of *maréchal des logis* [sergeant] serving in a reconnaissance group, he fought the Germans.

Like many from his generation, Littrey was impressed by his victors. They exuded order, force and faith in an ideal 'already glimpsed' in Spain. He was drawn to the infectiousness of the unknown and 'the passionate liturgy of the elite troops at the disposal of a new order' to reverse the decay of the old worm-eaten world. And yet he hesitated to don the uniform of the enemy of yesterday. But the death of his mother in an English air raid swept away any last reservations. The LVF made him an officer again and the Waffen-SS into 'one of its born leaders'. At the end of the war, he attempted to flee west by passing himself off as a STO conscript, but the tattoo gave him away. He was sentenced to fifteen years hard labour, had his property confiscated and was ordered to pay costs. Now, the BILOM offered him adventure and the opportunity to continue the fight against a detested ideology.

Also concerned about the 'menace coming from the East' was Roger Curzon.[7] In March 1942, not yet aged eighteen, he enlisted in the LVF. By that October, he was in action against the Soviet partisans in the forests. He joined an autonomous fifty-man commando of Frenchmen, Germans and Poles engaged most of the time as *enfants perdus* against the Soviet parachutists who trained and supervised the partisans. And then, one day, he met some French volunteers of the Waffen-SS. They spoke to him of 'Charlemagne' and suggested he should join. The idea did not displease him and his request for a transfer was agreed. Along with four or five other volunteers, he was sent to Wildflecken.

Sturmmann Curzon saw subsequent action in Pomerania. Finding himself at Kolberg, he managed to escape from the city in the company of a handful of other exhausted men. Withdrawing westwards, they were captured by Polish troops near to the town of Wollin (Wolin). He spent the next one and a half years in various prison camps throughout Russia before being repatriated in the summer of 1946. He was sentenced to 5 years in prison.

Others, like Barellon, had jumped at the opportunity to regain their freedom by means of enlisting in the BILOM. For him, it had all started in 1943 when, at the age of nineteen, he enlisted in the Waffen-SS because 'it seemed to him the only, the best, and the most appropriate solution, and the best choice for the future and the realisation of an ideal ... '[8] but above all he envied the men of the Waffen-SS. The superb recruitment posters for the Waffen-SS left him in no doubt that they were the best soldiers in the world. He wanted to belong.

Wounded in August 1944 with the SS-Sturmbrigade in Galicia, Barellon went on to see action with 'Charlemagne' in Pomerania and one of the few to make it out. Towards the end of the war, he found himself in Berlin with either Dutch or

7   Pseudonym.
8   Muelle, page 155.

Latvian SS troops and was transported out and to the west on one of the last trains, but his train journey was violently halted by an air attack. Captured by the British, he escaped, reached his region in France and was promptly denounced. In July 1945, he was sentenced to twenty years imprisonment.

Many others of those accepted had served in 'Charlemagne':

Becker: Alsatian, he held the rank of Unterscharführer

Bordon: *adjudant d'artillerie* in 'one of the heavy companies'

Irguiz[9]

L.G.: Grenadier, Company 5/58

Pierart: Oberjunker in the Signals platoon of a regimental Headquarters Company

Quagebeur[10]

Roubil: He held the rank of Sturmmann

Tillier[11]

A small number of the volunteers had served and seen action in other branches of the German war machine other than the Waffen-SS. For example, Robert Hernan[12] who had served as a Kriegsberichter [war correspondent] with the 3. SS-Panzer-Division 'Totenkopf. There was also Hervé Cormatin who had been with Skorzeny.

Rambert[13] had worn the *feldgrau* serving in the ranks of the *Bezenn Perrot* composed of extremist Breton separatists.[14] He believed in a sovereign and independent Bretagne. He worked alongside the SD. When the *Bezenn Perrot* evacuated Rennes for Germany he abandoned the *feldgrau* and made for Spain. However, in May 1945, he was arrested at Rabastens-de-Bigorre. On 21st September 1945, he was sentenced to life imprisonment.

Many were those who had not donned the *feldgrau*. André Cantelaube had been a prominent figure in the *jeunesse franciste*. Sentenced to fifteen years imprisonment, he was one of those who wanted out of prison at any cost.

Michel Robert[15] was a former *chef de trentaine* of the *Milice française*[16] who had done battle with the terrorists and maquis in Lyon. Arrested, he narrowly escaped

9   Pseudonym. From Kabyle, Amar Irguiz was ex-Sturmbrigade.
10   Francis Quagebeur was ex-Sturmbrigade
11   Pseudonym.
12   Pseudonym. A member of *Action Française*, Robert Hernan arrived at Sennheim on 13th August 1943 and left in February 1944 for Orianenburg where he was trained as a war correspondent.
13   Undoubtedly a pseudonym.
14   The name *Bezenn Perrot* was derived from father Jean-Marie Perrot, the parish priest of Scrignac, assassinated by terrorists on 12th December 1943. He was an outspoken advocate of collaboration with the Germans as a road to Breton separatism. The *Bezenn Perrot* was no more than one hundred strong and wore the field-grey. Armed with weapons captured from the terrorists, it took part in operations against the maquis.

summary execution. Interrogation and torture followed. After almost two years of ill-treatment and humiliation, he was sentenced to death for treason. His sentence was later commuted to life imprisonment. For him, the BILOM was a stepping stone to South America.

By late August 1948, a little less than five hundred volunteers had been accepted. Of note is that none had been the leading lights of collaboration; the powers that be had kept them under lock and key.

Many of the volunteers could not understand the irony of their new situation; they could 'make amends' by fighting international Communism and yet they had been languishing in prison for years because they had fought against Communism!

The volunteers were brought together at Fréjus, where they were dressed and armed, albeit poorly. The military training posed few problems. In fact, their young *encadrement* [Officers and NCOs], except for the *adjudants* and *adjudants-chefs* from the Colonial troops, had limited military experience and thus little to teach. Some were even former members of FFI units!

Adjudant-chef Pierre Duthilleul was posted to the BILOM as a '*tour colonial*'. A seasoned soldier, he had fought in North Africa in 1942, in the Italian Campaign with the 1st French Mountain Division as a gunner, in Provence in the late summer of 1944, ending WWII in Germany. In the BILOM, he served in the *section de commandement* as paymaster. He regarded and treated the volunteers as fellow serviceman, although his first impression of them was not good and he thought some were scoundrels. He would enjoy a good relationship with the volunteers.

In the meantime, the Communist Party had orchestrated a press campaign against this project, calling for vengeance, justice and punishment of the 'collabos', but France had need of *soldats* for Indo-China.

Finally, on 11th December 1948, the 1st Company of the BILOM, otherwise the 1/BILOM, 4 officers, 20 NCOs and 148 men, and elements of battalion headquarters, 5 officers and 5 NCOs, boarded the *Pasteur* bound for Indo-China. *Adjudant-chef* Duthilleul was satisfied with the preparation and the combat readiness of the volunteers. Fifteen days later, on the 26th, they disembarked at Saigon.

From 3rd January 1949 to 17th March 1949, the 1/BILOM was stationed in Cambodia and suffered its first losses. On 18th March 1949, the 1/BILOM was transferred to Sud Annam in the sector of Nha Trang. For the *réprouvés* [outcasts] of the BILOM, the war was one of patrols, ambushes, sudden and violent engagements, exhausting 'combing' operations, booby traps, malaria, dysentery, … and death. Losses mounted. And how did the *réprouvés* fight? They were not found wanting, proving themselves time and time as *soldats de qualité*.

On 6th April 1949, at Marseille, the first detachment of the 2/BILOM, 2 officers, 6 NCOs and 57 men, boarded SS *Compiègne*. This detachment arrived at Saigon on 8th May and joined the 1/BILOM nine days later. A further detachment of the 2/BILOM, 5 NCOs and 24 men, arrived in June.

The 20th June 1949 marked a milestone in the history of the BILOM. For the first time, *réprouvés* of the BILOM were decorated with the *croix de guerre*. This was

---

15   Undoubtedly a pseudonym.
16   Arguably, he was of the *Franc-Garde* of the *Milice française*.

proof, if proof was needed, of acts of courage. *Adjudant-chef* Duthilleul thought the decorations were merited. All now hoped for respect.

On 2nd July 1949, by order of the *général commandant en chef les Forces armées d'Extrême-Orient*, the 1/BILOM was dissolved to form the *1re Compagnie de Marche du Sud Annam*, otherwise the 1/CMSA, and the 2/BILOM the 2/CMSA. As a seasoned soldier, *Adjudant-chef* Duthilleul was little concerned with the dissolution of the BILOM. The former prisoners were told that henceforth they were soldiers in regular units of the *Corps expéditionnaire* and French soldiers in the service of their country. Nevertheless, it was not yet a question of discharge or the erasing of sentences.

The CMSAs would be hybrid, 75% local and 25% European. The surplus Europeans would form a commando, a shock unit, for each company. For the first time, some ex-prisoners were promoted to NCO rank. Also, some were assigned to positions of responsibility in the support services throughout Sud Annam. In this way, the process of their fragmentation began, but France was desperately short of *gradés* of worth.

On 1st January 1950, the 1/CMSA became the *3e Compagnie du 6e bataillon de marche d'Extrême-Orient* (BMEO) and the 2/CMSA the *4e Compagnie du 6e BMEO*.[17]

In February, some one hundred ex-BILOM soldiers were posted from the 3rd and 4th companies of the 6/BMEO; eighty went to other BMEOs [notably the 3/BMEO, the 4/BMEO and the 5/BMEO] and the remainder to different units and support services of the *Forces terrestres des Plateaux*. Thus, the spirit of the BILOM lived on throughout the whole of Sud Annam. And yet there was still no prospect of a pardon or amnesty on the administrative horizon.

On 31st December 1950, the BMEOs became *Bataillons montagnards*.

In March 1951, the first repatriations of ex-BILOM personnel started. Some would remain or return to Indo-China.

Giorgio Lave spent more than three years in Indo-China and it took the intervention of his superiors to get him, by now a Sergeant, to agree to leave his unit. Earning his paratrooper wings in France, he quickly returned to the Far East, winning more citations, the military medal and the respect of his *chefs*. In Algeria, the Red Berets made him an officer.

Amar Irguiz earnt his strips of *adjudant* and won the military medal. After a second tour of duty in Indo-China, he served in black Africa in 'confidential jobs'.

Cantelaube returned to Indo-China for his second tour of duty and came back a sergeant.

Henri Barellon was not in France long; he went straight off to fight Communism in Korea and when that war finished he set sail back to Indo-China. Sergeant Barellon was taken prisoner in July 1954 in the region of Ankhé and marched to a camp in Tonkin. He survived. Liberated, he then went to the war in Algeria that was just beginning.

Roger Curzon would remain loyal to the French Colonial Army for fifteen years. After Indo-China, he served in Algeria as a paratrooper with the Red Berets,

---

17   The BMEOs were created in response to the Viet-Minh threat on the mountains and plateaux of Sud-Annam.

and then in the Cameroon. He finished his military career in a unit born of the *2e D.B.*

Adjudant Hervé Cormatin became an excellent and respected NCO in Indo-China. He stepped on a mine in East Algeria and died hours later in a Parisian hospital. He was decorated with the *croix de chevalier de la Légion* on his deathbed.

For historical clarity, it should also be mentioned that some former volunteers of the LVF and the W-SS fought on the side of the Viet Minh. One even became an officer!

CHAPTER 19

The Postwar Years

Audibert, Roger. Brought before the courts, he was one of the few to be acquitted.

Appolot, François. Contrary to popular belief, Appolot did not die in the holocaust of Berlin. Dressed as a civilian, he returned to France and settled down. His family were unaware of his story, that is all except for his son who, after reading a book by Mabire, put two and two together and then spoke at length to his father. He lives somewhere in the east of France.

Bartolomei, Yvan. Died in February 1996 at the grand age of ninety-nine.

Bassompierre, Jean. After giving his captors the slip, he crossed France. With the help of Mme de S.[1] he passed into Italy. From Naples, he hoped to embark for the safe haven of South America. Under the false name of Joseph Bassemart he managed to obtain travel documents for Buenos Aires. However, after meeting up again with his comrade Jean de Vaugelas, also in a similar situation but without travel documents, he handed his over to him.

On 28th October 1945, Bassompierre was arrested aboard a boat that would have taken him to South America. Brought back to France, he was locked up in *la Santé* prison.

Hauled before *la Cour de justice de la Seine*, Bassompierre was charged on three counts: his attitude as *inspecteur général de la Milice* in the North Zone, his role in the assassination of Georges Mandel, as well as that in the repression of the mutiny at *la Santé* prison, Paris.

The case against him was flimsy and soon hinged on the third count: his role in the repression that followed at the prison of *la Santé*. On the evening of 13th July 1944, 'common criminal' prisoners at *la Santé* mutinied. The following morning units of the Paris *Franc Garde* led by Bassompierre restored order. As punishment, the German authorities wanted four hundred prisoners executed, which would have included 'political prisoners' (that is to say *Résistants*) who had refused to join the mutiny, but Bassompierre talked them down to fifty. He was preparing their execution when Knipping, the *délégué secrétaire d'Etat pour L'Intérieur en zone nord*, arrived and intervened. Knipping negotiated with the German authorities that the fifty would not be summarily executed, but appear before a court martial.

On the court martial sat *chefs milicien* Pierre Gallet, who was president, Max Knipping and Georges Radici [who would later serve with 'Charlemagne'].

---

1   A former *résistante*, Mme de S. first came to the assistance of the vanquished in 1945 as they sought to vanish from Europe and escape vengeance. In this way, she would help many other former members of 'Charlemagne'. It should also be noted that the case of Mme de S. was not unique. To cite one example of many, at Bordeaux, in peacetime, a former lieutenant of the F.F.I., considered 'a real hero', hid and helped several fugitives to escape. For more such examples see *"Historia # 32"*, page 180.

Forty-five common law criminals appeared before the court, of which seventeen were exonerated. Half an hour after the proceedings ended, the executions began by the police with guns supplied by the *Franc Garde* units present.

Despite the fact that Bassompierre had saved considerable life 'by opposing the murderous fury of the Germans',[2] two witnesses, Goujet, the *sous-directeur de la Santé* prison, and Vanegue, the *directeur adjoint de la police municipal,* swore on oath that Bassompierre had resigned himself to the execution of fifty mutineers. Following the dispositions of Goujet and Vanegue, the government commissioner concluded that 'Bassompierre had not attempted to lighten the sanctions and was willing to shoot as many Frenchmen as the Germans demanded', which is not true. Bassompierre pleaded his innocence in this bloody affair, reminding this court that he was not a member of the court martial that had handed down the death sentences.

Bassompierre's barrister, Charles-Ambroise Colin, opened the speeches for the defence and tried to prove that his client did not have blood on his hands and that he was an 'honourable, ardent and sincere man'. He spoke of the loyalty Bassompierre had sworn to the Maréchal, which 'he had kept to the end', and of the despair which had seized him after the armistice, later leading him to become a soldier.

On 17th January 1948, the jury, after just minutes of deliberation, sentenced Bassompierre to death. He replied: "The man you have just sentenced to death is not a criminal nor a traitor to his country." Despite pleas for mercy, despite the newspaper *L'Époque* publishing lists of former *résistants* ready to intervene on behalf of Bassompierre, despite a request from Reverend Father Bruckberger to *président* Auriol to take the place of the condemned, 'the only response was the salvo of the execution squad'.

In the early morning hours of 20th April 1948, Bassompierres was brought to fort de Montrouge for the execution of his sentence. At 0700 hours, accompanied by his Chaplain, he was marched before the butt. After receiving absolution, Bassompierre let himself be tied to the execution post but refused the blindfold. Bassompierre smiled to Bruckberger, who was now on his knees begging and crying, and then shouted out: "May God protect my family! May God protect France!" The firing squad, made up of *chasseurs alpins,* Bassompierre's former regiment, fired. A NCO administered the *coup de grâce.* It was a needless formality. Bassompierre was dead. He was buried in the cemetery of the *condamnés à mort* at Thiais. Later, he was moved and laid to rest in the family plot in Auteuil cemetery, Paris, under a marble cross carrying the inscription "J.B. 1914–1948".

Baudouin, Marcel. Died on 26th January 1969 in Bordeaux.

Bisiau, Michel. Murdered on 15th June 1953 in Ugarteche, Argentina.

Blanc, Robert. On his return to France he was locked up in Fresnes. On 18th May 1946, he was tried at the *Cour de justice.* There was brief mention of his service with the *Milice* in Paris, but nothing about Dijon. He was sentenced to six months in prison and ten years 'national unworthiness'. He was released that same day, having already served seven and a half months. He regrets nothing, except for the grief

2   Giolitto, *"Histoire de la Milice"* page 540.

and the worry he caused his parents, who saw him leave for a cause that they hated and saw as lost.

Boudet-Gheusi, Jean. Died on 19th December 1969 in Cagnes sur mer.

Boyer, Emilien. Died on 2nd January 1995.

Bridoux, Jean. It is said that he committed suicide on 14th July 1945 in Eichstatt prison following a visit from one of his former comrades of Saint-Cyr who had lent him his pistol. However, some believe that he was killed *sans jugement*. He is buried in Treuchtlingen cemetery.

Cance, Pierre. Died in August 1988.

Castrillo, Jean. In August 1946, he was brought to trial at the *Cour de justice*. Before the verdict the presiding judge asked him if he had any regrets. He replied: "*Monsieur le Président*, I have only one regret and it is losing the war." Reproached for swearing an oath of loyalty to Hitler, he was sentenced to four years in prison and 'national unworthiness' for life.

Cornu. On 18th May 1945, he was arrested at Bordighera. On 24th July, the *Cour de justice du Havre* sentenced him to ten years hard labour. Released in 1948, he continued to study medicine.

Désiré, Norbert. Died in May 1968 in Bordeaux aged fifty-nine.

de Genouillac, Michel. On 3rd August 1946, the *Cour de justice d'Orléans* sentenced him to two years in prison and a 50,000 Franc fine for harming the national defense. He served his sentence, which was not reduced at any time, and paid the fine to the last centime before a law of amnesty around 1950.

de Lacaze, Maxime. Wounded in Berlin, he was captured in hospital by the Russians. Although still weak, he escaped at night and wandered around the city before occupying an abandoned house in the quarter of Moabit. The following day, he found himself in danger yet again; the Russians had taken over the vacant apartments above and below his. Thereupon he decided to 'move house'.

He made his move in the middle of the night. After feeling his way down the building's stairway, he was on the landing when a grenade fell out of his pocket, noisily rolled down the steps and exploded in the road. Riddled with shrapnel, he was very lucky to be alive. His Russian 'neighbours' dashed to his assistance and, without asking him any questions, took him to a hospital. Even though he bore the tell-tale tattoo, he must have counted himself very fortunate that nobody actually thought of checking for this brand when he passed himself off as a conscripted worker.

Repatriated to France, he spent five months in Foch de Suresnes hospital and was then moved, still incognito and still 'carrying' pieces of shrapnel, to the Côte d'Azur for convalescence. At Nice, he was introduced to the former *résistante* Mme de S. who had already helped certain *vaincus de la Libération* escape from France. After recounting his story, she smuggled him into Italy at night in her motorboat. His next guardian was a Jesuit who took him in. Some time later, he reached South America.

de Lupé, Jean de Mayol. The end of the war found de Lupé and his ever faithful orderly officer Henri Caux in the American Zone of Occupation. Ignorant of the terrible political climate reigning in France, de Lupé wrote to his family and immediately received a reply from his nephew, Jacques de Mayol de Lupé, telling him to stop all correspondence. But his warning came too late; de Lupé had already sent a postcard to his home address on avenue Émile-Accolas, Paris, and was immediately denounced to the Police by the concierge with whom he had been on good terms. In September 1946, de Lupé and Caux were arrested by the Americans.

Transferred to Munich, de Mayol de Lupé and Caux were handed over to the French Police, who kept them under 'lock and key' for one month before sending them back to France. Upon their arrival, they were both incarcerated in Fresnes.

Caux was the first of the two to be tried. The Monseigneur came to his defence and maintained that his secretary had only ever acted on his orders. In February 1947, Caux received a two-year suspended sentence.

On 13th May 1947, de Mayol de Lupé appeared before the *cour de justice de Paris*. Struck down by illness months before, the seventy-four-year-old Monseigneur had to be brought into the courtroom on a stretcher carried by four guards. Yet the press immediately accused him of trying to move the public and the judges to pity. He was accused of collaboration, of being a National Socialist apologist and of wearing an enemy uniform and decorations.

In the face of government commissioner Coyssac demanding a sentence of hard labour for life, de Lupé's barrister, Mr. Véron, conducted a most brilliant defence with the help of numerous witnesses. Nevertheless, de Mayol de Lupé still received a fifteen-year prison sentence, the general confiscation of his possessions and the loss of (state) rights.

He was interned in camp Châtaigneraie at La Celle-Saint-Cloud, where, in June 1950, he celebrated his sacerdotal jubilee. On 24th December 1950, his great-nephew, Luigi de Lupé, of late ordained a priest, celebrated his first mass in the Monseigneur's cell.

In May 1951, four years into his sentence, de Lupé was released on parole.[3] He retired to his home on avenue Émile-Accolas where he died on 23rd June 1955. At his burial six former POWs who owed their release to him carried the coffin.

de Misser. Against all the odds, he slipped home undetected shortly after the end of the war. In June 1945, his mother reported him to the police. On 25th October 1945, he was sentenced to 20 years hard labour and the confiscation of means present and future. He spent almost three years 'inside'—Fresnes (from July 1945 to 6th January 1946), Clairvaux (January 1946 to 15th April 1946), camp Struthof (April 1946 to November 1947), Baugé (November 1947 to January 1948) and, lastly, camp Vierge at Epinal. On 8th May 1948, he was released conditionally.

de Rose. Died in 1981 in Périgueux.

de Vaugelas, Jean. After making good his escape from the train returning him to France, he managed to reach Buenos Aires in 1948 under a Red Cross passport and then took refuge in Argentina, where he built up a successful wine business by the

3   According to Landwehr, "*Charlemagne's Legionnaires*", page 192, de Lupé was released because of continuing bad health.

name of *Les Caves franco-argentines*. In 1957, he died from injuries received in a car accident near Mendoza, despite an operation to save him.[4]

Fayard, René. He managed to reach Spain 1945 and from there Argentina. He went into partnership with de Vaugelas in *Les Caves franco-argentines* and took over from him at the head of the firm after his death in 1957. Some time later, he escaped an assassination attempt and, in early 1960, discovered that his car had been sabotaged. On 3rd March 1960, he was playing bridge with his wife and friends out in the garden of his home in San Rafael, near Mendoza, when assassinated with a bullet in the nape of the neck.[5] The assassin has never been traced, but many believe that this was the work of the French *2e Bureau*.

Evrard, Jacques. After the war he became a *chef de service* (departmental head) in a Paris hospital. He died in December 1994.

Faroux, François. The end of the war found him in Austria. He decided to return to France and said of this:

> I attempted to make my way into Germany across the bridge over the river Inn at Passau. Because there were American and Allied checkpoints everywhere I decided to say I had no papers and explain the reasons for this. I was made prisoner, though more or less free. Then I was transported to a camp at Bamberg. Some French soldiers were there, but still I was free. And so it was until my return to France in the middle of June. I was brought back on a train with civilians, mostly from Alsace. After two days and two nights we arrived at Longuyon, along the border with Luxembourg, and a camp under the control of the FTP [Communists]. And so began two days of appalling ill treatment. Jail, but twenty to a cell … made to hold a can of shit above our head and then run like that … cigarettes extinguished on our skin (I still carry the marks sixty-one years later). Forty-eight hours later, I was taken to Nancy and the *Sécurité Militaire*. I was interrogated courteously by a Lorrain who had served in the German Army! He told me that I had only to enlist in the French Army for three years and go and fight in Indochina. Then he made me sign up for a regiment that was normally stationed near where my family lived. I was given thirty

4   However, claims have been made that de Vaugelas was murdered and his death made to look as though it was a car accident. See *L'Express*, 12th August 1993, which states that around ten Frenchmen were silently 'neutralised' in South America without any fuss and made to look as though it was natural death or the result of an accident, including de Vaugelas. Also, in a broadcast of "*A la recontre de Monsieur X*" on the French radio station *France-Inter*, late September 1997, an 'official' said: "You know, we murdered Jean de Vaugelas in Argentina!" But such claims are false. Told of the accident, Madame de Vaugelas rushed to her husband's side. She was able to speak to him before and after the operation and at no time did he think that the accident was the result of a 'deliberate wish to kill him'. (*Récit de la Mort de Jean de Vaugelas*, from Madame de Vaugelas to a family friend, 2000, which is in the author's possession.) Moreover, she is convinced that if her husband had any suspicions of malevolence towards him he would have told her.

5   *L'Aurore*, March 1960. This article, titled "A game of bridge, an assassin and a death", claims that Fayard was a former member of the Gestapo, which is untrue, and that he had swindled 30 million Francs out of his firm, which has never been substantiated.

days to report to the regiment at Rambouillet. This I did, but it was a trap. Two or three days later I was arrested and jailed again. I appeared on the list of 'wanted' and in this way I had given them time enough to find out. Besides if I had not reported then I could have easily been traced in my department, caught and jailed. And if I was not 'wanted' then service for three years. Anyway, other recruits came to see the jailed *Boche*. The following day, I was transported to Versailles. Two more days of ill treatment at the hands of the Police before I was presented to a judge. I was sentenced to a 'stretch' of six months, plus fifteen years of national indignity (no rights and more taxes to pay!) because I had not come of age when I enlisted … A lucky man!

Faroux would later reflect that he may have joined and served with the French Army, albeit for a matter of days, but he never wore its uniform, the very same uniform worn by those responsible for the murder of twelve of their fellow countrymen at Bad Reichenhall.

Fenet, Henri Joseph. His stay in Soviet captivity was short-lived. First he was taken to a POW camp and then admitted into a hospital north of Berlin for his foot wound. Days later, he was returned to the POW camp, but in the meantime it had been evacuated. Remarkably, the local Russians provided him with civilian clothes and let him go free. Thereupon he joined a group of French repatriates in south Berlin. Crossing into France at Valenciennes, he was arrested because he bore the telltale blood group tattoo. The soldier who caught him told him: "This letter is the insignia of killers, the most dangerous killers."[6] Sentenced to twenty years hard labour, Fenet was released at the end of 1949. He died on 14th September 2002.

Forez, René Jean. Denounced on his return to France, he was sentenced to two years in prison, plus banishment to Algeria for one year.

Fronteau, Jean. From Neuengamme, he was transferred to SS-POW Camp 357 at Fallingbostel. On 15th September 1945, he was handed over to the French authorities. On 13th March 1946, the *Cour de Justice de Poitiers* sentenced him to 20 years hard labour, later commuted to a prison sentence of five years. In August 1948, he was released conditionally.

Gonzales, Henri-Georges. From Valenciennes, he was moved to Douai prison, dating from the time of Napoleon, and then to his native Marseille. Processed through the Law Courts, he was sentenced in his absence to death, which was later commuted to four years imprisonment. His time in prison was hard, but made bearable thanks to the support from his parents. On 29th June 1948, after some two and a half years in prison, he was released conditionally.

Grenier, Jean. The *Cour de Justice* of Bordeaux sentenced him to three years in prison and ten years loss of national rights. He was released on 12th May 1948 and granted an amnesty in 1950. At that time the French Army was in need of junior *cadres*, and although exempt from military service, he was at the end of 1951 called before the Military Authorities, who proposed that he undertake training of his own free will to become an *sous-officier de réserve*. He agreed to this. He enlisted at the end of July 1952 and was appointed *sergent* one month later, then *sergent-chef* in

6   Roch, page 149.

the reserves at the end of 1955. In June 1956, he asked to serve in Algeria and here he would remain on active service until March 1957. On 1st October 1956, he was appointed *sous-lieutenant de réserve*. After Algeria he continued to train in the reserves, reaching the rank of *chef de bataillon*. As a member of a combatant unit in Algeria, he was decorated with the *Croix de la Valeur Militaire*.

Halard, Jean. Not tattooed, he managed to make it back to France by passing himself off as an S.T.O. deportee. Called up, he found himself back in uniform! He chose to go to Indo-China for the duration of his military service. That was two years. On his return to France in 1947 he was arrested by the Military Police; the Czechs had passed to France all the dossiers of the French volunteers of the Waffen-SS held in Prague. He was brought before a *Tribunal pour enfants* [Juvenile court]—he was a minor when he enlisted—but the charges against him of harming the national defence were dropped because of the *loi d'amnistie* [law of amnesty] of 1947. Today, he still remains very proud of having fought for Europe in the ranks of the Waffen-SS.

Hennecart, Lucien. Died in 1996 in Avignon.

Hersche, Heinrich. He spent two and a half years in American captivity, passing through thirteen POW camps. On 27th September 1947, the Americans freed him and gave him the choice of staying in the US zone or returning to Switzerland. He chose the latter. On his return home, he was tried and sentenced to one year in prison and loss of citizen rights for two years. He died on 9th February 1971.

Hug, Pierre. After the war he exiled himself to Argentina.

Jauss, Hans Robert. After the war he studied philosophy and history at Heidelburg where he became a professor in 1957. One of the founders of the University of Constance, he obtained in 1966 the chair of Romance literature. He died in 1997.

Kreis, Henri. Died on 9th May 1990.

Krukenberg, Gustav. On 9th May 1945, Krukenberg and ten other prisoners were brought before a Soviet lieutenant who, to the great surprise of all, asked them if anybody could play an accordion he had just found in his lodgings. One man came forward and, after a one hour long concert, the Soviet officer freed them all, including Krukenberg. He went north to Wittenau where they had agreed to meet up, but 'nobody else was there'. Then he made his way to the suburbs to the west of Berlin. In Dahlem he rested at a friend's residence.

Krukenberg had much to think about: he had seen a poster from the Soviet *Kommandantur* of Berlin ordering all German officers to come forward. What should he do? While convinced that he could get through to the west he chose to share the fate of the European volunteers placed under him at Berlin.[7] He felt morally bound in particular to the French volunteers who had held to the end beside him.

So, on 12th May 1945, Krukenberg presented himself of his own free will to the Russian authorities at Berlin-Steglitz, indicating his rank and service record. A Soviet military tribunal sentenced him to the loss of liberty for twenty-five years.[8]

---

7   According to Saint-Loup, page 495, Krukenberg was naive to surrender. This is incorrect,
     for he knew full well what awaited him in Soviet captivity (Krukenberg, page 21).

His crime was 'damages caused to the Red Army by his military resistance in Pomerania and Berlin'. After eleven years in Soviet captivity in East Berlin,[9] including three in solitary confinement, he was finally released.

In the years that followed, Krukenberg continued to work for reconciliation between Germany and France. He died on 23rd October 1980 in Bonn.

Lefèvre, Jean-Pierre. From his release to his death of a heart attack on 26th February 1994, he devoted himself to the care of his former comrades in arms.

Louis-Paul, Henri. Died on 22nd December 1979.

Mailhe, Jean. Died on 12th June 1997 in Paris.

Malardier, Jean. Captured in Berlin, he was repatriated to France where he was sentenced to two and a half years imprisonment. He served his sentence in full, refusing conditional release; he spent more than one year in Cuincy, near Valenciennes, and the remainder at Noë. He was released in March 1948.

Martret, Christian. Handed over to the French Army, he was transported under escort to Lille. He was in the company of a deportee. His true identity was not known until his tattoo was discovered. On his arrival at Lille, he was locked up in a cage at the zoo. People from the local area came to insult and spit at him and the other prisoners. And then one day a 'visitor' to the zoo approached his cage and pointed him out as the 'biggest bastard' whereupon he was pulled from his cage by a large crowd and badly beaten up.[10] The guards did not intervene. Only then was Martret transferred to prison Loos-les-Lille.

Martret was tried before the *tribunal militaire de Paris*. He feared the worst when he learnt that the representative for the prosecution was a Communist whose son had been executed by German Waffen-SS Division 'Das Reich' in the Limousin. The defence argued that Martret was very young and likened 'Charlemagne' to the Brigade 'Jeanne d'Arc' [that had fought on the side of Franco during the Spanish Civil War]. He was sentenced to seven years imprisonment. Surprisingly, his property—as an only child he had inherited the property of his parents killed by an English bomber shot down by FLAK—was not confiscated. Was this an oversight? The answer is undoubtedly yes. He served two years in a number of prisons—*la Santé* in Paris, Fresnes,[11] Versailles and le Struthof—before his release at the end of 1947. The BILOM approached him, but he did not want to fight, calling it a 'regiment of forced combat'. Today, he has no regrets.

Mercier, Raymond. From Valenciennes, he was moved to Douai prison, where he was imprisoned on 27th November 1945. Compared to the Soviet camps he had been through, Douai, although rather rustic, was paradisiacal. At first, the prison-

---

8   Krukenberg, page 22, Mabire, page 313, and "*Historia #32*", page 137. However, according to Saint-Loup, page 496, and Landwehr, page 169, Krukenberg was sentenced to twenty-five years hard labour.

9   Krukenberg, page 22, Mabire, page 313, and Landwehr, page 169. Incorrectly, his time in captivity has appeared as thirteen years (Saint-Loup, page 496, and "*Historia*" # 32, page 137).

10   'A monumental correction' is how Martret described the beating up!

11   Martret was at Fresnes when Laval was shot.

ers shared five to a cell, which later became three. Mercier shared with Std.Ju. Louis
Salmon and Charles M. (ex-LVF, captured at Bobr). On 28th May 1946, *la Cour
de Justice de Valenciennes* sentenced Mercier to four years in prison and 'national
unworthiness'.

In early 1947, Mercier was transferred to Noé prison. For the journey he was
chained to Paul Viaud, a former *Milicien* who was also 'Charlemagne'.[12] Once
again he found himself among friends, Blonay, Enselme, Edmond Faudemay
(Sturmmann, Company 8/58), Malardier, Raoul Martin, Pierre Million-Rousseau, Vincenot and many others. Never would he forget *la messe des Rameaux*
(Palm Sunday) at Noé that year, for the Gospel of the Passion was read by Robert
Le Vigan, one of the greatest actors of French pre-war cinema.

In early August 1947, he was moved to a new prison: Saint Sulpice la Pointe in
the Tarn. It came as a great surprise to him to find that the men who ran the prison
were intelligent and humane, more so because the prison governor was a communist militant. There was much talk of Quicampoix, the Spiess of Fahrschwadron B,
who had made good his escape from the camp and then sent a postcard to the
prison governor on the day of his departure for South America!

With over half his sentence served, Mercier was released conditionally on 23rd
February 1948, but asked and obtained permission to leave the next morning so
that he could to spend one last evening with the comrades whose friendship and
loyalty had got him through captivity. He may have gained liberty, but *rien n'était
fini*. He entered a world that he had left some seven years before and which he no
longer knew.

Métais, Pierre-Marie. Died on 13th September 1973 in Bayonne.

Mongourd. In 1946, he was shot in Lyon for his activities in the *Milice*.

Nelly. In November 1944 she was sent to a hospital in Bavaria where she met and
befriended a young Fleming girl. At the end of the war they fled to Austria and took
to the hills with soldiers. Captured by the English, they were made prisoners on parole because the English 'did not want to believe that they were volunteers'! The
English left and were followed by the Americans who handed them over to the
French on île de Mainau, lake Constance. Her Flemish friend was handed over in
turn to the Belgians.

Taken to Lyon, she was incarcerated in fort Paillet in a dungeon and chained
to a young Alsatian girl. 'The handcuffs rather amused us. Well we were young and
idealists'. Four or five months later, thanks to her lawyer, a close family friend, she
was transferred to Paris and Fresnes. After finding herself in a cell with six others, a
situation that lasted a matter of days, she shared a cell with the niece by marriage of
General de Lattre de Tassigny. The cell was so cold that one sudden warm night
waterlogged their straw mattress.

When brought before the courts she could not keep quiet, remarking that she
regretted nothing. This drove her lawyer to despair, but eventually he managed to
get her out because of her fragile health. She looked like a skeleton. Months later,
she appeared before a civic court at which only her lawyer had the right to speak.
Found guilty of collaboration, she was sentenced to 20 years of 'national

12   Viaud would later present Mercier to his family as his *compagnon de chaîne*.

unworthiness' and the confiscation of possessions. This sentence did not concern her. She had taken the nationality of her wartime fiancé, that of Denmark, and, being rather spendthrift, she had few belongings. Today she lives in Germany and still regrets nothing.

Pignard-Berthet, Paul. In September 1946, he was tried and sentenced to five years hard labour. This was later commuted to three years. In mid-October 1948, he was released conditionally.

Puechlong, Jean-Louis. On 24th June 1945, because of his severe injuries, he was repatriated. He was hospitalised in Paris and underwent further surgery 'to regularise' the stump. In mid August 1945, he escaped from the hospital. Remaining in Paris, he went underground. At the end of September 1946, he was arrested and imprisoned in Fresnes. Brought before the *Tribunal militaire de Paris*, he received a two-year prison sentence. He served his sentence in full.

Radici, Georges. Sentenced to death by the *cour de justice de la Seine* for his activities in the *Milice*, he was shot on 24th July 1947.

Raybaud, Emile. Captured and repatriated to France, he was imprisoned at Limoges. On 8th September 1946, he was very nearly murdered in his cell when former *résistants* invaded the prison. Tried, he was sentenced to death for his service in the *Franc-Garde de la Milice*. His sentence, however, was not executed. Pardoned, he was released after serving six years in prison.

In 1970, much to his surprise, he learnt from a former secretary serving on the headquarters staff of Waffen-Gren. Regt der SS 58 that late into the Pomeranian campaign he had been promoted to the rank of Obersturmbannführer and awarded the Iron Cross 1st Class. This Krukenberg confirmed.

He died on 7th September 1995 in Provence.

Rigeade, Yves. Died on 5th August 2005.

Salle, Louis. Died in 1953 in Briançon, in the department of Hautes-Alpes.

Santeuil, Marc. In early May 1945, dressed as a civilian, he set off back to France, but without identity papers he did not get far. Crossing the Rhine, he was stopped at a police checkpoint and questioned. He explained that his identity papers had been stolen, which were kindly replaced in a Breton name, made up by him, and with a place of birth in a village near Brest whose town hall he knew had been bombed and set on fire by the Anglo-Americans, destroying all records.

En route for Brittany, he decided to stop in the town of a fellow countryman by the name of Lucien[13] he had met in Germany some weeks before. Lucien had championed the politics of the 'New Europe' in this town and had left with the Germans in August 1944. Sainteuil hoped for help from Lucien's family, whose address Lucien had given him to pass on news. What innocence! Lucien's wife greeted Sainteuil with the 'welcome': "If you knew what trouble Lucien caused us I would rather that he were dead." She went and denounced him to the police.

In the evening, he went in search of female company and 'scored', spending that night and most of the following day in the bedroom of a small hotel. Almost dark when they left, they failed to spot that they were being followed. Two

13   Pseudonym.

plain-clothes policemen arrested them and took them to the local police station for questioning. Knowing that the woman was married, he wanted to protect her honour and see her go free with the minimum of fuss and delay. He thought about persisting with his Breton identity, but that meant the police would keep hold of her until such as time as he checked out. He thought about escaping at night, but that meant leaving her in the hands of the police. And so rather than give his real identity he gave a second false name, that of a Swiss man, also an actor, well known in the theatre circle of Paris, who had enlisted in the Waffen-SS at the same time as him. Sainteuil was aware that this Swiss man, full of Nietzschean ideas, had asked Hersche after fifteen days at Sennheim to leave and return to Switzerland, which was granted. To support his new identity, Sainteuil even gave the police the address of this Swiss man's mother in Paris, which by chance he had remembered.

When the police phoned 'his' mother in front of him she confirmed that her son had enlisted in the Germany Army and that he was in flight. Thus, the police could not prove any connection between the woman and this Swiss man. Asked how they knew each, Sainteuil replied by way of an explanation that they had met quite by chance in the street. And so she was released after some two hours in detention.

As for Sainteuil, he spent the night at the police station to the outside accompaniment of car horns, laughter and lights to celebrate victory. It was the 7th May 1945 and Germany had just capitulated. The following day, he was handcuffed and moved to the town's prison. Finally, he admitted his real identity. One month later, he was transferred to Fresnes.

Once at Fresnes, through his lawyer, he requested of the Ministry of Justice authorisation to fight in the war in Indo-China, which had just started. The response came: "Your client must be judged first." With disappointment, Sainteuil reflected: 'In this way, France refused to turn the page, to reinstate into the national community a young Frenchman who perhaps had made a wrong choice, but who was ready to risk his life to show quite simply that he was a Frenchman'. Moreover, he thought it ironic that at the same time the Foreign Legion was opening its ranks to hundreds of Germans from the Wehrmacht and the Waffen-SS with 'no questions asked'.

In early 1946, Sainteuil was tried. When asked by the judge 'if the accused had anything to add' he spoke of his convictions and reasons for enlistment in May 1944 when victory was not assured. This he did in reaction to those also in the dock who 'rewrote history' to get out of this spot. Sentenced to ten years in prison, he was unexpectedly released in early October 1946. He had his lawyer to thank who, in collusion with his parents, had conspired to prove that he was mentally ill. Nevertheless, he had already served some sixteen months at Fresnes.

Sainteuil returned to acting, but then one day the police arrested him again. Due to an administrative error, his name still figured on a wanted list. While the matter was sorted he spent four days in *la Santé* prison, which were worse than the five hundred or so of his first captivity. But his secret was now out and the Communist *Union des Artiste* made sure that he never set foot on the boards again. Bitterly, he recalls that his second arrest took away from him another love, that of the theatre.

Simon, Henri. Died 24 April 1997.

Soulé, Pierre. Wearing a Russian jacket and chapka, he made it out of Berlin, passing himself off as a French partisan. Captured by the Americans, he escaped and made his way to the region of Innsbruck-Salzburg where he joined up with 'elements of all nationalities determined to continue the fight'. From the mountains, they harassed the Russians, inflicting some damage. Out of ammunition and hungry, they surrendered to the Americans, but the Americans refused to take them prisoner because the POW camps had been emptied. Soulé was given a German identity card and taken on as an auxiliary. 'Weary of their congenital stupidity', he left them and made it back to France. Denounced, charged, sentenced, he served one year in prison.

He died on 22nd December 1992 in his native Bordeaux.

Vaxelaire, Jean-Louis. Escaping from the Americans, he chose to go straight back home to his parents, arriving in Paris on 21st May 1945. He had wanted to stay in Germany, but could not speak the language and was concerned about the constant threat of being 'shopped'.

Verney, Albert. Died on 20th July 1965 in Carpentras.

Vincent, Roger. Died on 2nd September 1974 in Strasbourg.

Addendum

The following information, kindly provided by Jules Dissent, became available too late to include in the main body of the text. Because little is known about the Medical Company of 'Charlemagne', the information is appended here.

Jules Dissent joined the *Milice française* in late May 1944. Along with his family he was virulently anti-Communist. In the years before the war he had been appalled by the innumerable massacres and atrocities committed by the Bolsheviks against their own people. And yet, the people of his generation would later claim, after the death of Stalin, that they had no such knowledge of Communist crimes. He was not a member of a political party, but his father was a member of the royalist *Action Française* and read the daily newspaper of the same name. The family detested the Republic and the shady politicians who represented it.

For Dissent, who 'was brought up in admiration of the heroism shown by the French Army during the First World War', the defeat of May 1940 represented a disaster of an unimaginable scale.

Following the defeat of May 1940, he pledged his loyalty, like his parents, to *Maréchal* Pétain, who had saved France from total collapse. Under the terms of the armistice, France retained its Navy, which he greatly admired. Indeed he had once dreamt of becoming a Navy officer.

Dissent was not anti or pro German, but his father, a World War One infantry officer who had been captured, respected some of their qualities. The English attack on the fleet at Mers-el-Kebir turned him against a country he considered as a friend and towards another, that of Germany. Nevertheless, he was a young Frenchman who was just trying to get on with a normal life and much of his time was spent in books. He passed his Baccalauréat in 1942 and went on to study medicine.

He followed political events and, by the spring of 1944, a veritable climate of terror reigned in parts of France that he largely attributed to the maquis and the communists and not to the *Milice* and not to the Germans. In the Limousin the Communists assassinated two family members on his mother's side, who had demonstrated their support for Pétain. The assassination of a well-known and devoted local doctor in particularly vile circumstances angered him. His crime had been to profess anti-Communist opinions and belong to the P.P.F. He was moved to action.

Life as a *Milicien* was quiet, despite being mobilised after the Allied Normandy landings. He did not participate in the single operation conducted by the *Milice de Poitiers* against the maquis. He carried an old revolver, but never used it in anger or practise with it. Nevertheless, it gave him comfort. His duties became those of a medic, but there were 'no wounded and few sick among the young men we were'.

On 23rd August 1944, Dissent departed his native Poitiers. He finally reached Ulm on 11th October. His journey had taken him via Strasbourg and Wiesbaden and not Belfort like many other *Miliciens*. While at Ulm he greeted the prospect of transferring to the Waffen-SS with little enthusiasm. Although it was a question of amalgamating Frenchmen from various units into one he had no wish to volunteer.

Before leaving France his father had told him: "Do what you are told, but don't volunteer'. In this way, he let destiny and the forthcoming medical decide. Though a little short sighted he was declared fit for military service.

On 6th November 1944, singing *La Madelon*, he was 'admitted' into Wildflecken camp.[1] He was dressed in the feldgrau of the German Army and an Italian overcoat, which greatly displeased him. Not only was the Italian overcoat less warm and comfortable than its German counterpart, but it made him look Italian, and the military reputation of Italy was inferior. Like most *Miliciens*, he wore blank right collar insignia. Curiously, he was not issued with a *Soldbuch*.

With René Gaultier, a fellow *Milicien* he knew well, he was allocated to the Assault Gun Company. In the absence of assault guns his training consisted of arms drill *à l'allemande*, exercises and some shooting practise with the old, but efficient Mauser rifle. The Company sang German, as well as French songs when it marched.

Towards the end of November 1944, as a medical student of one year, he requested a transfer to the newly formed Medical Company. He nearly blew his chances of a transfer when he and two other comrades went in search of food and were confronted on the way back to camp by Feldgendarmes. Luckily he was not carrying anything, but his two comrades were. They were promised punishment.

On 4th December 1944, he celebrated a rather miserable twentieth birthday, remarking: "I belong to a generation whose youth was not marked by many celebrations." On the 20th of the same month, he joined the Medical Company, becoming good friends with a fellow *Milicien*, Jean Cardaliat, a Breton. He was promoted to the rank of Sturmmann. One of the French NCOs in the Medical Company was named Mauver, whose father was one of the pioneers of thoracic surgery. Only the officers and some NCOs were armed.

At Wildflecken he encountered no hostility from the other factions that made up 'Charlemagne', but there was one occasion when he was ordered by French NCOs from the SS-Sturmbrigade to do a series of push-ups. He no longer recalls the reason for this, but he felt it was unjust and left him unhappy.

On 21st February 1945, the Medical Company left Wildflecken for the Eastern Front on a convoy Dissent believed to be the last. The convoy passed Erfurt on the 22nd, Berlin on the 23rd and Stettin on the 24th. In Pomerania, whist parked up in a station, the train was attacked once by Russian fighters, but received little damage. On 25th February 1945, towards two in the morning, the convoy finally arrived at Hammerstein.

The Medical Company was sent to the POW camp, which had recently been evacuated, and there it remained unemployed hour after hour. Dissent got the distinct impression that 'nobody knew what they should do'. Eventually, in the late afternoon, the Medical Company set out on foot eastwards and took up position in a house. Several volunteers left to try and get news and orders. At ten in the evening, the company set out westwards in the direction of Neustettin, arriving early next morning.

In the early morning hours of 27th February 1945, the Medical Company evacuated Neustettin for Belgard. Some memories of this march have remained

---

1   He does not recall being 'kept in waiting' in the valley for several days before gaining admittance to Wildflecken.

with Dissent. Shortly after leaving Neustettin, he was aboard a horse-drawn wagon when he caught sight of his friend Cardaliat as he passed him by on foot. They saluted each other and Cardaliat, who seemed in good shape, continued on his way faster than before. That was the last Dissent saw of him.

While crossing a village Dissent was caught up in an attack from the air. Towards the late afternoon, such was his exhaustion and that of those around him that they had to stop some moments in a house. They napped, but fearing that they might fall behind and into Russian hands, set out again. Dissent also recalls another memory of 'a rather surreal vision in this world of chaos': a trainload of Panther tanks and their crews heading eastwards towards the front.

Finally, on the morning of 28th February 1945, the Medical Company arrived at Belgard. It was no longer at full strength, but was still intact and officered, including a number of Germans. Among them was a doctor with the rank of Sturmbannführer and two NCOs with the ranks of Hauptscharführer and Scharführer.

On the evening of 1st March 1945, the Medical Company relocated from Belgard to Kowanz, where divisional headquarters had been sited. The men were quartered in a cattle farm. The animals suffered terribly because they were in need of milking.

On the morning of 4th March 1945, the Medical Company crossed Körlin and moved into position along the road to Kolberg, where it spent most of the day. At the end of the afternoon, Dissent was told that the Division was going to try and cross the Russian lines towards the west. He was ordered to carry as little as possible, which did not bother him because he only had on him a haversack holding a little food, as well as a bayonet, used for the most part to open tinned food!

On the evening of 4th March 1945, the Medical Company crossed the town of Körlin once more and took the road to Belgard. Dissent believes that the Medical Company followed in the wake of the I/RM and divisional Headquarters and was not with the RR. His company crossed Belgard to the south, bore south-west, followed the Persante[2] and crossed over a bridge 'in the middle of the country'. Daybreak found the company in front of a road it had to cross, but it was a road traversed by Russian lorries.[3] The order was thus given to cross in small groups and as quickly as possible. This was carried out, but the company now started to break up.

Dissent said of what happened next:

Shortly after having crossed the road, we reached a small wood with the hope of resting there awhile; but barely had we stopped than several mortar shells fell on the wood, forcing us to set off again. Finding myself close to two German NCOs of my company, I then decided to follow them, thinking that they were perhaps the most capable ones of getting out of this spot (and me with them).

We ran to the edge of the wood and came under fire, with bullets whistling unpleasantly above our heads. I heard shouted at a certain point 'the Sturmbannfüher is dead' and I ended up lying flat on my stomach between the

2   Dissent recalls following a pathway along the river.
3   Dissent believes the road was that from Belgard to Standemin.

two Germans. One had a rifle and the other a sub-machine-gun (my only weapon was a bayonet!) and they exchanged fire with the Russians. A moment later, which seemed long when the bullets are whistling above your head making a very particular sound, I noted they were no longer firing: one was dead and the other seriously wounded in the arm. I saw the Russians come out of the wood and come towards me, with weapons pointed and shouting ... I then got up and said 'camarade!'

They approached and took the weapons, including my bayonet that they casually threw away; one of them immediately stole my watch. I then tried hard to bandage the wounded German who was saying nothing but who must have been suffering greatly because a bullet had certainly fractured the humerus. I helped him walk to some nearby buildings where they separated us. I still don't know if he pulled through.

Dissent was captured in the vicinity of Standemin. First he was marched to Arnswalde, which took twelve days. Here he remained until 10th April 1945 when he was moved to Landsberg. Days later, he was on the move again to Posen. On 20th April 1945, he left for Russia. His destination was Voronej on the left bank of the Don. He passed through various camps. In the last a German doctor diagnosed him with tuberculosis and got him admitted into the camp's rough and ready 'hospital'. Nevertheless, this probably saved his life. He spent two months in hospital, which enabled him to grow strong and avoid passing through Tambov.

On 30th September 1945, Dissent began the return journey home. Prison awaited him. Still suffering from tuberculosis, he was hospitalised for a further two months. On 14th January 1946, he learnt that he had been released conditionally. He may have been free, but his health still continued to fail him and he spent two months in a Paris hospital, which was followed by two years in a sanatorium. In 1950 he was granted an amnesty without going before the courts.

Bibliography

Unpublished manuscripts

Cera, Jean-François, *Les raisons de l'engagement des volontaires français sous l'uniforme allemand, juillet 1941 mai 1945* (1992)

Marotin, Émil, *La longue marche*

Roch, Sabine, *La Division Charlemagne* (1990)

Soulat, Robert, *Historique de la Division Charlemagne*

Soulat, Robert, *Histoire des volontaires français dans l'armée allemande 1940–1945*

Books

Angolia, John, *Cloth Insignia of the SS* (Bender Publishing, 1983, 2nd printing)

Aron, Robert, *The Vichy regime 1940–44* (Putnam, 1958)

Auvray, Jacques, *Les derniers grognards* (Editions Irminsul)

Barger, Charles, *The SS family* (Ulric, 1998)

Bassompierre, Jean, *Frères ennemis* (Amiot-Dumont, 1948)

Bayle, André, *De Marseille à Novossibirsk*, (Histoire et Tradition, 1992)

Bayle, André, *San et Persante* (Self-published, 1994)

Bender, Roger James and Taylor, Hugh Page, *Uniforms, organization and history of the Waffen-SS*, volume 4 (Bender Publishing, 1982)

Brissaud, André, *Les derniers défenseurs d'Hitler: des Français* (Histoire pour tous NO 95, 1968)

Brunet, Jean-Paul, *Jacques Doriot* (Balland, 1986)

Cazalot, Georges, … *Et la terre a bu leur sang!* (Éditions de l'Homme Libre, 2005)

Colin, Charles Ambroise, *Sacrifice de Bassompierre* (Amiot-Dumont, 1948)

Conway, Martin, *Collaboration in Belgium* (Yale University Press, 1993)

Dank, Milton, *The French against the French* (Cassell, 1978)

Davis, Brian Leigh, *German uniforms of the Third Reich* (Blandford Press, 1980)

Davies, W.J.K., *German Army handbook 1939–1945* (Purnell Book Services, 1974)

Delperrié de Bayac, Jacques, *Histoire de la Milice* (Fayard, 1969)

Deniau, Jean-François, de l'Académie française, *Mémoires de 7 vies* (Plon, 1954)

Deniel, Alain, *Bucard et le Francisme* (Jean Picollec, 1979)

Duffy, Christopher, *Red storm over the Reich* (Atheneum, 1991)

Duprat, François, *Les campagnes de la Waffen-SS* (Les Sept Couleurs, 1992 and 1993, 2 Volumes)

Ertel, Heinz and Schule-Kossens, Richard, *Europäische Freiwillige im Bild* (Munin Verlag, 1986)

Fosten, D.S.V. and Marrion, R.J., *Waffen-SS* (Almark publications, 1974, 4th edition)

Fournier-Foch, Henry, *Tovarich Kapitaine Foch* (La Table Ronde, 2001)

Gaultier, Léon, *Siegfried et le Berrichon* (Perrin, 1991)

Giolitto, Pierre, *Histoire de la Milice* (Perrin, 1997)

Giolitto, Pierre, *Volontaires français sous l'uniforme allemand* (Perrin, 1999)

Jurado, Carlos, *Foreign volunteers of the Wehrmacht* (Men-At-Arms Series, 1983)

Jurado, Carlos, *Resistance warfare 1940–1945* (Men-At-Arms Series, 1985)

Klietmann, Dr. K.-G., *Die Waffen-SS eine Dokumentation* (Verlag 'Der Freiwillige' G.m.b.H. 1965)

La Mazière, Christian de, *Ashes of Honour* (Tattoo, 1976)

Labat, Eric, *Les places étaient chères* (La Table Ronde, 1953)

Lambert, Pierre P. and Le Marec Gérard, *Organisations, mouvements et unités de l'état français, Vichy 1940–1944* (Jacques Grancher, 1992)

Lambert, Pierre P. and Le Marec Gérard, *Partis et mouvements de la collaboration, Paris 1940–1944* (Jacques Grancher, 1993)

Lambert, Pierre P. and Le Marec Gérard, *Les Français sous le casque allemand* (Jacques Grancher, 1994)

Landwehr, Richard, *Charlemagne's Legionnaires* (Bibliophile Legion Books, 1989)

Littlejohn, David, *Foreign Legions of the Third Reich*, volume 1 (Bender Publishing, 1979)

Le Tissier, Tony, *The Battle of Berlin 1945* (Jonathan Cape, 1988)

Lefèvre, Eric and Jean Mabire, *La LVF 1941: Par–40° devant Moscou* (Fayard, 1985)

Lefèvre, Eric and Jean Mabire, *La Légion perdue* (Jacques Grancher, 1995)

Lefèvre, Eric and Jean Mabire, *Sur les Pistes de la Russie Centrale* (Jacques Grancher, 2003)

Lindenblatt, Helmut, *Pommern 1945* (Verlag Gerhard Rautenbeg, 1993, 2nd edition)

Logusz, Michael, *The Waffen-SS 14th Grenadier Division 1943–1945* (Schiffer Publishing, 1997)

Mabire, Jean, *La Brigade Frankreich* (Fayard, 1973)

Mabire, Jean, *La Division Charlemagne* (Fayard, 1974)

Mabire, Jean, *Mourir à Berlin* (Fayard, 1975)

Mabire, Jean, *Mourir pour Dantzig* (L'Aencre, 1995)

Mabire, Jean, *La Division Nordland* (Fayard, 1982)

Madeja, W. Victor, *Russo-German War 25 January to 8 May 1945* (Valor Publishing Company, 1987)

Malbosse, Christian, *Le soldat traqué* (La Pensée Moderne, 1971)

Mehner, Kurt, *Die Waffen-SS und Polizei 1939–1945* (Militar-Verlag Klaus D. Patzwall, 1995)

Mollo, Andrew, *Uniforms of the SS Volume 7* (Historical Research Unit, 1976)

Mounine, Henri, *Cernay 40–45* (Editions Du Polygone, 1999)

Muelle, Raymond, *Le Bataillon des réprouvés* (Presses de la Cité, 1990)

Munoz, Antonio, *Forgotten Legions: Obscure Formations of the Waffen-SS, 1943–1945* (Paladin Press, 1991)

Munoz, Antonio, *Hitler's Eastern Legions volume 1: The Baltic Schutzmannschaft* (Axis Europa)

Neulen, Hans, *Europas verratene Söhne* (Bastei Lubbe, 1980)

Oertle, Vincenz, *Volontaires suisses* (Thesis-Verlag, 1997)

Ophuls, Marcel, *The sorrow and the pity* (Paladin, 1975)

Ory, Pascal, *Les collaborateurs* (Le Seuil, 1977)
Lavigne-Delville, *Pour la Milice, justice* (Editions Etheel, 1955)
Rostaing, Pierre, *Le prix d'un serment* (La Table ronde, 1975)
Rusco, Pierre, *Stoi!* (Jacques Grancher, 1988)
Saint-Loup, *Les Volontaires* (Presses de la Cité, 1963)
Saint-Loup, *Les Hérétiques* (Presses de la Cité, 1965)
Schneider, Jost W., *Their Honor Was Loyalty* (Bender Publishing, 1993, 2nd
    edition)
Schneider, Russ, *Götterdämmerung 1945* (Eastern Front Warfield Books, 1998)
Schulze-Kossens, Richard, *Militärischer Führernachwuchs der Waffen-SS Die
    Junkerschulen* (Munin Verlag, 1987, 2nd edition)
Silgailis, Arthur, *Latvian Legion* (Bender Publishing, 1986)
Slowe, Peter and Woods, Richards, *Battlefield Berlin* (Robert Hale, 1988)
Soucy, Robert, *French Fascism: The Second Wave 1933–1939* (Yale University,
    1995)
Sweets, John, *Choices in Vichy France* (Oxford University Press, 1986)
Thomas, Nigel, *Wehrmacht Auxiliary Forces* (Men-At-Arms Series, 1992)
Tieke, Wilhelm and Rebstock, Friedrich, *Im letzten Aufgebot 1944–1945, Band
    1* (T.K. 18/33, 1994)
Trevor-Roper, Hush, *The Last Days of Hitler* (Macmillan, 1947)
Williamson, Gordon, *The Waffen-SS (4) 24 to 38 Divisions, & Volunteer Legions*
    (Men-At-Arms, 2004)
Yerger, Mark, *Waffen-SS Commanders Volume 2, Krüger to Zimmermann*
    (Schiffer, 1999)

Magazines, periodicals and articles

Les Archives Keystone sur la LVF (Editions Grancher, 2005)
Various issues of:
Axis Europa
Barnes Review
der Freiwillige
Historia
Revue d'histoire de la Deuxième Guerre Mondiale
Siegrunen
39–45 Magazine

The author is interested in obtaining copies of the following:
Bassompierre Jean, *Frères ennemis* (Amiot-Dumont 1948)
The unpublished memoirs of *abbé* Vernay
The unpublished memoirs of Dr. Métais
The unpublished memoirs of Emilien Boyer
Also, the author is interested in hearing from ex-Division members.

Stackpole Military History Series

Real battles. Real soldiers. Real stories.

Stackpole Military History Series

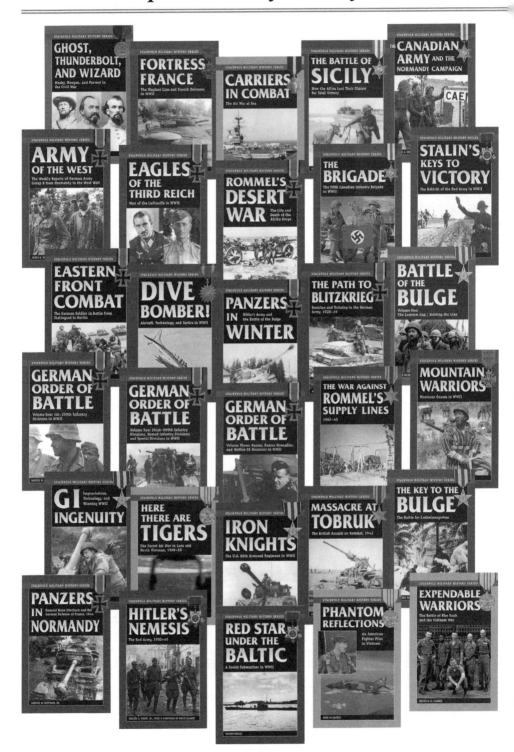

Real battles. Real soldiers. Real stories.

Stackpole Military History Series

STACKPOLE MILITARY HISTORY SERIES

BATTLE OF THE BULGE

Volume Two:
Hell at Bütgenbach / Seize the Bridges

HANS WIJERS

STACKPOLE MILITARY HISTORY SERIES

FOR THE HOMELAND

The 31st Waffen-SS Volunteer Grenadier Division in WWII

RUDOLF PENCZ

STACKPOLE MILITARY HISTORY SERIES

FOR EUROPE

The French Volunteers of the Waffen-SS

ROBERT FORBES

NEW for Spring 2010

STACKPOLE MILITARY HISTORY SERIES

IN THE FIRE OF THE EASTERN FRONT

The Experiences of a Dutch Waffen-SS Volunteer, 1941-45

HENDRI

STACKPOLE MILITARY HISTORY SERIES

SHIP-BUSTERS

British Torpedo-Bombers in WWII

STACKPOLE MILITARY HISTORY SERIES

KNIGHT'S CROSS PANZERS

The German 35th Panzer Regiment in WWII

STACKPOLE MILITARY HISTORY SERIES

D-DAY BOMBERS

The Stories of Allied Heavy Bombers during the Invasion of Normandy

STEPHEN DARLOW

STACKPOLE MILITARY HISTORY SERIES

TYPHOON ATTACK

The Legendary British Fighter in Combat in WWII

NORMAN FRANKS

STACKPOLE MILITARY HISTORY SERIES

CYCLOPS IN THE JUNGLE

A One-Eyed LRP in Vietnam

STAFF SERGEANT DAVID P. WALKER, USA (RET.)

Stackpole Military History Series

FOR THE HOMELAND

THE 31ST WAFFEN-SS VOLUNTEER GRENADIER DIVISION IN WORLD WAR II

Rudolf Pencz

Formed in the fall of 1944, the 31st Waffen-SS Volunteer Grenadier Division was composed mainly of ethnic Germans living in Hungary. After a brief period of training, the division endured its baptism of fire against the Red Army in the Hungarian sector of the Eastern Front in late 1944. The 31st then participated in the battles southeast of Berlin, where the division fought until its battered remnants surrendered to the Soviets in May 1945. Rudolf Pencz's carefully researched account records the complete history of this rarely covered Waffen-SS formation.

$21.95 • Paperback • 6 x 9 • 304 pages • 27 b/w photos, 11 maps

WWW.STACKPOLEBOOKS.COM
1-800-732-3669

Stackpole Military History Series

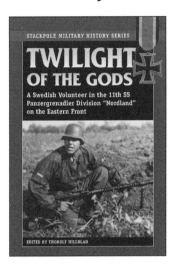

TWILIGHT OF THE GODS
A SWEDISH VOLUNTEER IN THE
11TH SS PANZERGRENADIER DIVISION "NORDLAND"
ON THE EASTERN FRONT
Edited by Thorolf Hillblad

This is the exciting true story of Erik Wallin, a Swedish soldier who volunteered for the Waffen-SS during World War II. Wallin served in the Panzer Reconnaissance Battalion of the 11th SS Panzergrenadier Division "Nordland," a unit composed largely of men from Denmark, Norway, and Sweden. Sent to the Eastern Front, the 11th SS fought in the Courland Pocket in late 1944 and then battled the Red Army along the Oder River and in Berlin, where the Soviets destroyed the division. Few memoirs of non-Germans in the Waffen-SS exist, and *Twilight of the Gods* ranks among the very best.

$18.95 • Paperback • 6 x 9 • 160 pages • 16 b/w photos, 1 map

WWW.STACKPOLEBOOKS.COM
1-800-732-3669

Stackpole Military History Series

PANZER GUNNER
A CANADIAN IN THE GERMAN
7TH PANZER DIVISION, 1944–45
Bruno Friesen

Six months before World War II erupted in 1939,
young Bruno Friesen was sent to Germany by his father,
a German-speaking Mennonite who came to Canada
from Ukraine and believed the Third Reich offered a
better life than Canada. Friesen was drafted into the
Wehrmacht three years later and ended up in the 7th
Panzer Division. Serving as a gunner in a Panzer IV tank
and then a Jagdpanzer IV tank hunter, Friesen fought the
Soviets in Romania in the spring of 1944, Lithuania that
summer, and West Prussia in early 1945.

$18.95 • Paperback • 6 x 9 • 240 pages • 56 b/w photos, 4 maps

WWW.STACKPOLEBOOKS.COM
1-800-732-3669

Also available from Stackpole Books

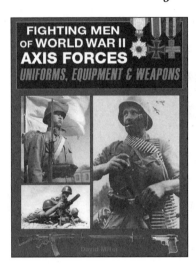
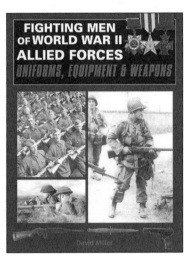

FIGHTING MEN OF WORLD WAR II
VOLUME 1: AXIS FORCES
VOLUME 2: ALLIED FORCES
David Miller

These comprehensive volumes present a full-color
look at Axis and Allied soldiers in World War II,
covering their weapons, equipment, clothing,
rations, and more. The Axis volume includes Germany,
Italy, and Japan while the Allied volume presents
troops from the United States, Great Britain, and the
Soviet Union. These books create a vivid picture of
the daily life and battle conditions of the fighting
men of the Second World War.

$49.95 • Hardcover • 9 x 12 • 384 pages • 600 color illustrations

WWW.STACKPOLEBOOKS.COM
1-800-732-3669